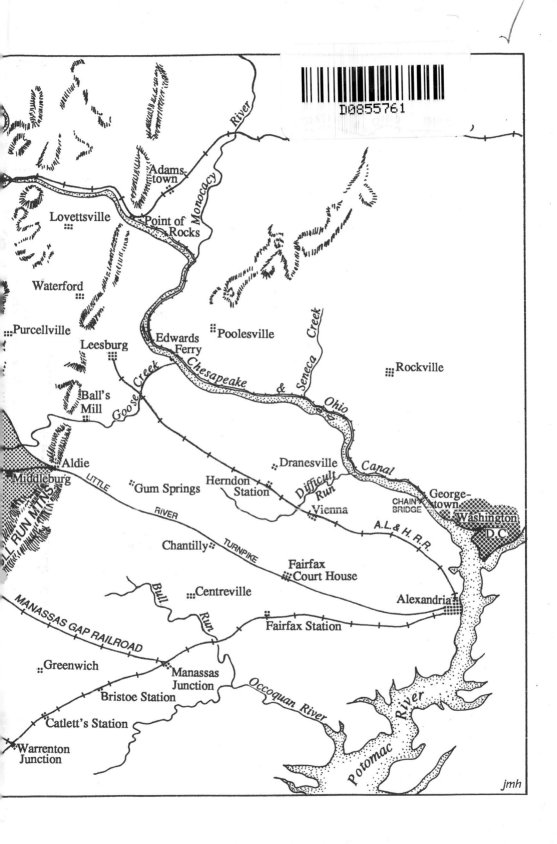

D0855761

Adams-
town

Lovettsville
Point of
Rocks

Monocacy River

Waterford

Purcellville

Leesburg

Edwards
Ferry

Poolesville

Rockville

Seneca Creek

Chesapeake

&

Ohio

Ball's
Mill

Goose Creek

Aldie

Dranesville

Canal

George-
town

Middleburg

LITTLE

Gum Springs

Herndon
Station

Difficult Run

CHAIN
BRIDGE

A.L.&H.R.R.

Washington
D.C.

BULL RUN MTNS.

RIVER

Vienna

Chantilly

TURNPIKE

Fairfax
Court House

Alexandria

Bull

Centreville

Run

MANASSAS GAP RAILROAD

Fairfax Station

Greenwich

Manassas
Junction

Occoquan River

River

Bristoe Station

Catlett's Station

Potomac

Warrenton
Junction

jmh

# Gray Ghost

68745

KB
Mose    Ramage, James A.
        Gra  Ghost              30.00

KB
Mose    Ramage, James A.     63745
        Gray ghost            30.00

JAN 24 00
AUG 23 88
SEP 23 88
NOV 8  00
MAY 4  01
OCT 27 81

Ann Bowling
Frank Ward
G  6793
F 24299
G  6491
G 178725

**GREENUP COUNTY PUBLIC LIBRARY**
614 Main Street
Greenup, Kentucky 41144

# Gray Ghost

The Life
of
Col. John Singleton Mosby

## JAMES A. RAMAGE

THE UNIVERSITY PRESS OF KENTUCKY

Publication of this volume was made possible in part
by a grant from the National Endowment for the Humanities.

Copyright © 1999 by The University Press of Kentucky

Scholarly publisher for the Commonwealth,
serving Bellarmine College, Berea College, Centre
College of Kentucky, Eastern Kentucky University,
The Filson Club Historical Society, Georgetown College,
Kentucky Historical Society, Kentucky State University,
Morehead State University, Murray State University,
Northern Kentucky University, Transylvania University,
University of Kentucky, University of Louisville,
and Western Kentucky University.
All rights reserved.

*Editorial and Sales Offices:* The University Press of Kentucky
663 South Limestone Street, Lexington, Kentucky 40508–4008

03 02 01 00 99   5 4 3 2

*Frontispiece*: One of the best scouts in the Confederacy, Mosby posed as a
regular cavalry scout, with boots, binoculars and saber, in Richmond early in
1865. (Library of Congress.)

Library of Congress Cataloging-in-Publication Data

Ramage, James A.
    Gray Ghost : the life of Col. John Singleton Mosby / James A. Ramage
        p.    cm.
    Includes bibliographical references (p.    ) and index.
    ISBN 0-8131-2135-3 (acid-free paper)
    1. Mosby, John Singleton, 1833-1916. 2. United States—History—Civil
War, 1861-1865—Underground movements. 3. Guerrillas—Confederate
States of America—Biography. 4. Soldiers—Confederate States of
America—Biography. 5. Diplomats—United States—Biography. I. Title.
E467.1.M87R36   1999
973.7'45'092—dc21
    [b]                                                              99-13688

This book is printed on acid-free recycled paper
meeting the requirements of the American National Standard
for Permanence of Paper for Printed Library Materials.

To Ann

# Contents

# 1

# Mosby's Weapon of Fear

Union cavalry charging with whirling sabers against Mosby's men suddenly realized that nothing in their drills or training had prepared them for this, for Mosby threw away the rules and never fought fairly. Here was no gentlemanly thrust and parry, but revolver bullets, noise, and smoke; men falling to the ground wounded and dead; and riderless horses jumping around out of control. The Union commander was usually one of the first down, and in shock and confusion his men had the urge to drop their reins and allow their horses to behave naturally and run away. "We considered that to meet Mosby and his men at close range meant certain death," and "often wondered what kind of a man he was that he could give us such warm receptions," recalled an 8th Illinois Cavalry veteran.[1]

John Singleton Mosby had no military schooling but was a lawyer and student of history and literature, quoting lines from the poetry of his favorite author, Lord Byron. He was a small, thin man—5 feet, 8 inches tall and 128 pounds—and an outstanding horseman who could handle a horse as smoothly as a steeplechase champion. Mounted on a magnificent gray horse, one of the fastest in the column, he led the assault, bridle reins in one hand, Colt revolver in the other. His eyes flashed, and he yelled in a high-pitched, powerful voice. In the heat of battle a transformation came over his face: deep and powerful emotions welled up, and his thin lips opened on his perfect white teeth as a satirical smile illuminated his countenance. He was no hedonist—his only luxury was freshly ground coffee—but these Civil War melees were the highest pleasure in his life.

The mounted charges and countercharges of Mosby's 43rd Battalion Virginia Partisan Rangers seemed spontaneous and unorganized, but every detail of his warfare and tactics was the result of extremely careful planning and execution by one of the most brilliant minds in the history of guerrilla war. Mosby was one of the most self-disciplined, focused, and indefatigable individuals who ever lived, and his goal was to win the crowning laurel of guerrilla war by penetrating the minds of the enemy and using fear as a psychological force multiplier. He created the illusion of ubiquity, the fear that he might appear anywhere at any time, and used this edge to operate for more than two years and three months behind enemy lines within a day's ride of Washington and still had the tactical initiative when the war ended.

Mosby specialized in overnight raids with men and horses rested and well nourished from a few days of freedom between operations. For him a perfect mission included entering the target area undetected, rapidly executing the mission, and withdrawing quickly, with no alarms raised and no fighting. He accomplished all of these goals in his most famous raid. Guided by a Union cavalry deserter, he infiltrated Union lines in Fairfax County with twenty-nine men on the night of March 8, 1863, captured Union general Edwin H. Stoughton and thirty-two men, and withdrew undetected with no shots fired. Confederate cavalry commander Gen. James Ewell Brown "Jeb" Stuart declared the operation a "brilliant exploit" and issued a special order proclaiming: "The feat, unparalleled in the war, was performed, in the midst of the enemy's troops at Fairfax Court-House, without loss or injury."[2]

Practicing the goal of never fighting fairly, Mosby ambushed the 6th Michigan Cavalry twice on the same overnight raid, and their commander, Col. George Gray, said: "Mosby did not fight fairly. He surprised me, and the night before had bushwhacked some of my men." Mosby understood that success depended on accurate reconnaissance and therefore had some of the best scouts in the Confederacy, local men familiar with every road and by-path and acquainted with the people living in the target area. He often scouted himself as well, both a few days before a raid and again immediately before deciding whether or not to attack. Only he knew his plans; he told no one, and the men had no idea whatsoever where they were going until they arrived. Once the march was underway he would tell the guide, and him alone.[3]

Adopting the fastest transportation available, Mosby's men had the best Thoroughbreds the Yankees could provide. Each Ranger had several and rotated them to have a fresh mount for each raid. Most were jumpers, accustomed to leaping high fences and dashing across fields for rapidly getting away. Union troops who watched them scatter into the woods said their horses jumped like deer, and Gen. Wesley Merritt reported: "The guerrillas, being few in numbers, mounted on fleet horses and thoroughly conversant with the country, had every advantage of my men."[4]

Normally, cavalry on the march sent up a humming sound that could be heard for hundreds of yards at night. Sabers and scabbards clanked, canteens jingled, and hooves clattered. Mosby, carefully practicing stealth, forbade sabers, canteens, and clanking equipment; his column moved so quietly that civilians lying in their beds in houses next to the road recognized when Mosby's men were passing in the night—the only sound was the pounding of hoofbeats. Near the target he would veer off into soft fields or woods, and it was so quiet that the men could hear whippoorwills calling in the distance. "Silence! Pass it back," he ordered, and from that point he directed only with hand signals. If attacking dismounted he would have the men remove their spurs and leave them with the horses and horse-holders. He walked in soft snow or used the sound of the rain and wind to cover footsteps, and once timed his final pounce with the sound of coughing by a Union horse. "We made no noise," he wrote, and one of his men recalled, "Our men were in among the prostrate forms of the Yankees before they were fairly awake, and they assisted some of them to unwind from their blankets."[5]

Modern military studies of sleep deprivation indicate that cognitive skills deteriorate after one night without sleep; after two or three nights, performance is considerably impaired. Confederate general John Hunt Morgan's men were falling asleep in the road on his Indiana-Ohio Raid, and his exhausted scouts failed him at Buffington Island by reporting that the ford was guarded by regular forces when they were only a few frightened home guards. Abel D. Streight became groggy from exhaustion and sleep deprivation on a raid in Alabama in the spring of 1863, and Nathan Bedford Forrest deceived him into surrendering to a force less than half his size. H. Judson Kilpatrick became worn down and lost his nerve in his raid on Richmond, Virginia, with Ulric Dahlgren early in 1864 and was driven away by defenders that he outnumbered six to one. But Mosby carefully saved the energy of his men and horses, moving slowly into a raid for maximum performance in the fight and hasty withdrawal. He preferred to strike at about 4:00 A.M. when guards were least alert and reserves most sound asleep. He said that it was easy to surround sleeping men and that it took five minutes for a man to awaken and fully react out of a deep sleep.[6]

Mosby and his men wore Confederate uniforms on missions so that they could claim their rights as prisoners of war if captured. But using disguise and perfidy was just as illegal as being out of uniform—under international law the penalty was to be shot or hanged. Ignoring this provision, Mosby and his men frequently masqueraded as the enemy. During cold weather they wore Union overcoats, and when they had Union prisoners they would place them in front to create the appearance of Union cavalry. They usually marched in leisurely go-as-you-wish style like friends out for a ride, but for disguise they would form in column of fours and appear to be well-drilled blueclads. When it rained they wore rubber ponchos convenient for approaching the enemy with revolvers drawn, concealed under the rain garments.

Mosby achieved the objective of using fear as a force multiplier, diverting several times his own number from the Union army and creating disruptions and false alarms. "A most exaggerated estimate of the number of my force was made," he wrote. He seemed to possess a sixth sense, enabling him to sense enemy weaknesses. Like an entrepreneur forecasting the business cycle, he had a tremendous instinct to select targets at the opportune time and place for maximum impact. Part of it was vigilance and alert scouting, but Mosby's record of locating and attacking weaknesses in enemy defenses was almost uncanny. A Union cavalry officer in the Army of the Potomac recognized it when he wrote: "Even now, from the tops of the neighboring mountains, his hungry followers are looking down upon our weak points."[7]

Time and again Mosby danced on the nerves of opponents where they were most vulnerable. Philip Sheridan had great personal pride in his ability as a supply officer, and one of the last things he wanted was to have some of his wagons captured by guerrillas. Henry W. Halleck feared that Mosby would make headlines on his watch defending Washington and stain his reputation. Elizabeth Custer worried that Mosby might capture her beloved new husband, George. Mosby's psychological war even went to the extent of sending a lock of his hair to Abraham Lincoln; even though it was only a joke, it reminded Lincoln that outside the Washington defense perimeter Mosby reigned.

Mosby realized that making his name feared would give his warfare greater emotional impact. He insisted that his men make it clear when they attacked that they were "Mosby's men." Rangers learned that the word "Mosby" was so powerful that it was useful in subduing a guard and preventing him from yelling or shooting. "I am Mosby," a Ranger would whisper, and sometimes the captive would go into a daze, bowing his head and trembling in fear. When ordered to walk, one prisoner staggered as if drunk, another became nauseated and vomited, and another fell on his knees and raised his hands, pleading for life. When a Union soldier disappeared, his friends would say, "Mosby has gobbled him up," or "He has gone to Andersonville."[8]

Union opponents said Mosby's men seemed to be "almost intangible" demons and devils, and myth claimed that when they scattered into the mountains the tracks of their horses suddenly disappeared. "Nobody ever saw one;" a Union officer wrote, "they leave no tracks, and they come down upon you when you least expect them." Northern journalists characterized them as "rebel devils," horse thieves, "skulking guerillas," "these nuisances that go on legs," gang of murderers and highway robbers, accursed poltroons, cutthroats, "picket shooting assassins and marauding highwaymen," "worse than assassins," and "lawless banditti." Union horsemen named their area "a nest of guerrillas," "Devil's Corner," "The Trap," and "Mosby's Confederacy."[9]

By the close of the war he had made himself the single-most-hated Confederate in the North. Northern newspapers designated him "the devil," Robin Hood, horse thief, bushwhacker, marauding highwayman, murderer, rebel assassin, notorious land pirate, and guerrilla chief. *Jack Mosby, the Guerrilla,* a dime novel published with a yellow paper cover in 1867, described him as a tall and powerful desperado with a black beard, a cruel, remorseless man who enjoyed cutting men apart with his tremendous saber and riddling them with bullets from a varied assortment of pistols on his belt. In the book, he had his sweetheart make love to Union officers to lure them into his hands and delighted in hanging them by their arms and kindling a fire under their feet to force them to talk. In the cheap woodcut on the cover he appeared in a room in the Astor House in New York City, pouring Greek fire on his bed. Mosby was so well hated that into the next generation Northern mothers quieted their children with, "Hush, child, Mosby will get you!"[10]

On the other side, Southerners admired Mosby as a great hero. His portrait appeared in the book *The War and Its Heroes,* published in Richmond in 1864. Southern journalists considered him a "daring and distinguished guerilla chief" who made the country seem literally alive with guerrillas. Southern people named babies for him and told the tale that one day in the Shenandoah Valley a Union officer knocked on the door of a plantation house. A woman slave answered the door, and he asked if anybody was home. "Nobody but Mosby," she answered. "Is *Mosby* here?" he inquired excitedly. "Yes," she answered, and he jumped on his horse and rode away. Shortly, he returned, surrounding the house with a company of cavalry. He came to the door and asked if Mosby was still there. "Yes," the woman said, inviting him in. "Where is he?" he demanded, and she pointed to her infant son in a cradle and proudly announced: "There he is. I call him 'Mosby,' Sir, 'Colonel Mosby,' that's his name."[11]

On slow news days during the weeks of lull between battles, newspaper editors satisfied the hunger for war news with blockade-runner and guerrilla stories. Minor dispatches on Mosby were clipped and reprinted, making national news on both sides. Many days the same newspaper had several different accounts of his exploits, and the *New York Herald* probably set the record on October 15, 1864, with nine Mosby articles, most reporting his Greenback Raid on the Baltimore and Ohio Railroad the previous day. He encouraged publicity, attempting to counter the myth that his men were criminals. When he captured Northern war correspondents he provided them fine food and cigars and turned on his charm, giving them some of their most colorful copy.[12]

John Hunt Morgan became a romantic hero of the Southern people, the symbol of guerrilla war and primary model for the Confederate Partisan Ranger Act. Mosby was the most successful partisan commissioned under the law. Morgan was killed September 4, 1864, and three days later the *Richmond Examiner* proclaimed Mosby "our prince of guerillas." Southern news reports on Morgan were heroic in tone; Mosby articles were businesslike and factual like market reports. Under the banner "Mosby at Work," statistics ticked off how many wagons he had burned and how many Yankees he had killed, wounded, or captured. Recounting the story of his capture of an infantry company guarding Duffield's Depot on the Baltimore and Ohio Railroad without firing a shot, the *Richmond Dispatch* related that, when the besieged Federals inquired what terms of surrender he offered, Mosby said: "Unconditionally, and that very quickly."[13]

Morgan and Stuart won the hearts of young women and Thomas J. "Stonewall" Jackson the adoration of grandmothers; Mosby had female admirers, but they made him feel uncomfortable. When the Confederate capital extended Mosby a hero's welcome in late January 1865 and the

Virginia legislature and Confederate House of Representatives honored him, young women from the gallery rushed to obtain his autograph, and he wrote his wife Pauline that it was more frightening than being in battle. "If there had been any decent way of doing so I wd. have backed clean out," he declared. Many young men daydreamed of fighting by his side, and Southern civilians identified with his attitude of defiance and irrepressible perseverance. "The whole Yankee army harks to Jack Mosby," wrote Confederate Bureau of War chief Robert G.H. Kean in his diary.[14]

Probably the highest praise that Mosby received in the war appeared in the *Richmond Whig* on October 18, 1864. He had been in Richmond recently, convalescing from a wound, and a few days later had returned to duty and raided Salem, temporarily halting Union construction on the Manassas Gap Railroad, and he had struck the B&O Railroad with the Greenback Raid.

> The indomitable and irrepressible Mosby is again in the saddle carrying destruction and consternation in his path. One day in Richmond wounded and eliciting the sympathy of every one capable of appreciating the daring deeds of the boldest and most successful partisan leader the war has produced— three days afterwards surprising and scattering a Yankee force at Salem as if they were frightened sheep fleeing before a hungry wolf—and then before the great mass of the people are made aware of the particulars of this dashing achievement, he has swooped around and cut the Baltimore and Ohio road—the great artery of communication between East and West, capturing a mail train and contents, and constituting himself, by virtue of the strength of his own right arm, and the keen blade it wields, a receiver of army funds for the United States. If he goes on as he has commenced since the slight bleeding the Yankees gave him, who can say that in time we will not be able to stop Mr. Trenholm's machine, and pay our army off in greenbacks. If he has not yet won a Brigadier's wreath upon his collar, the people have placed upon his brow one far more enduring.[15]

After the Stoughton Raid gossip spread among Union troops at Fairfax Court House, where the raid had occurred, that Mosby had come into town a few days before in disguise and toured the homes where Stoughton and his officers slept. Later a tale went abroad that, one day when he was surrounded by Union troops in a town, he had changed his uniform for "the coarse spun habiliments of a non-combatant" and joined the crowd of civilians watching the Yankees search for him. Stories circulated that he wandered about Union camps at night, a tall man with a flowing beard and long staff, sometimes dressed as a beggar. "Yet rumor made him every thing—A farmer—woodman—refugee," wrote Herman Melville.[16]

Stories placed him in disguise in Alexandria and Washington. Raconteurs said that he went into Alexandria one evening and had dinner at the Marshall House Hotel on the corner of King and Pitt Streets. Another tale had him dressing as a Union officer and crossing the Long Bridge to shop on Pennsylvania Avenue. One morning the rumor circulated that the previous evening he had been drinking at Willard's Hotel; and becoming friendly with a real Union officer, Mosby said, "I am often in Washington." The officer invited him to spend the night in his room, and Mosby accepted. The next morning Mosby departed before dawn, leaving a note on the bureau informing his host that he had spent the night with Mosby. In April 1865, shortly before Lincoln's assassination, Grant's wife, Julia, was out to dinner with Mrs. Rawlins, wife of Grant's chief of staff, John A. Rawlins. They noticed two men at a nearby table staring at them and attempting to hear their conversation. Mrs. Rawlins said, "I believe they are a part of Mosby's guerrillas." But Mosby's favorite was the official report by Secretary of War Edwin Stanton that he was in Washington with John Wilkes Booth on the night of Lincoln's assassination. "I never went to a place in disguise in my life," he said.[17]

In the Army of the Potomac men developed an inordinate desire to see him. A Union soldier captured by Mosby's men said, "Well, boys, you are a rare set of fellows. Is your colonel along? For of all men I desire most to see him." On September 1, 1864, Sheridan's army was camped in a wooded ravine near Charlestown, West Virginia. Suddenly about twelve men from the 23rd Ohio Infantry came running between the tents into the open ground, swinging their hats and yelling, "See the prisoners! Mosby a prisoner." Men dropped their letter-writing and card-playing and joined the crowd rushing toward Sheridan's headquarters nearly a mile away. Officers left their tents on the ridge and joined the stampede, major generals and all. Soon, about ten thousand men were running, and when they reached headquarters they learned that it was only a "sell," a joke. All joined in laughing and shouting, including Col. Rutherford B. Hayes, who had no idea that one day he would be president and would meet Mosby and appoint him to an office in his administration.[18]

After Lee had surrendered and when Mosby was negotiating his own surrender with Gen. Winfield S. Hancock, he sent his surgeon, Aristides Monteiro, and second-in-command, Lt. Col. William H. Chapman, to meet with Hancock in Winchester. A rumor circulated in Hancock's army that Mosby was coming, and the men gathered in the streets, shoulder to shoulder, a sea of blue uniforms, making it difficult to pass. "Mosby, which is Mosby?" they shouted, and Monteiro and Chapman pointed at each other. They reached Hancock's house and had a cordial meeting. When it was over and Hancock accompanied them to the front door, the crowd had increased, and soldiers were pressed against the iron fence on the lawn and blocking the gate. "It is rumored that Colonel Mosby is here," Hancock said with a smile. "Observe the curiosity of the army to see your leader. Gentlemen, it is impossible for you to go out by the front gate." Two Union colonels escorted them through the alley behind the house.[19]

People expected his men to be huge, hard-looking, and ferocious. When a group of women from New England saw a few of them as prisoners under guard in the slave pen in Alexandria, one exclaimed: "Good Gracious! They look just like our people!" In reality they were young, intelligent, smart-looking soldiers with clean uniforms, ornate saddles and bridles, and splendid horses that they rode with accomplished familiarity. They wore high cavalry boots, gray or blue trousers, gray uniform jackets, and gray felt or slouch hats, some with ostrich plumes. They looked very self-confident, and their eyes had the sharp glint of hunted men, ready to shoot. One night three of them stood around the bed of a *New York Herald* reporter they were capturing, and he feigned illness. The one pointing his revolver in the man's face quietly said, "You get up or I'll blow your brains out."[20]

When people finally had a look at Mosby, they reflected that they would never have imagined him a dashing hero. "I could scarcely believe that the slight frame before me could be that of the man who had won such military fame by his daring," wrote one of his men. He was a young man, twenty-seven years old when the war began and twenty-nine when he went partisan. He appeared to be of medium height, and his movements were brisk and sprightly, his steps energetic. He had small feet and hands and light-brown hair, wore a full beard at times and was clean-shaven at times, and was so thin his uniform looked several sizes too

large. Caring nothing for military bearing, when standing around talking to his men he clasped his hands behind his back or folded his arms in
front, whatever felt comfortable. Legend said that he wore a scarlet cape
and hat with an ostrich plume, and he had such outfits and wore them a
few times in action, but usually when raiding he dressed like his men. He
looked his best on a moving horse, for he rode like an aristocratic Southern gentleman, with elegance and grace.[21]

People who knew Mosby considered him unique; they had never
seen anyone like him. Those who knew him best and loved him most felt
entirely comfortable in his presence, but they realized that there was something mysterious about him that seemed beyond comprehension. Why
did he have such extraordinary inner strength, such tremendous self-
discipline? What constantly flowing spring gave him such uncommon
ability to turn adversity into opportunity? And why did he seem to possess two natures so strikingly obvious that one could distinguish them
on his face? With his soldiers and with friends and family he was kind
and generous, and when his gentle side was ascendant his smile was warm,
his dark blue eyes twinkled with charm, and he spoke in a voice low and
soft. On these occasions his conversation was that of a classical scholar
and professional attorney, with a winning sense of humor.

But in the presence of the enemy or in times of conflict, Mosby's
appearance and manner changed. His eyes burned with a piercing glow
and shifted quickly, side-to-side, and his voice rose, loud and high-pitched;
his smile became grim and firmly set. When his conflict side arose, a fire
burning deep within came into his expression, turning his sharp-pointed
nose and thin face into the appearance of a very angry hawk. His manner
became taciturn, and his enemies said he was cold-hearted and cruel. In
a fight, "he looked like a different man," observed his friend and surgeon
Monteiro. "He seemed to possess two distinct and separate natures."
Understanding this mystery provides the key to appreciating the strengths
and weaknesses of this great man.[22]

# 2

# The Weakling and
# the Bullies

Mosby was weak, frail, and sickly in childhood and youth, and he heard family doctors telling his parents that he had a predisposition to consumption, the nineteenth-century term for tuberculosis. "In my youth I was very delicate and often heard that I would never live to be a grown man," he wrote.[1] His persistent cough and weakened condition brought relief from farm chores and unusual pampering from his mother and other family members. But in antebellum Southern society, people measured worth by appearance, and at school he became a victim of bullies. He could have withdrawn into shyness and lost self-esteem, but instead, with great strength and self-confidence derived from his home sanctuary, he fought back, ferociously counterattacking every challenger and developing a deep sense of justice and an unusual pattern of life.

The most influential person in Mosby's childhood and youth was his mother, Virginia Jackson McLaurine Mosby. Born in Powhatan County, Virginia, May 15, 1815, she was small and attractive, with dimples in her cheeks and a friendly smile, and eyes that beamed with spirited brilliance. She was intelligent, witty, and charming, a kind and generous neighbor and friend. With extraordinary physical and emotional strength, she had eleven children and lived to the age of eighty-one. Her birth came four months after the battle of New Orleans, and it was appropriate that her middle name honored heroic Andrew Jackson, for she had the same iron will as "Old Hickory." Nearly everyone recognized her "great decision and strength of character." Mosby said she had a "strong individuality" that "impressed itself on all around her" and declared that, if she had been in command of the Confederate army, the South would have won the war. An unconfirmed story circulated that a few weeks after Appomattox she was on a train that stopped at a trestle in hazardous disrepair. All the other passengers got off to walk across the bridge rather than risk the danger of the train falling into the chasm, but she refused, insisting that she had a through ticket. According to the tale, the engineer and Virginia crossed safely, and the next day the bridge collapsed.[2]

She was a devoted mother, an ideal exemplar of the significant changes in child-rearing and family relations that had occurred in America by her generation. Helena M. Wall, in *Fierce Communion: Family and Community in Early America,* wrote that in the late eighteenth century there arose a new emphasis on the mother's role in child rearing; patriarchy declined, and the mother moved to the forefront and began practicing the doctrine of the "best interests of the child." In *Inside the Great House: Planter Family Life in Eighteenth-Century Chesapeake Society,* Daniel B. Smith agrees that, in eighteenth-century Chesapeake society, authoritarianism declined and children became the center of attention of the family. Parents became friends and hoped that the emphasis on early childhood nurturing would develop self-reliance, independence, and strength.[3]

Virginia married Alfred Daniel Mosby, born in Nelson County, Virginia, on December 9, 1809. He attended Latin Grammar School in Buckingham Court House and according to family tradition attended Hampden-Sydney College. There is no record of his enrollment, but he may have studied informally under one of the professors. An admirer of Thomas Jefferson, he believed in education; and, once he could afford it, for the younger children, he hired Abby Southwick, a tutor from Massachusetts. He was physically strong, quiet, and gentle, with enough self-confidence to marry and be satisfied with a strong, articulate wife who dominated family life. He agreed with Virginia that the children were the greatest reason for living and the most important source of happiness and comfort in life. Nine of their eleven survived past the age of five, and the highlight of Alfred's life was going to church on Sunday morning in a carriage brimming with babies and young children, two sons dressed like him with cravat and vest, and six or seven daughters arrayed in bright dresses and hair in curls and bright ribbons.[4]

Alfred and Virginia came from well-established families of the middling gentry in the Virginia Piedmont. According to family historian James H. Mosby, the Mosbys traced back to Edward Mosby, who emigrated from England to Charles City County, Virginia Colony, in 1635. Edward

Mosby (1665–1742), born in Henrico County and possibly Edward the immigrant's son, married Sarah Woodson, and they lived in Henrico County, where they had seven sons and one daughter. Two of the sons, Hezekiah and Jacob, married sisters from Goochland County, and the father of the brides, Nicholas Cox, gave the couples land as wedding presents. He gave Hezekiah Mosby, John S. Mosby's great-great grandfather, and his bride, Elizabeth Cox, seven hundred acres and gave Jacob Mosby and Susannah Cox six hundred acres. In about 1735 both couples settled down to farm their land along the Middle Road, U.S. Route 60 today, about thirty-five miles west of Richmond, the future capital of Virginia. Eventually Goochland County was divided and the area became part of Cumberland County; in 1777 the locality became part of Powhatan County, named for Chief Powhatan, father of Pocahontas.[5]

Hezekiah and Jacob were soon joined by their younger brother Benjamin Mosby, who opened "Mosby's Tavern" on the Middle Road and became the most prominent member of the Mosby family in America in his generation. An entrepreneur, Benjamin knew how to attract business—besides locating the tavern on the road into the frontier, at his own expense, on the site of his tavern he erected and provided Cumberland County its courthouse, jail, pillory, and stocks. This made the tavern the center of the community on court days, militia training days, and race days scheduled in the racetrack across the road.[6]

Hezekiah, on his farm a few miles west of the tavern, practiced diversified farming; and, with exports increasing and the population of Virginia expanding, he eventually owned 950 acres and 11 slaves. He bequeathed 475 acres to his son Daniel Mosby, the great-grandfather of John S. Mosby. Daniel moved to Albemarle County by 1782, and in 1789, to Amherst County, in the part that became Nelson County in 1807. There, on the waters of Dutch Creek, Daniel farmed 641 acres and owned 22 slaves. He married Sarah Hankins and they had seven children, including John H. Mosby, John S. Mosby's grandfather. John H. Mosby was attentive to his parents, who deeded him three hundred acres in gratitude.[7]

John H. Mosby was mindful generally, eventually becoming one of the most successful farmers in Nelson County. On 2,627 acres, with 35 slaves, he grew tobacco, corn, and wheat and raised livestock. He married Jane Ware of Goochland County, April 11, 1799, and an unconfirmed family tradition held that Jane was a cousin of William Henry Harrison, future president of the United States. John S. Mosby's father, Alfred, believed the tradition and named his younger son William Harrison Mosby and a daughter born in 1841, Isabella Harrison Mosby, for President Harrison. When John H. Mosby died in 1839, his executors were bonded at $70,000, and he willed 988.5 acres in separate plots to son Alfred, John S. Mosby's father.[8]

Mosby's mother's family, the McLaurines, proudly claimed a Scottish heritage. When Mosby was a child, his mother kept the McLaurine plaid in a frame over the mantel and on the wall a picture of the McLaurine monument in Edinburgh. Family tradition told of a marriage connection to Rob Roy MacGregor, the hero of Scottish history made famous in Sir Walter Scott's novel *Rob Roy.* "I suppose we are descended from that Union," Mosby wrote, "& that we have the blood of the Highland Chief." In the Civil War he was proud to be called a "modern Rob Roy."[9]

The first of the family to move to America was J. Robert McLaurine, who was born in Scotland and as a young man left for Virginia in 1750. John S. Mosby's maternal great-grandfather, he lived in Williamsburg where he soon married Elizabeth Blakely, daughter of a local merchant. Then, on May 16, 1752, he became rector or pastor of Southam Parish, the parish of the Anglican church that included Hezekiah and Jacob's farms and Benjamin's tavern. The glebe, a plantation provided by the church for the pastor's home and support in addition to his salary, was a few miles east of the Mosby tavern and farms. The central church in the parish was the Peterville Church, on the Middle Road a few miles from the glebe. Robert served as pastor for over twenty-one years, and the parishioners loved him and his wife Elizabeth, finally honoring them with burial under the chancel of the church.[10]

As pastor of the established church, Robert was a prosperous gentryman. With his salary of cash and tobacco and earnings from the glebe, he purchased 633 acres of land and 21 slaves. The Anglican churches in Virginia were self-governing; and in the absence of a bishop, laymen served as vestry, hired the pastor, repaired the glebe, and assisted with the political, moral, and social welfare responsibilities of the church. This brought Robert together with the Mosby family, who along with a few others dominated ecclesiastical and political matters in the community. Benjamin Mosby erected a gallery in the Peterville Church. Benjamin's son Littleberry Mosby Sr. served as vestryman and church warden, supervised repairs on the glebe, and took charge of building an almshouse. The church paid another of Benjamin's sons, Poindexter Mosby, to take a destitute man into his home.[11]

The church required educated clergy, and Robert was a pastor-teacher, with emphasis on the teaching. One symbol of his love for teaching was the decoration on the lengthy wall of the dining room of the glebe. He purchased linen wallpaper of life-size scenes from the 1699 romance novel *Les aventures de Telemaque* by French Bishop Fenelon. The novel adapted the story of Homer's *Odyssey* with the goal of teaching the young grandson of King Louis XIV how to meet the challenges of life. Robert used another room for a library and, with his collection of books, taught many young scholars in the parish, including his son James.[12]

In addition to an appreciation for learning, James McLaurine, Mosby's grandfather, inherited 316.5 acres from his father, land that Robert had purchased from Poindexter Mosby. On this property in the Mosby neighborhood, James erected "Edgemont," a farmhouse north of the Middle Road, by then called Old Court House Road. The house was near the western county line in Powhatan County, and the farm was in both Powhatan and Cumberland County to the west. Today the site is located west of Ballsville Road and north of U.S. Route 60. James grew tobacco, oats, and wheat and raised cattle and sheep. He accumulated 1,345 acres in 3 plots, had 19 slaves, and invested in manufacturing with Littleberry Mosby Jr. The family dining room had fine china, silverware, and walnut furniture, and the master bedroom was furnished in mahogany. He loaned money to several people, including his children.[13]

James married Catherine Steger, a neighbor from a prominent Powhatan County family. One of her brothers, John H. Steger, was a justice and sheriff; and his son, John O. Steger, Catherine's nephew, later became an attorney in Richmond and married a sister of John Esten Cooke, the famous novelist and historian who served with Mosby as a member of Stuart's cavalry. James and Catherine McLaurine had two sons and seven daughters, and the youngest daughter was Mosby's mother, Virginia.[14]

Mosby was born at Edgemont on December 6, 1833, when it was still the home of his mother's parents. Virginia was eighteen years old and had already borne one child, Cornelia, who had failed to gain weight and soon died. For this second lying-in she turned to the most popular alternative medicine in the South at the time—Thomsonianism. Thomsonians followed the theories of Samuel Thomson (1769–1843) of New Hampshire, who taught that in cases of difficult deliveries the taking of the laxative calomel and the use of bleeding prescribed by the regular physicians were to be avoided. Instead, the Thomsonian midwife encouraged natural labor and delivery without intervention. If a problem developed, she would calm the patient with vomiting induced by the emetic *lobelia inflata,* commonly known as Indian tobacco. Thomson's method of childbirth was more natural and less hazardous for the mother and child. Five weeks after John was born, Virginia wrote, "I suffered greatly during my confinement, being threatened with the milk leg and would have had it dreadfully if I had not have had a Tomsonian [sic] attendance. I never got out of my room until my month was out. I am now very well and fat and I have one of the finest children I ever saw at its age. He is a remarkably fine child larger now than my dear little Cornelia was at her death. . . . He has fair skin and hair and very dark blue eyes. Some say it will be black though I don't think so myself. He is right pretty, but not as much so as my other baby was."[15]

The baby was born in Powhatan, but Alfred and Virginia made their home in the Mosby community in Nelson County, about fifty miles west of Powhatan, near Murrell's Shop. It was off the beaten path in the foothills of the Blue Ridge Mountains. Alfred worked diligently and succeeded, paying taxes in 1836, the year John was three, on four slaves, four horses, and a carriage. Three years later, when John was six years old, Alfred's father died, and he received his inheritance. He and Virginia might have remained in Nelson County except for John's education. The boy attended a small country school and learned the alphabet at the age of six, but, one day about four weeks into the term, the schoolmaster went home for lunch, became intoxicated, and walking back to school fell down beside the road and went to sleep. The older boys found him, gathered him up, and carried him to school, and in a drunken state he taught the remainder of the day. John had never seen a person under the influence before, and the experience left him a teetotaler. At the age of twenty he attended a temperance camp and was never tempted by alcohol.[16]

Another more basic pattern began forming in his life in his first month of education. He was so frail and sickly, his mother sent a young male slave to escort him to and from school. One day Mosby asked the servant to stay all day, and at playtime the older boys forced the African American onto a block and "auctioned" him to the highest bidder. Mosby thought it was a real sale and felt terrified, helpless, and abused. The school closed after the incident of the drunken teacher, and, while John had learned to spell, he could not read. Later, the family would employ Abby Southwick, but that was beyond their means for now. Therefore, when John was seven years old, they moved to Albemarle County, which had abundant opportunity: eighteen academies and the University of Virginia.[17]

On January 4, 1841, Alfred borrowed money to purchase "Tudor Grove," a 397.5-acre farm four miles south of Charlottesville on the Old Lynchburg Road. The land was fertile; and, by growing wheat, corn, and oats and raising cattle, hogs, and sheep, he paid the debt in three years and held clear title. The sun shone on the Mosbys of Tudor Grove, nestled peacefully on a ridge with fields sloping behind the house toward the pine-covered Blue Ridge Mountains, their lofty summits rising in regular succession in the west, mingling with the blue sky. From the back porch John watched clouds envelop the mountains and saw thunderstorms sweeping across and rolling off into the horizon in the southwest. From the front lawn he had a clear view of Thomas Jefferson's Monticello and at night saw the lights in the windows of the mansion. When he came home from school and turned into the lane and passed through the large black oak and white oak trees that sheltered the house from the view of passersby on the road, he had a feeling of separation from the outside world. This was home, and it was an ideal sanctuary, just as his parents had intended.[18]

He learned to read in a nearby log schoolhouse but was still frail and still a victim of bullying. The widow teacher gave him the only whipping he received in school, for fighting with her son. At the age of ten he attended college preparatory school in a small brick building at "The Grove," a home on the south side of Main Street in Charlottesville. He rode to school on his mare with his horse's feed on one side of the saddlebags and his lunch on the other. He failed to study regularly, hated sports, and was not a good student, except in literature, which he enjoyed. His ill health made him irritable, and this made him an even more inviting target of bullies. Many years later, during one of his visits to Charlottesville after he was famous, he recognized Charles Price in the crowd of hero-worshipers gathering to see him. Mosby laughingly recalled that in school at "The Grove" he had had many fights, and the only one he did not lose was the bout with Charlie. "I suppose you would have licked me too, had we not been parted. Boys, Charlie, are the meanest things in the world. At least I think so. The larger ones invariably take advantage of the smaller ones."[19]

The contrast between his experience at school and life at home made a great impression on him. At school they called him "John" and regarded him as an unpopular, crabby, "hard student," but at home he was "dearest Jack," the center of attention. From the beginning, his mother, having lost little Cornelia, gave him an unusual share of attention and care. He was the eldest surviving child, "our dearest one," she said. The attention continued because he never gained weight—no matter how much he ate—and he remained sickly and delicate. Dr. John C. Hughes treated him for years and advised his mother to always provide him the most favorable circumstances or he might develop consumption and die.[20]

At home everyone pampered Jack. It was not difficult because with family and friends he was unselfish, gentle, and kind, with a sprightly personality that gave him the ability to enter a room and light it up with his buoyant wit and invigorating charm. The next child was Victoria, born in Nelson County five or six years after him. Then came Isabella Harrison, who was born in 1841 and died in 1846, followed by Eliza, Blakely, Lelia, William Harrison, Lucy, Florence, and Ada—seven sisters who lived and a brother, all considerably younger. As the sickly older brother, he was excused from farm work and left free to play with the youngsters, swinging on grape vines, romping with them in the house, and racing around the lawn with one of the children on his back, pretending to be a runaway horse. He caught his first fish in the creek near the road with a line and pin hook made by his mother, and, when he rose before daybreak to hunt squirrels in the hickory and oak forests, a slave cook had coffee ready for him in the kitchen.[21]

Mosby therefore developed an extremely dynamic bipolar personality. His internal evaluation of himself formed at home contradicted and was threatened by the external opinions at school. A home environment of love and support gave him self-confidence and great self-esteem. His mother loved him intensely; she was right, and the outsiders were wrong. He looked to her as the strongest person in his family and selected her as his mentor, his champion and oracle. Some victims of bullying turn inward and become shy and withdrawn, but, with his tremendous inner strength, he always counterattacked. He lost the fights physically but showed himself and the bullies that he was fearless. Virgil Carrington Jones, in his classic biography *Ranger Mosby,* published in 1944 a..d based on interviews with Mosby's children and others who had known him, pointed out that Mosby's dominant trait was his tendency to fight. Jones entitled his chapter on Mosby's birth "To Virginia a Fighter Is Born." Mosby entered the adult world with the pattern of behavior to react to opposition or criticism with an all-out attack. As a victim of bullying, he developed an unusually keen sense of justice that gave him a lifelong sense of deep resentment at the slightest injustice or dishonesty. He came to identify with the underdog striving against a stronger opponent. At about nine or ten he read Mason L. Weems's biography of Francis Marion, the guerrilla Swamp Fox of the American Revolution; and, reading in bed in his room, he would cry aloud with delight when Marion, with a few men, defeated larger detachments of the superior British army.[22]

Mosby's self-esteem was so strong that it gave him very unusual self-confidence and courage. He expected difficulties in life but was confident that he could overcome them. With an almost perfect self-reliance, in a crisis he was calm and cool and clear in judgment, all within his point of view. He was so strong that he never needed a morale boost in the form of leisure time or self-indulgent pleasure. There was never any decadence or corruption or dishonesty in his life; Mosby had no skeletons in his closet. But herein lay his great weakness—he felt so invulnerable that he had no need for the approval of society. His tendency toward confrontation overshadowed his desire for approval. In his inner circle of family and friends he had lasting intimacy, and he responded with totally unselfish generosity, loyalty, and love. But everyone outside that circle of intimates he regarded differently. He viewed the outside as hostile, a world to be attacked and conquered; the way to order and control his world and maintain his self-esteem was to conquer antagonists. This is why throughout his life Mosby's opponents considered him an indefatigable adversary.

Mosby spent most of his time at home reading literature and history, particularly from ancient Greece—"I was born a Greek," he said. At the age of sixteen, still living at home, he enrolled in the University of Virginia and emphasized Greek language and literature under Dr. Gessner Harrison in the School of Ancient Languages. Mosby was outstanding in Greek and Latin but barely passed his other courses. As he admitted, he was not regular in study habits, preferring to read Greek literature. He joined the Washington Society, a literary club, and completed the Greek program with honors, receiving a certificate on June 29, 1852. Under Thomas Jefferson's plan, the university gave no degrees; a student simply completed the basic curriculum in a school and then took whatever courses he desired. Mosby finished Greek at eighteen years of age and remained another year to round out his education in mathematics and other subjects.[23]

As a university student he earned the reputation of troublemaker.

It was illegal to ride fast on a horse through the streets, but in a "spirit of pure deviltry" he defied the ordinance by racing into town at full gallop. On campus the professors were in charge of discipline, and the students delighted in disobeying their strict rules. The great symbol of resistance to authority was the "calathump," a noisy student party, where, at night, the young men would don masks and parade along the walks of the pavilions and through the streets, calling each other Ezekiel, Jeremiah, Judas, or other Bible names, and yelling and blowing horns and whistles. One Saturday night they found a supply of empty crates and erected a large pyramid in front of the courthouse and placed a squealing pig on top. On Fool's Day, April 1, 1851, when Mosby was seventeen and still in his first year, he participated in a calathump. The fun was underway when George Slaughter, the town sergeant, grabbed one of the students, threw him down, and began pummeling him. Considering this unjustly brutal, Mosby struck Slaughter with his fists, kicked him, and broke a gun stock on his head. The authorities indicted Mosby; a jury found him guilty, and the court fined him ten dollars.[24]

For his second year, Mosby moved from home into Brock Boarding House on Main Street, a few blocks southeast of the campus, and, in October 1852, marched in another calathump. This time, his friend Charles Wertenbaker, later a Charlottesville cigar maker, struck Slaughter over the head with a pine table leg. Slaughter charged Wertenbaker with assault and summoned Mosby to testify as a witness. Mosby refused to appear, and the circuit court summoned him to appear at the next term and show cause or be fined for contempt of court. The charges against both were eventually dropped. The university and the city officials had been lenient, but the farmers and country people could not understand why such behavior should be tolerated; many citizens thought strong disciplinary action should be taken.[25]

Mosby became the scapegoat for the people's resentment, but it all began not with a calathump, but with a party at his parents' house on Saturday night, March 26, 1853. He invited several fellow students and included as a guest John Spooner, an accomplished violinist, and another young man who also played the violin. This caused conflict because George R. Turpin, a fellow student and son of a Charlottesville tavern keeper, wanted the musicians on the same night. When Spooner told Turpin that they had already accepted Mosby's invitation, Turpin replied, "Don't you know that Mosby don't care any thing for you, but he only wants you for your musical accomplishments?" The musicians kept their commitment, and Mosby's party was successful, but Spooner told Mosby what Turpin had said.[26]

Turpin was a notorious campus bully. He had slashed Frank Mannoni with a knife and beaten Fred H. Wills so badly with a rock that for a while it appeared that Fred would not recover. Turpin was large and athletic, and his modus operandi was to send an oral warning to the victim to prepare himself for a thrashing upon the next encounter. Undaunted, Mosby followed the code duello in defending his reputation and family honor; he wrote a letter to Turpin demanding an explanation and on Tuesday morning, March 28, sent it by a friend. Turpin read the letter and exploded, speaking of Mosby with contempt and issuing his usual notice: "I will see the damn rascal and eat him up, blood raw, on sight."[27]

At first Mosby decided to fight Turpin and absorb his customary beating. "I must be prepared to take the fare that others have received at his hands," he said upon receiving Turpin's response. He remained calm and, later that morning in mathematics, his worst subject, performed so well under Professor Courtenay's oral grilling in differential calculus that a classmate declared: "Jack, old boy, I believe you have made your examination. You curled old Profes!" Then, when Mosby went to the noon meal at his boardinghouse, there was Turpin, dining as a guest of a friend. Mosby knew this was the fateful meeting, and his deep sense of justice, reinforced by so many fights at school, overcame the restraint of his judgment. He borrowed an old pepperbox pistol, an early type of revolver with revolving barrels that looked like a pepper shaker. He loaded the gun and waited in the back porch, near the door of his room, at the top of the stairs to the dining hall on the floor below.[28]

Turpin was one of the last to leave. When he ascended the steps, there stood two of Mosby's friends and Mosby, with his right hand inside his jacket, holding the pistol. "I understand you have been making some assertions," Mosby began. Immediately, Turpin rushed at his frail victim, and Mosby took out the weapon and shot him, the bullet making a round hole in Turpin's high shirt collar, passing into his jaw and lodging in the muscles of his neck. Turpin claimed that Mosby drew the pistol before he attempted to seize him, but three witnesses testified that Mosby did not draw until Turpin rushed forward. "I did not wait to be eaten up," Mosby said. Some of the students took Turpin into one of the rooms, and a medical student stopped the bleeding until Dr. James L. Cabell of the medical school faculty arrived. The wound bled a great deal, but the bullet was removed and Turpin recovered. Through the years Mosby reflected on the shooting many times, and he could never see anything in his action other than crystal-clear justice—the underweight weakling had finally, with a gun, defeated a bully. In his seventy-seventh year he gave his final conclusion: "I have never done anything that I so cordially approve as shooting Turpin."[29]

Mosby and a friend went to Mosby's parents' home, and that evening he was arrested at Tudor Grove and committed to the county jail and denied bail. The grand jury indicted him on two counts—malicious shooting, a felony punishable by one to ten years in the state penitentiary, and unlawful shooting, punishable, at the discretion of the jury, by one to five years in the penitentiary or confinement in the county jail for not more than twelve months and a fine not exceeding five hundred dollars. Mosby's parents employed three of Charlottesville's most able and expensive attorneys for his defense. Alexander Rives and Egbert R. Watson would eventually rise to judgeships, and the leader, Shelton F. Leake, was a brilliant and witty criminal lawyer who had served in Congress and was now lieutenant governor of Virginia. The prosecutor was William J. Robertson, the youthful and talented commonwealth's attorney for Albemarle County who would later serve on the Virginia Court of Appeals and as an attorney would represent the family of Robert E. Lee in the case against the United States government for seizing Arlington. In 1888 Robertson would be elected first president of the Virginia Bar Association.[30]

Nineteen-year-old Mosby was arraigned in circuit court before Judge Richard H. Field at ten o'clock in the morning, Tuesday, May 17, 1853, and he pled not guilty. Three days later, on Friday, the jury was sworn and sequestered and the trial began. Testimony was heard that day and on Monday; on Tuesday, May 24, closing arguments were made and the jury retired. Three student eyewitnesses testified, two for the defense and one for the prosecution. All three swore that Mosby did not fire until Turpin lunged forward. Mosby's lawyers argued that he should be acquitted on the grounds of self-defense. Robertson's eloquent opening and closing statements lasted a total of seven hours, but he bore no ill will for Mosby. The difference in size and strength of the two men was obvious, and Turpin's reputation was well known. Mosby said later that there was nothing in Robertson's statements that offended or rankled him or his father. Robertson told the jury that he was doing his duty but that he wished this cup might have passed from him. Later, during the

Civil War, Mosby learned that even the judge had been on his side. On that occasion, Mosby was passing through Charlottesville, and Judge Field invited him home for dinner. "Well Mosby," he declared during the meal, "I always believed you did exactly right in shooting that fellow." Mosby gasped: "Why in the devil, then, didn't you tell the jury so?" "Ahhh," Field replied, and they both laughed heartily.[31]

The jury deliberated, and they were unable to agree. Four members argued that Mosby acted in self-defense and should be acquitted. Six were in favor of conviction of unlawful shooting with a lenient sentence of a brief imprisonment in the local jail. But two jurymen insisted that Mosby was guilty on both counts and should be sentenced to the penitentiary as a felon. Late in the day, the jury returned without a verdict. Field recommitted them to the sheriff overnight, with instructions to return the next morning at ten o'clock. He told them that, if they could not reach a verdict, Mosby would be kept in jail for six months awaiting another trial. Reflecting overnight on that fact, nine of the ten men who favored lenience decided that it would be no favor to Mosby to end in a hung jury; therefore, during the deliberations on Wednesday, May 25, they compromised and came into the courtroom with a verdict.[32]

Court Clerk Ira Garrett directed Mosby to stand, and Mosby rose and looked at the jury, eyes bright and clear, showing no sign of penitence or regret. The foreman read the verdict: innocent of malicious shooting, guilty of unlawful shooting, with a sentence of twelve months in the county jail and a fine of five hundred dollars. This was as lenient as the two hold-outs would accept. Under Virginia law this was the maximum sentence that could be given under the category of misdemeanor; if Mosby had been sent to the penitentiary for one year or more, he would have been a convicted felon. At the formal sentencing on May 30, Field ruled that the term of twelve months would date from May 25, and Mosby had to pay court costs. If, at the end of the twelve months' imprisonment, the fine and expenses were not paid, Mosby would remain in jail for the maximum of another six months.[33]

Mosby felt no guilt, but he was deeply hurt. Many years later, he wrote one of his grandsons that all the state of Virginia ever did for him was throw him in the Albemarle jail. Once, when he was wounded in the Civil War and on the way to Lynchburg to recover, he had an hour layover at the train station in Charlottesville. He was famous by then, and a crowd gathered. Among the sea of adulatory faces he saw Ira Garrett, the court clerk. "I felt then," he said, "that I was revenged for the verdict the people of Albemarle had pronounced against me." He felt vindicated with the county and the state, but almost to the end of his life he could not forgive the university for expelling him when he was in jail. He had someone check the records and learned that the faculty unanimously expelled him on April 5, 1853, eight days after the shooting and well before the trial. In 1915, when he was eighty-one, he found it ironic that the faculty invited him to speak on campus as an honored guest. "I am a no better person now than when I shot Turpin," he declared.[34]

The shooting represented Mosby's passage into manhood, and, while he would always intensely adore his mother, during the trial he found a new mentor, one who would enable him to make going to jail a positive experience. The jail was a small building on the public square, toward the rear, between the courthouse and the two-story row-house shops and stores that stood where Jackson Park is today. Jailor Wash Childs and his wife and their slave, Margaret, lived in the building, and at first Mosby stayed in the front, in the debtor's room. Nearly every day little boys walking by stopped at the window to talk briefly with him.[35]

A few days after the trial Robertson called and was surprised when Mosby came to the door with a book in his hand and greeted him pleasantly.

"What are you reading?" asked the prosecutor.

"Milton's *Paradise Lost*," Mosby answered, "and I hope soon to enjoy *Paradise Regained!*"

"You should do some writing," said Robertson. "John Bunyan, you know, wrote *The Pilgrim's Progress* in a prison cell."

"No, I have determined to study law. The law has made a great deal out of me. I am now going to make something out of the law."

"Fine. You may have the use of my library whenever you want it."[36]

During the remainder of Mosby's incarceration, Robertson taught him and became his friend and mentor. After the Civil War, Robertson associated with Mosby on cases in Warrenton, Virginia, and, when he was there, used Mosby's library. For many years Mosby kept Robertson's portrait on the wall of his home and, after the judge died in 1898, referred to his noble character and remembered him with lines from Byron's "Manfred": "The dead but sceptred sovereigns, who still rule / Our spirits from their urns."[37]

In the meantime, while Mosby read law, three of the jurors asked Leake to write a petition from the jury requesting a pardon, and nine jurors signed it. The petition reported on the division among the jurors, described their reasoning, and indicated that one of the two hold-outs "avowed in the Jury room feelings of the strongest dislike and prejudice" toward Mosby's father Alfred. The defense lawyers met and decided to circulate a separate petition among the citizens and send Alfred Mosby with the two petitions and other documents to Governor Joseph Johnson in Richmond. Alfred went to the university and throughout the community, obtaining 298 signatures, including those of at least 105 university students. Leake wrote a letter to the governor stating the facts of the case and requesting a pardon. He declared that under the circumstances nine out of ten men would have acted as Mosby did. "I do not hesitate to say that I would," he wrote. He indicated that Alfred Mosby was his friend and that the family was "of the highest respectability." Rives wrote a letter recommending Alfred as "one of our most respectable and amiable citizens, and all who know him, yearn for a speedy respite to the distress of himself and family." The attorneys emphasized that by June 21, 1853, after less than three months in jail, Mosby had developed a cough; and his health, and possibly his life, were in serious danger. They obtained certificates from Mosby's family physician and two other doctors well acquainted with his case. Dr. W.E. Bibb certified that Mosby's strongly developed predisposition to consumption might well kill him if he remained in jail. Dr. John C. Hughes agreed that the jury's sentence might be a sentence to death. Dr. J.W. Poindexter, the family physician, certified that, with Mosby's frail constitution, continued confinement would "produce *premature death.*"[38]

Late in June, Alfred went to Richmond and saw Governor Johnson. A respected and popular governor, he was born in New York, but had lived in Harrison County, in today's West Virginia, for many years and was the first Virginia governor from west of the mountains. He studied the documents and met with Alfred, telling him that the statements were *ex parte,* from only one side. He promised that if Alfred would obtain a certificate from the clerk of the court, the judge, or the prosecutor corroborating Leake's summary of the testimony, he would grant a pardon. Alfred returned to Tudor Grove with a glad heart, assuming that the pardon was won. There was great joy over the "*Glad Tidings*" in the governor's promise. "But alas!" wrote Mosby's mother, "our hopes & expectations was turned into grief." The court clerk refused to sign the required statement, claiming that he had heard only snatches of the testimony, and Field and Robertson also refused. If there had been a transcript, it could have been sent to the governor, but, sadly, there was none.[39]

On the other hand, the governor received a letter from D.W. Maupin, one of the jurors, opposing the pardon. And Joseph Points, an Albemarle resident who had not been on the jury, asked Johnson to deny the pardon and make an example of "a very troublesome young man." He claimed that many of the students who had signed the petition were minors, including one boy of age thirteen or fourteen who had signed "M.D." after his name. Nevertheless, Johnson had Secretary of State George W. Munford draft a pardon message, and he told Munford that, when the certification arrived from Charlottesville, he would approve the pardon.[40]

All of the efforts of Alfred and the lawyers and doctors had produced nothing but an impasse. Now, Mosby's mother took up her pen and wrote a classic letter of application for clemency for her beloved son. Using literature and history and a perceptive understanding of human nature, she pressed her case. She had heard that Johnson was "a man alive to all the finer feelings" and therefore would consider her plea. She requested that he use his authority to balance the tyranny of the jury that was swayed by one juror's hatred of Alfred and therefore had dealt as harshly with John as "in the days of the Bastile [sic] or the reign of Terror," and, while she lacked the eloquence of Cicero or the Magi, her love for her son sprang from as deep a fountain of feeling. She had dreamed the night before that she was meeting with the governor and he rebuffed her, but, just as she was leaving his office, he called her back and said that he would approve the pardon. In the dream she fell to her knees "with a heart overflowing with gratitude and love for you which were so very power full as to awaken me." Her whole family, she wrote, including eight children, were "in the deepest distress," all from the perfidy of one man, Turpin. "And now most Honourable Sir if you have any mercy left do if you please relieve my son from the bonds put upon him by injustice. I can say no more but only Hope."[41]

Answering for the governor, Munford wrote that Johnson felt deeply for her and that he would reconsider the case upon receiving a statement from the judge, prosecutor, or court clerk. The Mosbys reported this to their lawyers, and Leake wrote Munford, pointing out that such a statement could not be obtained and that there was no transcript of the trial. Pleading for Munford's intervention, Leake promised that if Munford was ever in jail, he would turn him out at the first opportunity. Leake mentioned that his efforts for Mosby's pardon were not for a fee. "The truth is I feel deeply for the young man & his family—all people of high standing." Munford and the governor reviewed the case again, and, in the absence of the requested document, Johnson decided on August 16, 1853, not to grant the pardon.[42]

When Virginia visited John in mid-September, she found him not in the debtor's room as before, but in the back room where there was no window and it was cold and damp. He had a cold, and his eyes were irritated from reading with inadequate light. She decided to write a second letter to the governor. This time she stressed that it was not John's fault that the clerk did not make a transcript of the trial and that hold-out juror John N. Hamner should be punished for prejudice against Alfred rather than young John, who "was acting in self defense from a bully of notorious character," a ruffian. She feared that he might die in the cold, damp jail. "My son is of a very weak delicate constitution . . . he has been delicate from his birth." She wrote that people were saying that Johnson had decided never to use the pardon power again, but she had confidence that he was more independent than that. She warned that a final rejection "would be too over power to my heart," but if he approved the pardon she would pray for him and his family for the rest of her life.[43]

At that point, Johnson was called home to Bridgeport to the bed-side of his wife, who was critically ill. On December 6, 1853, two days before she died, he decided to pardon Mosby and asked Munford to write to Virginia requesting that Leake's first letter be returned as evidence. When Munford's letter arrived at Tudor Grove, it brought great rejoicing. With "overflowing gratitude," Virginia immediately sent the letter to Jack and thanked Munford: "Your letter was indeed and in Truth a messenger of glad tidings and great joy, and has brightened up many sorrowfull hearts, it is as a ray of sunshine in our hitherto overcast & burdened minds, and I can never feel gratefull enough to our Noble Governor for what he has done." The pardon came on December 23, and on February 16, 1854, the legislature remitted Mosby's fine.[44]

Mosby's great emotional strength had turned misfortune into opportunity. After being in jail almost nine months he prepared to enter the practice of law and take on any challenge. He had selected a new mentor outside of his family, and Robertson was included in Mosby's inner circle. He entered adulthood with tremendous self-confidence, matched only by his accompanying weakness.

# 3

# "Virginia is my mother."

Mosby's conviction and incarceration had shattered the serenity of life at Tudor Grove; soon after his release from jail, the family moved to a farm in Fluvanna County. He continued reading law and on September 4, 1855, passed the bar under the examination of Judge Field and two other judges. Leaving home at the age of twenty-two, he opened a law practice in Howardsville on the James River in Albemarle County. There were few clients, and he was half-starved and homesick; but then an attractive nineteen-year-old woman from Kentucky came visiting relatives, and his mood brightened.[1]

When he first met Mariah L. Pauline Clarke, he knew immediately that she was unlike any other young lady that he had known. He noticed that Pauline's hairstyle and clothing were in fashion and she was attractive, with a well-shaped body, strong chin, well-proportioned nose, and comely mouth with a pretty little dimple in her upper lip. Her eyes gleamed with intelligence and zest for life, and when she smiled her face illuminated with congeniality. Mosby thought that, like his mother, here was a person who radiated affection, warmth, and love for family and friends.

Mosby soon learned that here was a rare woman whose self-confidence matched his own. And what was most astounding was that she could match him in conversation. She had a lively sense of humor and had read literature and history. She enjoyed talking about the Crusades and gossiping about King Henry VIII, Lady Jane Grey, and other English kings and queens; and she was interested in Robert the Bruce of Scotland, Rob Roy, and Robin Hood. Pauline had keen interest in newspaper editorials on national politics and world affairs, and Mosby was impressed that her father had been a member of Congress and in the last election was an elector for President Franklin Pierce.

Pauline's father was Beverly L. Clarke, a Virginia native who had moved with his parents to Kentucky at about fourteen years of age. Beverly was a handsome, well-educated attorney who ran for office and became one of the most respected statesmen in the Bluegrass State. He was known for sterling integrity, gentlemanly manners, and polished oratory. He served in the Kentucky House of Representatives from Simpson County and in 1847 began a single term in the United States House of Representatives. In 1855 he won the Democratic nomination for governor but lost to Know-Nothing or American Party candidate Charles S. Morehead.[2]

Beverly married his first cousin, Mariah Louisa Clarke, a devout Roman Catholic. They had a son, George W. Clarke, and three daughters. Following a Catholic tradition, they named all three in reverence for the Virgin Mary: Mariah (Pauline), Maria (called Delia) and Mary. Pauline was born on March 30, 1837. When she was eleven years old, her mother died. Beverly then married Zenobia Turner, also a Roman Catholic, and they had a son, Thomas H. Clarke. Beverly did not join the church himself until near the end of his life, but during the emotional 1855 governor's campaign, his opponents condemned him for having a Catholic wife. In 1858 President James Buchanan appointed him minister to Guatemala and Honduras, and his wife accompanied him to Central America. He was serving when he became seriously ill and was not expected to survive. A few months before his death on March 17, 1860, he was baptized, and when he died he was temporarily buried in the Church of San Francisco in Guatemala City. In 1868 the Kentucky legislature had his body reinterred with honors in Frankfort.[3]

Pauline visited Howardsville and met Mosby in June 1856, and that winter he visited her in Kentucky. They married on December 30, 1856, in the City Hotel in Nashville, Tennessee, with Father J. Schacht officiating.[4] The newlyweds lived in Howardsville, creating a harmonious, loving home. Pauline was entirely comfortable being married to a lawyer, the same profession as her father. Having grown up surrounded by politics and accustomed to the commotion and hubbub of political campaigns, she thrived on meeting new people and welcoming guests into their home. Like him she had great inner strength that gave her courage and composure and enabled her, on a daily basis, to live a buoyant life in good humor and with the conscious goal of making a loving home for her husband and children.

With no barriers of selfishness between them, John and Pauline formed an inner circle of total honesty and devotion. He enjoyed buying her candy, dresses, and other gifts. When away, he wrote frequently, addressing her as "My Dearest Pauline." She had two beautiful children before the war: May Virginia, born March 10, 1858, and Beverly C., born October 1, 1860. Later, when the two were fourteen and twelve, she beamed with pride in a letter to a relative: "I enclose May's and Bev's pictures for you all. I am sure this will make mine a welcome letter." Faithful to the Roman Catholic Church like her mother, she prayed with the children and enrolled them in convent schools when possible. When the seventh son, George Prentiss Mosby, died at the age of ten months, she had his monument engraved: "Gone to play with the Angels in Paradise."[5]

Pauline's deep religious faith, a source of her strength and serenity, was the only characteristic that Mosby did not share. Family tradition holds that he was baptized in the Methodist church, but he never gave much attention to religion. He sometimes talked of going to Heaven and after Pauline died said that he never had "gloomy views" of eternity, that it was the separation that was painful. When he was sixty-six years old, a relative asked him what church he attended and he answered, "I rarely go to any. Occasionally to the Catholic, because my wife was a Catholic & my children were educated Catholics." It never bothered him that the Roman Catholic church was a minority institution in the Protestant South, and he sincerely supported Pauline in her faith and her desire for a Catholic education for the children.[6]

Apparently Mosby continued practicing in Howardsville until November 1858, when he and Pauline and May moved west to Bristol on the Virginia-Tennessee border. Howardsville had too many lawyers and not enough business, but in Bristol Mosby was only the third attorney to hang a shingle, and the small town was booming. It was an unusual place, sitting half in Virginia and half in Tennessee, and for a hungry lawyer this doubled the opportunity. The railroad connecting East and West had opened six months before, and passengers heading west stepped off the cars of the Virginia and Tennessee Railroad in Virginia and walked across Main Street—the state border—into Tennessee to take the East Tennessee and Virginia Railroad going west. On both sides of the street new buildings were going up, including a third hotel, opened the year Mosby arrived. He rented space for his home and office on the Virginia side near the railroad depot and attended court in both Washington County, Virginia, and Sullivan County, Tennessee. In 1860 he purchased a town lot for four hundred dollars but was still renting when he left for the war. He paid state taxes on one slave, $150 of furniture, a clock, and one horse. Beverly was born, and they welcomed into their home two teenage girls: John's sister Blakely Mosby, and Pauline's sister Delia Clarke.[7]

As far as his income was concerned, when the election of 1860 came he should have supported either the Southern Democrat, John C. Breckinridge, or the Unionist, John Bell—nearly all of Washington County's voters voted for one or the other. But Mosby considered Bell's third-party campaign nothing more than a tea party. As a slave owner and the son of slave owners, he might have favored Breckinridge, but he was a former Henry Clay Whig and a Unionist opposed to secession. Therefore he announced for the Northern Democratic candidate, Stephen A. Douglas, and took a leading role in the local campaign. When Alabama secessionist William L. Yancey came to Abingdon to campaign for Breckinridge, Mosby went to see him to invite him to debate with a Douglas orator. He called at the home of former Virginia governor John Floyd, and someone introduced him to Yancey in the library. Yancey curtly said "No" and contemptuously brushed Mosby aside. "I shall never forget the arrogant & insulting way in wh. he treated me," Mosby wrote in 1902. By then Mosby wished that Yancey had not died during the war and could have lived to see the ruin that his fire-eating had wrought on the South.[8]

When the election occurred on November 6, Virginians voted viva voce, by voice vote, so it became general knowledge that Mosby was the only voter in his precinct to vote for Douglas. Washington County cast 1,178 votes for Breckinridge, 916 for Bell, and 56 for Douglas. Breckinridge carried all of the slave states except Virginia, Kentucky, and Tennessee— they voted for Bell. "I voted *against* the people with whom I lived," Mosby recalled. But voting for Douglas was one thing; opposing Virginia on secession was another matter entirely.[9]

South Carolina seceded on December 20, 1860; and by February 1, 1861, six additional states had left the Union. One morning in mid-January 1861, Mosby met his friend J. Austin Sperry, editor of the *Bristol News,* and challenged Sperry's editorial in that day's issue advocating secession. Mosby predicted that secession would mean a lengthy, bloody war, followed by a century of border feuding, and teased that he would like to be the hangman some day and be able to hang a secessionist. Sperry asked which side Mosby would fight for if war came. "I shall fight for the Union, Sir,—for the Union, of course, and you?" Sperry replied that he would fight for the South, and if they met in battle, he would run his bayonet through Mosby. "Very well," said Mosby and, paraphrasing Shakespeare's *Julius Caesar,* declared: "We'll meet at Philippi." In Act IV of the drama,

Caesar's ghost appears to Brutus in his tent and promises to reappear at Philippi, where in Act V the great battle of 42 B.C. occurs. Mosby was telling Sperry, a former teacher, that he would meet him in battle—Mosby in blue, Sperry in gray.[10]

Despite the vote against Lincoln in 1860, most of Mosby's neighbors in Washington County and most Virginians opposed secession until after the attack on Fort Sumter on April 12, 1861. But on April 15, Lincoln called for seventy-five thousand volunteers to invade the South, and two days later the Virginia convention passed an ordinance of secession. In the state referendum that followed, Washington County overwhelmingly approved. Now that Virginia was out of the Union, Mosby, like Robert E. Lee and many others opposing secession, could not bring himself to fight against his home state. In fact, three months before Virginia seceded and shortly before the conversation with Sperry, in late December 1860, Mosby had enrolled in the state militia. His friend and former University of Virginia classmate, William Blackford, invited him to join the Washington Mounted Rifles, a volunteer cavalry company forming in Abingdon. At the time, to stand for Virginia was to stand for the Union, and Mosby agreed, but he and most of the recruits seldom attended drill. Then upon Virginia's secession, Capt. William E. Jones called the company to arms, issued Confederate uniforms, and instructed the men to put their affairs in order.[11] Mosby went home to Bristol and walked into Sperry's newspaper office.

"How do you like my uniform?" he asked.

"Why, Mosby!" exclaimed Sperry. "This isn't Philippi, nor is that a Federal uniform."

"No more of that," Mosby said. "When I talked that way, Virginia had not passed the ordinance of secession. She is out of the Union now. Virginia is my mother, God bless her! I can't fight against my mother, can I?"[12]

Many years later he declared that states' rights were unconstitutional, and the only cause of the war was slavery, an institution that in retrospect he abhorred—one of the saddest sights he ever saw was the public auction in Abingdon in the summer of 1860, when several families were separated. In his postwar view, Lincoln freed more whites than blacks because he overthrew the "oligarchy of slave holders."[13]

After a few weeks of drilling in Abingdon, the company received orders to march to Richmond, and Mosby went home to say goodbye. He never forgot how difficult it was. Many years later during a visit to

Bristol, Mosby and Joseph W. Owen, one of his former Rangers, walked past the house where Mosby had lived. Pointing it out, Mosby said, "Joe, it was there I fought my hardest battle of the war, when I left my wife and children." The company departed Abingdon on horseback on May 30, 1861, marching the first day in the rain and mud. A person standing by the road watching the column pass that day could have easily selected him as the man most likely to drop out first. He weighed only 122.5 pounds, and he was the most frail and delicate soldier in the unit. He was a slouchy rider, and his indifference and distaste for military courtesy hung over him like a cloud. For all that he knew, getting wet and sleeping on the ground might bring on his predicted early death.[14]

But behold, to his great surprise his lungs cleared up, he could breathe freely, he enjoyed eating, and he began gaining weight—conditions that he had never experienced in his entire life. Describing how he slept on the ground, he wrote to his mother, "I never before had such luxurious sleeping." The homesickness lifted, and by the time they reached Richmond on June 17, 1861, after eighteen days of marching, he realized that military life thoroughly agreed with him. After a few pleasant days in Richmond, the command moved north a few miles to the camp of instruction at Ashland. There Mosby's parents visited, bringing a box of food, a daguerreotype of May, and a slave, Aaron, to serve as his body servant.[15] Aaron would cook, curry his horse, and care for his personal needs throughout the war.

And Pauline, back home in Bristol, was a bulwark of support. She wrote frequently, and he eagerly looked forward to her letters. She enclosed "dictated" notes from May and gave details of everyday happenings. She reported that she had planted a garden and that her teaching of literature with Blake and Delia was going well. She said that Delia had become so caught up in the war that like her brother-in-law she wanted to sleep outside. One day Pauline dressed in her finest outfit and took May and Beverly to have a daguerreotype made of the three of them to send him, and she sent him a lock of May's hair. She collected bills from his law practice and made investments. He sent her money and urged her to inform him if she needed anything. "Kiss my babes a thousand times for me & tell precious May to dream about me every night until I return," he wrote. "My love to Blake & Deal. Make them write to me."[16]

In camp most enlisted men preferred the company of other enlisted men. Mosby made friends with one private, Fountain Beattie, and they remained close to the end of their lives. However, for a second friend,

Mosby chose the company commander. When dismissed for the day, he would go to Captain Jones's tent, and they would talk far into the night. Both men hated sham and red tape, both neglected their personal appearance, and both had tasted life's suffering. Jones was nine years older, at thirty-seven years of age, and Mosby identified with him as the epitome of a trained military leader. A native of Washington County, he had graduated from West Point in 1848 and gone on duty with the Mounted Rifles on the frontier. After a few years he came home on furlough to marry his hometown sweetheart, Eliza M. Dunn, on January 13, 1852. Less than three months later, on their honeymoon voyage to his new assignment in Texas, a storm blew up at Pass Caballo and swept Eliza out of his arms and overboard, and she drowned. Jones was never the same; he remained a widower and could not forgive himself for not saving his bride or dying with her. In 1857 he resigned from the service and returned home to operate a large vineyard on his father's farm and live apart from society.[17]

He was short and scruffy-looking, in blue jeans and a tattered homespun coat, with an unkempt beard and receding hair line. He had piercing eyes and a surly expression, and usually seemed irascible and grouchy. Strict in discipline, he had inspection every morning, harshly scolding any man who had an ungroomed horse. In a high-pitched voice, he would scream: "Stand up firmly!" "Ragged! Ragged! It must be smooth! Some of you damned farmhands haven't got out of the bulrushes!" Later in the war during a march, he punished two men for pillaging dry goods—he forced the first to wear a hoop skirt around his neck and the other to ride around all afternoon holding his stolen umbrella over Jones's head.[18] But his men saw through the gruff exterior, realized that he cared deeply for them, and affectionately named him "Grumble Jones."

Mosby could not have selected a better mentor for his introduction into military life. He taught Mosby the importance of vigilance, showed him how to enforce discipline fairly, and by example demonstrated that the men appreciated efficient administration. In the beginning, somehow, he obtained the latest cavalry carbines, the scarce Sharps breechloaders that fired three times faster than muzzle-loaders. He acquired new uniforms from the state penitentiary, and as far as he was concerned their dun, or dull brownish-gray, color was fine. But when the men tried them on, everyone except Mosby and Beattie declared them too ugly to wear, took them off, and cast them in a heap. Wisely, Jones accepted their verdict and returned the garments. Mosby was so attentive, he even learned to avoid Jones's shortcoming of openly disagreeing with and disobeying his superior officers. He valued Jones's teaching so highly that, when a friend offered to obtain Mosby a commission, he declined, preferring to train as private under Jones.[19]

Eventually Mosby and Jones parted, and Mosby moved on to identify with Jeb Stuart as his next mentor. It seems unusual that in succession he became the protégé of two such opposite personalities. Stuart loved fancy uniforms, ostrich plumes, prancing horses, and elaborate parades, and he was dashing and handsome. Jones hated display and was surly and unattractive. But both were fighters and both realized that beneath Mosby's timorous exterior abided a soldier of great ability and strength, a fighter burning for a fight.

# 4

# Scouting behind Enemy Lines

Mosby distinctly remembered the first time he saw Jeb Stuart; he had never before seen such a gallant man. He thought Stuart looked like a Greek god or a hero from a romantic novel come to life. It was at Bunker Hill in the Shenandoah Valley at sunset on July 9, 1861, and Jones's company was arriving from Richmond to join Stuart's 1st Virginia Cavalry regiment screening the army of Gen. Joseph E. Johnston. The column topped a rise, and Mosby looked down on Stuart's camp in a little canyon between two slight ridges. He noticed that, instead of the holiday atmosphere of camps he had seen before, here everything was neat, orderly, and businesslike. The tents were in even rows, with the horses haltered to picket ropes and a flag waving over headquarters. Before the tents about forty-five men were standing in a straight line, and walking back and forth in front was Lieutenant Colonel Stuart, speaking in a clear and powerful voice—these were the relief guards and he was giving final instructions before they went on picket for the night.[1]

Stuart was twenty-eight years old, ten months older than Mosby; and, although they were both from non-aristocratic backgrounds in the Virginia Piedmont, they were worlds apart. Stuart had graduated from West Point and fought Indians and now was in charge of Confederate cavalry in the Valley. Above average in height, he was broad-shouldered and athletic, weighing 180 pounds, with auburn hair, a full beard, and blue-gray eyes that sparkled with good humor. He wore high cavalry boots and a Union cavalry blouse and foraging cap, with linen havelock. Mosby had never seen anyone move so gracefully nor anyone so comfortable with being in charge. An aura of romance surrounded him; he was a romantic cavalier in the truest eighteenth-century meaning of the term, a brave fighter so gentle that on the western frontier he collected tiny flowers and feathers of small birds and pressed them into a scrapbook with clippings of cheerful, optimistic poems. Stuart was so unique that he "seemed able to defy all natural laws," Mosby concluded. "I did not approach him, and little thought that I would ever rise from the ranks to intimacy with him."[2]

Two days later, Mosby participated in his first scouting expedition. Jones led fifty men a few miles north, toward the Union camp at Martinsburg. Soon they happened upon a small foraging party of Union cavalry, who fled into a cornfield. Jones led the main body forward on the road and sent a squad of five, including Mosby, galloping through the woods to intercept them. The squad caught two Union men and forced them to surrender. "Since then," Mosby wrote, "I have witnessed the capture of thousands, but have never felt the same joy as I did over these first two prisoners." They sent the captives back with one man, and Mosby and the others went on to the Union picket line. "We scoured about the woods & fields fully two hours in full view of their tents & they didn't dare to come out & attack us," Mosby informed Pauline. Riding out on his own the next day, he learned what a help the local civilians could be—a family gave him "a great treat," two gallons of buttermilk.[3]

They had been on duty only ten days when they participated in Stuart's successful screening of Johnston's withdrawal from the Valley and reinforcement of the main Confederate army under Gen. Pierre G.T. Beauregard for the battle of First Bull Run. On the evening of July 20, the night before the battle, Jones's company camped on the southern bank of Bull Run, near Ball's Ford, almost two miles downstream from the Stone Bridge where the Warrenton Turnpike crossed the creek. Mosby lay down in the broom sedge under a pine tree, looked up at the stars, and said to Beattie: "Well, 'Font,' old boy, this, perhaps, will be our last night on earth." The next morning they awoke to picket firing on the Confederate left at Sudley Springs, about four miles upstream. The battle with the Union army of Gen. Irvin McDowell was beginning. After breakfast, Stuart sent the company on a reconnaissance across Bull Run. Ordering the men into column of fours, Jones assigned Mosby as the first man in the first set of four, and he rode in that position all day, an honor he always cherished.[4]

Beginning around noon, the company supported Gen. Thomas J. Jackson's famous stand on Henry House Hill that turned the tide of battle in favor of the Confederates. For two hours, Jones's men remained on horseback in reserve on Jackson's right, taking artillery fire that they could not return. Jones commended them for standing like veterans, but it was difficult. Thinking of Pauline and the children, Mosby took May's daguerreotype from his pocket, and this was a mistake: "For a moment the remembrance of her prattling innocence almost unfitted me for the stern duties of a soldier," he wrote Pauline. Then the Union attack faltered, and the invaders began a panic-stricken retreat. Mosby and his companions pursued for six or eight miles, taking overcoats and tents and other items and capturing prisoners until dark. Early the next morning Mosby telegraphed Pauline that he was safe.[5]

The Union army retreated to Washington, and Lincoln appointed Gen. George B. McClellan commander of the newly named Army of the Potomac. McClellan posted two divisions in Virginia on the right bank of the Potomac, with Gen. William F. Smith's division near Chain Bridge. Johnston's Confederate army moved north and by mid-October established headquarters at Centreville, with Stuart's cavalry at Fairfax Court House, fifteen miles from Washington. For seven and one-half months, except for reconnaissance missions and small-scale demonstrations, it was "All Quiet along the Potomac" just as described in the popular song. For Mosby this was a valuable time of training as a scout, attracting Stuart's attention, and gaining appointment as Jones's adjutant.[6]

Generally in the war, both sides deployed cavalry as pickets or guards to serve as a trip-wire defense to warn of an approaching enemy force. A line of companies stretched across the front, with each company headquarters designated as the reserve and outposts or picket posts of four to six men thrown forward one-half mile. The only one who stayed alert and mounted was the vidette, a man from the outpost positioned about a hundred yards forward, toward the enemy. Mosby enjoyed duty as a vidette, much preferring it to camp life, which he considered irksome. At a crossroads in Fairfax County he would sit alone on his horse from midnight to daybreak, listening to the owls and night-hawks. He ate breakfast with the local people and, on scouts with the company, learned how to set an ambush among the dense pines and, when ambushed, remain calm and aim low.[7]

Unbelievably, he stayed in good health. "My health is as good as it can be," he wrote Pauline. A month later he informed her: "I live very well & enjoy perfect health. Aaron relieves me of all the drudgery of camp—is a very good cook." Then came his first winter, and he still did not cough. "It is quite cold now," he wrote. "Night before last what little time I had to sleep was lying out-doors wringing wet (it was severely cold) with my gun in my hand. My health is better than it ever was in my life." Once in November, seven months into his military service, he stood guard all day in a drenching rain and returned for six hours at midnight in below-freezing temperatures. "It is surprising," he exalted, "that I never have had the least sign of a cold."[8]

During this period he was absent from duty only for a few days, and that was when he was hospitalized. On a dark, rainy night in late August he and another man were posted on the road near Falls Church. At sundown Jones rode out to inform them that no friendly patrols were out, and if any troops approached from the direction of the enemy they were to fire without warning. A few hours later, Mosby was asleep when his companion on duty screamed, "The Yankees are coming!" Mosby sprang up and mounted; and when the body of horsemen approaching from the direction of enemy lines came within fifty yards, Mosby and his comrade fired their carbines, wheeled, and raced back toward the re-serve. Running headlong in the darkness Mosby's horse stumbled and fell over a cow lying in the road, toppling him forward, falling on him, and knocking him unconscious. The column turned out to be Confeder-ates, sent out on a different road by an officer at Stuart's headquarters who forgot to notify Jones that they would be re-entering the lines. They gathered up Mosby and took him to the toll keeper's house in Falls Church, where he regained consciousness the next day. Jones sent him in an am-bulance eight miles to the hospital in Fairfax Court House. "I was bruised from head to foot, and felt like every bone in my body had been broken," Mosby remembered. Jones gave the forgetful officer a well-deserved curs-ing and relieved Beattie to stay with Mosby in the hospital.[9]

Fully recovered, one night he was on picket within four miles of Washington when he struck up a conversation with his Union counter-parts. He invited them to supper, and under flag of truce they accepted and ate with him and spent the night. Off duty, he rode on his own to Munson's Hill, about six miles from Washington, to enjoy the view of the city, with its fortifications under construction and the Stars and Stripes floating over the capitol. International law prohibited shooting pickets except during a demonstration or attack, but he ignored the rule. For sport he would ride out with the hay wagon and shoot Union guards on the opposite hill, then adjust the sight on his Sharps carbine by checking with a local woman for a report on the effect of his bullets. "One of them was killed dead - shot through the head," he wrote Pauline. Describing the pleasure of shooting men in a cornfield, he declared: "I took a deliberate aim & fired at them with more eagerness than I ever did at a squirrel." When a man stepped into the road to return fire "it took several to carry him back." Once on a scout near Falls Church with about eighty men, Mosby and Beattie became separated and were riding through a pine thicket when they came upon two Union soldiers. Mosby demanded their surrender, but they commenced firing. Mosby and Beattie each selected an opponent, and both sides exchanged several shots without effect. "I then jumped down from my horse," Mosby related, "and as the fellow turned to run I rested my carbine against a tree & shot him dead. He never knew what struck him. . . . After the fight was over I went & looked at the man I killed. The bullet had passed entirely through his head."[10]

On September 11, Union colonel Isaac Stevens, 79th New York Infantry, led an eighteen-hundred-man reconnaissance to Lewinsville, about four miles from Chain Bridge, and Stuart countered with a small force. Mosby went along and was thrilled when they made contact and began exchanging artillery fire. Then, as the Federals started to withdraw, he aimed his carbine at Stevens, dressed in a fancy uniform and riding a beautiful horse. Stuart saw it and ordered him not to shoot, giving the excuse that the colonel might be a Confederate. "I never regretted anything so much in my life as the glorious opportunity I missed of winging their Col.," Mosby wrote Pauline. On the other hand he told her: "I never enjoyed anything so much in my life as standing by the cannon & watching our shells when they burst over them. One of our men had his head shot off by a shell & another wounded."[11]

Confederate officers relied on Northern newspapers for news, and Mosby competed with other scouts to be first to bring a paper with some momentous story. When the news broke in Washington of the capture of Confederate diplomats James Mason and John Slidell at sea, Mosby brought the first paper, a copy of the *Washington Star* taken from a prisoner. Stuart was away, so he gave it to Lt. Col. Fitzhugh Lee, Stuart's second in command. Mosby had no idea that Lee despised him, but he was about to get that message. Fitz was a nephew of Robert E. Lee and an impressive cavalry officer, two years younger than Mosby, but he was a West Point man, all spit and polish, and he disapproved of nearly everything about Mosby: he used a civilian saddle, wore red artillery facings on his uniform instead of the cavalry buff, and most essential, practiced irregular tactics. Completely in the dark, Mosby said proudly, "Colonel, here's a copy of to-day's paper." Refusing the paper and staring at Mosby, Fitz replied in an icy tone, "The ruling passion strong in death." Mosby was stunned. He recognized this as a phrase from the poem "To Lord Cobham" in Alexander Pope's *Moral Essays*. Cobham was the English religious dissenter hanged and burned in 1417. To Mosby there could have been no more stinging rebuke—with literature and history, his favorite subjects, Lee was saying that Mosby would get what he deserved when the Yankees shot or hung him as a spy.[12]

Stuart respected Fitz Lee but disagreed with Lee's antipathy toward irregular warfare and his disapproval of Mosby. Indeed, Stuart saw much of himself in Mosby. Like Mosby he hated the boredom of inactivity of camp life. Out on the picket line one morning he suggested that some of his men pick fresh corn for breakfast: "You don't want to go back to camp, I know; it's stupid there, and all the fun is out here. I never go to camp if I can help it." Like Mosby he abstained from alcohol, never seemed fatigued, and could think and act quickly in a crisis. The two men had so much in common that when one described the other he was in essence describing himself. Mosby wrote after the war that Stuart had been a soldier made in Heaven, a natural military genius who hated red tape and ignored the narrow rules taught in military school. "Stuart was not a mathematical general. He knew that war cannot be reduced to rules." Stuart wrote of Mosby: "He is bold, daring, intelligent, and discreet. The information he may obtain and transmit to you may be relied upon, and I have no doubt that he will soon give additional proofs of his value." Every word in these quotations applies with equal accuracy to both men.[13]

Stuart realized that the strategic value of cavalry was in reconnaissance and screening, in dispelling the fog of war by gathering vital information on enemy strength and movement and covering one's own army to deny the enemy such information. He became Robert E. Lee's eyes and ears, one of the best cavalry reconnaissance officers in the war. He had scouted Native Americans on the frontier, and now he was running a scouting school, teaching himself and his men to conduct overnight missions behind enemy lines, to masquerade as the enemy and use ruses like placing blueclad prisoners of war in front of a column to make it appear Union. In the Valley on July 2, 1861, a week before Jones's company arrived, Stuart pretended to be a Union officer and single-handedly captured forty-six infantrymen. He would eventually recruit some of the best scouts in the army—men such as William Farley, Frank Stringfellow, and Channing Smith. He would send them behind enemy lines over-night, singly or in small squads, and when they returned he would as-similate their reports and make conclusions. In Fairfax County, Stuart realized that he had never seen a scout any better than Mosby.[14]

Stuart had been promoted to brigadier general in command of the cavalry brigade of Johnston's army, and Jones had moved up to colonel of the 1st Virginia Cavalry regiment. Stuart was now on the lookout for scouts for his staff, and he wanted an opportunity to observe Mosby up close. His chance came at army headquarters in Centreville on the stormy night of February 12, 1862. After dark Mosby arrived to report to Stuart that he had completed the errand of driving two young ladies to Frying Pan, a few miles north. Stuart was staying at army headquarters in the Grigsby house, and, since several inches of snow had fallen and it was still snowing and a cold wind was blowing, he insisted that Mosby spend the night rather than going to his camp on Bull Run about four miles away.[15]

This was highly unusual and took Mosby by surprise—Brigadier General Stuart was inviting a private to join him around the fireplace with Gen. Gustavus W. Smith and General Johnston, the army com-mander. "I felt just as much out of place and uneasy as a mortal would who had been lifted to a seat by the side of the gods on Olympus," he recalled. They had dinner in the dining room, and the next morning at breakfast Mosby was honored to talk with Johnston, "whom I would have regarded it as a great privilege the day before to view through a long-range telescope." Stuart totally approved of Mosby. After breakfast he loaned him a horse and sent along a courier to lead it back to head-quarters. When Mosby rode into camp at mid-morning, on Stuart's horse and escorted by one of Stuart's staff, Jones realized that he must act quickly if he expected to keep Mosby in the regiment. He ordered Mosby to his tent and promoted him to first lieutenant and adjutant (administrative assistant). "I had had no more expectation of such a thing than of being translated on Elijah's chariot to the skies," Mosby wrote.[16]

From February 13 to April 23, 1862, Mosby served as adjutant of the 1st Virginia Cavalry. He assigned the administrative duties to a clerk and, now excused from picket duty, scouted for Stuart. In early March Johnston withdrew from Centreville to a more defensible position south of the Rappahannock River. McClellan countered by secretly moving the Army of the Potomac to the Virginia Peninsula between the York and James Rivers. On March 15, 1862, the first fleet of transports left Alexandria for Fort Monroe, but the Confederate high command would not determine McClellan's move until April 5.[17] The intervening time of uncertainty and suspense provided Mosby an opportunity, for a moment, to dispel the fog of war.

In order to mask his move, before starting, McClellan first marched his army south to Manassas, arriving there on March 11, four days before the first embarkation. As far as the Confederates knew, McClellan's army remained along Bull Run, preparing to attack. On March 24 Stuart predicted that McClellan would withdraw and go by water to the Peninsula or some other landing site along the coast, but he had no reliable intelligence to confirm it. As far as Stuart or Johnston or any other Confederate leader knew, McClellan's army of over a hundred thousand was preparing to march directly against the Confederate army.[18]

This theory seemed confirmed on March 27 when a large Union force came down the roadbed of the Orange and Alexandria Railroad, appearing at Cub Run, just east of Warrenton Junction, eleven miles from the Rappahannock River. Stuart had sent Jones's regiment to observe, and Mosby was leading the advance picket post of ten or twelve men. He ordered them to dismount and form a skirmish line on a hill on the west bank. When the Union advance of about ten or fifteen cavalry, sabers drawn ceremoniously, crossed Cub Run and dismounted, the Rebels fired, sending them back across the creek in wild confusion. "We ceased firing, threw up our caps & indulged in the most boisterous laughter," Mosby recalled. The Union column halted in a large open field on the east bank and formed in battle line, unlimbering their artillery and parking their long train of 450 supply wagons. The artillery opened on Mosby's position and he withdrew. Jones reported that it appeared to be a grand display to prove that they were in force and estimated their strength at ten thousand men.[19]

The Union force was most of the corps of Gen. Edwin V. "Bull" Sumner, sent by McClellan to make a demonstration to cover the move underway to the Peninsula. After crossing Cub Run on March 27, Sumner's men marched to Warrenton Junction, where they began arriving at 8:30 P.M. Johnston was concerned but not alarmed because he still had the Confederate army on this front. Stuart's cavalry screen of eleven hundred men fell back from Warrenton Junction to Bealeton Station, four miles in advance of the Rappahannock where Gen. Richard S. Ewell's division of eight thousand infantry was stationed. Johnston's headquarters and his remaining main force were south of the Rapidan River. He had the enemy outnumbered unless this was McClellan's main offensive, and that was what he wanted to know—was this the advance of the Union army or a feint?[20]

The next morning, March 28, Sumner remained at Warrenton Junction with his main body but sent Gen. Oliver O. Howard forward to the Rappahannock with a brigade of infantry and regiment of cavalry. Stuart and his men were mounted and on alert in the vicinity of Bealeton Station, when Howard's advance skirmish line came in sight. He turned to Mosby and said, "General Johnston wants to know if this is McClellan's army, or only a detachment." Mosby replied, "I will find out for you, if you will give me a guide." Stuart quickly designated one; and Mosby, the guide, and two other men set out for the Union rear. They went beyond Warrenton Junction and by the end of the day Mosby had learned all that he needed to know. He headed back and rode nearly all night.[21]

While Mosby was gone Stuart withdrew across the Rappahannock and extended Ewell's defensive line, bringing the force on the south bank to ninety-one hundred men. Howard reached the other bank and fired artillery across the river, then at dark pulled back from the bank, out of cannon range, and bivouacked for the night. When daylight came on the twenty-ninth, a heavy fog limited visibility to only a few yards, and it was drizzling rain. Stuart knew that at least a brigade had driven him back, but he did not know how many there were or whether other units were moving in support, and now in this weather he could not see the enemy. Then suddenly, out of the fog came Mosby, soaking wet but beaming— he had intelligence that would dispel the perplexity in Stuart's mind. He said that he saw Sumner's large wagon train moving back toward Washington, the main force at Warrenton Junction was unsupported, and the relatively small detachment on the opposite bank had separated yesterday from the main body, and, not only were they unsupported, they were beginning to leave, covered by a weak rear guard of cavalry. Greatly relieved, Stuart immediately ordered his men to ford the river and attack. Finding the situation exactly as Mosby described, they captured fifty prisoners of war.[22]

Reporting these events, Stuart commended Mosby and David Drake, Stuart's chief musician and scout, who may have scouted separately or may have been the guide assigned to accompany Mosby: "Adjutant Mosby and Principal Musician David Drake, of the First Virginia Cavalry, volunteered to perform the most hazardous service, and accomplished it in the most satisfactory and creditable manner. They are worthy of promotion and should be so rewarded." Tactically they revealed that the force immediately across the river was small and falling back, and strategically that the entire enemy expedition was unsupported and therefore a feint. They did not prove that McClellan was going elsewhere, only that his army was not heading this way now. Four days later, on April 2, Stuart learned from a citizen that large numbers of McClellan's men were departing Alexandria on transports. Three days after that, when the Union army began advancing on the Peninsula on April 5, the Confederate high command finally concluded that McClellan's main thrust was there.[23] Mosby's report had not predicted the Peninsula campaign, but the information that he had obtained pointed in that direction, and later events confirmed it. Mosby's scouting had no grand strategic impact, but Stuart realized that Mosby had been correct, and he was very grateful. Thus began a pattern in Mosby's intelligence reports—viewed from hindsight his reports correctly portended future enemy movements.

Along with Johnston's army, Stuart's cavalry moved to the Peninsula to defend Richmond. They were camped a few miles inside Confederate lines near Yorktown on April 23, 1862, the date for the election of regimental officers required by the Conscription Act recently passed by the Confederate Congress. The act established the first military draft in American history and extended present one-year enlistments to three years. Bending over backward to make amends to the men given extensions, Congress allowed them to elect their own officers. Throughout the army the men tended to vote for the most popular men available, and it was the case with the 1st Virginia Cavalry—they voted out Jones and elected Fitz Lee. By now Mosby knew that Fitz hated him and would not retain him as adjutant. One day not long before, Jones had been absent and had left Mosby in charge of preparing the regiment for inspection. When everything seemed ready, in his non-regulation uniform Mosby sauntered up to Lee and said, "Colonel, the horn has blowed for dress parade." Livid with rage, Lee screamed, "Sir, if I ever again hear you call that bugle a horn, I will put you under arrest!" Now, an hour after the election Mosby handed Lee his resignation, and Lee accepted it.[24]

Mosby would never again think of Yorktown without remembering his disappointment in being demoted to private. "I lost my first commission on the spot where Cornwallis lost his sword," he wrote. Starting over at the bottom, he determined to make something positive of the situation. The day after he resigned he met with Stuart, and Stuart appointed him to his staff as a courier, which meant scout. For the next eleven months Stuart would refer to him as a lieutenant or captain, but officially he was a private, and it was humiliating. Many years after the war when his grandson Spottswood Campbell was frustrated with slow career advancement, Mosby wrote that he could sympathize: "You know how long I served as a private in our war & what the judgment of the world on me was at its close."[25]

He hated his life on the Peninsula anyway. He felt hemmed in by the close proximity of the two armies, there were no opportunities to scout, and there was too much boring time in camp. Stuart's cavalry served as the rear guard for Johnston's withdrawal toward Richmond, and once McClellan deployed within five miles of the city the cavalry went inactive. On May 31 Johnston attacked in the battle of Seven Pines and was himself severely wounded. The next day Davis named Robert E. Lee commander of the newly named Army of Northern Virginia. Mosby read of these events in the Richmond newspapers, but he was more interested in the news on the enactment of the Partisan Ranger Act on April 21 by the Confederate Congress. The law, modeled primarily on the career of John Hunt Morgan, authorized the organization of units to conduct guerrilla war behind the lines of the enemy invader. They were to be part of the army, subject to the same regulations and with the same pay and rations, but as an incentive the government paid them cash for captured munitions—they could officially profit from the spoils of war. Capt. John Scott, a former editor of the *Richmond Whig* from Fauquier County and after the war the first historian of Mosby's raiders, advertised for recruits, promising action and relief from the tedium of camp life. A *Whig* editorial warned that Turner Ashby and Morgan had best "look to their laurels." Mosby decided that the partisan life was for him; he would break away and go to the Shenandoah Valley and apply as a scout for Stonewall Jackson. He respected Jackson and hoped that Jackson might sponsor him in a partisan operation. "I always had the grandest admiration for his genius and the most unbounded faith in his star," he reflected.[26]

Then early in the morning on June 9, he finally received a break— Stuart invited him to a private breakfast. During the meal Stuart informed him that Lee was considering an offensive on the north side of the Chickahominy River and needed to determine the disposition of troops there on the Union right. He asked Mosby to take two or three men and scout behind the lines as far as Totopotomoy Creek. "That was the very thing I wanted; an opportunity for which I had pined," Mosby recalled. Within a few minutes he and four men rode away. The next afternoon

Stuart was seated on the ground under a tree when Mosby rode up all out of breath, dismounted, and lay on the grass beside him. It was unconventional for a private to report to a general in such an informal manner, but it would have been fine with Stuart if Mosby had hung from a limb by his heels—the important thing was that he had intelligence from behind enemy lines. He revealed that McClellan's right was up in the air, unsupported by infantry, and that, according to local civilians, the Union supply line on the Richmond and York River Railroad was thinly guarded by cavalry.[27]

Stuart asked Mosby to write and sign his report; as soon as it was finished, he galloped away to Lee's headquarters. Lee read it and ordered Stuart to lead a reconnaissance to confirm the information. Stuart said that this appeared to be an opportunity to carry out one of his favorite schemes—a ride around McClellan's army; Lee did not rule out the idea. Stuart's father-in-law, Philip St. George Cooke, had remained in the Union army and was in command of McClellan's Cavalry Reserve defending the Union rear. Stuart considered Cooke a traitor to Virginia and hoped to embarrass him.[28]

The raid began at 2:00 A.M. on June 12, and for three days Stuart's twelve hundred men rode a hundred miles around McClellan's army just as Stuart had dreamed. Before daylight on the second day, he prepared to enter Union lines by summoning Mosby and placing him in the advance, with the task of riding on ahead to scout Hanover Court House. Mosby and a few men rode to within a few hundred yards of the village and made the first contact with Union troops on the raid, a squadron of about 150 cavalry who soon retreated in haste. Next, at Haw's Shop the advance came to the Union cavalry picket line. These Yankees fled as well, and the Rebels followed in a running fight for several miles. The chase paused momentarily near Linney's Corner, where on the crest of a hill about a hundred Union cavalry made a stand. Stuart ordered a mounted saber charge, and Mosby participated. The fighting was hand-to-hand; the brave Union men scattered and ran but not until one of them had shot and killed the leader of the charge, Capt. William Latane. The Union horsemen retreated beyond their camp at Old Church, and Mosby participated in the looting of their tents.[29]

Old Church was the jumping-off point for the expedition, so, while the men gathered spoils, Stuart met with his two lieutenant colonels. Now that they had completed the mission of reconnaissance on the Union right, should they turn around and return to camp or proceed around

the enemy army, changing the nature of the expedition from a reconnaissance to a raid? They had routed the Union pickets, and the way lay
open into McClellan's rear, with an opportunity to strike his railroad
supply line nine miles away. William H.F. "Rooney" Lee, of the 9th Virginia Cavalry, a Harvard graduate and son of Robert E. Lee, enthusiasti-
cally approved. Fitz Lee, however, opposed. This was exactly the response
that Stuart wanted—Fitz's shock at the idea of such a guerrilla raid confirmed for Stuart that his father-in-law would react with the same disbe-
lief and by the time he recovered the raid would be over. Stuart had not
learned it at West Point, but he appreciated the harassing nature of hit-
and-run warfare.[30]

Moving from Old Church, Stuart turned to Mosby and said, "Mosby,
I want you to ride some distance ahead." Mosby replied, "Very well. But
you must give me a guide; I don't know the road." Stuart detailed two
men familiar with the vicinity, and Mosby led the way, riding ahead of
the main body one or two miles. After about four miles he surprised a
sutler and captured him and his wagon. Sutlers—forerunners of today's
base exchange—were merchants authorized to sell the army groceries
and personal items not available as rations or government issue. Mosby
left a man behind to guard the prize and proceeded. Where the road
came near the Pamunkey River, he saw at Garlick's Landing the masts of
two Union supply schooners that were being unloaded onto army wagons. He sent the other man to inform Stuart, who detailed men to burn
the wagons, ships, and supplies. Meanwhile, Mosby went on alone. Rounding a bend near Tunstall's Station on the railroad, he came upon a Union
quartermaster wagon. The driver and a vidette surrendered immediately,
giving up their supply of Colt revolvers, boots, shoes, and blankets. Then
one-half mile west of Tunstall's he bluffed a company of Union cavalry
into withdrawing without firing a shot. He waited for the main body and
then fought in the saber charge that quickly overwhelmed the small force
at the station.[31]

The raid confirmed for Mosby that the life of a partisan was for
him. In *Our Masters the Rebels,* Michael C.C. Adams sets forth that Northern soldiers were at a disadvantage because they assumed Southerners
were superior fighters. Mosby saw this played out before his eyes on this
raid. The raiders had the advantage of surprise, but Mosby thought it
went deeper. As evidence of "the panic that reigned," he described how
at one point twenty demoralized Union cavalrymen raced to overtake
the raiders so that they could surrender. The only explanation Mosby

had for such unusual behavior was "They were dumbfounded." The driver of the quartermaster wagon and the vidette with him went into a stupor, with bedazzled looks on their faces like they had just seen a ghost. The small contingent of Union infantry at Tunstall's were so surprised that several did not even have their guns loaded. But the most outstanding incident was his bluff of the pickets near Tunstall's Station. They were a company of Pennsylvania cavalry, mounted and drawn up in line in the road. Mosby was alone and it was nearly sunset and his horse was exhausted from riding all day. He knew that if he turned to flee they could overtake him with their fresh horses. He halted in the middle of the road, purposefully drew his saber, and turned in the saddle to wave it in the air, as if beckoning to imaginary followers. "Come on, boys! Come on!" he shouted. The Pennsylvania men did not wait to see who this Rebel might be addressing; they turned and quickly vanished.[32]

How could anything be this much fun? He loved getting the upper hand on his opponents and seeing the fear in their eyes; finally the weakling was putting the bullies in their place. Stunning and befuddling the foe was more pleasure than wounding or killing him. And partisan raiding was certainly more profitable than regular warfare. Acquiring and consuming spoils cast a holiday atmosphere on the raid. In the abandoned Union camp at Old Church, Mosby took a carpet for Pauline from an officer's tent, and by the end of the raid he also had two revolvers and a horse with equipment, spoils that totaled $350 in value—almost 32 months' salary for a private at $11 per month. Mosby was not greedy, but he knew that avarice could be harnessed as a means to success. At the courtesy of the sutlers, the raiders feasted on such luxuries as fruit, cakes, candy, beef tongue, and Rhine wine. Later, he recalled his pleasure in the pillage of sutler stores at Talleysville during the night of June 13: "That summer night was a carnival of fun I can never forget." The next morning while Stuart waited on the northern bank of the Chickahominy for his men to build a bridge to cross, Mosby spread a picnic for him and served sausages, canned meat, figs, champagne, and other delectables. Summarizing the entire experience, he observed, "I never enjoyed myself so much in my life."[33]

And the raid brought attention. Stuart's report recommended Mosby for a commission, commending him and scout William Farley for their distinguished records of daring and usefulness since the beginning of the war. Lee's congratulatory order mentioned Mosby as one of seven privates who had earned "special commendation" from their com-

manders. Of course the raid made Stuart a great Southern hero, and
Mosby shared a bit of the limelight. The *Richmond Dispatch* published a
detailed account of his ruse at Tunstall's and referred to him as "the gallant Lieutenant." The *Abingdon Virginian* mentioned his scouting and
riding in the advance and concluded: "We hold this a bright record, alike
for bravery, intelligence and enterprise. Mosby is evidently of the same
stuff that Morgan and Ashby and such men are made of." Clearly the way
to emotional satisfaction, fortune, and fame lay in guerrilla raids behind
enemy lines.[34]

Mosby considered transferring to the new Virginia State Line under former governor John Floyd, who had known Mosby before the war;
but Stuart advised him to remain in the Confederate army, promising
that now a commission would be no problem. On June 20, 1862, Stuart
wrote a letter to Secretary of War George W. Randolph recommending
him in highest terms for a commission as captain of a company of sharpshooters in his brigade. Mosby took the letter to Randolph's office but
never received approval. On June 26, Lee's offensive began, initiating the
Seven Days' battles. The cavalry were not involved. Stuart was not present
at the battle of Malvern Hill on July 1, nor was Mosby, who had his horse
shod that day. Failing to conquer Lee, McClellan went on the defensive at
Harrison's Landing on the James River, and Stuart's cavalry went on picket
duty north of Richmond near Atlee's Station in Hanover County. In camp
again, Mosby's frustration resumed. "I never could rest inactive," he said
later, for "quiet to quick bosoms is a hell."[35]

He met with Stuart and requested a detail of twelve men to go with
him for partisan raiding in the rear of the newly designated Army of
Virginia organizing in Washington under Gen. John Pope. Stuart answered that he needed all of his men for the spring campaign, and he
could not approve, but he would recommend Mosby to his friend Jackson; no doubt he could spare a few men. Jackson's corps had fought on
the Peninsula and had recently moved north to Gordonsville to defend
against Pope. On July 19, 1862, Stuart wrote a letter to Jackson highly
recommending Mosby as a scout but not mentioning his desire for partisan service. Actually, Stuart may have feared the operation would fail.
When Mosby talked about irregular warfare behind the lines for an extended period of time, Stuart could not comprehend how it would succeed. Mosby was not proposing a brief raid; he was proposing to live off
the land in enemy-occupied territory. How would he re-supply and re-
arm? Five months later, after Mosby had demonstrated that he could

raid, and when winter was beginning, Stuart would give Mosby temporary use of the men he wanted, but not now. Stuart had promised him anything he wanted, then assured him that he could have a command, and now he would not detail him a small squad. The closest Mosby's memoirs came to criticizing Stuart was the passage on this issue. At the end of his life, he wrote that it still seemed strange. "I had to beg for the privilege of striking the enemy at a vulnerable point."[36]

Then when Stuart realized Mosby was really going, he gave him a club-footed man named Mortimer Weaver, one of his couriers from Fauquier County, the area where Mosby proposed to operate. "I accepted the letter to Jackson—the best I could get—and with a club-footed companion, an exempt from military service, I started off," he related. Mosby planned to ride to Beaver Dam Station on the Virginia Central Railroad and there send Weaver with the horses to Jackson's camp at Gordonsville. His parents were now living at "Idle Wilde" at McIvor's Station on the Orange and Alexandria Railroad just north of Lynchburg, and Pauline and the children were visiting there. He would take the train to Lynchburg, see them, and then report to Jackson. The two men left Stuart's camp on July 19, rode to Beaver Dam, and spent the night with a farmer. The next morning, with Mosby's horse, Weaver left the depot. Mosby unbuckled his two Colt revolvers, placed them and his haversack in a storage room, and sat down outside to wait for the train. Weaver had just ridden out of sight when someone yelled, "Here they come!" Mosby sprang to his feet and saw a regiment of Union cavalry approaching at a trot, less than one hundred yards away. He started running, but they quickly captured him, confiscating his pistols, haversack, and Stuart's letter. They allowed him to keep the copy of Napoleon's *Maxims* that Stuart had sent as a gift to Jackson.[37]

Pope had issued an order to his men declaring that he would attack and not pay any attention to his rear. Mosby had boasted that he would mind Pope's rear for him, and ironically Pope had captured Mosby. Pope had sent the 2nd New York Cavalry under Col. J.M. Davies to cut the Virginia Central Railroad, and they were as surprised as Mosby at his capture. Assuming that he was a captain, they took him to Fredericksburg; then he was sent by steamer to Washington and the Old Capitol Prison. He spent the next ten days studying Napoleon's *Maxims*, then was exchanged under the recently approved cartel of exchange.[38]

With a few hundred prisoners he was placed on a steamer to Hampton Roads, where it anchored for four days before proceeding up the

James River. The other prisoners remained at leisure during the wait, but Mosby noticed something that inspired him to spring to work as a scout. Across the bay at Newport News lay a fleet of transports loaded with Union troops. He knew that if the boats went up the James River the men would be going to reinforce McClellan for a renewal of the Peninsula campaign; but if they sailed out of Hampton Roads and went north, they would be going to Aquia Creek to reinforce Pope, and the next Union offensive would feature Pope in northern Virginia, not McClellan on the Peninsula.[39]

Mosby had become acquainted with the captain, a Southern man from Baltimore, and he told Mosby that the troops were Gen. Ambrose E. Burnside's army, just arrived from North Carolina. Mosby requested that when he went ashore on the last day he inquire as to Burnside's destination and that he purchase one dozen fresh lemons. On that day the captain left, and Mosby saw the fleet pass out of Hampton Roads by Fort Monroe. Then the captain returned, and as he handed Mosby the lemons he whispered, "Aquia Creek on the Potomac." That nailed it— McClellan's drive on Richmond was over; Pope would command the next offensive. That evening the steamer got underway, and Mosby was so excited he could not sleep; he sat on deck in the moonlight, watching the morning star. "I knew the momentous news I was carrying," he stated.[40]

The vessel arrived at Aiken's landing, the point of exchange, at about ten o'clock in the morning, and Mosby was the first man off. He went to Robert Ould, Confederate commissioner of exchange, and whispered that he had important information for General Lee; could he leave for headquarters at once? Ould approved, and he quickly made his way to Mary Dabbs's house, Lee's headquarters near Richmond. With difficulty he convinced Lee's staff that he must see Lee immediately, and he was taken into Lee's office. Lee was alone, seated at a table studying maps and attempting to anticipate the enemy's next move. The great hunger of the Civil War commander was for accurate information that would dispel the fog of war and reveal enemy intentions. Lee had this desire stronger than anyone. He had scouted in Mexico, and now he employed a coterie of scouts or spies to report from behind Union lines. He wanted to know about every cloud of dust, boats moving up or down the Potomac River, trains on the Baltimore and Ohio Railroad—everything. He would sit at his table; study the maps and analyze the separate pieces of information from the scouts and from civilians, prisoners, and newspapers; and project himself across the lines, into the mind of the opposing commander, divining his thoughts. His biographer Douglas S. Freeman wrote that one of the keys to Lee's greatness was his synthesis of military intelligence; he could visualize a problem like a three-dimensional model on the table.[41]

When Mosby walked in that day, Lee was about as frustrated as he could be. He wanted to *know* what Lincoln's new general in chief, Henry Halleck, was planning. Would McClellan renew the Peninsula campaign or would Pope advance overland? He had expressed his frustration two days before, on August 3, when he ordered Stuart to penetrate Pope's lines around Fredericksburg to ascertain "if possible the veiled movements of the enemy." The previous day he had written Jackson: "It is important the strength of the enemy at Fredericksburg should be ascertained, or your communication might be cut." And in defending Richmond himself, he was worried with McClellan. It had appeared two days before that McClellan might be advancing on Petersburg, and then yesterday gunboats had moved up the James River to Malvern Hill, possibly in preparation for a landing of troops and a repeat of the advance on Richmond. "In a day or two their object may be disclosed," he reflected. Then suddenly in walked an angel—in shirt sleeves and covered with dust—but a messenger from Heaven nevertheless. It was as if Mosby had jumped off the map and now stood there, an answer to prayer, a surprise visitor with an unexpected piece of the puzzle.[42]

Lee asked the stranger to sit down, and his gentle and kind manner set Mosby at ease. After the war ended and Lee died, Mosby would have no part in the Lee cult that made Lee a legend, but he regarded Lee as the most impressive person he ever met; he never forgot the awe and veneration he felt in this first meeting. He regarded Lee as the most prominent man in the world and imagined that he was talking with one of the heroes from Homer's *Iliad* and *Odyssey*. "I felt like a man looking at a fixed star through a telescope," he stated.[43]

Mosby described what he had seen and what the captain reported and then said, "General Lee, you do not know me, and don't know whether to place any dependence in the information which I have given you." Then he gave his name and told how he was a scout for Stuart and one of the men mentioned in Lee's general order on Stuart's ride around McClellan. "Oh, yes," Lee answered, "I remember." Lee called for an aide and asked him to alert a courier to stand by to take a message to Jackson, and then he asked Mosby why he was gobbled up. "Couldn't you run away?" he inquired. "Yes," said Mosby, "but not as fast as a horse." Then Mosby was highly honored by the next question: where did Mosby expect the next enemy advance on Richmond? He confidently replied that the reinforcement of Pope indicated that it would be from the line of the Rappahannock. After a few minutes, as Mosby rose to leave, he took the dozen lemons from his haversack and placed them on the table. "Oh," said Lee, "you had better give them to some in the hospitals." But Mosby left them, realizing that Lee would enjoy giving them to the wounded.[44]

That same day Stuart sent Lee a report from south of Fredericksburg indicating that interrogation of captured prisoners revealed that Burnside had arrived in Fredericksburg with sixteen thousand men. That evening McClellan occupied Malvern Hill in considerable force, and to Lee it looked like a general advance. The next day, August 6, Lee moved his army against McClellan's line, and there was brisk skirmishing. That night, even though it seemed that McClellan was taking the offensive, Lee wrote Jackson warning that Burnside was probably in Fredericksburg and urging that he consider attacking Pope's right flank immediately.[45]

Then on the morning of August 7 the picture began coming into focus for Lee, and it was according to Mosby's prediction. Lee discovered that McClellan had withdrawn from Malvern Hill in the night. Early on the same morning Jackson began marching north from Gordonsville, moving against Pope before he was reinforced by Burnside. When Jackson moved, one piece of the intelligence that he acted on was Mosby's report. It was not as significant as Stuart's report or possibly other information that Lee and Jackson had, but it was one piece. Jackson's advance resulted in the battle of Cedar Mountain on August 9, four days after Mosby had met with Lee.[46]

After the war, Mosby claimed that his report sent Jackson on his way, bringing on the battle of Cedar Mountain. From his single point of view it did, but his claim was an exaggeration that failed to take into account the synthesis of intelligence from several sources. Still, Mosby's claim calls attention to the long-term value of his report in influencing Lee to have confidence in him as a scout. Mosby's report looked toward a Union advance in northern Virginia rather than on the Peninsula, and that prediction proved true. Burnside's army had moved as Mosby predicted, and on August 13, eight days after Mosby met with Lee, Lee learned that McClellan's army was transferring north, and he initiated the campaign that culminated in the Confederate victory at Second Bull Run. After eight days, Mosby's prediction was entirely fulfilled.[47]

When Mosby left the meeting with Lee he went by Stuart's headquarters and then took the packet-boat up the James River Canal to Idle

Wilde to visit Pauline and get a horse. He remained for about ten days and left to report to Jackson on August 17, 1862. On the way he ran into Stuart and his staff direct from a meeting with Lee at Orange Court House. Lee had ordered Stuart to raid in Pope's rear, and Mosby accepted Stuart's invitation to join him. Stuart's cavalry were expected from Hanover Court House, but they still had not arrived the next morning when a Union cavalry force surprised the staff sleeping on a porch at Verdiersville on the Confederate right. The Federals captured Chief of Staff Norman R. Fitzhugh and took Lee's instructions for the raid, Stuart's plumed hat, cloak, sash, and gloves and Mosby's haversack and telescope. For five days the men teased Stuart with the query: "Where's your hat?" Then on August 22, after Pope had fallen back across the Rappahannock River, Stuart was starting on a raid on Pope's headquarters at Catlett's Station when he galloped by Mosby in the column. "I am going after my hat!" he shouted. The raiders did not find the hat, but they captured Pope's letter-book, money-chest, cloak, and hat; and Mosby acquired two Colt revolvers to replace the pair lost at Beaver Dam Station when he was captured.[48]

Remaining with Stuart's cavalry during the battle of Second Bull Run, Mosby had his horse wounded by a ball in the shoulder, and a bullet passed through his hat, slightly grazing the top of his head. He captured nine Union soldiers, a horse, two saddles, and two pistols. In the battle of Antietam he served as a courier for Stuart, who was screening on the extreme left, on Jackson's left flank in the West Wood. At about ten o'clock in the morning he paused a moment to watch Jackson, "transfigured by the joy of battle," directing his artillery fire against the last Union infantry charge north of Dunkard Church. The Union lines withdrew, leaving the ground covered with dead and wounded men. Stuart saw among the wounded a Confederate lieutenant bending over a Union officer, demanding his formal surrender. The officer was severely wounded in the left shoulder, and Stuart ordered the lieutenant away. Mosby dismounted, placed a rolled blanket under the man's head, and handed him his canteen. Mosby asked his name, and he said, "Colonel Wistar of the California regiment." He was Col. Isaac J. Wistar, commander of the 71st Pennsylvania Infantry, known as the California Regiment in honor of its first colonel, Edward D. Baker from San Francisco. Wistar recovered and was named brigadier general later that year. After the war he became president of the Pennsylvania Canal Company, and in 1869 a friend took Mosby to his office in Philadelphia. Mosby identified himself as the private who had given him water at Antietam.[49]

Mosby's horse became disabled in the battle, and he went to his parents for a remount and to visit them and Pauline and the children. He rejoined Stuart on November 5, at Barbee's Cross Roads in Fauquier County, when Stuart was screening the withdrawal of Longstreet's corps from the Valley to Culpeper. Stuart established headquarters near Culpeper and sent Mosby and two men on a scout behind McClellan's army at Rectortown. On that mission, on November 10, Mosby was standing near the track of the Orange and Alexandria Railroad at Catlett's Station when a special train passed bearing McClellan to Washington. He learned that McClellan had been replaced by Burnside and sent one of the men to Stuart with the news. He and the other man went forty miles behind the lines to Fairfax County and learned that Union troops were not leaving Alexandria for the Peninsula. On November 15, Burnside began moving from Warrenton to Falmouth, opposite Fredericksburg, on the campaign that culminated in the battle of Fredericksburg. He masked the maneuver so successfully that Lee could not determine what was happening. Lee furiously dispatched several individual scouting expeditions. Mosby and one companion scouted and reported correctly to Stuart that Burnside was moving toward Fredericksburg, information that Stuart had already received from at least one source. Within a few days, the report was confirmed by events.[50]

Finally, Mosby conducted a scout that demonstrated to Stuart that he could raid independently with a few men behind enemy lines in northern Virginia as he had proposed five months before. When Burnside moved to Falmouth he arranged to defend Washington by leaving Gen. Franz Sigel north of the Rappahannock with Sigel's 11th Corps and Gen. Henry Slocum's 12th Corps. On November 20, Halleck ordered Sigel to withdraw closer to Washington, and he moved his headquarters to Fairfax Court House, with cavalry pickets thrown out several miles to the west. During Sigel's movement Lee in Fredericksburg worried that Sigel might be headed to Alexandria to embark on boats for the Peninsula. Therefore, before Stuart left Culpeper for Fredericksburg, he detailed nine men to Mosby for a reconnaissance to determine where Sigel was going. Mosby succeeded, not only in correctly analyzing Sigel's move, but also in driving in Sigel's pickets. At Bull Run bridge Mosby's squad found a regiment of Union cavalry on patrol out of Centreville taking a break with ten men on picket a short distance toward the bridge. Mosby dismounted his nine men as skirmishers, and they charged, firing their carbines and screaming the Rebel yell while Mosby galloped about on horseback shouting orders to imaginary squadrons. Assuming that Stuart's entire brigade was upon them, the ten pickets fled in panic and stampeded the regiment. Stuart forwarded Mosby's report to the War Department, and Lee sent Mosby a message of gratitude for easing his anxiety. The *Richmond Dispatch* reported that the Yankees lost one dead, five wounded, and two missing. And Stuart enjoyed describing "with great glee" the comic spectacle of Mosby routing an entire regiment with only nine sharpshooters. By turning a scout into a raid, Mosby demonstrated that he could operate independently thirty-five miles behind enemy lines with no Confederate force nearby.[51]

By his twenty-ninth birthday on December 6, 1862, Mosby had been in the Confederate army almost twenty months, and, while he had been a first lieutenant and adjutant for less than three months, he was now a private. He had won commendations and praise as an excellent scout for Stuart, now a major general and commander of the cavalry of the Army of Northern Virginia. He had made Stuart his latest mentor and had earned his respect and friendship. He had earned the confidence of Lee. But Mosby was very dissatisfied. Scouting with the regular cavalry required too many hours of boring camp life and did not provide the emotional satisfaction that he felt in the practice of irregular warfare. His need for conflict greater than his need for being Stuart's protégé, he had left Stuart for Jackson, to enter partisan service in July 1862. He was captured and after he was exchanged happened upon Stuart, who was actively on campaign, and rejoined him, determined somehow to prove to Stuart that he had the required abilities to succeed as a guerrilla. Finally Stuart had detailed him nine men for a reconnaissance, and in that minor operation Mosby emulated Stuart on the ride around McClellan on the Peninsula—he turned a scout into a raid behind the lines and used an irregular ruse to rout the enemy. As soon as winter weather postponed regular operations, he would ask Stuart again for the loan of a few men, and he would demonstrate that he could fight a continual guerrilla war behind enemy lines.

# 5

# Capturing a Yankee General in Bed

Lincoln and the War Department were extremely sensitive about the defense of Washington, D.C. The army had enclosed the city in thirty-seven miles of forts and connecting earthworks mounting the most powerful cannon made. For a field of fire the trees and brush were cleared, leaving a one-mile strip of bare ground, tree stumps, and brush piles separating the capital and Alexandria from the no-man's-land beyond. Corps commanders of the Army of the Potomac, meeting as a board of defense, recommended, in addition to artillery, twenty-five thousand infantry for the forts and three thousand cavalry for the early warning line across Fairfax County twenty miles from Washington. If the main army was not in covering distance, fifty thousand men were required in the defenses. When Mosby began his raids in January 1863, with the two armies facing each other on the Rappahannock at Fredericksburg, there were more than sixty thousand men inside the Washington defenses, and on the screen were thirty-three hundred cavalry and fifty-two hundred infantry. The system was designed to protect against strong incursions, and Mosby recognized its vulnerability: "A small force moving with celerity and threatening many points on a line can neutralize a hundred times its own number. The line must be stronger at every point than the attacking force, else it is broken."[1]

When Stuart's cavalry raided into Fairfax County on the Dumfries Raid, December 26–31, 1862, Mosby asked Stuart to leave him behind a few days with nine men. Stuart approved, and Mosby lodged the men in the area of Middleburg, twenty miles west of the cavalry screen. He knew this was a trial, and he had to succeed to win approval of a longer-range assignment. He recruited a guide from Fairfax County, a man familiar with every road and footpath behind the Union picket line. John Underwood was the best guide Mosby ever had—"a second Kit Carson," Mosby called him. He was twenty-five years old, short and stocky, with a tuft of white hair waving on top of his head. He was intelligent and alert and had ever-moving eyes. He scouted for Mosby almost a year—his only military experience—and was killed late in 1863 by a Confederate deserter. Guided by Underwood, in two nights Mosby and his squad surprised three outposts from the rear, capturing twenty Union cavalrymen and twenty horses. In Middleburg he had the prisoners sign paroles (promises to remove themselves from the war until exchanged) and divided the horses and accoutrements with Underwood and the men. Then he and the nine men returned to Stuart.[2]

Delighted, Stuart detailed Mosby fifteen men of the 1st Virginia Cavalry for the winter. There was no problem obtaining volunteers, but many in the camp laughed at Mosby, calling him "The Don Quixote of the War," about to be captured chasing windmills. He knew, however, that he was on the verge of destiny; he went to Richmond and posed in a captain's uniform for what became his favorite wartime photo of himself. Since his demotion in April 1862, he had been known as a lieutenant or captain, and now he used the title, without commission. On January 24, 1863, he and his men set out from Stuart's camp near Fredericksburg and returned to the Middleburg area. He dismissed them to find lodging in homes and to meet the morning of January 26 at Mount Zion Church one mile east of Aldie for their first raid.[3]

On schedule, Underwood guided them about twelve miles to the picket post at Chantilly Church in Fairfax County. Arriving at 4:00 P.M. they captured two videttes without firing a shot and surprised their ten dismounted companions, with their horses unbridled for feeding. All surrendered but one, and when he mounted and started to ride away, Mosby shot him through the arm and in the side, wounding him too seriously to move. The raiders took the other eleven and the horses to Middleburg, where Mosby divided the spoils among the men and paroled the prisoners. He asked them to tell their commander, Col. Percy Wyndham, to arm his pickets with Colt revolvers; their obsolete carbines were not worth capturing.[4]

Wyndham was commander of the cavalry brigade in the center of the screen, with headquarters in Fairfax Court House, and Mosby sensed that guerrilla harassment would exasperate him and create fear and frustration in his command, producing weaknesses to exploit. Wyndham was an English officer knighted in Italy for distinguished service under Garibaldi and had served well as commander of the 1st New Jersey Cavalry, taking over when the regiment was in disarray and restoring discipline and morale. He was twenty-eight years old, energetic, and effective when he applied himself, but he felt slighted being on guard duty and was doubly insulted by the requirement of reporting to the overall screen commander, Col. R. Butler Price, a man of equal rank whom Wyndham despised. In his frustration, instead of inspecting his picket posts and doing his work, Sir Percy spent most of his time in Washington, where he was the darling of the press corps.[5]

As soon as he learned of Mosby's attack, Wyndham ordered his brigade to prepare to march into the night—they would pursue and capture the Rebels. He led them to Middleburg, arriving at daybreak the morning after Mosby's raid, surrounding the town, searching the houses, and arresting all the males. He warned that if the raids continued he would burn Middleburg. His troops rounded up twenty-one males, all civilians, for none of Mosby's men were staying in the village. Mosby and Beattie, one of the fifteen volunteers, were asleep in a house nearby when a male slave awakened and warned them that the Yankees had come. Mosby gathered about twelve men and attacked Wyndham's rear guard when they started to leave. The Rebels captured one man and three horses, but Wyndham counterattacked and captured Beattie and two other Mosby men. Mosby's fast horse enabled him to escape, and he sat on his horse down the street, daring the Union men to shoot at him. Then he retreated to a nearby hill and sat still on his horse, watching them leave.[6]

Middleburg had never been in such danger before, so a few residents petitioned Mosby to halt his warfare. He responded in writing that they could tell the Union authorities that he refused to degrade himself by acceding to Yankee demands and that his warfare was legal and would continue. Quietly, however, he lessened the pressure on Middleburg by shifting his rendezvous to Rector's Cross Roads four miles west on Little River Turnpike. Wyndham's next move was to set a trap for Mosby by posting a squadron of cavalry in reserve near a thirteen-man picket post on Difficult Run, near Herndon Station, an abandoned depot on the Alexandria, Loudoun, and Hampshire Railroad that operated only within Union lines in Fairfax County during the war. To lure the guerrillas the pickets built a large campfire. The night was dark, and there were several inches of snow on the ground, enabling Mosby's men to approach noise-

lessly and easily capture the ten men around the fire. Two mounted
videttes attempted to escape; one was captured and the other killed with
a shot through the heart. The raiders were gone by the time the reserve
reacted. "Have had a gay time with the Yankees," Mosby wrote Pauline.[7]

Then Wyndham imitated tactics from Greek literature and sent a
"Trojan horse" to Middleburg in the form of a lightly guarded wagon
train that appeared to be laden with army supplies. Inside each white-
topped wagon were six 13th Pennsylvania Infantry, called "Bucktails," as
each recruit was supposed to shoot a deer to qualify. The Bucktails were
armed with the most advanced weapons, Spencer seven-shot repeating
rifles. When the wagon train neared Middleburg, fourteen of Mosby's
men charged the cavalry guards in front, causing them to panic and gallop back to the wagons. The infantrymen inside heard the sound of hoofbeats and assumed Mosby's men had arrived. They threw back the canvas
tops and opened fire—on their own cavalry. After the war Mosby wrote
that Wyndham's counterguerrilla tactics were "as ineffective as the blind
Cyclops beating the air."[8]

By February 15, unable to stop Mosby, Union pickets on the cavalry screen began pulling in their outposts at night, withdrawing to the
security of fifty-man reserve camps, where they posted videttes, built
fires, and went to sleep. On the night of February 26, forty-four men of
the 18th Pennsylvania Cavalry went to sleep in the schoolhouse on Ox
Road at Thompson's Corner, less than three miles from regimental headquarters at Chantilly. Their horses were haltered to nearby trees, and they
had three videttes out. It was raining and sleeting. "As only a raccoon
could be supposed to travel on such a night," Mosby noted, "I knew the
pickets would feel safe and would be sound asleep, so that a single shot
would create a panic." The day before, he had left Rector's Cross Roads
with twenty-seven men, including local civilians, convalescents from the
Confederate hospital in Middleburg, and cavalrymen home for mounts.
They approached the school from the front; when the vidette challenged
them, Mosby's man in the advance answered "Friends." The vidette fired
his carbine and raced back to the school. "Close on them, men," shouted
Mosby. They gave the Rebel yell and charged on horseback, firing their
revolvers. It was 4:30 A.M., "when our men generally get pretty sleepy
headed," wrote Pvt. William H. Martin, who was in the regiment but not
on duty that night. "The men had leisurely laid by thinking that they
were perfectly safe," he explained. The Union men fired a few shots with
their carbines, panicked, and scattered into the darkness. One Federal

was killed and two wounded, one with a severe leg wound that required amputation. Mosby's men acquired forty horses and equipment and captured five or six prisoners. To the Union men the lesson was clear: If fifty men were not safe, certainly ten were not, and outposts should continue to withdraw every night.[9]

Wyndham had been ordered away on a scout to the Rappahannock in support of the Union army and would be gone until March 3; he was unavailable to retaliate. Colonel Price ordered that a force be sent to Aldie to capture Mosby. Maj. Joseph Gilmer, 18th Pennsylvania Cavalry, marched with two hundred cavalry to Middleburg during the night of March 1; once again at daylight, the citizens were surrounded by Union horsemen. Gilmer's men searched the buildings and arrested the elderly adult males. These were probably most of the same men that Wyndham had taken away. The Washington authorities usually released civilians after a few days. When they repeated the threat to burn the town, one woman said that she could not stop the raiders. "You harbor them," a captain answered. Soon they left, riding double, with the male citizens and several slave women and children on the horses behind them. They had left when Mosby and seventeen men arrived and found the women in the street in tears. "There are Yankees enough to eat you up," they cried. Undaunted, Mosby and his men rode on, apparently to be captured attempting the impossible.[10]

Meanwhile, Gilmer's column passed through Aldie, five miles eastward. A few miles farther, Gilmer's advance saw mounted soldiers ahead, drawn up in battle line, across the road. Gilmer assumed they must be Mosby's men and panicked. He left the solid turnpike and turned to the right, leading a wild retreat down the muddy road toward Centreville. His men dumped the civilians and joined in the race for camp. Later, Gilmer learned that the force was a fifty-man detachment of the 1st Vermont Cavalry under Capt. Franklin T. Huntoon—Gilmer had fled without a fight from fellow Union cavalrymen. Before the month ended he was court-martialed and found not guilty of cowardice in fleeing from a small body of friendly cavalry, but guilty of drunkenness on duty. On July 23, 1863, he was cashiered from the army.[11]

After Gilmer had left, Huntoon marched into Aldie and directed his men to dismount and to unbridle and feed their horses at the large, historic Aldie Mill beside the turnpike. The horses were eating and the men were lounging around when suddenly Mosby and his men charged in at full gallop, firing their revolvers. A few of the Vermonters returned fire, wounding two of Mosby's men, but most mounted and retreated. Mosby captured Huntoon and eighteen men and twenty-three horses. The raiders were gathering these trophies and helping dust the flour from the captives, who had hidden in the flour hoppers, when into town walked the adult males of Middleburg, having been dropped by Gilmer's men in their panic. They had been freed by the 1st Vermont Cavalry; but, as far as the women of Middleburg were concerned, Mosby had rescued their fathers and grandfathers.[12]

By this time Mosby's effort to instill fear in the minds of the Union pickets provided him the greatest opportunity for an ideal raid that he would ever have. When the outposts started pulling in for the night, they left open a gap in the center of the screen, between the 18th Pennsylvania Cavalry camp at Chantilly and the infantry fortification at Centreville three miles south. The telegraph operator at Centreville noticed the opening and on March 4 reported it to Maj. Gen. Samuel P. Heintzelman, commander of the Washington defenses. Heintzelman warned Price and probably assumed that Price notified Wyndham, who was in charge in that section. Wyndham had returned from his scout on March 3. It is not known whether Price informed Wyndham; but, whether or not, Wyndham's cavalry did not close the hole in the picket line.[13]

Mosby learned of the gap, and then he heard something that thrilled him with excitement. From prisoners of war he learned that, five miles inside the hole in the line, Wyndham and General Stoughton, commander of a brigade of infantry, had fallen to the temptation of "headquarterism." It was the widespread practice in both armies of setting up headquarters in a comfortable hotel or house in town with the command camped a few miles away on the outskirts. Wyndham and Stoughton were sleeping in Fairfax Court House separate from their men. Wyndham had two regiments of cavalry in winter quarters of log huts with tent roofs and crude fireplaces on a pine knoll at Germantown, one mile west of town, and a third regiment, the 18th Pennsylvania, at Chantilly, four miles beyond Germantown on the Little River Turnpike. There was a small infantry regiment at Germantown and a brigade of infantry with artillery at Centreville, in all over twenty-five hundred troops, but none of them reporting to Stoughton; his closest men were at Fairfax Station three miles away.[14]

Before the war Fairfax Court House was a beautiful little town on a long rolling hill, and Fairfax County was the location of many landscaped and well-trimmed plantations, including George Washington's Mount

Vernon down on the Potomac River. But now much of the area around Fairfax Court House was in ruins, houses deserted and ransacked, fences gone, and fields overgrown with bushes and thorns. The hotel in the center of town was an army hospital, and there was a tent on the courthouse lawn for the Union telegraph operator. And yet, there were several large houses around the public square still occupied, and here a commander and his staff could sleep in feather beds, have fine meals in the dining room, and entertain guests. But then, as John Morgan experienced, there would come a surprise incursion; and the commander, separated from his men, would be captured or killed. Stonewall Jackson usually slept surrounded by his men, and Turner Ashby sent his regrets and stayed in camp when invited to parties.

Stoughton was twenty-four years old, the youngest general in the Union army. A graduate of West Point and member of an influential family in Vermont, he had proved himself as colonel of the 4th Vermont Infantry on the Peninsula and had come to Fairfax Court House in December 1862 as commander of the Second Brigade of Gen. Silas Casey's Division in the Washington defenses. For headquarters he selected the two-story brick house of Dr. William P. Gunnell on Main Street opposite and a few yards west of the courthouse. Wyndham stayed in the home of Judge Henry W. Thomas a block south of the courthouse on the Chain Bridge Road, and when out of town left Lt. Col. Robert Johnston, 5th New York Cavalry, in charge. Johnston stayed with his wife at the home of Joshua C. Gunnell, near Wyndham's headquarters.[15]

Stoughton's brigade had been in Fairfax Court House when Stuart's cavalry came in late December, and Stoughton effectively repulsed Stuart's attack. Then, on January 20, 1863, he received orders to move his infantry onto the outer picket line at Wolf Run Shoals, about eight miles south, and to Fairfax Station three miles south to guard a supply depot. At that time he should have gone with his men, and Wyndham should have moved his headquarters to his cavalry camp at Germantown. But Stoughton, his staff, and his band remained in town with a few guards to protect them and Wyndham and Wyndham's staff. Stoughton's mother and sister came to visit, and they moved in with three of his aides in a house one block from headquarters in the home of twenty-three-year-old Antonia Ford and her father, Edward R. Ford, a prosperous merchant. For meals the general's staff and guests gathered at headquarters, where Stoughton and an aide slept on the upper floor.[16]

Stoughton somehow heard of a breach in the screen several miles north, where Wyndham's right on Ox Road connected with Price's left from Dranesville. On March 1 he warned Heintzelman's headquarters that spies could freely pass through the opening. He reported that a spy had been questioning his servants on the number of troops in the vicinity and whether he kept his horse saddled at night, and he recommended that all civilians within the lines be required to take the loyalty oath. "It is absolutely essential to the security of the command in this vicinity," he wrote. The record does not indicate any response by Heintzelman. Stoughton's men realized that he was in danger. How could they protect him when he was so far removed? On March 5 one of Stoughton's men wrote home, stating that he had no idea what Stoughton would do in case of an attack, and besides, a general should be with his men: "If he is so fancy, that he can't put up with them, the Government had better put him out." Stoughton's superior, Casey, was in no position to disapprove— he was in charge of the infantry division on the screen, and his headquarters were in Washington.[17]

It was a raider's dream—within a three-block diameter were the headquarters of a general and a colonel, protected only by a few headquarters guards. The target was enticing but risky because, even though there was no body of troops in town, it would mean marching within one and one-half miles of over twenty-five hundred men in the vicinity. Mosby had become familiar with the streets early in the war, but he needed a guide familiar with the gap and the present encampments. Exactly the man he was looking for, James F. Ames, had deserted Wyndham on February 10, 1863, and asked to join Mosby. He was a sergeant in the 5th New York Cavalry, and he came from Germantown, the closest encampment to Fairfax Court House, one mile away! He was a huge, muscular man, and his gleaming black eyes and articulate conversation showed that he was intelligent. He said that he deserted because Lincoln freed the slaves. Mosby's men did not trust him, but Mosby wrote later: "I felt an instinctive confidence in his sincerity." Mosby was an excellent judge of character, and he was never more correct. "Big Yankee" Ames became a lieutenant and one of his most valuable men. He fought with unusual zeal, especially against his former regiment. Once in close fighting, one of the 5th New York men said, "How are you, Sergeant Ames?" "Well," he answered, and shot the man with his pistol. When he deserted he came without a horse. After interviewing with Mosby, he and Walter E. Frankland from Warrenton walked through the gap in the screen on Sunday night, March 1, took horses from the 5th New York stable in

Germantown, and rode back through the line without a challenge. Mosby decided to trust Ames as his pilot.[18]

The challenge was to penetrate the screen, passing between the cavalry at Chantilly and the infantry at Centreville, avoiding the cavalry and infantry at Germantown. Mosby would cut the telegraph wire between Centreville and Fairfax Court House and capture the general's guards before they could yell or fire a weapon to alert the camps. If the alarm sounded, Mosby might be captured by the two cavalry regiments at Germantown or the regiment at Chantilly. The time frame was narrow; he needed to arrive after the soldiers went to sleep and pass back through the gap before daylight. He knew it was hazardous. "My fate was then trembling in the balance," he recalled. "If we should get caught it would end my career as a partisan; everybody would say that I had tried to do what I ought to have known to be impossible." When the raid began, he said, "I am going to mount the skies to-night or sink lower than plummet ever sounded."[19]

Twenty-nine men followed his directions and had a home-cooked dinner on Sunday, March 8, and then reported late in the afternoon at Dover, two miles west of Aldie. There was melting snow on the ground and a mist hanging in the air; at dark it began drizzling rain. They rode on the turnpike to within three miles of Chantilly and veered off to the right into the pines and open fields and moved silently, jumping rabbits and listening to the hooting of owls. It was a perfect night for raiding, so dark that a man could hardly see the horse in front of him. The column became separated, and the group in the rear got lost and began circling blindly. Mosby went back and located them; the delay cost him two hours of darkness, but he was still on schedule. They proceeded through the gap in the screen, midway between Centreville and Chantilly. Going southeast, they came to the road between Centreville and Germantown and cut the telegraph wire. Then they took the road to within one-half mile of Germantown and headed into the pines again, seeing the fires of the Union pickets on their left. They struck the Chain Bridge Road running north from Fairfax Station and entered Fairfax Court House from the direction of "friendly Union" territory to the south.[20]

The surprise was complete, even for Mosby's men. He had told none of them where they were going except Ames, and they were now amazed to find themselves riding into Fairfax Court House. Some of the Union men captured were so surprised they laughed, thinking it was a practical joke; then reality took hold and they seemed disoriented and dumb-

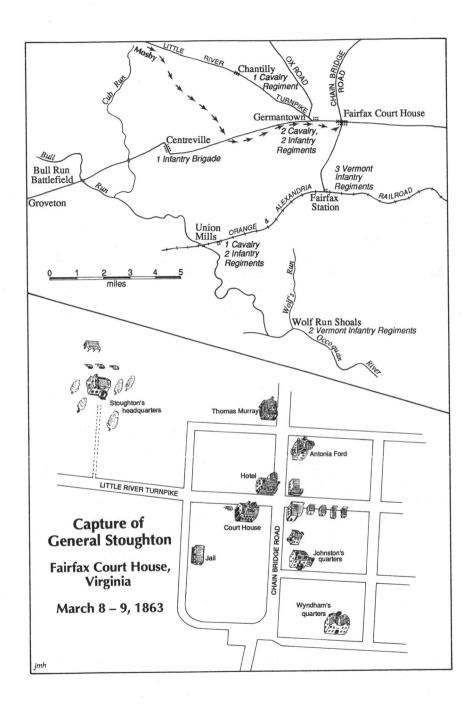

Mosby

LITTLE          RIVER

Cub Run

Chantilly
1 Cavalry
Regiment

OX ROAD

CHAIN BRIDGE ROAD

TURNPIKE

Germantown

Fairfax Court House

Centreville
1 Infantry Brigade

2 Cavalry,
2 Infantry
Regiments

Bull

Bull Run
Battlefield

Run

3 Vermont
Infantry
Regiments

RAILROAD

Groveton

ORANGE & ALEXANDRIA

Fairfax
Station

Union
Mills
1 Cavalry
2 Infantry
Regiments

Wolf's Run

0  1  2  3  4  5
miles

Wolf Run Shoals
2 Vermont Infantry Regiments

Occoquan       River

Stoughton's
headquarters

Thomas Murray

Antonia Ford

Hotel

LITTLE RIVER TURNPIKE

**Capture of
General Stoughton**

Court House

CHAIN BRIDGE ROAD

Johnston's
quarters

**Fairfax Court House,
Virginia**

Jail

**March 8 – 9, 1863**

Wyndham's
quarters

jmh

founded. Ames rode beside Mosby in front and guided every step. It was a classic overnight Mosby raid, with men and horses rested and well-fed. As usual, Mosby and his men wore Confederate uniforms but had rain gear over them; the night was so dark, one could not distinguish blue from gray anyway. Mosby ordered the men to move quietly and speak in whispers.[21] They moved into town at 2:00 A.M. without a single challenge. Mosby left Ames and Frankland at the square and led the column farther along the street to the house of Thomas Murray, where he mistakenly thought Wyndham had his headquarters. Murray informed him that Wyndham lodged back down the street a couple of blocks, but he did not know where Stoughton slept. When the column returned to the square, Ames and Frankland had captured the sentinel in front of the hotel-hospital, across from the courthouse. "Halt, who comes there?" he had demanded. "Fifth New York Cavalry waiting for the return of Major White, of the Fifth," Ames answered, putting his pistol to the man's head and whispering, "You are Mosby's prisoner." Upon Mosby's return the raiders captured the telegraph operator asleep in his tent and seized a soldier who said he was one of Stoughton's headquarters guards.[22]

Now Mosby knew the location of Wyndham's quarters and had a prisoner who could guide him to Stoughton's; he could set to work. He divided the men into squads of four or five men and gave them assignments, upon completion of which they were to report back to the courthouse. Ames led the squad that searched Wyndham's house, another took the horses from Wyndham's stable, a third searched the provost marshal's office, and a fourth cleared his stable. Ames discovered that Wyndham had gone to Washington the day before, but he took Sir Percy's uniform and horse and two members of his staff, including Capt. Augustus Barker, Ames's former company commander and now Wyndham's adjutant.[23]

Mosby headed the party of five or six men who went to General Stoughton's headquarters. Dismounting in front of the house, he sprang up the steps and gave a thundering knock on the door. An upstairs window opened and a man said, "Who's there?" "Fifth New York Cavalry with dispatches for General Stoughton," Mosby replied. He heard footsteps on the stairs; and Lt. Samuel F. Prentiss, Stoughton's aide, in his nightshirt, opened the door and held out his hand. Mosby seized him by the collar and told him to lead the way to the general's room. Prentiss struck a light, showed them upstairs, and went into Stoughton's room with Mosby and two of his men. Walking over to the bed, Mosby pulled down the bedclothes and gave Stoughton a shake.

"Is this General Stoughton?" he asked.

Stoughton, waking up and seeing three men with pistols pointed in his face, said, "Yes, what do you want?"

"You are my prisoner."

"The hell I am."

"Jackson is at Centreville and Stuart is in possession of all your camps. You may have heard of Captain Mosby. I am Mosby."

"Oh yes, I have heard of him, but Jackson is not at Centreville, nor could Stuart be in possession of the camps about here without my hearing of it. I think you are a raiding party and a small party at that. Is Fitz here?"

"Yes."

"Well, take me to him. We were class mates."

"Certainly, but be quick."[24]

While Stoughton dressed, Mosby performed an act that symbolized his psychological war—he went to the fireplace, took a piece of coal, and on the wall wrote "Mosby." Outside, Rangers captured the guards, mounted them on horses from the stable, and were standing in front of the house when Mosby brought out Stoughton. At the courthouse, the street was crowded with horses and riders; when Mosby came, Ames introduced Captain Barker, and they started off.[25]

They were turning right at the corner of the courthouse when a man standing on the front porch of the house on the left shouted, "Halt! The horses need rest. I will not allow them to be taken out. What the devil is the matter?" There was no reply, and louder still he yelled, "I am commander of this post and this must be stopped." It was Lieutenant Colonel Johnston, commander of the cavalry brigade in Wyndham's absence. Mosby ordered two men to dismount and capture him; but when they entered the house and burst into the bedroom they found his wife in bed and his uniform on a chair, hat on the table and watch hanging on the wall, but no commander. They searched the house but did not find him—he had escaped out the back door in his nightshirt and was hiding under a barn.[26]

When Stoughton saw that Stuart's cavalry were not present and observed how few men Mosby had, he said, "This is a bold thing you have done; but you will certainly be caught; our cavalry will soon be after you." In a quiet voice, Mosby answered: "Perhaps so." They set off in column of fours, pretending to be Federal cavalry. It was so dark and there were so many prisoners that Mosby's men had more than they could handle—and some escaped, including Stoughton's aide, Prentiss. Mosby assigned William Hunter, one of his first fifteen veterans, a single duty: keep a firm grasp on the bridle reins of Stoughton's horse. Stoughton took it in good humor; Cub Run was high, and he was drenched at the ford, along with everyone else. "Captain," he joked, "this is the first rough treatment I have received."[27]

The infantry pickets at Centreville challenged the column, but Mosby did not answer. Captain Barker broke away and attempted to escape into the fort, but his horse fell in a ditch, and one of Mosby's men recaptured him. Until Centreville, Mosby remained in the rear, listening for pursuing cavalry. Then he moved to the front and led the advance around Centreville and across Cub Run, scouting ahead to the Manassas battlefield. He and George Slater, another of the original fifteen, were sitting on their horses on the heights of Groveton looking eastward when the column, with Hunter and Stoughton in the lead, came into view just as the sun rose on the horizon behind them. Mosby rarely referred to history with his men, but in this moment of jubilation he said, "George, that is the sun of Austerlitz," thinking of the brilliant sunshine that had scattered the mist for Napoleon's great victory at Austerlitz on December 2, 1805. Mosby had captured a brigadier general, a captain, a telegraph operator, thirty men, and fifty-eight horses, without firing a shot or losing a man.[28]

The next day, March 10, Mosby and his men took the prisoners to the Confederate cavalry camp at Culpeper Court House, and Mosby turned Stoughton over to the commander, his nemesis Fitz Lee, now a general. Lee was sitting at a table writing. "General," Mosby said, "here is your friend General Stoughton, whom I have just captured with his staff at Fairfax Court House." Astonished, Lee looked at Mosby and at Stoughton, then jumped to his feet and shook hands with Stoughton and invited him to have a seat by the fire and dry out from the ride in the cold rain. Mosby was dripping wet and cold as well, but Lee just stared at him as though he should leave. "It was plain that he was sorry for what I had done," Mosby related. "I was very mad at such treatment." Ignoring Lee in turn, Mosby shook hands with Stoughton, told him goodbye, and left. Fitz probably had the same thought as later, when, endorsing a subsequent Mosby report, he wrote, "Such performances need no comment." Mosby never openly broke with Fitz; he was too close to Stuart and too well respected, but in private letters after the war he delighted in deflating Fitz's image. For example, when Fitz became a national hero in the

Spanish-American War, Mosby ridiculed: "The raging crazes now are baseball, reunions & Fitz Lee."[29]

Morgan was killed when his headquarters house was surrounded; Stoughton was not physically harmed, but his life was wrecked. Sensational headlines began on March 9, the day of the raid. "A Union Brigadier General and Several Officers Gobbled Up," announced the *Washington Star* and suggested: "There is a screw loose somewhere, and we need a larger force in front." A *Star* editor accused Stoughton of putting personal comfort over efficiency and preferring the dulcet music of his band to the sound of men drilling. People made much of the fact that he had stayed in a brick house, and they seized the opportunity to condemn Lincoln's boy-generals. Repeating a false rumor that Stoughton was only twenty-one years old, a Union soldier wrote to the *Baltimore American* declaring that nothing better could be expected from "these *boys,* fresh from schools, without experience, without judgment" or common sense.[30]

The *New York Times* called the capture "utterly disgraceful." The *Baltimore American* styled Stoughton "the luckless sleeper at Fairfax" who was "Caught Napping." The image of Mosby pulling down the covers and spanking him on the bottom became fixed in the popular mind. A humorous howl went up, and Lincoln joined in by making a statement to the reporters. He said that he did not mind losing a brigadier as much as the horses, "for I can make a much better Brigadier in five minutes, but the horses cost a hundred and twenty-five dollars apiece."[31]

Stoughton was taken to Libby Prison in Richmond, where he lost his health. Exchanged in May, he practiced law in New York City with an uncle, but the capture weighed on his mind. On June 1, 1867, he wrote Mosby requesting a statement that Antonia Ford had not been involved and denying the widespread stories that, in his surprise, Stoughton had used profanity. Apparently Mosby complied, because several years after Stoughton's death on Christmas Day 1868, when Mosby was under consideration for the consulate in Hong Kong, Stoughton's brother wrote Mosby a strong letter of recommendation. Stoughton was dead when Mosby revisited the headquarters house in Fairfax Court House and, standing in the bedroom, reflected that the capture left young Stoughton, like the tragic hero Count Manfred in Byron's poem "Manfred," "a blighted trunk upon a cursed root."[32]

Equally humorous with the spanking was the image of Lt. Col. Robert Johnston fleeing from his bed in his nightshirt while his wife, in her nightgown, confronted the Rebels. A *New York Times* editorial condemned the cavalry for attracting the enemy rather than warning of enemy raiders and, as far as Johnston was concerned, lamented: "We regret exceedingly that he was not caught, then and there, and carried into Dixie's land, in *statu quo*. The appearance of a National cavalry officer, taken when on outpost duty in his night-shirt, paraded through a rebel town in the same airy costume, would not only have supplied the unfortunate inhabitants with some amusement, but have served as a severer warning to his comrades left behind than they are likely to receive in any other way." The story was too entertaining not to be amplified, and it was. Mrs. Johnston became a lioness, the only Federal who resisted in the entire raid, and in the tale her husband jumped out the window naked and hid under a privy. He was labeled "Outhouse Johnston," and it was more than he could stand—he fled to Washington and on December 5, 1863, was cashiered from the service, pleading guilty of being absent without leave and breach of arrest.[33]

Wyndham was to blame for the gap in the picket line even though he was absent the night of the raid. He too was ridiculed and after one week relieved to rejoin the 1st New Jersey Cavalry. He was severely wounded in the battle of Brandy Station and resigned from the Union army. He returned to Italy and served again under Garibaldi, later meeting his death in a ballooning accident in India.[34]

Seldom in military history has an overnight raid by thirty men caused so much enemy activity. The infantry at Germantown moved into Fairfax Court House and constructed rifle pits and patrolled the streets. The cavalry brigade in the center of the screen moved inside the infantry lines and, reinforced by a Michigan cavalry brigade from Washington, for weeks picketed only in regimental strength. The brigade headquarters of Stoughton's infantry brigade moved to Fairfax Station, where the Vermonters, determined not to lose another commander, dug rifle pits and threw up breastworks for miles, entirely encircling the depot. Fifty miles west in Winchester, Gen. Robert Milroy ordered a regiment of cavalry to move forward from near Winchester to Berryville to prevent Mosby's men from entering the Shenandoah Valley.[35]

Taking action to avoid another such incident, Halleck ordered Brig. Gen. Julius Stahel, an infantry division commander in Sigel's 11th Corps in the Army of the Potomac, to report to Fairfax Court House in command of the cavalry screen, which was reorganized and strengthened. Stahel was promoted to major general, and the command confusion of having two brigade commanders on the picket line was cleared up. By

April 30, Stahel's cavalry was enlarged from two brigades of thirty-three hundred men to a division of fifty-two hundred, three brigades and one battery. Price became commander of Stahel's second brigade. Casey's infantry division headquarters moved from Washington to Centreville, and his men on the line were reinforced with one brigade of infantry, stationed in the former hole in the line at Chantilly, directly in front of Fairfax Court House. On April 17, Casey was replaced by Gen. John J. Abercrombie.[36]

Stuart's reaction greatly contrasted with Fitz Lee's. He issued an order commending Mosby for "boldness, skill, and success" and "daring enterprise and dashing heroism" in several forays. Lee, who had commended "Lieutenant Mosby" on February 28 for capturing many prisoners and boldly harassing the enemy, now on March 19 had him appointed captain of Partisan Rangers, effective March 15, and, within another week, promoted him to major, effective on March 26. The appointment as an officer of Partisan Rangers was only temporary until he could recruit a company to be mustered into the regular cavalry. Then he would be a major in the regular cavalry. Lee believed that he was doing what was best for Mosby, for by now partisans had a reputation for pillaging the farms of their friends more than enemy camps. They were considered harmful and on the way out. Stuart advised, "By all means ignore the term 'Partisan Ranger.' It is in bad repute. Call your command 'Mosby's Regulars.'" Mosby went against this advice and against public opinion—he wanted a company of Rangers, not regulars. He wrote to Stuart that he could not accept the appointment on Lee's terms, that his men had joined him under the impression that they would be entitled to spoils under the Partisan Ranger Act. He demanded the authority to enroll his men as partisans.[37]

Aiding him in his campaign to remain a partisan was the phenomenon that the capture of Stoughton made him famous and a hero of the Southern people. "Your praise is on every lip," Stuart wrote. The *Richmond Enquirer* published Stuart's commendation and a letter from Mosby describing the raid, and the editors praised him as a "gallant Captain" who had performed a "brilliant act." "Capture of a Yankee Brigadier," ran the headline in the *Richmond Dispatch,* and the front-page report stated that Mosby rousted thirty men, a captain, and the general from their beds. The dialogue in Stoughton's bedroom was repeated over and over; and, by the time it reached Richmond, a touch of profanity had been added. The story was mythical, but it went that when Mosby asked

Stoughton if he knew him, Stoughton said: "Yes, have we caught the son of a bitch?" "No," Mosby supposedly replied, "we haven't, but he has caught you, so get up and prepare to ride." Another version had Stoughton asking, "Have you caught the damned rascal?"[38]

In the North newspaper editors and army officials investigated and concluded that the loose screw was headquarterism, but also that Antonia Ford and other civilians had spied for Mosby and that Mosby's men had dressed in Union uniforms and had the countersign. On the picket line the men had a good deal of discussion about Ford. Many decided that Mosby had sent a spy into the picket line at midnight, and, when the "grand rounds" patrol passed, the spy overheard the countersign. A rumor circulated and appeared in the newspapers that a few days before the raid Mosby had come through the lines in disguise, toured strategic sites guided by Antonia, and spent the night in the Ford house. At least ten people, including Antonia Ford, were arrested and imprisoned in the Old Capitol Prison for about two months. None of the accusations were valid except headquarterism. Mosby did not have the countersign, and, while he often relied on information from citizens, this time the residents were not involved. In 1900 he wrote to a friend that he met Ford when he was a private on picket duty early in the war but did not communicate with her again until after the war: "She was innocent as Abraham Lincoln."[39]

Eight days after the capture of Stoughton, Mosby struck the screen again, this time in the daylight in the northern sector about nine miles north of Fairfax Court House, at Herndon Station. On March 16 he met with forty men at Rector's Cross Roads and rode fourteen miles to Ball's Mill on Goose Creek, rested overnight with friends, and the next day moved against the twenty-five-man picket post of the 1st Vermont Cavalry. John Underwood guided the raiders to the rear of the village, and they entered from the north at noon. This was the direction and time for the relief of the guards, and Mosby had his men masquerade as the Union relief party. He had the two men on the point dressed in blue overcoats, and they captured the vidette before he could sound a warning. When Mosby's men appeared, the Union lieutenant and his men were dismounted and resting at a sawmill. At one hundred yards, Mosby ordered a saber charge, and several bluecoats fled into the upstairs of the sawmill. Mosby jumped down, ran in, and demanded that they surrender or he would burn the building—they quickly surrendered. In a house nearby, the raiders captured a Union cavalry investigating committee having lunch. They were in town to investigate charges that the pickets were stealing from civilians. One member of the committee was Maj. William Wells, later a general. Mosby's report, which Lee sent to President Davis, stated, "I brought off 25 prisoners—a major (Wells), 1 captain, 2 lieutenants, and 21 men, all their arms, 26 horses and equipments. . . . My loss was nothing." "Still Gobbling Them Up," reported the *Washington Star*. Heintzelman pulled back the screen five miles southeast, from Dranesville and Herndon Station to Difficult Run.[40]

When Mosby disbanded at the end of the Herndon Station Raid, he asked the men to meet again at Rector's Cross Roads on March 23, after six days of rest. Meanwhile he and Underwood scouted toward Fairfax Court House, and he decided to make a daylight attack on the one-hundred-man reserve picket-post of the 5th New York Cavalry at Chantilly, where the camp of the 18th Pennsylvania Cavalry had been during the Stoughton Raid, five miles west of Fairfax Court House on the Little River Turnpike. He hoped to slip through the same fields that he had used on the Stoughton Raid and approach Chantilly from the rear. Fifty-five men showed up, and that was so many they would likely attract attention, but Mosby accepted them all—he was in no position to turn men away.[41]

They marched forth on the turnpike to a point six miles west of the picket line at Chantilly and turned to the south and went parallel to the road, in the woods and fields. By this time they had come about twenty-three miles at a steady pace, and Mosby realized that the horses were jaded. He had made a mistake in arriving at the target without rested horses. Then two videttes spotted them and took the alarm into Chantilly. Mosby canceled the raid, but about seven or eight men from his party broke away and, on their own, attacked the advance picket post of seven men west of Chantilly. They killed one of the pickets with a shot through the forehead and captured the other six. Rejoining Mosby and the column on a hill to the west overlooking Chantilly, they watched as about seventy men of the 5th New York mounted, formed in column, and headed toward them.[42]

Mosby realized that he was in great danger because the Union horses were fresh and his were exhausted. He knew that if he retreated they would overtake and stampede his men. As a student of ancient history, he was familiar with the tactic of false retreat used by Titus Labienus, Julius Caesar's commander in Gaul. Mosby decided to take a page from the history of 53 B.C. and pretend to withdraw. He led the raiders at a trot, back up the pike three miles west of Chantilly to a place where the road passed through a slip of woods about one-half mile wide. Within the woods Union troops had cut down trees and erected an abatis, or barricade of fallen trees perpendicular to the road, with sharpened tree branches facing west. Here he halted and sent five of his men home with the seven prisoners and ordered the others to draw sabers and prepare to charge. Concealed behind the abatis, he heard the hoof strokes and the loud cheers of the approaching enemy. When they came within one hundred yards, he ordered the charge. Completely surprised, the Federals halted; but before they could wheel, Mosby's men were among them. In the melee, Mosby's men returned their sabers to the scabbards and used their "death-dealing" revolvers. The result was three dead Union cavalrymen, one mortally wounded, and thirty-six captured, including one lieutenant, and fifty horses captured. "Hurrah for Mosby!" Lee exclaimed. "I wish I had a hundred like him." Mosby had turned a potential stampede into a rout of the enemy by using a mounted countercharge from ambush and melee with revolvers. His maxim henceforth would be to never stand still and receive a charge but always take the offensive. He had learned the uselessness of the saber against the revolver and not to make contact with the enemy when his horses were jaded.[43]

In three months as an independent, Mosby had forced major rearrangements on the early-warning screen in the defenses of Washington, he had attracted forty temporary volunteers to reinforce his fifteen men on loan from Stuart, he had created fear in the enemy minds, he had become a Southern hero, and he had learned valuable tactical lessons. He had moved up from private to major, but somehow he had to convince Stuart and Lee to give him and his men permanent status as Partisan Rangers. He had no knowledge of it but would learn later that he had a silent admirer high in the Confederate government—Secretary of War James A. Seddon was reading every one of Mosby's reports and cheering to himself. Eventually he would overrule Stuart and Lee and, in spite of the negative reputation of Rangers in general, would give Mosby what he wanted.

# 6

# Miskel's Farm

There was a Union signal station on a hill on the left bank of the Potomac River in southern Maryland, and the men had a clear view of the farm across the river in Virginia. A few minutes after sunrise on April 1, 1863, they began cheering at the top of their voices, for they saw a detachment of 150 Union cavalrymen surround Mosby's 69 men inside the high plank fence around the barn. The Union horsemen were mounted and in ranks, and all was steady and in order, while in the barnyard everything was commotion and confusion—the Rebels were just waking up and rushing to saddle their horses. In the farmhouse, the pro–Southern farmer looked out a window and thought to himself, "They've got old Mosby this time sure." Mosby was surprised, surrounded, and outnumbered over two to one. Then the boys in blue charged, and in a ferocious fight Mosby's men broke out of the trap, killing, wounding, or capturing 74 percent of the attackers. Across the river the men on the hill fell silent and the wind came up, swirling and making a sorrowful sound. They watched Mosby's men gathering up the wounded and dead and for the rest of their lives wondered how in the world Mosby turned disaster into triumph in that barnyard that morning.[1]

It began the day before, a gloomy wintry day with snow falling thick and fast all morning and dark clouds hovering on the horizon until night. Mosby's men rendezvoused at Rector's Cross Roads, and this was the largest group yet. Besides the squad detailed from Stuart, there were Confederate cavalrymen on furlough to get horses, infantrymen absent without leave, and several recruits from the area. Ames appeared, along with brothers Samuel and William Chapman from the disbanded Dixie Artillery Company. A few were convalescents from the Confederate hospital in Middleburg, like infantryman Samuel Underwood, wounded in the left foot and riding with crutches tied to his saddle. Sam, a brother of scout John Underwood, would become one of Mosby's favorites and one of the few that he had officially transferred to him.[2]

Other than Stuart's detail they were conglomerates, a scratch outfit come together for one raid. There was no adjutant, and there were no lieutenants or sergeants. Mosby had met only twelve of them before, and most of them were strangers to each other. In a reference to Shakespeare, he wrote that they were "almost as motley a crowd as Falstaff's regiment." He was referring to the lack of organization, not their appearance—they were clean-cut, intelligent men, well-dressed and well-mounted. Mosby refused to enroll them as regulars and operated for over five months without organization, until June 10, 1863, when he received approval for partisan status. Union prisoners of war captured by the raiders during this period were amazed that the band had no subordinate officers. "Each man is in himself a commander," one said. "In a charge the order is given, and each man acts for himself."[3]

Mosby characteristically told no one the objective, which was the Union picket post at Dranesville, on the Northern sector of the cavalry screen twenty-eight miles away. The snowing stopped by mid-afternoon, and at sundown they arrived at Herndon Station, two miles south of Dranesville. Mosby learned from residents that the picket post had withdrawn behind Difficult Run, five miles toward Alexandria. Later in his career, after his men were mustered in, he would cancel missions that were failing, but now he hesitated. "I knew that if I dispersed the men without trying to do something I would never see them again," he wrote.[4]

It was cold and the men and horses were tired, so he decided to find forage and food and a place to spend the night and rest the horses. He marched to Dranesville and turned left on the Leesburg and Alexandria Turnpike. Four miles later, at almost midnight, he turned right into Miskel's farm, the nearest place with adequate shelter and provisions. The horses were placed in the barnyard and fed, and after supper the men went to sleep in the house and barn loft. Mosby slept on the floor by the fireplace in the front room of the house. The nearest Union cavalry camp was nine miles away, and he felt safe. He had no guards on the turnpike and only one sentry watching the horses. "My authority over the men was of such a transitory nature that I disliked to order them to do anything but fight," he remembered.[5]

Mosby was unaware that a trap was closing around him. Miskel's farm was nine miles southeast of Leesburg, where Broad Run flows into the Potomac River. The farmhouse was only a few hundred yards from

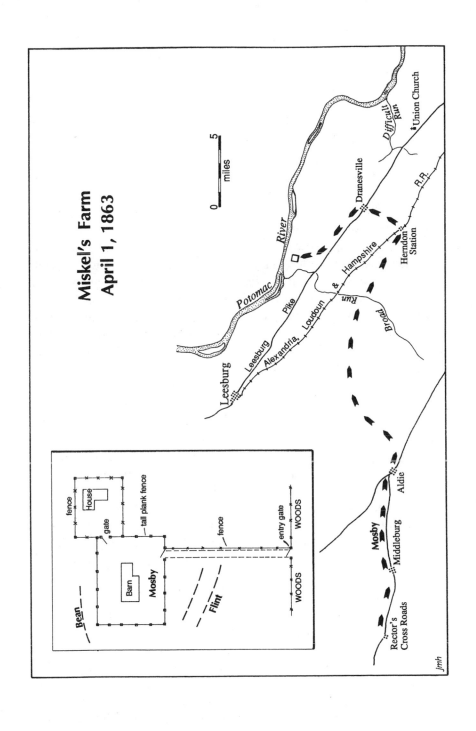

## Miskel's Farm
## April 1, 1863

Potomac River

Leesburg

Leesburg Pike

Alexandria, Loudoun & Hampshire R.R.

Dranesville

Herndon Station

Difficult Run

†Union Church

Broad Run

Mosby

Aldie

Middleburg

Rector's Cross Roads

0 — 5 miles

### Inset

Bean

fence

House

gate

tall plank fence

Barn

Mosby

Flint

fence

entry gate

WOODS

WOODS

jmh

the Potomac River, and he was hemmed in by streams on two sides and fences and woodlands on the other. The only exit was the way he had come in, the lane to the turnpike. The farm entry gate was in a fence corner formed by a fence running parallel with the pike and another along the eastern side of the farm. The horses were unsaddled and tied inside a high plank fence surrounding the barn.[6]

While Mosby slept the Union cavalry searched for him. When the raiders left Herndon Station, a Unionist civilian proceeded to the Union camp and reported that Mosby was about and that his men would probably spend the night in homes in Dranesville. Maj. Charles F. Taggart, in charge of the northern section of pickets, selected a detachment of 150 men from his most experienced and efficient regiment, the 1st Vermont Cavalry, placed them under his best, most resolute officers, and sent them to search for Mosby in Dranesville. The Vermonters had been organized in 1861 and had fought Turner Ashby, served at Second Bull Run, and had been on picket duty here since the previous fall. Later they would fight at Gettysburg, Cedar Creek, and other battles. Tonight, they had scores to settle—Mosby had surprised them at Aldie Mill and Herndon Station, capturing five officers and thirty-eight men.[7]

Taggart appointed Capt. Henry Flint in charge, and at 2:00 A.M. the party set out from camp at Union Church, five miles from Dranesville. In Dranesville they separated into two columns and surrounded and searched every house, finding no Mosby men but learning that Mosby was at Miskel's. Flint secured a civilian volunteer to guide them. By morning the sky was clear and the sun was rising over the snow-covered fields when they stopped at the farm of Isabella Reed two miles south of Miskel's. Seated at the kitchen table was Dick Moran, one of Mosby's men who was a family friend and had spent the night. Dick jumped up and hid under the stairs and listened as someone, probably a slave, confirmed that Mosby was at Miskel's. Moving on, Flint shouted: "All right, boys; we will give Mosby an April fool!" and they responded with a hearty cheer. Moran, forty-nine years old and the father of ten children, ran to the barn, saddled up, and rode across the fields to warn Mosby.[8]

Flint led the first squadron of one hundred men and Capt. George H. Bean the rear squadron of fifty men, at an interval. As Flint rode through the entry gate and into the enclosure of the farm, he believed that he had Mosby in a cul-de-sac from which he could not escape. All of Mosby's horses were still inside the barnyard fence. Flint ordered Bean to have his men close the gate behind them and barricade it with fence rails.

Then he sent Bean and his squadron to the left, around to the rear of the barn. Flint formed his men in two ranks in a semicircle at the front of the barn, and spontaneously they began shooting their carbines, splattering bullets into the front of the barn and the boards of the fence.[9]

Mosby had awakened at sunrise, put on his boots, and stepped into the backyard, where he heard Moran, coming at full speed, waving his hat and yelling with his foghorn voice, "Mount! Mount! The Yankees are coming!" He ran to the barnyard and, looking through the plank fence, saw Flint's advance coming through the entry gate. The outlook seemed dim, yet he recalled that Napoleon's *Maxims of War,* numbers eighteen and twenty-three, counseled that when enveloped one should quickly assemble his forces and go on the offensive, disconcerting the adversary. The Chantilly fight had taught him the superiority of the revolver over the saber in a melee. He told his men they must fight their way out and ordered them not to shoot but saddle and mount.[10]

In the field, Flint finished his deployment and shouted, "Draw sabers!" "Charge!" He took the lead, and they galloped forward, sabers flashing in the sunlight. On his own Mosby recognized the truth in what Stonewall Jackson once told Gen. Richard Ewell: "Shoot the brave officers and the cowards will run away and take the men with them." Mosby ordered the men to kill Flint. The Union horsemen dashed up to the high plank fence, apparently expecting to slice off Mosby's ears or give him sunburn from the beams reflecting off their whirling blades. Mosby and several of his men, standing behind the fence, waited until they came within revolver range and then commenced firing with both pistols, emptying saddles right and left. Flint fell in the snow and mud a few yards from the fence, killed immediately by six bullets. Lt. Josiah Grout went down with a bullet in the hip and one in the abdomen. Between twelve and fifteen enlisted men fell, leaving at least fourteen riderless horses jumping and running and dodging the men at their feet.[11]

One of Mosby's men who had saddled up in the barn came riding out the door and saw Mosby standing in the barnyard on foot, a smoking Colt in each hand. Now, with the enemy stalled and with about twenty of his men mounted, Mosby threw open the gate, and still on foot, ordered: "Follow me! Charge 'em! Charge 'em! and go through 'em!" The men who witnessed this said later that they had never seen such audacity— Mosby was leading a cavalry charge on foot. Then one of the men dismounted and gave Mosby his horse, and he proceeded, mounted. He and his men screamed the Rebel yell and closed with the already stunned right wing of Flint's squadron, and now it was the Colt versus the saber, and no contest. One of Mosby's men emptied five saddles. "The remorseless revolver was doing its work of death in their ranks," wrote Mosby, "while their swords were as harmless as the wooden sword of harlequin."[12]

The men in Flint's second rank saw the riderless horses and the wounded and dead on the ground and realized that Flint was down. Suddenly they panicked and raced for the gate, wishing now they had left it open. As they fled, on their right they saw a horse and rider coming at full gallop, racing with them for the gate—it was Captain Bean. From his position in the rear of the barn, he could not see everything, but he heard and saw enough to convince him to abandon his men and save himself. Almost in hysterics, he and others pressed their horses against the locked gate until it gave way. Bean had a good horse, and he was one of the first to arrive back at camp in Union Church. Within the month he was dismissed for cowardice.[13]

The gate was down, but everyone tried to go through at the same time, and they became wedged in the enclosure. Mosby and his men followed down the lane close behind, and in the corner moved among them, shooting at close range. Once they emptied their revolvers they used them as clubs. The Vermonters who escaped followed Bean in the race for camp. "They never drew rein or looked back to see how many were behind them," Mosby wrote. "I got pretty close to one, who, seeing that he was bound to be shot or caught, jumped off his horse and sat down on the roadside. As I passed him he called out to me, 'You have played us a nice April fool, boys!'" Mosby lost one man killed and three wounded; the Vermonters had a 74 percent casualty rate, with seven killed or mortally wounded, twenty-two wounded, and eighty-two men and ninety-five horses captured.[14]

Having seen the power of the Colt revolver in this second melee against the saber, never again would Mosby order a saber charge. He had carried a Colt since before the battle of First Bull Run but had not realized what it could do in close until the Chantilly ambush and this fight. Like John Hunt Morgan, he appreciated the increased firepower of infantry and, when appropriate, would deploy a squad of dismounted sharpshooters armed with long-range rifles. Yet his characteristic tactic was the mounted charge, given increased shock and killing power by replacing the saber with two Colt revolvers per man. He said that the saber was as out of date as a coat of mail, as worthless as a cornstalk, and good for nothing but roasting meat over a fire. To attack with a saber you had to get close enough to strike the enemy; to hit an opponent with a .44 caliber six-shooter, you had to be within thirty feet. By coming into close quarters to use their sabers, the Union cavalry were playing Mosby's game—they were coming within range of his pistols.[15]

Flint should have dismounted his men, giving them the firepower and discipline of infantry skirmishers like Morgan usually did. On foot, he should have advanced to within fifty yards—still out of range of Mosby's revolvers—and demanded a surrender. Mosby might have cut his way out, but it would have been costly, and Flint would have avoided panic. By using the saber charge Flint played into Mosby's hand and lost the advantage. After the skirmish Mosby's men took the wounded of both sides into the farmhouse, and Mosby visited the bedside of Lieutenant Grout and granted his request that one of his friends among the prisoners be allowed to stay behind with him. Grout recovered and in 1896 attended William McKinley's inauguration as the Republican nominee and soon-to-be-elected governor of Vermont. Mosby called on him and his family at the time, and they became friends.[16]

During the next few days Mosby tested the Fairfax cavalry screen and found it vigilant. He led and sent dry runs into the Shenandoah Valley to the rear of the Union force in Winchester. The Orange and Alexandria Railroad had opened in March for the first time since Mosby had gone independent. In April the trains extended to Warrenton Junction, delivering supplies to cavalry units on Gen. Joseph Hooker's right flank and, beginning in mid-April, to Hooker's cavalry corps under Gen. George Stoneman, who were preparing to cross the Rappahannock to raid Lee's communications. The Chancellorsville campaign was beginning, and Hooker was so successfully masking his flanking movement against Lee at Fredericksburg that Stuart anxiously wanted to know where Hooker was going. When Mosby proposed a raid in Fairfax County in the Union rear, Stuart sent him a reply on April 25 encouraging the idea and asking him to watch for troop movements. The next day, April 26, Stuart ordered Mosby to capture one of the railroad trains supplying Stoneman and emphasized again that Mosby should watch for moving enemy divisions. Mosby called a meeting at Upperville on April 28 and with eighty men set off to obey Stuart's orders, when a Union cavalry raid from Fairfax Court House blocked his way. By the time Mosby could organize another raid, Stoneman had departed to raid Lee's rear, and the Confederates had located Hooker in Chancellorsville.[17]

When Mosby learned that Stoneman had taken the Union cavalry out of the campaign, he recognized an opportunity to strike Hooker's communication line. Early in the morning of May 3 he and one hundred men, including twenty South Carolina cavalry on leave to find horses, were moving in that direction when near Warrenton Junction they captured a few prisoners from a small detachment of infantry guarding the railroad. Interrogating them, Mosby learned that there was a small cavalry camp at the junction. After this he would scout before attacking, but this time he acted blindly: "I had no idea whether I was attacking a hundred or a thousand men." At about 9:00 A.M., with the roar of cannon in the battle of Chancellorsville in the distance, he led a mounted charge with pistols against the camp of one hundred 1st West Virginia Cavalry. The Union men fired a few shots, then surrendered. Mosby's men spread out to gather up the scattered Union horses when suddenly down the track came two hundred of the 5th New York and 1st Vermont Cavalry at full speed, sabers drawn. Their camp was only one mile northeast, and they had heard the gunfire. Mosby ordered a Chantilly countercharge, but his raiders ignored him and fled in panic. It was his first defeat—he lost three dead, seventeen wounded, and six captured. "I learned wisdom from experience, and after that always looked before I took a leap," he wrote. Stahel congratulated his cavalry for breaking up the gang of guerrillas that had long infested the area. "Splendid Affair at Warrenton Junction," and "The Rebels Completely Routed," ran Northern headlines.[18]

Mosby was not discouraged; he still had faith that he could organize a command, but it would be difficult. On about May 1 he had returned the original fifteen to Stuart, and in his assembly on about May 10—the first after Warrenton Junction—only thirty-seven men appeared. The need for a Fairfax scout had passed, but he attempted to carry out Stuart's order to attack the railroad. He burned the small railroad bridge at Cedar Run, cut the telegraph line, and set fire to Kettle Run bridge. Union infantry from a passing train extinguished the blaze on the trestle at Kettle Run before it was damaged. On the return, the men complained that, since there were no spoils, the raid was a failure, a "water-haul." Mosby realized that to keep his men he had to furnish spoils: "War to them was not an abstraction; it meant prisoners, arms, horses and sutler's stores; remote consequences were not much considered." Therefore, on May 19, 1863, he asked Stuart for a mountain howitzer. With it he could capture a train, satisfy Stuart, and provide spoils from the train. Actually Stuart was asking too much of Mosby. Stuart knew that it would be complicated, given Mosby's need to allow his men time to collect spoils, and therefore he had warned him to avoid attacking near the camp of an enemy cavalry brigade.[19]

Hooker's main supply line ran from Aquia Creek; only one train each day used the Orange and Alexandria Railroad, leaving Alexandria each morning with supplies for the cavalry converging on the Rappahannock River for the June 9 battle of Brandy Station. General Heintzelman in Washington had been given charge of defending the railroad for 38.5 miles from Alexandria to Cedar Run, one mile south of Catlett's Station. He had the 12th Vermont Infantry guarding the 16.5 miles from Bull Run to Cedar Run. The regiment had two companies at Catlett's and eight at Manassas Junction. He had a cavalry detachment of 170 men under Col. William D. Mann, 7th Michigan Cavalry, camped at Bristoe Station and sending out mounted patrols. A company of the 15th Vermont Infantry rode as guards on top of the cars.[20]

Mosby's challenge was to avoid the infantry and cavalry camps and cavalry patrols and drive the company of infantry away from the train after it was derailed. He needed the cannon to scatter the infantry and destroy the boiler on the engine. By May 27 a cannon had arrived from Stuart, and Sam Chapman drilled some of the men in its use. Mosby realized later that what he was about to attempt was "not only hazardous but foolhardy." This time he scouted carefully and selected a hill one mile east of Catlett's Station, far enough away from the infantry at Catlett's, and 6.5 miles from the cavalry camp at Bristoe Station. And he avoided cavalry patrols; one passed an hour before the attack. But one thing he failed to consider—the booming of the cannon would immediately alarm the cavalry camp at Bristoe Station.[21]

Mosby had failed to realize that the cannon changed the nature of his guerrilla operation. For one thing it attracted attention and violated his rule of having headquarters in the saddle. As soon as it rolled into Fauquier County, Mann learned about it from his scouts and made a report. It was a twelve-pound brass mountain howitzer and was light for fast travel, with no caisson and only fifteen rounds of ammunition in the limber chest, plenty to stop a train but not enough for a skirmish. And more important, now he could not run from a stronger enemy force by scattering into the woods and mountains; he had to defend the cannon. Morgan had light artillery, but he raided with one or two thousand men or more. At the time Mosby would have needed at least two hundred well-organized cavalry to defend the gun, rather than the forty-eight conglomerates who showed up. With this small, unorganized force, the cannon was a millstone around his neck.[22]

On the bright and sunny morning of May 29, Mosby met his men at John W. Patterson's mill on the Little River south of Middleburg. The birds were singing, the trees had new bright green leaves, and corn was coming up in the fields. They marched fifteen miles past farms and woodlands to Greenwich, about four miles from the target, and paused for supper. Then they moved two more miles and spent the night, within about two miles of the track. The next morning they moved to within one hundred yards of the track and concealed themselves in the thick scrub pines and high undergrowth. Some of the men cut the telegraph line, loosened a rail, and attached a telegraph wire. Hidden in the grass, the wire extended to a tree, where one of the men was to tug it just as the train drew near, removing the rail. The site was on a slight hill where the train would be running downgrade and would be difficult to brake. The howitzer was hidden on the edge of the tree line ready to fire once the train derailed.[23]

At 7:00 A.M. the train left Alexandria with nine cars of forage and rations and one car filled with sutler's supplies. It came down the grade at full speed. The fireman, watching the track, saw the rail move and shouted to the engineer, but it was too late. The locomotive ran off the track and fell over on its side, injuring the fireman and breaking the leg of a newsboy. The lieutenant and thirty infantrymen on the cars fired a volley that killed the horse of one of the raiders. Then the cannon boomed, and a shell crashed through one of the cars. The guards quickly jumped down and ran away into the woods on the other side of the track. The second shell struck the boiler of the engine, sending steam and hot water into the air and creating a loud whistling sound. Mosby's men ran to the sutler's car, broke in, and seized boxes of oranges and lemons, candy, leather for boots, and especially fresh shad. Fish was a rare delicacy in the blockaded Confederacy, and each man took several. They captured the Union army mail, used hay to set fire to all of the cars, and departed, heading back up the narrow path in the woods from which they had come.[24]

At Bristoe Station they heard the cannon. Mann, who would soon lead a cavalry charge under Custer at Gettysburg, assumed immediately that it was Mosby attacking the train. Some of his men said it was Stuart, but he knew about the cannon and knew that Mosby would hit and then run north toward his boarding area. This was the key; he knew how to organize a pursuit, how to act quickly and correctly. He sent a detachment of about forty-five men of the 5th New York Cavalry under Lt. Elmer Barker west to intercept Mosby. The 5th New York had been humiliated by Mosby several times, including Chantilly and the capture of Stoughton, but they, like most Union cavalry by now, were gaining self-confidence. Their saber charge at Warrenton Junction had scattered Mosby's men. Mann himself took 125 men along the track directly against Mosby. Most were 1st Vermont Cavalry, the regiment whipped by Mosby at Miskel's. These men had no way of knowing it, but this would be their last fight with Mosby; they only knew that it was an opportunity to even the score.[25]

Mosby and his raiders struck the road to Greenwich and had gone only about one mile from the track when the advance saw Union cavalry in the road ahead. It was Barker's detachment. If Mosby had not had the cannon, he could have scattered his men across the fields and through the woods and escaped. But the cannon had to be escorted along the road through the enemy troopers. Mosby halted and had Chapman deploy it in the road and open fire. Chapman threw a few shells, killing one of the Union horses, and Barker retreated to a nearby hill off the road. Mosby then advanced, moving past the dead horse and leaving Barker's detachment behind. But they had not gone far when Mosby, bringing up the rear, saw Barker closing in pursuit. Back on the hill after Mosby had passed, Barker had asked for twenty-five volunteers to chase Mosby, and here they were again, galloping forward, following the trail of fresh fish dropped in the road. They overtook the rear guard of Mosby himself; Capt. Bradford S. Hoskins, an English captain and veteran of the Crimean War who had joined Mosby; and three other men. The Union men charged with bayonets and pistols—they had the momentum and a five-to-one advantage. Hoskins, thrusting with his sword, was mortally wounded by a revolver bullet, and one of Mosby's men was killed. Two of the Union men were wounded and their horses shot.[26]

The rear guard fight caused Barker to halt, enabling Mosby to rejoin his men. By now he realized that, since he was confined to the road and slowed by the cannon, he could not outrun the enemy. And worst of all, he saw that, without his permission, his raiders were leaving; they were unwilling to fight for the cannon. Later he condemned them for deserting to go on a picnic, fry shad, and eat confectioneries. Left with only a few men, he determined to save his honor and stand by the gun and not surrender it without a struggle. He directed Chapman to turn the cannon into a narrow lane, sloping upward, with high fences on both sides, and unlimber and shell the enemy until they came up the lane and then load with canister—if the Federals wanted the gun, they would have to charge up the lane into its mouth.[27]

Barker and about twenty men, unfazed by the shells exploding around them, saw the challenge and realized that, if they could capture Mosby's piece, it would go a long way toward settling accounts; the captured gun would be a trophy, physical proof of victory over an elusive enemy. "I think we can get that gun before they can fire again," he told the men. "Let's go," they answered. With sabers drawn, in column of fours they charged and were only twenty feet away when it fired. A twelve-pounder shooting canister was like a huge shotgun with a twelve-pound shell; the "boom" was accompanied by the hissing and whistling of more than two dozen lead balls. Three men were killed, one shot through the head. Barker was hit by two balls in the left thigh, and his horse was struck by four or five. An additional seven men were wounded.[28]

Barker and his men withdrew to the main road, and at that moment Mann and his men arrived. Now his detachment charged the cannon, and it fired again, killing one and wounding seven. The unharmed Union men continued fighting, emptying their revolvers and then using sabers, determined to capture the gun. Chapman had been outstanding, but he was out of ammunition and wounded with a bullet in the thigh— he continued fighting with the rammer of the gun. Mosby and one man countercharged and ran through the Union ranks to the Union rear. This was a mistake. He had to pass back through to escape, and as he did a large cavalryman struck him on the shoulder with a saber and almost knocked him to the ground. He shot the man with his pistol and clung to the saddle, his horse brushing against tree limbs, knocking off his hat and scratching his face. He could hear the Union men cheering as he rode away. He stopped at a nearby house to wash the blood from his face.[29]

He had lost the cannon on the first raid; Hoskins was mortally wounded; two were wounded, counting himself; and eight were captured, the wounded Chapman among them. Mosby would carry the scar from the saber wound the rest of his life. He had wrecked a train, burned ten cars, captured four days of mail for the troops at Bealeton Station, and stopped railroad traffic for twenty-four hours. The *Richmond Dispatch* ran the headline, "Mosby again at Work," and praised him for defending the cannon. It was no humiliating defeat, but he learned that capturing trains was complicated and that having a cannon required a strong force of organized, disciplined men. Stahel wired Heintzelman: "We whipped him like the devil, and took his artillery. My forces are still pursuing him." The *New York Times* commended the cavalry for giving "the guerrilla chieftain the soundest thrashing he has yet received." Stahel had the cannon polished and placed in front of his headquarters in Fairfax Court House, where it glistened in the sun, a symbol of the newfound courage and persistence of the Union cavalry.[30]

Mosby made an even greater exception to his rule of having headquarters in the saddle when he sent for Pauline and the children to join him in Fauquier County. On March 16, 1863, one week after the capture of Stoughton, he wrote her that he had arranged with his friends James and Elizabeth Hathaway for their room and board. The Hathaways had a large plantation and three-story brick house about five miles north of Salem in the heart of "Mosby's Confederacy." They had a large family and owned 760 acres and 31 slaves in 1860. Fount Beattie was boarding there and would marry one of the daughters, and they would have twelve children. Pauline, May, and Bev arrived; and at the Hathaways' she conceived her third child, born December 8, 1863, and named John Singleton Mosby Jr. She would stay in northern Virginia for five months and then in August would go south to visit at Idle Wilde and sojourn with other relatives and friends.[31]

Pauline and the children were at the Hathaways' when on Monday night, June 8, 1863, the Union cavalry searched the house and found them. The raiders were a detachment of the 1st New York Cavalry, scouting from Berryville through Snicker's Gap and down into Mosby's land. At 8:00 P.M. in Salem someone told Capt. William Boyd that Mosby was staying at the Hathaways. He and his men surrounded the house at about midnight. They found Pauline and the children in a bedroom upstairs but no Mosby. She took it good-naturedly, commenting that she could not imagine how they found her. "Mrs. Moseby is decidedly handsome, and converses with more than ordinary intelligence," one of the party reported. They arrested James Hathaway and took him away as a prisoner, along with several horses from the stable. A contemporary newspaper article stated that Mosby had been warned by one of his men and had left the house for the night. John Scott, in his 1867 history of Mosby's command, a book based on interviews with Mosby, gave the incorrect date of May 28, but obviously described the same event. He wrote that Beattie awakened Mosby with the warning that the enemy were coming, and Mosby slept the rest of the night in a woodland near the house and did not learn about the search until the next morning after the New Yorkers were gone.[32]

Two days after the Hathaway raid, Mosby finally received authority to enlist his men as partisans. After Stuart and Lee had turned him down, he had appealed to Secretary of War James Seddon. Seddon was a civilian with no military training who understood and appreciated classic guerrilla warfare. Forty-seven years old, he was born in Fredericksburg, graduated from the University of Virginia with honors, and became a wealthy lawyer and politician in Richmond. He was tireless, independent, scholarly, and a good judge of character. When he took office on November 21, 1862, he investigated complaints against the partisan rangers and reported on January 3, 1863, that the program had failed. Not only had partisans developed an odious reputation, they had set up permanent camps, neglecting to take advantage of the home ground by finding quarters among the civilians and disbanding and reassembling upon call. He was reluctant to disband them but was avoiding approval of new commands and attempting to convert existing units into the regular army.[33]

Seddon had completely turned against partisans before Mosby went independent. However, when Mosby's reports began coming in, he read them and noticed that Mosby was boarding his men in homes, disbanding and reassembling in the manner of a classic people's war. Receiving Mosby's appeal, he went against his own rule and gave Mosby authority to recruit a new Ranger command. He stated that Mosby's commission as captain of Rangers implied the authority to organize a company of Rangers, and Lee and Stuart acquiesced.[34]

The command met on June 10 at Rector's Cross Roads and was for the first time organized as Company A, 43rd Battalion Partisan Rangers. The law required Mosby to allow the men of the company to elect their officers. This provision had unseated him and Jones, and he realized that combining democracy with discipline was "as dangerous as mixing acid and alkali." Throughout the war he would appoint all of his officers and force the men to approve. He would draw the company up in line, nominate an officer, call for "ayes," and quickly declare unanimity. Once, when there were rumblings against what the men called "Mosby's elections," he nominated a man and declared that anyone who disagreed should step forward and he would send him to the regular army. No one did, and he declared the candidate elected.[35]

There was great apprehension in the North and in Washington over an expected Confederate invasion, and Mosby realized that a raid in southern Maryland would have multiplied impact. Scouts reported that a small force of cavalry guarding the border on the northern bank of the Potomac had a camp at Seneca Creek, twenty miles up the Potomac from Washington, near a bridge over the Chesapeake and Ohio Canal that ran alongside the river. At daylight on June 11, Mosby and one hundred men—seventy of his own and thirty Prince William County Rangers under Capt. William G. Brawner—attacked and routed eighty men of the 6th Michigan Cavalry, plundering and burning their camp, seizing their colors, and killing and wounding five, and capturing seventeen men and thirty horses, plus four mules taken from a canal boat. Mosby had two men killed including Brawner and two wounded. He had sent Stuart Stoughton's saddle; now he sent him the captured banner. Endorsing Mosby's report, Stuart recommended him for promotion to lieutenant colonel. During the raid Mosby found his new authority over the men very valuable: he was able to order and maintain the attack and enforce discipline during the looting and the retreat.[36]

Six days later, on the afternoon of June 17, 1863, Mosby and his men were again heading toward Seneca. Lee had begun moving his infantry into the Shenandoah Valley in the beginning of the Gettysburg campaign, and a raid in Maryland would serve as a diversion. Stuart's cavalry had arrived in Fauquier County the day before, screening Lee's right flank, and Mosby had met with him in the morning at Kitty Shacklett's and earlier in the afternoon at Middleburg. Now the raiders stopped to rest in the Catoctin Mountains north of Aldie and were enjoying the view for miles around, when they saw clouds of dust rising in the east and realized that Hooker's army was moving from the vicinity of Fredericksburg to Fairfax and Loudoun Counties to counter Lee. Mosby knew that the arrival of the Union army in his area presented an opportunity to capture couriers and stragglers.[37]

Canceling the raid, after dark he and three men rode onto Little River Turnpike, in the camp of Gen. George Meade's corps at Gum Spring, six miles east of Aldie, and fell in with the stream of wagons and troops moving west along the road. In the darkness, their gray uniforms were indistinguishable from blue. They passed the last of Meade's infantry picket posts at 10:00 P.M. Four hundred yards beyond, at the front gate of Union sympathizer Almond Birch, they saw three horses, an orderly holding the bridles. Pretending to be a Union officer, Mosby asked the man whose horses these were, and he said Major Sterling and Captain Fisher of General Hooker's staff, direct from Hooker's headquarters with dispatches, inside having supper. Mosby called him over, leaned down and took him by the collar with one hand, thrust a revolver in his face with the other, and whispered, "You are my prisoner. My name is Mosby." Soon the officers came out, and Mosby captured them and took Sterling's satchel of letters. Maj. William R. Sterling was a member of Hooker's general staff, and Capt. Benjamin F. Fisher was the Army of the Potomac's chief acting signal officer. Mosby took them a short distance to a friendly farmhouse, called for a light, and quickly realized that these were important documents, especially a letter from Hooker's chief of staff, Gen. Daniel Butterfield, to Gen. Alfred Pleasonton, the Union cavalry commander at Aldie. He wrote a note to Stuart and sent a man with it and the dispatches and prisoners to Stuart.[38]

The captured letter took Stuart directly into the mind of Hooker; it was as if Stuart had overhead Hooker giving a briefing to his cavalry chief. He learned that Hooker's headquarters were at Fairfax Station, General Meade's corps was at Gum Spring, and General Howard's corps was north of Meade's. The letter confirmed that Stuart's cavalry screen was working, which was crucial because that night Lee's army was on the move into Maryland and strung out from there southeast to Culpeper. It confirmed that Hooker did not know the location of Lee's army or Lee's plans and that Hooker was not crossing the Potomac in pursuit and that he had no immediate plans to cross or to move at all until he obtained further information on Lee's movements. The letter directed Pleasonton to push against Stuart the next day and revealed that two cavalry regiments were heading on a scout the next day toward the Rappahannock. This enabled Stuart to counter with cavalry and prevent the expedition from possibly discovering Lee's infantry. Lee received the letter only after it was nearly forty-eight hours old, but for him it confirmed what he had recently reported to Davis based on scouting reports. Another valuable dispatch gave the number of divisions in Hooker's army, enabling Stuart and Lee to estimate enemy strength. Once more Mosby had proved to be a valuable scout.[39]

The capture of Hooker's two staff members in the midst of their own army made front-page news in the North. "Gobbled Up," ran the headline of the *Washington Star*. The next morning, Butterfield ordered Meade, the nearest corps commander to the Birch house: "Catch and kill any guerrillas, then try them, will be a good method of treating them."

Hooker warned couriers and reconnaissance parties to take strong escorts: "The country is reported full of guerrillas." Meade moved his picket line west to include the Birch house. Three days later, Pleasonton, having driven Stuart out of Middleburg, concluded that everyone in the town supported Mosby. He ordered all adult males arrested and ruled that the women must keep indoors; and in the future when Union lines advanced, his men were to search all houses for concealed enemy soldiers.[40]

Stuart's report on Gettysburg commended Mosby for capturing the dispatches and for scouting reports that informed him of enemy movements: "In this difficult search, the fearless and indefatigable Major Mosby was particularly active and efficient. His information was always accurate and reliable." In the nine days from June 16 to June 24, Mosby scouted behind the lines for Stuart five times, activity that involved him in Stuart's decision to ride around the Union army on the march to Gettysburg. When he returned to Stuart's headquarters at Rector's Cross Roads from the fourth scout on the night of June 22, Stuart was in the process of deciding what route the cavalry should take into Maryland. Lee had suggested that, if Hooker was moving north, Stuart should move on Gen. Richard Ewell's right, but Lee had not recommended any route. A message from Longstreet suggested that Stuart sweep around to the rear of Hooker to avoid tipping off Lee's invasion, and he indicated that Lee agreed. Mosby was in the room during Stuart's discussion with his staff, and he spoke up that he knew that the camps of the different corps of Hooker's army were so spread apart that Stuart could easily pass between them and proceed to Seneca Ford, which he knew to be passable because he had used it on his raid eleven days before.[41]

Stuart proposed Mosby's plan to Lee and sent Mosby on his fifth scout to reconfirm that Hooker was not moving and that the cavalry could pass between the corps. Mosby left and the next morning was again between the camps in Loudoun and Fairfax, and found all quiet. He sent one courier and then another to Stuart and then scouted alone. On a farm near Frying Pan he captured two unarmed Union cavalrymen picking cherries. It was raining and under his gum cloth he drew his pistol and rode up to them. "What regiment do you belong to?" he asked. As they answered he brought out his pistol and told them he was Mosby. The name "put them under a spell," he observed, and they surrendered. Returning to Stuart late in the day with his prisoners riding alongside, he found the turnpike blocked by a Union wagon train moving west, with a strong cavalry escort. Intent on reaching his pathway through the Bull

Run Mountains before dark, he decided to masquerade as a Union officer and proceed. "So I concluded to take the greatest risk that I took in the war—to ride with my prisoners through the wagons and column of cavalry." For two hundred yards they trotted forward, passing the wagons and cavalrymen, Mosby's pistol drawn and in hand under his cape. Once his right elbow struck a Union cavalryman as they hurried past. After two hundred yards he turned left onto the next road and, before crossing the mountains, paroled the prisoners and kept their horses. As one of them signed his name he was still in such a daze that he asked Mosby whether the column they passed through was Union or Confederate.[42]

The next morning, June 24, Mosby reported to Stuart that Hooker's army had not moved; the route was still clear. In the night Stuart had received Lee's final instructions. Stuart was to cross the river, selecting a route at his own discretion. "You will however be able to judge whether you can pass around their army without hinderance." Stuart told Mosby that he would follow his suggestion and asked him to meet him with his command the next morning, June 25, on Little River Turnpike about ten miles east of Aldie to guide the way.[43]

The idea of crossing the Potomac somewhere other than in the path of the Confederate army west of the Blue Ridge Mountains seems to have already been under consideration by Stuart when Mosby arrived from his fourth scout on the night of June 22. Mosby suggested the route through the Federal army to Seneca Ford, and he felt personally responsible for Stuart's raid. Later, when Stuart was blamed for contributing to Lee's Gettysburg defeat by being away, Mosby felt that the critics were attacking him as well.

The morning of June 25, when Mosby and his men arrived at the meeting place, he found that Hooker's army was moving toward the Potomac; the roads were filled with marching infantry. He heard artillery firing in Stuart's direction and correctly assumed that Stuart had run into General Hancock's corps moving north from Thoroughfare Gap and Gainesville. Separated from Stuart by moving Union troops, Mosby assumed that Stuart had canceled the march through Hooker's army and headed back toward the Valley to cross the river in the path of Lee's army. "I supposed that Stuart had returned," he wrote, and "I concluded that he had gone back and I did the same." He assumed that, since the route to Seneca was blocked, Stuart had turned back.[44]

In the postwar Gettysburg controversy, Mosby quoted several times from Lee's final order of 5:00 P.M., June 23, 1863; and after the debate intensified he started deleting Lee's request that Stuart "judge whether you can pass around their army without hinderance." Mosby knew that herein lay the most vulnerable part of his lawyer-like defense of Stuart. Without question Lee left it up to Stuart to judge whether there was a hindrance. On that day Mosby judged that there was a hindrance and that Stuart had canceled the ride and gone back. If Mosby had imagined that Stuart was still in his Confederacy, searching for the quickest way around Hooker's army and preparing to make headlines by passing between Hooker and Washington, and moving to finally cross at Seneca Ford where Mosby had suggested, certainly he would have found his way to Stuart. Mosby's judgment was so sure that Stuart had turned back, he did not even look for Stuart. The Lee cult condemned Stuart for disobeying Lee's orders by not turning back after meeting a hindrance. But, again, Lee clearly left it up to Stuart to judge whether there was a hindrance. Stuart was not guilty of disobeying orders; he was guilty only of a mistake in judgment, a mistake that Mosby did not make that day.[45]

Mosby dispersed his men and three days later on June 28 at noon, nine hours after Stuart had crossed at Seneca at 3:00 A.M., came together again near Upperville with thirty men. They went through Snicker's Gap into the Valley and crossed the Potomac River near Hancock on July 1 and raided Mercersburg, Pennsylvania. They captured 218 cattle and 15 horses and returned to Virginia.[46]

Since Stoughton's capture, Mosby had learned several valuable lessons. He had recognized the superiority of the revolver over the saber in a mounted charge and melee. He had learned to arrive at the objective with rested horses, scout before attacking, and avoid bivouacking in a cul-de-sac. What he had known all along about his men demanding spoils had been confirmed, and he realized what Stuart meant when he warned him to avoid raiding near strong enemy cavalry camps to allow his men time to plunder. He had learned that the Orange and Alexandria Railroad was so heavily guarded that capturing a train with a small force was complicated and dangerous. He had seen that a cannon announced its presence, required a strong force to defend, and eliminated the tactic of scattering to escape from a superior enemy. Now that he was organized under the Partisan Ranger Act he had authority over his command and could exert his special style of leadership.

# 7

# Featherbed Guerrillas

Mosby fixed his mind on the goal of success as a partisan raider and determined to remain independent. With almost incredible stamina and self-confidence he rejected traditional procedures and used several unconventional keys to success. He carefully followed the advice of Stuart and Lee "to be extremely watchful as to the character of the men" he enlisted. Except in the fall of 1864 when the battalion increased to nearly four hundred men, he insisted on meeting and interviewing each recruit. He would stare into a man's face, watch his eyes, and instinctively judge his worth. Disregarding regulations, he accepted many unauthorized transfers from the regular army, but only if they appeared in person and submitted to an interview. He ignored official transfer orders and if he disapproved of an applicant treated him with icy contempt. One such man appeared with orders, and Mosby had heard a rumor that he had robbed a civilian. "I don't want you with me," he said, ripping up the order, casting it on the ground, and turning his back and walking away.[1]

He attracted some of the most outstanding horseback riders and gentlemen in Virginia. At least thirty-nine were former cadets at the Virginia Military Institute. James Monroe Heiskell was a grandson of James Monroe, and John S. Mason of George Mason. Frederick W. Smith was the son of Virginia governor William Smith. A few were from Canada and Europe, and, among those whose antebellum residence is known, over 8 percent were Maryland natives, but mostly they were Virginians. Over 28 percent were from Loudoun and Fauquier Counties, and over 80 percent were from Virginia. Many had served previously in Confederate service, mostly in the regular cavalry or other partisan commands. Reports were frequent that they looked unusually youthful, and it was true; Mosby attracted more than his share of young recruits. In 1864 they averaged about twenty-three years of age, when the average for the regular armies was about twenty-six. Teenagers were common in both armies, and Mosby had at least seventeen men under age sixteen when the war ended, including one Ranger aged fourteen.[2]

He expected a man to be loyal and self-motivated, able to seize the initiative and respond individually during go-through-style assaults and when scattering into the mountains on retreat. But his number-one requirement was courage—he expected a man to fight fearlessly. In colonial America reportedly the best gamecocks were the offspring of blue hens, and the people of Delaware colony and one of their best regiments in the Revolution became the "Blue Hen's Chickens." Mosby called his best fighters blue hen's chickens. Nineteen-year-old Joseph Bryan, preparing for his first skirmish, asked, "How can I make a reputation in Mosby's command?" A veteran replied that, when Capt. Richard Montjoy gave the command, Bryan should break from the ranks and ride into the enemy as fast as his horse could run. Bryan did, and Montjoy exclaimed, "He will do, he is one of the Old Blue Hen's chickens, won his spurs on the first round."[3]

When Mosby yelled "Charge!" victory was usually at hand, and the men knew that he would not recklessly expose them to danger. Repeated victories and collection of spoils created a winning tradition, stimulated a high pitch of anticipation, and instilled pride in the unit. Having handpicked all of the officers, he quickly removed any who proved incompetent, and he gave much attention to rest and food for the men and horses. With discipline he had two simple rules: behave like a gentleman off duty and show up for announced raids. "I had every man on his honor," he said. "If he violated the trust that was placed in him, I lost no time in getting him back to the main army again." To the men, being returned to regular duty was equal to being sentenced to "Mosby's Botany Bay."[4]

Other than dictating officer elections and enforcing strict adherence to his simple rules, Mosby practiced goal-oriented democratic leadership that contributed to esprit de corps. He cultivated team spirit by fairness in dividing spoils and commending and rewarding courage under fire. He permitted freedom in off-duty time and on raids allowed each man to make full use of his talents. There was no saluting or addressing officers by rank except that everyone called Mosby by his rank. There were no inspections, no guard duty, and no drills. The only time they marched in ranks was when masquerading as Union cavalry on raids. Passing through Loudoun County on his return from Gettysburg, Union general Carl Schurz saw eight or ten Rangers riding toward him and later noted, "They looked rather ragged, and I took them for teamsters or similar folk." Stuart first saw Mosby's men in June 1863. He was standing on the street in Middleburg when Mosby and thirty or forty of his men rode leisurely into town. Mosby halted, dismounted, and asked what he thought. Stuart answered with a reference to the familiar story of "Captain Scott's Coon," a tale about a raccoon, a dog, and famous frontier marksman Capt. Martin Scott. One day the dog treed the raccoon, and when the raccoon saw Scott coming through the woods he hurriedly surrendered to the dog. Scott was a real person killed in action as a lieutenant colonel in the Mexican War. Stuart told Mosby that when the Yankees saw Mosby's men coming they would say with the raccoon, "Don't shoot, I'll come down."[5]

Mosby wrote that men joined him because they were "attracted by the chance of booty and desire for adventure, without the irksome duties of camp life." He admitted that they were "Feather-bed" cavalry but insisted that, if nourishing food and sound sleep made them "such a terror to their foes," who could object? On raids before reaching enemy territory he allowed a "go-as-you-please march," with the men moving about in the column, joking, singing, and telling stories. They would chase each other and kick the horse of a recruit just to watch it buck and see if the new man could stay in the saddle. Often Mosby would laugh with them. Addressing Monteiro, "Major of Calomel," for the popular cure-all, he would tease the surgeon about a certain widow who had flirted with him. One day during the tense time at the end of the war when the decision on whether to surrender was under consideration, Mosby suddenly asked, "Doctor, what do you think of the widow?" Monteiro answered, "Confound the widow. What in the name of the paternal ancestors of all the mules in creation has the widow to do with the serious question before us?"[6]

Like Stuart and Morgan, Mosby attracted camp clowns and enjoyed their revelry. On the way into a raid, resting in the woods, he would ask John Sinclair, a great mimic, to give his description of the capture of a sutler's wagon train. "How was it, John?" he would ask. "Let's have it about those sutlers." Sinclair would jump up and flutter about, and throw his arms in the air in a dramatization of panic and confusion. Quoting the sutlers, he would shout, "Drive on! Don't you run your mules into my wagon. Now, we're all tangled up. They've got us all!" Mosby and the entire camp would roar with laughter.[7]

Welcomed into the family life of their hosts, the men enjoyed the pleasures of soldiers on furlough. Elizabeth Edmonds and her daughter Amanda "Tee" boarded eight men on their plantation of "Belle Grove" near Paris. Elizabeth had three sons in Mosby's command; and Tee, single and about twenty-four years of age, enjoyed hosting parties in the evenings for Rangers from nearby houses. One of Mosby's men would play the banjo or fiddle for singing and dancing, and in the summer a group would gather on the front lawn under the pear tree or fish in the pond. In the winter they went sleigh riding, played cards, and drank eggnog and apple toddy. When the men returned from a raid it was like a holiday. Every raider wanted to talk at once as they related their adventures, teasing and laughing about humorous incidents on the expedition. And when they shared their booty it seemed like Christmas—sometimes every member of the household received a gift. There were shoes, hoop skirts, fruit, cans of meat, cakes, candy, and other items normally unavailable. "The boys return this evening," Tee wrote on January 19, 1865, "loaded with good rio coffee and oysters—the latter one of the greatest treats I have had since the war."[8]

Elizabeth and Tee Edmonds and the other civilians of Mosby's Confederacy were vital to his continued operation. Mosby said that if he had gone into camp he and his men would have been captured. For more than two years they boarded in homes, usually two per family. Every few days he would call a rendezvous, and the men would gather like "Children of the Mist." When an expedition ended he dismissed them, and they dispersed into the population. This approached the people's war described by nineteenth-century military philosopher Carl von Clausewitz when he recommended meeting for raids and dispersing like mist or vapor, and it made Mosby the truest guerrilla in the Civil War in the classical sense. A Union trooper observed that Mosby's men "would scatter like wild geese, and disappear." A Loudoun County Unionist declared that searching for him was useless—Union columns passing were like ships at sea; the water closed behind them when they left, and nothing was changed. Mosby praised the civilians for sacrifices and dedication comparable to one of the great people's wars of Medieval Europe; he said they were comparable to the people of Flanders who supported Guy de Dampierre, Count of Flanders, in repelling the invading French army of Philip IV early in the fourteenth century. Mosby proclaimed his Confederacy "The Flanders of the South."[9]

Historian Drew G. Faust theorized that Confederate women in general became tired of sacrificing and withdrew their support of the war effort. On the other hand, recent studies demonstrate that there actually may have been little civilian disillusionment until near the end of the war. William A. Blair found that Union army depredations on civilian property united Virginia society against the Yankees. Daniel Sutherland concluded that most Confederates in Culpeper County remained loyal and actively resisted until near the end, when discouragement set in based on many months of occupation by the enemy army. The experience of civilians behind Mosby seems to support the theses of Blair and Sutherland. Mosby's friends remained loyal to the end, but special situations in their lives probably gave them higher morale than civilians farther south. They could trade through the leaky blockade with merchants in Baltimore until Sheridan closed trade on December 8, 1864, and participation in Mosby's war gave them an active role in the war. And strengthening Blair's theme, Mosby's supporters did not blame Mosby for the Union depredations on raids caused directly by the attacks of Mosby's men. Instead they blamed the Yankees and considered Mosby "our safe guard." They gave Mosby and his men credit for diverting the Union raiders and lessening depredations. In March 1865, when a large Union force came to Middleburg searching for Mosby, Catherine Broun wrote in her diary, "They did not do any damage. Col. Mosby kept them too busy skirmishing."[10]

Letters to the Virginia and Confederate governments confirm that, after the first few weeks when they realized that the Union army would not burn their homes, Mosby's hosts welcomed his men. Word went out from Mosby's Confederacy into nearby areas of Virginia behind Union lines that partisan bands were a protection of property from deserters and stragglers and Union raids. This was in contrast to the dominant reputation of the Rangers, as in other areas of the Confederacy they were considered harmful. And the reputation of Mosby's men reached the high command. Stuart endorsed a Mosby report: "Major Mosby continues his distinguished services in the enemy's rear, relieving our people of the depredations of the enemy in a great measure." Lee wrote, "Lieutenant-Colonel Mosby has done excellent service, and from the reports of citizens and others I am inclined to believe that he is strict in discipline and a protection to the country in which he operates."[11]

Early in the war Mosby observed that the area was densely populated with slave-owning families loyal to the Confederacy. Loudoun County's white residents were mostly yeomen farmers marketing wheat and other crops and practicing diversified agriculture. In the northwestern section the German-Americans and Quakers did not own slaves, and they opposed secession and remained loyal to the Union. Their presence lowered the percentage of African Americans in the population of Loudoun County to 31 percent, lower than Virginia's 35 percent. But in 1860 the county had 670 slave owners, most of them in Mosby's Confederacy. Only thirty-one, less than 5 percent of the slaveholders, were gentry with twenty or more slaves; 40 percent of the owners had three or fewer slaves, about the same as for Virginia at 41 percent of slaveholders.[12]

Fauquier County had only a few Unionists, and in 1860 African Americans made up 51 percent of the population, 48 percent being slaves and about 3 percent free blacks. This percentage of blacks was higher than Virginia's 35 percent and greater than the Deep South states of Louisiana, Alabama, Florida, and Georgia. More than 40 percent of the white families in Fauquier owned slaves, which was considerably higher than the 25 percent in Virginia and the entire South. More than 13 percent, 128 families, owned twenty or more slaves, a greater proportion than 11 percent for Virginia and 12 percent for the South. Together, Loudoun and Fauquier had 161 gentry with 20 or more slaves and 449 middling slave owners with 8 to 19 slaves, Loudoun with 165 and Fauquier with 284. Thus, both counties had 610 slave-owning families with 8 or more slaves. Not all of these families were located within Mosby's Confederacy, but they could provide assistance when he came scouting or marching through. Mosby had selected this base of operations for his people's war very effectively; he depended on a concentration of slave owners true to the Southern cause.[13]

The families who boarded his men became directly involved in the Confederate war effort on a daily basis. They prepared and cooked food, laundered and mended uniforms, and cared for horses. A myth developed in the Union cavalry that they assisted the raiders with an organized early-warning system to notify of approaching enemy forces. A Union colonel wrote, "The universal sympathy of the inhabitants in their favor, made every citizen their courier, and every house their signal-tower." The Federals assumed that laundry hanging on the line and lights burning in garret windows were secret signals. But this was imaginary; there was no organized warning system. For a few days in February 1864 Mosby's men picketed the roads but soon realized that was a mistake because the guards became targets to be captured. In fact, individuals sometimes spontaneously warned Mosby's men by grapevine telegraph or passing the news by word of mouth. When this happened usually there would be a five- to ten-minute notice and then the soldiers would ride house to house alerting each other. On February 20, 1864, Mosby was having breakfast at Joseph Blackwell's when a young boy, brother of one of his men, burst in reporting that the enemy were about one mile away: "The Yankees are on the pike: It's just blue with 'em."[14]

The host families were quite active in concealing the raiders from searches of their homes by Union cavalry. They built secret closets and trapdoors and hid the raiders under porches, in hogsheads, and in water tanks on the roof. In an upstairs bedroom during one search, the children jumped out of bed, and the Ranger boarding with the family got in between the cords and the feather mattress; the children lay on top of the mattress, under the quilts, pretending to be asleep. When the Union men came the slave Mammy met them in the hall with a candle and admonished them not to awaken the children. Ranger Hipkins was courting a young lady in the Faulkner family between Upperville and Ashby's Gap when the Union cavalry appeared. "Follow me," said Aunt Em, the black Mammy, "I may fool them Yankees yet." Hurrying down the steps of the front porch, she led him to the corner of the house and pointed toward a large rain barrel, half full of water. "Quick! Jump in there," she said, and he obeyed. She placed a board on top and sat on it, perching there through the search and saving Hipkins from capture.[15]

With the civilians behind him, Mosby used irregular tactics to give his men an initial advantage, and once a fight began he usually won through his innovative use of the mounted charge with Colt revolvers. In the regular cavalry on both sides the *arme blanche* remained the weapon of choice throughout the war and into the twentieth century. In World War I both sides had large cavalry forces in spite of barbed wire and machine guns. Tanks began replacing horses in the American cavalry in 1933, but horses were still used on U.S. Army maneuvers in 1940. Some horse cavalry units fought in Europe and Asia in World War II.[16]

Eighteenth-century European cavalry relied on the shock of the saber charge to throw the enemy into confusion and retreat. From opposing armies, well-ordered ranks of horsemen ran toward each other, horses seeking intervals on their own, and riders engaging in hand-to-hand combat in a melee. Napoleon's cavalry usually charged in a trot or controlled canter and, while they used guns a few times, relied mostly on sabers. Usually one side or the other soon developed an infectious panic and fled, with the enemy in pursuit attempting to seize captives.

Mosby reported once that he led a charge, "the shock of which the enemy could not resist." He heightened the shock effect by substituting revolvers for sabers and by breaking through the orderly blue ranks at full speed in a nontraditional formation that resembled a horse race or an Indian attack.[17]

The mounted charge involved taking the offensive. "It was a rule from which, during the war, I never departed, not to stand still and receive a charge, but always to act on the offensive," he recalled. When possible he would begin a charge by ordering the men into a column of fours, and it was an honor to be selected to ride in the front rank of four. Then he would silently signal or yell, "Boys, go through 'em!" and the race started with each man for himself, clapping his spurs and holding the bridle reins in one hand or dropping them and firing a revolver in each hand. "Which are our men and which are the Yankees?" asked a recruit. "Damn the difference! Go right in!" shouted a veteran. Standard cavalry tactics required staying in line in correct alignment, and against Mosby it was impossible. "The enemy were amidst the men," reported a Union commander, "and both parties were so mixed up that it was impossible to get the men into line."[18]

Mosby scheduled no target practice, but the men frequently trained on their own, with the goal of hitting a tree trunk three times when riding by in a full run. "My men had no superiors in the saddle and were expert pistol shots," he said. Since the Colt was accurate only for a few yards, he ordered them to hold their fire until they could distinguish the eyes of an opponent. The enemy using sabers cooperated by closing to arm-and-blade length, and sometimes after a fight men gathering up the wounded and dead noticed powder burns on their uniforms. He and the men attempted to wound or kill the enemy commander in the first contact to cause loss of confidence and demoralization. On their own, after using all of their bullets, some men would pistol-whip the enemy with empty revolvers. In one fight a Ranger had been taken prisoner and just freed, and he stood in the road swinging an empty Union carbine, whacking his former captors as they retreated past him.[19]

Mosby recognized that his men would fight this way if he followed one of the cardinal rules of irregular warfare, the principle that there are no rules. He was a maverick anyway and enjoyed casting aside the narrow, rigid rules of the military manuals. He never blinked at disobeying regulations forbidding him to recruit eligible conscripts or requiring officer elections. Instead he concentrated on factors that were vital to success such as spoils, continued civilian support, accurate intelligence, and irregular tactics. Civilians assisted him in maintaining discipline by applying social pressure, but the operation depended on his strength of character and leadership ability. It is amazing that he led his men for the first five months with no organization whatsoever and continued for almost two more years with no training cycle and no military courtesy and only his own personal discipline. Elsewhere in the South the amount of freedom allowed partisans broke down in indolence and brigandage. "We did not drill ourselves into a machine that could not operate when any part went wrong," he said. "We just maintained our individuality and at the same time a cohesiveness and went to the task."[20]

And that he did when Meade's Army of the Potomac returned into Virginia from Gettysburg and established a supply line running through Mosby's Confederacy. Mosby could lead men, but he would soon find that he had a lesson to learn about capturing sutler wagons.

# 8

# Unguarded
# Sutler Wagons

Mosby's plans to mind the rear of Pope's army were realized one year later against Meade. After the battle of Gettysburg, Meade positioned the Army of the Potomac about where Pope's army had been when Mosby had attempted to go partisan the first time. He carefully guarded his main supply line on the O&A Railroad but, for a few weeks, provided no escorts for sutlers coming from Washington on the Warrenton Turnpike. Less than seven miles into Virginia the merchants would come to a cavalryman standing in the road beckoning them to turn into a by-path; it was Mosby in broad daylight directing traffic from both directions into a ravine where his men were waiting to unhitch the horses and plunder the goods. One warm day, dressed in a shirt and blue trousers, he rode into a sutler's camp and ordered a beer and a slice of cake. From the unsuspecting sutler he obtained intelligence useful for locating that day's roadblock. In two weeks with thirty men, he captured at least 118 sutler and army wagons, adventures dramatized on the stage in Alexandria as "The Guerilla; or, Mosby in Five Hundred Sutler-wagons."[1]

Stuart approved, but Lee questioned whether Mosby was giving too much attention to spoils and neglecting military objectives. The acquisition of spoils was at the heart of Mosby's operation and was the basic motivator in the Partisan Ranger Act. In the American Revolution Thomas Sumter, under "Sumter's Law," allowed his men to keep plunder from the enemy. The Partisan Act went a step further and made it official through government reimbursement. Since the Partisan Rangers were independent, the Confederate Congress sought to encourage them by applying the principle of maritime prize law, without the procedure of condemning the seized property in prize court. Like privateering, the act harnessed avarice for the cause. The law and its regulations and practices authorized payment for captured arms and munitions, infantry and cavalry accoutrements, horses, mules, and cattle. Beef cattle were turned over to the commissary and the other items to any quartermaster.[2]

After a raid Mosby would sometimes award the best horses to men who had acted with uncommon bravery, and the remainder were divided by lottery, only among the men who had participated in the raid. The men then sold their extra horses to the quartermaster. In 1863 the Union government paid $110 for a cavalry horse; a revolver was worth a minimum of $12, a rifle $10. Therefore, including accoutrements, a Mosby raider could earn more than $132 by capturing one Union cavalryman. This was more than twelve months' pay for a private. The Confederate government paid in gold and greenbacks, protecting Mosby and other partisans from the inflation suffered by Confederates in general.[3]

Frederick the Great of Prussia warned that pillage was "the source of the greatest disorders." Napoleon's Maxim 107 declared that plundering would disorganize and ruin an army. Lee and Stuart worried that Mosby might attract unsavory characters, but Mosby took a potential negative and turned it into a positive. Gerald Linderman in *Embattled Courage* wrote that, in the absence of discipline, Civil War armies used courage to keep men in battle; for Mosby it was spoils. He stated that his early 1863 "conglomerates" were "held together by the cohesive power of public plunder." He brought discipline and order to the looting by requiring that the men turn in captured horses to him for distribution. His system was fair and encouraged each man to fight.[4]

The most valuable item was horses, so the Rangers preferred to attack enemy cavalry. Mosby often heard them before an assault, arguing about who should have a certain beautiful horse seen in the enemy column. When he saw that he was outnumbered or entering a hard fight, he would encourage them by promising captured horses. Once, when the Union force had them outnumbered two to one, he said, "Now we'll get two horses apiece instead of one." And another time he shouted, "Boys there's a horse a piece for you." He allowed the men to keep as personal property the goods taken from sutlers and money and other items seized from prisoners and male passengers on trains. When the fighting was over, in a play on words of his customary order to attack, Mosby would yell, "Boys, go through 'em!" and now it meant go through their saddlebags, knapsacks, and pocketbooks for cash and take their watches, boots, and clothing as you wish. "Now I want your greenbacks," a Ranger would say. "Fork it over. Fork it over," meant hand me your cash. "Give me your pocket-book," Pvt. Samuel Alexander demanded. "I have not got any pocket-book," the prisoner replied. "Well then, surrender," said Sam, taking his weapons. "Here you damn Yank, hand over your watch," said a raider to a passenger from the train on the Greenback Raid. Nearby Pvt. Billings Steele started robbing a passenger who said, "Why Billings, I am your brother; besides, they have robbed me twice already." The robbery violated international law, but both sides in the war adopted Mosby's philosophy: "We plunder the enemy, as the rules of war clearly allow. 'To the victors belong the spoils' has been a maxim of war in all ages."[5]

When a sutler was captured and it was safe, Mosby would encourage the men to celebrate in wild abandon. Sutlers usually charged high prices, and they had the ability to attach a man's pay, making them the natural enemy of the men on both sides. Capturing them was a delight. "A sutler at last!" a Ranger said when one came up the road with a heavy load. Closing in, the raiders all talked at once: "If you get hold of a pair of number seven high boots, save 'em for me, and I'll give you some of the flannel shirts I get, and don't forget to save me some figs and candy, and some cigars."[6]

In the Confederacy the Union blockade and wartime economic dislocations caused serious shortages and hardships. In Lynchburg coffee disappeared from the stores, and people substituted hot rye. In 1863 families auctioned off heirlooms to purchase shoes for fifteen dollars and flour for twenty dollars per barrel. In 1864 bacon, beef, butter, and beans were scarce, and flour was $160 per barrel. In Richmond in February 1864 friends gathered for starvation parties with music and nothing to eat but bread and butter. By April 1, 1864, white sugar could not be purchased in Richmond, milk was scarce and high-priced, and coffee was twelve dollars per pound. A clerk in the Treasury Department fainted at her worktable—she had not eaten for two days and had no shoes. During the last year of the war, Lee's army ran short of shoes and blankets. When the bacon and meal rations were unavailable in August 1864, the men survived on "Hopping John," a soup of bacon, peas, and okra or rice.[7]

Given the deprivation, capturing one of the sutler's rolling retail stores was like a child's fantasy. Mosby's men would sing:

When I can shoot my rifle clear,
At Yankees on the roads,

I'll bid farewell to rags and tags
And live on Sutlers' loads.[8]

There were cans of turkey, peaches, tomatoes, cheese, and cakes and pies. "The men would eat and drink a little of everything that came within their grasp." Pvt. Sewell Williams was so dazzled that he filled his sack with playing cards and cigars even though he neither smoked nor gambled. Sutlers were forbidden to sell liquor, but they did, and the Rhine wine captured in the rear of Gen. Carl Schurz's corps in July 1863 was so fine that even Mosby joined the party. "For an hour or so we had a high jinks," he recalled. The men named several of the raids for the spoils acquired: First Calico Raid, Great Calico Raid, Ice Cream Raid, Coffee Raid, Boot Raid, and Greenback Raid. Returning from the Wagon Raid, some wore captured Union uniforms turned inside-out to show the colorful lining, and some played captured musical instruments. They were so laden with merchandise after the First Calico Raid that a woman asked to purchase calico from Mosby. "Madam, you have mistaken my profession," the guerrilla chief answered. "I am a soldier."[9]

Shrewdly, Mosby refused to participate in the division of spoils. He used captured weapons and rode captured horses, but there was apparently only one instance of him selling horses on his own account. On October 1, 1863, he sent Aaron home to Pauline with horses to be sold for two thousand dollars and the money invested in tobacco. The record does not reveal how he acquired these horses; he may have bought them. He was careful to avoid any appearance of impropriety, going to the extreme of not owning or wearing a watch until after the war. When he captured $173,000 in greenbacks, his men insisted that he take a share. He refused, but when the money was distributed the men took up a collection of eight to ten thousand dollars and gave it to Pauline. She gave it to him, and he divided it among the men: "Boys, I didn't go into the Confederate service for money or plunder," he said. "Come and receive your Christmas gifts." Finally the men used the money to purchase "Coquette," a horse that he had been admiring; and, since a horse was a military necessity, he accepted. And he could not refuse when they presented him a pair of scarlet slippers with gold embroidery for his swollen foot, which had been injured.[10]

Three sutler wagons were among the spoils that Mosby and his men captured during the march of Meade's army through his Confederacy after Gettysburg. Behind the Union columns Mosby and 30 men captured 186 prisoners, 6 times their own number, and so many that he established a temporary holding station in the Bull Run Mountains. Camp Spindle, his only camp, held the prisoners until men could be spared to escort them south to Confederate lines. When the first party of forty-seven arrived at Lee's picket line, there were so many blue uniforms the pickets thought it was a flank attack. Mosby harassed so effectively that one wagon train passed through Fauquier County escorted by cavalry riding single file alongside the wagons. The Rangers also captured 9 army wagons, 50 cavalry accoutrements, and 123 horses and mules—4 for each man. "Mosby has richly won another grade," Stuart noted, and Lee forwarded Mosby's report to the War Department "as evidence of the merit and activity of Major Mosby and his command."[11]

Meanwhile, as Meade's army marched toward the Rappahannock, engineers repaired the Orange and Alexandria Railroad, and Heintzelman organized to defend it as far as Bull Run. The Washington cavalry screen had been stripped for the Gettysburg campaign, but Heintzelman had retained 462 men of the 2nd Massachusetts Cavalry under Col. Charles Russell Lowell. Now he gave priority to the railroad and left the cavalry screen down. On July 15 he ordered Gen. Rufus King's division of 2,799 infantry and Colonel Lowell, with his men plus two companies of the 6th New York Cavalry, to guard the rail line. Both headquarters were at Centreville north of the railroad on the Warrenton Turnpike.[12]

By leaving Fairfax Court House and Little River Turnpike unguarded, Heintzelman gave Mosby an invitation. On the night of July 30 there were twenty-eight loaded sutler wagons in Fairfax Court House, stopping overnight, and one was on the road west of town. One of them had ice cream, and therefore this expedition was the Ice Cream Raid. To avoid Lowell's cavalry at Centreville, Mosby and twenty-seven men moved in after dark and cut the telegraph wires from Fairfax Court House to Centreville. He succeeded until he abandoned the hit-and-run principle and attempted to bring out all of the wagons. For even though the warning screen was down, the Union officers had been warned. By 8:30 P.M. word had come to General King that Mosby's men were moving in his direction, and he notified Lowell. Rather than attempt to locate Mosby on the way into the area, Lowell wisely prepared to intercept him on his return.[13]

Lowell, a member of the Lowell family of Boston, was a nephew of poet James Russell Lowell and Mosby's most distinguished wartime opponent. He graduated valedictorian at Harvard and was managing an iron works in Maryland when the war began. He served on the Peninsula and on McClellan's staff at Antietam and, in the fall of 1862, organized the 2nd Massachusetts Cavalry, a regiment with five companies known as the California Battalion, several of the men having moved to California and made passage back to Boston to enlist. Lowell was a model officer: slim, handsome, and intelligent-looking, with a well-trimmed mustache and tailored uniform that fit and looked clean and fresh. Always calm and fearless, he had twelve horses shot from under him. "I do not think there was a quality I could have added to Lowell. He was the perfection of a man and a soldier," Sheridan stated.[14]

He was twenty-eight years old and engaged to Josephine Shaw, sister of Col. Robert G. Shaw, who had been killed on July 18 attacking Fort Wagner in Charleston Harbor with his famous African American regiment, the 54th Massachusetts Infantry. Charles and Effy were married on October 31, 1863, and she came to the camp in Vienna in Fairfax County on November 8, 1863. Fighting Mosby was difficult work and not much appreciated. He wrote home about the men he had lost, and a relative observed that Lowell was fighting "inglorious warfare." He replied that he would prefer regular duty; but this was his assignment, and it was all in a day's work. "You must not exaggerate the danger. Mosby is more keen to plunder than to murder,—he always runs when he can."[15]

On the night of the Ice Cream Raid, Lowell took about 170 cavalry to the woods near Mt. Zion Church one mile east of Aldie and camped at 1:00 A.M. The next morning at daylight, when Mosby's men came up the road with their spoils, Lowell had them outnumbered six to one. It was perfect strategy; he easily scattered Mosby's men and recaptured the wagons. "We retook them all," he wrote Effy, "but didn't take Mosby."[16]

After that Mosby left captured wagons behind and, for the next two weeks, hit and ran. Unhitching the teams from the wagons, looting the goods, and paroling the drivers and sutlers, he and his men would hasten away with the mules and horses and what spoils they could carry. It did not matter if wagons were loaded and moving west or empty going east; he would order them to park and unhitch. One driver answered as he jumped down, "Unhitch it is." A *New York Herald* correspondent in Washington reported that almost every day Mosby was capturing wagon trains between Washington and Warrenton. One sutler lost six thousand dollars, and another had been captured three times and lost seven thousand dollars. An estimated $1 million in property was lost, and the whole thing was "a stigma upon our arms." A reporter at Meade's headquarters stated that the army was seriously inconvenienced by the shortage of sutler goods and that Mosby had made it so dangerous that only "the most venturesome and greedy" merchants dared the trip. The story circulated in the Union army that a Virginia man and wife happened along the road during a Mosby raid, and she told him, "Go in, Bill, and help the Major, if you do get killed."[17]

A sutler was asleep on a buffalo robe at Warrenton Junction a month later. When told "The guerrillas are coming; you had better hitch up," he said, "Damn the guerrillas; I have been bothering myself to death, ever since the army began to move, to keep out of their way, and now I don't care much if they do catch me." Exaggerated tales circulated and appeared in the newspapers. For example, the New York Herald reported that Mosby captured fifty sutlers' wagons in one raid. Southerners were highly amused. They celebrated the story that he once captured 150 mules and laughed at the tale that on a Sunday afternoon "almost within range of the guns on the Washington fortifications" Mosby's men halted and took the horses from a funeral procession on its way from Lewinsville to Washington, leaving the Yankee mourners standing in the road beside the hearse.[18]

Lowell finally ended the hilarity when on August 12 on his own he established a system of escorted convoys going both ways between Alexandria and Centreville, using thirty to fifty cavalry and leaving on an irregular schedule. Then the War Department awakened to the plight of the sutlers and took over. Henceforth, the provost marshal general's office would not sign a manifest required to prevent alcohol shipment until a convoy was available with an escort of one regiment of cavalry. The convoys left Washington on Mondays at 9:00 A.M. and returned from Warrenton Junction on Thursdays at 9:00 A.M. On August 21, Meade complained to Halleck that his cavalry was as exhausted as if they were in active operations because they had to protect his flanks and his long line of supply.[19]

When Lee received Mosby's August 4, 1863, report with Stuart's favorable endorsement, there was a false rumor making the rounds that Mosby had recently held an auction in Charlottesville and sold thirty thousand dollars' worth of spoils. Consequently, endorsing Mosby's report, he wrote that, while he greatly commended Mosby for "boldness and good management," he was concerned that he was taking too few men on his raids and giving too much attention to merchants and not enough to military targets. On the same day he sent a letter to Stuart stating that Mosby had a large number of men but only used a few on his expeditions and directing Stuart to order Mosby to keep his men on duty, hold no more auctions, and attack enemy outposts and communications, especially the Orange and Alexandria Railroad, which would divert troops to the rear and weaken the Union army.[20]

Stuart had a deeper appreciation of guerrilla warfare than Lee, and he was unconcerned. He realized that attacking unguarded sutler wagons was part of hitting the enemy where he was weak and harassing him like a gnat. Lee's reprimand also warned Mosby that Lee failed to appreciate the principle that a force of a few men using stealth can operate more effectively in hit-and-run raids than a large force. Mosby felt indignant that Lee assumed that the auction rumor was true without inquiring, and obviously Lee was misinformed on how few men he had. He had increased to about eighty men before Gettysburg, but afterwards had only thirty and still had only thirty. Mosby realized that to keep Lee's approval he would have to combine attacks on vulnerable sutlers with attacks on the railroad. What seemed unjust was that Lee did not appreciate that the wagon attacks were diverting and wearing down regiments of Meade's cavalry, depriving Meade's men of ice cream and creating great embarrassment in Washington. He determined to meet with Lee when possible and for now place enough emphasis on regular military objectives to satisfy Lee.

It was almost unreasonable to expect Mosby and thirty men to cause any significant damage to the rail line. Morgan could raid the Louisville and Nashville Railroad with twenty-four hundred or thirty-nine hundred men and artillery, but how could Mosby raid the heavily guarded and shorter O&A with thirty? In the first week of August, Meade ordered an inspection of the railroad defenses, and the report came on August 7 that it was "very unsatisfactory." Heintzelman was in charge of guarding the track to Manassas Junction, and the Army of the Potomac was to picket from there to the front. However, the officer in charge at Manassas Junction had no communication with Heintzelman's men assigned to the other section. He had no idea how many miles of unprotected track lay between the two sectors. Quickly responding, Meade's chief of staff directed that the line be closed up and "strict vigilance" and frequent inspections be the rule, with four-man posts located within sight of each other, every quarter mile. The connecting point was clearly specified as Bull Run, and Meade ordered that no train was to move without infantry guards on the cars. Then he assigned General Howard's 11th Corps to guard the 24.25 miles from Bull Run to Bealeton Station. Before August 7, Mosby might have loosened a rail in the gap in the defenses, but after the guard was closed up and strengthened he was wise to direct his efforts toward Heintzelman's section.[21]

And that was his objective on August 24, to take thirty men somewhere east of Bull Run and burn railroad bridges in obedience to Lee's command. Mosby expected the raid to be a water-haul, and he knew that the small trestles would be immediately repaired and the impact would be negligible, but orders were orders. East of Fairfax Court House beside the turnpike he concealed the raiders and scouted with three men, finding three trestles unguarded. But at about 2:00 P.M. as he returned to bring up the men from the woods, he saw a drove of one hundred Union cavalry horses heading west on the pike, guarded by twenty-five of Lowell's 2nd Massachusetts Cavalry. This was too good to be true, so Mosby decided to first take the horses and burn the bridges later. It was a proper decision, using the irregular tactic of changing the goal of the mission when a better opportunity appeared. The horses were replacements for Meade's cavalry, which had a severe shortage due to an outbreak of the foot-and-mouth disease that killed horses by the hundreds and left several brigades only half mounted.[22]

The cavalrymen driving the horses proceeded a short distance to Billy Gooding's Tavern three miles east of Fairfax Court House, dismounted, and were watering the horses when Mosby's men attacked from both directions on the road in front of the tavern. A party of nine of the 13th New York Cavalry happened to be passing, and they joined in the fight, increasing Union strength to about thirty-five men. Several Federals used their revolvers, and a few fired from windows of the tavern, but Mosby's men had the momentum and a crossfire. After a brief, sharp fight, all the Union men ran away or surrendered. Mosby's men captured twelve prisoners and eighty-five horses. The Union had two dead and five wounded; Mosby had two dead and three wounded, including himself.[23]

One bullet pierced his side and passed around his ribs, and the other went through his right thigh, killing his horse. After the war Mosby said that the California Battalion was the best body of men that he fought in the war, and they got a leg up on that impression in this fight. Fortunately, neither bullet hit bone. Wisely Mosby had recruited Dr. William L. Dunn as assistant surgeon of the command. Dunn and three men took him to a nearby pine woods, where Dunn immediately treated the wounds. Before being taken away Mosby ordered Lt. William T. Turner to take a few men and burn the trestles. They succeeded in burning one. A few days later some of the men took Mosby to Idle Wilde near Lynchburg to recuperate.[24]

The Union cavalrymen who escaped reported that Mosby was wounded, perhaps mortally, and a rumor said that he was dead. An infantry and cavalry force sent to find him reported that he had been taken away, presumably to the graveyard. On August 29, five days after the fight, the *Washington Star* published an eyewitness account of a woman who allegedly saw Mosby passing through Upperville two days after he was wounded, in a wagon guarded by nine men, with Mosby lying on pillows with umbrellas shielding him from the sun, his face with "the ghastly hue of death upon it." Many in the North and in Meade's army concluded that he was dead. Then, on August 31, one week after the fight, the *New York Herald* reported that he had died three days before in Dranesville and ran his obituary, "Sketch of Mosby, Guerilla Chief." In Washington a new rumor started nearly every day. Some said that he was nearly well, others that his leg had been amputated, and then came the report that he had a severe back wound and would never ride again. The *New York Herald* correspondent in Washington decided on September 8 that it was impossible to determine whether he was alive or dead.[25]

Union Secretary of War Edwin M. Stanton probably barely noticed that guerrillas burned the small railroad trestle, but he became quite upset over the disappearance of the drove of one hundred badly needed horses worth eleven thousand dollars. Mistakenly thinking that the party of 13th New York Cavalry who had happened into the fight were responsible, he ordered a court of inquiry. If he had known that he was accusing the Massachusetts regiment of the prominent Colonel Lowell, he might not have acted. The court soon met with Gen. George Stoneman as president, and Lowell took full responsibility, apparently admitting that he should have detailed a stronger escort. The court deliberated and came to the conclusion that Lowell should be more careful in the future. Lowell accepted the warning, but in a letter to Effy explained that he had not been careless, that the only reason Mosby escaped was because one of Lowell's captains, not named, "went insane" during the skirmish, and the delay gave time for Mosby to withdraw. He regretted that the court of inquiry would be a blemish on his record. "All such courts hurt a fellow's chances," he worried, and this may be the reason that his promotion to brigadier general seemed slow. It came only after he was mortally wounded commanding a brigade under Sheridan in the battle of Cedar Creek on October 19, 1864.[26]

When Mosby was nearly recovered, he traveled to Richmond and met with Secretary of War Seddon. He probably expressed appreciation for Seddon's approval of his partisan status. Seddon said that he had read all of Mosby's reports and "spoke in the highest terms of the services" of Mosby's command. Before he left Richmond, Mosby ordered a shipment of percussion torpedoes, planning to use them to blow up a railroad train. He received the bombs by October 1, 1863, but there is no record of their use. Over a year later Lee sent more, and Mosby had them planted as of November 6, 1864. Apparently the only Union report of torpedoes that might have been set by Mosby's men came in December 1864 when Union cavalry found a few in the road in Ashby's Gap. The technology was still experimental, and Mosby's torpedoes probably failed to explode.[27]

Next he visited Lee at his headquarters at Orange Court House. It was their second meeting and the first since Mosby had gone independent, and it helped that he had been wounded. Lee treated him kindly and said that he was greatly satisfied with Mosby's conduct. He apologized for jumping to a conclusion on the rumor of the Charlottesville sale. Then they discussed how Mosby could give greater priority to the O&A, and Mosby probably told Lee about the torpedoes. Lee suggested that he attempt to capture prominent Union officials. After the meeting Lee wrote an order listing these special instructions for Mosby and sent it to Stuart.[28]

Mosby returned to duty and on the night of September 21 attempted to raid the O&A. He took more than forty men to a wooded area near Warrenton Junction and camped for the night. At daylight the next morning, they moved to within two miles of Bealeton Station, to a point about fifteen miles in the rear of Meade's headquarters at Culpeper. Mosby concealed the main body in the pines and with three men was scouting the railroad track, when he heard from the east the rumble and clatter of a large wagon train from the direction of Washington. Peering through the underbrush, he saw a mule train transporting a large pontoon bridge. There were twenty trucks, each with eight mules, and the convoy was heavily guarded and headed toward Meade as fast as the mules could go. Mosby saw that Meade was planning to cross the Rapidan and flank Lee's army, which had the favorable defensive position on the south bank. The bridge was six hundred feet long, and the Engineer Brigade was delivering it from Washington. Mosby sent a message by courier to Stuart, and

Stuart sent the intelligence to Lee. Meade canceled the plan, and the report had no strategic impact, but once again he had provided a potentially valuable glimpse behind the lines.[29]

Mosby realized that he had taken care of business as far as regular partisan work was concerned, and Lee would be satisfied. He was free to turn to guerrilla war. True to his hit-and-run instincts, he canceled the raid on the heavily guarded railroad, dismissed half of his men, and headed into Fairfax County with twenty. This violated Lee's wishes for larger parties, but it was true to the principles of irregular war. Near Bull Run he concealed his men in a stand of oak trees and ambushed a twenty-two-man detachment of the 19th New York Cavalry, out from camp at Manassas Junction to search for a lost horse. Their horses bolted, and Mosby took nine prisoners and thirteen horses. They were from Col. Alfred Gibbs's regiment, in the Army of the Potomac, guarding the farthest section of the O&A where Meade's guards connected with Heintzelman's. Moving on after daylight, the raiders seized eight quartermaster mules from a woodcutting party near Burke's Station in Heintzelman's sector of the railroad. The infantry protecting the wood-cutters watched in amazement as Mosby's men cut the animals from the herd in a pasture in plain view of their camp. It was out of range of their muskets, and they could only stand and watch.[30]

Then Mosby sent all but four of the men home with the prisoners and animals. With the remaining four, on the afternoon of September 22, he rode to the vicinity of Alexandria, and on hills overlooking the town he took out his field glasses and studied the roads and defenses. He was scouting for the next part of his instructions—the capture of Union officials. The raid was a success. He had scouted for Lee, captured railroad guards, and acquired spoils for his men: $2,420 in mules and horses, plus arms and accoutrements. The *Richmond Sentinel* reported the arrival of the nine prisoners in Richmond and concluded: "Mosby's troopers are busy in the enemy's rear."[31]

Five days later, on Sunday, September 27, he and eight men returned to Fairfax County and slept in the pines between Fairfax Court House and Alexandria. The next day they captured six stragglers, and Mosby sent them off guarded by four of his men. With the other four, after dark he penetrated the ring of capital defenses and entered Alexandria to capture Lincoln's man in Virginia, the Father of West Virginia and now Restored Governor of Virginia, Francis H. Pierpont. He had led the movement for the creation of West Virginia and, when statehood was achieved in 1863, had moved to Alexandria. Officially the United States recognized him as governor of the entire state of Virginia, but in reality he had authority only in areas occupied by the Union army. Mosby called him the "bogus Governor" of the state. The five raiders called at the City Hotel where Pierpont leased a suite, but he had gone to Washington that evening.[32]

When Pierpont learned how close he had come to being captured, he was incensed, especially in light of the message he received, supposedly from Mosby: "You did not see the farmer who rode by your hotel on a hay wagon yesterday, did you Governor? My driver pointed out your window, and I marked it plain. It's just over the bay, and I'll get you some night, mighty easy." Pierpont complained to Secretary of War Stanton: "This conduct on their part is impudent and Wicked and must be stoped or the whole Union sentiment with in our lines will be demoralized." At least he felt comforted in his previous decision to keep his family in Pennsylvania and Maryland, safe from guerrillas.[33]

The raiders rode south out of town on the Telegraph Road to "Rose Hill," the home of Pierpont's aide, Col. Daniel H. Dulaney, four miles from town. They had no difficulty locating the house because one of them was Pvt. French Dulaney, the colonel's son. They dismounted and approached the door, and Mosby knocked. Someone threw open an upper window, and Mosby said quietly, "Is Colonel Dulaney in?" The answer was yes, and Mosby explained that he had dispatches from Pierpont that he must deliver in person. Presently the colonel opened the door. "Is this Colonel Dulaney?" Mosby asked. "Yes Sir. Walk in, gentlemen, and be seated." Mosby stepped in first and said, "My name is Mosby." The colonel realized that he was captured, and then his son stepped through the door. "How do Pa?" said French, "I'm very glad to see you." "Well, Sir," the colonel replied, "I'm damned sorry to see you."[34]

On the return, they set fire to the railroad bridge at Cameron's Run, less than three miles from Alexandria and within range of the artillery of two of the forts west of Alexandria. Guards extinguished the flames without much damage, but Mosby had, with eight men, fulfilled his special instructions from Lee. His September 30 report stressed that the value of his operation was the diversion of Union troops to the rear to guard communications. Stuart wrote on it that Mosby was "faithfully carrying out" his instructions, and Lee gave him great credit for "boldness and skill." The *New York Herald* reported Dulaney's capture with the complaint: "Guerillas seem to be about as plentiful in Fairfax County as our own troops and much more active. Until a regiment is stationed at Fairfax Court House, and another at Vienna, we may anticipate the continued and frequent depredations of these bands."[35]

For the remainder of the war Mosby and his men continued watching for opportunities to capture high-ranking enemies. On a snatch raid in Fairfax County on the night of June 9, 1864, Mosby prepared to enter Alexandria again. After capturing the pickets on Telegraph Road, he planned to divide his force of thirty-five men into three detachments to capture Pierpont; apprehend Gen. John P. Slough, Military Governor of Alexandria; and round up horses. Somehow Union officials learned about the raid and went on alert, and Mosby canceled the mission.[36]

Twice in August 1864, Mosby's men attempted to snatch Gen. Philip Sheridan. Leading a spare horse for the general, one night Valley scout John Russell took six men inside the camp of Sheridan's army in Jefferson County, West Virginia. They arrived at his headquarters, but before Russell could silence the sentinel he fired his carbine and alerted the guards. A few nights later Adolphus E. "Dolly" Richards led a small force into the camp, but they were unable to locate Sheridan's headquarters. Dolly captured a soldier and attempted to force him to guide them, but instead he screamed and awoke his comrades, and the Rebels withdrew.[37]

Lt. Walter "Wat" Bowie and about eight men attempted to capture Maryland governor Augustus Bradford. Safely reaching his father's home in Prince Georges County a few miles west of Annapolis, Bowie left the men there and scouted the capital alone. He found Bradford too well-guarded and canceled the mission. On the return he was mortally wounded in Montgomery County, Maryland, and died the next day, October 7, 1864. Bowie's raid and the other failed attempts showed how careful Union commanders and officials were after Stoughton's capture. Mosby would succeed in capturing only one other general—Alfred Napoleon A. Duffie—and that was not a planned capture but resulted from Duffie's unusual negligence. More typical was the alert that Gen. Winfield S. Hancock in Winchester gave to Gen. John D. Stevenson in Harpers Ferry on March 10, 1865. Hancock had heard that Mosby planned to visit Stevenson's room that night and capture him in bed. "You had better be careful," he warned.[38]

No evidence has been found that Mosby planned to capture Lincoln. When Jesse McNeill captured two Union generals on the same night in Cumberland, Maryland, Mosby joked, "The only way I can equal this will be to go into Washington and bring out Lincoln." One morning he was scouting in Fairfax County across the Potomac from Washington, sitting on his horse on a hilltop with a view of the city, when Mrs. Barlow appeared, driving a farm wagon loaded with vegetables. She was the wife of a Union soldier and had a pass into Washington to deliver her produce. She and Mosby were acquainted from stops he had made at her house to drink coffee. He saw a pair of scissors hanging from her apron and asked to borrow them. Cutting a lock of his hair and handing it to her, he said, "Please take this lock of my hair right into Lincoln and say to him that I am coming in to see him soon and will expect a lock of his hair in return." The story circulated in Washington that she made the delivery and Lincoln laughed heartily.[39]

In minding Meade's rear with thirty men, Mosby had embarrassed the enemy by seizing unguarded wagons in broad daylight, taking ice cream from the mouths of the men in the Army of the Potomac, seizing a drove of horses, and snatching an aide of the governor from his home, all within a few miles of Washington, D.C. He had forced the Union army to convoy sutler wagons with a strong escort. He might have scouted the O&A more carefully and discovered the unguarded gap in the Union defenses in early August, and he could have given greater priority to attacking the small bridges in Heintzelman's sector east of Bull Run. But true to classic guerrilla tactics, he had remained flexible on missions, concentrated on enemy weaknesses, and preserved his command for further service. He had learned the valuable lesson that to satisfy Lee he must continue making scouting reports and give future raids and official reports a strong tone of contribution to the main army effort.

# 9

# Masquerading as the Enemy

The best opportunities to masquerade as the enemy came in the immediate rear of main armies where soldiers felt secure and moved alone or in small detachments. When Meade's army withdrew to Centreville to counter Lee's advance during the Bristoe Station campaign in October 1863, Stuart sent Mosby to scout in Meade's rear between Centreville and Washington, and the Rangers used the opportunity to masquerade as Union cavalry. The battalion had increased to two companies on October 1 but still had only about fifty men. On about October 17 Mosby concealed them in a woodland near Frying Pan and after dark went with seven men to Chantilly, about three miles north of Meade's headquarters. They were hiding in the pines on Little River Turnpike watching for prey when a wagon train came with no escort. They let it pass and fell in behind, pretending to serve as the rear guard. Passing through an infantry camp, they saw enemy infantry on each side of the pike, gathered in small groups around blazing fires cooking supper. The sky was cloudy, and no one suspected that the cavalry "escort" wore gray. Beyond the last picket post, Mosby gave a signal, and the raiders drew their revolvers and surrounded the wagons, forcing the drivers to unhitch. They captured thirteen prisoners, seven horses, and thirty-six mules. The event probably inspired the tale that appeared in the *New York Herald* that one night Mosby went into a Union infantry camp at Centreville and ordered the teamsters to hitch their supply wagons and move out under his escort, and once outside the camp captured the wagons.[1]

During the six days that Meade's army was at Centreville, Mosby captured between seventy-five and one hundred prisoners and more than one hundred horses and mules. On October 19, the day that Meade's army began moving toward Warrenton, Mosby sent two scouting reports indicating that infantry were moving southwest from Fairfax Court House and Centreville. On October 20 at 10:30 A.M., Stuart forwarded the intelligence to Lee, and it demonstrated again that Mosby was a useful pair of "eyes" behind the lines, making accurate, prognostic reports. When Meade's army camped at Centreville, Mosby was in Meade's rear toward Washington and could probably be counted on to notice significant troop movements.[2]

The Army of the Potomac had barely settled into camp near Warrenton when on the seventh night, October 26, 1863, Mosby's men pretended to be Union soldiers in the middle of the army, only two miles from headquarters. At 6:00 P.M. fifty Rangers left Salem and after dark rode ten miles inside the Union cavalry screen in Meade's rear, aiming for the stream of supplies going from the Gainesville supply depot southwest to Warrenton. Using prior reconnaissance, intimate knowledge of the area, and the cover of darkness, they reached a secluded stretch of the Warrenton and Gainesville Turnpike with trees on each side. Before long a wagon train of about forty wagons appeared, guarded by cavalry, infantry, and artillery. Mosby noticed that the escort was divided in the front and rear and the center was unprotected. The challenge was to quietly stop the wagons in the center, unhitch the teams, set fire to the wagons, and leave before the escort could be alerted. If he had simply attacked, the teamsters would have spread the alarm, and the escort would have driven off the Rangers. Mosby directed Capt. William H. Chapman to take ten men and stop the column by pretending to be Union soldiers.[3] William had joined Mosby over seven months before, at the same time as his older brother Sam, and both had fought at Miskel's Farm. Up to this point, William had been in Sam's shadow, for Sam was a Baptist minister and was more outspoken. Sam sang hymns in a loud voice and loved fighting almost as much as Mosby. He fought so ferociously at Miskel's Farm—emptying both revolvers and standing in his stirrups to slash right and left with his saber and ending up with a saber cut on his head—that the enemy assumed he was Mosby. Mosby liked Sam and appointed him adjutant, but he lacked William's gift of discretion, the ability to judge when an enemy force could be attacked and defeated. This would be more clear to Mosby later; for now he risked the expedition on William's ability to portray a Union provost marshal.[4]

William rode alongside a wagon and asked the driver who was in charge of this section of wagons and obtained the name of the commissary of the artillery reserve, a lieutenant. Then he rode forward, found the lieutenant, and arrested him under orders from headquarters, identifying himself as a captain of the 18th Pennsylvania Cavalry on provost marshal duty. He ordered the teamsters to park along the road and unhitch their mules. At that point, amid the clatter and jangle, Mosby and the other Rangers came out and joined in the roundup. Suddenly a Union cavalry detachment appeared, and there was no time to fire the wagons; the raiders left in haste. They obtained 103 mules, 42 horses, and about 30 prisoners without firing a shot.[5]

Meade wrote Halleck: "Last night a supply train coming from the depot at Gainesville was attacked between New Baltimore and Warrenton and some one hundred animals taken from it. The train had an escort, which was in front and rear, but was unable to reach the center of the train before the guerrillas had made off with the animals. The wagons were left untouched." Army gossip reported that Mosby had made off with four hundred mules, and a *New York Herald* correspondent at Meade's headquarters wrote, "Despite the precaution of strong pickets, the inevitable and inscrutable Mosby manages to break through our lines occasionally."[6]

Mosby divided the horses among his men and had the mules delivered to Stuart. At $110 in Union currency, the drove was worth $11,330. When Stuart saw them, he said, "Hurrah for Mosby! This is a good haul. Mules! and fat, too!" He forwarded Mosby's report to the War Department with the endorsement: "This is but another instance of Major Mosby's skill and daring in addition to those forwarded almost daily." And Seddon wrote, "Noted, with admiration at the fearlessness and skill of this gallant partisan." Within the month William Chapman was unofficially commanding a separate company of Mosby's men and within two months, on December 15, 1863, was elected commander of new Company C.[7]

On November 7, Meade moved from Warrenton across the Rappahannock toward the north bank of the Rapidan; the day before Mosby had filed a reconnaissance report that portended the march. With three men he had scouted to Catlett's Station, ten miles from Warrenton, and had reported on November 6 that two days before Gen. John Sedgwick's corps remained stationary but "a good deal of artillery" had moved toward the front from Warrenton. For seventeen days, until the Mine Run Campaign began on November 26, the two armies faced each other across the Rapidan River. During this time, while operating around Warrenton, fifteen miles in Meade's rear, Mosby captured about seventy-five cavalry, more than one hundred horses and mules, and six wagons.[8]

On November 22 Mosby reported on these and other successes and stated that the O&A was so well-defended, with sentinels on the track in sight of each other and guards on all the trains, that he found it "very difficult" to assault. Three days later Stuart approved: "Major Mosby is ever vigilant, ever active. The importance of his operations is shown by the heavy guard the enemy is obliged to keep to guard the railroad from his attacks." By November 19 the O&A had opened to Meade's head-quarters at Brandy Station, and Gen. John Newton's first infantry corps was stationed at Warrenton Junction guarding the line. When the army left on the Mine Run campaign on November 26, Meade left Gen. John R. Kenly's division from the first corps on duty as railroad guards, along with five hundred men of Gen. David M. Gregg's cavalry division. Mosby, however, did not deserve full credit for this vigilance; Frank Stringfellow, a former Stuart scout, and James C. Kincheloe of the Prince William County Partisan Rangers were active as well. Mosby's goal was to satisfy Lee, and Lee was pleased. On November 17 he noted that Mosby had with boldness and skill inflicted "repeated injuries" on the enemy, keeping him "in constant apprehension." Then Lee gave what to Lee was the highest compliment—he suggested that Mosby increase his battalion to regimental strength and muster into the regular cavalry. Seddon endorsed Mosby's November 22, 1863, report: "Noted, with satisfaction and appreciation of the energy and valor displayed."[9]

Meade left the O&A strongly defended when he took his army away from the railroad and across the Rapidan to flank Lee on the Mine Run campaign. Kenly's division and Gregg's detachment of cavalry protected the track from Manassas Junction to Rappahannock Station, and from there Col. Thomas C. Devin's brigade of Merritt's cavalry division had responsibility. The only problem was that the two did not connect. Devin's men were camped about two miles northeast of Culpeper, ten miles from where Kenly's line ended. They were ordered to guard the twelve miles from Culpeper to the linking point with Kenly at Rappahannock Station. About midway was Brandy Station, but since Meade had abandoned it as his supply center, Devin's cavalry did not patrol it the first night; they left a gap between them and Kenly of five or six miles.[10]

Meade left at 6:00 A.M. on November 26; Mosby noted the move and by sundown Mosby had found the gap on the O&A. With 125 men—

his most thus far—he proceeded to the northern bank of the Rappahannock in the afternoon, concealed the battalion, and scouted with three men. Late in the afternoon they reached Brandy Station and saw a large wagon train escorted by a few infantry loading at the former supply depot. Relying on audacity to mask the color of their uniforms in the fading light, Mosby and his scouts rode into their midst. Sitting calmly on his magnificent gray horse, he talked with the teamsters and the guards, determining for certain that the wagons were guarded very lightly. Upon their leaving the perimeter a sentinel challenged them and Mosby answered, "We are a patrol." The man again ordered "Halt!" and fired as they rode away. It was fully dark when Mosby returned with all of his men and re-entered the camp. A quartermaster thought they were Union cavalry and said, "Have they gone?" meaning the lead wagons. "No, just going," Mosby replied. Mosby's men started unhitching the mules, and suddenly a sentinel fired a shot and all was bedlam as guns fired from various directions and mules and drivers ran in circles. One driver asked Mosby which way he should run, and Mosby pointed to a wagon and shouted, "Unhitch them mules!" The raiders burned between 30 and 40 wagons and made off with 112 mules, 7 horses, and 20 prisoners.[11]

Meade's turning movement failed, and his army returned north of the Rapidan and went into winter quarters, huddling around fireplaces in their crude huts. During the first week of the new year, winter took over. On Monday, January 4, it snowed all day; two nights later, soldiers threw extra logs on the fire when the arctic jet stream shifted south out of Canada, dropping temperatures to below zero. Sheets of ice formed along the riverbanks, and the Potomac froze over for the first time in three or four years. On Thursday evening at about 8:00 P.M. it started snowing again and snowed all night, covering northern Virginia with several inches of drifting, blowing snow that refused to melt. Temperatures remained around zero, and the people of Alexandria filled their ice houses with three-inch chunks of ice. In Baltimore by Friday evening youths were skating on the lakes and ponds, and sleigh bells were ringing on four-horse sleighs on the streets downtown. Steamers kept the channel open south from Washington, but immense fields of floating ice accumulated in Chesapeake Bay at the mouth of the Susquehanna River, halting commercial side-wheeler traffic and driving up the price of oysters in Baltimore from seventy-five cents to a dollar and a half per bushel.[12]

It was ideal weather for a raid, and Mosby accepted Frank Stringfellow's invitation to combine in an overnight expedition to capture Maj. Henry A. Cole's cavalry recently moved onto Loudoun Heights just south of Harpers Ferry. Stringfellow had scouted the camp and offered to take Mosby and his men into Cole's rear and capture the entire battalion without a shot. He had guided Mosby's men on a raid toward Warrenton on November 21, and they had captured two ambulances and three wagons of medical supplies. He was twenty-four years old, a native of Culpeper County, and before leaving Stuart had earned commendation for conspicuous gallantry. As a guerrilla he preferred high-risk operations, but his actual accomplishments were not nearly as colorful as described in his sermons as an Episcopal minister after the war. He said that he donned a Union colonel's uniform, entered Union lines, and had dinner with Union general Sedgwick and his staff; and he boasted that he spied in Washington, sleeping in the hotel where Vice President Andrew Johnson boarded. "Most of Frank's tales would have been equally true if told of the Argonaut," wrote Mosby. "He was a brave soldier, but a great liar."[13]

Cole's cavalry was one of two Union cavalry units organized along the border of northern Virginia and given authority by Secretary of War Stanton to conduct independent operations. The other was one of the most persistent and long-standing opponents of Mosby's men, the Loudoun Rangers. Cole recruited his men from Maryland, Pennsylvania, and the Unionist area of northern Loudoun County. Like the Loudoun Rangers, they had the disadvantage of conducting independent warfare surrounded by hostile civilians once they left Maryland or northern Loudoun County. As they were local rivals, Mosby and his men usually underestimated both units.

Major Cole, from Frederick, Maryland, was about twenty-nine years old, strong, brave, and earnest. In December 1863 he received orders to move his battalion out of Harpers Ferry to serve as an early-warning screen against regular Confederate forces that might advance northward on Hillsboro Road in the Loudoun Valley and to protect the bridge on the Shenandoah River. The camp was on a shelf on the eastern base of Loudoun Heights, a half mile from Harpers Ferry, on the left of Hillsboro Road as one proceeded north. Cole stayed in a two-story house, and his men camped in tents in the level area beside the house to the north. Here on the northern edge of the Blue Ridge Mountains, over twelve inches of snow had accumulated, casting a blanket of white on the cedar and pine trees above and on the rock ledges and evergreens of Maryland Heights towering over Harpers Ferry and the icy Potomac River.[14]

Cole had pickets on the road about a quarter-mile from camp on the bridge over Sweet Run. This was the only road from the south, and he expected these guards to warn of any enemy appearance. The road north ran along the crest of the shelf, and at the road's edge the mountain continued its descent in a sharp grade covered with trees, vines, and thick bushes. Cole felt confident that the only way an enemy force could approach would be north on the Hillsboro Road; and if they did his men would be ready to respond to a rifle-fire warning from the pickets—he ordered the men to sleep on their arms, as he always did on expeditions. "We felt very safe," one of Cole's troopers wrote in his diary.[15]

One reason Mosby agreed to Stringfellow's plan without scouting himself was that some of his men had given one of Cole's detachments a thrashing on New Year's Day at Five Points in Fauquier County. What he failed to take into account was that Cole was not on that raid and that Cole himself was strong and efficient.[16] Another mistake was in misjudging Stringfellow. Mosby had been teaching his officers not to fight unless they could win, and he was about to learn that Stringfellow lacked such discretion. Stringfellow had found a route through the woods, around Cole's pickets to the rear and up the steep cliff, and he believed that, since Cole felt so secure that he did not have sentinels posted around the tents, a surprise coming on the road from Harpers Ferry would easily force a surrender. Mosby should have scouted himself and realized that the camp, laid out as it was on the shelf, hemmed in on the base of the mountain, would give the enemy no place to run. To attack Cole's camp was to enter a tiger's cage; when the tiger awoke, fighting him would be comparable to making a mounted cavalry charge against veteran infantry—something that Mosby always attempted to avoid.

On Saturday, January 9, having agreed to meet Stringfellow and his men on the Hillsboro Road south of Cole's pickets, Mosby rendezvoused with about one hundred Rangers at Upperville and set out on the twenty-two-mile trek. The air was calm, but it was so cold that some of the men cut holes in the middle of their blankets and threw them over their shoulders. Now and then a man would dismount and run beside his horse to restore his numbing feet. Near Round Hill, about halfway, they stopped at the home of James Heaton, father of Ranger Henry Heaton, for a hot meal and to get warm. At 10:00 P.M. they set out again, and about two miles south of Cole's camp they met Stringfellow and ten men, bringing the force to about 110. Mosby estimated that Cole had 175 to 200 but hoped that surprise would make up for the numerical disadvantage.[17]

Stringfellow guided as planned, off the road to the right and along the western base of the Short Hill Mountains. There they halted, and Stringfellow and Mosby reconnoitered for two hours. They observed that Cole's men were asleep in their tents north of the headquarters house, with no sentinels to be seen anywhere in the camp. They rejoined the men and led them north to the Potomac and west along the riverbank to a path leading up through the trees to the road. The cliff was so steep they had to dismount and lead their horses single file and grasp bushes to keep their footing in the snow. Reaching the top, they came out on the road midway between Cole's camp and the river. Mosby sent a small party south on the road to capture the pickets on the bridge and dispatched Stringfellow and his men to go down the road as well, past the tents to the headquarters house, where he would capture Cole in keeping with Mosby's maxim to capture or kill the enemy commander. Mosby would take a dismounted detachment into the tents to quietly round up the prisoners.[18]

It was between 3:00 and 4:00 A.M., and the rows of tents were still unguarded. Mosby and his detachment entered the camp and began forcing the surrender of men in the first row of tents, when the crack of a carbine echoed along the mountain. In their scout a few hours before, Mosby and Stringfellow had not seen a single sentinel; but there was one now, standing in front of the headquarters house. He ordered Stringfellow and his men to halt, then fired and ran. Cole heard the shot, ran out the back door, and began waking his men. Confederate captain William R. Smith, still mounted on the road behind Mosby, yelled, "Charge them, boys! Charge them!" and led several men galloping into the camp in a mounted charge. At the same time, Stringfellow and his men came charging on horseback from the other direction. Mosby mistook Stringfellow's men for the enemy and shouted encouragement to Smith. Incredibly, men from Mosby's task force were charging each other on horseback in front of the tents of the enemy, who emerged from their beds shooting at both mounted columns.[19]

Cole's troopers had removed their boots and coats, and some had taken off their outer clothing, but they scrambled out into the snow, carbines and revolvers blazing. Certain that all of the mounted men were Rebels, Cole shouted, "Shoot every man on horseback!" and others repeated the cry. A Confederate pointed his pistol at a man and said, "Surrender!" and the Union man answered, "No, I won't! You surrender!" It was point-blank shooting, and in the darkness one could not see the faces of the enemy, but the Union troops could clearly see the outline of mounted Rebels. Men cursed and yelled, a wounded horse shrieked in pain, and riderless horses plunged and kicked and ran wild. "It was a perfect hell!" one of Cole's men recalled. Union captain George Vernon rushed to the edge of the tents, and a bullet struck him in the face, passing through his left cheek and destroying his left eye. He grasped his face, fell into the snow, and screamed, "Rally here men; they're nothing but a set of damn horse thieves!" Several of Cole's men withdrew higher on the mountain behind the tents and fired from there. Confederate lieutenant Thomas Turner was shooting from his horse when a bullet struck him in the abdomen. He threw up his hands and cried, "I am shot." Two of the men from his company pulled alongside and led him and his horse to the road. After about fifteen minutes, Mosby's shrill voice rang out, "Retreat, boys; they are too many for us!"[20]

Afterward, Mosby accused Stringfellow of firing the first shot and awakening the camp, and he criticized Stringfellow for charging into his men. He would never again use Stringfellow as a guide or combine on a raid with him. The raiders had used the guerrilla tactics of an overnight raid with rested men and horses, Mosby had scouted the site immediately before the assault, he had used inclement weather and timed the attack when the enemy were most sound asleep, and he had approached from the enemy rear. But as he said in ordering the retreat, there were too many bullets; the enemy was surprised and had no choice but to fight in their stocking feet. In *The Art of War,* Chinese philosopher Sun Tzu wrote, "In a desperate position, you must fight." Cole's cavalrymen, all dismounted and in rows outside their tents or scrambled farther up the mountainside, became in essence a skirmish line of infantry firing at mounted cavalry. In the cold air they awoke quickly and fought ferociously.[21]

The "Gallant Repulse of Mosby's Guerrillas" made front-page news in the North. Reporters emphasized that Mosby left his dead lying in the bloodstained snow in the camp and that his line of retreat was marked by drops of blood in the snow-covered road. Mosby lost four men killed, four mortally wounded, three wounded, including Fount Beattie shot in the thigh, and one captured. Cole had four killed and sixteen wounded. For Mosby the casualty rate of 10 percent was unusually high, but the damage was greater than numbers revealed. He lost both Smith and Turner, his handpicked protégés who had graduated from his informal school of guerrilla tactics and had become replicas of himself. He had taught both discretion on when to attack and when to run, and both had commanded successful raids on Union pickets in Warrenton. "Billie" Smith was captain of Company B, the father of four children, and he died only two days short of his twenty-eighth birthday. Tom Turner, first lieutenant of Company A, was from Prince Georges County, Maryland, and he had been one of the original fifteen from Stuart's cavalry. During the retreat his companions took him to a house on the Hillsboro Road a short distance south of Cole's camp, and Mosby stopped to see him and stood by the bed, weeping like a child. Turner died the next day.[22]

Northern journalists elevated the size of Mosby's force to four hundred men and praised Cole for vigilance. His superior officer, Harpers Ferry commander Gen. Jeremiah C. Sullivan, sent him and his men twenty gallons of whiskey. In Cumberland, Maryland, Gen. Benjamin Kelley praised Cole and his troops for watchfulness, discipline, and bravery in repelling "a murderous attack, made by an overwhelming force at 4 o'clock on a dark, cold morning." Halleck gave the soldiers "high praise for their gallantry in repelling this rebel assault." They received a thirty-day furlough, and the people of Frederick, Maryland, honored them with a parade, speeches at City Hall, and a banquet. Cole was promoted to lieutenant colonel on March 5, and to colonel on April 20.[23]

Mosby's men always regarded the fight as "a little Waterloo." But ironically, the defeat earned Mosby the highest praise that he ever received from Stuart. Endorsing Mosby's report, Stuart wrote, "His sleepless vigilance and unceasing activity have done the enemy great damage. He keeps a large force of the enemy's cavalry continually employed in Fairfax in the vain effort to suppress his inroads. His exploits are not surpassed in daring and enterprise by those of *petite guerre* in any age. Unswerving devotion to duty, self-abnegation, and unflinching courage, with a quick perception and appreciation of the opportunity, are the characteristics of this officer." He recommended promotion to lieutenant colonel, which was officially approved effective January 21, only eleven days later. Seldom has a defeated commander received promotion and such high accolades for a defeat.[24]

Lee's idea for Mosby's advancement was to increase his command to regimental strength and bring him into the regular cavalry. Mosby's goal was to clone himself with company commanders who would be able to apply his guerrilla tactics in simultaneous raids at different locations. He had hand-picked and trained Billie Smith and Tom Turner, and they had proven their ability with successful raids when Mosby was not present. They had learned Sun Tzu's maxim, "He will win who knows when to fight and when not to fight."[25] Now others would have to step forward and become Mosby clones.

# 10

# Seddon's Partisans

Secretary of War Seddon was in frail health and looked much older than forty-eight. The doctors said he had chronic neuralgia, and some people said that he would never survive the workload of a cabinet position. His wife Sally stayed at home on the plantation in Goochland County, and he lived quietly in the Spottswood Hotel. He wore a skullcap, had a prominent nose and straggling hair, and was so thin it was said that one could hear his bones rattle when he descended the hotel stairs. John B. Jones, the war clerk who saw him every day, wrote in his diary, "Mr. Secretary Seddon, who usually wears a sallow and cadaverous look, which, coupled with his emaciation, makes him resemble an exhumed corpse after a month's interment, looks to-day like a galvanized corpse which had been buried two months. The circles round his eyes are absolutely black!"[1]

There were too many dull reports to read and too many lengthy meetings with President Davis. But Seddon was a disciple of John C. Calhoun and an ardent secessionist. He rarely laughed and meant it when he quipped that the South would provide hospitable graves for all the Yankee invaders "six feet to each" with "a few inches more to their leader." After the war he destroyed his papers to keep them out of the hands of the Radical Republicans. He did not read all of the reports from the far-flung Confederate armies, but with much pleasure he read every one from partisans John H. McNeill and Mosby. Their successes in guerrilla warfare behind enemy lines filled his heart with good feelings and gave him hope that the Southern people still had the will to fight and establish a nation. Two of the highlights of his life were visits in his office with each man.[2]

McNeill came first, in early March 1863, calling to propose a raid on the B&O trestle on the Cheat River in West Virginia. McNeill was a successful cattle farmer, a native of Moorefield, West Virginia. One month older than Seddon, he was six feet tall, with blue eyes and a huge gray beard that reached almost to his waist, and he wore a black hat with a black plume. His partisan rangers never increased beyond one company, and his highest rank was captain, but with sixty or eighty men he was effective at surprising enemy camps and capturing prisoners several times his own number. Seddon considered him "a very brave and enterprising partisan officer," and his proposal appealed because it involved only six hundred men, a relatively small number for the raid. Seddon may have been the only official in the Confederate high command who understood the value of stealth in guerrilla operations. He agreed with McNeill that "a sudden and unexpected dash of a small force" was less likely to attract opposition and more likely to succeed. Seddon recommended the plan to McNeill's superiors in the regular army, but they expanded it into an unsuccessful expedition of over six thousand men.[3]

Seddon, McNeill, and Mosby had no previous military experience, but all three had an appreciation for stealth in guerrilla warfare. It was not so with the West Pointers in command. When the Confederate Senate debated the Partisan Ranger Act, Kentucky senator Henry C. Burnett stated that guerrilla tactics were superior to what was taught at West Point and the president needed authority to begin a people's war, in spite of the West Point generals. The grassroots movement for guerrilla war championed by journalists came from outside the military establishment. Encouraging Congress to move, the *Richmond Enquirer* declared, "'A People in Arms' cannot be conquered."[4]

It was not public knowledge, but two West Point commanders in the Confederate army had opposed the movement before the act passed. On March 5, 1862, Joseph Johnston complained that someone was passing out handbills in his camps and advertising in the newspapers for partisan recruits, and he disapproved because such bands would encourage desertions and cause discontent and mutiny in the ranks. On April 2, Gen. Henry Heth disbanded two Virginia State Ranger units in his district of western Virginia, condemning them as robbers and plunderers and the system as a loophole to avoid duty.[5]

Before the law passed, Secretary of War Judah P. Benjamin turned down requests to raise guerrilla companies by pointing out that they were not part of the military organization of the Confederacy and could not be authorized by the War Department. George W. Randolph, Secretary of War when the law passed, was the grandson of Thomas Jefferson, a Richmond lawyer, and the first Secretary of War with military experience. In his youth he served in the Navy for six years. Well read in military history, earlier in the Civil War he had drafted Virginia's manpower procurement system and had served as an artillery officer. Taking over from Benjamin, he worked with Davis to finish writing the first Confederate Conscription Act enacted on April 16, 1862, five days before the Partisan Act. In Senate debate on partisans, his views were stated by senators who objected that partisan units would attract men needed for the regular army.[6]

In charge of implementing both laws, Randolph gave priority to conscription and restricted the guerrilla movement. In less than three months after enactment of the Partisan Act he ruled that authority to raise a command of partisans would not be granted without a recommendation from the general commanding the department. On July 31, 1862, Randolph issued General Orders no. 53 prohibiting future enrollment of conscripts in Ranger service. He believed that there were already too many partisan units, and many were not enrolled with the department. His ruling and general order severely limited the organization of new units as far as the War Department was concerned. Commanders would authorize few units, and even if they did, with males from eighteen to thirty-five ineligible, the Rangers would be restricted to young boys and old men. In practice, however, all over the Confederacy new units were organized in complete disregard of Randolph's rules. In his general report of August 12, 1862, he recommended that partisan commands deemed superfluous be brigaded as troops of the line, "although nominally partisans." Later, by 1863, Lee would agree, but in 1862 he approved new units for local service with the understanding that they would be subject to the orders of the general commanding the department.[7]

Randolph resigned in November 1862 to return to active duty, and Seddon took over. By then not only were partisans impeding recruitment, complaints were pouring in that, rather than attacking the enemy, Rangers were stealing from and terrorizing Southern civilians. In Knoxville, for example, they stole horses from Unionist citizens and rode the old men out of town on fence rails. As mentioned above, Seddon reported on January 3, 1863, that the program had failed and that he was refusing to approve new commands and attempting to bring existing units into the regular army.[8]

Then after making an exception for Mosby, he was pleased that Mosby continued disbanding and that Mosby and McNeill still practiced stealth with small detachments. He decided by November 26, 1863, to close the program, except for Mosby and McNeill. He reported that the partisans had proved inefficient and had committed grave depredations on the Southern people and had caused dissatisfaction in the army. The trained soldiers were envious of the lighter discipline and the opportunity for profit. He recommended that the partisan corps be merged into the troops of the line or be disbanded but that the War Department should have discretion to preserve the ones who were "daring and brilliant," rendering "eminent" service, as "valuable coadjutors of the general service"—McNeill and Mosby.[9]

On Christmas Day 1863 he received a letter from North Carolina governor Zebulon V. Vance complaining that partisans were illegally seizing property and committing depredations more outrageous than the plagues of Egypt. Then a letter came through military channels from the Shenandoah Valley, through Stuart and Lee, and Seddon realized that it was time to draft repeal legislation. The letter was written on January 11, 1864, by Gen. Thomas L. Rosser, commander of the Laurel Brigade, Ashby's famous cavalry. Rosser was born in Virginia, grew up in Texas, and was two weeks short of graduation at West Point when he resigned to join the Confederate army. He was six feet, two inches tall, a large, proud man full of swagger. His subordinates admired his bravery but considered him incompetent. Always receiving more attention than he deserved, he later became the "Savior of the Valley," and the nickname held even after his crushing defeat at Tom's Brook on October 9, 1864. Nonetheless, Stuart respected him, and Lee promoted him to major general.[10]

From personal experience within the month, Rosser had come to hate partisans. His brigade was picketing on the Rapidan when on the night of December 14, 1863, about sixty of his men deserted to go home to Loudoun County for winter clothing. They were from Lt. Col. Elijah "Lige" V. White's 35th Battalion of Virginia cavalry. White was born in Poolesville, Maryland, and lived on a farm in Loudoun County before the war. He recruited his men from Loudoun County and Maryland for a border war but mustered them into the regular cavalry. He was an aggressive fighter, charging with sabers and revolvers, but informally like Indians, so Rosser called them "Comanches." White and his men hated camp life and preferred detached duty in Loudoun County, north of Mosby's Confederacy.[11] Rosser believed that the life enjoyed by Mosby's men had enticed the Comanches to desert.

Two days after the desertions Rosser received orders to report to the Shenandoah Valley, where in the first week of January the Laurel Brigade participated in Fitz Lee's foraging expedition to Moorefield, West Virginia, and Rosser ordered McNeill to advance with his company over an ice-covered mountain road. As a guerrilla McNeill refused to abuse his horses in this way—he did not say a word but silently shook his head. Rosser argued and fumed, but still McNeill quietly defied him. Rosser could not believe that an old cattle farmer would refuse to obey an order by a general who lacked only two weeks finishing at West Point. The raid ended in frustration and disappointment, and Rosser blasted partisans.[12]

His letter stated that experience had convinced him that the partisan corps was an evil nuisance that should be closed down. It kept men out of the regular ranks, lowered the morale of the regulars who were jealous, and caused desertions. It was almost impossible to keep the men of his brigade from the counties of Mosby's Confederacy on duty. They wanted to join Mosby and live at ease, sleeping in houses and turning out in cold weather only for the leisure-time pleasure of plundering. He wrote that he respected the gallant Mosby, but turned one of Mosby's accomplishments on its head by stating that Mosby's men were "of inestimable service to the Yankee army in keeping their men from straggling." And, probably referring to McNeill's insubordination, he stated, "They never fight; can't be made to fight."[13]

Stuart endorsed the letter on January 18, 1864, agreeing that partisans were generally detrimental and pointing out that Mosby was the only efficient partisan that he knew and even Mosby usually operated with only one-fourth of his strength. When Mosby had gone independent, Stuart had recommended that he avoid the word partisan, and he agreed with Lee's desire to bring him into the regulars. Now Mosby had operated for one year, and still Stuart did not recognize that there was safety in dividing into small squads for raids. By sanctioning Rosser's recommendation he was threatening Mosby's operation.[14]

Lee agreed with Rosser and Stuart: "As far as my knowledge and experience extends, there is much truth in the statement of General Rosser. I recommend that the law authorizing these partisan corps be abolished. The evils resulting from their organization more than counterbalance the good they accomplish." Lee's solution was to do away with spoils reimbursement and bring worthy partisans such as McNeill and Mosby into the regular service for assignment on detached duty. Lee meant to make a temporary exception in Mosby's case, and he was not at all meaning to criticize Mosby. The day before, he had written a letter with a single subject—the promotion of Mosby to lieutenant colonel in the Partisan Corps to "encourage him to still greater activity and zeal" in harassing the rear of the Union army. He enclosed two Mosby reports showing that Mosby had started the new year with "considerable zeal." Lee wanted Mosby to follow the model of Virginian John D. Imboden, who organized the 1st Virginia Partisan Rangers, brought them into the regulars, became a general, and continued on duty in the Valley. Lee hoped that Mosby would increase to a regiment so that he could at least promote him to colonel.[15]

Ironically, Mosby's mentors Stuart and Lee, in attempting to reward and honor him, were threatening to shut him down because if he lost the reimbursement system he would be unable to raid successfully. Seddon received the letter with its endorsements and used it with Congress as support for his bill of repeal. In drafting the bill he gave himself the authority to make exceptions—he was not going to allow McNeill and Mosby to be brought in. The bill passed on February 14, 1864, with the exemption provision intact. The next day Seddon endorsed Mosby's latest message: "A characteristic report from Colonel Mosby, who has become so familiar with brave deeds as to consider them too tedious to treat unless when necessary to reflect glory on his gallant comrades."[16]

On April 1, 1864, Lee began carrying out the reorganization by recommending that all partisans reporting to him be disbanded immediately, except Mosby. Lee wrote, "I am making an effort to have Colonel Mosby's battalion mustered into the regular service. If this cannot be done I recommend that this battalion be retained as partisans for the present." He commended Mosby for excellent service and for enforcing discipline and protecting civilians. He excepted Mosby but made it clear that he wanted Mosby's status as a partisan to be temporary, only until he could be brought into the regulars.[17]

Seddon received Lee's letter, and on April 21, approved, *except* he wrote, "Mosby's and McNeill's commands I prefer to have retained as partisan rangers." The permanent partisan status of Mosby and McNeill was saved by Seddon, who had given it on a permanent basis to Mosby in the first place. Stuart and Lee had approved the end of the system, and Lee was attempting to bring Mosby into the regular cavalry, which would have closed his operation. Stuart and Lee failed to appreciate the essence, the cement of Mosby's operation. They agreed that Mosby was great, and they both recommended his promotion and continuance where he was.

They regarded it as a compliment and favor to make him regular, but he feared being returned to regular duty as much as his men.[18]

Mosby did not learn of Rosser's letter until after the war when he read it in the Confederate archives in Washington. He responded: "There was scarcely a day that our command did not kill & capture more Yankees than Rosser did the whole time he was in the Valley." Seddon was vindicated in both cases by McNeill and Mosby. Numerous instances confirmed his faith in the value of small, efficient raids. For example, on May 3, 1864, with sixty men, McNeill captured a B&O train, rode it into Piedmont, West Virginia, and burned seven railroad shops and destroyed fifteen locomotives and more than one hundred loaded freight cars.[19]

Soon after the repeal law passed, Mosby's superiors received his report of his great planned ambush of February 22, 1864. Ambuscades were the greatest fear of small Civil War cavalry detachments marching along contested roads. The keys to success in executing an ambush were accurate intelligence, intuition on enemy intentions, and, of course, surprise. On this occasion the Union cavalry were so surprised they raised their hands to their faces in a reflex action to ward off the bullets. One of Mosby's men described the onslaught as "the jaws of death." It was about mid-morning, and Mosby and 160 men were concealed in the dense pines across from Anker's blacksmith shop on the Alexandria Turnpike near Miskel's farm. The sky was clear, it was just cool enough for blue overcoats, and the air was still. Most of the men were mounted, and they knew the enemy was approaching when their horses' ears went forward and began twitching; then as they drew closer the animals' legs tightened in anticipation, like Thoroughbreds just before the starting gate clangs open.[20]

In the ambush at Anker's shop, Mosby himself had scouted the night before and returned to the men well after midnight in "excellent humor," anticipating victory. The Union force was bivouacked on a farm about six miles away, toward Leesburg, and they were on their return to their camp in Vienna, having scouted to Rector's Cross Roads the day before. Capt. James S. Reed was in command, and he had 150 men, most like himself, from the California companies of the 2nd Massachusetts Cavalry. Mosby knew that during the night they had been joined by a 150-man force of the 16th New York Cavalry, led by Maj. Douglas Frazar and also returning to camp in Fairfax County.[21]

Shortly after sunrise, before breaking camp, Mosby gave a briefing: "Men, the Yankees are coming and it is very likely we will have a hard fight. When you are ordered to charge, I want you to go right through them. Reserve your fire until you get close enough to see clearly what you are shooting at, and then let every shot tell." Then he deployed the complicated ambush. Down the road about 2.5 miles at a fork in the road, he positioned a man to observe whether the enemy came straight along the pike or turned off on the alternate road to their right. If they turned, Mosby planned to fall back through the pines and re-set the ambush on the other route. He placed twenty dismounted men with carbines in the dense pines near the turnpike opposite the blacksmith shop. Mosby took about seventy men toward Alexandria, over a slight hill, and concealed them in the woods south of the pike, ready to attack the front. He sent William Chapman with the remaining men to hide in the woods and assault the rear.[22]

Mosby had observed the day before that Reed took the precaution of throwing out a twenty-five-man advance guard about two hundred yards to the front and three videttes two hundred yards still farther to the front. Mosby wanted to halt the videttes and the advance until the entire column bunched up alongside his dismounted riflemen, and then he would attack. In any event he determined to move in himself on their front rather than between their advance and main body, which would leave his rear vulnerable. In order to bunch them up, he ordered Lt. Frank H. Rahm to take two men and sit on their horses in the road on top of the hill opposite Mosby's detachment. Rahm was to strike up a parley with the videttes and this would halt the advance; once the column bunched, Mosby would blow a whistle and everyone would attack: the dismounted men on the enemy's right flank, Mosby in the front, and Chapman in the rear.[23]

Soon the man down the road came with word that Frazar had taken the other road and Reed's column was advancing on the pike in the same formation as yesterday. The moment before an ambush was the most tense time for Mosby's men. There was no talking or moving around, and they leaned forward in the saddle, almost holding their breath to keep silent. "There was an unnatural, an unearthly stillness around us at that moment—a stillness which seemed to creep over our flesh like a chill, and to be seen and felt," one man recalled. In the quiet they heard the booming of the siege guns in the forts around Washington, firing in celebration of Washington's birthday.[24]

Reed's three videttes passed Chapman and the dismounted men and halted below the hill. "Who are you? What command do you belong to?" their spokesman demanded.

"Fifth New York Cavalry. What command do you belong to?" said Rahm.

"We are the California Battalion, but believe you are Mosby's Men. If you are not, advance and make yourself known," said the Union man.

"If you are the California Battalion, you advance and make yourself known, but we believe you are Mosby's Men," Rahm said.

"I'll find out damned quick who you are," said the man, raising his carbine to fire. Mosby heard all of this and quickly blew the whistle.[25]

At this moment the twenty-five-man advance was in the road beside Mosby's dismounted men; they were completely surprised when the volley of carbine-fire came out of the trees and undergrowth. These were the men who threw their hands over their faces in surprise. Reed halted the main body in the road behind and prepared for action. Mosby attacked the advance from the front, and Chapman came in on the right flank of Reed's main body, all of the Rebels screaming like demons. The Union men attempted to stand firmly, but several saddles were emptied by the first volley, and then came the mounted melee and the bullets from the Rebel revolvers. Rapidly the road began filling with dead and wounded men, and the horses shied away, breaking down a fence beside the road and stepping into the field north of the road and into the woods on the other side. Reed was shot in the left lung and died immediately. In the first contact Mosby's horse, a fine mare, was shot twice and severely wounded in one leg. He had to halt, but Baron Von Massow, a Prussian officer who had joined the command, rode on into the fight. He wore a glittering uniform with a long cape lined in scarlet and had a large ostrich plume in his hat and waved a German saber that flashed in the sunlight. The Union troopers thought he was Mosby and, singling him out as special target, shot him in the lungs. One of Mosby's men, William B. Palmer, had told him before the fight, "Baron, unless you are ready to die this morning, use your pistols and put back that sabre," and he replied, "Palmer, a soldier should always be ready to die." The wound removed him from the American war, but he recovered and returned home to Europe.[26]

After a few minutes the Federals broke and ran, scattering in all directions. The Union lost ten dead, seven wounded, and seventy captured, for a casualty rate of 58 percent. Mosby had one dead and five severely wounded, including Von Massow. Stuart wrote on Mosby's report: "This is another of the many brilliant exploits of this gallant leader. His boldness and skill are highly commended, as evidenced by the complete rout of the enemy with so small loss." And Lee responded: "Respectfully forwarded, uniting in the commendation bestowed by General Stuart."[27]

A few weeks later Lee sent word through Stuart to have Mosby keep a close watch on the B&O and O&A Railroads for any evidence of enemy troop movements. Lincoln had made Grant his new general in chief and supreme commander, moving Halleck to chief of staff, and the million-dollar question for Lee was, where would Grant locate his spring offensive? Lee studied the reports of his scouts with care, determined to outwit Grant, referred to by Lee's aide Walter H. Taylor as "the present idol of the North." Grant's grand plan was to send William T. Sherman from Chattanooga toward Atlanta and, in the East, launch three advances. Meade's Army of the Potomac would cross the Rapidan into the Wilderness and attempt to turn Lee's right in the main thrust. Gen. Benjamin F. Butler would threaten Richmond from the south with his Army of the James, and Gen. Franz Sigel would be ordered to advance from West Virginia south up the Shenandoah Valley to deprive Lee's army of the vital produce of the Valley farmers.[28] Due to unusually lucky circumstances, Mosby accidentally forecast one of Grant's three offensives, Sigel's move up the Shenandoah Valley, three days before Grant ordered it and one month before it began.

Mosby could not have asked for better luck than he had on March 26, 1864, when he received Stuart's message ordering him to scout the B&O. He had just returned from a reconnaissance in that direction the day before. He had gone to the Shenandoah Valley with six men and returned in a snowstorm with two Union cavalry prisoners. Arriving back in Fauquier County, he stopped at Benjamin Triplett's house and went inside. The two prisoners escaped from the guard and took Mosby's horse and pistols. But he was not discouraged, for he had intelligence to report: "I received a few moments ago Major [Henry B.] McClellan's note with reference to the movements of the enemy along the Baltimore and Ohio Railroad. I made a reconnaissance over there yesterday with a few men." Something significant must be happening on the B&O, he revealed. Heretofore the Union cavalry had all been camped at Halltown, three miles south of Harpers Ferry, but now they had moved to about seven or eight miles south of Harpers Ferry, in an unusual chain of pickets stretching across the Valley through Charlestown and Smithfield to Little North Mountain. The pickets were unusually vigilant in preventing ingress and egress from their line, and Mosby assumed they must be screening some movement. Union engineers had recently surveyed the inoperative Winchester and Potomac Railroad and had begun laying rails to repair the road from Harpers Ferry to Winchester. Mosby stated that he did not know what was happening, but lower-Valley citizens believed that the enemy was preparing to advance.[29]

Stuart sent Mosby's report to Lee, and on March 30 Lee wrote Davis: "It is stated that preparations are making to rebuild the railroad from Harper's Ferry to Winchester, which would indicate a reoccupation of the latter place. The Baltimore & Ohio Railroad is very closely guarded along its whole extent. No ingress or egress from their lines is permitted to citizens as heretofore, and everything shows secrecy & preparation." In reality Grant had ordered none of what Mosby saw. Lincoln had appointed Sigel commander of the Department of West Virginia, and Sigel on his own, without any instructions from Grant, made the preparations described by Mosby. On March 29 Sigel received Grant's orders to set aside infantry for an offensive, and on April 29 Sigel began marching south. Mosby portended the advance, but he was not so lucky on the opening of the Winchester and Potomac Railroad; it was not opened until later in the year. On April 18 Lee interpreted that the railroad survey Mosby reported had been a Union feint.[30]

Lee had come to place confidence in Mosby's scouting; he had made the right call so many times that now when he made a mistake on the more crucial question of Grant's main offensive it caused Lee much concern and contributed to a false alarm in Richmond. By March 30, Lee knew that Grant was present with Meade's army at Culpeper and that O&A trains were bringing recruits to Meade and preparations were underway for a strong Union advance across the Rapidan. One thing bothered him, however, and that was what was happening with the large army Gen. Ambrose E. Burnside was organizing in Annapolis. This was the most well-kept secret in the Union army—not even Burnside knew where his own command was going. Following Grant's instructions, Secretary of War Stanton directed Burnside to take the 9th Corps of less than four thousand men coming to Annapolis from Tennessee and recruit it up to fifty thousand in preparation for "special service." Lee wanted to know how many men were coming from the West and whether they were joining Burnside or Meade. On March 31, Longstreet informed Lee that the Union 9th Corps was en route to Virginia, and, on April 7, Lee ordered Longstreet to transfer to the eastern theater with his command.[31]

At his headquarters near Orange Court House Lee synthesized

the intelligence reports from his scouts and until Saturday evening April 9 he believed that he had successfully divined Grant's main thrust. Two of his most reliable scouts had reported from behind the lines: S. Franklin in Alexandria and Channing Smith from Meade's headquarters in Culpeper. The two were not in communication with each other; they were on opposite ends of the O&A Railroad, and their reports supported each other. They saw thousands of Union soldiers moving south on the cars, recruits and men returning to Meade's army from furlough, with new uniforms and new overcoats, deep blue and unfaded by the sun, and cannon, larger ones than usual. They reported that all was quiet on the Potomac and at Aquia Creek. They had heard a rumor that troops were coming from Charleston to Ft. Monroe, and a story afloat in Meade's army claimed that the 11th and 12th Corps were en route from the West to Culpeper. Nothing was settled in Lee's mind, but thus far the evidence seemed to support his belief that the "approaching storm . . . will apparently burst on Virginia."[32]

Additional eyewitness spy reports came in from Meade's camps that the number of tents was increasing and every day new troops were disembarking from the cars, separating into squads and moving off to different corps, indicating that they belonged to different units. Then on Saturday evening, April 9, Lee received a report from Mosby that threw him into a quandary. Mosby related that a civilian from Shepherdstown, West Virginia, had told him that the 11th Corps had passed eastward on the B&O the previous week. Lee guessed correctly that Mosby was mistaken, that the troops on the B&O were the 9th Corps going to Burnside, but he could not be certain. Mosby also reported that a man living near Fairfax Station had said that no reinforcements had come up to Meade from Alexandria on the O&A, but that every night troops with artillery were passing down toward Washington from Meade's army. Lee wrote Davis that this Fairfax Station man was not as reliable as his own scouts, but it bothered him that Mosby was completely contradicting his intelligence synthesis. "We have to sift a variety of reports before reaching the truth," he wrote Davis.[33]

Two days later, at 4:00 A.M. on April 11, Mosby wrote to Stuart that he had just returned from a reconnaissance in Fairfax County. "Think I have obtained the information you desire concerning Grant." He declared that no reinforcements had gone to Meade and that the rumors of such were the result of a Federal campaign of misinformation to mask the real movement. Actually Grant had transferred infantry and artillery with wagons and cannon on the O&A to Washington, where they had united with soldiers stripped from the Washington and B&O defenses—replaced by veterans of the Invalid Corps and black regiments—and combined they had gone to Annapolis to join Burnside. It was understood in Washington that Navy transports were to take this army to Butler's department for an advance on Richmond from south of the James River. Mosby promised to report again in two days. "You may place the most implicit reliance in this information," he concluded.[34]

Mosby had been deceived and had failed as a scout, especially on the reinforcement of the Army of the Potomac. But Burnside's destination was so secret that it was not surprising that Mosby was mistaken. Burnside himself was hoping that Grant would send him into Lee's rear on the Atlantic coast; that was why Burnside had selected Annapolis as the mobilization center for his expanding corps. At this time the only thing Burnside knew was that he must be ready to move by April 20—he did not know where. Finally, when the corps of more than twenty thousand men broke camp on April 23 and marched through Washington on the afternoon of April 25 for attached "special" duty with Meade's army, Lincoln's attorney general, Edward Bates, had no idea where they were going.[35]

By the time that Stuart received Mosby's April 11 letter, he had asked scout S. Franklin what he thought of Mosby's idea that Grant was transferring large numbers of infantry back to Washington at night. Franklin replied that he was on the O&A at about the same time as Mosby and that he had information that Mosby lacked; Franklin knew about Meade's order sending sutlers, men who were sick, et cetera, to the rear. Thus Franklin interpreted that the men on the cars on the return trips were convalescents and men going home to reenlist because their enlistments had expired. Nevertheless, in spite of Franklin's written rejoinder, on April 12 Stuart endorsed Mosby's new report: "I think Mosby's statements must be correct."[36]

On the same day, Lee replied to Stuart: "I have read Mosby's letter. He seems to be confident of his information, and he may be correct. But it is strange that among all the other scouts none should have discovered this counter movement." He ordered Stuart to find out if a corps had left Grant, because if it had, he wanted to attack. "Can you find it out?" he asked. This was extraordinary—all of the information Lee had involving movement on the O&A contradicted Mosby, but he had enough confidence in Mosby to ask Stuart to determine.[37]

Also on April 12, Lee wrote Davis repeating Mosby's April 11 report, point by point. He was concerned that additional intelligence seemed to support the idea of a campaign on Richmond: troops were leaving Halltown and Harpers Ferry, farmers were forbidden to bring fresh produce into Harpers Ferry to sell, and ten steamers had gone up the Potomac on April 9, possibly to transfer Burnside to City Point to capture Drewry's Bluff. With everything considered, Lee decided to alert Seddon. He immediately informed the Secretary of War that an investment of Richmond was possible, and "no time should be lost" in moving prisoners of war, Confederate men on parole, and other nonessential persons from the capital to allow adequate provisions for troops defending the city. Seddon wrote to Lee on April 14 that the prisoners had been removed and he was speedily evacuating the last of the paroled Confederates. "The hospitals and work-shops will be cleared of all who can be spared," he promised. Seddon approved a secret plan for removing twenty thousand residents by April 16, and it leaked out and caused a great commotion. Braxton Bragg was in favor of sending all the government clerks to South Carolina or Montgomery, Alabama, or somewhere, but after two lengthy cabinet meetings on the subject, the idea was deferred.[38]

While Mosby was failing he did it wholeheartedly—next he asserted that, in addition to the 9th Corps, the 11th and 12th Corps had been consolidated and transferred over the B&O as one corps to Burnside. This may have been a misinformation plant by the Union army, but, whether or not, Mosby had made another mistake; the only troops moved were the 9th Corps. By this time, Lee had reconciled the contradictory scouting reports in his mind by deciding that Grant planned two strong offensives: the main assault on the Rapidan and one by Burnside south of Richmond. He believed that Grant had taken a corps from the Washington defenses and along the B&O and moved them to the Rappahannock in the daylight, and moved an equivalent corps at night back to Washington and on to Annapolis for Burnside. In a letter to Davis, he did not explain how it made any sense that Grant would make such a switch rather than simply sending the B&O and Washington troops to Burnside, which is what in reality had happened. The reason was, this was the only way that he could reconcile Mosby's reports with the other information.[39]

Finally, after nine days of confusion, on April 18 Lee received a message from Mosby correcting himself. He had examined the O&A more closely and found that the troops sent back to Alexandria from the Rappahannock consisted not of a corps but of furloughed regiments that had re-enlisted, invalids, sutlers, and retainers. What had appeared to be cannon were only disabled guns and broken carriages. Lee was much relieved that Mosby's intelligence now coincided with the other scouts on this point, but the questions of how many men Burnside had and where he was going were still open. Lee now thought that Mosby was correct, that Burnside had the 9th Corps and a consolidated 11th and 12th Corps and that a fleet would take them to the James River.[40]

By April 28, the grass was green, the buds were swelling on the trees, and the frogs were singing at night. Lee drew his cavalry and artillery nearer to him, still expecting two offensives. On April 29, he informed Davis that a scout in Washington, not Mosby, had reported that Burnside had taken twenty-three thousand men from Annapolis through Washington to Alexandria on April 25. This was correct, and Mosby had not achieved the scoop correcting his forecast of Burnside's direction. Lee believed that, since Burnside had marched overland to Alexandria, he was bound for the Rapidan frontier, not Richmond, but this was not certain; Burnside could still take boats from Alexandria.[41]

Then at last, in the climax, Mosby came through in his usual dramatic fashion. At 1:45 P.M. on April 30, Lee received a message from Mosby that he had seen Burnside's force pass through Centreville on April 28. Lee immediately telegraphed Davis renewing his request for reinforcements. He followed with a letter that stated in part: "Lt Col Mosby, who was within a mile of Centreville on the 28th, the day that Burnside passed through, learned from prisoners that no troops were left at Annapolis except convalescents." Lee had already concluded that the 11th and 12th Corps had not left the Western theater, and he had concluded that Burnside had only the expanded 9th Corps. Now Mosby's eyewitness report put the last piece in the puzzle—Burnside was definitely joining Meade; the major offensive would be on the Rapidan. When Mosby wrote his summary report on this period, Lee endorsed: "The services rendered by Colonel Mosby and his command in watching and reporting the enemy's movements have also been of great value."[42]

Mosby had to walk a thin line to stay in operation. Lee and Stuart did not understand the value of stealth in small numbers, and Lee did not appreciate the value of spoils for cohesion. If not for Seddon, Mosby might not have gained full partisan status in 1863; and if not for him in 1864, Lee might have succeeded in making him regular and closing him off to the spoils system. From their point of view, Stuart and Lee were complimenting Mosby and attempting to provide him the opportunity to expand and win higher rank. They respected him for enforcing strict discipline over his men and for protecting his civilian supporters from roving bands of stragglers, and they greatly appreciated his scouting and his incessant headline-making raids behind enemy lines. Finally, Lee made an exception of Mosby and acquiesced in Seddon's decision to allow Mosby and McNeill to use the spoils system for the duration.

# 11

# Mosby's Clones in the Valley

General Lee finally conceded that Mosby's vision of his command, with separate small raiding forces attacking at different places simultaneously and commanded by Mosby clones, was effective. He congratulated Mosby for successfully multiplying himself many times. After the loss of Smith and Turner, he had William Chapman; and by April 29, 1864, when Sigel's offensive began in the Valley, he had three additional replicas serving as officers in the battalion, now increased to four companies and over two hundred men. Like Chapman the new clones were young, handsome, intelligent, and proficient in masquerading as the enemy, organizing an ambush, and sensing whether a fight would succeed. Dolly Richards was so much like Mosby that enemy commanders deceived and surprised by him often reported that he was Mosby. He was born in Loudoun County near Upperville and had fought under Ashby and, like Mosby, served on the staff of General Jones. Mosby made him captain at the age of nineteen and major at twenty.[1]

Richard P. Montjoy, a Mississippi native who entered Confederate service in the Louisiana Infantry, rode the finest horses and dressed as fastidiously as the men he commanded in Company D, Mosby's company of "dandies," Marylanders who wore elaborate uniforms. He sang happy songs and was loved by everyone, especially the ladies. He was twenty years old when killed in action, in a moment of triumph, racing on his horse along a farm lane in Loudoun County pursuing four Union cavalrymen fleeing in a rout. As he came close, one of the Federals turned and fired his revolver, hitting Montjoy in the brain. Mosby issued a special order memorializing him as "an immortal example of daring and valor," and after the war the men erected a monument at his grave in Warrenton. Alfred Glascock of Fauquier County, a veteran of Ashby's cavalry, once said to his men masquerading as Union cavalry, "Now, boys, I am going to show you how to capture Yankees in the regular Mosby style," and with fourteen men captured twenty-nine. He succeeded Montjoy in command of Company D.[2]

Others would fail the test of experience. Lt. William L. Hunter conducted a frontal assault on a stronger enemy force on April 22, 1864, and was captured. Capt. Walter E. Frankland disobeyed Mosby's order to set an ambush and conducted a disastrous frontal assault on the 8th Illinois Cavalry dismounted and in a strong defensive position; Mosby relieved him from command and wrote years later, "It was a perfect massacre & I can never forgive him." Second Lt. Joseph Nelson conducted a Mosby-like charge at Charlestown, West Virginia, during Mosby's June 29, 1864, raid on the B&O Railroad and captured twenty-five prisoners and twenty-eight horses. "Good Joe!" Mosby shouted, waving his hat and slapping Nelson on the shoulder. "Good for old Company A!" But one month later Nelson allowed discipline to break down on a raid to Adamstown, Maryland. Two men became intoxicated and were captured, fighting each other with fists in the middle of the road. Later he would allow his men to be surprised and suffer defeat.[3]

Mosby and his duplicates determined that Franz Sigel was an ideal target for guerrilla harassment. He was thirty-nine years old, a native of Germany and graduate of the military academy at Karlsruhe. Exact and rigid, he emphasized drill and sham battles, and when things failed to conform to set patterns he became anxious and hesitant. Evidence that he was in over his head was his error of putting into practice what Pope said he intended in 1862; Sigel did not mind his rear. He left Martinsburg on April 29 with nine thousand men, having stripped bare the defenses of the vital B&O Railroad and leaving inadequate escorts for his supply wagons. During the next sixteen days, Rebel partisans and former partisans numbering 1,100 harassed him in the rear, ambushed him on his right and left, and attacked his front so effectively that they eliminated or diverted 1,650 of his cavalry from the campaign; and, more significantly, they got inside his mind and eliminated his self-confidence. On May 13 at Woodstock, he notified his superiors: "My forces are insufficient for offensive operations in this country, where the enemy is continuously on my flank and rear." The guerrillas slowed him down and gave Confederate general John C. Breckinridge vital time to gather a force to defeat him at the battle of New Market on May 15.[4]

McNeill, Imboden, and partisan major Harry W. Gilmor were involved, and Mosby's men struck the first two blows. On May 2, five miles south of Martinsburg, Mosby and ten men attacked an empty wagon train heading north; two nights later he and twenty men raided Martinsburg, capturing fifteen horses. Sigel reacted by ordering eight hundred of his cavalry to the rear to search for Mosby and remain on guard duty in the rear. On May 9, when Sigel was marching from Winchester to Cedar Creek, two separate Mosby forces of about twelve men each attacked his supply line. In a total of at least five attacks, Mosby's men captured wagon trains, both loaded and empty, and several stragglers and small cavalry detachments. McNeill's Piedmont Raid caused Stanton and Halleck to bring over thirty-four thousand Ohio one-hundred-days militia to guard the B&O and Sigel's department in his absence. After his defeat at New Market, Sigel withdrew to Cedar Creek, where he was relieved on the night of May 21.[5]

Halleck suggested Maj. Gen. David Hunter as Sigel's replacement, and Grant agreed. Hunter was sixty-one years old, a native of Washington, D.C., West Point graduate, and career army man with a record strewn with duels and personal controversies. He was a tough man who seemed almost ruthless. He had a long mustache and prominent nose, and wrinkles on his face formed a permanent scowl. He was of medium height, broad-shouldered, and wore a black slouch hat with holes punched in it for ventilation, an old linen coat, coarse trousers, and government-issue shoes. Regarding the war as a crusade against slavery, he was overruled when in April 1862 he liberated the slaves in his Department of the South. On his own he approved the first black troops, and the Confederate government declared him a felon and ordered him executed if captured.[6]

Hunter considered guerrilla warfare "unlawful and uncivilized," and his solution was to burn the homes of civilians supporting guerrillas. His own troops considered this too harsh and nicknamed him "Black Dave" for the black smoke that rose in the sky from the houses he ordered burned. When his army reached Lexington and he learned that former Virginia governor John Letcher, whose home was in the town, had issued a proclamation urging the citizens to conduct guerrilla warfare against him, he ordered the burning of Virginia Military Institute and Letcher's home. Later, after he returned north from his expedition and while still in command of the department, he ordered the burning of several Rebel homes, the first of which belonged to his prominent West Virginia cousin Andrew Hunter.[7]

Hunter was so thick-skinned and determined, guerrilla harassment had no effect on him; he was so bullheaded, he refused to be intimidated by anything. Trimming the army into shape, he ordered all sutlers and camp followers to Martinsburg and closed his lines to passage by civilians, without exception. Still at Cedar Creek, the pickets arrested a young woman attempting to pass, and when they brought her to the provost marshal she began wringing her hands, pulling her hair, and crying that she must get home to nurse her six-week-old baby or it would starve. In private the provost marshal examined her breasts and determined that she was lying. He informed her that she was to be detained as Hunter had ordered. At that point she broke out in laughter and took a seat under a nearby tree, calmly smoking her clay pipe and watching the activity at headquarters.[8]

When orders came from Grant to live off the country, Hunter had already decided to do that for the most part. He ordered each man to take one hundred rounds of ammunition and an eight-day supply of rations. Supply wagons would follow, but when rations ran low designated companies would forage for livestock and if necessary they would eat the horses and mules. It was not always enforced, but he ordered severe punishment for straggling or pillaging. Ten days into the expedition many of the men were out of rations except coffee, sugar, and salt. On the sixteenth day, when they were at Staunton, 110 miles from base, a supply train arrived with hardtack, coffee, and sugar, and some of the men had their first square meal in a week. The rations ran out again, and on June 22, on the return march through West Virginia, some of the men discovered a farmer's beehives. They broke them open and took up large chunks of honeycomb and shoved them in their mouths, resulting in streams of honey flowing down their chins onto their uniforms. Now and then they would stop to swat the bees buzzing around their heads and resume "eating like a herd of grizzly bears," wrote one man in his diary.[9]

Compared to Sigel, Hunter organized and moved up the Valley with lightning decisiveness and speed. He arrived at Cedar Creek on May 21, 1864, at 7:00 P.M. and at 9:30 wrote a message ordering Gen. George Crook and Gen. William W. Averell in West Virginia to move immediately with their troops toward a conjunction in Staunton. On the same night, he strengthened the pickets on his left by sending 150 cavalry under a field grade officer to Guard Hill, a wooded ridge on the north bank of the Shenandoah traversed by the road from Winchester to Front Royal. Maj. Henry Roessle, 15th New York Cavalry, took a detachment from that regiment and posted a 30-man picket post on the hill in the pines to the extreme left and kept the reserve of 120 men one-half mile in the rear, to the west. Early in the evening Capt. Michael Auer, in charge of the picket post, became ill and asked Roessle for permission to go lie down in a nearby farmhouse. Roessle agreed; after all it seemed useless to be out here anyway with the Shenandoah River running high and swift. Surely the new general was overly cautious.[10]

But earlier that day, Mosby and 103 men had marched through Ashby's Gap and crossed the river in skiffs, horses swimming behind. They arrived at Guard Hill after dark, and two men scouted. After midnight, when the pickets were asleep, William Chapman sent fifteen dismounted carbineers charging through the bushes, firing and shouting like Indians. The mounted men followed, and most of the pickets scattered into the woods and escaped. The noise aroused Auer, and he rode up demanding, "What the blankety blank does all this fuss mean?" One of the raiders replied: "It means that Mosby has got you." Auer said, "Well, this beats hell, don't it?" Besides Auer, the raiders captured ten other men and forty-five horses.[11]

Enraged, Hunter wrote a general order and on the second day after the attack had each regiment form in line to hear it read aloud. The document dishonorably discharged Auer for being disgracefully surprised and captured without firing a shot and warned that in the future negligent pickets would be given no mercy but would be discharged for their crime against the command. Then the next day, having investigated, he issued another general order commending Auer for bravely riding to the scene, but reaffirming his discharge and now also dishonorably discharging Roessle for gross neglect of duty.[12]

Auer was actually a brave soldier. He was a twenty-five-year-old cigar maker from Syracuse, New York, a native of Switzerland. He had been wounded in the ankle in the Antietam campaign and medically discharged. Re-enlisting in the cavalry, he had been wounded three months earlier in a skirmish with Mosby's men near Upperville, when his horse fell on him. He spent the rest of the war in Confederate prison camps and after his release informed Hunter what had happened that night, whereupon Hunter promoted him to major and changed his discharge to honorable. When Auer applied for a veteran's pension, he wrote to Mosby asking him for a letter certifying that his horse fell on him in the Upperville fight.[13]

Two nights after the capture of Auer, Hunter was still at Cedar Creek when someone near Newtown, about eight miles in the rear, fired a rifle from the yard of a house at a passing wagon train. Hunter immediately sent a detachment of cavalry to burn the house and outbuildings and warn the community that, if this happened again, every Rebel house within five miles of the incident would be burned.[14]

Completely undeterred, he departed Cedar Creek at 8:30 A.M. on May 26, having been with his men only five nights and four days. On May 29, he reached Rude's Hill, 24.5 miles south of Cedar Creek, when at Newtown, now about 32 miles in the rear, the guerrillas struck again. In the late afternoon Gilmor's men captured a loaded southbound train of sixteen wagons; the next morning, May 30, Mosby's men attacked the rear guard of an empty northbound wagon train, killing two Union cavalrymen, capturing two men, and seizing eight horses. "This bushwhacking has got to be stopped," said Hunter. The next morning he sent back a detachment of two hundred cavalry with orders to burn every Rebel house, store, and outbuilding in Newtown and on each side of the road south to Middletown, a distance of about five miles. Maj. Joseph Stearns led the burning expedition, but the townspeople convinced him and his men that they had not been involved but that the attackers were Confederate soldiers. Stearns and the force rejoined the army on June 3, and Hunter accepted his explanation.[15]

On June 5 at Piedmont, Hunter's command defeated the five-thousand-man force of Mosby's friend Grumble Jones, killing Jones and taking more than a thousand prisoners. On June 6, he arrived at Staunton on the Virginia Central Railroad; and on June 8, Crook and Averell joined him, bringing his force to about 18,500. Grant had given him discretion, once he reached Staunton, to move toward Richmond via Charlottesville or Lynchburg. In deciding what to do next, Hunter failed to give adequate consideration to the fact that, after the battle of Piedmont, his men were running short of ammunition. He sent General Stahel, who had been wounded at Piedmont, for more ammunition from Harpers Ferry and reported that he and his army would "move south immediately to perform our work." He should have remained where he was until the ammunition arrived, but it would take over a week to bring the ordnance 110 miles from Martinsburg, and at the moment Lynchburg was unguarded; he hoped to capture it before enemy forces arrived.[16]

Lee acted quickly to defend Lynchburg, a vital rail center. He sent Breckinridge's division of two thousand men and Gen. Jubal A. Early's eight thousand veterans of Stonewall Jackson's old corps, and, by the time Hunter attacked, Lynchburg was defended by ten thousand men with an ample supply of ammunition. During the skirmishing, Hunter received the dreaded message from one of his commanders: "I am almost out of ammunition." Grant had been worried that this might happen. After Hunter's offensive was well under way, he sent Sheridan and his cavalry north of Richmond to attempt to unite with Hunter, but Sheridan's force had been defeated and driven back at the battle of Trevilian Station. When Halleck and Grant learned that Sheridan was turned back, they realized that Hunter had extended beyond his ammunition supply, and they knew he would have no choice but to escape into West Virginia. Grant reported later that Hunter's "want of ammunition left him no choice of route for his return but by way of Kanawha."[17]

So Hunter went out of the Valley, eastward from Lynchburg, into the Kanawha Valley of West Virginia, committing the unpardonable sin of leaving the Shenandoah Valley open to a Confederate invasion and leaving Washington weakly defended and exposed to attack. Hunter gave Early a clear pathway to fulfill Lee's orders to go down the Valley, cross the Potomac, and threaten Washington. Hunter in his own estimation had been "extremely successfull, inflicting great injury upon the enemy," and his friend Stanton congratulated him on his "brilliant victory" at Piedmont. But Hunter would never be able to justify the mistake of leaving the Valley highway open for Early's raid. He wrote to Grant: "I was not informed that I had any thing to do with the defense of Washington, and supposed General Halleck had made ample provision for this purpose." This was valid; Grant and Halleck should have ordered him to give priority to defending the Valley.[18]

Hunter had not been defeated by the guerrillas. Grumble Jones had used up his ammunition at Piedmont, Lee had checkmated him at Lynchburg, and he had defeated himself by outrunning his ordnance supply. But the guerrillas were still hovering, watching and waiting for vulnerable targets. When General Stahel left Staunton on June 9 to fetch the ammunition, he took the long way around through West Virginia, probably to avoid the Valley guerrillas, and once he arrived in Martinsburg, it took him four days to organize an escort that he considered strong enough to make it through the Valley's guerrilla gauntlet. But even if he had been uninjured and there had been no guerrillas, he could not have caught up with Hunter 180 miles away in Lynchburg in time for the fighting on June 18, when the ordnance ran out.[19]

Hunter had relied mostly on the Ohio militia to defend the B&O Railroad in his absence. When Stahel returned to the rear for the ammunition, he took many of the guards from the railroad for a 4,650-man escort for the ammunition wagon train. Fear of the guerrillas caused him to organize such a strong force, and Mosby took advantage of Stahel's weakening of the garrisons on the B&O. The wagon train and escort left Martinsburg on June 25, and when Stahel learned that Hunter had withdrawn he ordered it to halt at Bunker Hill. Four days later, on June 29, the escort still had not returned to the railroad; it was divided and camped at Smithfield and Bunker Hill. Stahel had opened the way for a Mosby raid on the B&O: Charlestown was unguarded, Harpers Ferry had a few hundred infantry and only 108 cavalry, and Duffield's Station west of Harpers Ferry had only 45 infantry.[20]

Mosby's scout for the Valley, John Russell, discovered this and told Mosby. Russell was born and reared in the Shenandoah Valley, in Clarke County, Virginia, near Berryville; and he was familiar with the people and the roads. He had served in the Confederate infantry and joined Mosby on October 10, 1863, at the age of twenty-two. After the war he and his wife Harriet and their ten children lived near Berryville, where by the time of his death on February 21, 1932, he became well known as "Mosby John." His parents had given him no middle name, so he named himself "John Singleton Russell" in honor of Mosby.[21]

Mosby had learned the year before on the O&A that he needed more than two hundred men and artillery to successfully raid a railroad. Now for the first time he had the manpower, so he acquired a twelve-pound Napoleon. With Hunter's army on their northward trek through West Virginia and no Union army present, he changed his tactics from dividing into small forces for safety to raiding in strength, with more regular tactics. He used the cover of darkness on the night of June 28 to cross the Blue Ridge Mountains and the Shenandoah River and march to the vicinity of Charlestown, where he bivouacked. The next morning he left Lt. Joseph Nelson with a detachment at Charlestown to watch for cavalry from Harpers Ferry five miles away. In broad daylight, the main body proceeded to Duffield's Depot; and at 2:00 P.M. they unlimbered the cannon with much flourish, and Mosby demanded their surrender. They submitted without resistance; the cannon and Mosby's superior numbers made fighting seem futile.[22]

Mosby's men looted and burned the camp and depot and plundered a few small retail stores. The engineer of an eastbound train approaching two miles away saw the smoke, halted, and reversed to Martinsburg. One of the merchants from Pennsylvania had just arrived with a large supply of groceries and dry goods, and the raiders filled the limber box and artillery carriage with bags of coffee and gathered mounds of calico and female apparel and stacked them on their horses, making this the "First Calico Raid." When the column reached Charlestown they learned of Nelson's victory over a fifty-man cavalry detachment from Harpers Ferry. Mosby's men returned to Fauquier in triumph with no losses themselves and seventy-four prisoners and thirty-four horses. Traffic on the B&O was delayed for eighteen hours, and the telegraph line was cut, but the raiders did not attempt to damage the track.[23]

Meanwhile, Early's army marched north down the Valley, toward Washington. Early did not contact Mosby, but on July 2 Mosby learned that Early's thirteen thousand men would bivouac that night at Winchester, and he recognized this as an opportune time to raid the B&O at Point of Rocks, between Harpers Ferry and Washington, and multiply the fear. Point of Rocks was a small town and depot where the Potomac River, Chesapeake and Ohio Canal, and B&O Railroad came together to pass through the gap in the Catoctin Mountains. For travelers the cut through the rocks on the 350-foot-high granite bluff rising on the north side made the defile a landmark, a "point of rocks." Here, twelve miles east of Harpers Ferry, eastbound trains left the river and rolled inland through beautiful southern Maryland toward Baltimore. Now the place was defended by two companies of the Loudoun Rangers and two companies of infantry, a force about equal to Mosby's in numbers. Crossing the Potomac would have a greater impact than when Mosby raided Seneca on June 11, 1863, and White raided Point of Rocks on June 17, 1863. Now with the Union army away and the capital weakly defended and Early approaching, Mosby knew that a Point of Rocks raid would get inside the enemy's mind and sting like a bee. He ordered his men to tell everyone they met that this was an advance force of scouts for Longstreet's corps, rapidly marching toward the Potomac River.[24]

At noon on July 4, 1864, Mosby attacked with conventional tactics. He positioned the cannon on the southern bank in Virginia on a hill 180 feet in elevation, where it could fire at the canal, the railroad track and the enemy pickets where he prepared to cross with most of his 250 men. Once the cannon began shelling the pickets he sent forward a party of dismounted sharpshooters firing and wading the river, followed by mounted men. The pickets threw down their weapons and ran, scrambling up the rough mountainside and disappearing among the trees. Then the cannon opened on a boat that just happened to be passing in the canal. It was the *Flying Cloud,* chartered by seventeen clerks from the Treasury Department in Washington for a July 4 excursion. They had been to Harpers Ferry and were on the return trip, enjoying lunch on board, when the excitement began. The first shell fell short, splashing in the river, and the next two passed overhead. By then the boat had reached a lock, and there was no one to operate it, and Mosby's mounted raiders were racing toward them on the towpath. "Finding it useless to try to save the boat, we jumped for the hills," one of the clerks said later. The raiders took their lunch, liquor, and cigars and burned the boat.[25]

Then an eastbound passenger train came steaming along and stopped just before it reached the logs stacked on the track by the raiders. The cannon fired four shots at it, and the sharpshooters fired a volley that wounded the fireman in the arm. The engineer reversed and withdrew to Sandy Hook. The Rebels plundered and burned the infantry and cavalry camps, captured seven men and wounded two, and looted four retail stores and two sutlers. Mosby sent a detachment of twelve men south on the towpath to the mouth of the Monocacy River, six miles east, and they plundered a camp of the 8th Illinois Cavalry, burned four canal boats, plundered a store, and captured two prisoners and two horses. Mosby recrossed the afternoon of July 4 but remained on the right bank with the cannon until after 5:00 P.M. the next day.[26]

Mosby's timing was consummate. At the same hour as the assault, the telegraph operator in Harpers Ferry saw Early's men forming in line on Bolivar Heights on the edge of town. The day before, in the expectation of Early's invasion, the pickets at Point of Rocks had been alerted and ordered to fall back ten miles to Frederick, Maryland, if attacked in force. Mosby's appearance, with the booming of the cannon and dismounted sharpshooters splashing across the river, created the exaggerated impression that regular Confederate infantry were advancing. The telegraph operator at Point of Rocks reported "rebels in force," disconnected his instrument, and headed for the mountains. The officer of the day said afterward that he could not fight the entire Rebel army and he was not going to have his men cut up by shell and canister. Generals Max Weber in Harpers Ferry and Lew Wallace in Baltimore telegraphed to Halleck that the enemy had crossed in force at Point of Rocks.[27]

"We have no idea of the extent of the enemy's force," reported the *Washington Star,* and the reporter lamented that, with the telegraph down, there was no way to know. There was great excitement in Frederick and Hagerstown, with merchants sending their goods into Pennsylvania at reports of the enemy advancing on a fifty-mile front and seven thousand cavalry crossing at Muddy Branch, driving the pickets there back twenty miles to Washington. In Harrisburg, Pennsylvania, Governor Andrew G. Curtin reported a rumor that twenty thousand men had crossed at Point of Rocks. Panic-stricken canal boatmen rushed into Washington with word that between twenty and forty thousand men had crossed the Potomac at every fordable point as far downriver as Muddy Branch.[28]

On the night before the raid, B&O president John W. Garrett set aside a fifteen-car train to take five hundred troops to reinforce Harpers Ferry. At noon on July 4, the time of Mosby's attack, the train left Washington with 470 unarmed artillery troops. By midnight Halleck knew that it was only Mosby at Point of Rocks, but the Mosby raid had cut direct communications and prevented transport of the 470-man force to Harpers Ferry. The train had reached Monocacy, east of Point of Rocks, halted, and returned to Monrovia and unloaded to await the clearing of the track. In order to deliver the 470 men and reestablish communications, Halleck rounded up 2,800 dismounted cavalry from the Washington defenses and sent them under Gen. Albion P. Howe "to force his way to Harper's Ferry." By the time that Howe reached Point of Rocks, Mosby was gone; but he proceeded to Maryland Heights, and Halleck ordered him to remain there.[29]

As soon as Howe left, Halleck telegraphed Grant, asking for reinforcements for Washington. Sending the Howe force had reduced by one-third the available infantry on the defensive perimeter north of the Potomac and left Washington with only ninety-five hundred men, less than Early's force. The sending of Howe contributed to the decision by Halleck and Grant to divert two corps from Grant to Washington. The 6th Corps came from Grant's army at Petersburg, and the 19th Corps en route from Louisiana came to Washington instead of going to Grant. There would have been panic without Mosby's raid, and Halleck would have asked for reinforcements even if there had been no Mosby raid, but Mosby had heightened the anxiety, contributed to the diversion of twenty-eight hundred from Washington, and strengthened Halleck's request for transfers from Grant.[30]

With 250 men, Mosby had diverted 2,800 from Washington, and

that was more than eleven times his own number. With timing and an audacious midday attack, punctuated with the booming of the cannon and the charge of the dismounted men, Mosby's 250 created the impression of 20,000 and in the enemy minds extended the invasion front to fifty miles, from Shepherdstown to Muddy Branch. The raid closed the telegraph connection with Harpers Ferry and shut down traffic on the canal and railroad for over twenty-four hours. And as they had done at Duffield's Station, the men plundered the Point of Rocks stores, gathering candy, women's shoes, calico, and other dry goods. In celebration the men decorated themselves and their horses with red-and-white bunting, hung boots and shoes over their horses' necks, stacked bolts of calico in front and in back of their saddles, and some draped crinoline dresses and hoops over their shoulders and stuffed women's bonnets on their heads. This was the "Great Calico Raid."[31]

On July 6, still active from the Point of Rocks raid, Mosby conducted a mounted frontal assault on an almost equal force of Union cavalry in what became known as the Mount Zion Church fight. The Union commander was Maj. William H. Forbes, 2nd Massachusetts Cavalry, serving on the Fairfax cavalry screen out of Falls Church and reporting to Lowell. He was a member of the prominent Forbes family of Boston and Mosby's most wealthy opponent in the war. His uncle Robert B. Forbes was a founder of the China trade, and his father, John M. Forbes, had accumulated a fortune in China and in American railroads. William had attended Harvard University and at the age of twenty-one in 1861 had entered the cavalry. After the war he invited Mosby to dinner in Washington, and they became close friends.[32]

Mosby had 175 men present and the cannon; Forbes had 150: one hundred 2nd Massachusetts Cavalrymen and fifty 13th New York. The Union men were veterans of over one year's service, and they were armed with Spencer repeating carbines, but they and their horses had never come under artillery fire. They had been scouting toward Aldie for two days, watching for Early, then Mosby. Each night, as Lowell had instructed, they had carefully slept under arms with bridle reins in hand ready to mount at a moment's notice. This afternoon they rode south from Leesburg, and at 5:30 P.M. stopped at Mount Zion Church, east of Aldie on the Little River Turnpike, to rest and eat supper. They were about to remount at 6:30 P.M. and return to camp when Forbes heard the pickets firing on the pike one-fourth mile to the east, toward Falls Church.[33]

Mosby and his men had been waiting in ambush two miles in that direction, but somehow Mosby sensed that with the cannon he could be just as successful with an open attack. He positioned a party of mounted sharpshooters in a patch of woods to his left and deployed the cannon in the road, supported by one company. The sharpshooters galloped ahead, exchanging fire with the pickets and driving them back.[34]

When Forbes heard his pickets firing, he immediately ordered the men to mount and form two battle lines, one behind the other. They were east of the church on a slight slope, their left in the road and their line extending into a field on the right. The field had a rail fence running along the road for about two hundred yards, and on the Union right it ended in the woods. The Union men formed in straight, textbook alignment, the officers in position with sabers drawn and the men ready to fire their Spencers. They watched as their pickets withdrew from the woods and into the open field before them. Then suddenly the cannon boomed, and a shell came whistling over their heads and exploded in the air behind the second rank. Mosby's advance came along the road, reached the corner of the field, and halted while a couple of men dismounted and took down two panels of the fence. Then Mosby dashed into the field and galloped forward, leading the charge. The Union cavalry had not trained for such an unconventional frontal assault—they had never seen anything like this. The oncoming Rebels resembled an Indian war party or a gang of cowboys, every man yelling and holding his pistol in one hand and bridle in the other.[35]

Forbes's front rank fired their Spencers, and some of the second rank fired pistols, but Mosby's men broke in, helter-skelter, every man for himself, mingling into the first rank. Forbes's chaplain, Charles A. Humphreys, shouted: "Major, what shall we do?" and he said, "We will form again—in the edge of the woods." Raising his saber, he rode to the front, pointed to the woods on the right and to the rear, and shouted, "Form in the woods! Form in the woods!" Both ranks turned by the right flank, and Mosby knew he had won. One of Napoleon's maxims was that, if your adversary hesitates, take advantage of it. Mosby ordered his reserve to charge, and all of Mosby's men were on the Union vulnerable flank as it turned.[36]

Forbes attempted to create a rally by turning his horse toward the Rebels and yelling, "Now rally round your leader." He thrust his saber at Mosby, but Thomas Richards, Dolly's brother, spurred his horse and threw himself between, receiving the thrust in the shoulder, the saber flying from Forbes's hand. Mosby fired his revolver at Forbes, but Forbes's horse reared and the bullet went into the horse's face, knocking the animal down with Forbes pinned beneath. The field was littered with dead and wounded men, and wounded horses were dashing wildly about in pain and fright. Chaplain Humphreys escaped on his fast roan horse, outrunning Mosby's men in a pursuit of several miles. More than thirty years later when Mosby spoke at Tremont Temple in Boston, Humphreys attended and introduced himself and described his horse and his flight and said, "Do you remember me?" Mosby answered, "No, but I remember your horse."[37]

Mosby lost one mortally wounded and seven wounded; Forbes had fourteen dead and thirty-seven wounded, ten too severely to move, and fifty-five captured, including himself. Mosby's men captured about one hundred horses. Mosby's casualty rate was 4.5 percent, and Forbes's was 70 percent. Lowell was not present, but his explanation was that Forbes had made a mistake by remaining on the defensive; he should have ordered a saber charge. That would have given Forbes some momentum and a shock effect, but in the melee they would have found their sabers less effective than their carbines. In practice, if Lowell had been present on the expedition he would have had a strong body of infantry as well as cavalry, and that would have prevented Mosby's attack. Forbes said, with tears in his eyes, that Mosby's helter-skelter charge was "unprofessional."[38]

Meanwhile, Early's army had crossed the Potomac and was in Maryland, advancing toward Washington. Early's raid would reach the Union defensive line five miles north of the White House and demonstrate there on July 11 and 12 and then withdraw. Stuart had been mortally wounded at Yellow Tavern on May 11 and had died the next day, and now Mosby was reporting to Lee, as was Early. During the expedition Mosby and Early remained on friendly terms. But months later, after Early had been driven out of the Valley and had come under criticism for failing to capture Washington, Mosby learned that Early had turned against him. Mosby asked a member of Early's staff why Early did not notify Mosby in advance of his surprise attack on Sheridan's army at Cedar Creek on October 19, 1864, so that Mosby could have raided the wagons in Sheridan's rear. Early replied, "I wasn't going to do the fighting & let Mosby do the plundering." When Mosby heard this a few days before the war ended, for the first time he realized that Early was "my malignant enemy."[39]

"Old Jubilee" was a forty-seven-year-old curmudgeon who hated cavalry and condemned partisans for threatening organization and morale. He was tall and stoop-shouldered, with black hair, a scruffy black beard, and flashing black eyes. He was born in Franklin County, Virginia, graduated from West Point, and had fought Seminoles in Florida. Upon the coming of war, he was a lawyer and member of the state legislature from Franklin County. He cursed blue streaks, and Lee called him "my bad old man." Mosby said that he had the morals of a hog and agreed with Richard Ewell that he "was as brave as a lion and as mean as a dog." After the war he became the chief spokesman for the Lost Cause and the Lee cult and a baiter of Longstreet, Mosby, and other "traitors" who turned Republican. Mosby reacted in private by comparing Early to Bombastes Furioso, a bombastic character in a contemporary drama, and he thought it ironic that Early, who fled to Canada, became so popular in the South: "Early is the first man who ever got the reputation of a hero for running from danger."[40]

After the Point of Rocks Raid, Mosby sent Beattie and Henry Heaton, who had been an aide for Early, to find Early and give him a written message. Mosby's letter reported the Point of Rocks Raid, provided intelligence on enemy strength, and, even though he was not in Early's command, promised, "I will obey any order you will send me." On July 6 or 7 Beattie and Heaton found Early at Sharpsburg and gave him Mosby's letter. He had no comment on the Point of Rocks Raid but gave them the oral message that he intended to capture Maryland Heights across the Potomac from Harpers Ferry and then march on Washington. He requested that Mosby support him by crossing the Potomac, cutting the railroad and telegraph, and reconnoitering in Maryland toward Washington.[41]

It was common knowledge that Early was difficult to work with, and now Mosby knew it. He had felt slighted that Early did not notify him in advance of the invasion; Mosby learned about it when he ran into one of Early's commissary officers in Rectortown on July 2. Now Early sent no word of congratulations or gratitude for the Point of Rocks diversion but made the ridiculous request that he repeat the raid, as though it had not been done. If Early wanted Mosby's cooperation, he should have commended him for the already accomplished diversion, thanked him for the information on the enemy, and requested that if possible Mosby should gather further intelligence on enemy strength and dispositions in Maryland and Washington.[42]

But Mosby was more offended by the fact that the message was oral; that was why he disobeyed. "Genl. Lee & Stuart always wrote to me when they wanted me to do anything," he declared. A few months later, during Sheridan's Valley campaign, Early sent Mosby another oral message by Private George, an aide to Early who became a physician in Danville, Virginia, after the war. It was a ridiculous request that Mosby guard the gaps in the lower Valley and protect Early's flanks, and Mosby ignored it as well. "If Early wanted me to do a thing he should as Genl. Lee & Stuart always did - send *written* instructions & not by the word of mouth of an unknown man."[43]

Now, instead of following Early's oral instructions, Mosby marched toward the Potomac in an attempt to unite with Early on Maryland Heights. He soon determined that Early had failed to maneuver the enemy off Maryland Heights and realized that strong Union forces separated him from Early's army. Still receiving no written orders, he did not know where Early was until he heard the roar of the guns on July 9 in Early's victory at the battle of Monocacy in Maryland.[44]

Two days later, on July 11, when Early was threatening the Washington defenses the first day, Mosby crossed the Potomac with his men, probably about 250, and passed through Poolesville and camped for the night. On the morning of July 12, the day that Lincoln came under enemy fire at Fort Stevens, Mosby's men raided the camp of the 8th Illinois Cavalry picket post at Muddy Branch, twenty miles up the Potomac from Washington and fifteen miles in Early's rear. They found the camp deserted; the raiders were plundering the possessions of soldiers that Early was pinning down, essentially as Early later complained. The raiders took thirty cattle and burned the camp. Mosby's postwar explanation for why Early turned against him was that he resented Mosby's positive press while his was negative. The newspapers would report Early's failure to conquer Washington, but in the *Washington Star,* Mosby's 30 captured cows became 950, and in the *Philadelphia Inquirer* and *New York Times,* nearly 1,000.[45]

Early withdrew across the Potomac and passed through Loudoun County and Snicker's Gap, where Mosby found him and saw him for the first time in his life. It was a friendly meeting, and Mosby offered to reconnoiter, but Early gave no instructions. He gave Mosby a small rifled cannon and complimented him for his energy and bravery. Even without instructions, within the next forty-eight hours, Mosby reported to Early that Union general Horatio G. Wright's corps had crossed the Potomac and was heading toward Snicker's Gap in pursuit. Early mentioned in a letter to Breckinridge on July 20 that Mosby's intelligence had been part of the information that enabled him to retreat up the Valley in safety. Wright's corps moved to Berryville and within a few days returned to Washington, opening the way for Early to attack and defeat Crook on July 24 at the second battle of Kernstown and send John McCausland's cavalry raiding across the Potomac again. Early camped at Bunker Hill in early August, and there Mosby met with him the second time. This time Mosby asked why Early had not told him that he planned to attack at Kernstown so that Mosby could have raided Crook's rear. Mosby did not indicate Early's reply, but he was probably smiling to himself that he had prevented Mosby from plundering while he did the fighting.[46]

In his first war memoir, published in 1867, Early attempted to justify his decision not to attack the Washington fortifications. In the midst of a lengthy paragraph discussing how little he knew at the time about the enemy forces in Washington, he related how in Sharpsburg he had requested that Mosby create a diversion and attempt "to find out the condition of things in Washington, but he had not crossed the river and I had received no information from him." Thus he partially blamed Mosby for his lack of intelligence on enemy strength in Washington and implied that Mosby had neglected his duty. Later that year, Scott's book on Mosby's command was about to appear, and Early heard that it would not agree. He wrote to Mosby explaining that he had been "severely and unjustly criticized" for not conquering Washington and that he was attempting to clear himself and Mosby. Mosby replied with a detailed explanation of his attempts to cooperate with Early and reconnoiter for him. Scott's book appeared with a reply to Early's book included in the appendix at Mosby's request. The statement defended Mosby for attempting to meet Early on Maryland Heights.[47]

Early was correct that Mosby did no scouting for him north of the Potomac. Mosby had not assisted Early before or during the battle of Monocacy or during the approach to Washington and the withdrawal from north of the Potomac. If Stuart had still been alive and leading the raid, he would not have asked Mosby to repeat a diversion just completed, and he probably would not have ordered Mosby to reconnoiter in Maryland or Washington, which were beyond his area of familiarity and civilian support. But if Stuart or Lee had asked or if Early had requested properly, what would Mosby have done? He would probably have at least sent Walter Bowie, his scout from Maryland, on a reconnaissance mission. Scott wrote that Mosby sent Bowie and nine men on such a mission, but they became involved in a skirmish in Loudoun County and returned without scouting. And Mosby would probably have attempted to scout himself, with a few men. But Early failed to coordinate with Mosby and therefore deprived himself of Mosby's scouting. He knew this and made no complaint at the time and should not have attempted to blame Mosby for his paucity of intelligence on July 11 and 12. During the Washington raid and in the Valley campaign against Sheridan, the only instructions that Early gave Mosby were the two oral messages. "I had always to guess at what he wanted me to do - that he never once ordered or requested me to do anything," Mosby wrote later.[48]

When Wright's nineteen thousand men and Crook's nine thousand were in the lower Valley, Mosby temporarily sent his artillery into the mountains and divided the battalion into five parties for stealth raiding; from July 17 to 21, they captured three hundred prisoners and three hundred horses. The Union army departed, and Mosby organized a fifth company and an artillery company and acquired a third cannon. On July 30, the day that McCausland burned Chambersburg, Pennsylvania, Mosby took the artillery and two hundred men on the raid that Lieutenant Nelson led to Adamstown, Maryland. Mosby remained south of the Potomac with the cannon and dispatched Nelson with a detachment that cut the telegraph line on the B&O at Adamstown at 2:00 P.M., closing communications for ten hours. This was a nuisance to Halleck, who was attempting to direct forces to intercept McCausland; he had to send messages via Harrisburg.[49]

By early August, Mosby had 250 men and 4 cannon, and he was ready to harass the next phase of Grant's offensive in the Shenandoah Valley. He had John Russell's excellent scouting, and with four clones he could divide into five parties for simultaneous forays. Or he could march with his entire force and arrange an attack with artillery, dismounted sharpshooters, and mounted men with revolvers. He had raided the B&O once in West Virginia and twice in Maryland and could again. He had succeeded in creating fear in the minds of Union commanders in Washington and had contributed to Sigel's defeat, but the next commander in the Valley would be Grant's hand-picked man.

# 12

# The Night Belonged
# to Mosby

By 1864 Mosby and his men were achieving his goal of producing fear in the minds of the enemy as a force multiplier. Clausewitz, in his book *On War,* wrote that local bands of guerrillas should surround the invading army with a feeling of uneasiness and dread. Che Guevera taught that invaders should be made to feel, day and night, that everything outside of camp is hostile, that they are "inside hostile jaws." Mao Tse Tung identified the enemy's mind as the target and proposed that it was more important to attack his will than his body. Guerrillas should, he declared, cause the invader "constant mental worry," with harassment as irritating as a swarm of "innumerable gnats."[1] William Cullen Bryant's "Song of Marion's Men" mentioned the fear created in the minds of the British invaders by Francis Marion in the American Revolution:

> And they who fly in terror deem
> A mighty host behind,
> And hear the tramp of thousands
> Upon the hollow wind.[2]

Union cavalrymen on duty against Mosby on the Washington, D.C., cavalry screen felt surrounded even though they far outnumbered his small force. "Bands of guerrillas like so many ravenous beasts and birds of prey, hover around our lines, attacking wherever an opportunity offers plunder," one wrote in May 1863. Col. Henry S. Gansevoort wrote his father on October 1, 1863: "In fact, the whole country, in our rear, front, and flanks, is full of guerillas," and in July 1864: "He is continually around us." A trooper informed the *Baltimore American:* "In fact, we are surrounded by guerillas."[3]

When a Union cavalry force marched into Mosby's Confederacy, they saw outlined on the sky silhouettes of mysterious riders mounted on seemingly giant horses and sitting, motionless, on the surrounding hills. It was useless to fire at the Rebels because they were just out of range. They were at home and thoroughly familiar with every byway, traveling light, with no blanket, knapsack, or canteen. As the Union column moved along, the figures would disappear and appear again on hills farther along. Sometimes, when the column slowed to ford a creek, snipers would fire long-range rifles, sending bullets pit-patting into the trees by the road. A horse or a man would fall, wounded or dead, creating the stress of constant alert. Mosby would gallop his fast horse within shooting range of the advance, fire a few shots from his revolver, and yell "Come on, Yanks," attempting to draw a few men into ambush.

Besides the danger of being killed by sniper fire, one of the foremost thoughts in a man's mind was the hope that his horse would hold out and he would not become separated. He knew that Mosby's men were watching for horses with drooping heads and trembling knees, for when a horse staggered and broke down and a man fell behind, he was gobbled up. Or if a man with an uncommonly speedy horse rode ahead of the advance, they would capture him. If the column unbitted the horses to feed at a grist mill or dismounted to water the animals at a tavern, Mosby's men would attack. One horseman forgot to buckle on his saber after dinner in Chester's Gap and had to go back alone to fetch it and was captured.[4]

Toward night, when the shadows of the trees lengthened and the dark deepened in the forest, one imagined sinister, lurking danger so that riding between patches of woods close on each side of the road was a gauntlet of fear. One night in the winter of 1863-64, about 150 men of the 1st Rhode Island Cavalry scouted for Mosby north of the Rappahannock River. They were veterans, and the expedition was unremarkable until their return toward camp at 11:00 P.M. The night was cold and clear, and as they approached a wooded area they heard the sound of horses approaching, hoofbeats pounding on the frozen road. Drawing their sabers they charged and captured two trembling African American men on two "poor woe-begone mules." The regimental historian wrote, "The spectre of Mosby and his gang had vanished." One night Pvt. John N. Wilson, 7th Michigan Cavalry, rode along the O&A Railroad on courier duty and approached a camp that he assumed were Mosby's men. He rode safely past two mounted videttes without being challenged. "To say I was scared is to speak mildly," he recalled. "I am not sure but that my hair stood on end."[5]

It was a mistake to stay overnight inside Mosby's Confederacy unless the detachment had a strong commander and a contingent of infantry to provide a feeling of security, for the night belonged to Mosby and his men. Rangers would roll wagons toward the camp and shout commands to imaginary artillery and infantry and, when everything seemed prepared, yell, "Are you ready to surrender now Yankees?" They attempted to lure men into ambush by sending a civilian into the camp with word that Mosby himself was present and this was their chance to capture him. They would keep the Federals awake by firing revolvers and lighting fireworks; and when it was time for the changing of the guard, a few Rangers pretending to be Union soldiers would march up to a picket and announce with authority, "Corporal of the guard with third relief," and take the man captive. "How we longed for daylight!" one man exclaimed. "Drenched with rain, half-frozen, not daring to make a fire, having nothing to eat but dry hardtack, and not even cold water to wash it down, we were miserable, indeed."[6]

One of the most effective uses of hovering was against the "Owl Shoot Raid" led by Stahel when he was in command of the Washington cavalry screen. Attempting to capture Mosby, on April 27, 1863, at 6:00 A.M., he left Fairfax Court House with a brigade of two thousand cavalry, four cannon, and five days' rations. Marching west on Little River Turnpike, he turned left on the road to Ashby's Gap, preparing to spend the first night in Middleburg. The column was an impressive sight, with fine horses and dark uniforms in orderly ranks and Stahel riding a beautiful white horse and issuing and receiving orders from mounted orderlies. It was quite an array of military force to use against Mosby and his eighty unorganized conglomerates.[7]

At 5:00 P.M. when the column neared Middleburg, about twelve of Mosby's men appeared, hovering on the hills and reminding Stahel that he was entering hostile territory. In Aldie Stahel had arrested all of the males and in Middleburg rounded up several more, for a total of thirty-five, including six Mosby men and one seventy-year-old civilian who had walked on crutches all of his life, and sent them to Washington under guard. For a campsite Stahel selected a wooded area one mile west of town, but before ordering the men to make camp he unlimbered the

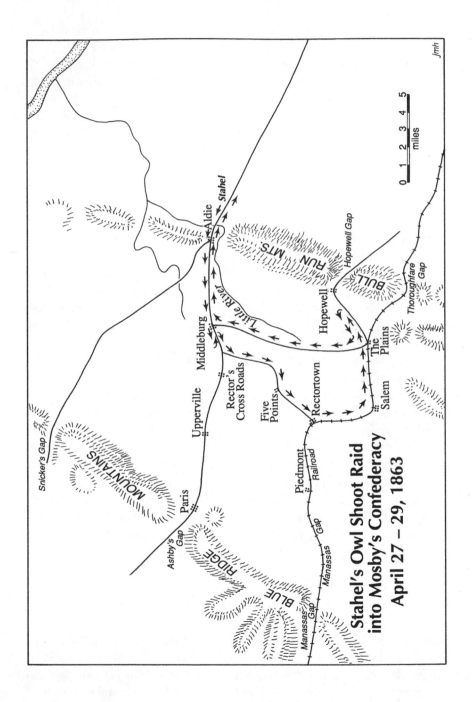

Stahel's Owl Shoot Raid
into Mosby's Confederacy
April 27 – 29, 1863

artillery and fired eleven shots into the trees to clear the woods of Rebels. This shelling greatly amused Mosby and the Rangers, and they ridiculed Stahel for bombarding nothing but bats and owls. Then, moving into the woods, Stahel deployed a dismounted skirmish line on the perimeter with cannon loaded in support. He prohibited the building of fires and allowed only half of the men to unsaddle and sleep at a time.[8]

The next morning, without coffee, they marched south into Mosby's land, and late in the day headed east from The Plains, moving toward Hopewell Gap in the Bull Run Mountains. Suddenly Mosby and about eighty men appeared in the road at the top of a hill one hundred yards ahead. Stahel halted, formed in line, and deployed the battery. For about an hour the two forces watched each other: eighty Rebels holding two thousand Federals at bay. This was such a memorable occasion that Mosby's men named the site "Stahel's Hill." Finally darkness arrived, and Mosby withdrew and disbanded his men for the night. Stahel fell back to The Plains and went into bivouac, but late in the night he panicked and ordered a night march to Middleburg, a distance of about eight miles. During the trek he had his rear guard cut trees and place them in the road as barriers. At one point a citizen asked an officer, "Why, sir, where in the world are you going?" "Ah, sir!" came the reply, "This is too unhealthy a country for us."[9]

In Middleburg the next day, Stahel's troops searched houses and pillaged and then marched to Aldie and settled down east of town for the night. At 10:00 P.M. a squad of Mosby's men opened fire on Stahel's pickets, and Ranger Dick Moran shouted in his deep, booming voice: "Here they are General. Bring up the Reserve." By now, Stahel's nerves could stand no more; he ordered the men to break camp immediately, and the second night of marching brought them safely to base. Someone asked Mosby why he failed to pursue on the first night's march, and he replied that the movement took him by surprise; he said that he could not believe that the Union army had placed an idiot in command of a brigade of cavalry and four cannon.[10]

Eleven months later, when Mosby's command had increased to about 200 men, on March 28, 1864, Maj. George F. McCabe and 234 men of the 13th Pennsylvania Cavalry came searching for them. McCabe's station was at Nokesville on the O&A Railroad, and his assignment was to guard Meade's supply line. He and his men arrived safely in Middleburg and started searching homes for Mosby's men. They found none, but civilians said that Mosby was waiting west of town with a force that outnumbered them three to one. McCabe believed it and withdrew to Aldie, now followed closely by Mosby's men, hovering on the hills. In Aldie the Rangers attacked his rear guard, and with a sense of "great danger to the safety of the command," McCabe returned to base.[11]

The seventy-five-man detachment of Cole's Cavalry that Mosby's men defeated at Five Points exercised more courage but, without the strength of Cole's presence, were vulnerable. Cole sent them on December 30, 1863, under Capt. Albert M. Hunter, to hunt for Mosby. They rode from Loudoun Heights to Leesburg and on the third day, January 1, 1864, moved toward the heart of Mosby's Confederacy. Hunter had been confident thus far, but passing through Upperville in a cold rain he heard the crack of a rifle and one of his men fell in the road, killed instantly by a shot in the head. Leaving the man's body with civilians, Hunter marched to Rectortown, where several riders appeared on the hills. The rain had stopped, but a cold wind was blowing and the temperature dropped below freezing. Deciding to withdraw before dark, he was leading his men through Five Points when thirty-two Rangers attacked from the rear. They killed Hunter's horse, captured him, and forced his men into headlong flight. In panic the Union men splashed across Cromwell's Run, and several men's boots filled with water. Afraid to halt and dry out in homes, they rode on. When they reached camp several had frostbitten ears and faces, and those with frozen feet had to have their boots cut off and later their feet or toes amputated. Hunter broke free and escaped but lost fifty-seven men killed or captured. Cole explained to the *Baltimore American* that there was no reason for Hunter's "utter rout and discomfiture," for if a commander kept his wits there was less danger from Mosby's guerrillas than from regular cavalry.[12]

But Hunter's fear was real and his feelings, and those of other Union cavalrymen were brought to life in a poem by Herman Melville, who went as a civilian observer on a raid led by Lowell, April 18-20, 1864. Melville was a friend of Lowell and a cousin of one of Lowell's regimental commanders, Henry S. Gansevoort, 13th New York Cavalry. Melville's great dream was to become a famous writer and support himself by writing books that would sell, but thus far he had failed. Like many Americans, Melville recognized the deep significance of the Civil War and began writing war poems, hoping at last to become famous as the poet laureate of the Civil War. But he had no military experience and needed to have a taste of the war firsthand. He was visiting Lowell's brigade headquarters on April 18, 1864, when Lowell started on a scout for

Mosby and his men and invited him to ride along. There would be fighting, and this would be Melville's only war experience.[13]

He could not have been in more careful hands. Lowell was the most cautious, successful opponent that Mosby faced on a continual basis. He cared for his men and took care not to lose them carelessly. In order to protect his officers, he encouraged them to avoid wearing insignia of rank distinguishable at one hundred yards. He always assumed that he might be killed from a rifle shot behind the next fence but wore his uniform nevertheless, preferring, he said, to die in uniform rather than out of it. At the time Mosby had about 200 men, and on the raid Lowell took 500: 250 infantry and 250 cavalry. He had learned that it helped him remain calm and prevented his men from getting spooked when he used strong detachments and protected them from attack with infantry or dismounted cavalry—he knew that Mosby would not knowingly come near infantry. This time he sent the infantry on ahead to set up a secure camp at Ball's Mill on Goose Creek, northeast of Aldie. He departed Vienna between 9:00 and 10:00 A.M. on April 18 with the cavalry detachment, including Melville, riding horseback in the column.[14]

They proceeded with extreme caution, stopping every ninety minutes to adjust saddles and rest the horses. Joining the infantry at Ball's Mill at 4:00 P.M., they dismounted, fed the horses, ate supper, and at 5:00 P.M. mounted, crossed Goose Creek, and marched toward Leesburg, where some of Mosby's men were reported foraging for corn. They were nearing Leesburg at about dusk when a few of Mosby's men fired on the advance from woods south of town. Lowell ordered a saber charge, and the Rebels withdrew and Lowell's men rode into town without further opposition. They searched the town, but, finding no Rebels, Lowell expected that Mosby might be gathering for an attack. He took his men to a narrow side road just outside of town and kept them on alert—they did not light fires or make camp but all night stood to horse in the road in column of fours. If a man wanted to lie down he did so with bridle reins in hand, and sometimes his horse lay down beside him. But as soon as one dozed off, Mosby's men would send signal rockets into the sky from the nearby hills or open fire on the pickets, causing everyone to stand to horse, ready to mount if the order came.[15]

At daylight after a cold breakfast and no fires to make coffee, Lowell sent parties into the woods, and they surrounded a party of Mosby's men, capturing eleven and mortally wounding one. At 10:00 A.M. Lowell marched to Goose Creek, and his cavalry were in camp protected by the

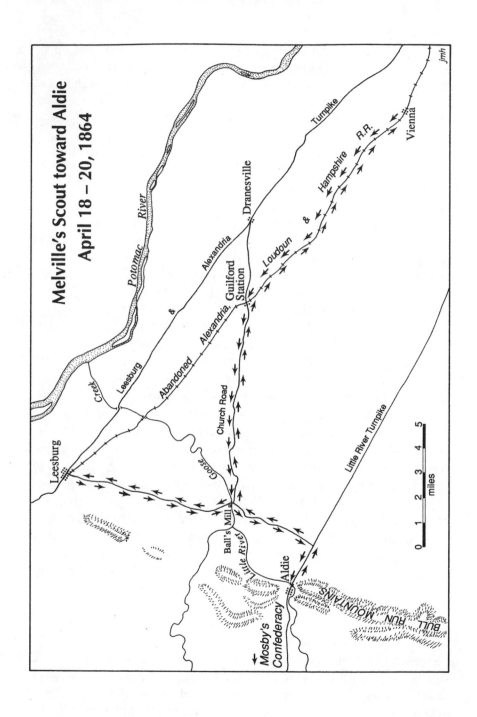

Melville's Scout toward Aldie
April 18 – 20, 1864

infantry when at 4:00 P.M. a Unionist civilian rushed in and reported that Mosby himself had just passed through the fields not two miles away. Lowell had the bugler sound "Boots and Saddles," and they galloped to Aldie, where the citizens confirmed that Mosby had been there and had left a message of regard for Lowell. At this time, according to Lowell's report, he decided that since Mosby knew of his presence it seemed useless to proceed with plans to send a force that night to Rectortown or Upperville, because the element of surprise was lost.[16]

Instead he decided to take advantage of intelligence probably provided by a civilian informer that several of Mosby's men would be attending a wedding in Leesburg that evening. He sent seventy-five cavalrymen to surprise the Rebels at the wedding; and to insure that his men would remain calm, he sent them dismounted. Marching on foot brought them to the party thirty minutes after it had ended, but they started a fight with some of the Rangers who were departing, and the Union men lost one killed and three wounded. It is not certain whether Melville marched on this expedition, but he was included when the cavalry mounted at dawn the next morning, the third day, and Lowell marched them with an ambulance to Leesburg to gather the Union wounded. At 10:00 A.M. they marched back to Ball's Mill and returned to Vienna. Lowell's chaplain, Charles A. Humphreys, described how he felt after three days and two nights of hunting Mosby: "I had slept only two hours, and was so stiff from a cold caught the first night that it seemed as if I could count by its special ache each muscle in my body."[17]

Lowell had conformed to his conservative raiding style, avoided panic, and protected his men from ambush. His men had appeared three times in Leesburg, where Mosby's men had been reported. Losing one killed and three wounded and mortally wounding one Rebel and capturing eleven, the mission seemed successful. On his next raid ten days later, with Melville gone, he took twice the force—five hundred infantry and five hundred cavalry—and went to Rectortown, searched homes at night, and captured twenty-one Mosby men and one infantryman and twenty horses. Mosby's men hovered and skirmished with the column, and in three days the blueclads lost three killed, two wounded, and three captured. Lowell's men killed two Mosby men and wounded four. On this April 28-30, 1864, raid, since he outnumbered Mosby's men by five to one and had a strong infantry force, he marched with greater self-confidence. His superior, General Christopher C. Augur, commended him for displaying "zeal and ability" on this and two previous raids that included the Melville expedition.[18]

Melville returned home and wrote "The Scout toward Aldie" and included it in his book of war poems, *Battle-Pieces and Aspects of the War,* published in 1866. But again he was disappointed; the book failed on the market, selling only 468 copies by 1868. Finally he gave up attempting to earn a living by writing and took a job as a customs inspector in New York. In his excellent book, *The Civil War World of Herman Melville,* Stanton Garner postulated that "The Scout toward Aldie" is "a small-scale version of *Moby-Dick,*" with Mosby as the great white whale, the symbol of evil. Literary critic Edward W. Goggin viewed the poem as an allegory of war in general. Like the raid, all warfare is frustrating, futile, and filled with deadly misperceptions. In general combat, soldiers envision danger everywhere, and uncertainty contributes to despair. The Union soldiers in the poem see Mosby as a shark, snake, bird, demon, and satyr's child; and, wrote Goggin, they fear finding him, and "transfixed by their fear, they begin to see him everywhere. He captures their febrile imaginations, infecting every aspect of their existence. 'Rumor' makes him 'every thing'; he is not merely 'everyone' but every tree, stream and house."[19]

Melville's poem is a fictional tribute to Mosby's success in creating fear in the minds of the enemy. Unrestrained by the discipline of history, Melville used the freedom of poetry to dramatize the fright of the Union cavalry. Referring to their fear of wandering from the safety of the Union stockade in Vienna, he wrote:

> Unarmed none cared to stir abroad
> For berries beyond their forest-fence:
> As glides in seas the shark,
> Rides Mosby through green dark.[20]

Regarding the fear of being killed by sniper fire, Melville considered writing that the Union men worried that Mosby would see the bright gold lace on their blue uniforms, but for the final draft he substituted shiny buttons for gold lace.[21] He portrayed the apprehensions called forth by hovering:

> And five gigantic horsemen carved
> Clear-cut against the sky withdrawn;

Are more behind? an open snare?
Or Mosby's men but watchmen there?[22]

The poem captured the fear of ambush from the woods, identified as "Mosby's hall." Not in reality, but in the poem, an ambush occurs and suddenly Mosby:

Speaks in a volley! out jets the flame!
Men fall from their saddles like plums from trees;
Horses take fright, reins tangle and bind;
"Steady—dismount—form—and into the wood!"[23]

Melville may have made the only contemporary association of Mosby and his men with the word "ghosts" when he compared them to ghosts in a haunted house and mentioned "fear for the gleaming ghost!" And when an officer in the poem said that his men would next see Mosby in their dreams, Melville suggested that the weary soldiers would have nightmares of Mosby.[24]

Melville described the hostility of Mosby's civilian supporters to the Union men and mentioned that Mosby had no camp and used hit-and-run tactics. He emphasized that the Union goal was to capture Mosby himself, recognized the use of pro–Union civilian guides and intelligence from prisoners of war, and noted the physical and mental exhaustion resulting from the scout. At the end, the horsemen hardly seemed the same column as three days before:

Foot-sore horses, jaded men;
Every backbone felt as nicked,
Each eye dim as a sick-room lamp,
All faces stamped with Mosby's stamp."[25]

Union sergeants of the guard warned pickets going on duty, "Now don't let old Mosby get you." In Washington one night Pvt. James H. Haight, 11th New York Cavalry, was guarding the quarters of Secretary of War Stanton, and toward morning he saw his horse's ears lift and felt him bracing his legs on alert. Through the darkness, Haight saw what he thought was a squad of Mosby's cavalry charging toward him. He fired his revolver, and the advancing column wheeled and galloped away. On the break of day he saw that he had shot at a herd of horses in the adjoining pasture.[26]

On dark and rainy nights, pickets would see Mosby everywhere. A New York cavalryman challenged two images on his front and, receiving no reply, aimed and fired several shots, awakening the reserve. Morning light revealed that he had been frightened by two cedar trees. An owl hooting, a night hawk screeching, a rabbit jumping through the leaves, and other mysterious sounds in the scrub oak and pine forests filled men with terror. A cowbell clanging in the distance and slowly coming closer might be a guerrilla. One night on the cold wind a Union picket heard a hollow, pounding sound, steady like a drum, and he feared it might be a scout calling Mosby's men to capture him. The next morning he saw that it was a broken limb beating against another limb. Infantry pickets were sitting by a campfire near Catlett's Station, and they heard the sound of a child crying in the woods. One man rose to investigate, and the others told him to sit down, that if he went out he would never return. On picket, Aaron E. Bachman, 1st Pennsylvania Cavalry, heard what sounded like men whistling back and forth to each other, with short and long blasts. He sounded the alarm and awoke the reserve; they scoured the woods but found no guerrillas. Upon his relief, he recalled, "The man who was placed on my post was so scared he shook like a leaf."[27]

Mosby's goal was to cause the enemy to waste his strength chasing an imaginary foe, "a Jack-o'-lantern." It would be impossible to calculate the number of hours of lost sleep caused by false alarms from fear of Mosby's men. An infantry picket wrote home that a false alarm had awakened him and forced him into line to watch for guerrillas. "I did not sleep at all last night. Today I Dont feel so wel." Early in 1863 the 7th Michigan Cavalry rode over the Long Bridge and camped in the snow in Fairfax Court House. Snug in their "dog tents" the first night, they heard, "Hark, Mosby, Mosby. Hurry up, for God's sake, men, hurry up." They pulled on their boots, saddled and mounted, and rode into the dark, "but Mosby was like Pat's flee, he was not there; at any rate we did not get our fingers on him or our eyes either, so we bid farewell to the old cuss and went back to quarters—it was only a false alarm." Lt. Rawle Brooke, 3rd Pennsylvania Cavalry, was in charge of a picket reserve post near Warrenton on August 23, 1863, when he recorded: "The third night with-out sleep. . . . I never passed a more anxious night, expecting to be 'gobbled.'" After Stoughton's capture, a company of the 18th Pennsylvania Cavalry became demoralized from the heavy guard duty and lack of sleep and mutinied rather than go on picket.[28]

Sometimes Union cavalry guards stretched telegraph wire across the road at the height where horses could pass underneath, but riders would be thrown. Around their camp at Bealeton Station in December 1863, the 1st Rhode Island Cavalry erected a barricade of poles and tree tops and at night stretched telegraph wires across the entrance. In Warrenton a rumor said that Mosby would come charging up Winchester Street on Sunday night, April 26, 1863, and the small Union cavalry force in the town went into a panic. They hurriedly erected a barricade of wagon beds, logs, and other objects across the street a few feet forward from a large mud hole in front of Bragg's Carriage Shop. In their imaginations they saw Mosby's guerrillas galloping along in the dark, jumping the barricade, and splattering in the mud. On top of the works they placed a fake cannon, and the townspeople gathered and doubled over in laughter at what they dubbed "Bragg's Battery" and "Fort Warrenton."[29]

Union soldiers relieved the tension by joking and teasing. Aaron Bachman was saddling his horse to go on picket one night, and his friends said, "Bachman, you will be the lucky boy tonight. You will surely be stolen tonight. Goodbye! Give us a lock of your hair. This is the last time we will see you." Theodore Gerrish went with a friend outside Union lines early one morning to milk a cow. Suddenly they heard a loud scream, and a person leaped over the fence into the barnyard behind them. "I thought Moseby, and his whole gang of cut-throats were upon us," Gerrish recalled. He sprang to his feet, spilling the milk, and he and his friend ran across the barnyard and jumped the fence. Looking back they saw a woman slave, bending in laughter at the two frightened Yankees.[30]

Fear took on a life of its own, and imagination multiplied Mosby's force far beyond its actual strength or presence. He said that three hundred men skillfully led in the rear equal ten thousand on the fighting front, and he was speaking in terms of disruptions and false alarms. His small battalion was never a threat to Washington, but a cloud of dust or plume of smoke would rise in the sky along the Potomac, and civilians in southern Maryland would go into a panic, and the commanders in Washington would alert the defenses and order pickets to take up the planks on Chain Bridge to prevent Mosby's men from entering the capital. Chain Bridge was built in 1808 with huge chains attached to stone abutments, and, when it was rebuilt with timber trusses on masonry piers, it was still called "Chain Bridge." It was inside the defensive perimeter, guarded by Fort Marcy and Fort Ethan Allen and their connecting rifle pits. When Mosby was expected, soldiers would move artillery to the riverbank on the Washington side—two mountain howitzers aimed across the deck of the bridge and two rifled six-pounders on a hill a few yards to the rear. On the Virginia side of the bridge there was a loopholed gate, and on both ends of the bridge eight or ten planks were kept loose; at 9:00 P.M. the lieutenant in charge would close the gate and have guards remove the planks.[31]

On May 14, 1863, when Mosby had about forty unorganized raiders, a rumor swept into Baltimore and down to Washington that Mosby's force had suddenly increased to nine hundred men and they were charging toward Chain Bridge or Aqueduct Bridge. The rumor arose when a two-hundred-man Union cavalry detachment from the Shenandoah Valley marched into Loudoun County, hunting for Mosby. General Milroy, who had sent them, had neglected to inform Washington; and someone mistakenly reported them as Mosby's men. In this imaginary emergency, commanders alerted the pickets, and for several nights they took up the Chain Bridge planks. With Mosby doing nothing, fear had multiplied his force to the fantasy number of nine hundred, twenty-two times actual strength.[32]

More than a year later, when it was well known that Mosby had artillery, on July 7, 1864, a rumor circulated that he and Gilmor with a large force and two cannon were in Dranesville, rapidly advancing along the thirteen miles to Chain Bridge. The pickets were alerted, but they were already taking up the planks each night just in case. After the war Mosby believed that the Chain Bridge precaution proved that his psychological war succeeded. He celebrated Hooker's testimony before the Joint Committee on the Conduct of the War that "the planks on the chainbridge were taken up at night" solely because of Mosby's men.[33]

Fear invaded the mind of Lincoln's chief of staff, General Halleck, and gave him some of the most uncomfortable hours of his career. Halleck was forty-nine years old and had achieved success in life. He was a West Point man, attorney, businessman, and the author of important scholarly books, including an important two-volume study of international law. He had commanded in the field in this war, and his natural tendency toward caution was heightened by his goal of avoiding embarrassment and guarding his reputation. His troops had named him "Old Brains" for his gruff, arrogant manner, and to clerks in the War Department he was "Old Wooden Head."[34]

Halleck took command of the defenses of Washington in the emergency created when Early, on his withdrawal from Maryland, turned back down the Valley and won the battle of Kernstown on July 24, 1864, and again threatened Washington. Grant directed Halleck to send Gen. Horatio G. Wright and nineteen thousand men to Harpers Ferry to counter Early. Halleck rounded up a 1,363-man scratch force of cavalry to guard Wright's long supply wagon train, and on July 26 the column left Washington and marched westward on the Rockville and Frederick Pike. Now, as the man in charge of this important movement, Halleck took unusual interest in the cavalry screen on the north bank of the Potomac. These men were protecting the left flank of Wright's wagons.[35]

Beefing up the cavalry line, he moved the six-hundred-man 2nd Massachusetts Cavalry from Washington out to Poolesville to picket twenty-eight miles of riverbank to the mouth of the Monocacy River. To defend beyond that point he alerted the six-hundred-man 8th Illinois Cavalry at Monocacy Junction to be extra vigilant. Everything seemed in order until the morning of July 29, three days into the march, when a report came in from the Union cavalry at Poolesville that Mosby and White with four hundred cavalry and three cannon were in Leesburg, planning to cross the Potomac. Assuming that this force had by now reached the river, the report placed Rebel raiders within twelve miles of the route of Wright's supply wagons.[36]

But Halleck did not panic until 12:20 in the afternoon when the rumor came that the Rebels had crossed and were in Maryland. Reason would have counseled that the first-rate 2nd Massachusetts Cavalry would have seen and challenged them. But since there was no word from the cavalry, fear whispered that Mosby had slipped through the picket line; some of the heavier wagons had fallen behind, and Mosby had captured them and was already on the way to the B&O Railroad to punctuate the headlines by seizing a train. Worked into full panic, Halleck telegraphed Gen. Lew Wallace, middle department commander in Baltimore, that Mosby and White had crossed. "Send out immediately your cavalry, a battery, and some infantry to protect the railroad, and also any of Wright's trains on the Rockville and Frederick pike," he ordered. Ten minutes later he wired Hunter in Harpers Ferry. There was nothing Hunter could do, but maybe some of the blame could be laid on him. "As no cavalry has yet arrived here," he wrote, "General Wright must look out for his trains." Then he alerted "Any Officer at Monocacy Station," the jump-off point of the last leg of the trip, to hurry forward the wagons to protect them from Mosby.[37]

Wallace ordered infantry to deploy along the B&O and ordered a regiment of cavalry, a regiment of Pennsylvania militia, and a battery of artillery under Gen. Erastus B. Tyler to take a special train to the area. Tyler's force was gathering when nine hours and forty minutes into Halleck's scare, at 10:00 P.M., Wallace canceled the orders to Tyler and sent Halleck word that Union cavalry pickets had driven Mosby back across the Potomac and Wright's wagons were secure. Assistant Secretary of War Charles A. Dana informed Grant: "Wright got to Harper's Ferry to-day with all his train safe. Halleck had been much alarmed for fear Mosby might cross at Edwards Ferry and cut off Wright's road." Stanton told his friend, B&O president Garrett, "The great difficulty is to know the exact truth & to avoid being misled by Stampedes & groundless clamor or being surprised by real danger."[38]

Mosby was operational and at the moment when Halleck lost control was camped with two hundred men and three cannon ten miles northwest of Leesburg and six miles south of the river, at Morrisonville. On the night of July 29 he sent a few men to scout the fords in preparation for the July 30 Adamstown, Maryland, Raid, but he had no intention of attacking Wright's wagons. White and his command were with Lee's army in Petersburg; but Company B, from Maryland, had deserted to go home when they learned of Early's Raid, and this probably gave rise to the rumor that White's men were present.[39]

Mosby's Adamstown Raid of July 30 inconvenienced Halleck, as discussed previously, but he remained calm. Two days later, however, on August 1, 1864, the third day after the scare over the wagons, he joined Augur in another panic. At this time Mosby was forty miles away in the Valley, marching in the opposite direction from Washington. The fright began when citizens of Rockville, Maryland, saw a cloud of dust sent up by a Union cavalry patrol. Rockville was on the pike to Frederick ten miles northwest of the Washington defensive perimeter. Jeb Stuart had raided the town on June 28, 1863, on his Gettysburg foray, and on July 9, 1864, the citizens felt vulnerable when Union forces retreated through town from the battle of Monocacy and withdrew into the safety of Washington, leaving them to the mercy of Early's army on July 10. Like the citizens of Indiana and Ohio raided by Morgan, the people of Rockville realized that the Union army could not protect their homes. On July 13 Early's army passed back through on the withdrawal, and after that Rockville residents were thoroughly demoralized. From then on, Rockville invasion panics were a joke in Washington, but it was easy to laugh when one lived behind secure fortifications.[40]

On Monday, August 1, with tension high because Early's cavalry were across the Potomac and had burned Chambersburg, Pennsylvania, on Saturday, the rumor started that Mosby and two hundred men were across the Potomac and marching toward Rockville, a few miles away. The raiders had captured the mail carriers in Poolesville and Hyattstown and a stagecoach in Clarksburg. By nightfall the story had grown into a report that Mosby's men were the advance for Longstreet's corps, now paused on the right bank of the Potomac, ready to invade Maryland. Soon after dark citizens in Rockville gathered a few belongings, rounded up their livestock, and headed down the road toward Tennallytown inside the Washington defenses and protected by Fort Reno. At 10:30 P.M. Gen. Martin D. Hardin, commander of defenses north of the Potomac, alerted the pickets and ordered a regiment of infantry to "move at once" to Tennallytown to fight the approaching cavalry. At 11:00 P.M., upon Augur's recommendation, Halleck ordered all reserves to the front and directed Gen. Cuvier Grover to march "at once" with all available men in his division to Tennallytown. Grover's division of the 19th Corps was arriving on boats from the Army of the Potomac and was scheduled to go to Harpers Ferry. At the moment, four thousand had reached Washington. Halleck ordered that, as soon as more units landed, they were to move immediately. The next morning the sun rose over Fort Reno, and Mosby was not there; Halleck and Augur realized that they were victims of a groundless invasion panic. Assuming that their fantasies estimated Longstreet's corps at ten thousand men, fear multiplied Mosby's force forty times.[41]

Two months later, when Augur departed Washington in the middle of the night to rescue the work crew that Mosby had cut off on the Manassas Gap Railroad (MGR), he left Halleck solely in charge of the defenses of Washington and the Maryland border. Halleck's reputation was on the line again, and he felt vulnerable because Augur took with him the cavalry of the early-warning screen on the Potomac and in Fairfax County. If Mosby crossed into Maryland now, there would be no warning. Twenty-four hours after Augur departed, Halleck received a dispatch at 11:45 P.M., October 7, from Gen. John Stevenson at Harpers Ferry, reporting that Mosby's command had suddenly increased to eight hundred men with four cannon, and they were advancing toward the Potomac to invade Maryland and rob a bank in Annapolis. Actually, Mosby's three hundred men and four cannon were still operating against the MGR in Fauquier County.[42]

Stevenson's message filled Halleck with the same concern that had prompted him the previous year to retain the 2nd Massachusetts Cavalry in Maryland during the Gettysburg campaign—he feared that Mosby would attack the B&O or the Washington Branch Railroad connecting Washington and Baltimore. The next morning he ordered all available cavalry to Rockville and strengthened the infantry guards on the railroads. In a turmoil, he made the blunder of ordering a twenty-five-man battery of the 3rd Pennsylvania Artillery to immediately move south from Monrovia to Rockville. The small force arrived in Rockville with its four cannon before the cavalry, and for fourteen hours Halleck anxiously fretted; he could imagine the headlines if Mosby captured the cannon. "Save your guns at all hazards. Report very often," directed Tyler. The cavalry arrived on the second day of the scare and saved the guns, and after three days Halleck canceled the alarm.[43]

Mosby knew from reading Northern newspapers that fear of him and his men frequently disrupted and harassed Union officers. In October 1864, when the Union Quartermaster Department in Washington ordered a work crew to clear the trees on the Manassas Gap Railroad to deprive Mosby's guerrillas of cover, forty-seven workers were arrested for refusing to go because they feared capture. Surgeon John H. Brinton, in charge of Sheridan's wounded at Winchester in late September 1864, wrote in his memoirs that it was unsafe to forage outside of camp for fresh food to serve men in the hospital. He had a female nurse who pestered him for fresh eggs for her favorite patient, and he recommended that she go herself to a farmhouse outside Union lines. "I was much in hopes that some of Mosby's men would catch her," he joked, but she was wise enough not to venture out.[44]

When Ulysses S. Grant was on the O&A Railroad returning to his headquarters in Culpeper, Virginia, from one of his meetings with Lincoln in April 1864, he saw a cloud of dust ahead at Warrenton Junction and stopped the train. He sent a man into the station, who returned with word that Mosby's men had just passed and were gone. "I breathed a sign of relief when I heard it," he told Mosby after the war. About the same time, Gen. George Custer's wife, Elizabeth, worried that Mosby's men had captured her husband traveling on a train through the same area. Custer and "Libby," his "dear little Army Crow," were honeymooning, and they were together as much as possible. On September 11, 1864, he was in the Valley without her, looking forward to their next reunion. "Not even the supposed proximity of Mosby's gang could drive away my happy thoughts of you," he declared in a letter to her.[45]

The apprehensions of soldiers on picket or in Mosby's area were real, for to fall into Mosby's hands was to go to a dreaded prison camp. But reasonable fear became exaggerated, and Mosby made one of his greatest irregular contributions by appearing in the fantasies of enemy soldiers, commanders, and civilians. In early August 1864 as he minded the Union rear in the Shenandoah Valley, he was about to face his strongest opponent in the war, a fighter and Grant's handpicked man, General Sheridan.

# 13

# Blue Hen's Chickens and Custer's Wolverines

Sheridan understood the psychology of guerrilla warfare and comprehended as well as anyone in the Union, except perhaps Lincoln, that public opinion in the North would not support extreme counterguerrilla measures that threatened to bathe the country in blood. Therefore when one of his reactions to Mosby's first raid involved the hanging and shooting of prisoners of war assumed to be Mosby's men, he kept it so quiet and secret that the victims remain still unidentified today. He welcomed Grant's more moderate orders to arrest Southern males of draft age and burn the crops and outbuildings of civilians who supported guerrillas. Nevertheless, after Sheridan and Grant had rejected retaliation, the clash of Mosby's Blue Hen's Chickens with Custer's proud Wolverines resulted in the breakdown of civilized warfare and some of the most inhumane acts of the Civil War.

"Little Phil" was 5 feet, 5 inches tall and 135 pounds, with a large head, square shoulders, and abnormally short, duck legs. A soldier, seeing him and his staff for the first time, asked a companion which was Sheridan. "The one with the big boots," he said. "What!" exclaimed another man, "you don't mean that little rat terrier?" Like Mosby, in boyhood Sheridan's appearance had attracted bullies, and he too had developed a killer instinct that many thought was visible on his face. His friend Gen. William T. Sherman said he resembled "a persevering terrier dog." His normal voice was a croak, but when he became excited or scolded with sharp words, as he often did, it changed to a deep rasp. Few were excluded from his biting criticism. In 1864 he became fed up with false alarms in West Virginia and during one Rebel raid snapped at powerful

B&O president Garrett in Baltimore: "I will advise you when to commence running."[1]

Sheridan was energetic and able to inspire confidence in his men. On his huge black horse Rienzi, his short legs did not matter; he looked impressive and powerful. Like Grant he moved through camp quietly, and men who had not been with Grant considered Sheridan the first professional soldier they had ever seen; there was a sense that he was in charge. A West Point graduate born in New York and having grown up in Ohio, he began the war as a chief quartermaster and commissary and was as familiar with wagon trains as anyone. He was known to keep his wagons snugly guarded when parked and securely escorted on the road. He realized that success depended on morale and provided the best water, food, and clothing available, along with rest and forage for the horses. One of his infantry officers, future president Rutherford B. Hayes, recorded in his diary, "We are a happy army."[2]

Grant had brought Sheridan from the West and made him commander of the cavalry corps of the Army of the Potomac. Now he was only thirty-three years old, and many feared that it was a mistake to appoint him commander of the new Army of the Shenandoah and the Middle Military Division. His assignment was to destroy Early's army, advance up the Valley 110 miles to Staunton, and open a second front that would divert forces from Lee's army at Petersburg. Grant considered the mission "of vast importance" and wanted him to follow Early "to the death," but it was a tall order to send a man who insisted on secure supply lines into a valley infested by guerrillas.[3]

Sheridan arrived at Harpers Ferry to take command at 7:30 P.M. on August 6; within forty-eight hours, Mosby's men had his attention. On the afternoon of August 8 he alerted Gen. Christopher C. Augur, in Washington, that two hundred of Mosby's men were across the Shenandoah River only five miles from his headquarters. It was true; Mosby's men were foraging corn among the Unionist civilians of northern Loudoun County. This prompted Sheridan to ask Augur for a status report on the cavalry screen. Augur reported that he had six hundred of the 8th Illinois cavalry north of the Potomac and another cavalry force of 916 men at Falls Church in Fairfax County. Like Grant, Sheridan hated to divert manpower from the fighting front to guard the rear, but he decided to strengthen the cavalry screen north of the Potomac before starting his offensive. He temporarily (August 8 to 26) assigned six hundred of his own cavalry to reinforce the 8th Illinois Cavalry. This screen was still almost 900 short of the recommended 3,000 and was comparably stingy; but with 250 men Mosby temporarily diverted 600 from Sheridan's army, over twice Mosby's own strength.[4]

Sheridan could live with this, he thought, but one of the last things he did before departing at 5:00 A.M. on August 10 was to leave instructions with his adjutant to further strengthen the Potomac screen by ordering the scattered companies of the 8th Illinois Cavalry to report to Muddy Branch for picket duty. He moved his army swiftly, issuing the men three days' rations and leaving the subsistence and headquarters wagons safely parked on Bolivar Heights, one mile south of Harpers Ferry and guarded by Gen. John R. Kenly's small infantry brigade headquartered at Halltown, two miles farther south. Early was at Bunker Hill and Sheridan hoped to flank his right by a fast move to Berryville, head him at Winchester, and defeat him in battle within three days, before the supply wagons were required.[5]

Everything went smoothly except that Early withdrew up the Valley in front of Sheridan and escaped. On the night of August 11, camped eight miles south of Winchester, Sheridan wrote Grant that Early's "precipitate retreat" had frustrated the plan. Now the campaign would be extended beyond the three days' rations of his thirty thousand men. On the day before at the end of the first day's march, he had ordered that the three days' rations be extended to four days, supplemented by fresh beef. This meant that the food would be consumed on the thirteenth, and he wanted the supply train to catch up by that fourth day so that rations could be issued for the morning of the fifth day.[6]

Therefore, on the night of August 11 he sent Capt. Andrew J. McGonnigle, acting chief quartermaster of the Middle Military Division, on a thirty-mile, all-night ride to Harpers Ferry to bring the wagon train escorted by Kenly's brigade and a battery of artillery of Gen. William H. Emory's 19th Corps that had been left behind. He stressed to McGonnigle that he must hurry and the wagons must rush to Winchester by the evening of the twelfth. The next morning Sheridan sent a brigade of infantry back to Winchester to meet the wagons and then moved his army south to Cedar Creek, where Early showed resistance with minor skirmishing. For the night of August 12, Sheridan was camped at Cedar Creek, with Early four miles south on Fisher's Hill.[7]

Now, on the evening of the third day, Sheridan was thirty-six miles from Bolivar Heights, and he expected that his supply train was en route. Several reports came in that Longstreet's corps was on the way from Petersburg to the Valley, and one of the telegrams, from Gen. Max Weber at Harpers Ferry, included a sentence that related to the supply wagons. "Mosby is already between Harper's Ferry and your command," Weber wrote, "and last night [August 10] captured and paroled the [New York] Tribune correspondent, as he [the reporter] reports." Suddenly, Sheridan realized that he had made a mistake—he should have brought the wagons with him. Kenly's brigade had only 931 men, about half the number required to escort 525 loaded supply and headquarters wagons, and, furthermore, Kenly's was Sheridan's least effective brigade; that was why he left it behind on guard duty. Sheridan could imagine the headlines if Mosby captured one of Emory's cannon.[8]

At 9:30 P.M. Sheridan sent an order to Washington and Baltimore that the 8th Illinois Cavalry was to be concentrated "without delay," and Augur was to send them south toward Middleburg "to exterminate as many of Mosby's gang as they can." This extermination order was unusual for a West Point general, and it indicates the level of Sheridan's anxiety—Mosby had gotten inside his mind. Sheridan had not been on duty in the Valley seven days, and he was already swatting the guerrilla gnats swarming around his supply line.[9]

At midnight he wrote Grant, informing him that he would wait at Cedar Creek for the wagons, due before noon the next day. He shared that he was worried about the reports of Longstreet and was concerned that all of his cavalry had not arrived. He complained that, if Grant had not detained Gen. Cuvier Grover's infantry division in Washington, Sheridan could have used them to escort the supply train. Grant had by now approved sending Grover to Sheridan, but it was too late for this situation. Sheridan felt uneasy that Kenly's brigade was "very small" and reported that he had sent an infantry brigade back to Winchester to bolster the escort for the march from there to Cedar Creek.[10]

Early that morning McGonnigle had galloped into Harpers Ferry and arrived at the post quartermaster's office. He gave Sheridan's written order to Kenly to an orderly and directed him to deliver it to Kenly at Halltown. It placed Kenly in entire control, directing that he would be held responsible for the safety of the wagon train, and it gave the order of march and emphasized that he was to reach Winchester that evening. Normally McGonnigle would have been finished, but there was such a rush and so great a fear of displeasing Sheridan that on his own authority he wrote an order appointing Capt. James C. Mann, assistant quartermaster of the 1st Division, 19th Corps, in charge of preparing the wagons for departure "at once." This order made no mention of Emory's artillery. Without notifying Kenly that he had appointed Mann, McGonnigle went to bed, leaving word with the post quartermaster's office that he must not be disturbed, except by Mann once the wagons were ready.[11]

Mann began rounding up assistant quartermasters, commissary officers, teamsters, and wagon masters; soon the parking ground on Bolivar Heights became a scene of great confusion as men scrambled to harness and hitch up. The drivers of the Cavalry Reserve Brigade were inexperienced and the mules new to harness. Several of the cavalry forage wagons were empty, and forage had to be acquired and loaded.[12]

It was 9:40 A.M. when Kenly received Sheridan's order in Halltown. He was a respected lawyer and lifelong resident of Baltimore, a hero of the Mexican War. He had been severely wounded and captured in the battle of Front Royal on May 23, 1862, and had commanded a division in the Bristoe Station campaign in the fall of 1863. His brigade included 581 men in the 3rd Maryland Potomac Home Brigade and 350 men of the 144th and 149th Ohio militia. These foot soldiers were joined by a small detachment of cavalry escorting the army paymaster Maj. Nathaniel C. Sawyer and $112,000.[13]

He immediately called a meeting of his staff and, while the troops were being called out, sent his aide, Lt. John Huidekoper, to Bolivar Heights to "hurry out the trains and bring up the battery." Kenly had seen the parked wagons the day before but was "totally ignorant" of the number of wagons. He organized the escort and waited with them at Halltown. Finally, at 11:00 A.M. the first wagon appeared, followed by eight more during the next hour. He held these nine, waiting for others, and at 1:00 P.M. Huidekoper returned and said that everything was confused in Bolivar Heights: the wagon masters of the trains of the separate corps refused to listen to him, insisting that they already had their orders from someone, but they would not tell him who. He asked to see McGonnigle but was told that he could not be disturbed. He asked around for the artillery battery, but nobody could tell him anything about it. Rather than going into Bolivar Heights himself, Kenly assumed that whoever was issuing orders must have notified the artillery battery and continued waiting.[14]

At one-thirty several more wagons came, and he started the lead wagons south out of Halltown. He rode down the road about 1.5 miles and watched as the convoy passed. By three o'clock only a few more had arrived, and they were coming slowly, with gaps between. Therefore, he sent a lieutenant forward to stop the lead wagons before they reached Charlestown. At that point Capt. John K. Russell, assistant quartermaster of the 6th Corps, rode up and said the wagons were coming awfully slow. Kenly agreed and said there must be some problem, but neither of them knew who was in charge. Russell pointed out that he was the senior quartermaster with the train; and in a rare moment of decisive action, Kenly appointed him, and Russell sprang on his horse and galloped back to Bolivar Heights. Twenty minutes later Mann appeared and identified himself as the man in charge and showed him McGonnigle's order. Finally, at 3:20 P.M. Kenly was meeting the man who had been organizing the convoy since morning. He dispatched Mann to rush the wagons and sent countermanding orders to Russell notifying him that he was to cooperate with Mann. At 4:15 Kenly received a note from Mann that the rear of the train was ready—he left seventeen forage wagons behind, unable to find forage to load them; and, since he knew nothing about Emory's artillery, he had not notified their commander.[15]

The harness creaked and the drivers shouted and the white-topped wagons moved up the Valley, but Kenly was leading one of the most vulnerable supply expeditions in military history. Sheridan had placed Kenly in command, but McGonnigle appointed Mann in charge of organizing the wagons, without telling Kenly. As far as Kenly had known when the day began, he was in total command of everything. Instead of going into Bolivar Heights himself to start the train, he sent Lieutenant Huidekoper, and the wagon masters gave him the brush-off, telling him they already had instructions. When the expedition was still stalled at 1:00 P.M. and Huidekoper returned with his report, Kenly learned that some unidentified man other than Huidekoper was organizing the march and everything was frightfully confused, but he still did not go into the staging ground. Huidekoper had been unable to find the artillery unit, but Kenly assumed the unidentified man would notify them. Still ignorant of who was in charge, at about three o'clock he appointed Russell and for about twenty minutes the expedition had three commanders: Kenly, Mann, and Russell. The general soon straightened that out, but the command confusion and his hesitancy caused time to be wasted and resulted in inadequate protection. Sheridan ordered the bringing of the artillery to strengthen the escort—Napoleon required one cannon for every 120 wagons, and Kenly had directed that, if the battery reported for duty, the guns would be interspersed along the convoy in four sections.[16]

The train of more than five hundred wagons was strung out three and one-half miles when it started, and by the time the lead wagon reached the watering stop at Buck Marsh Creek one mile north of Berryville at 10:00 P.M., it was extended to five miles, with a significant gap of three miles, or one and one-half hour, between the wagons of the infantry in front and the cavalry in the rear. It took two and a half hours for the train to pass a given point on the road. At Berryville Kenly ordered the lead section to halt, park, and water the mules. The advance guard of two companies of infantry sat down in the road two hundred yards to the front, with twenty men thrown forward a few yards. They had walked fifteen miles, and soon they went to sleep. Kenly noticed a few mounted men passing through the camp and asked who they were. The strangers replied that they belonged to the Signal Corps, and he posted them as videttes.[17]

Kenly should have remained at Berryville until all of the wagons arrived and were ready to proceed, but at 11:30 P.M. he had the men awakened and ordered to start the wagons. Before he left he ordered Mann to remain until the last wagon had passed. "I consider this the most dangerous point in the route," he said. The cavalry corps train did not arrive until after all of the infantry wagons and their escort had left. Now they parked their wagons, watered their mules, and fell asleep, protected by the Ohio infantry, who also slept. By about 6:00 A.M., thirty minutes after sunrise, Kenly was approaching Winchester, eight miles beyond Berryville, while at Berryville Mann had begun waking up the officers and men of the cavalry wagons. The first wagons were pulling out, and some were crossing the creek. The drivers of the Cavalry Reserve Brigade in the rear were hitching the wheel mules and harnessing the swing and lead mules, but the rear guards were still asleep, with no pickets out. Suddenly, a cannon boomed, and an artillery shell came out of the fog and exploded on one of the wagons in the road. The drivers mounted their saddle mules and fled.[18]

Two days before, on August 11, Mosby's scout Russell had reported that Sheridan's army had passed through Berryville, and Mosby recognized this as an opportune time to raid Sheridan's rear. On August 12, when Kenly was organizing the convoy, Mosby met with about 250 men, and they marched with two howitzers through Snicker's Gap and crossed the Shenandoah River. Soon after dark they halted a few miles beyond the river and bivouacked at the barn of a supporter. Mosby sent Russell and two or three others to scout and went to sleep. In the middle of the night, Russell returned and awakened Mosby with word that a large wagon train was passing through Berryville. "Saddle up, Munson," Mosby said to John Munson, "and come along with me." Mosby, Munson, Russell, and a few others mounted and rode forward. When they arrived at Buck Marsh Creek Kenly's section had left, and they found Mann's section watering mules and resting. They rode among the guards and drivers asking questions and chatting in a friendly manner. Munson filled his pipe with tobacco and lit it with a Union cavalryman's match. They scouted carefully, but the vulnerability of the convoy was obvious, and Mosby sent Munson to bring the battalion.[19]

At about dawn Mosby posted the cannon on a hill about two hundred yards south of the creek. Shortly after 6:00, when it fired its third shot, that was the signal to charge. The men rushed from the slope in their characteristic horse-race attack, screaming and firing their revolvers. It was a scene of wild confusion as teams of mules ran wildly about, crashing their wagons into trees or other wagons, and running away with their harness clanging. The Union infantry guards fled into the woods southwest toward Berryville and formed in line behind a stone fence and houses on the edge of town. Mosby's men charged and routed them and another party that had retreated into a brick church. The raiders killed 6 Union men, wounded 9, and captured 200; they looted and burned 40 to 42 wagons and seized 420 mules, 200 cattle, and 36 horses. Mosby had two dead and three wounded. A few days later Mosby read in a Northern newspaper that he had overlooked the paymaster's cash in one of the burned wagons. He dropped the paper and exclaimed, "There's a cool million gone after it was fairly earned! What other man could sustain such losses with so little embarrassment?"[20]

The first thing Sheridan did when the raid was reported to him was to send a detachment of his headquarters cavalry to Berryville. He required that couriers have an armed escort of eight to ten cavalrymen, and he immediately detailed one of his best infantry brigades to the rear on permanent duty as wagon train guards. They were Leonard D.H. Currie's 3rd Brigade, 1st Division of Emory's Corps, and they numbered eighteen hundred men. Mosby's Wagon Raid diverted seven times Mosby's own number from Sheridan's fighting force, and Currie's brigade would remain in the rear guarding wagons during all three of Sheridan's battles in the campaign. This diversion was Mosby's most strategic contribution in the war.[21]

Another problem was dealing with the impact on morale and the embarrassment of the newspaper reports. During the morning of the day of the raid the rumor started in the army that the Rebels had burned 11 wagons, but by 7:00 P.M., when the wagon train arrived with food, the estimate had increased to 170. Later that evening Sheridan received Grant's letter informing him that he should go on the defensive because Early was being reinforced. He replied and concluded with, "Mosby attacked the rear of my train this morning, en route here from Harper's Ferry, and burned six wagons." It was too painful to admit that all but one of the wagons of the Cavalry Reserve Brigade were destroyed. Six days later the news had come to Halleck's attention, and he asked if it was true that the Rebels had burned seventy to eighty wagons and captured five hundred horses and mules. Sheridan replied correctly that it was about forty wagons and understated the loss in animals at two hundred mules.[22]

Northern newspapers reported the number of wagons lost from twenty to seventy-two and disclosed that the guards panicked, threw down their guns, and fled in all directions. And when Sheridan withdrew down the Valley back to Halltown because of Early's reinforced army, not because of Mosby or the guerrillas, the *New York Times* nonetheless named Mosby as one of the causes of Sheridan's retrograde movement. "The great openings in the mountain ridge at Thoroughfare and Snicker's Gap had to be closed before his rear could be considered safe. The presence of MOSBY's men in the counties east of the Blue Ridge, within an easy day's ride of the highway for our wagon trains, in the Shenandoah Valley, had been less an element in the calculations than it should have been." Sheridan exploded and ordered all war correspondents out of his department. A reporter responded that they had permits, and he told them to go to hell. "But, general," the man answered, "I believe that place is in your department too." Mosby had not caused Sheridan's retrograde movement, but he heightened Little Phil's embarrassment.[23]

In his report of the Wagon Raid, Sheridan told Halleck that the one-hundred-days men ran without fighting, but he did not blame anyone. Then after the raid made the newspapers, he ordered a board of inquiry, and it met for eight days over three months and reported on November 13, 1864, after Sheridan had won the campaign and had become one of the most popular generals in the Union army. Therefore the board dodged the bullet and named a scapegoat. They concluded that the guard was insufficient for the number of wagons, which was a criticism of Sheridan without naming him, and they blamed Capt. Edward P. McKinney, commissary of subsistence of the Cavalry Reserve Brigade, in charge of the rear wagons, for going into park and allowing the men to sleep, without orders. The only criticism of Kenly was that "no sufficient picket" was established at Berryville.[24]

Sheridan was to blame for the small, inefficient escort and for ordering the men to rush and reach Winchester by night. McGonnigle caused confusion by writing his own orders placing Mann in charge of organizing the train without notifying Kenly, and he slept while Mann and Kenly needed his help. Kenly's follow-up report charged that the officers in charge of the rear wagons were guilty of "neglect of duty and disobedience of orders," but he himself had neglected his duty in not going into Harpers Ferry and Bolivar Heights to use his authority to organize the train. He should not have started until the convoy was closed up, and when a gap developed he should have halted until it closed. At Berryville he should have kept the advance pickets alert, and he should have waited for all of the wagons.[25]

Grant seemed almost as upset as Sheridan when he received Sheridan's letter informing him of the loss of six wagons. Historian Mark E. Neely Jr. wrote in *The Fate of Liberty: Abraham Lincoln and Civil Liberties* that generally Grant's first reaction to a crisis tended toward excess, and then, when he cooled down, wisdom would overrule. That is what happened on August 16. Excess ruled as he wrote his first letter of reply; then two hours later wisdom took over, and he wrote a more mild message. In the first he wrote, "The families of most of Mosby's men are known, and can be collected. I think they should be taken and kept at Fort McHenry, or some secure place, as hostages for the good conduct of Mosby and his men. Where any of Mosby's men are caught hang them without trial." But Grant was very interested in conscription and by now any male Confederate between seventeen and fifty was subject to the draft and logically a Southern soldier; therefore, in the second letter he ordered Sheridan to arrest all males under fifty and hold them as prisoners of war. And, following his policy of destroying the economic support of the enemy and orders he had issued on August 5 to destroy food and forage in the Shenandoah Valley, he directed Sheridan to attack Mosby by freeing the slaves and destroying and confiscating the crops and livestock of his civilian supporters.[26]

Sheridan received the first message on August 17 in Berryville and replied, "Mosby has annoyed me and captured a few wagons. We hung one and shot six of his men yesterday." Sheridan's initial reaction had paralleled Grant's, and he began the killing the day before he received Grant's first order. On August 19 he wrote Grant, "Guerrillas give me great annoyance, but I am quietly disposing of numbers of them." On August 22 he reported, "We have disposed of quite a number of Mosby's men." After that Sheridan still made references to exterminating Mosby's gang, but apparently he discontinued the practice of killing prisoners.[27]

Mosby was shocked when he read these reports in the *Official Records* after the war. He accused Sheridan of murder and compared him to Jack the Ripper and the Master of Stair who conducted the treacherous massacre of Glencoe in Scotland in the seventeenth century. Yet, he was puzzled because none of his men captured in the Valley had disappeared; he had seen them come home at the end of the war. At times he believed that the killings were only Sheridan's "spectres of imagination," and at other times he thought the men killed were prisoners from Early's army. The victims were probably men from some of the other partisan bands or, as Mosby wrote, regular Confederate troops.[28]

Sheridan's killings remained secret until years later, but soon the violence broke out in the ranks and escalated out of control. On the night of August 18, five days after the Wagon Raid, Sheridan was in Charlestown on the retrograde and had Custer's cavalry covering his right rear at Berryville. Mosby raided in three separate parties: he and Richards led separate attacks near Charlestown, and William Chapman took about 150 men to try Custer's Wolverines. Chapman concealed his men in the woods near the Shenandoah River and was scouting after dark with another man when they attempted to capture a lone vidette of the 5th Michigan Cavalry. The plan was to surround the man, front and back, but Chapman's comrade was delayed. When Chapman demanded the man's surrender, he fired, and Chapman returned fire and killed him. None of the man's fellow troopers saw the shooting. When they found his body they assumed he had been bushwhacked.[29]

Custer cared deeply for the men of his Michigan Brigade and refrained from exposing them needlessly; they knew that he would lead them effectively, selecting to fight when they could win. He was proud of their skill with the saber charge, and they took pride in him. "With Custer as a leader we are all heroes and hankering for a fight," a man wrote in his diary. Custer regarded Mosby's men as bushwhackers, beyond the pale of legitimate warfare, and his answer, like Hunter's, was to burn the homes of civilians. On August 19, the morning after the killing, he ordered Col. Russell A. Alger, commander of the 5th Michigan Cavalry, to send men to burn the houses of five prominent citizens near the site. Alger assigned Capt. George Drake and fifty men.[30]

A light rain was falling that afternoon, and Chapman and his raiders were still in the area when at about 2:00 P.M. they saw above the trees a column of heavy smoke rising in the sky toward Berryville. Riding to investigate they came to a house fully ablaze, but they rode on toward the next farm where the flames had burned into the attic of the house and the roof was collapsing. The women and children were standing in the yard in the rain, and a woman said, "We are rebels still if we are burned out of house and home." She pointed toward Benjamin Morgan's farm, and there were Drake's men, surrounding the house and outbuildings, setting them on fire. "No quarter! No quarter today!" shouted the raiders, and dashed on toward Morgan's.[31]

Chapman outnumbered the enemy about three to one, but Custer's men saw them coming and formed in line, holding their fire until the Rebels were within forty yards. Chapman's men charged the center of the line; the Union men were thrown into confusion, and most retreated along the stone-fenced lane leading to the road. A few escaped, but about twenty-five were trapped in a fence corner and surrendered. Mosby's men carried out his previous orders that no prisoners were to be taken among house burners—they shot all of the Union soldiers and rode away, leaving their bodies on the ground. "About 30 horses were brought off, but no prisoners," Mosby reported. "MOSBY has practically raised the black flag," declared the New York Times.[32]

Sheridan did not approve the house burning, but Custer had not consulted with him. When he heard the news he had just the night before received Grant's second message recommending the more moderate procedure of dealing with Mosby. He welcomed the opportunity to use it now. Hopefully it would avoid further atrocities. He sent a copy of the Grant letter to Augur and countermanded his previous instructions to the 8th Illinois Cavalry to "exterminate" Mosby's men; now they were to arrest adult males and destroy crops and livestock but not burn dwellings. He issued a circular to his army ordering the arrest of all able-bodied males under fifty suspected of aiding the guerrillas. He sent a cavalry force to search the Berryville area, and they arrested twenty wagon-loads of males aged sixteen to sixty and escorted them to Charlestown. He set aside Capt. Richard Blazer's company of guerrilla fighters to hunt Mosby, increased courier escorts to fifteen enlisted cavalrymen and one officer, and directed that any soldier who went outside the camp unarmed would be arrested.[33]

While Sheridan concentrated at Halltown with no lines of communication, Mosby's men raided the pickets in Fairfax County. Then, on September 3, the very day that Sheridan's army moved south to Berryville again, the Rangers returned, raiding in three parties. They observed that the supply trains were securely defended, but the next day Mosby and five men captured an ambulance and thirteen horses from an unguarded train of thirty-five ambulances moving south a few miles from Charlestown. Northern newspapers reported that they took the entire train and ridiculed Sheridan for not securing his line of communication. The *Baltimore American* condemned the "negligence" of sending the train without escort through an area infested with a "herd of marauders" and chuckled at Sheridan for providing the guerrillas arms, horses, and mules, and now ambulances for their wounded.[34]

By September 13 the battalion had grown to three hundred men in six companies, and Mosby divided them and sent them in different directions. He went with a few men to Fairfax County and that night entered the camp of the 13th New York Cavalry near Falls Church and captured the regimental butcher in bed. Gansevoort and the regiment were gone toward Aldie searching for Mosby. Gansevoort had learned from Lowell that one of the keys to locating Mosby's men was the use of civilian informers. The next morning he and his men were returning on the Little River Turnpike east of Chantilly when his scouts learned from civilians that Mosby and two men had just passed through Fairfax Court House and turned toward Centreville. This was unusually timely and accurate intelligence. Gansevoort sent five mounted men, armed with revolvers, to intercept them.[35]

They met on the road east of Centreville and, within a few yards of each other, drew their revolvers and fired. Three of the New Yorkers quickly turned and fled, and the three Rebels also wheeled and galloped off in the opposite direction, pretending to retreat. The remaining two Union men followed in close pursuit, exchanging shots with the prey for about a mile. Then, suddenly, Mosby and his men halted and turned on their pursuers, firing in close, Mosby shooting rapidly with a revolver in each hand. A bullet shattered the handle of one of Mosby's pistols, and both of the Union horses fell dead in the road, almost side by side. One of the New Yorkers, scout Henry Smith, was lying in the road with his legs fastened under the body of his horse. With one charge left in his revolver, he rested his arm on the horse, took careful aim, and shot Mosby. The bullet entered his left groin, and he threw up both hands in pain and galloped away.[36]

The bullet was too near an artery for surgery, and he carried it the rest of his life. His men took him to the house of an elderly woman, and she assisted in dressing the wound. Less than three weeks later, having convalesced at his mother's and returned to duty on crutches,[37] Mosby stopped at the same house for information. From her window the woman asked who it was.

"It's Colonel Mosby; don't you remember me?"

"Oh no it aint? Colonel Mosby was here ten days ago badly wounded. I wouldn't believe you unless I saw the wound."

"You're as bad as Thomas who doubted his Lord, but I can't stop now to show you my wound," said Mosby.[38]

Meanwhile, fear spread and became general that the black flag was out and if you were captured you would be hanged or shot. The Morgan's Lane killings had unleashed, as Mosby said, "the bloody Molock of revenge," in reference to the god of the Ammonites to whom children were sacrificed. Custer's superior, lst Cavalry Division commander Gen. Wesley Merritt, was a West Point graduate from Illinois, a popular and intelligent young man. The day after the massacre he directed one of his brigade commanders to "stir up and kill as many of the bushwhackers as possible who are between you and the river." After the war he accused Mosby's men of cold-blooded murder and "wanton acts of cruelty." That night Merritt's superior, Cavalry Corps Commander Gen. Alfred T.A. Torbert, sent the lst Rhode Island Cavalry on a scout with orders "to bring in no Prisoners."[39]

Newspapers fanned the flames with violent rhetoric. "Massacre By Mosby—Rebel Treachery—Cowardly Cruelty," ran the *New York Times* headline on the story of Morgan's Lane. The account accused Mosby's men of surrendering to blood lust by firing repeatedly into the dead and dying on the ground, filling them with bullets and buckshot, and cutting two of the men's throats. A later *New York Times* story declared, on the other hand, that the thirty victims were not shot in the heat of battle but were all hanged—"Mosby Hanging Union Soldiers," was the headline. Many soldiers in Sheridan's Army of the Shenandoah agreed with the journalists that Mosby's men were a gang of robbers, murderers, and cutthroats who should be exterminated.[40]

These feelings came out in the open in Front Royal on the morning of September 23, 1864, when Torbert's cavalry killed six Mosby prisoners in retaliation for the mortal wounding of Union lieutenant Charles McMaster. Four men were shot and two were hanged, with a placard left on one of the hanged bodies: "Such is the fate of Mosby's men."[41] The placard was a black flag, a declaration that Torbert's cavalry meant to hang future prisoners from Mosby's command. That morning Torbert was retreating north down the Luray Valley, having been repulsed the day before by a Confederate cavalry force at Milford. Four days before, Sheridan had defeated Early at Winchester and, preparing to attack him again at Fisher's Hill, had given Torbert the assignment of taking a cavalry force south through Milford to New Market Gap to cut off Early's army if Early attempted to retreat. Torbert did not know that Sheridan had won again at Fisher's Hill the day before, and he was not aware that Early was pushing south beyond New Market with a clear path up the Valley, since Torbert was not in place. He would have been in an even worse frame of mind if he had known and if he had foreseen that Sheridan would never forgive him. But things looked dim enough; he had been turned back and was moving from the front in frustration.[42]

Torbert was young, handsome, and dapper—at thirty-one years of age he was six feet tall, always beautifully mounted and sharply dressed, with fancy Russian-style whiskers. Born in Georgetown, Delaware, he was a professional soldier, a graduate of West Point, and an infantry commander before Sheridan made him a cavalry man, and chief of cavalry. On this morning he was leading two brigades of Merritt's division: Custer's and the Reserve Brigade under Lowell, who had been finally transferred from the Fairfax screen. Torbert was not expecting an attack—the enemy army was behind, across the mountains—and at the head of the column he had a lightly guarded ambulance train of wounded men from the Milford skirmish. They marched along the Luray Road, heading toward Front Royal on the way to Cedarville in Sheridan's rear. The ambulances were followed by Lowell's brigade, then Custer's.[43]

Shortly after daylight when the ambulances neared town, a detachment of 120 of Mosby's men under Sam Chapman charged. Sam had scouted, but he had only seen the ambulance train; he had no idea that two brigades of cavalry were right behind. As soon as his assault began, he recognized his mistake and pulled away, retreating at full speed southeastward toward Chester's Gap. Union lieutenant Charles McMaster, 2nd United States Cavalry, in command of the escort of the ambulances, anticipated the move and raced along a side road with a small squad, arriving on Chester Road in the pathway of escape for the Rebels. What happened next was a matter of disagreement. Chapman's men claimed that McMaster stood dismounted in the road waving his saber in defiance, and they shot him and could not help but ride over him lying in the road. His comrades gathered him up, and he said that he surrendered and the Rebels robbed him and shot him as a prisoner of war. He was a popular young man—about twenty-seven years old, a native of Belfast, Ireland, and his version spread quickly through the Union column; some said that he was shot with his own pistol. Tee Edmonds, Mosby's friend from Fauquier County, wrote in her diary that he had surrendered and was pleading for his life when the Rebels shot him and ran over him. He was not expected to live and died within the next few months.[44]

The Federals retaliated on all of the prisoners they captured. Spontaneously, a group of Union soldiers stood Thomas E. Anderson under a tree near where he was captured south of town and shot him. A different group took Lucian Love and David L. Jones into the graveyard behind the Methodist church on the southern edge of town and shot them. Others took William T. Overby and a man named Carter to Torbert. "Take those men up to that tree and hang them," he said to Capt. Theodore W. Bean, provost marshal. Bean was in charge, but men from McMaster's regiment hanged the two men side by side on a walnut tree on a hill by the road to Cedarville about one mile north of the courthouse before a large crowd of taunting soldiers.[45]

Last was Henry C. Rhodes, a seventeen-year-old Front Royal resident who had borrowed a neighbor's horse to join Chapman's raid, hoping to acquire a horse of his own. During the retreat the horse broke down, and he was running on foot along Happy Creek when some of Custer's men captured him. They tied his arms to the rear straps of the saddles of two mounted men, who began pulling him along between them, walking their horses at a fast pace, almost faster than he could run. They went north on Chester Street through the center of town. Rhodes's mother ran out at one point and clasped her arms around his neck, but they halted and pulled her aside. They turned into an open field northeast of town near today's baseball field. A large crowd of soldiers gathered, many of them Custer's, and Custer's brigade band struck up "Love Not, The One You Love May Die," and the crowd marched in a circle around their victim. One soldier volunteered to kill him and emptied his pistol in Rhodes, and they left him dead in the field. A citizen picked him up and placed him in a wheelbarrow; someone threw a sheet over him, and they delivered him to his mother.[46]

Torbert ordered the hangings, and nobody ordered the four

shootings. However, camp talk in Sheridan's army attributed all six to "the incensed comrades of the men of CUSTER's brigade who had similarly suffered a few days previously," and years after the war many still blamed Custer. The residents of Front Royal and Mosby and his men firmly believed that Custer ordered all six killings. It was Custer who ordered the house burnings, and it was his men shot on Morgan's farm; it seemed reasonable that he was now retaliating. Custer and his staff marched through the center of town just before the hangings, halted at the hanging site, and were present on the hill during the hangings. Custer was the most flamboyant officer in the Union army, and seeing him was like watching a circus act. Beautifully mounted, he wore a black velvet uniform trimmed in gold lace and an immensely broad-brimmed black felt hat; his long blonde curls bounced on his shoulders, and the ends of his long red necktie streamed along behind his shoulders. He was the most colorful officer in town and probably the only commander present at the hanging. His Wolverines were easily distinguishable as well, with their bright scarlet neckties. There were many witnesses to Rhodes's capture, dragging, and killing; and it was completely obvious that the men involved wore beautiful neckties of red. There is no record that Custer ever publicly responded to the charge; but in the 1870s, during the construction of the Northern Pacific Railroad, former Confederate general Rosser asked him about it, and Rosser declared that Custer "often stated that he was in no way responsible for the execution or murder of those men."[47]

In Sheridan's first seven weeks in the Shenandoah Valley, Mosby had penetrated his mind. He was embarrassed that the Wagon Raid took advantage of his mistake and hated it that Mosby caused him to divert valuable men from the fighting. But after an initial extreme reaction he controlled himself. Then, beyond his control, the clash of Mosby's men and Custer's troops broke into bloody retaliation. Mosby and his men refused to adjust their tactics or mitigate the effects of their raiding. They continued treating captured prisoners who were not house-burners with dignity and kindness. But the specter of retaliation hung in the background, and Mosby knew that he had to somehow force the Union officers and men to put away the black flag; he would eventually have to retaliate for the Front Royal killings with similar acts of inhumanity.

# 14

# The Lottery

Vehement rhetoric and inhumane acts continued in the Shenandoah Valley into November 1864, and eventually Mosby retaliated for the Front Royal killings; but in the meantime Union forces reopened the Manassas Gap Railroad through Mosby's Confederacy. He interdicted the railroad, diverting cavalry from the picket line on the Potomac River and opening the way for a raid on the Chesapeake and Ohio Canal and the B&O Railroad. Mosby's attacks annoyed Sheridan, but as long as Early's army threatened he focused on it, waiting to operate against Mosby's civilian supporters.

Mosby was recovering from his September 14 wound when he hobbled on crutches into Lee's headquarters near Petersburg for a meeting. Lee stood and walked toward him, extending his hand: "Colonel," he said, "I have never had but one fault to find with you—you are always getting wounded." On the return trip to his mother's house, he learned about the Front Royal hangings; and, even though he was not recovered and had to be lifted onto his horse, on September 29 he returned to duty.[1]

By then Sheridan's supply line extended over one hundred miles into the upper Valley, and Mosby was preparing a raid when scouts reported construction on the MGR. Before the war the rail line had extended from Manassas Junction on the O&A, westward into Fauquier County and through Manassas Gap into the Valley, seventy-seven miles, from Manassas Junction to Mount Jackson. It had been used by the Confederate army to transfer men from the Valley to Manassas for the battle of First Bull Run. But when the Confederate army withdrew south in March 1862, the troops burned the trestles on the South and North Forks of the Shenandoah River, and they were never rebuilt during the war. It had been partially restored by the Union for four brief periods but had been abandoned for fourteen months, since Meade's army used it for supplies after the Gettysburg campaign in the summer of 1863.[2]

Mosby claimed after the war that his operations against the reopening of the railroad and in the Valley at the time were his most strategic contributions in the war. He asserted that his men prevented Sheridan from conquering Richmond and preserved the Confederacy for six months. These claims should be evaluated in light of the decisions made by Sheridan and the Union high command regarding the railroad. To begin with, Sheridan did not request the project. He had viewed his Valley campaign from the start as a raid against Early's army and its civilian supporters; and, now that he had defeated and driven Early out of the Valley, he wanted to finish burning the crops and barns in the upper Valley as Grant ordered and withdraw toward Winchester, sending his infantry to reinforce Grant. He never planned to cross the Blue Ridge Mountains to capture Charlottesville as Grant suggested; Sheridan knew that "a line of communication from 135 to 145 miles in length" was untenable.[3]

But before Sheridan could communicate his decision—it took two or three days for messages to reach Washington and two or three to receive a reply—he learned on October 1 that Grant still expected him to push forward to Charlottesville and therefore had ordered the opening of the O&A through Culpeper; but if Sheridan decided to withdraw down the Valley, the O&A would be re-built only to Manassas Junction and the MGR opened for his supply line.[4]

Sheridan replied that he was not going to Charlottesville and therefore did not need the O&A, and he attempted to discourage the rebuilding of the MGR by estimating that, given the threat of Mosby's guerrillas, it would take a corps of infantry to defend the O&A and another corps to defend the MGR. This was a great exaggeration, but he was attempting to discourage the idea; opening railroads implied extended operations, and his plan was to terminate the campaign. Before receiving this message from Sheridan, Grant had responded to a letter from Sheridan a few days earlier, before he had fully stated his plans, in which Sheridan indicated that he would withdraw to near Front Royal. Assuming that Sheridan would cancel the advance on Charlottesville but would need the MGR for supplies in Front Royal, on October 2 Grant ordered work stopped on the O&A south of Manassas Junction and the crew transferred to the MGR. Then, when Stanton and Halleck learned that Sheridan did not plan to operate out of Front Royal but wanted to terminate the campaign and send his men to Petersburg, they suggested that, even though the MGR would not be needed for supply, it could be used to transfer Sheridan's men to Alexandria for water transportation to Grant. Without consulting Sheridan, Grant agreed. Thus, without Sheridan's approval the MGR was to be restored.[5]

On October 3 the construction crew, under Col. George S. Gallupe, guarded by about two thousand infantry and forty-three cavalry serving as couriers, transferred to the MGR and began replacing cross-ties and fastening rails. Mosby scouted for two days, waiting for the work to advance and extend the guards along several miles of track. When the crew and its two construction trains reached Rectortown, thirty miles from Manassas Junction, and the guards were spread ten miles from Rectortown back to Gallupe's main camp at The Plains, Mosby recognized that it was time to strike. He attacked at Salem, midway between The Plains and Rectortown, separating the trains and construction crew from Gallupe's headquarters.[6]

Mosby placed two cannon on a hill south of Salem overlooking the camp of the battalion of a few hundred of Gallupe's infantry, and at 3:00 P.M., October 5, opened fire with the artillery and sent sharpshooters forward, supported by the remainder of his two hundred raiders. The Union men fled from their tents, fleeing toward Rectortown. Mosby captured about fifty prisoners and seized the railroad, cutting off about a thousand men forward from that point. His men looted the camp and ripped up several yards of track.[7]

Gallupe was unaware of the attack until the next morning when he came to Salem with a locomotive and a few cars, moving his headquarters to Rectortown and delivering building supplies to the construction team. Suddenly, cannon fired from a hill overlooking the track, and two shots came through the air, barely missing the smokestack of the locomotive. Gallupe withdrew and soon returned with two hundred infantry. He halted and, immediately in front of the train, formed the men in battle line across the track, bayonets gleaming in the sun. Mosby's cannon opened fire again, and Gallupe's bluecoats hastily reboarded and retreated to The Plains. With this detachment and the men he left behind, Gallupe had eight hundred infantry in The Plains and could have easily retaken the railroad, but instead he ordered his men to entrench. He sent all of the trains still under his control back to Manassas Junction for safety and telegraphed Washington that he was cut off and needed reinforcements. "Hear artillery firing, supposed to be between Salem and

Rectortown, a distance of eight or ten miles. It is absolutely necessary that I have at least a section of artillery, in order to dispossess the enemy," he wired. Mosby had moved to Rectortown and was shelling the construction crew, which had fled with the trains into a deep railroad cut for natural protection.[8]

Augur received the alarm in Washington at 5:20 P.M. and went into action. A veteran of the Mexican War and frontier Indian fighter, he prepared immediately to go to the scene to take charge. He ordered every cavalryman who could be spared from the cavalry screen to move without delay, and 1,875 men responded. Then he took a special train through the night, arriving at The Plains at seven o'clock the next morning, October 7. He sent Gallupe's infantry forward, and they easily reoccupied Salem and, ignoring Mosby's harassment, reestablished communication with the workers and guards in Rectortown. The railroad reopened by 9:50 A.M., October 8, and Augur remained at Rectortown until Sheridan ordered him to close the road and take up the track a few weeks later. Mosby had delayed construction for two days, but, with Augur's cavalry arriving, he sent his artillery to the top of Little Cobbler Mountain and divided his command into three detachments for raiding mostly elsewhere. With the enemy present in force it was time to avoid the railroad. By October 10 the rebuilding was complete to Piedmont, the farthest it would extend.[9]

One of Mosby's detachments made one other significant raid on the railroad. On the morning of October 10 near The Plains, Alfred Glascock and a few men loosened a rail and attached a wire. Concealing themselves in the heavy undergrowth near the track, they heard a train coming and pulled the rail loose. The train was an eastbound doubleheader, using two engines to make up for the loss of traction from grass on the track. It ran down an embankment with a crash, killing four crew members and mortally wounding M.J. McCrickett, military superintendent of the railroad. McCrickett's death made headlines and compelled Stanton to order counterguerrilla measures.[10]

Augur decided to erect stockades "to command the entire track" and proposed the use of civilian hostages on the trains. A few days later authorities in Alexandria arrested about twenty prominent civilians and incarcerated them in the slave pen and military courtrooms along with a few prisoners from Mosby's command. Two trains ran each day; beginning on October 17, each had seven male civilians and three of Mosby's men riding in a boxcar behind the engine. Northern newspapers applauded—the *Washington Star* having recommended the year before that Southern civilians be tied to the cowcatcher of each locomotive. On one trip a guard's rifle accidentally fired, mortally wounding Fauquier County's Jamieson Ashby, venerable uncle of Turner Ashby. The program was pronounced a success, but Mosby had previously discontinued operations against the railroad.[11]

Secretary of War Stanton decreed that McCrickett was murdered and ordered fire-and-sword destruction within five miles on each side of the track. Houses were to be burned, livestock seized, and residents relocated to the north or south. He had notices printed that hereafter persons found within five miles of the track would be shot on sight as "robbers and bushwhackers," and if the depredations continued, he threatened to extend the five miles to ten. Officers in the field ignored the orders, but the Quartermaster Department took laborers from Washington to Manassas Junction and cleared and burned trees and undergrowth within one-half mile of the MGR on each side for ten miles. As with the use of hostages, this program had no impact either, other than to satisfy Stanton's need to do something.[12]

Sheridan had not proposed the opening of the railroad, but, when he returned from the upper Valley and began planning to send his infantry to Grant, on October 10 he wrote to Halleck, reporting that the 6th Corps would soon reach Front Royal and requesting that if the railroad was finished to that point he needed cars for ten thousand men. The next day, October 11, he wrote that he had decided instead to hold the 6th Corps for another couple of days and that, instead of breaking up their organization for the train trip, he preferred sending them through Ashby's Gap to Alexandria. He ordered Augur to stop construction at Piedmont and withdraw to Manassas Junction.[13]

Mosby said in an 1898 interview: "If Augur had succeeded in rebuilding the road in a few days, as intended, Sheridan and Grant would have overcome Lee, and Richmond would have fallen early in October, 1864, instead of April, 1865. Thus my 300 men prolonged the war at least six months." He asserted that he not only "neutralized" Augur's work crew and guards but also "Sheridan's army of 60,000." But if Mosby's men had not existed and there had been no interruption of construction, the MGR still probably would not have reached Front Royal by October 11. The construction superintendent estimated that it would take eight days to build the trestles required on the last sixteen miles from Piedmont to Front Royal. If his estimate proved correct, without

Mosby's two- or three-day interruption, construction would have reached Front Royal about October 16, well past Sheridan's decision not to use it. Even so, there is no evidence that Sheridan's decision on October 11 to hold the 6th Corps for another couple of days related to the railroad. Instead, Sheridan was worried about Early's army.[14]

Two days later, on October 13, Sheridan's caution proved well founded when Early's army reappeared. Therefore, Sheridan canceled the march of the 6th Corps to Alexandria and directed Augur to resume construction. Sheridan wanted the railroad kept open for supply now that it was uncertain how long he would have to continue campaigning against Early. As soon as Sheridan defeated Early at the battle of Cedar Creek on October 19, he ordered the railroad closed and its rails taken up for use in rebuilding the Winchester and Potomac Railroad in the lower Valley. There is no evidence that he considered the MGR unsafe. On October 16 he traveled on it himself from Rectortown to Washington for his conference with Halleck and Stanton.[15]

Roy Morris Jr., in *Sheridan: The Life and Wars of General Phil Sheridan,* wrote: "Mosby was a remarkably daring and resourceful ranger, but he was just a ranger, and, as such, was tangential to the larger strategic picture." This was true, and it was the proper role of a guerrilla. Sheridan never seriously planned advancing on Richmond, and his strategic decisions were based on the movements of Early's army, not the reality or threat of guerrilla attacks. Mosby's thesis was based on the premise that the MGR was critical in Sheridan's strategic decision-making, but it never was.[16]

Mosby's strategic contribution was diverting manpower from Sheridan's army to guard his communications. Little Phil preferred keeping the entire rear guard as lean as his defense of the B&O. "There is no interest suffering here except the Baltimore and Ohio Railroad," he wrote Grant early in the campaign, "and I will not divide my forces to protect it." But during the battle of Fisher's Hill, September 22, 1864, he had fifty-four hundred men in the rear guarding communications. The night before the battle, regretting that Col. Oliver Edwards's infantry brigade was in the rear at Winchester, he ordered five thousand reserve troops to be rounded up in Washington and sent as a Provisional Division to guard the rear and free his fighting men for the front. These reinforcements soon arrived, but at the battle of Cedar Creek on October 19, he had sixty-one hundred men guarding his wagons and communication lines, with Edwards's brigade still at Winchester. As previously mentioned,

Mosby's most strategic achievement was the diversion of Currie's brigade from all three of Sheridan's battles.[17]

Mosby's activity against the MGR did not save Richmond, but it forced Augur to strip bare his cavalry screen and opened the door for Mosby to raid the B&O in Maryland and create embarrassing headlines for Sheridan when he reached Washington on the morning of October 17. The October 14 Maryland raid occurred simultaneously with the Greenback Raid on the B&O in West Virginia, and this made it seem that Sheridan was negligent in defending the Union lifeline to the west. The idea for the Greenback Raid began when Mosby's scouts reported an eight-mile gap in the B&O picket line beginning one mile west of Harpers Ferry and extending through the favorite target area for Confederate guerrillas at Duffield's Station. Confederate lieutenant colonel Vincent A. Witcher had conducted a cavalry raid to Buckhannon, West Virginia, in September, and Halleck had ordered reinforcements sent from Harpers Ferry. The commander at Harpers Ferry, suffering from Sheridan's parsimonious assignments to the B&O, had transferred three hundred men of the 74th Pennsylvania Infantry guarding Duffield's Station to West Virginia, leaving the gap in the line.[18]

As in the Wagon Raid, Mosby took advantage of the enemy weakness. The absence of guards meant that with a small party and no cannon he could capture a train and give his men adequate time to plunder. With eighty-four men he went to Quincy's Siding, one mile west of Duffield's, and at 2:30 A.M. on October 14 derailed Locomotive No. 27 and eight cars, westbound with about two hundred passengers. The wreck ripped the smokestack off the locomotive and burst the boiler, scalding two crew members. At about the same location on February 11, 1864, Gilmor and twenty-five men had captured a westbound express and robbed the passengers without taking prisoners or burning the train. When Lee learned about it he was upset that no military object was achieved. He had Gilmor court-martialed for train robbing, but he was acquitted. Mosby allowed his men to rob the male passengers, but they burned the cars, killed a Union officer who drew his pistol, and captured fifteen prisoners on the ingress in the Valley and eleven on the train. Among the captives were two Union paymasters on their way to Sheridan's army with $173,000 in greenbacks. Lee reported to Seddon that Mosby destroyed a "U.S. military train."[19]

On the same day William Chapman and eighty men took advantage of a second hole in Sheridan's picket line, a twenty-five-mile gap along the Potomac from Great Falls to the Monocacy River. This vacancy developed when a battalion of cavalry left with the Provisional Division; a three-hundred-man detachment of the 8th Illinois Cavalry went to Port Tobacco, Maryland, to chase blockade-runners; and the remainder of the 8th Illinois went with Augur to protect the MGR. With no challenge Chapman crossed at White's Ford, burned five empty canal boats, and at Adamstown, Maryland, on the B&O cut the telegraph line and plundered two stores. No trains were running, as Mosby's raid early that morning had halted traffic. On the return to the Potomac the raiders skirmished with a party of the Loudoun Rangers, but, as with Mosby's party, Chapman had no casualties. Halleck ordered the paymasters in Martinsburg to return to Harpers Ferry, and Sheridan's army had to wait a few days for their pay.[20]

Canal boat companies were behind in stockpiling West Virginia coal in Washington for the winter because of Early's raids, and they were rushing to fill orders. Nevertheless, realizing that the canal was unprotected, Supt. George W. Spates declared, "Boating must stop unless a guard is placed on the canal" in the twenty-five-mile vacancy. Under headlines such as "Guerilla Raid on the Ohio and Chesapeake Canal" and "Rebel Raiders across the Potomac," war correspondents condemned the authorities for lack of vigilance. B&O executives suggested an investigation into why the guard was down.[21]

News of the two raids rivaled the Wagon Raid and Stoughton's capture in notoriety. The stories came at a low point for Southern morale, and this gave them greater impact in the South. Atlanta had fallen on September 1, and on September 4 John Hunt Morgan was killed. The Confederate cavalry lost at Tom's Brook on October 9, and on October 19 Early was defeated at Cedar Creek. In contrast, Southerners delighted in the knowledge that Mosby had struck the mighty B&O and delayed Sheridan's payday. Northern reporters inflated the amount of cash taken to four hundred thousand dollars and criticized Sheridan for failing to defend the railroad. The *Baltimore American* told of a woman passenger on the captured train who threw her arms around the neck of one of the raiders and said, "Oh my love, my dear man, you will not kill me." Pushing her away, he said, "Confound you, let me go, I will lose my part of the plunder with your stupidity."[22]

Meanwhile, on the same day as the two raids, Augur's cavalry captured Mosby's four artillery pieces. John Lunceford, eighteen years old, deserted from Mosby's command and informed Gansevoort that the cannon were on Little Cobbler Mountain only one mile south of Gansevoort's 13th New York Cavalry headquarters at Piedmont. In a night raid, Gansevoort's men climbed through the dense vines in the darkness and seized the guns. This was great news in the North and embarrassing for Mosby, but he had no further need for the pieces for the duration of the war. He had found his first brief use of artillery in 1863 to be a liability and in 1864 used cannon for about four months, from June to October. Since there had been no strong enemy force in the area and he had over two hundred men to safeguard the pieces, he used them effectively. Now, however, Augur's cavalry on the MGR and Sheridan's forces in the Valley made the guns a hindrance.[23]

Rumors still floated on both sides that the black flag was raised. Mosby's men loaded their pistols with care, purchased faster horses, and wondered how and when Mosby would respond to the Front Royal killings. Sheridan curbed his anger against guerrillas, losing restraint only once after discontinuing the executions in reaction to the Wagon Raid. This time it involved the killing of his chief engineer, Lt. John R. Meigs. Mosby's men were not involved, but the nature of the incident caused Sheridan to regard it as a guerrilla action. On October 3, during the burning of the upper Valley, Meigs and two assistants were conducting a survey near Dayton within Union lines and less than two miles from Sheridan's headquarters. It was raining, and they wore rubber ponchos. Three of Early's cavalrymen, also in rain gear, fell in with them and rode alongside. According to the Confederates they drew their pistols and demanded that Meigs and his men surrender, and when they resisted both sides began firing. Meigs was shot under the right eye and in the left breast and died immediately. The other two Federals were wounded, and one of them rode into Sheridan's headquarters a few minutes later and stated that the Rebels had masqueraded as Union men and were talking in a friendly manner when all of sudden they opened fire, without warning.[24]

Meigs, eldest son of U.S. quartermaster general Montgomery Meigs, was twenty-two years old, top graduate in the West Point Class of 1863, and had been mapping the Valley since Sigel's campaign. He was popular and a close friend of Sheridan. What bothered Sheridan was that he was killed on the nonviolent mission of surveying well inside Union lines, and it was not a fair fight. Sheridan called it an "atrocious act" of murder and ordered Custer's cavalry, in charge of screening the area, to burn every house within five miles of the killing, including the village of Dayton. The burn order went out at 2:00 A.M. the next day, and several houses were burned; but, before the torch reached Dayton, Sheridan relented and suspended the order. Falling back on Grant's suggestion, he directed the arrest of all able-bodied males in the vicinity. To Grant he complained, "Since I came into the Valley, from Harper's Ferry up to Harrisonburg, every train, every small party, and every straggler has been bushwhacked by people, many of whom have protection papers from commanders who have been hitherto in this valley."[25]

Sheridan exaggerated, but Mosby's Rangers were a nuisance on his communication line. "Numerous guerrilla parties in his rear frequently interrupt communication with him," Halleck wrote Grant. Reporters complained that the roads swarmed with guerrillas, and by the time their dispatches reached their editors the news was stale. At Harpers Ferry the commander copied messages to Sheridan in duplicate and sent them by separate couriers. Signal Corps officers wanted a telegraph line from Cedar Creek to Winchester; because of the guerrillas they set up stations on the mountaintops and sent messages with flags. A large shipment of mail was captured by Mosby's men on October 11. The next night, Sheridan sent important letters to Augur with a courier escorted by a regiment of cavalry. He carefully protected the prisoners, cannon, and flags captured in the Union cavalry victory at Tom's Brook on October 9 by sending them from Cedar Creek to Martinsburg guarded by a brigade of infantry. On October 16, on his trip from Front Royal to Piedmont to take the MGR to Washington, Sheridan had an escort of a regiment of cavalry. At Piedmont, he told Maj. Augustus P. Green, 13th New York Cavalry, that he had "great contempt" for Mosby and his men. "He told me to be careful of my men," Green recalled, "and to have my pickets well out, and for them to be very careful and not to be ambushed." When Sheridan marched south from Martinsburg on Oct 18, he had a seven-hundred-man regiment of cavalry; and at Bunker Hill he ordered out advance, rear, and flank guards to comb the woods and keep a sharp lookout for guerrillas.[26]

The killing of Meigs occurred south of Mosby's range of operations; but when Sheridan returned to the area opposite the Blue Ridge gaps, two other members of his staff were mortally wounded by Mosby's men. On the morning of October 11, Chief Quartermaster Lt. Col. Cornelius W. Tolles and Surgeon and Medical Inspector Emil Ohlenschlager were on their way south from Winchester to Sheridan's headquarters at Cedar Creek. They were riding in an ambulance escorted by twenty-five men of the 17th Pennsylvania Cavalry. When they reached about midway, about eight miles north of Cedar Creek, they were attacked by Dolly Richards and thirty-two raiders, who demanded their surrender. Tolles and Ohlenschlager jumped from the ambulance and fled on foot, and the Rangers shot them, mortally wounding both. They were brought to headquarters, and sympathy for them extended throughout the army. Ohlenschlager was very popular, and when he died three days later from his stomach wound his last words were that he was killed after he had surrendered. Tolles was shot in the back of the head; part of his brain was missing and tissue was protruding from the wound. A gruesome physical description of his injury spread throughout the camp. Within a few days his wife came, having been delayed on the train that Mosby derailed at Quincy's Siding, and she stayed by his side until his death on November 8.[27]

A *New York Tribune* reporter happened to witness the fight, and he called it "one of the bloodiest little attacks of guerillas on record." "Bloody Work of a Guerilla Party," stated the *New York Herald,* claiming that the officers surrendered and then were shot. Sheridan reported to Grant that the guerrillas were "becoming very formidable and are annoying me very much," and he would "exterminate them," but it could not be done with search parties because the Rebels would only escape on fleet horses into the mountains. When free of Early's army he would burn out their supporters. One of Ohlenschlager's fellow surgeons, Alexander Neil, wrote in a letter two days after the attack that he heard that Mosby's men were killing all of their prisoners "and they have raised the black flag. But there are two sides that can play this game and our boys remember every one they catch. but tis best to tell no tales."[28]

On October 13, one of Sheridan's commanders made it no secret when he hanged one of Mosby's men. Col. William H. Powell, head of a cavalry division, was in Rappahannock County southeast of Front Royal when some of his men brought in the body of a man reputed to be a Union soldier. Investigating, he concluded that the man had been murdered by two Southerners, Chancellor and Myers, reported to be Mosby's men. He captured Albert G. Willis, who truly was one of the Rangers, and ordered him hanged in retaliation. Powell was a large, powerful man, blind in one eye and manager of an ironworks in Ironton, Ohio, before the war. He considered Mosby's men a "gang of cut-throats and robbers" practicing "willful and cold-blooded murder." At Flint Hill, thirteen miles from Front Royal, he had Willis hanged and a placard left on his body:

"A.C. Willis, member of Company C, Mosby's command, hanged by the neck in retaliation for the murder of a U.S. soldier by Messrs. Chancellor and Myers." In fact, Chancellor and Myers, Confederates from Fauquier County but not Mosby's men, arrested the unidentified Union man as a spy and were taking him to the provost marshal at Gordonsville when he attempted to escape and Chancellor shot and killed him.[29]

A Mosby detachment under Montjoy entered Falls Church and were taking horses from the stables on October 18 when civilian J.B. Reed blew a fox horn to alert the nearby cavalry camp. Montjoy's men captured Reed and an African American home guard and, on the return march seven miles west, took them into the pines and shot them. Reed died immediately, and the home guard's ear was shot off. He lived to tell the story, and the newspapers declared that Reed was murdered and his throat was cut, proving that the black flag was out. Mosby admitted that his men killed Reed but denied that they cut his throat.[30]

Leading a raid in the Valley on the morning of October 25, Mosby captured another general. He had 375 men, the largest number that he ever had on an expedition, and his purpose was to operate on Sheridan's communications. He divided into small parties and, with a few men, was reconnoitering the pike north of Winchester, when a light wagon appeared, racing north with an escort of ten cavalry. It was Gen. Alfred Napoleon Alexander Duffie, the dapper little Frenchman whom Sheridan had relieved of command of a cavalry division and assigned to remount camp in Hagerstown, Maryland, where he was going. His full escort was a force of fifty cavalry, and he would have been safe if he had remained with them. But in the wagon he impatiently rode forward, leaving most of the escort behind. Mosby's men captured Duffie and three enlisted men, and Sheridan remarked that Duffie was taken "by his own stupidity." A rumor spread among Unionists that Duffie surrendered and was murdered "in cold blood" and his body left by the road. The *Richmond Sentinel* declared that if Mosby's men had not yet killed him, they should place him in front of their next charge, and this would be proper retaliation for the Yankee use of hostages on the MGR.[31]

The violence had escalated into a life of its own, and, since Sheridan did not appear to be leaving the Valley, Mosby decided that he must act. "If I had not retaliated, the war in the Valley would have degenerated into a massacre," he wrote later. Moving with judicial deliberation, he wrote to Lee on October 29 requesting authority to hang seven of Custer's men when he could capture them. Retaliation was well established in international law, and Lee replied on November 3 that he fully approved.[32]

The Rangers targeted Custer's division, and, when Richards returned with fourteen prisoners a few days later, that made a total of twenty-seven believed to be from Custer's command or to have served under Custer at the time of the Front Royal killings. Mosby called a meeting of the battalion for 11:00 A.M. November 6 at Rectortown, for the purpose of having a lottery to select seven prisoners to be hanged. The prisoners were held in a corn crib on a hill near town, and through the cracks in the board walls they watched Mosby's men gathering from all directions and noticed that the Rangers were not laughing or joking but were unusually quiet and somber. It was pleasant sunny weather, but a dark cloud of dreaded duty hovered over the little hill. Every one of the Rangers felt that it was necessary, but every heart was filled with pathos. Mosby was present in town but did not meet with the men or see the prisoners or watch the lottery.[33]

All of the prisoners had been captured within the last few days, and each had been questioned as to his connection with Custer; therefore, they knew what was coming when Mosby's officers brought them out and formed them in a single line in front of the corn crib. An officer announced that seven men must be selected by lot to be hanged in retaliation for the shooting and hanging of seven of Mosby's men. Most of the prisoners bowed in prayer, some weeping, but they all stood in place as one of Mosby's men passed down the line with a hat held at eye level. Each prisoner took a slip of paper and opened it—if it was marked, he was to be hanged. If the paper was unmarked the man sighed with relief; if it was marked, he groaned in despair. "Tell my mother I died like a man," said one. James Daley, a drummer boy, drew a marked paper and fainted. Some of Mosby's men wept, tears running down their faces.[34]

The man with the hat reached the end of the line, and only five had been selected—two marked papers remained in the hat; they had miscounted and prepared two extra papers. A second lottery was required. Someone informed Mosby that a drummer boy had been selected, and Mosby excused him, making a total of three men still to be chosen. By now, recalled one of the prisoners, "we more than ever wanted to go home to our parents." Three men were selected in the second drawing, and the seven were coffled together with a wrist tied to a rope and taken away toward the Valley in Sheridan's rear. Passing through Ashby's Gap, the party met Montjoy returning from a Valley raid with more prisoners.

Two of the condemned men saw Montjoy's Masonic pin and gave him the Masonic distress signal. He substituted two of his prisoners who admitted that they were in Custer's command and stated that they were not Masons. Later, when Mosby heard of this, he told Montjoy, "I want you to understand that my Command is not a Masonic lodge."[35]

The eight-man detail assigned the task of carrying out the hangings did not have their hearts in it. They went through fields and byways to Beemer's woods, one mile west of Berryville on the road to Winchester. On the way, one of the prisoners, 5th Michigan Cavalry private George H. Sowle, who had been in Custer's command at the time of the Front Royal killings but was not now, loosened his binding. It had started raining and it was very dark in the early hours of the morning of November 7 when they arrived. While crossing the field toward the trees, Sowle dropped into a ditch and escaped. Mosby's men tied the hands of the six remaining behind their backs and hanged three of them, all of whom remain unidentified today. They stood the other three in line, and one Ranger with a loaded revolver stood in front of each man and fired. On the left, Pvt. Melchior H. Hoffnagle, 153rd New York Infantry, was shot in the right elbow and fell to the ground, pretending to be dead. He survived with the loss of his right arm. On the right, Cpl. James Bennett, 2nd New York Cavalry and currently in Custer's division, took a bullet in the left shoulder. "For God's sake kill me if you are going to!" he screamed. "Don't torture me to death." The Confederate moved closer and placed his revolver in Bennett's face and fired again, and Bennett fell to the ground. Meanwhile, on the first fire, the pistol aimed at the prisoner in the center, Cpl. Charles E. Marvin, 2nd New York Cavalry in Custer's command, clicked. Marvin, a large, powerful man, had managed to free his hands behind his back; when he heard the snap, he struck his guard in the face, ran into the woods, and climbed a hickory tree.[36]

Mosby's detail left, and Marvin climbed down and helped Hoffnagle to the house of a civilian and then to the army hospital in the Lutheran church in Winchester. Bennett was also still alive. The second bullet entered his left eye and passed through, destroying his right eye. He dragged himself to a tree and was sitting there with his back against the trunk when a civilian passed and took him to a local doctor, who treated him and took him to the same hospital as Hoffnagle. Bennett's left arm was paralyzed for life, and he could see with greatly impaired vision with his left eye.[37]

When Mosby learned that four of the prisoners had escaped, two wounded and two unharmed, he was pleased. "I was really glad they got away as they carried the story to Sheridan's army which was the best way to stop the business," he declared. In Winchester, fifteen miles in the rear of Sheridan's headquarters at Cedar Creek, Col. Oliver Edwards reported the incident to Sheridan and sent him the placard that a civilian had found pinned to the body of one of the hanged men. It was Mosby's answer to the Front Royal and Flint Hill posters: "These men have been hung in retaliation for an equal number of Colonel Mosby's men hung by order of General Custer, at Front Royal. Measure for measure." *New York Times* correspondent E.A. Paul interviewed Marvin and filed dispatches with detailed accounts of the executions.[38]

Mosby's target for the hangings was not Sheridan—the situation had gotten beyond Sheridan's control. He was waiting for the day when the strategic situation would allow him to send his cavalry to burn out Mosby's supporters. On November 11 he reported to Grant that a small division of cavalry had been to Rectortown and had taken livestock and horses and the raid would warn Union citizens in Loudoun County to flee the coming wrath.

The real audience was Sheridan's officers and men, especially the cavalry. Mosby wrote a letter to Sheridan warning that the executions were in retaliation for the murder of his men and announcing that since the Front Royal affair he had captured seven hundred Union prisoners and not harmed any of them except these seven. He promised to order no more executions unless retaliation became necessary. He sent a copy to the Richmond newspapers, knowing that Sheridan's men would read the reprints in the Northern papers. "I wanted Sheridan's soldiers to know that, if they desired to fight under the black flag, I would meet them," he stated.[39]

The retaliation appeared to be successful, but probably equally important was the closing of the Valley campaign a few days later. In mid-November Lee began transferring troops from Early to Petersburg, and Sheridan withdrew north into winter quarters at Kernstown. On November 24 he opened the Winchester and Potomac Railroad to Stephenson's Depot, three miles north of Winchester, and had a supply line that was relatively secure and a less-inviting target. Mosby continued raiding and still annoyed Sheridan, but there were fewer opportunities for bloody confrontation. With Early's force shrinking, Sheridan prepared to send the 6th Corps to Grant and to give more attention to hunting Mosby.

# 15

# Sheridan's Mosby Hunt

Sheridan and other commanders hunting Mosby were limited in that the Union had already used and shrank back from an extreme counterguerrilla policy. In attempting to stop the bloody border war in Kansas and Missouri, the army had gone to the heart of the matter and taken the war to the civilians in the most extreme counterinsurgency program of the war. Reacting to Confederate William C. Quantrill's bloody raid on Lawrence, Kansas, Union general Thomas Ewing on August 25, 1863, issued Orders no. 11 removing about twenty thousand residents from four counties in Missouri and turning their homes into a burned wasteland. Soon it became obvious that this policy of depopulation and devastation accomplished nothing. The violence continued, and people in the North considered the measures outrageous and uncivilized. Halleck defended the order as legal but suspended its execution, directing that such measures should be used again "only in case of overruling necessity."[1]

Extremists recommended such methods against Mosby. Col. Horace B. Sargent, 1st Massachusetts Cavalry, guarding Meade's right flank near Warrenton on September 2, 1863, suggested that civilians supporting Mosby be relocated and their land laid waste: "Attila, King of the Huns, adopted the only method that can exterminate these citizen soldiers." Unionist citizens in Fairfax Court House reacted to Stoughton's capture by demanding that Confederates be removed from inside Union lines. At Sheridan's headquarters in Winchester on January 8, 1865, New York reporter Charles Farrell declared, "There is but one remedy where people have determined upon such diabolism, and that is to smoke them out and drive them with fire and sword until not a vestige of them or their places remain to blot the fair face of the earth."[2]

Union army commanders issued harsh orders, but officers in the

This previously unpublished photograph depicts Mosby as a lieutenant colonel in 1864. (From the collection of Kent Masterson Brown.)

Mosby's reputation as a troublemaker at the University of Virginia went against him during his trial for shooting a fellow student. This daguerreotype was made before he was expelled for the shooting. (University of Virginia Library.)

This portrait of Mosby as a University of Virginia student, depicting the gentle, scholarly side of his personality, contrasts so greatly with his daguerreotype of the period that he looks like a different person. (University of Virginia Library.)

*Above,* Mosby shot fellow University of Virginia student George R. Turpin in Brock Boarding House, later renamed the Cabell House. (The Albemarle County Historical Society.) *Below,* Bristol, Tennessee/Virginia, in 1856 was on the verge of a building boom that would attract Mosby in 1858. (Courtesy of V.N. "Bud" Phillips.)

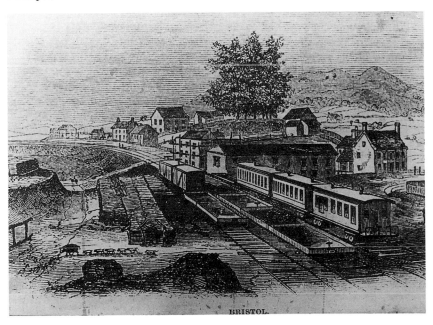

Mosby's wife, Pauline Clarke Mosby, enjoyed reading and discussing literature with her husband. She was a beloved wife and mother, and a dedicated member of the Roman Catholic Church. (The Virginia Historical Society.)

*This picture is a copy of one taken in Richmond in January 1863. The uniform is the one I wore on March 8th 1863 on the night of General Stoughton's capture*

Just before beginning his guerrilla warfare and perhaps sensing that he was on the verge of destiny, Mosby posed for his favorite wartime photograph of himself. (Russell, *Memoirs.*)

Union general Edwin H. Stoughton (left), a graduate of West Point and descendant of a prominent Vermont family, never recovered his reputation after Mosby captured him in bed in this house (below) in Fairfax, Virginia. (The National Archives; The Virginia Historical Society.)

House in which Col. John S. Mosby captured Gen. Stoughton.
FAIRFAX, VA.

After he became famous for capturing Stoughton, Mosby was promoted to major, a rank he held from March 26, 1863, to January 1864. (The National Archives.)

Union soldiers such as these in southern Maryland searched for Mosby's men in the bedrooms of his civilian supporters. (Frank & Marie-Therese Wood Print Collections, Alexandria, Virginia.)

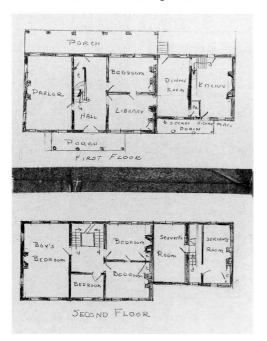

Families boarding Mosby's men concealed them in secret hiding places such as the hidden cellar under the dining room at Belle Grove. (The Virginia Historical Society.)

The first page of *Harper's Weekly,* September 5, 1863, featured Mosby's men raiding sutler wagons near Washington, D.C. (The Library of Congress.)

When he painted Mosby from life in Richmond in February 1865, Louis Mathieu Didier Guillaume may have portrayed the raider's silent hand signal to attack. (Courtesy of the R.W. Norton Art Gallery, Shreveport, Louisiana.)

*Above*, Union troops guarding Chain Bridge on the Potomac River in Washington, D.C. went on alert during invasion panics resulting from fear of Mosby. (The Library of Congress.) *Below*, Lightly equipped and superbly mounted, Mosby's men hovered just out of rifle range, scanning passing columns for stragglers and creating fear in the minds of the enemy. (The Western Reserve Historical Society, Cleveland, Ohio.)

During this October 11, 1864, attack by Mosby's men in the Shenandoah Valley, Sheridan's chief quartermaster, Lt. Col. Cornelius W. Tolles, and surgeon and medical inspector, Emil Ohlenschlager, jumped from the ambulance in which they were riding and attempted to escape. Both were mortally wounded. (The Western Reserve Historical Society.)

Robert E. Lee told Mosby that his only fault was that he was always getting wounded. During his convalescence from his September 14, 1864, wound Mosby posed for this photograph in Richmond. (The Virginia Historical Society.)

Sheridan set aside a hunter-killer team of 100 men under Capt. Richard Blazer with one mission—kill or capture Mosby and his men. Here, Blazer and his men hunt for Mosby. (The Western Reserve Historical Society.)

When Mosby's Rangers emptied their revolvers, they used them as clubs. In this image Pvt. Sydnor G. Ferguson strikes the blow that knocked Capt. Richard Blazer to the ground and brought his capture on November 18, 1864. (The Western Reserve Historical Society.)

*Above*, Fear of Mosby intruded on the honeymoon of Union general George A. Custer and his wife, Elizabeth, portrayed by newspaper artist James E. Taylor on a visit in 1864 to Sheridan's headquarters in the Shenandoah Valley. (The Western Reserve Historical Society.) *Below*, Gen. Philip H. Sheridan nearly always succeeded, except in capturing Mosby. In this postwar photo he confers with subordinates, left to right: James W. Forsyth, Wesley Merritt, Thomas C. Devin, and George A. Custer. (The National Archives.)

Prominent Richmond, Virginia, sculptor Edward V. Valentine created this bust of Mosby from life in August 1865. He captured Mosby's fighting spirit and Mosby was most proud. (The Valentine Museum.)

Portrait artist Edward Caledon Bruce, painting Mosby's portrait from life in February 1865, portrayed Mosby's kind and gentle side. (The Museum of the Confederacy.)

Mosby was a prosperous attorney in the time immediately after the Civil War.
(The Valentine Museum.)

Mosby's assignment as federal land agent for the Nebraska Sand Hills enabled him to take the lead in enforcing federal laws against illegal fences on public land. The region was unsuitable for homesteading, but ideal for cattle such as these. (Nebraska State Historical Society.)

Mosby initiated charges of violating federal land laws against great Nebraska cattle rancher Bartlett Richards (center), shown here in Wyoming in 1882. (Nebraska State Historical Society.)

In his last twelve years, Mosby lived in Washington, D.C., where he became a familiar figure on the streets. He was seventy-three and assistant attorney in the Department of Justice when he posed for this 1907 snapshot. (The Western Reserve Historical Society.)

Late in life Mosby took pride in funding the education of two of his grandsons, Spottswood (left) and Mosby Campbell (right). He was eighty-one years old in this 1915 photograph. (University of Virginia Library.)

*Above*, Mosby became a subject of silent films such as *The Pride of the South*, released in 1913. In this scene actor Joseph King, portraying Mosby, leads his men on a raid against Fairfax Court House, Virginia. (The Library of Congress.) *Below*, "Don't shoot! He is my husband!" says Mosby's fictional daughter to her father in this scene from *The Pride of the South*. The film abandoned reality and portrayed Mosby's daughter as having married a Union officer. (The Library of Congress.)

field refused to enforce them. General Pope, in command in Virginia in the summer of 1862, directed that guerrillas were to be shot, residents within five miles of a raid were to pay damages, and all disloyal males were to be arrested and required to take the loyalty oath and give security for good behavior. Pope's orders were ignored. The next year, when Mosby went into operation, one method of retaliation was to arrest the adult males supporting him. They were soon released, and Mosby's warfare continued.[3]

When Meade was using the O&A as his supply line after the Gettysburg campaign, Herman Haupt, director of Military Railroads, requested that he prevent raids against the railroad by threatening civilians. Accordingly, on July 30, 1863, Meade ordered that citizens along the track who aided guerrillas were to be arrested and confined or expelled from Union lines; residents within ten miles of the track were to pay for repairs; and if the attacks did not cease, all inhabitants would be removed and their property confiscated. Mosby continued, and Heintzelman directed Lowell to remove residents on the north side of the railroad from Alexandria to Manassas Junction and burn the houses of guerrilla supporters. Lowell had a few males arrested but stopped when he observed that prison authorities quickly released them. He burned two mills and the house of a thief and sent a message to Mosby notifying him that he would not burn the boardinghouses of Mosby's men. It required emotional restraint, but Lowell considered Mosby an honorable foe and refused to create a situation of bloody retaliation.[4]

In Warrenton in the winter of 1863-64, Union commanders accused citizens of spying for Mosby, enabling him to penetrate Union picket lines and attack posts from the rear. Therefore, to separate the people from "the guerrillas who infest the country about," on November 17, 1863, David M. Gregg completely sealed the town from the outside world. Citizens were not allowed to pass in either direction for any reason, not even to make necessary trips to grist mills outside of town. On January 8, 1864, Gregg realized that he had made a mistake and canceled the order; some of the people were almost starving, and Mosby's attacks were unabating.[5]

After Wyndham's failed attempts to ambush Mosby by using decoys, others used the same tactic. On May 6, 1863, Gen. Robert H. Milroy in Winchester sent four hundred infantry and thirty 1st New York Cavalry to ambush Mosby in a stand of trees on the road north of Upperville. The cavalry succeeded in luring about fifteen Rangers into the trap, but, like Wyndham's men, the Union infantry fired into their own cavalry, killing one, mortally wounding two, and wounding three. "It was a fearful blunder," wrote the lst New York Cavalry historian. "That more were not killed was due to the wild, excited firing of the infantry." Gen. James H. Wilson, one of Sheridan's most distinguished cavalry commanders, on August 16, 1864, in the lower Shenandoah Valley, ordered one of his brigade commanders to "leave some wagons with picked men concealed in them somewhat in rear as a decoy for bushwhackers."[6]

On the night of June 24, 1863, the night before Hooker ordered his army to cross the Potomac toward Gettysburg, Pleasonton told Hooker, "I shall try Mosby to-morrow." He set an area ambush—an ambush in an area frequented by the enemy—on Mosby's usual path over the Bull Run Mountains. The next morning Mosby came along but had two men well in advance, and they triggered the assault. Mosby heard the firing and took a different trail in safety. He was wary because a few days earlier, just over the mountain, Meade had ambushed him with a planned ambush—one with accurate intelligence on where and when Mosby would appear. On June 21, a male slave had come to Meade's headquarters in Aldie reporting that he knew exactly where Mosby would be the next morning. The man had seen Mosby and heard him tell Dr. Jesse Ewell that he was going west over the mountains but would return this way and greet him here at sunrise the next morning. Mosby was usually secretive about his plans but this time was careless.[7]

Meade recognized the opportunity and sent his best men: 33 of the 17th Pennsylvania Cavalry and 103 of the 14th U.S. Infantry, under Capt. William H. Brown. The force left camp at 1:00 A.M. on June 22, marched to Ewell's, and set a perfect ambush in the lane that Mosby would use after he came down the mountain and greeted Dr. Ewell. Brown posted half of the infantry behind Ewell's Chapel and had the others lie on the ground behind a fence on the opposite side of the road. To lure Mosby into the crossfire, he placed the cavalry in the road in full view. As expected, Mosby and about thirty-five men appeared; when Mosby saw the Union horsemen and their valuable horses, he led a mounted charge. The Union cavalrymen pretended to retreat and withdrew beyond the Chapel out of the line of fire of the infantry. Everything had gone perfectly so far, and Mosby and his foremost men were only ten yards away when the infantry fired. The problem was that the infantry were so nervous at seeing Mosby, they "did not hit a rebel," according to Meade. Mosby wheeled and escaped into the mountains. "And thus the prettiest chance in the world to dispose of Mr. Mosby was lost," Meade lamented. Actually, Brown's men wounded three Rangers, including John N. Ballard, whose leg was amputated. Brown lost one man killed.[8]

Several Union commanders conducted hammer-and-anvil circular hunts, alerting or sending large forces into Mosby's Confederacy from different directions at once. The first was by Heintzelman when he arrested the men of Middleburg in retaliation for Mosby's Seneca Raid. He sent cavalry from three directions: Maryland, the Shenandoah Valley, and from along the O&A; they converged on Middleburg at different times, between ten and twenty-four hours after Mosby had dispersed. The first detachment into town on the night of June 11, 1863, captured Mosby's Capt. J. William Foster, six men, and ten horses.[9]

Military historian Antoine Jomini wrote that effective guerrillas can turn a large invading force into a blind man, a Don Quixote attacking windmills. Thus it was with a brigade of over twelve hundred cavalry with artillery that Col. J. Irvin Gregg sent after Mosby and his fewer than sixty men on September 10, 1863. The Federals marched from camp west of Warrenton to Middleburg, spent the night, and returned to camp the next day. They saw nothing, heard nothing, and accomplished nothing. Mosby was convalescing from his August 24 wound, and his men did not harass the column. "I came to the conclusion," one of the Pennsylvania cavalrymen wrote, "that hunting guerrillas with four regiments of cavalry and four pieces of artillery, was very much like shooting mosquitoes with a rifle,—very mashing to the little bird if you hit him."[10]

On December 28, 1863, at 2:30 P.M., Meade had fresh intelligence that Mosby would meet his battalion at Rector's Cross Roads that night and attack Union pickets in Fairfax County. With great urgency he sent telegrams and mounted couriers with orders to close the net on Mosby from two directions. From his camp in Vienna, Lowell sent out parties to Upperville and the Blue Ridge Mountains, and from Warrenton Lt. Col. John W. Kester, 1st New Jersey Cavalry, came with five hundred mounted men. Two companies of infantry patrolled the road from Fairfax Court House to Flint Hill "in order to intercept him." Lowell captured nineteen Rebels, ten of them Mosby's men, and twenty-five horses. Kester's men captured eight horses and one hundred uniforms with no men in them at Rectortown and countercharged twice against Mosby's men, but both times the Rebels escaped on fleet horses. Less than two months later, as shown below, Kester would be much more successful using more efficient tactics.[11]

The key question was "Where is Mosby?" and the most effective Mosby hunters developed friendships with Unionist civilians and used them as guides. But by far the most effective pilots were deserters from Mosby's command—they knew which houses contained sleeping Rangers. Union officers learned to distrust white adults in Mosby's Confederacy and asked directions only of children and African Americans. Captured Rangers were no help; they answered nothing. Walter Frankland refused to tell where Mosby was, and his Union interrogators forced him to "walk a circle," marching around the perimeter carrying a fence rail. John Puryear remained silent even when his captors put a rope around his neck and twice pretended to hang him.[12]

Mosby hunters used Jessie Scouts—Union soldiers in Confederate uniforms—to gather intelligence. In early August 1863, Pleasonton infiltrated Mosby's rendezvous with two Jessies and upon their report sent a cavalry force; they captured two Rebels and fifteen to twenty horses, but Mosby's command was gone. Sheridan had a company of Jessie Scouts, and the Union cavalry in Fairfax County had scouts in Confederate uniforms. False Confederates became so common in Mosby's Confederacy that at one point Mosby issued membership cards so that genuine Rangers could identify each other. By the last year of the war, any stranger in a Confederate uniform was assumed to be a Union spy until proven genuine.[13]

Augur employed Pardon Worsley, a peddler, blockade-runner, and double agent, as a spy; and when Worsley confirmed that Mosby frequented the home of Joseph Blackwell, Augur ordered it burned. The most ridiculous counterinsurgency operation was Pleasonton's attempt to bribe Mosby to turn his coat. In the second week of June 1863, when Pleasonton was desperate to penetrate Stuart's screen of Lee's army moving toward Gettysburg, he somehow had the idea that one of the most incorruptible men who ever lived could be bought for cash. "There is a chance for him, and just now he could do valuable service in the way of information as well as humbugging the enemy," he asserted. Chief Quartermaster Rufus Ingalls replied that money was forthcoming. But apparently Pleasonton came to his senses, because Mosby never heard of the bribe until he read it in the war correspondence after the war.[14]

Special forces today practice capturing important enemies by studying the subject's daily routine in a targeting process known as "Figure Eight." Since most individuals are creatures of habit, one studies when a target's day begins, where he goes, and who he sees, looking for a pattern and an ideal opportunity to capture him. This would not have worked against Mosby, because, except in the Ewell's Chapel ambush, his movements were varied and unpredictable. He told no one where he planned to spend the night, and he settled down for the night only after dark so that potential informers had no idea where he was. Often he slept alone or with one or two men in the woods or in orchards or fence corners, lying on the ground with a buffalo robe for cover. Mosby "is an old rat and has a great many holes," Lowell observed.[15]

Custer experienced the frustration of sending a hunter-killer force after Mosby without intelligence or an informer. His Michigan Cavalry Brigade was camped at Warrenton Junction on August 1, 1863, when he organized an expedition of 250 hand-picked men under Col. William D. Mann, 7th Michigan Cavalry, and sent them on a special mission to capture or drive Mosby from the country. They traveled light and lived off the land and for three days found nothing. Then on August 4 they struck the trail of Mosby's men returning from a sutler raid in Fairfax County, attacked and scattered them, freed about fifty prisoners, and recaptured eighty mules and captured about twelve of Mosby's men. At the end of seven days they returned to camp, and Mann reported that he did not lose a man or a horse. With active patrolling he succeeded in intercepting the Rangers but failed to capture Mosby or close down his warfare.[16]

Lowell's most successful raid, November 18-23, 1863, involved the use of a Unionist civilian and a deserter from Mosby's command as guides. He had no problem recruiting Alexander F. "Yankee" Davis, a civilian who lived near Aldie and always seemed eager to lead Union columns against Mosby. The deserter was Charles Binns, a native of Loudoun County who had left Mosby's battalion when Mosby had him and another man arrested for kidnapping two African American women and preparing to sell them as slaves. He volunteered to show Lowell where Mosby's men were boarding. With 250 cavalry, half of them dismounted, Lowell arrived at the richest hunting ground after dark on Sunday night, November 22, and with four parties searched homes, capturing eighteen card-carrying Rangers, thirty-five horses, thirteen saddles and bridles, and twenty-five revolvers. Binns guided several additional raids and in Virginia was viewed as a traitor for the rest of his life. In 1909, at the age of seventy-seven, he announced in a newspaper that he wanted to rest and hear no more of the war. Mosby replied that Binns was like Banquo's ghost in *Macbeth;* he would never find rest but would forever hear, ringing in his ears, the raven calling "Nevermore," and in 2009 A.D., would still be wandering the hills crying "Respite, respite, Nepenthe."[17]

Gansevoort copied Lowell's tactics of using strong raiding forces accompanied with dismounted men and obtaining intelligence from civilians and deserters. He fought Mosby for twenty months, from July 1863 to the end of the war, except for a few weeks of medical leave now and then to rest from typhoid fever. He despised guerrilla war and pleaded for a transfer that never came but nevertheless scored a number of successes. With up-to-the-moment intelligence from civilians, he learned Mosby's location and sent the party that wounded him on September 14, 1864. He burned Blackwell's home and captured Mosby's four cannon. After the war he was brevetted brigadier general of volunteers for "faithful and meritorious service."[18]

Any tactics that captured or killed Mosby's men were effective, but the most efficient Union cavalry raids combined overnight raiding, midnight searching, and use of deserters as guides in tactics that paralleled Mosby's. The single-most-effective raid against Mosby in the war used these tactics. It occurred February 17-18, 1864, when Meade's army was in winter quarters south of the Rappahannock. All of a sudden, the quiet at Pleasonton's cavalry headquarters was interrupted by the appearance of a deserter from Mosby's command. He just rode in and said that he knew where Mosby would be that evening and it would give him great satisfaction to pilot a force to the very house. Pleasonton sent him to Gen. David M. Gregg, guarding the rear at Warrenton, and ordered Gregg to send a scout, guided by this man, to capture Mosby in his hideout. "Please report by telegraph as soon as the party returns," he wrote.[19]

Gregg was impressed that the man was articulate, well-informed, and full of resentment against Mosby. He was Pvt. John Cornwell, and the record does not indicate whether he aired his grievances, but it is known that he had disagreed with Mosby over an expense account. Mosby had sent him to Charlottesville to bring a wagon-load of ammunition; when he returned and submitted his expenses, Mosby said they were excessive and refused to authorize payment. Filled with resentment, when he heard that Mosby was returning from Richmond and would attend a party that night in Markham to celebrate his promotion to lieutenant colonel, he decided to betray him. Gregg ordered Lieutenant Colonel Kester, the same officer who had participated in the December 28 circular hunt, to move out with 350 cavalry, traveling light with one day's rations and returning to camp the next day. It was twenty miles to

Markham, and by the time they arrived the party would probably be over, but hopefully, with Cornwell's help, they could capture Mosby in bed.[20]

The expedition left Warrenton at 11:00 P.M. in the middle of a three-day cold spell, one of the worst that winter. The temperature had dropped well below freezing, and a cold north wind was blowing hard, chilling their faces and making them turn aside every time they topped a hill. The creeks and ponds were frozen, and now and then men would dismount and walk to restore feeling in their feet. But the howling wind covered their sounds, and the cold would keep Mosby and his men inside and make surprise more likely. They marched ten miles to Salem, on the southern edge of Mosby's Confederacy, and divided into six teams of fifty to seventy-five men, fanning out on separate roads; when more than one team covered the same road, they leapfrogged to the next house. Cornwell guided the detachment that searched Markham. The next afternoon at 1:00 P.M. they met in Paris, on the other side of Mosby's land, took an hour for lunch, and returned in one column. They had no time to become spooked, and, on the egress through the center of the hostility they had stirred up in the night, they remained calm in spite of severe harassment by Mosby's men. At one point Rangers fired at them across a field from behind a stone fence, and the Union rear guard charged with revolvers and drove Mosby's men away.[21]

Kester had one man wounded and two horses killed, but he captured twenty-eight Rangers and fifty horses. The raid was not perfect because one of the fifty-man search teams got lost in the night and made no captures, and they did not find Mosby—he had delayed his return one day because of the weather. Nevertheless, Meade proudly reported the captures to Halleck at 10:00 P.M. on February 18, as soon as he had the news.[22]

Sheridan wrote in his memoirs that he had delayed hunting Mosby until after defeating Early. He stated that he "had not directed any special operations" against partisans as long as the campaign was active. It is true that he gave priority to fighting Early; but, as we have seen, he began operating against Mosby at Cedar Creek at 9:30 P.M. August 12, the night before the Wagon Raid. About a week later, withdrawing from the extreme measure of executing prisoners of war, a key component of his more moderate program was the detachment of a hunter-killer team under Capt. Richard Blazer with a single mission—capture or kill Mosby and his men. "I have 100 men who will take the contract to clean out

Mosby's gang," he wrote Augur on August 20. "I want 100 Spencer rifles for them."[23]

Thus, on his seventeenth day in the Valley, Sheridan created an irregular, special force with nothing to do except hunt Mosby and his men. Blazer was the man for the job; he was the best guerrilla hunter in the Union army because he used irregular tactics himself. Thirty-five years old and a native of Gallipolis, Ohio, he had enlisted in the 91st Ohio Infantry and earned a reputation fighting guerrillas in West Virginia under Gen. George Crook. Mosby's men respected him so much they called him "Old Blaze," and Mosby gave him the highest compliment he ever gave an opponent by departing this one and only time from hit-and-run tactics and ordering his men to go after Blazer in continual operations and not return until the task was finished.[24]

Blazer consciously cultivated friendly relations with the civilians in the Valley north of Snicker's Gap, and the people responded with so much admiration that Mosby said he feared they were about to make him a naturalized Confederate citizen. He used civilian informers and interrogated captured Mosby prisoners. He dressed a few of his men as Jessie Scouts and had them masquerade by name as 12th Virginia Cavalrymen. He became intimately familiar with the terrain, used mountains to mask his movements, and appreciated the value of surprise and ambush. He discarded the saber and armed his men with revolvers and Spencer rifles, and therein was his first weakness. Spencers were new, and a man could fire seven rounds before reloading, but they were not equal to revolvers in a mounted melee. Emphasis on the repeaters made it necessary for Blazer to fight at rifle range with part of his men dismounted in order to reap the advantage. Firing rifles in ordered ranks from horseback frightened the horses and caused confusion. Blazer would have been more of a terror if he had used overnight raids, but instead he would take his seventy-five to one hundred men on three-day missions, going into camp late at night and breaking camp and moving on before daylight. His campfires left evidence, and three-day operations gave Mosby's men opportunity to find him.[25]

Blazer had been in operation two weeks when he gave Mosby's men their worst defeat in the war. At 2:00 P.M. on September 4, 1864, he surprised seventy-five men of Company A at Myer's Ford on the east bank of the Shenandoah River south of Charlestown, West Virginia. Lt. Joseph Nelson, who had allowed discipline to break down on the July 30, 1864, Adamstown Raid, was in charge. Mosby had left him and his men to go forward and scout, and Nelson had pickets on the river but none in his rear toward the Blue Ridge Mountains. Blazer learned of their location from two civilian informers, slipped through the mountains, and suddenly attacked Nelson from behind, taking him completely by surprise. Some of the Rangers were asleep. Blazer had part of his company dismounted and firing from the woods across an open field. "The seven-shooters proved too much for them," Blazer reported. The Rebels scattered, jumping over a fence and running through a cornfield. Blazer and his men killed thirteen Rangers; wounded six, including Nelson, in the thigh; and captured five men and seventeen horses. Sheridan proudly reported the victory to Halleck the next evening; when the defeated men told Mosby, he said, "You let the Yankees whip you? I'll get hoop skirts for you! I'll send you into the first Yankee regiment we come across!"[26]

Mosby recognized that sooner or later he would have to remove Blazer, and about two months later he knew that he could wait no longer when Blazer whipped his men again in a planned ambush based on accurate intelligence. Montjoy and thirty men were coming home from a raid in the Valley with seventeen prisoners, when suddenly Blazer's men stood up in the undergrowth by the road and opened fire with their rifles, wounding four or five Rangers, one mortally, and freeing the prisoners. It was four miles west of Ashby's Gap, farther south than Blazer usually worked, and it showed that Blazer was threatening Mosby's operation. "I was a great deal vexed about the affair of Montjoy's, which I attributed to carelessness," Mosby said after the war.[27]

On November 17, 1864, he divided and sent his battalion into the Valley in two forces: Dolly Richards and 110 men passed through Snicker's Gap, and William Chapman with about 100 went through Ashby's Gap. Mosby wanted to go himself: "I intended to camp on his trail until we closed in on him. On the day my command got ready for the expedition I was suffering with a severe cold and fever." His final order was: "Wipe Blazer out! Go through him." This was unique; becoming a hunter he was dispatching two hunter-killer teams for continual operation. "It was black-gum against thunder, but I knew what the result would be," he wrote.[28]

On the first night, Dolly's scouts located Blazer's camp in its usual location near Kabletown, south of Charlestown, West Virginia. Quietly closing in early the next morning, November 18, Dolly saw smoke rising above the trees from the campfires of Blazer's men. But when the Rangers arrived, Blazer and his seventy-five men had left, searching for

Richards, whose presence his scouts had reported. Blazer had defeated Mosby's men twice, and he and his troopers were confident that any one of them could whip two of Mosby's men.[29]

Both captains wanted a fight, and both wanted to surprise and ambush the other. Blazer needed to fight at rifle range with some of his men dismounted, and Richards required an in-close mounted melee. Richards left Kabletown and headed south on the road to Myerstown, pretending to retreat toward Snicker's Gap, and Blazer followed. Using tactics Mosby had taught, Richards turned left at the crossroads in Myerstown, went one-fourth mile toward the river, and arranged an opportunity ambush, one set with the mission in progress. He turned his men to the right, through a stand of trees beside the road and into an open field beyond that dropped sharply over a hill and rose again on another hill at the back of the field, with a rail fence on the far side. Using the topography, he left a few men near the road as decoys pretending to be his rear guard; and just over the brow of the hill, hidden from the road, he positioned Company B, half of his men. They remained on their horses, facing the road, ready to charge. He took Company A to the far end of the field and prepared them, upon the appearance of the enemy, to move up the hill in the rear of the field, open a gap in the fence, and pretend to be retreating into the woods beyond, in haste.[30]

At 11:00 A.M. Blazer and his men came to the crossroads, and civilians told them that Mosby's men had just departed, in a hurry. Taking the bait, he galloped east, hoping for a fight before the Rebels escaped. His advance exchanged a few shots with Dolly's decoys, and Blazer halted and formed in line toward the field. At that moment, Company A "retreated" up the far hill and seemed to be fleeing in fright. Blazer ordered a mounted charge; and just as his horsemen broke out of the trees into the edge of the field, Company B gave a yell and countercharged, closing and shooting their revolvers. Company A turned and dashed back across the field. When they closed on the Union left flank, the blueclads retreated in a rout, back to the crossroads. Blazer attempted to rally and form an ambush from behind the buildings, but his men ignored him and raced away, some north toward Kabletown and others, including Blazer, straight west toward Rippon.[31]

Blazer had a fleet horse, and he soon took the lead, racing along the muddy road. But Ranger Sydnor G. Ferguson, an eighteen-year-old from Fauquier County, had a faster horse, and he came alongside, emptying both pistols. Blazer threw himself forward in the saddle, spurring his horse and refusing to surrender. Finally, Ferguson stood up in his stirrups and struck Blazer with an empty revolver, knocking him to the ground and capturing him. Syd had no idea that the man was Blazer. The Union force had twenty-one dead, twelve wounded, and twenty-two captured, for a casualty rate of 73 percent. Dolly had at least eight wounded, one mortally, and he captured fifty horses.[32]

Blazer went to prison in Richmond and then to Danville, Virginia, where he developed kidney disease that left him partially disabled. Sheridan did not report Blazer's defeat for three days; when he did, he understated the casualties, giving only twenty-two killed and wounded, and understated Blazer's strength at sixty-two men. Evaluating the fight later, Mosby wrote, "As an illustration of pluck and tactical skill, nothing in the war surpassed it."[33]

Blazer the hunter became Mosby's prey; but with the threat of Early's army gone, Sheridan prepared to operate against Mosby's civilian supporters. Ten days after Blazer's capture he sent his Burning Raid into Mosby's Confederacy.

# 16

# Sheridan's Burning Raid

Sheridan's cavalry came through Ashby's Gap on Monday afternoon, November 28, 1864, with four days' rations and forage, ample ammunition, and plenty of matches. Descending the eastern slope of the Blue Ridge Mountains into Loudoun Valley, they divided into columns of two regiments each; and beginning at 3:00 P.M., for four days residents could trace their line of march by the great columns of black smoke rising in the sky and hovering over the country, almost shutting out the sun. A woman watched from her window in the mountains and counted over twenty barns burning at once. The flames crackled and roared, and the air smelled of burning hay, corn, and wheat. At night the sky lit up in a red glare plainly visible at Point of Rocks. In Harpers Ferry a Union soldier wrote, "I can see from the window now the reflection of the fire glowing on the horizon, showing how completely the work of devastation is being carried out."[1]

Mothers and young women tore their hair and shrieked in despair; children stood in windows, their faces pale with fright. A mother in Upperville stood by her front gate, crying as her two milk cows were taken and she had no milk for her children. In Middleburg the next day women heard the lowing of their frightened milk cows being driven away and rushed into the street, pleading for their release. Sometimes after dark a Union private would return with a family's milk cow. "All in fearful anxiety expecting them with their firebrand any moment. See immense fires very near us," wrote a woman in Middleburg two days later. Sheridan hoped Mosby's supporters would blame him for the destruction, but instead they held it against the invaders. "The Yankees burned our barn!" protested Tee Edmonds.[2]

The purpose was to destroy Mosby's economic support, just as the previous burning in the Shenandoah had deprived Confederates of supplies from the fertile Valley farms. Grant had first ordered the Loudoun-Fauquier burn on August 16 in reaction to the Wagon Raid. He had directed Sheridan to send a division of cavalry into Mosby's Confederacy to arrest all males under fifty years of age and destroy or bring off all crops, livestock, and slaves. Now Sheridan sent Merritt's Cavalry Division of five thousand men with orders to destroy all forage and subsistence, burn all barns and grist mills and their contents, and drive off all livestock. As in the Valley, they were to burn no dwellings.[3]

They applied the torch not only to Mosby's Confederacy but to the Unionist Quaker and German-American areas of northern Loudoun County. Sheridan ordered the men to burn and seize livestock regardless of loyalty to the Union, but it was difficult for the Union cavalrymen to set fire to the barns of families who welcomed them by cheering and waving the United States flag. "It was a cruel but necessary measure," one soldier recalled. In the Quaker town of Waterford a large crowd gathered in the street, and when the blueclad horsemen appeared they cheered at the top of their voices. At a nearby farm two young women perched on the entry gateposts waving flags and watching the soldiers apply matches to their hay crop. "Burn away, burn away," one said, "if it will prevent Mosby from coming here." They took every animal from the farm of Levi Waters two miles south of Harpers Ferry: nine milk cows, two fat cattle, one horse, and two sheep. Waters's son John Waters went after one of the milk cows, and they let him have it. The son estimated the loss at $584. Another Unionist farmer lost fifteen cattle, four barns, and seventy tons of hay but proclaimed, "Well, they can't make a Rebel of me yet."[4]

They usually took the livestock but sometimes sought excuses not to burn the mills and barns of Unionists. Sparing the barn of prominent abolitionist and Quaker leader Samuel Janney, near Hamilton in Loudoun County, they said it was so near the house that flying embers might ignite the dwelling.[5] Gen. Thomas C. Devin, commander of the second brigade, was a stern and brusque man from New York City, but he had a kind heart. He and his staff had earlier visited and made friends with Mr. Mansfield, a Quaker with a flour mill and large house. When Devin and his staff arrived this time, Mansfield invited them to dismount and have refreshments. Devin refused and ordered his adjutant, Capt. John H. Mahnken, to set fire to the mill. Turning to his friend, he said, "Mr. Mansfield, you had better have some buckets of water ready in case your *house* should take fire." Then he turned, spurred his horse, and rode away without looking back. Mahnken stacked dry wood against the outside wall of the mill, lit it, and presently caught up with Devin.

"Mr. Mahnken, did you fire that mill?"

"Yes Sir."

"Did you see it burning?"

"Yes Sir."

"Very well, very well," concluded Devin, comforted in the knowledge that Mansfield had used the water to extinguish the blaze and save his mill.[6]

Sheridan knew what he was about, but to some loyalists it seemed unfair that they had to pay the price for the destruction of Mosby's support system. Some complained that Mosby's foraging was not all that extensive and that north Loudoun residents could not be accused of boarding his men because Rebels seldom stayed in the area overnight. Others asked if this was how the Union awarded loyalty. "Well, if it does any good let it go," one man answered, "but I can't see it."[7]

Merritt estimated that his men brought in more than five thousand cattle, more than three thousand sheep, nearly a thousand hogs, and more than five hundred horses. They burned haystacks and shocks of corn in the fields, took the oxen and other farm animals, and destroyed outbuildings, farm equipment, and harness. The aspect that struck at the center of Mosby's operation was the destruction of corn and the ability to produce corn. Mosby's horses were corn-fed, and, by depriving him of this vital supply, Sheridan struck him with a direct hit. Beginning in the spring of 1864, when the battalion had increased to over two hundred men, Mosby had come to rely on corn from the Loudoun Unionists. Now he had almost four hundred men, and Sheridan had destroyed not only the present supply but the work animals and production equipment for the next crop.[8]

And Sheridan was still not finished; his next blow against Mosby's civilian supporters also had a severe impact. The Union blockade against trade with the Confederacy, declared August 16, 1861, had been only loosely enforced and some of the time not at all before Sheridan came to the Valley. In 1863 the Lincoln administration had recognized the need to open limited trade in occupied territories to allow loyal civilians to purchase subsistence. The Treasury Department issued permits to merchants to sell to loyalists in Union-occupied areas of the Confederacy, a program that applied perfectly to the Loudoun Unionists. Selected merchants were required to sell only to persons who took the loyalty oath, but those with stores in southern Maryland and Loudoun County illegally sold to secessionists as well.[9]

Sheridan had heard rumors of this and directed Merritt's men to watch for blockade-runners on the Potomac River and burn their boats. Merritt's raiders captured no smugglers but reported that an extensive contraband trade was underway in Berlin and Point of Rocks. Therefore, on December 8, within a week of the burning raid, Sheridan closed all trade under the jurisdiction of Harpers Ferry, including the Treasury Department stores. Smuggling continued, but this order and Sheridan's enforcement of the blockade made the last four months of the war the most difficult for Loudoun Unionists and Mosby's supporters.[10]

In ordering the burning, Sheridan dropped Grant's idea of arresting males under fifty years of age capable of bearing arms. He emphasized that there was to be no "personal violence" to civilians but that the raiders were to "clear the country" of Mosby's men. Merritt directed the division to attempt to run down, ambush, or decoy the guerrillas, and after the raid admitted that such efforts failed because the Rangers were familiar with the country and easily escaped on their fleet horses into the mountains.[11]

On the first day of the burning, General Stevenson at Harpers Ferry received late intelligence relating to the skirmish in which Montjoy had just been killed and assumed that he knew where to find and capture Mosby and his command—he had a report stating that Mosby and his entire command were in the vicinity of Hamilton, "and will in all probability remain there for the night." Hamilton was between Snicker's Gap and Leesburg; and, since Merritt's division was already sweeping through Mosby's Confederacy, Stevenson proposed a "grand drive" to surround him. For months Sheridan had hoped for an opportunity to organize "a circular hunt for the whole gang," and it was convenient that Merritt's Reserve Brigade had already been ordered to move from their camp in the Valley to Snicker's Gap the next morning to join the raid. Sheridan replied that Snicker's Gap would be occupied early in the morning and he would notify Merritt. At 10:17 P.M. he wired: "Go on with your programme."[12]

In the night Stevenson moved infantry and cavalry into position in the Blue Ridge Mountains and by daylight had sealed the passes at Gregory's Gap and Keyes's Gap south of Harpers Ferry. The commander at Point of Rocks closed all communication across the Potomac into Maryland. Augur learned about the effort from Halleck and volunteered to send eight hundred cavalry from Fairfax County, and Sheridan directed them to march through Leesburg to a conjunction with Merritt at Snicker's Gap. Everything went smoothly in all directions, and the roundup was a grand failure. Sheridan blamed Stevenson's faulty intelligence, and he was right—Montjoy's party south of Point of Rocks numbered only thirty-eight men. Mosby and his men were not campaigning that day, and Mosby knew better than to call them together during the burning.[13]

He realized that the destruction was so great the area would not support the horses of his almost four hundred men through the winter. As soon as the Union cavalry departed, he headed for Petersburg to ask Lee's permission to reorganize and divide his command so that half could be sent to the Northern Neck of Virginia between the Potomac and Rappahannock Rivers in Chesapeake Bay. On December 6, his thirty-first birthday, he shared a dinner of leg of lamb with Lee at his headquarters, and Mosby reflected that Grant's headquarters were only about a mile away across the lines. Years later he recalled, "I little dreamed then that I wd. ever sit down to dinner with Grant—'What mortal his own doom can guess.'" Lee heartily approved of the transfer to the Northern Neck. He had a deep concern for the protection of Southern citizens behind Union lines such as those on the Northern Neck, and he believed that partisans could enforce law and order and discourage small enemy raids.[14]

However, Lee could not approve Mosby's proposed reorganization because it was not allowed in army regulations. Mosby wanted to reorganize his seven-company battalion into a regiment of two battalions with himself as colonel and Richards and William Chapman as battalion commanders, each with the rank of major. Lee recommended that he consult Seddon. Mosby presented the plan to Seddon, and he recommended a regiment with Mosby as colonel, with the men divided for the winter under a lieutenant colonel and a major. Mosby agreed and named Chapman lieutenant colonel and assigned him to take half of the men to the Northern Neck. All of this became official on January 9, 1865, with Mosby's rank as colonel effective December 7, 1864. The command thus became the 43rd regiment of Virginia Cavalry but never campaigned together as such because Chapman's detachment left on January 3 and remained until the end of the war.[15]

Sheridan never let up in his attempt to capture Mosby or destroy his means of support. When he sent his cavalry corps under Torbert on a raid toward Gordonsville from December 19 to 28, he instructed Torbert to return through Mosby's Confederacy and search for the large number of beef cattle apparently overlooked on the Burning Raid. And in the hope that Mosby might rendezvous in response to Torbert's expedition, Sheridan ordered Augur to send a cavalry force through Thoroughfare Gap, north to Middleburg and Aldie; perhaps they might happen upon Mosby and his men. The plan came very near success, not because Mosby reacted to Torbert's raid—he did not—but at last a military movement ordered by Sheridan and conducted by Augur's horsemen wounded Mosby and captured him, at least for a moment.[16]

The force from Fairfax Court House, a thousand men under Lt. Col. David R. Clendenin, 8th Illinois Cavalry, went through Thoroughfare Gap and on December 21 reached The Plains and divided. Clendenin took four hundred men north toward Aldie and sent Maj. Douglas Frazar, 13th New York Cavalry, west toward Rectortown with six hundred men. He directed Frazar to turn north from Rectortown and march that evening to Rector's Cross Roads, reuniting with him around midnight in Middleburg. Frazar's column arrived at Rectortown in the early evening and dismounted to make fires and cook supper.[17]

When someone brought Mosby word of Frazar's approach, he was two miles on the other side of Rectortown at the home of Clotilda Carter attending the wedding of one of his men, Jacob "Jake" Lavinder, to Judith Edmonds. Without interrupting dinner, Mosby and Thomas R. Love excused themselves and went to reconnoiter. For the wedding Mosby wore his finest uniform, recently smuggled through the Potomac blockade: new gray trousers and jacket; black beaver overcoat; a drab hat with gold cord, star, and ostrich plume; and a fine gray cape lined in scarlet. The Union men in Frazar's force who saw him sitting on his horse on a hill overlooking their position noted that he was beautifully mounted, and, with the wind swirling his cape, they dubbed him "Scarlet Cloak."[18]

Two days before, it had turned cold; for twenty-four hours it had been raining and sleeting, and ice covered the trees and hung in icicles from the eaves of houses. Now it was freezing rain, and the wind chill made it seem bitterly cold. Mosby and Love saw that Frazar's men had built fires and assumed they were camping for the night. Leaving the scene, Mosby sent word to his men at the wedding to prepare to harass Frazar's column in the morning, and he and Love rode north toward Rector's Cross Roads planning to spread word of tomorrow's gathering. Four miles along they saw a light at Ludwell Lake's house, and Mosby thought about the fresh-baked rolls and other delicious dishes that Lake's wife, Mary, was well known for serving; he told Love that they would stop and eat. Love offered to stand watch outside, but Mosby said there was no danger. He felt so secure that he and Love left their pistols on their horses tied at the front gate.[19]

Mary Lake was true to her reputation; she served one of the best dinners Mosby ever had—spare ribs, rolls, and the hot coffee that he loved. Lake's son, Ludwell Lake Jr., was a private in Mosby's command; and Ladonia, one of his daughters with his first wife Sophia, was married to Ranger Benjamin Skinner, captured and in a Northern prison camp. At home that evening were Lud, Mary, Ladonia and her two children, and Sarah, another daughter. The house was a midsized stone building, two and one-half stories, located on the road between Rectortown and Rector's Cross Roads one mile south of the Ashby's Gap Turnpike.[20]

At about 9:00 P.M. Mosby heard the tramp of horses, rose from the table, opened the dining room door to the backyard, and saw that the house was surrounded by Union cavalry. Frazar had not camped in Rectortown but had resumed the march, following the same road that Mosby and Love had taken. The advance guard had seen the two horses at the front gate and encircled the house. Mosby closed the door and was walking toward the front when several Union cavalrymen walked in the front door. Mosby's hat, cape, and overcoat were lying in a corner, but the jacket he wore had the two stars of a lieutenant colonel on the collar, his promotion to colonel not yet official. He raised both hands to cover the insignia, and in answer to their demand for his name and regiment, he said: "Lieutenant Johnston, 6th Virginia Cavalry." For the first time since 1862, he was captured. Then a strange thing happened in Ludwell Lake's dining room; Pauline believed that it was a miracle in answer to her prayers, divine intervention invoked by the Agnus Dei medallion that she had hung around his neck when he left for the war.[21]

Abruptly, the horsemen in the backyard began firing their revolvers, and a bullet came through a window and struck Mosby in the abdomen. "I am shot!" he shouted, not from the pain, for he felt only a stinging sensation, but to create panic. To avoid being shot themselves, the Yankees scrambled out the door, turning over the dinner table, and extinguishing the candle. Mosby's wound was bleeding. Beginning to feel faint, he walked into the adjoining bedroom and took off his coat with the insignia of rank and shoved it under the bureau. "Then I lay down and began to give an imitation of a man about to die," he said later. "I put my hand on the wound and smeared it over my mouth, thus giving me the appearance of having an internal hemorrhage and too far gone to take away."[22]

The front of his light-blue cotton shirt was saturated with blood, and when Frazar and two other officers walked in he was moaning and gasping for breath. Frazar asked who he was, and he whispered, "Lieutenant Johnston, 6th Virginia Cavalry." Frazar told him that he must examine the wound to determine whether to take him in, and Mosby had no objection. Frazar found that "a pistol bullet had entered the abdomen about two inches below and to the left of the navel; a wound that I felt assured was mortal." He and his companions left the room; and on his way out he remarked to Ludwell Lake, "He will die in twenty-four hours." One of the soldiers stripped Mosby of his boots and trousers, "evidently supposing that a dead man would have no use for them," Mosby said later with a smile.[23]

In light of modern surgery, Pauline was sagacious; Mosby's deliverance still seems miraculous. The bullet entered the abdomen, passed above the fascia, the sheet of fibrous tissue under the skin, and deflected, passing around the abdomen to the right side. Frazar wrongly assumed, in modern medical terms, that the bullet penetrated the peritoneum, the serous membrane lining the abdominal and pelvic walls and investing the viscera, and that peritonitis had begun, and therefore Mosby would be dead in about twenty-four hours. Today's surgeons, familiar with gunshot wounds to the stomach, estimate that only five percent are deflections like Mosby's.[24]

When the door closed and all of the Yankees had left, Lake said, "We have to get Mosby out of here. I don't want my house burned down and that is what they will do if they come back and catch him here." He shouted for his slaves to yoke the oxen and place straw in the ox-cart, and they wrapped him in quilts and took him a mile and a half to the southwest, to the home of Mrs. Aquilla Glascock. Lying in the cart on his back he could hear the wind whistling through the trees and could feel the sleet and rain falling on his face. "When we reached there, I was almost perfectly stiff with cold, and my hair was a clotted mass of ice," he recalled. Ranger George Slater boarded at Glascock's, and he helped bring Mosby in and laid him by the fireplace. Slater had been with Stuart when Stuart was mortally wounded in the abdomen by a bullet that perforated his stomach, taking his life in twenty-seven hours. Mosby asked Slater to examine him and see if his wound was similar. Slater did and stated accurately that this was different, that the bullet had passed around Mosby's body.[25]

The next morning Mosby's surgeon, William Dunn, administered chloroform and extracted the bullet. Mosby remained in bed, and over the next few days his men moved him frequently; he was still in the area on December 27 when Torbert's cavalry came through on their return march. Sheridan had learned that Mosby was wounded and had ordered them not only to seize cattle but also search thoroughly for the downed guerrilla chief. They seized a thousand cows but left without finding anyone who would tell them anything about Mosby's location. The next day Frazar returned with three hundred men and searched for three days, looking under every bed and checking every chimney, icehouse, and chicken coop. Once they came close, and one of Mosby's bearers asked him, "What shall we do with you?" and he replied, "Bury me." When he was able they took him to his mother's home, where he arrived on January 3, 1865.[26]

The wounding of Mosby was one of the most sensational news stories of the Civil War. A rumor on the streets of Richmond, Virginia, five days after the event avowed that he had died, and the next day the *Richmond Dispatch* published the report. The *New York Herald* endorsed the story, announcing on December 28 that he was "dead and buried." An editorial in the *Baltimore American* proclaimed, "We hope the report may prove true." On December 29 the *New York Herald* confirmed the death and on the thirtieth published an obituary, "The Fate of Mosby: Death of the Notorious Pirate of the Valley." The writer declared, "Like Morgan, Anderson and other guerillas of like character, Mosby has met with a dog's death."[27]

At this point the editors of the *Baltimore American* momentarily succumbed to wish fulfillment and reprinted the New York story of the death with the heading: "The Death of Moseby, the Guerilla Chief." Then on December 31, ten days after the event, the journalists corrected themselves, but the *New York Herald* editors did so reluctantly: "Mosby is not yet dead. He may possibly recover, 'the devil takes care of his own.'" The new year began with a series of updates on his condition and follow-up pieces. The *Baltimore American* of January 2, 1865, had six articles on the subject.[28]

For Southerners the story seemed too exciting to be true. First they heard that Mosby was mortally wounded and dead; then word came that he was alive, having outwitted the Yankee who had shot him. Word was that when the Union officer saw that the gallant Mosby was alive, he kicked him to roll him over to examine his wound, then robbed him of his clothing and remarked as he left that this man would do no more harm. Stories circulated that when the Union cavalry searched for him the people concealed him; no one told where he was, not even the servants under interrogation. The *Richmond Dispatch* reported that once Torbert thought he had located Mosby at a miller's house near Upperville and dispatched a captain from his staff and a detachment of dragoons with an ambulance to bring him away, but they soon returned with the ambulance empty. "At one time they were nearly upon him," stated the *Richmond Sentinel,* "and his escape seemed very improbable."[29] And finally, more than two weeks after the event, when they reported him safe and recovering at his father's farm, Confederate journalists warned that this daring and gallant man would retaliate. "Let the Yankees look out, as he is a military Shylock," declared the *Richmond Whig,* "and will demand of them the debt they owe him, to the last farthing." Tee Edmonds agreed with Pauline: "Oh! how kind Providence shielded from their demon clutches our Moseby."[30]

Sheridan first officially reported, eight days after the shooting, that Mosby was mortally wounded. Then the next day, December 30, he received a remarkably accurate report, which he believed true, that the ball passed around the abdomen and the wound was not mortal. But that night he received a telegram from Augur informing him that the Richmond newspapers were reporting Mosby dead in Charlottesville. Therefore, on December 31, Sheridan congratulated Augur for sending the party from his command that killed him. In a day or two Sheridan would learn the truth, but during his celebration on December 31 he wrote General Emory, 19th Corps Commander, "I have no news to-day, except the death of Mosby. He died from his wounds at Charlottesville."[31]

The night of the shooting, when Frazar joined Clendenin in Middleburg around a campfire, they examined the wounded officer's hat. "I then immediately knew it must be a field officer," Frazar reported. He showed the hat to Love and seven other prisoners they had captured and asked if it belonged to Mosby. They all stated that it was not the colonel's hat. Frazar decided that, whoever the man was, his wounds were mortal; and when he arrived in Fairfax Court House on December 22 he reported that his men had mortally wounded an unidentified major. Frazar came under intense pressure for allowing Mosby to trick him. Less than two months later he was court-martialed and found guilty of disobeying orders to correct and return charges against one of his privates. On March 13, 1865, he resigned from the 13th New York Cavalry and accepted an appointment in the United States Colored Troops.[32]

Continuing his counterguerrilla campaign, on January 1, 1865, Sheridan stationed Devin's cavalry brigade of two thousand men in Loudoun County for the remainder of his occupation of the Valley. They camped at Lovettsville in the German-American community and foraged off the civilians, using up supplies to deprive Mosby of them and discouraging smugglers. Through January and until his departure, Sheridan sent cavalry raids into pro–Southern areas in the Valley and in Mosby's Confederacy, searching homes at night and reporting the killing or capture of 150 guerrillas. Where they found a Rebel soldier, the men were to burn or haul away all of the farm's fence rails, confiscate the livestock except one milk cow, and warn the people that if depredations continued the area would be devastated and all civilians relocated elsewhere. He celebrated on February 5 when his Jessie Scouts guided a cavalry raid to Moorefield, West Virginia, and captured Gilmor in bed.[33]

Sheridan hoped that with Mosby away he could prevent raids on the B&O with a strong infantry picket line on the Winchester and Potomac Railroad and with Col. Marcus A. Reno's 12th Pennsylvania Cavalry posted near Charlestown. He relieved the 2nd Eastern Shore Infantry regiment of Maryland from guard duty at Duffield's Depot and sent them to Baltimore for consolidation with another small regiment. Richards, by now so close a replica of Mosby that Mosby might as well have been present, learned about the weakness and on the frigid night of January 18 slipped through Sheridan's pickets with more than sixty men and derailed a freight train a mile and a half east of Duffield's. The raiders acquired canned oysters and other luxuries, including a large shipment of coffee beans, making this the Coffee Raid. Sheridan ordered an investigation and had the troops burn all ferry boats on the Shenandoah River.[34]

A few weeks later, on the early morning of February 4, an unidentified party of Rebels derailed a freight train one mile east of Richards's attack, robbed the crew, and plundered the cars. This time Reno's scouts gave him advance warning, notifying him when the raiders crossed the Shenandoah River. Reno, a handsome West Point graduate with a reputation for gallantry, later became famous for his role in the battle of Little Big Horn. At 10:00 P.M. on February 3 the alarm came, and he quickly dispatched two parties of fifty cavalrymen each commanded by Lt. Harlow

M. Guild and Lt. Deloss Chase. He emphasized that they were to ride in different directions so as to avoid shooting each other in the dark. Guild lost his way, and, sure enough, the two columns attacked each other. Reno relegated all of the blame to Guild, who, as a habitual substance abuser, was drunk as usual. "When not stupefied with whiskey he is with opium," Reno reported. Secretary of War Stanton, a friend of B&O president Garrett, scolded Sheridan for the chronic derailments at Duffield's, and finally Sheridan protected the station with a strong regiment of cavalry and a hundred infantry.[35]

By mid-February 1865 Sheridan's cavalry had learned the value of overnight raids and tactics used twelve months before by Meade's men, tactics paralleling those of Mosby. Guided by a deserter or spy and traveling light with no forage or wheels, going silently with no jangling sabers, and refraining from stopping in Mosby's Confederacy to eat, make coffee, or feed the horses, they could surprise Mosby's men and capture them asleep in bed. Torbert was on leave, and Merritt was in command of the Cavalry Corps on February 18 when two deserters from Mosby's command offered to serve as pilots. Merritt's headquarters issued orders incorporating what had been learned. Maj. Thomas Gibson, 14th Pennsylvania Cavalry, was to leave camp after dark, at 6:00 P.M., and with 237 men pass through Ashby's Gap. Then he was to divide into separate columns with Capt. Henry Snow, 21st New York Cavalry, in charge of the other force, search houses in separate directions, and reunite in Upperville one hour before daylight to withdraw from Mosby's land before the guerrillas could rendezvous and intercept or harass.[36]

It was a sound plan, but on the road to Ashby's Gap Gibson decided that Piedmont would be a more productive linking point and sent orders back through the column to Snow in the rear, changing Upperville to Piedmont. He assumed that Snow received the message, but the record does not indicate whether he did or not. Beyond the Blue Ridge Mountains they separated as planned, and Snow proceeded to Upperville with a hundred men. He left most of them in town to search the houses and went with a small squad to the home of Dolly Richards's father on a nearby farm. Snow had successfully slipped through the informal grapevine warning system, and his men surrounded the house while Richards and two other Rangers slept inside. However, by the time Snow entered and searched the house, Richards and his companions were concealed behind a trapdoor, watching and smiling. Snow rode back to town and to his disappointment saw that his men had captured two barrels of liquor. About one-third were drunk, six so dead drunk he had to leave them behind. With three prisoners of war he proceeded immediately back to headquarters camp in the Valley.[37]

Meanwhile Gibson had gone south to Markham; and, even though he had lost eleven of his men on the confusing roads, he captured eighteen Rebels and fifty horses. He reached Piedmont on time, but Snow was not there. Thinking that Snow might be waiting in Upperville, he took his detachment to Upperville and learned that Snow had departed hours before. The confusion had delayed Gibson, and it was about 10:00 A.M. when he reached Paris at the entrance to Ashby's Gap. The Rebels had gathered behind a stone fence on elevated ground, and as he marched by they fired rifles into his column. Due to the nature of the terrain he refrained from ordering his men to return fire.[38]

At that moment Dolly Richards arrived, and the Rangers on the hillside greeted him with three huzzahs. He counted forty-three Rangers, and he knew that the enemy had about 125; but, like Mosby, he sensed that an attack would succeed. He expected that Gibson would pass through the gap and turn right at Mount Carmel Church onto Shepherd's Ford Road, a narrow path running north between the Blue Ridge Mountains on the right and impenetrable rocks and undergrowth on the left. The pathway led to Shepherd's Ford on the Shenandoah River, but it was so narrow the Union column had to pass single file.[39]

When Gibson's blueclads disappeared up the mountain, Richards advanced and on the path assaulted the rear guard, driving them in panic into the main body. In the narrow pathway, Gibson could not form a defensive line or arrange an effective countercharge. In close, the Union carbines were no match for the Confederate revolvers. Gibson reported that he was "unable to engage in a mêlée successfully with an enemy armed with at least two revolvers to the man." When it ended, Richards had freed the prisoners of war, recaptured the horses and killed or wounded twenty-five of the enemy, and captured sixty-four men and ninety horses. Gibson lost eighty-nine men, a casualty rate of 71 percent. Mosby wrote in a letter after the war, "I have always said it was the most brilliant thing our men ever did."[40] Sheridan gave a preliminary report to Grant the next day stating that the prisoners were recaptured "and some of our own men were also taken," but it was impossible to tell how many. Two days after the event Stanton heard the rumor in Washington that an entire detachment of 110 of Sheridan's men had been captured, and reports came in that overnight in Sheridan's region of responsibility young

Jesse McNeill and a small force of guerrillas had captured Generals George Crook and Benjamin F. Kelley in Cumberland, Maryland. Stanton telegraphed Grant, "The frequent surprises in Sheridan's command has excited a good deal of observation recently." He asked, "Can you excite more vigilance?"[41]

Five days after the Mount Carmel skirmish, Stanton's office sent Sheridan a message notifying him that the Secretary of War was yet waiting for an explanation of how the 110 men were lost: "The frequent disasters in your command have occasioned much regret in this Department, as indicating a want of vigilance and discipline which, if not speedily cured, may occasion greater misfortune." Sheridan replied the next day—February 25, two days before leaving the Valley—that his raids had generally been successful but "this party was stampeded, and the whole affair badly managed."[42]

Sheridan delivered a heavy blow to Mosby's economic support and forced Mosby to winter half of his men elsewhere. By not burning houses and not arresting civilians, he avoided accusations of inhumanity from the Northern people. Soldiers under his direction seriously wounded Mosby himself and took him out of action for the duration of Sheridan's command in the Valley. But Mosby would return and his men were well mounted and well equipped and still had the tactical initiative. Sheridan weakened Mosby, but his counterinsurgency program failed. Later, when he reflected on the loss of Currie's brigade to guard wagons, it seemed extreme; and in writing his official report he vented his frustration with sour grapes. In the fable of the sour grapes the fox decided that the luscious bunch of ripe grapes beyond his reach were sour anyway; the fox disparaged what he could not attain. Sheridan reported that he had refused to operate against guerrillas because they assisted him in keeping his wagons closed up and prevented straggling. It was true that he kept his priority on Early's army and delayed the full force of his anti-Mosby campaign until Early was defeated; but, as shown, even before the Wagon Raid he began operating against Mosby.[43]

Sheridan stated in his memoirs that, when he advanced to Cedar Creek the first time, detachments necessary to protect his communications in a "hostile region" depleted his line of battle strength to less than Early's army. This was an exaggeration to justify his retrograde movement, but Mosby declared it "the highest tribute ever paid to the efficiency of my command." In an interview in 1911 he said jokingly that Sheridan had made him "the greatest general in history, not even except-

ing Caesar, Hannibal, or General Grant himself," for Sheridan's statement meant that, even though Sheridan "had an army of 94,000 men
effective for service, and Early but 15,000, that when these generals met
Sheridan's force was no larger than Early's because of the detachments
out of action which had to guard attacks and skirmishes from behind."
Tongue in cheek, Mosby was laughing that Sheridan had credited him
with neutralizing seventy-nine thousand Union soldiers with his three
hundred guerrillas.[44]

The only way Sheridan could have defeated Mosby would have been
to capture or kill him or remove his sanctuary of civilian support, and
the Missouri experience made this politically impossible. Like American
forces in Vietnam, Sheridan fought a limited war against Mosby, a fight
with one hand tied behind. After the war, Louis N. Boudrye, chaplain
and historian of the 5th New York Cavalry, wrote that the Union army
should have burned all of the houses in Mosby's Confederacy. John C.
Hoadley, Melville's brother-in-law and editor of Gansevoort's papers,
declared that "the true moral" of the Mosby story was that the army should
have given suitable notice and desolated Mosby's Confederacy. But a remnant of chivalry survived, and at the end of the war travelers going south
from Washington into Virginia saw a symbol of Mosby's victory. In the
last eleven months of the conflict the Union cavalry on the early-warning screen had been on the defensive, pinned down by Mosby's men in a
thirteen-mile line of stockades, two or three miles apart.[45]

# 17

# Apache Ambuscades, Stockades, and Prisons

By the final months of the war, Union commanders in the lower Shenandoah Valley and on the Washington early-warning screen had lost so much sleep from Mosby's raids and false alarms that they went on the defensive. Sheridan's successor, General Hancock, attempted to seal the lower Valley and defend the B&O Railroad with a heavy line of infantry and cavalry pickets, and his counterguerrilla tactics harked back two years to Stahel's methods. In Fairfax County the Union cavalry appeared to be defending the nation's capital from hostile Indians. They had erected a line of stockades for defense; and when they dared to venture into Mosby's Confederacy, they took strong patrols of six to eight hundred cavalry. In Washington officials were conducting their own counterguerrilla campaign, convicting Mosby's prisoners of war as outlaws, and, when that failed, discriminating against them in prisoner exchange.

Apparently when Sheridan departed on February 27, 1865, he left no advice to Hancock on how to hunt Mosby's men—or if he did, Hancock ignored it. Hancock was a friend of Stanton, and Stanton selected him because he wanted a man who would efficiently defend the B&O. In that way he was an ideal choice; Hancock was one of the most efficient Union generals, handsome, honest, and popular with his troops and the public. Born in Pennsylvania, he graduated from West Point and commanded gallantly at Fredericksburg, and at Gettysburg became a hero for defeating "Pickett's Charge." He suffered a serious thigh wound, and during his recovery Stanton assigned him to recruit a new reserve corps of veterans in Washington. The recruiting was disappointing, but Hancock hoped it would pick up and enable him to lead a new army up the Valley to participate in the final victory over Lee.[1]

He won Stanton's gratitude for closing the guerrilla throughway to Duffield's Station tighter than it had been in the war. Indeed, one of his first acts was to post the 1st Veteran Infantry regiment, 800 men under Lt. Col. Charles Bird, at Keyes's Ford about 3.5 miles south of Harpers Ferry. This was his banner unit, and placing them on the Shenandoah River to support Reno's cavalry at Charlestown demonstrated his commitment to defense of the B&O. Rebel raiders avoided infantry pickets and knew to stay clear of Bird's regiment. Hancock also closed Union lines south of Harpers Ferry, prohibiting civilian passage except in urgent cases.[2]

But his counterguerrilla strategy failed. He considered Mosby's Rangers marauders living off the plunder of defenseless citizens and wanted to shut them down, but he ignored what Sheridan's cavalry had learned about the value of overnight raids and midnight searches. Instead, he organized a circular hunt by eighteen hundred infantry, cavalry, and artillery and ordered them to surround and capture Mosby's two hundred Rangers and burn their supplies at Upperville. Like Stahel's owl-shooting expedition, this was as ineffective as using an AK-47 to shoot a mouse. He placed Reno in command of a hammering force of a thousand men: three hundred of Reno's cavalry and seven hundred of Bird's infantry with two cannon. Carefully guarding their rations in a supply wagon train, at 9:30 A.M. on March 20 they crossed the Shenandoah River at Harpers Ferry and moved south through Loudoun County. Meanwhile Hancock posted an infantry regiment in Ashby's Gap and another at Snicker's Ferry to seize fleeing Rebels, and from Fairfax Court House he brought five hundred cavalry and two cannon to prevent escape in that direction.[3]

On the first day Reno's infantry marched through the Unionist area of Loudoun Valley between the Blue Ridge and Short Hill Mountains. The cavalry moved on a parallel route east of the Short Hills, and they bivouacked together that night near Hillsboro. On the second day the cavalry went to Leesburg and swung back to rejoin the infantry in Purcellville on the outskirts of Mosby's Confederacy. With all of this warning, Mosby's men had gathered and were hovering on the hills in every direction. Rather than moving into the enemy land, Reno organized his task force in the standard formation, with the cavalry riding in advance, on the flanks and in the rear, and withdrew along the turnpike toward Leesburg. Two miles along, at Hamilton, called Harmony then, Mosby attacked and altered Reno's marching order for the remainder of the mission.[4]

Mosby had gathered 128 men, and in this his last significant engagement in the war, prepared an ambush. One mile south of the turnpike, beside the road leading to today's Lincoln, he concealed the men in a wooded hollow and sent six horsemen into the edge of Hamilton as decoys. Presently a detachment of the 12th Pennsylvania Cavalry under Lt. John H. Black took the bait and came galloping after the decoys. Mosby's men charged, killing nine, wounding twelve, and capturing thirteen men and fifteen horses. The Union remnant retreated into town and found protection behind a line of Bird's infantry formed behind an osage orange hedge. Some of Mosby's men rode directly into the face of a volley by the infantry, costing Mosby two men dead, six or seven wounded, and six captured.[5]

Reno camped that night about one mile west of Hamilton and for the remaining three days of the raid, under intense harassment and sniper fire, marched to Snickersville, Bloomfield, Upperville, and Middleburg, keeping his cavalry drawn in behind the infantry to protect them and their horses from the guerrillas. In his official report he estimated Mosby's command at five hundred men; a few weeks later, when the war had ended, he asked one of Mosby's officers how many Confederates were in the Hamilton ambush. "One hundred and twenty-eight, all-told," the man said, and Reno exclaimed, "Twenty-eight thousand, you mean." This was one of the highest compliments Mosby's force-multiplying received—in Reno's memory, Mosby's detachment was expanded over two hundred times. When Hancock received Reno's report and reflected, he was mystified that with such a strong force the mission "accomplished much less than I had expected it to do."[6]

By the end of March, Hancock estimated that he had twenty-five thousand infantry and three thousand cavalry almost in shape for taking the offensive against Lee. In the meantime, he used an infantry division to seal the lower Valley with infantry pickets. Along with forces from Harpers Ferry, he ordered Gen. John R. Brooke's 4,913 men of the First Provisional Division to picket the Shenandoah River from Harpers Ferry south along fourteen miles of bank to a point on the river east of Kabletown. He meant this to last for a few weeks, until he began his march southward, but the Valley had a way of spooking Union generals, causing them to imagine phantom enemy armies. Sheridan worried that

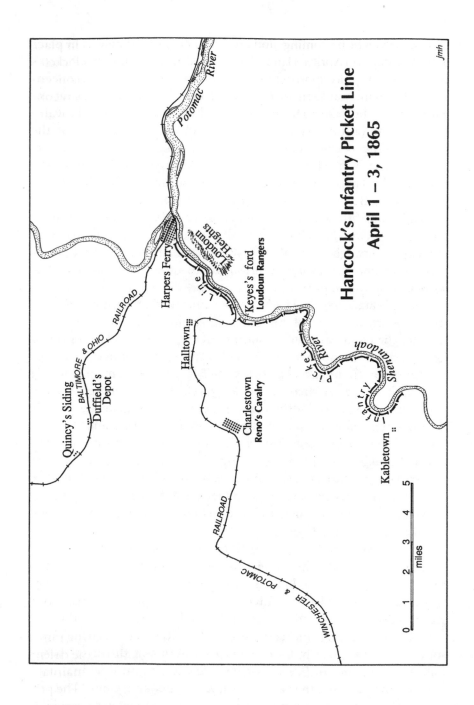

Hancock's Infantry Picket Line
April 1 – 3, 1865

Longstreet might be coming; and after his new picket line was in place only three days, on April 3, Hancock swallowed a false rumor that Pickett's Division was rapidly approaching. He withdrew from the river, concentrated the infantry at Kernstown, and dispatched the cavalry on a reconnaissance up the Valley. This left only five hundred dismounted cavalry guarding the railroad near Halltown northwest of the camp of the Loudoun Rangers who were leisurely picketing Keyes's Ford.[7]

Two days later, when Mosby organized his eighth and last company under Capt. George Baylor, he sent Baylor and his fifty men to exploit the weakness. Baylor learned on the way that the Loudoun Rangers were vulnerable and crossed the river and approached from the direction of Harpers Ferry with his advance dressed in blue overcoats. In the daylight they passed through the picket line of dismounted cavalry without challenge. The Loudoun Rangers were lounging around, expecting any time to hear of the end of the war, and several were resting and fishing on the riverbank. Baylor surprised and scattered them, killing two men, wounding four, and capturing sixty-five men and eighty-one horses.[8]

Mosby rendezvoused the raiders on April 8 and divided into two detachments. He took about one hundred through Ashby's Gap and captured a small picket post near Berryville, and he ordered Captain Glascock to take the other force of about 115 men to Burke's Station on the O&A Railroad inside Union lines and capture mules from a wagon train hauling wood. Glascock was to be married within a few days and decided that, since Richmond had fallen, the war was over. He took the force to Salem, dismissed them, and went home. The next day most of the men reassembled at The Plains on the call of Baylor and continued the mission. On April 10 Baylor marched south around the left flank of the Union line and arrived at Burke's Station but found the mules too well guarded. He canceled the mission and returned three miles southwest to Arundel's Tavern and halted to rest and feed the horses. Arundel's was only 2.5 miles south of the southernmost Union fort at Fairfax Station, and the commander sent a force of 8th Illinois Cavalry that surprised and routed Baylor's men. A few days later Baylor apologized for tarnishing the honor of his new company.[9]

Baylor violated the hit-and-run principle within easy striking range of a Union cavalry screen that had concentrated and gone on the defensive. One of Mosby's goals was to divert men from the front to maintain a strong force on the warning screen to prevent his incursions. "The primary object of partisan war should be to neutralize as large a portion as possible of the enemy's force by keeping up a continuous alarm for the safety of his communications and his line of supply. Every man detached from the front to guard the rear of an invading army is so much subtracted from its aggressive strength." In a letter to a newspaper he declared that three hundred men operating efficiently in the rear equal ten thousand in the front. During an interview he estimated that his command had forced twenty to thirty thousand Union troops to be stationed in Washington and another time said, "It took fifty thousand soldiers on the other side to keep us in check." Mosby's estimates were greatly exaggerated, and, as has been described, his most strategic diversions occurred on Sheridan's communications in the Valley. And yet, even on the more complicated Washington front, he diverted several times his own number from the regular fighting.[10]

First, it is important to consider what a small investment in manpower Mosby's operation was to the Confederacy. At any one time he never had more than 400 men, and the largest number that he led on a raid was 375 on October 25, 1864. For the first eight and one-half months he had only one company, and he had fewer than one hundred men until November 1863, fewer than two hundred until April 1864, and fewer than three hundred until August 1864. He had one cannon for one raid in May 1863 and up to four guns for about four months, from June to October 1864. His highest rank was colonel, and his highest organization was one regiment of eight companies. Seldom in military history has a government received such a significant return on such a minor investment.

The best reading on how many men Mosby diverted from the Union army to guard against him on the Washington–southern Maryland front came during the Gettysburg campaign. At other times, such as when Mosby first went independent in January 1863, it is impossible to credit Mosby because the screen of thirty-three hundred cavalry was already in position before he came, to warn of raids by regular Confederate cavalry or infantry. But during Gettysburg both armies went to Pennsylvania, and the only organized Confederate force threatening Washington and the Potomac River border was Mosby's. Hooker, before departing, absorbed Stahel's cavalry division into the Army of the Potomac and took them with him. Hooker's headquarters directed Lowell's 2nd Massachusetts Cavalry regiment of 462 men guarding the Potomac at Poolesville, Maryland, to go as well. Heintzelman ordered Lowell to disobey and remain where he was and asked Halleck to support him on the ground that if Lowell departed a small band of guerrillas would be able to raid into Maryland and cut communications on the canal and on the railroad to Baltimore. Halleck upheld Heintzelman and thus Mosby with 30 men denied the Union army 462 men at Gettysburg. This was fifteen times Mosby's own strength.[11]

Grant stripped the cavalry screen for his spring 1864 offensive, and when Lowell and his 2nd Massachusetts Cavalry departed in July 1864 it left less than one-third the recommended three thousand men in Fairfax County. Lowell's successor, Col. Henry M. Lazelle, 16th New York Cavalry, reported on July 19 that the area beyond Aldie was "the enemy's country" and "nothing but an overwhelming force of 500 or more men can march with impunity in his country." Therefore it was necessary to cancel search-and-capture missions and erect three stockades "to concentrate our strength to occupy a defensible position." He proposed that his two regiments, now camped on hills near Fort Buffalo in the vicinity of Falls Church, build stockades with abatis at Falls Church headquarters, Lewinsville four miles north, and Annandale four miles south. Constant mounted patrolling between the stockades would provide communication, and, in times of alert, each fort would keep two horses saddled around the clock so that, if Mosby attacked, two riders could be dispatched in different directions to bring reinforcements.[12]

And "in order to prevent the constant annoyance arising from small parties of guerrillas," Lazelle applied a tactic that he had learned fighting Indians before the war. He was a Massachusetts native, graduated from West Point in 1855, and after the war would return as commandant of cadets, 1879-82. After West Point he served on the frontier in Arizona and New Mexico, fighting Apache. In the Sacramento Mountains on February 8, 1859, he had been severely wounded in the lungs and had learned first-hand respect for the Apache tactic of the night ambush by a small number of dismounted warriors. He now reported that, since he had "some little experience in Indian maneuvers, which bears a certain analogy to this warfare," he would create a secret ambuscade line of five-man posts to intercept Mosby's raiders. Augur had no objection, and Lazelle ordered his plan into effect. He established the ambush line forward from the stockades two to five miles, extending from the Potomac River on the north, eleven miles to the Braddock Road south of Annandale. Twenty ambush posts were concealed in the forest after dark with two days' rations. Their assignment was to remain concealed in the day and in the night ambush Mosby's men on the roads and bypaths.[13]

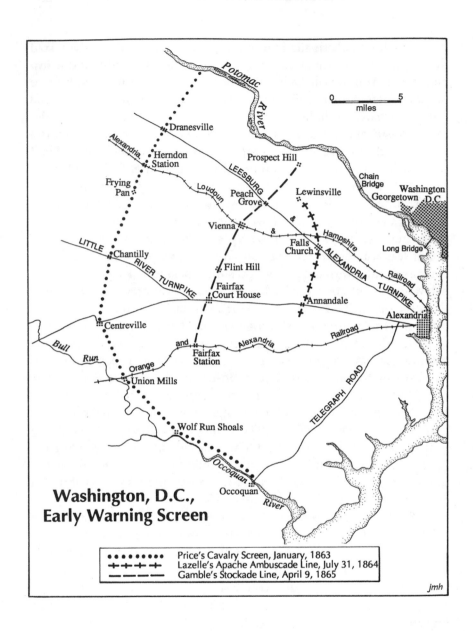

Washington, D.C.,
Early Warning Screen

•••••••••  Price's Cavalry Screen, January, 1863
+++++  Lazelle's Apache Ambuscade Line, July 31, 1864
– – – –  Gamble's Stockade Line, April 9, 1865

jmh

Lazelle's stockade tactic was completely successful. Mosby tested the weakest fort at Annandale with an overnight raid and found it impenetrable. At noon on August 23, 1864, he left Rectortown with three hundred men and two cannon and the next morning in heavy fog and only a few yards' visibility arrived at the stockade at 5:00 A.M. and demanded a surrender. There were only 170 men in the walls because Lazelle had been ordered to dispatch a long-range scouting expedition and had sent half of his force. Capt. Joseph Schneider, 16th New York Cavalry, replied: "A German commands this fort and he will never surrender." Mosby ordered his artillery to fire over the wall into the stockade, and they began a barrage that delivered between thirty and forty shells, wounded two horses, and destroyed some quarters and an old barn used as a stable. Mosby ordered the firing to cease and sent in under flag of truce a second demand of surrender, and Schneider answered, "Tell Colonel Mosby I will not surrender, and if he sends that rag up here again I'll shoot it to hell." Mosby and his men withdrew, and Lazelle sent one hundred men from headquarters to restore the stockade to "a defensive state."[14]

But it was a different story with the Apache ambuscade line. Mosby's raiders captured one of the outposts on the morning of August 24 and another the following morning, and on succeeding nights Ranger parties of twenty to thirty men returned to easily gobble the five-man teams. When two posts were taken on the night of August 31, Lazelle ordered the next shift to "build a cribwork of fallen trees to intrench themselves by day," and continue ambushing at night. The *Washington Star* reported, "Our scouts are on the alert on the hills, valleys, and through the dense woods, but are unable to catch these picket-shooting assassins and marauding highwaymen."[15]

Duty on the ambush line exhausted the men, and there was no rest because on July 30 Augur ordered Lazelle to begin sending daily long-range scouts to the Blue Ridge Mountains and the Rappahannock River to investigate regular Confederate cavalry movements. Lazelle had requested at least six companies of infantry to help occupy two of the stockades, but none came. Severely undermanned, Lazelle's men were driven into the ground by scouting, ambush duty, and Mosby's attacks. "The duty has been the incubus to the cavalry here," Gansevoort complained. It had destroyed "the spirit, drill, and efficiency of the soldier." Finally, when Augur stripped Lazelle's screen to take the men to guard reconstruction of the MGR, Lazelle resigned on October 18, 1864.[16]

Gansevoort was temporary commander for one month, and on

November 19, 1864, Augur appointed Col. William Gamble, 8th Illinois Cavalry, in charge and ordered him to return the screen to the fifteen-mile line where it was before May 24, 1864. Gamble brought his 8th Illinois regiment and was assigned two infantry regiments, giving him at least eighteen hundred men, which was still about one-third less than recommended. He was a forty-six-year-old Irish immigrant and had served as an enlisted man in the regular army, fighting the Seminoles in Florida. When the Civil War began he was a civil engineer in Chicago. He was an able and respected colonel, having been wounded at Malvern Hill and having commanded a brigade of cavalry at Gettysburg.[17]

With headquarters at Fairfax Court House, Gamble erected a new line of eight stockades with abatis, thirteen miles long and extending from the Potomac to Fairfax Station on the O&A Railroad. There were three structures at headquarters and single stockades at Prospect Hill, Peach Grove, Vienna, Flint Hill, and Fairfax Station. He organized flag communication between headquarters and Vienna and daily mounted patrols of twenty cavalrymen along the full extent of the line.[18]

Gamble requested two twenty-pound Parrott guns for Fairfax Court House, but Augur's headquarters replied that he had no use for guns of such caliber. Mosby had no artillery and could not assault the stockades, but small parties of his men attacked and defeated two of the cavalry patrols in the first two weeks of March. Gamble reacted by ordering that each patrol be guarded by a second patrol thrown out as flankers into the fields and woods one mile toward Mosby's Confederacy. He sent large detachments of cavalry numbering six hundred and eight hundred men to search Mosby's boardinghouses at night. They captured some of Mosby's men, and morale in the 8th Illinois regiment was high when the war ended, as illustrated by their attack at Arundel's on April 10. But even in its success, Gamble's elaborate defensive network and scouting in strength confirmed that Mosby was still in control of his Confederacy.[19]

During the last year of the war, Mosby hunters had two powerful allies in the Lincoln administration attacking Mosby's command with the weapons of military justice and imprisonment. Secretary of War Stanton and Judge Advocate General Joseph Holt agreed that partisans were felons not entitled to the privileges of prisoners of war and regarded it as their duty to bring them to justice. They were already directing the administration's sweeping effort to arrest and try Northern civilians accused of disloyalty, and now they worked together to use the system of military commissions to prosecute Mosby's men. Military commissions were essentially courts-martial of civilians, and they were not kangaroo courts; but with the same commission of army officers meeting for weeks to try case after case, it was a quick and convenient method of producing guilty verdicts. In 1866 in *Ex parte Milligan,* the Supreme Court ruled that such military trials of civilians were unconstitutional where civil courts were functioning.[20]

Stanton and Holt's prosecution of Mosby's men illustrates how tempting it was to use military commissions to circumvent the law. They knew that Confederate Partisan Rangers were legal—the issue had been officially decided nearly two years earlier. Halleck wrote in his book on international law, published in May 1861, that partisans were criminals "subject to the punishment due to their crimes." However, as general in chief, in August 1862 he practiced commendable restraint by asking Francis Lieber, professor of history and law at Columbia College, to write an opinion on guerrilla warfare. Lieber responded with an essay that drew a distinction between partisans and outlaws based on the military nature of the unit. Lieber defined partisans as legal practitioners of irregular tactics because they were enrolled in the army and wore uniforms. Self-constituted, unauthorized irregulars, on the other hand, were "brigands" and "freebooters" with no rights as belligerents. Halleck had Lieber's essay printed and distributed in the army.[21] Then, in December 1862, Halleck appointed Lieber to a committee to write a set of instructions on the conduct of the Union army. The influential document that resulted, Halleck issued from the War Department on April 24, 1863, as General Orders no. 100, and it became known as "Lieber's Code." Like Lieber's essay, the code provided that partisans in the Confederate army who wore the uniform were legal and entitled to all of the privileges of prisoners of war.[22]

Historian Mark Neely describes how difficult it was to convict Confederate irregulars in Missouri and Tennessee, even in trials by military commission. Defendants were accused of actions such as burning bridges, stealing horses, and plundering; and it was easy to obtain witnesses to such behavior. But the defendants would argue successfully that, yes, they committed the acts, but as soldiers of the Confederacy. So the cases usually hinged on the military nature of the group to which the man belonged. Rarely could a witness be found who could testify on this, because how could one know whether the man's group was authorized by the Confederate government or was simply an outlaw band? Therefore judge advocates prosecuting the cases usually abandoned attempts to prove the men were guerrillas and fell back on violations of the oath of allegiance or documented violations regarding subscription or parole.[23]

When the Bureau of Military Justice discovered a witness willing to testify that Mosby had no formal organization but operated a gang of men united only for plunder, Holt recognized an unusual opportunity. The witness was deserter Charles Binns, the man who had been guiding Lowell's raids. He had served as a private under Mosby for four months before deserting on November 3, 1863. With Binns as star witness for the prosecution, Holt set out to prove in court that Mosby was leading a band of felons. He began arraigning and trying Mosby prisoners of war before a military commission of six army officers in session in Washington. The president was Gen. Abner Doubleday, later famous for supposedly having created the game of baseball in Cooperstown, New York.

The first trial began on February 10, 1864, and the defendant was twenty-two-year-old Pvt. Philip Trammell, captured November 11, 1863, in Loudoun County. He was charged with "Violation of the laws of war in carrying on a guerrilla warfare," and specifically robbing from citizens and waging "a private warfare against the lawful Government of the United States, for the purposes of plunder, and in total violation of the laws and customs of war." General Orders no. 100 stated that men not enrolled in the army who intermittently returned to their homes and avocations and took off their uniforms "shall be treated summarily as highway robbers or pirates."[24]

As the first witness, in answer to queries by Judge Advocate John A. Foster, prosecuting the case, Binns testified that when he joined Mosby's command he was not formally enrolled and he assumed none of the men were. He stated that he drew no pay, only spoils; and, when raids ended, Mosby dispersed the men, and Trammell went home to his father's farm near Frying Pan and the others went to their homes or to boardinghouses. An unidentified member of the commission asked if Mosby's men were under any obligation to reassemble for the next raid. "No sir," Binns said, "They could meet him if they chose. They were under no obligation to meet him but if they did they shared the proceeds if anything was captured."[25]

A defendant before a military commission, as with courts-martial at the time, had the right to counsel, but one's attorney was strictly prohibited from speaking, examining witnesses, or addressing the court. Speaking for himself, a defendant could make statements and cross-examine witnesses. Trammell may have had an attorney, but none is indicated in his trial record. Whether he had legal advice or not, he did not cross-examine Binns or reply. Trammell, with his lawyer if he had one, concentrated his defense on the specification of armed robbery; he had no idea that the case hinged on the testimony of Binns that Mosby's band was illegal.[26]

The next prosecution witness, Julius Morse, stated that he was in his room in the house of Walter H. Erwin in Falls Church when Trammell came in and at gunpoint robbed him of a hundred dollars in greenbacks. Trammell asked Morse if he could swear that he was the man. "I would not swear positively but I think you are," said Morse. Then D.O. Munson testified that he was captured by some of Mosby's men on the night in question and escaped. He did not identify Trammell as one of them, and Trammell had no questions for him. Next, Erwin testified that he saw the robbery and had no doubt that the robber was Trammell, and Trammell did not cross-examine. Foster closed his case, and Trammell requested that John B. Fortner of Herndon Station be summoned as a witness because he could prove that on the night of the alleged crime Trammell was not in Falls Church but at the house of an uncle. At this point Foster called and gave the oath to Thomas T. Johnson, a detective of Col. Lafayette C. Baker, provost marshal for the War Department. Johnson stated that Fortner lived outside Union lines and "the process of the court could not safely be served on him," and reports were that Fortner was "a disloyal citizen." The court rejected the request, and Trammell closed, "I have no statement to make except that I am not guilty of the charges preferred against me, and I deny the statement of the last witness. I was never at Falls Church in my life."[27]

In his closing argument Foster said, "It appears by the evidence before us that this Defendant was a member of Moseby's guerilla force. The evidence is abundant that this force is in the habit of stealing, robbing & marauding through the country, that they are not a regularly organized, military force, that these parties are not mustered in to any service, are not organized but are in the habit of meeting together for a raid, & afterwards of dividing the plunder they take among themselves, which is the only payment they receive. It appears that when a raid is over they disperse to their various homes, no one being under any obligation to rejoin them again except at his pleasure." Then after summarizing the testimony on the robbery, he said, "The crime is clearly defined by the War Dept. in Gen. Order, No. 100, and leaves no discretion on the part of the Court as to the punishment to be inflicted."[28]

The court unanimously found Trammell guilty and sentenced him "to be shot to death." Holt reviewed the case and approved, confirming that Mosby's command "is shown to have no regular organization but is made up of men who without being mustered into any service, join together and make a raid capturing whatever plunder they can; dispersing to their homes at any time they choose; being under no obligations to serve again, and receiving no pay except a share of the plunder." Based on Binns's testimony, Foster's summary and Holt's review were correct; Mosby's men were illegal guerrillas under Lieber's definition in General Orders no. 100. Of course, Mosby's men were officially enlisted in the Confederate army, were eligible for the same salary as regular Confederate cavalry, and had to report for raids or Mosby would return them to regular duty. But the trial set a precedent and established grounds for charging more of Mosby's prisoners on the same charges.[29]

The next case before the Doubleday Court was of another Mosby prisoner, and his trial seemed to confirm the precedent. John H. "Jack" Barnes, captured in Fairfax County with Robert M. Harrover on October 22, 1863, was the defendant. Barnes had been captured twice before and exchanged, and this time his prison record described him as a "celebrated guerrilla." He was charged with four crimes: breaking an oath of allegiance, violating parole by fighting without being exchanged, "waging unlawful and guerrilla warfare against the United States" through "many acts of robbery, theft and murder," and spying. He was found not guilty of spying and not guilty of breaking an oath of allegiance but guilty of breaking his parole and guilty of guerrilla warfare. In the trial Binns submitted a deposition and an alleged deserter named Lyne testified that the Rangers were not enrolled and not paid but divided their plunder and dispersed after raids. Closing, the judge advocate said, "The Government has gone to great length to show the character of this famous Band of Moseby."[30]

In his defense Barnes submitted a deposition inquiring, "If it is sought to charge me on the ground of being an accomplice in a felony, why not indict me in the civil tribunals of the country? But if it is to be regarded as a military offence to belong to Moseby's Battalion, I answer that the organization, being a part of the military force of the Confederacy" is legal and exchanges prisoners. Regardless, the commission sentenced him to be hanged. In July Lincoln commuted the sentences of Trammell and Barnes to ten years in prison, and on July 26 they were sent to the penitentiary in Albany, New York.[31]

Holt wrote a bill making it easier for field commanders to execute guerrillas and spies and presented it to Congress. When these men were convicted by courts-martial, commanders already had the authority to execute them without approval of the president. Under Lincoln this was significant, because he usually commuted death sentences. Holt's bill extended this authority to exclude Lincoln's mercy to guerrillas and spies convicted by military commission, and it passed on July 2, 1864, as "An Act to provide for the more speedy punishment of guerrilla marauders, and for other purposes."[32]

Robert M. Harrover, about twenty-two years old, was tried by Doubleday's commission on July 29 and August 1. He had been recommended for exchange, but Stanton had suspended his release and ordered him to stand trial. He was charged with violating his registration for conscription in Washington by joining Mosby's "irregular and unlawful band of Guerrillas." He called as a witness Col. Daniel H. Dulaney, Governor Pierpont's aide who had been captured in September 1863 and held by Mosby's men for seven days. Dulaney was a respected Unionist, and his testimony carried weight with the members of the commission. He stated that his son, Pvt. Daniel French Dulaney, was mustered into Mosby's command as were all of Mosby's battalion and that he witnessed one of the musters. When asked about pay, he said, "They were paid just as the Virginia Cavalry were paid." This made a strong impression on some of the commissioners, and after the court adjourned for the weekend they told Foster that he had "failed to prove Mosby's band an irregular organization as charged." The verdict was not unanimous; but since the charge of being a guerrilla was combined in the same charge as violating draft registration and Harrover was truly guilty of that, the commission found him guilty and sentenced him to be shot. He escaped from the Old Capitol Prison on August 15 and was at large on September 27, when Lincoln commuted his sentence to ten years' hard labor in the penitentiary.[33]

Next was twenty-one-year-old Pvt. Charles F. Beavers. Captured June 3, 1864, he was truly guilty of giving himself up, taking the oath, spying in Washington, and then returning to fight with Mosby. The notation on his prison admission record stated, "He is besides a noted outlaw. Should be tried." He was found not guilty of spying but guilty of violating his oath of allegiance and sentenced to be hanged. At about 11:30 A.M. on August 26 he was taken to the scaffold in the southwest corner of the Old Capitol Prison Yard. Many Confederate prisoners watched from windows looking out upon the yard. "Good-bye, father," he said and, looking toward his comrades in the windows, called out "Good-bye, boys." At 11:45 the trap door fell with a dull sound, and his body dangled in the air. Sensational headlines celebrated "A Guerrilla Executed" and "One of Mosby's Guerrillas Hanged."[34]

By now Mosby could imagine the collar around his own neck becoming slightly uncomfortable. He had no knowledge that in Harrover's trial Dulaney had exploded the grounds of Holt and Stanton's campaign; as far as he knew, the military commission trials would continue and with Holt's new legislation field commanders would approve the hanging and shooting of his men. One of his basic goals was to have his men treated as prisoners of war, and here the Union government had convicted four, two of whom were in the penitentiary, one had escaped, and one had been hanged. It appeared to him that Holt and Stanton were campaigning to prove him and his men outlaws.

On August 25, 1864, the day before Beavers was hanged, he sent a message to Lazelle in Falls Church notifying him that, in retaliation for the imprisonment of Trammell and Barnes, he was directing that two of his Union prisoners, Maj. William H. Forbes and Capt. William C. Manning, both of the 2nd Massachusetts Cavalry, be sent to a similar Confederate facility. On September 9, Robert Ould, the Confederate exchange agent, complained to his Union counterpart about Trammell and Barnes and declared that Mosby's men "are as regularly in our service as any soldier in General Lee's army." Unless the men were released, he threatened to retaliate on Forbes and Manning by sending them to a similar prison.[35]

But the Confederate prison camp system was vastly overcrowded, and, as far as Mosby determined, Ould's threat was not carried out. Forbes was confined in several different prison camps and exchanged in December 1864. Manning was placed in close confinement in Libby Prison in Richmond, and it may have been on Mosby's behalf. On December 5, 1864, Union authorities retaliated for Manning by placing a Confederate officer in the same conditions. Ould protested on November 8, 1864, that Trammell was in Albany for "being a guerrilla" and on January 18, 1865, complained about the confinement of Barnes, Trammell, and Harrover, being unaware of Harrover's escape. On April 4, 1865, Mosby objected that Trammell and Barnes were still in Albany and stated that he had pleaded in vain for retaliation on Forbes and Manning. Trammell and Barnes were not released until after the war.[36]

After the grounds for the trials collapsed, Union authorities realized that it was not necessary to hang Mosby's men to be rid of them—it was equally effective and more efficient to keep them in prison. The cartel of prisoner exchange had broken down in May 1863, but exchanges continued. After February 1, 1865, under Grant's direction, thousands of men were exchanged, including prisoners held in close confinement as hostages for retaliation. As exchanges occurred, Mosby's men sometimes noticed that none of them were included. This discrimination, which was made against other partisans as well, had begun for Mosby's men by the time he was in operation less than five months. On May 13, 1863, Ould was receiving exchanged prisoners from the Old Capitol when he discovered that twelve of Mosby's men had been excluded under the allegation that they were "bushwhackers and guerrillas." He pointed out that Mosby's command was in the regular army and entitled to exchange and threatened to retaliate if they were not released immediately. Col. W. Hoffman, commissary-general of prisoners in Washington, replied that his policy was to exchange all irregulars who were not spies, and he overruled the suspension order and released the men five days after Ould's protest. At least five of the twelve had entered prison with the notation "not subject to exchange" entered by their names.[37]

Many of Mosby's men were exchanged, some more than once, but if Augur had been in control none of them would have been released until the end of the war. In early May 1864 he requested a list of guerrillas confined in the Old Capitol Prison during the last three months. On May 4, 1864, Lt. Col. Henry H. Wells, provost marshal general for Defenses South of the Potomac, forwarded the names: "They are all of them men of bad character and ought not to be exchanged, but confined in some prison remote from Virginia, where they will not be likely to escape. They are generally rebels, cut-throats, and thieves, and only await a release to return to their old avocation." Augur forwarded the list to the adjutant-general's office "with the request that these men be not exchanged, but kept closely confined during the war. . . . One of them would give more trouble to us than half a dozen ordinary soldiers."[38]

Increasingly from that time Mosby's prisoners entered confinement with special notations on their prison records and were denied exchange. Thomas J. Thompson was identified as "a well known rascal"; John E. Rowzee, "a noted cut-throat"; and Robert L. Spindle, "a guerrilla bushwhacker and horse thief." Spindle was sent to Camp Chase in Columbus, Ohio, and Thompson and Rowzee were in a group of about fifteen Mosby Rangers sent from the Old Capitol to Fort Warren in Boston Harbor

September 20, 1864. Fort Warren, on George's Island, had been constructed as a Civil War fort and then transformed into a military prison camp. Conditions were better than many Civil War prisons—the men had blankets and three days per week a solid meal of bread, soup, and meat. But they soon realized that they had been sent to Boston Harbor for the duration.[39]

In January 1865 several were on a list of prisoners recommended by the surgeon for medical exchange; the non-Mosby men were exchanged, but the Rangers who were ill were not. On February 6, a group of eighty-seven prisoners from the commands of Mosby, White, and Kincheloe were transferred from the Old Capitol to Fort Warren. A special train was scheduled and a rumor circulated in Washington a few days before that these "desperate characters" planned to escape. This caused officials to take extra precautions: they were handcuffed in pairs, and on the train an armed soldier sat in every other seat and a squad stood at the back and front of each car. When they passed through New York City they had to walk through the streets to change railroads, and a large crowd gathered on the sidewalks. Mosby's sergeant Alexander G. Babcock recognized the famous editor Horace Greeley and, raising his arm to show how he was manacled, shouted, "How are you Horace? What do you think of such treatment of prisoners of war?"[40]

On March 2 another group of thirty men from Mosby's and Kincheloe's commands were sent to Fort Warren and told that they would not be exchanged. On April 4, when Mosby complained to Ould about Barnes and Trammell, he also protested that all of his men in Union custody had been taken to Fort Warren and that Northern newspapers were reporting that they would not be exchanged. Keen and Mewborn's roster has at least 180 of Mosby's men in prison camps when the war ended, 136 of them in Fort Warren, for about 75 percent of those identified. Others were in Fort Delaware, Elmira, New York, and others. Several of the Rangers were exchanged in February and March, including some who had been in prison since 1863. Including fourteen men listed by Keen and Mewborn as dying in prison or in an enemy hospital, there were at least 195 men whose services Mosby lost in the last months of the war. His maximum active strength was less than four hundred, and thus his numbers may have been depleted by about one-third by captures, death in prison, and denial of exchange. The Union cavalry night searches of boardinghouses denied him many valuable men. "Keeping my men in prison weakened us as much as to hang them," he wrote.[41]

Sheridan's economic war cost Mosby two hundred men for the final months. When the Union cavalry captured his men and Union prison officials denied them exchange, this cost Mosby almost two hundred additional soldiers. But the attraction of spoils and adventure brought more recruits than he needed. On April 5, 1865, he organized Baylor's new company, and on April 12, William Chapman's force returned from the Northern Neck. At the end of the war he had between three and four hundred men in a regiment of eight companies. He and his men and their civilian friends were winning their guerrilla war, and they were emotionally unprepared for the end. When Lee surrendered, Catherine Broun recorded, "It is a *terrible disappointment,* so unlooked for." Since he was not defeated, Mosby approached the close of his warfare from a position of strength, and that made his surrender unusually complicated and challenging.[42]

# 18

# "All that the proud can feel of pain"

Mosby's men had seen him cry only once, standing by the deathbed of Tom Turner at Loudoun Heights. But when he read about Lee's surrender in the *Baltimore American* and realized that the war was over, he broke down again, in "the very image of despair." Sitting on a log outside the house where he had spent the night, he laid aside the paper and said, "I thought I had sounded the profoundest depth of human feeling, but this is the bitterest hour of my life." He had never been physically healthy in peacetime, and he loved fighting so much that he spoke of coming under fire as a "marvelous experience." He could not bring himself to surrender as long as General Johnston's army remained active in North Carolina and as long as there was a shred of hope of continuing the fight. He disbanded the regiment but delayed his own surrender until after Johnston, and by then the Union army was offering a five-thousand-dollar reward for his capture.[1]

When Lee surrendered on April 9 and Stanton and Halleck instructed Hancock to offer the same terms in his department that Grant had given Lee's men, they ordered that Mosby was to be excluded. Therefore, on the morning of April 10, Hancock issued a circular to the public announcing that Confederates could surrender except: "The Guerrilla Chief Mosby is not included in the parole." That afternoon Stanton asked Grant for his opinion. Should the terms offered Lee's army be extended to Mosby's men and others? Stanton was surprised when Grant replied that all should be given the same terms, including Mosby. Now backtracking, on the following day Hancock's chief of staff Charles H. Morgan wrote Mosby a letter informing him and proposing a meeting between Mosby and an officer of equal rank to discuss Mosby's surrender.[2]

At Winchester Hancock waited for two days for an answer. When none came, he issued a second circular on April 13, mentioning that Mosby had not replied and threatening that, if he did not come in, Hancock's forces would desolate Mosby's civilian supporters. Meanwhile, he began organizing a second circular hunt to capture Mosby. He issued orders for the mobilization, on the morning of April 15, of about eight thousand infantry and cavalry in an operation designed to seal off the Potomac River and the Blue Ridge Mountains, sweep into Mosby's Confederacy to arrest all able-bodied adult males, confiscate all livestock, and destroy Mosby's "haunts" with the torch, leaving the people in poverty. He still had no reply from Mosby when at 1:00 A.M. on April 15, only a few hours before the raid was to begin, he received notification of Lincoln's assassination and had to cancel the operation.[3]

Mosby was stalling—he had decided to continue the fight as long as Johnston had an army in the field in North Carolina—and he had sent Channing Smith and four men to Richmond to find out and to ask Lee's advice. Smith had not returned, but on the fifteenth, the same day that Hancock canceled the raid, Mosby wrote a letter proposing a conference to discuss a brief suspension of hostilities to allow time for him to communicate with Confederate authorities. He sent the letter to Hancock with a delegation of four officers that included William Chapman, returned from the Northern Neck, and Aristides Monteiro, Mosby's surgeon during the last few months of the war. As the four entered Union lines in the Valley and identified themselves, a Union picket shouted, "Thank God! The war is over. I know the end has come when Mosby's men surrender." Chapman and Monteiro presented the letter to Hancock, and he seemed amazed that they did not have the appearance or demeanor of outlaws but were both educated and cultured gentlemen.[4]

They left, and Hancock thought this was going to be easy. He had his chief of staff reply on April 16 that armistice talks were not required, that a forty-eight-hour cease-fire was now in effect, until noon, April 18, to give Mosby time to communicate with his government. At that hour, a Union officer of equal rank would meet Mosby in the hotel in Millwood in the Valley, a site between Hancock's headquarters and Mosby's Confederacy, and receive Mosby's surrender if that was his decision. Mosby had received this letter when on April 17 Smith returned from Richmond. Smith said that he saw no indication in Richmond that Johnston had surrendered and that Lee had told him that he could give no advice since he was on parole. "But, General, what must I do?" Smith persisted. "Channing, go home," Lee said. "All you boys who fought with me, and help to build up the shattered fortunes of our dear old State."[5]

Hancock had no doubt that Mosby would surrender with his entire command at the Millwood meeting. To insure success and manage the situation with flair, he gave Mosby probably the highest open compliment the Union army gave him during the war—he sent not a colonel equal to Mosby but a general, Brig. Gen. George H. Chapman. He had commanded a division of cavalry under Sheridan and was now second in command of Hancock's cavalry. He was from Indianapolis and, like Mosby, he was a lawyer and not a West Point man, and Mosby and his men respected Chapman. Hancock had done his usual efficient work.[6]

The meeting went pleasantly, with Mosby and several of his officers on one side of a long table and Chapman and his delegation on the other. Lincoln's funeral was scheduled for the next day, and Mosby and his companions expressed regret over his death. Mosby was honored that Hancock had sent a general, and, in the atmosphere of mutual respect that marked the meeting, he spoke openly and truthfully. He said that he had already told his men that they could come in and give their parole as individuals. He stated that he was not convinced that the Confederate cause was hopeless and that he wanted to propose an extension of the truce to allow time for him to determine whether Johnston's army was still engaged. He indicated that, if Johnston should surrender, he would disband the regiment and allow each man to be paroled individually. And he said that he planned not to surrender but to go into exile outside the United States.[7]

Chapman agreed to extend the suspension of hostilities for forty-eight hours, until noon, April 20, and gave conditional approval of a further extension beyond that of ten days, contingent upon the approval of his superiors. If the extra ten days had been granted, Mosby would probably have been spared a great deal of difficulty, for Johnston surrendered on April 26, well within the period. Hancock was now convinced that Mosby would not surrender as an individual until after Johnston, but he was very favorably impressed. He much approved of Mosby's notification of his men that they were free to surrender individually, and several had in Winchester. He was moved by the positive report he received from the Millwood meeting and especially that Mosby and every one of his officers expressed regret over Lincoln's death. Hancock, therefore, came close to recommending the ten-day extension in his letter to Halleck on April 19 asking for instructions. But Grant had lost patience with Mosby. He had given him nine days, and upon the end of the latest forty-eight-hour truce it would be ten days. "If Mosby does not avail himself of the present truce end it and hunt him and his men down," he ordered Hancock. "Guerrillas, after beating the armies of the enemy, will not be entitled to quarter." Hancock informed Mosby that he had only until noon, April 20.[8]

The second Millwood meeting was quite different from the first. Hancock sent a staff officer, probably a colonel, but his name and rank are unknown. He and his contingent arrived early and were seated on the other side of the table when Mosby and about twenty of his men arrived. The officer warned Mosby that, if he did not surrender his regiment immediately, Hancock's army would destroy Loudoun and Fauquier Counties. Furious, Mosby answered in a loud voice, "Tell General Hancock it is in his power to do it, and it is not in my power to resist it; but I will not accept a parole before Joe Johnston has surrendered." He stood up and thrust his arm over the table and with his hand gave the gesture familiar to his men as his silent hand signal to attack. Then, with no further word, he stepped briskly to the door, followed by his men. "Mount and follow me," he said, and they galloped away.[9]

Riding back through Ashby's Gap into his Confederacy for the last time, he was heartbroken. He probably suspected that the happiest, most self-actualizing part of his life was over. Never before had he been this fulfilled or this healthy, mentally and physically, and from this point up to the last year of his life he would attempt to duplicate the psychological world he had experienced as a Civil War guerrilla. It was time to bid farewell to this stage of life and pass to the next, a passage marked by the ritual of disbanding and issuing a farewell order. The following morning he sat at the breakfast table at "Glen Welby," the mansion of Richard H. Carter. As he attempted to write his thoughts on paper, he paused for a moment; and as he usually did in times of great celebration or deep pain, he escaped into literature. He thought of Washington Irving's book *The Alhambra* and the tragic fall of Boabdil, the last Muslim sultan of Granada, and how, defeated and departing into exile, Boabdil turned for one final look at his palace-fortress "Alhambra" and sighed with the deepest agony.[10]

He had called the last rendezvous at noon in nearby Salem, and the Rangers gathered in an open field north of town. It was raining and there was a thick fog and it was cold. Mosby stood on foot beside the road near the field, quietly shaking hands as they arrived. At about noon the officers ordered the men to mount and form in line. Mosby rode up and down the line, halted, and sat on his horse in front as Chapman and Richards read his farewell address:

> Fauquier Co:, April 21st 1865.
> Soldiers -
> I have summoned you together for the last time. The vision we cherished of a free and independent country has vanished, and that country is now the spoil of a conqueror.
> I disband your organization in preference to surrendering to our enemies. I am no longer your commander. After an association of more than two eventful years, I part from you with a just pride in the fame of your achievements and grateful recollections of your generous kindness to myself. And now, at this moment of bidding you a final adieu, accept the assurance of my unchanging confidence and regard. Farewell!
> Jno. S. Mosby
> Colonel.[11]

The men would hold annual reunions in their senior years, but Mosby attended only one. Almost thirty years after the parting, on January 16, 1895, he met with them in Alexandria, Virginia, and in his carefully written speech recalled their suffering at the disbanding. He compared it to the intense torture of the Greek god Prometheus when he was punished by Zeus for attempting to give fire to human beings. Prometheus was chained to a rock in the Caucasus Mountains where every day either a vulture or eagle ate his liver and every night it was restored. Mosby quoted two lines from Byron's poem *Prometheus:* "The rock, the vulture, and the chain, / All that the proud can feel of pain." Then he stated that he would soon be saying goodbye again to return to San Francisco and that he had always felt "that life cannot afford a more bitter cup than the one I drained when we parted at Salem, nor any higher reward of ambition than that I received as Commander of the Forty-third Virginia Battalion of Cavalry."[12]

After disbanding, Mosby and about six volunteers went south, and when they reached the outskirts of Richmond he sent John Munson into town to obtain the news. While Munson was gone Ben Palmer acquired a newspaper from an outbound boat on the James River and Kanawha

Canal, and they read of Johnston's surrender. Munson returned with a report that several horses were hitched on Franklin Street just waiting to be taken. Mosby replied that it was too late: "It would be murder and highway robbery now. We are soldiers, not highwaymen." He disbanded for the second and final time, and they dispersed.[13]

The men surrendered under the terms of Appomattox, but Mosby's protraction had cost him. With Grant's offer withdrawn, Hancock had offered a reward of two thousand dollars for Mosby's capture. He knew of this price on his head and abandoned any thought of going into exile. "To have run away would at least have looked like a confession of guilt. So I took my chances and remained in Virginia." Traveling alone he went to his Uncle John Mosby's home in Nelson County, the land of his early childhood. He knew that he had done nothing wrong. During the meeting with General Chapman at Millwood he had said so, and Chapman reported, "For himself he said he had no favors to ask, being quite willing to stand by his acts, all of which he believed to be justifiable."[14]

Mosby remained in Nelson County for almost two months, except for a visit in May with his parents near Lynchburg. During that visit each night before bedtime he would leave to spend the night in the home of a relative. "I am an outlaw, and self-preservation is the first law of nature," he told his mother one night as he went out the door. "Mosby Still at Large," reported a *New York Herald* article on May 1, and rumor had him heading for Texas. On May 3, Hancock raised the reward to five thousand dollars, to be paid immediately upon Mosby's "apprehension and delivery at any military post."[15]

In May, probably on his journey back to Nelson County from near Lynchburg, he stopped briefly in Charlottesville to see his friend and former professor William H. McGuffey at the University of Virginia. He went to McGuffey's house, enjoyed a brief visit, and quietly rode away. After he was gone two companies of Union cavalry surrounded McGuffey's house and demanded that Mosby come out. McGuffey came to the front door and, shaking his fist, shouted, "You just came here to catch Colonel Mosby because you knew he was gone." The event inspired a local legend in several versions that had Mosby surrounded by Yankees, either being fitted for a suit in a tailor shop, having a shave in a barber shop, or talking with his mother in the home of the family she had reportedly come to visit. The tales usually climaxed with Mosby mounting and defiantly riding through a column of Yankees in the street attempting to block his escape.[16]

Sometime in May Mosby sent a letter to Lee asking him to intercede with Grant. Uncle John's friend, who delivered the letter, returned with word that Lee entirely approved of everything that Mosby had done in the war and that he would contact Grant. True to his word, Lee sent an oral message to Grant explaining that he held Mosby in the highest regard and requesting that Grant offer him parole. By June 6, Grant's chief of staff, Gen. John A. Rawlins, had sent notification that no exception would be made for Mosby.[17]

Then, developments involving Lee's own status worked in Mosby's favor. On May 29, President Andrew Johnson issued his proclamation of amnesty and pardon; this greatly relieved Lee's worry that his soldiers might be punished, but he wanted assurance that Grant agreed. Sometime after June 7, when Lee was indicted for treason by a federal grand jury in Norfolk, he made a verbal inquiry of Grant as to whether Grant would uphold the presidential pardons of Confederate soldiers and whether Grant would endorse his own application for pardon if he made one. Lee desired to set an example in reconciliation by cooperating with the president in making such an application. Grant answered that he would respect the paroles of the veterans, and he urged Lee to apply. On June 13, Lee applied for a pardon, contingent upon Grant's keeping his word not to prosecute the soldiers. Grant realized that Lee's application incurred the wrath of die-hard Confederates, and he greatly respected Lee for the action and was most grateful.[18]

In this atmosphere of reconciliation, authorities in Washington, probably under Grant's direction, ordered Gen. John Gregg, in command of a brigade of cavalry at Lynchburg, to offer Mosby parole. In several letters written after the war Mosby stated that he was certain that Grant gave the order. "Grant had the outlawry withdrawn," Mosby declared. Gregg notified Mosby that his parole was approved and he would be given safe passage into Lynchburg. A meeting was arranged in the law office of Charles L. Mosby, one of Mosby's relatives, and on June 13, Mosby and his brother Willie went into town in a borrowed carriage and were waiting in the second-floor office when Gregg's delegation arrived. Mosby had his pistols loaded and in the holsters on the floor at his feet. The spokesman said that Gregg had received an order from Halleck, now commander in Richmond, directing that Mosby was not to be paroled but arrested and held until the War Department could decide what to do with him. Gregg's provost marshal had felt insecure about paroling the famous guerrilla and had telegraphed Richmond requesting Halleck's confirmation.[19]

Mosby quietly bent down, picked up his revolvers, and placed them on the table, still in the holsters. "I am *ultimus Romanorum,*" he said. "I will not submit to arrest. I will kill the first man who attempts it." He was saying, with a reference to European history, that he was the last Confederate patriot. *Ultimus Romanorum,* "The Last of the Romans," was the honorary title given to Italian patriot Rienzi (1313-54) and later applied to Horace Walpole and others. Mosby threw the pistols over his shoulder, and he and Willie walked out and down the steps to the street. A large crowd had gathered to see him and celebrate his surrender, and when they saw that he was leaving in haste, they became aroused. A citizen came forward and told him that several of them would furnish money if he wanted to leave the country. He declined, and he and Willie jumped in the buggy and left town.[20]

The next morning at daylight Gregg's cavalry searched several homes in Amherst and Nelson Counties, including Alfred and Virginia Mosby's, in compliance with Halleck's order. After another couple of days apparently Grant had set Halleck straight because on June 16 Gregg informed Mosby that he had received authority to accept his parole. On June 17 Mosby and Willie returned to Lynchburg and, finally, Mosby surrendered.[21]

It had been a long and complicated process but had great signficance for Mosby's future, because it was the foundation for Mosby's friendship with Grant. Grant learned of Lee's great respect for Mosby, and Mosby knew at the time that Grant had ordered the parole and he was grateful. Then later, Grant intervened again. The parole agreement provided that paroled Confederates would not be disturbed as long as they remained at home and obeyed the law. When Mosby entered law practice in Fauquier County after the war, he was not disturbed as long as he remained in Fauquier County, but when he attended court in Alexandria in Fairfax County or Leesburg in Loudoun County, Union authorities arrested him. It was a matter of interpretation whether the parole allowed him to practice in adjoining counties.[22]

On the afternoon of August 10, 1865, he arrived in Alexandria, and word spread quickly. As he and a few friends walked along King Street, people gathered behind and set up a commotion, arguing loudly whether it was a murderer or cavalier in their midst. At the intersection of King and Royal Streets, he and his friends retreated into George Harper's tailor shop on the corner. The crowd pressed against the windows and door of the business, soldiers and civilians, men and women, shouting and threatening each other. Someone told Henry H. Wells, now a general and commander of the district, that a riot was in progress, and he ordered his soldiers to arrest Mosby, escort him out of town, and tell him not to return without permission. However, Mosby demanded to be taken to Wells and, when escorted into the general's office, demanded an explanation. Wells said that he did it to protect Mosby, that he feared that the Unionists in the crowd who were yelling that they wanted to kill Mosby as a horse thief and highway robber might carry out the threat. On about January 8, 1866, he was arrested in Leesburg and soon released.[23]

There may have been other instances, but in any case the arrests hindered his practice. Finally, Pauline came to the rescue, like his mother had when he was in jail. One day she told him that she and five-year-old Beverly were going to Baltimore to purchase furniture and, instead, went to the White House to ask the president to intervene. Johnson was a family friend from Tennessee, and it was well known that he was using the pardon power very leniently. But Pauline did not know that, as military governor of Tennessee, he had developed a deep hatred for guerrillas, and he treated her and Bev coldly, gruffly refusing to consider her request. She and Bev left and went immediately to Grant's office. There the reception was a total contrast. Based on Lee's recommendation, Grant now respected Mosby and warmly welcomed his wife and son. He listened sympathetically as she described the problem and said that he understood. He took out a blank sheet of paper and in his own hand wrote an order exempting Mosby from military arrest and giving him freedom to travel anywhere in the United States. He handed the note to Pauline and graciously escorted her and Bev to the door. That night, in their hotel room, after Bev said his prayers, he looked up at his mother and said, "Now, mamma, may I pray to God to send old Johnson to the devil?" Later, when Grant was president, Mosby told him the story. Grant laughed heartily and said, "A great many would have joined in Beverly's prayer."[24]

Grant's kindness had made an indelible impression on Mosby, and the handwritten order would be one of his most cherished possessions for the rest of his life. Later, he gave it to his daughter May, and she framed it and hung it on the wall of her parlor.[25] With the war over and Reconstruction ahead, Mosby would settle into his law practice. But eventually his deep need for conflict and for identification with a powerful mentor would take over, and he would fully satisfy both requirements by supporting Grant for president.

# 19

# Grant's Partisan in Virginia

Early in the mornings from houses on Main Street in Warrenton, people saw Mosby walking along on his way to work. Slowly putting one foot in front of the other, with stooped shoulders, faded coat, vest with two buttons missing, and white slouch hat pushed low on his forehead, he was the picture of a man who had known adventure but was now bored and frustrated. One could scarcely imagine that this clean-shaven, quiet lawyer was a former guerrilla chief.[1] For seven years his gentle nature remained ascendant, but then in the spring of 1872 his need for conflict and a powerful mentor came roaring forth, and he supported Grant's re-election.

For the rest of his life, in conversations with close friends he would justify his action by arguing that he meant to assist the South by reconciling Southern whites with Grant and the North. In 1904 his best friend, Joseph Bryan, gently informed him that his reasoning was based on a false foundation—there was no way Southerners were going to reconcile with Grant in 1872. Pinned down, Mosby opened his heart: "Admitting that to be true," he replied, "the question is, was there any apostasy in my attempting to achieve it? Was there anything wrong in Prometheus bringing down fire from Heaven for the benefit of men? . . . I may have attempted to attain the impossible." Then he repeated: "Again I ask you. Was it wrong for Prometheus to bring fire from Heaven for the benefit of men: & even if he failed was it right for mankind to abuse him for the failure?" Lord Byron admired Prometheus as an independent champion of freedom who suffered for his heroic actions. Mosby was confessing that like a Greek god he had defied conventional restraints. Unable to explain his motives rationally he retreated into literature and justified himself in the morality of Greek mythology.[2]

Ironically, the years from 1865 to 1872 were the most prosperous of his life. Many of the people of "Mosby's Confederacy" came to him for legal services, and he attended court in surrounding counties and handled a great deal of real estate and legal business for Baltimore merchants. By August 12, 1865, he had moved his family to Warrenton and opened a law office, and his reputation and fame propelled him into instant success. People requested his autograph and photo, and they recognized him on trains, in the streets, and wherever he went. When he entered a meeting all heads turned, and "Mosby, that is Colonel Mosby" buzzed around the room. In Washington, D.C., a showman opened an exhibit in the Old Capitol Prison where he had been imprisoned and charged twenty-five cents admission. One of the features inside was a charcoal drawing of Mosby's horse on the wall. A Mosby look-alike showed up in Philadelphia and Baltimore and received a royal welcome until the citizens discovered he was not the real Mosby. In Baltimore large crowds gathered to see the same impersonator's photo in a gallery and later, when they discerned the ruse, laughed that they had been humbugged by a "counterfeit guerilla."[3]

In 1866 Mosby earned an annual income of fifteen hundred dollars, and the next year purchased a house and four-acre lot on Main Street for thirty-seven hundred dollars. Pauline bought fine furniture in Baltimore and by 1868 had spent over a thousand dollars furnishing the house. She selected beautiful paintings for the walls, and he filled the library with new books. In 1871 he earned six thousand dollars in a decade when the average laborer made about six hundred dollars per year. But making money never gave him any satisfaction. He grieved for the war, and when he met a fellow veteran the old memories would flood his mind, making him feel almost overwhelmed. "I often recur to the memory of the good old times we had in the Quaker settlement. I wish they could return," he wrote Monteiro.[4]

For the first four years after the war he refrained from politics and then in the summer of 1869, when military rule under Congressional Reconstruction was about to end in Virginia, he came out exactly in the center of the political stand of the majority of white Virginians. The state Conservative Party (later the Democratic Party) that opposed Radical Republican Reconstruction nominated Gilbert C. Walker for governor. When he came to speak in Warrenton, Mosby met him at the train station and hosted and introduced him at the local rally. In his remarks Mosby said that Walker stood for civilization while the Republican Party represented "barbarism." Mosby actively campaigned for Walker and for his friend James Keith, a fellow Warrenton attorney, running for the state legislature. Both won, and the Conservative state legislature ratified the 14th and 15th Amendments, bringing an end to Reconstruction in Virginia.[5]

Mosby became an aggressive Conservative Party member, personally taking the offensive against carpetbaggers, Northern men who came into the South and worked for Radical Republican governments. Southerners considered them fortune hunters and knaves, and Mosby called them "bounty jumpers and jailbirds." He declared Fauquier County Sheriff William H. Boyd a carpetbagger and resolved to run him out of town. He accused Boyd of holding office illegally and defaulting financially by not accounting for revenue collected. Soon after airing these charges, Mosby heard that Boyd had been on a trip to Pennsylvania and there had said that Mosby was a highway robber. Mosby demanded a duel: "I now demand satisfaction, not explanation or equivocation. Will you fight?" Boyd's answer was to resign and leave town.[6]

On March 8, 1870, Mosby was in Richmond lobbying for Keith's nomination for state circuit court judge when he happened upon General Lee and visited him in his hotel room. Lee died seven months later, and, as it was their last meeting, Mosby described it in his *Memoirs* and related that soon after he left Lee's room he happened upon Gen. George Pickett. Pickett asked Mosby to return to Lee's room with him. Mosby agreed and observed that the discussion between the commander and leader of "Pickett's Charge" was formal, cold, and embarrassing for all present. He eventually published an account of the meeting, and Lee fans challenged him for describing Lee negatively. He wrote to a friend that his article could have been worse—that when Lee and his daughter Agnes checked out of the hotel, Mosby, Pickett, and James Keith were in the parlor; and Lee spoke cordially with Mosby and Keith but ignored Pickett. "So it is—but there is no inconsistency between the position he occupies in history and his freezing out a man he didn't like," Mosby concluded.[7]

Governor Walker split the Conservative Party, bringing widespread hostile reaction to two laws, one selling the state's stock in railroads to private investors and the other funding the state debt for internal improvements before the war. He won the "Bourbons," or ultra-conservatives, but alienated railroad entrepreneur William Mahone and many in the party. The state party was in disarray and so was the party system on the national level. Members of the Republican Party, reacting to corruption in Grant's administration, had broken away and created the Liberal Republican Party. They nominated Horace Greeley for president and adopted a platform of reconciliation with the South and civil service reform. Democratic delegates, including Mosby and Virginia Conservative Party representatives, met two months later, and most agreed to also nominate Greeley as the only hope to defeat Grant. Most white voters in Virginia refused to vote for Greeley or Grant and stayed home from the election.[8]

The confusion in politics gave Mosby an opportunity to culminate his friendship with Grant and become Grant's protégé and partisan in Virginia. In the last week of April, about one week before Greeley's nomination by the Liberal Republicans, Mosby told United States senator John F. Lewis of Virginia that he wanted to meet Grant. In his mind, he had crossed the Rubicon; he had decided to endorse the president. For months he had discussed the decision with Keith, who had been elected state judge and was serving in Warrenton. Keith warned that he would be separating from white Virginians and Southerners and that he would pay a heavy penalty. Regardless, as soon as the Liberal Republicans nominated Greeley, Mosby wrote to Lewis indicating that he would work for Grant. Lewis answered that he had mentioned Mosby to Grant and Grant wanted Mosby to come to the White House. Immediately, Mosby and Beverly, now eleven years old, left for Washington.[9]

Joseph Bryan pointed out that Mosby became a Republican not to associate with African Americans but "with the powerful men who controlled the Republican party in the North," the most powerful being Grant. Working for Grant provided Mosby both a powerful mentor and great conflict, and when he met him on Wednesday afternoon, May 8, he immediately felt regenerated: "I had never before been in the White House. When I walked in with my son into the room where Grant was sitting his presence inspired something of the awe that a Roman provincial must have felt when first entering the palace of the Caesars. His manner soon relieved me of embarrassment and restored my self-confidence." On the journey home he and Bev took the Aquia Creek steamboat for Alexandria, and they had a seat next to Mosby's friend from Stuart's cavalry, former Confederate general Wade Hampton. Mosby became so excited telling Hampton about the meeting that he forgot to disembark at Alexandria and did not realize it until the bell tolled when they passed Mount Vernon.[10]

The visit was a sensation that returned "the once famous Colonel J.S. Mosby" to the national spotlight. Southerners were shocked. Grant was the head of the abolitionist, pro–African American Republican Party, and many Southern whites regarded him as a threat to civilization. By endorsing him, Mosby was challenging the legitimacy of the rebellion and betraying the Lost Cause. "This business is a good deal meaner, than the hanging of those federal spies in the Valley," declared the *Bristol News,* and Mosby and Grant were both nothing but an "overrated pair of antipodal military hacks." Mosby said that the South would not have been more shocked if during the war he had deserted to the Union cavalry.[11]

Politically, Grant considered Mosby's desertion a symbol of reconciliation and a sign of hope that his strategy to win the votes of Virginia conservatives and moderates would succeed. Emotionally, he found in Mosby an emotional link to Lee's memory and a nostalgic connection to the glorious Civil War days. Grant needed to be around men who could carry a conversation; and Mosby's sharp wit, charming flattery, and ability to cut immediately to the core of issues elevated his morale. But it was not a companionship of equals; it was a mentor-protégé relationship. Grant was fifty, and Mosby was thirty-eight; and Mosby came humbly and in the quintessence of his gentle, inner-circle element. A reporter who saw him at the White House noted that he was a "pleasant spoken and mild mannered man," far different from what one expected in a guerrilla.[12]

In his memoirs Grant wrote, "Since the close of the war I have come to know Colonel Mosby personally, and somewhat intimately. He is a different man entirely from what I had supposed. He is slender, not tall, wiry, and looks as if he could endure any amount of physical exercise. He is able, and thoroughly honest and truthful. There were probably but few men in the South who could have commanded successfully a separate detachment in the rear of an opposing army, and so near the border of hostilities, as long as he did without losing his entire command." In a speech in Boston on April 27, 1906, Mosby said of Grant, "No man ever had a better friend than he was to me."[13]

In the meeting, Mosby promised to support Grant in Virginia and predicted that Grant would carry the state if he successfully persuaded Congress to enact the Amnesty Bill then under consideration. Congress had already removed the political disabilities of many former Confederates, and soon the bill passed and most of the remaining Rebels were pardoned, leaving only about five hundred still barred from holding political office. Mosby went home and started enlisting politicians in Virginia as "Grant Conservatives." His goal was to unite the Grant administration with the white voters in Virginia, nearly all of whom were in the Virginia Conservative Party. It was a quixotic crusade that would leave him, once party lines reformed, in the role of Grant's guerrilla warrior in Virginia politics.[14]

He enlisted John S. Wise, son of Gen. Henry S. Wise, former governor of Virginia, and a few others and made it a point to attend the Democratic convention in Baltimore in July. This was a disingenuous tactic to get involved with Virginia Conservatives in the campaign. He supported a "straight Democrat," which meant anyone other than Greeley; and, when the convention voted as expected for Greeley, he was present to shepherd disgruntled Virginians into the Grant camp.[15]

He began canvassing in Fauquier County by inviting voters to a public debate between himself for Grant and his friend Eppa Hunton for Greeley. He arranged the meeting not in Warrenton but in Salem, where he had disbanded his men. It was symbolic of his returning to battle, and no one who saw and heard him that day had any doubt but that he was again on the attack, now as a stump speaker. "Mosby Makes a Raid on Greeley," reported one headline. Hunton had been wounded leading his men as a colonel in Pickett's Charge and was later promoted to general. He had a law office in Warrenton in the same building as Mosby and was campaigning as a Conservative candidate for the United States House of Representatives. He would win and go on to a distinguished career as a Democrat in the House and Senate and would continue as Mosby's friend.[16]

Hunton spoke first and then Mosby rose to respond. His friends, several of whom were veteran Rangers, applauded and gave three cheers. He spoke for almost thirty minutes, and they interrupted him at least thirty-one times with cheering, laughter, and applause. He said nothing against Hunton but ridiculed Greeley and his adherents. The Democratic Party, he said, had surrendered to the enemy, the Liberal Republican convention, which was nothing but "a band of plunderers, bummers, foragers and dead beats" with only one principle, and that was spoils. He described how at the Baltimore convention he had seen the "oddest lot of bummers and shysters" imaginable; they resembled P.T. Barnum's exhibit "The Happy Family," a cage of wild animals, predator and prey, supposedly living together in peace.[17]

He called Greeley's *New York Tribune* a "perfect Vesuvius, belching forth and scattering the hellish lava of hate and discontent through the South." Greeley was a tool of Tammany Hall, he shouted, a scarecrow and "a man whose chief claim to distinction was his intolerant hate of the South, the wearing of a white hat, and walking down Broadway with one leg of his breeches stuck in his boot." Mocking Greeley's offer to clasp hands across the bloody chasm of Civil War, he said that he had never known a candidate who would not reach across any chasm, bloody or not, for a vote. He closed by urging everyone to vote for Grant, and for several minutes the grove rang with cheers for Grant and Mosby. A reporter commented, Mosby "speaks as fiercely as he fights. Take him all in all, he is an ugly customer to tackle, either in the field or on the rostrum."[18]

News of the debate spread quickly, and that evening when Mosby arrived home he learned that a rejoinder to his speech had already been delivered. At a Greeley rally that afternoon in Warrenton, former Confederate army private John B. Withers, now mayor and druggist, had said, "Colonel Mosby might drive Confederate generals, but he couldn't drive a Confederate private into supporting Grant." Mosby confronted Withers, and they broke into an argument that became so heated that Judge Keith had them arrested and set their bail at four thousand dollars each.[19]

Mosby continued speaking and writing in the same manner, and when it was announced that Republicans had carried Virginia he wired the White House: "Virginia casts her vote for Grant, peace, and reconciliation." Grant carried Virginia by about two thousand votes because most white voters stayed home and left the balloting to a minority of Republicans and Grant Conservatives. Mosby had not united the Conservative Party under the administration's banner and was not responsible for Grant's victory in Virginia.[20]

He admitted that Grant gave him more credit than he deserved. A few days after the election he was in Washington on business, waiting in the outer office of the treasury secretary, when in walked Grant. He shook Mosby's hand and said, "I heard you were here, and came to thank you for my getting the vote of Virginia." He offered to appoint Mosby to a federal job, but Mosby refused. He realized that accepting a position would make him a scalawag, a Southerner who cooperated with the Radical Republicans for private gain, and weaken his position as Grant's ambassador to Conservatives in Virginia, just as accepting spoils in the Civil War would have weakened him as a guerrilla chief. He also turned down offers to represent claimants before the Southern Claims Commission, keeping his record clear of "bartering my political influence" for fees, in order to work as Grant's patronage broker for his friends in Virginia.[21]

Party lines redeveloped for the Virginia governor's race in 1873, and Conservatives rallied under the banner of white rule. "Shall we be governed by Negroes?" they cried, nominating former Confederate general James L. Kemper, who still limped from a severe wound in Pickett's Charge. Republicans nominated Robert W. Hughes and identified with the cause of African Americans. This created a dilemma for Mosby. He could support Grant and align himself with Grant's administration but comprehended that he could not endorse Hughes or join the Republican Party of Virginia, for this would identify him with African Americans and destroy him in Virginia. In his speeches for Grant in 1872 he had repudiated the "negro party of Virginia," because identifying with them would bring "social degradation." In obtaining federal patronage for Virginians he never consulted with state Republican leaders and never asked for anything on their behalf.[22]

Embarrassed, he wrote Postmaster General John A.J. Creswell, explaining that he could not support Hughes. He claimed that he had succeeded thus far in using federal patronage to produce "a revolution in public sentiment in Virginia toward the Administration. I never could have done this if I had in any way identified myself with the radical organization in Virginia which is composed almost entirely of carpetbaggers and negroes. If I had gone into it, I would simply have destroyed myself without effecting any good for nobody would have followed me." He stated that he could vote with Virginia Republicans in national elections but could not put them in power in Virginia. Instead, he was for "our people," meaning the best white people in the state.[23]

He wrote Grant on August 31, informing him that he would campaign for Kemper. When Kemper won, as governor-elect he asked for Mosby's advice in writing his inaugural address and, before the ceremony, requested that Mosby arrange a meeting with Grant. Mosby was almost beside himself with jubilation that Virginia had a governor willing to consider Mosby's dream of uniting Conservatives for the Republican president. "If consummated it meant the death-knell to Negro government and carpet-baggery," he wrote later. Mosby went immediately on a secret mission to the White House, and Grant agreed; but word of the trip leaked out, and Kemper's friends raised a storm of protest and Kemper awakened to reality. When Mosby returned to Richmond, Kemper called at his hotel room and canceled the meeting. "I was very mad at the way I had been duped and never spoke to him again," Mosby complained.[24]

By 1874 the tide of white supremacy was running strong, and the free, disarranged situation in Virginia politics was over. The Conservative Party was in control, and they wanted nothing to do with Mosby's campaign to unite with the administration. Hunton was up for re-election to the House, and he was the clear choice of Conservatives who scheduled a state nominating convention for August 26 in Alexandria. Meanwhile, Mosby began campaigning for the office himself as an independent on a platform of alliance with Grant.[25]

He soon learned that he had vigorous opposition. In June he was in Salem when B.F. Rixey, a former state senator, started an argument and both men lost control. Standing in the street they began striking each other, one with a cane and the other with a carriage whip. Friends separated them, but, as Rixey's blows landed on his head, Mosby started to realize that the voters of the district did not want him for their Congressman. He persuaded his friend James Barbour, a Culpeper attorney, to run in his place and dropped out to take the offensive for Barbour.[26]

His strategy was to "raid" the Conservative state convention by organizing the selection of delegates in local districts that would pledge to vote for Barbour rather than Hunton. He succeeded in capturing the delegation from the district where Hunton resided, but this incurred the wrath of Hunton's friends such as Alexander D.F. Payne, a Warrenton attorney. Payne began exhibiting a document signed by Harry Bonen that accused Mosby of duplicity and deceit in attempting to raid the convention. On August 20, a week before the convention, Mosby challenged Payne to a duel; he accepted, selecting squirrel rifles at forty paces and naming a site in Fauquier County as the place. They chose seconds, and what followed was a fiasco and a sensation in the newspapers. Before he received Payne's letter of acceptance, Mosby got out of town, taking the train to Washington, leaving with his second a proposal that the dueling field would be in Prince Georges County, Maryland, opposite Alexandria. Mosby violated the code duello by not allowing Payne to choose the location, but all of this was nothing but bluster anyway. At 7:00 P.M. on the night before the fateful day of the scheduled duel, Judge Keith had Payne arrested in Warrenton and had detectives in Washington surround and capture Mosby in the lobby of the Congressional Hotel at 11:00 P.M. Soon Mosby returned home, and he and Payne both apologized.[27]

The convention met, and Hunton's faction refused to seat Mosby's

delegates on the ground that any man who had publicly announced support for Mosby was disloyal and had no right to attend a Conservative
Party meeting. Mosby called it an insult and an "insolence"; the party
"has excommunicated us all," he wrote. Then a newspaper editorial condemned him for bringing his guerrilla tactics into politics. Like in the
war, the writer declared, he attacked the convention from the rear and, as
Grant's partisan, spread discord and disorganization like a mischievous
boy thrusting a cocklebur under the tail of a gentle horse. Realizing that
open tactics will fail, "he slips into by-paths and, under cover of the darkness, spreads birdlime in the way people must tread."[28]

Mosby was now a man without a party. "I lost the confidence of
both but preserved my integrity & self-respect," he wrote later, in the
true spirit of independence. But he still had what he wanted most: the
relationship with Grant that gave him informal personal power. Exag-
gerating, he wrote, "I did attain such a power in Grant's administration
as never private individual had before." But there was a high price to be
paid.[29] Southern political leaders asked him for secret favors from Grant,
but, if it became public knowledge, they withdrew and apologized for
contacting the odious man in Virginia. Mosby felt used, like the brave
little mouse who belled the cat. In the fable the mouse risks his life to tie
a bell on the cat so that all mice will be warned of his approach. "Such a
duty is a shirt of Nessus to any one who wears it," he lamented. The shirt
of Nessus in Greek legend was the tunic given to Hercules by his wife,
who did not know it was poisonous. Hercules put it on, and it was so
painful that he killed himself by falling onto a funeral pyre. The shirt of
Nessus came to mean a fatal gift, a source of tragedy from which there is
no relief.[30]

On May 2, 1875, he wrote Grant that he had become so loathsome
in the public eye that he could not visit the White House; the criticism
would damage them both. Most of his law business dried up, and he had
to borrow money. At least Pauline was wonderfully understanding and
supportive. She discussed politics and current events with him and worried about the attacks on him by his enemies. Writing to a friend during
the 1872 campaign, she enclosed one of his Grant speeches and a clipping of a favorable newspaper editorial, "which Mr. Mosby says more
than compensates him for all the abuse he has had heaped on him by the
Greelyites." They remained close, and he cooperated in educating the
children in Roman Catholic schools, sending May and Beverly to boarding school in Montreal. Immediately after the war they welcomed his

sisters Blakely and Lucy to live in their home, and Pauline continued having children, giving birth eight times in eighteen years. Virginia Stuart was born in 1867; Pauline V., July 20, 1869; Ada B., May 10, 1871; George P., born August 27, 1873, and died July 17, 1874; and Alfred M., born March 9 and died June 30, 1876.[31]

Pauline never recovered from Alfred's birth, and she died of complications from childbirth at 6:00 A.M. on Ada's fifth birthday, May 10, 1876, at the age of thirty-nine. A large crowd gathered for her funeral, and Mosby had her grave marker engraved with a quotation from the eulogy of the priest in her funeral mass in the Catholic Church: "She died as she lived, a faithful Catholic."[32]

Mosby grieved, and he would never remarry. But not only had he lost his wife; in a few months he was about to lose his mentor. Grant was nearing the end of his second term and succeeding him would be either Democrat Samuel J. Tilden of New York or Republican Rutherford B. Hayes from Ohio. After the Republican convention, Mosby met with Grant and announced that he supported Hayes. On July 24 he sent Hayes a brief, carefully written letter in which he claimed to be one of the conservative class in Virginia who would vote for Hayes if he made a friendly overture to the South. The letter was completely in line with the goal of Hayes's Southern policy, which was to win the votes of Southern white Democratic/Conservatives who had been Whigs and Douglas Democrats.[33]

But declaring that he would work for Hayes was not enough to win Hayes's friendship and allow Mosby to continue as patronage broker in Virginia—he had to take the offensive and blast his way into the campaign. His opportunity came when the staff of the *New York Herald* invited him to write a letter in favor of Hayes to be printed in point-counterpoint to one written for Tilden by Robert Barnwell Rhett Jr., son of the famous South Carolina fire-eater who took John C. Calhoun's seat in the Senate. He accepted and rose to the challenge. Mosby produced his best writing in letters, and in my opinion this letter to the editor is his very best published writing. With concise and clear references to ancient Roman history, English literature, the history of the American Revolution, and the Bible, he justified Hayes's Southern policy and told why one should vote against Tilden for Hayes. How did Tilden propose to reform the civil service? "By a change in the system of appointments? Not at all; but by filling the offices with his partisans, who will flock to Washington 'as fierce as famine and hungry as the grave.'"[34]

Mosby had avoided becoming a member of the Republican Party; but, in order to gain favor with Hayes, he announced in this letter that he was doing what he had noted earlier would ruin him: he was joining the Republicans. Not only that, he endorsed "the political equality of the races"; and because it suited Hayes's goal, he stated incorrectly that the South had accepted equality. Actually, he was declaring war on most Southern whites. The Democratic Party, still called the Conservative Party in Virginia, had taken form throughout the South under the standard of white supremacy, and Democrats condemned the Republican Party as the party of black people: this made Mosby a traitor. He knew it and said so in the letter: "I know very well the measure of denunciation which the expression of these sentiments will receive from the people in whose cause I shed my blood and sacrificed the prime of my life. Be it so. I wait on time for my vindication."[35]

An editor of the *New York Herald* noted in an accompanying editorial that he was surprised that the guerrilla chief could write with such piquancy and power. "His letter is an able political manifesto, and will make a deep impression on the canvass," he wrote. Hayes's campaign staff had it printed as a handout, and it cemented Mosby's friendship with Hayes and made him a full-fledged, battered, suffering Southern Republican.[36]

The letter touched the very heart of Hayes's Southern policy. Mosby stated that the only way the South could gain its full share of benefits from the national government was to vote for Hayes. Historian Kenneth E. Davison wrote that Hayes's goal was not removal of the troops from the South nor return of home rule to Southerners; his great dream was to establish the Republican Party in the South. Hayes and most whites in the North agreed that African Americans were inferior and could not govern; therefore Hayes bypassed the blacks and carpetbaggers in the Republican Party in the South and appealed to white Southern Conservatives, hoping to recruit them as Republicans. This had been exactly Mosby's position since 1872. Hayes wanted to win white Southerners with federal funding for internal improvements, and, in turn, the strong white Republican Party in the South would protect the blacks out of good will, and Hayes would accomplish equality for blacks and reconciliation with Southern whites. In the election he hoped this strategy would win Virginia and a few other Southern states.[37]

In Warrenton people began calling Mosby a traitor. One day one of his sons, probably Beverly, engaged in a cheering match with Littleton S.

Helm, one of Alexander Payne's seconds in the 1874 dueling fiasco. Mosby's son cheered for Hayes, and Helm shouted, in obvious reference to the boy's father: "Hurrah for all traitors to their country," and "Hurrah for Aleck Payne." Mosby was in Washington at the time, and by his return a few days later a rumor was circulating that Helm had called Mosby a traitor for supporting Hayes and a coward for running from the duel with Payne. On October 15, 1876, Mosby challenged Helm to a duel, and Helm named as weapons double-barreled shotguns loaded with one-ounce balls at twenty paces. A few days later Helm wrote a letter to Mosby explaining that he had not specifically called Mosby a traitor or coward.[38]

Tilden activists published an article alleging that Mosby had appointed twenty-seven of his guerrillas to federal jobs in Washington and nine in the Naval Yard, including his brother Willie. Mosby published a denial, pointing out that Willie was farming and Grant had appointed only three of his Rangers to federal positions in Virginia. He did not mention that he had obtained Virginia men appointments as consuls in La Rochelle, Jamaica, and Palermo or that he had named a Confederate veteran as customs collector of the port of Norfolk or that he had obtained an appointment for one of his sisters on the Light House Board. Grant had given him a share of patronage in Virginia, and he had used it as spoils. "He appointed a good many of my friends in Virginia to office just to oblige me, and he never once asked a question about their politics," Mosby said later. "What do you want?" he wrote his former Valley scout, John Russell, "How would you like a mail agency on the Winchester [Rail] Road? Let me know."[39]

Some Southern Conservatives responded to Hayes's appeal but Tilden won easily in Virginia and in the nation won the popular vote by 250,000. But there were disputed returns in several states, and eventually an electoral commission declared Hayes the winner. Mosby had preserved his role as patronage broker and won a new mentor, but, just as he had predicted, he was destroyed in Virginia. After the Hayes campaign the people of Warrenton avoided him and his family as if they were stricken with an infectious disease. No one dared insult him, but the children became the offspring of Judas and nearly every time they ventured out of the house they were maligned with heckling and catcalls.[40] His clients dropped him, and his income decreased over 80 percent, from six thousand in 1871 to eleven hundred in 1876. By November 21, he had moved his law office to Washington and had shut up the house, taking the children to live with his mother. On court days he returned to Warrenton armed with a revolver in a holster on his hip. He sold the house for seventy-five hundred dollars to Eppa Hunton in 1878.[41]

When the gentle side of Mosby's personality dominated, he would lament that everyone in Virginia that he did not give a federal job condemned him as a traitor and that this period of his life was like passing through "the Valley of the Shadow of Death."[42] He would complain about belling the cat and wearing the shirt of Nessus. But when his fighting blood was up he would declare that the Southern people were wrong in persecuting him for being their friend and that he would do the same thing all over again. There was only one thing worse than being a traitor, and that was being a scalawag. Mosby had avoided this under Grant, but during the Hayes administration he would have to request a federal appointment and go away in what he considered a twenty-five-year exile from Virginia.

## 20

# Hayes's Reformer in Hong Kong

Eventually Mosby accepted a Republican appointment, consul in Hong Kong, and went into exile in "far Cathay," leaving his heart behind with his children in Virginia. Three were under twelve years of age; Ada, the youngest, was seven. They were beautiful, and he loved them dearly; but he would not see them for nearly seven years, except Beverly, who came to Hong Kong as his vice consul for the last two and one-half years. He left them in the care of his mother in Virginia and wrote to them frequently and sent gifts and money for their education and living expenses. When he returned they were nearly grown; Ada was fourteen.

The consulate was on the water's edge, and after dinner he would sit on the veranda and watch small launches coming and going to ships anchored in the harbor, flying the flags of every trading nation. He felt shut up on the small island, and, when he was lonely and homesick, his gentle side suffered. "I am anxious to see my children who are all that makes life dear to me," he wrote. And to the gentle Mosby it seemed amazing that conflict followed him here: "It seems that I am fated like Ulysses always to be in a storm, never to see sunshine & rest. I thought that if there was a spot on this earth where peace could be found it wd. be on an island on the China coast & here I expected repose for a short time from strife. But my doom has followed me until I begin to think that the curse of unrest has been pronounced on me as it was on Salathiel."[1]

In anguish, the gentle side of his personality identified with Ulysses, the hero of Homer's *Odyssey* who wandered for ten years; and with Salathiel, the Wandering Jew in medieval legend. Salathiel was living in Jerusalem along the Way of the Cross, and, when Jesus came by carrying the cross and stopped to rest, Salathiel chased him away. Therefore, in the story, Christ condemned him to live until the Second Coming, maturing to the age of one hundred and perpetually reverting back to age thirty, always a vagrant and stranger, wandering alone on the earth.

But the conflict side of Mosby's personality prevailed, and he charged into battle against corruption. Engrossed in strife, he identified with Hercules; he was cleansing the consular service of decades of corruption like Hercules flushed thirty years of filth from the floor of the Augean stables. Suddenly, the island did not seem so small, and he came to enjoy the jackdaw that sang on his windowsill each morning, the mild climate, the· diverse people, the New England sea captains that he had dinner with on their ships, and most of all the absorbing contention with a well-defined enemy. "I never enjoyed better health than I have here," he wrote. "I take a sea bath every night & sleep as sound as a log."[2]

Declaring war on the consuls who had banded together in China to steal from sailors, embezzle government funds, and bully the weak and defenseless, Mosby achieved reforms that touched the soul of the American reform ideal. The State Department, Mosby's employer, protected the Consular Ring; but the more powerful the opponent, the more Mosby enjoyed the fight. Refusing to be intimidated, he defied the Department and with the quiet, behind-the-scenes support of Hayes swept the China coast. Before it was over, Mosby's work caused the resignation or recall of the assistant secretary of state for Consular Affairs in Washington, the minister to China in Peking, the consul general in Shanghai, and the consul in Bangkok, and their replacement with honest, first-rate men. "While the Democratic orators in Virginia have been *talking* reform I have been *acting* it," he wrote.[3]

It had been relatively easy obtaining the appointment because he had become a friend of Hayes. He visited the White House, and they talked about the Civil War. Mosby hosted the president's tour of Montpelier, James Madison's home. Hayes rewarded Mosby with patronage, but to support his family he had to ask for a salaried position. He asked for employment as a lawyer in the attorney general's office, but there were no openings. Hayes offered him the consulate at Canton, which was not very desirable, and Mosby turned it down. Then on August 22, 1878, Hayes offered Hong Kong, and he accepted.[4]

History rates Hayes as a reformer at heart, and he was serious about it, including prosecution of corrupt government officials in his platform. Like most Americans he wanted honest men of character in the civil service. For some time, newspaper editors and Democrats in Congress had demanded consular reform, and he and Secretary of State William M. Evarts adopted the goal of hiring honest consuls with legal experience. When he recommended Mosby to Evarts he mentioned that Mosby was "a good lawyer."[5]

Mosby arrived in Hong Kong on February 2, 1879, on the steamer *City of Peking,* reported the next day to Governor General John Pope Hennessey, and on February 4 began work. As a British colony Hong Kong had the protection of the British flag; and, with an ideal, almost landlocked harbor, it was expanding as the commercial center of China. Junks came in from along the coast with cattle, fruit, and vegetables; and ships arrived from distant Asian ports with tea, cinnamon, and silk for transhipment in the world market. Boats went into China with consumer goods such as opium, rice, cotton, and salt fish.[6]

As consul, Mosby was to perform legal functions for United States citizens and businesses, but his main duty was to supervise and facilitate American commerce. The consul served as special counsel for U.S. sailors and shipmasters. He signed seamen onto American flagships and approved their discharge from the crews of ships. If a shipmaster had been cruel to a seaman, the consul could discharge the seaman from the ship; if a crewman had misbehaved or fallen ill, the captain could have the consul remove him. For U.S. seamen stranded in port he was to provide lodging, clothing, and passage home.[7]

Consular reform was sorely needed. When Secretary of State Thomas Jefferson recommended the first legislation authorizing consuls he insisted that, except for the Barbary States, they not be paid a salary but collect and keep "unofficial fees" for their income. Over the years Congress had approved salaries for some, but all still had authority to collect unofficial fees, and it was a tremendous temptation to keep not only the fees classed as unofficial but also to take money collected that belonged to the U.S. Treasury. By this time, all over the world incompetent consuls appointed for political influence were selling the flag. Consular Inspector De B. Randolph reported in 1882 that if the entire story were told "the most cold and indifferent citizen would blush for the name of his country." Almost everywhere, American merchants went to the British consul for help, knowing that the U.S. consul was either absent, worthless, or a thief. Mosby reported that ship captains in the Far East had the impression that each U.S. consul made his own law and noted that in Hong Kong the stealing of fees was worth more than a bonanza in Nevada.[8]

One of the greatest abuses involved the care of discharged seamen. Regulations required the consul to collect three months' extra wages for a discharged crewman and, if a U.S. citizen, give him two-thirds and deposit one-third in an account for the aid of destitute seamen. From this account the consul was to provide the man's living expenses in port and his passage home. The previous consul, David H. Bailey, friend of Treasury Secretary John Sherman, had deposited these funds in his private bank account and had not only stolen the extra wages of U.S. seamen but also had collected and kept the three months' extra wages due sailors of other nationalities discharged from U.S. ships. Before three weeks had passed, Mosby reported to the State Department that, based on two court cases, he had excluded foreign nationals from contributing to the destitute fund and was giving them all of their extra wages. He gave each U.S. sailor his two-thirds and placed one-third in the consular account designated for destitute seamen. Word spread quickly that an honest man had taken over in Hong Kong.[9]

But Mosby was not content to clean up his own operation; he resolved to expose the fraud that Bailey had practiced for seven years. He collected letters from ship captains who had discharged sailors and paid extra wages and discovered that none of these were reported in Bailey's quarterly statements. He found old discharge forms in a drawer and in a pile of rubbish on the floor and listed twelve hundred names of sailors shipped but not entered on Bailey's records. His suspicions were aroused when on his first day of work he met one of Bailey's partners in crime, Peter Smith, a scoundrel that Bailey had hired as "Shipping Master for the American Consulate" and provided an office in the consulate. Smith operated a boardinghouse, and Bailey assigned sailors there for a few days' lodging and board, a little grog, and a few old clothes. If a man hired onto a different ship, to obtain the required form, he had to pay Smith a bribe of two dollars and Bailey a bribe of one month's advance wages. Smith would go aboard a ship and stir up a fight among the crew, and Bailey would hold a hearing, discharge them all, and collect their extra and advance wages. The monthly pay for a seaman was between ten and twenty dollars, and Bailey robbed each man of forty to eighty dollars, "all consumed in the voracious maw of the Consulate." As described below, Mosby's first official act was to discharge Smith, and, in regard to lodging, he left it to shipmasters to select any boardinghouse.[10]

The door to the United States was open for Chinese emigration, and it was increasing because the Chinese people recognized that American public opinion was rising in opposition. In 1882 Congress would pass the Chinese Exclusion Act prohibiting immigration for ten years. One reason was the charge that California was filling up with "coolies," laborers allegedly coerced into labor contracts. Supposedly many were kidnapped or "shanghaied," and were slaves. To prevent the coolie trade, Congress had passed a law February 4, 1862, requiring that the U.S. consul at the point of departure in China certify that each man was leaving voluntarily. Hong Kong was not the only port of emigration, but it was the major one; in 1879 Mosby reported 8,919 emigrants and 7,304 in 1880.[11]

On his first day of work it was the busy season and the harbor was crowded. The *Oceanic* was preparing to leave for San Francisco with emigrants, and Mosby went aboard with Peter Smith to observe. He knew that Smith was required to interview each man through an interpreter and ask whether he was voluntary, stamp his ticket, and charge the ship twenty-five cents for each person interviewed. Mosby knew Smith was a reprobate as soon as he met him, and on the boat trip from the wharf in Smith's skiff he could hardly believe that this man represented the United States. On board Mosby watched as the emigrants came on deck and passed before Smith, seated behind a small table. He asked no questions but simply took each ticket, stamped it, and handed it back. When the process was completed, Mosby fired Smith for incompetence and refused to pay his wages of three cents per emigrant.[12]

Studying the regulations, Mosby saw that the system of "official" and "unofficial" fees was an open door to corruption. The certification of emigrants on U.S. flagships was an official duty, and the consul had to deposit the fees in the consular account of the U.S. Treasury. But the regulations allowed consuls to keep the fees collected from foreign vessels as "unofficial." He examined Bailey's records and learned that in seven years Bailey collected $28,465 in emigration fees and kept $13,729.60 without reporting it. For the $14,735.40 that he reported, he indicated exactly $14,735.40 in expenses incurred in the examination. One of the expenses was two hundred dollars per year for the hire of Smith's boat. The only other expense that had any validity was Smith's three cents per emigrant; the rest Bailey embezzled.[13]

Mosby nearly always examined the emigrants himself; when he could not, he sent his vice consul. He used an interpreter and asked each person whether he volunteered. He saved the boat hire by asking the ship to be inspected to send a boat. He deposited *all* fees in the U.S. Treasury, including "unofficial" emigration fees collected from foreign ships. Refusing to accept money that had not passed through government accounting, he deposited his unofficial fees in a separate account and officially requested the State Department's approval of returning the funds to him, washed clean by government accounting. The State Department refused, ruling that when he deposited the fees in the Treasury that made them "official," belonging to the government. Throughout his tenure he continued and afterward sued the government and received all of the fees that he had deposited for examining emigrants, $5,147.[14]

There were few women emigrants because U.S. law forbade Chinese laborers to bring their wives. Some single women emigrated, and with them consuls were required to enforce the law excluding prostitutes. Bailey had accepted bribes of ten to fifteen dollars each to stamp the applications of prostitutes, and agents in the business assumed Mosby would expect the same. When one of them offered Mosby a bribe, he had the man arrested. He called a meeting of the leading Chinese merchants and followed their suggestion to require females to apply one week in advance, have a photograph taken, and go to Tung Wan Hospital for an interview. Many were turned down, and he feared some were innocent. "A woman's virtue is a mystery which it is very hard to determine; even in American society it is very difficult, I may say impossible for any woman to prove her virtue," he wrote. Less than six months into his term, he received a letter from the collector of customs in San Francisco congratulating him for closing the traffic in prostitutes.[15]

Many Chinese individuals were addicted to opium, and they preferred the high-quality "foreign mud" imported from India, a trade reserved for British merchants. But after England defeated China in the Opium Wars and commerce in the drug became legal, farmers in China began cultivating the poppy, and merchants began exporting Chinese-grown opium. It was a relatively minor item, but demand was increasing as physicians recognized the unparalleled power of morphine to kill pain. They prescribed laudanum, a form of opium, and it appeared in patent medicines, sometimes as a liquid in eight-ounce bottles that some customers would open and start drinking before leaving the pharmacy.[16]

For years, Russell and Company, a large American company that pioneered in the China trade, had dominated the importation of Chinese opium in the United States. The company was founded by Robert B. Forbes of Boston, an uncle of William H. Forbes, Mosby's Union officer friend who now represented the company in Hong Kong. Before Mosby came, the company had lost its monopoly on the export of Chinese opium to the United States. Called the "Opium Farm," the monopoly was openly sold periodically by the governor of Hong Kong to the highest bidder. In the latest sale, Russell and Company had bid $201,000, but a rival had won with $205,000. Rather than abandon the business, the company moved its boilers from Hong Kong to Macao, a Portuguese colony a short distance to the West, and resumed processing, in competition with the new "farmer" in Hong Kong. There was no U.S. consul in Macao, and Bailey had been charging the company an annual bribe of ten thousand dollars to sign the required opium invoices. During Mosby's first few weeks, Forbes asked Mosby to sign invoices and offered him the same bribe. Mosby refused the $10,000 and signed for the regulation $2.50.[17]

About eight months later Forbes had an eighty-thousand-dollar shipment of opium in Macao ready for export to San Francisco. It was shipped in "cakes" or balls the size of twenty-pound cannon balls, several in a wooden chest. Governor Hennessey heard about it and warned Mosby not to sign, that Macao was beyond Mosby's jurisdiction. Mosby signed, and Hennessey, who was actually a warm friend of Mosby's, reported him to Secretary of State Evarts, accusing him of exceeding his authority and taking a huge bribe. Mosby fired off a telegram to Hayes denying the charges and wrote the colonial secretary pointing out that he had come to China to foster American trade, not destroy it. He avowed correctly that his action was perfectly legal, and if Her Majesty wanted to stop the shipments she should blockade Macao. "I deny the right of His Excellency to use me as a substitute for a blockading squadron," he wrote. The governor backed down, the *Hong Kong China Mail* praised Mosby's action, and the State Department upheld him with a mild scolding for using a tone of "derision and contempt" in replying to the governor.[18]

For his reform program in general the *China Mail* praised him for cleaning out "the utter rottenness" in the system. "The gallant Colonel has apparently adopted as his motto the well-worn words, *Fiat justitia, ruat coelum*," Latin for "Let justice be done though the heavens should fall." On his second day of work he had fired Vice Consul H. Seldon Loring and eventually replaced the shipping clerk and interpreter. On the morning after he dismissed Smith, Mosby was in a boat on the way to a ship when a man named Battles, a friend of the Ring, said, "Mosby, you have acted too hastily & made a mistake. You could have made the same arrangement with Peter Smith that Bailey & Loring did." A few days later he received an envelope addressed "U.S. Consul at Hong Kong," and he opened it and found that it was to Loring from Vice Consul J.W. Torrey in Bangkok. Torrey reported that the only "fat thing" he had made lately was a $480 bribe, and he congratulated Loring for making enough money in Hong Kong to retire.[19]

The corruption had been investigated and exposed several times, and Mosby realized that he was seeing firsthand what he had read about in the news and heard in Washington. During the winter of his appointment and before he left the United States, it appeared that action might be taken. The House of Representatives was investigating George F. Seward, the Ring leader, and Democrats were pushing for his impeachment. Seward had been consul and consul general at Shanghai and in 1876 was appointed Minister to China. He had been succeeded in Shanghai by a Hayes appointee, Republican lawyer and former congressman from Mississippi G. Wiley Wells. Like Mosby, Wells was horrified at the crimes of his predecessor, and he charged Seward with embezzlement, bribery, extortion, and defrauding the Chinese government. The House of Representatives called him home to testify, along with two of his former Shanghai staff members. In the hearings he defied Congress by refusing to turn over his accounts on the ground that he might be incriminated; and when the two staff members returned to Shanghai, Bailey fired them. The House Judiciary Committee recommended articles of impeachment, but the House vote failed.[20]

Mosby knew when he left Washington that the Senate had not yet confirmed Bailey's appointment as consul general to Shanghai, and therefore he hastened to officially blow the whistle on him in a dispatch to the State Department signed February 21, 1879, and sent on the first steamer leaving with mail after his arrival. The timing proved very significant. The letter exposed Bailey's embezzlement of an estimated "over $30,000" in emigration fees (later proved to be $28,465), and it arrived at the State Department before the Senate confirmed Bailey. The State Department tradition was "never anticipate trouble," and "in case of doubt, do nothing." In this situation the Department filed Mosby's letter and did not inform the Senate of his charges.[21]

Mosby was certain that the Department was ignoring his letter to shield the Ring. If Bailey's crimes were exposed it would increase demands for George Seward's impeachment, and all of this talk of corruption reflected poorly on George's famous cousin, Frederick W. Seward, assistant secretary of state for consular affairs. Fred was the son of the great secretary of state under Lincoln and Johnson, William H. Seward, and he had been in charge of consuls during his father's term. When Grant became president, he and his father had resigned, and Hayes had reappointed him. He was the official in charge of consuls and, as Mosby's supervisor and correspondent, was the addressee of Mosby's February 21 dispatch.

Mosby comprehended that he could blow the whistle on Bailey through channels to Fred until doomsday and there would be no action. Therefore, three days after his February 21 letter he went around Fred and Secretary of State Evarts and opened communication directly with President Hayes. He wrote to former Union general T.C.H. Smith, a clerk in the Treasury Department and friend of the president. By this time a U.S. Navy ship had come to Hong Kong from Bangkok, and the officers had confirmed that Vice Consul J.W. Torrey and Consul David B. Sickels were guilty of the type of extortion and bribery that Torrey had mentioned in the letter that Mosby had opened. Mosby requested Smith to inform Hayes. Then, in a first postscript to a second letter to Smith a few weeks later, Mosby wrote, "If the President does not clean out this Augean stable it will be the subject of Congressional investigation. Better let his administration get the credit of it than the Democratic party. I write this as his friend." In a second postscript, he concluded, "It is much better for the President to root out the corruption here than to leave it to a Congressional Committee. I intend to see that it is done."[22]

The evidence against the Bangkok consulate was corroborated when Grant visited Bangkok and Hong Kong on his world tour and told Mosby that the stories were true and Mosby should write Hayes directly. After that Mosby began sending letters to the White House addressed to William K. Rogers, the president's secretary. In the first letter, signed May 19, he called Sickels "a weak, incompetent fool" and declared Torrey as much of an outlaw as "Dick Turpin or Capt. Kidd."[23]

The Ring members shielded each other by refusing to testify against each other and by recommending a Ring member to succeed them as they left a position. Hayes had spoiled the arrangement by appointing Mosby, and they attempted to scandalize him to cause his recall. George Seward's secretary of the ministry in Peking sent a message to all of the consulates in the Far East requesting letters accusing Mosby of anything. The only dirt they found was quickly released to the press in the sensational story of "Mosby and his swallow-tail" coat. Gossip said that when he arrived in Hong Kong and received his first invitation to dinner at Government House, he refused to wear a formal jacket, showed up dressed in horseback riding clothes, and exclaimed that he would wear American clothes or none at all. The truth was that Mosby arrived without possession of a formal evening suit and had to decline an invitation to a reception until he could have one made. Governor Hennessey certified that Mosby's dress and behavior were exemplary: "I need hardly say there is no one in this country whose social qualities and high character I more fully appreciate," and Mosby gave this letter to the newspapers. Most editors agreed with the headline: "A Large Story Out of a Small Piece of Cloth."[24]

Meanwhile, in Washington Fred Seward attempted to ambush him. He requested "certain and clear specifications" of the charges Mosby made against the Bangkok consulate in his May 19 letter to the White House. Mosby recognized that it was an attempt to entrap him into making charges based on hearsay and replied that, yes, he had written to the president's secretary, but the evidence of criminal activity was not in his own letter but was documented in the letter of a ship captain that he had enclosed. Mosby stated that he had lost his own letter to Rogers, but "I believe that I said Sickles [sic] was an idiot and his Vice Consul Torrey who controls the Consulate was about as fit to be in the Consular service as Dick Turpin or Captain Kidd. I have no apologies to make for having expressed this opinion." Much to Mosby's satisfaction, he already had a letter from Fred in which Fred condoned all of Bailey's actions as consul.[25]

By late June 1879 it appeared that the Ring had won. Bailey had been confirmed, and renewed impeachment charges against George Seward had been sent to the House Judiciary Committee for a quiet burial. Therefore, Mosby the guerrilla warrior went where his Republican mentor Hayes dared not go—he secretly enlisted the aid of a Democratic newspaper editor. Mosby wrote a confidential, not-for-publication letter to Stilson Hutchins, founder and editor of the *Washington Post,* a new and hungry newspaper, less than two years old. He described the Ring and pointed out that his letter reporting that Bailey had stolen thousands of dollars in fees had been in the files of the State Department before Bailey's confirmation. He pointed out that the Ring was behind the attire scandal and stated that he had written to the president that if he did not reform Mosby would turn to the Democrats in Congress. Mosby was organizing but not yet on the attack, and Hutchins did not yet publish these revelations.[26]

Meanwhile, Mosby continued sending more details to Hayes and, finally, in July received his first mild signal that a reformer was alive in the White House. He learned that Hayes had appointed a special investigator to come to Hong Kong to investigate Mosby's charges. It was former Union general Julius Stahel of the Owl Shoot Raid, now consul in Hiogo, Japan, and friend of Bailey and the Ring. There had been more stringent investigators in Hong Kong before, and the Ring had survived and expected to again. On the way to Hong Kong Stahel visited Bailey in Shanghai and listened to his side of the story and after he came to Hong Kong received a lengthy letter from Bailey. In sentiment he was on Bailey's side.[27]

Mosby knew that Stahel's investigation would produce no reform unless it had the support of a second frontal assault. The American people needed to know that the State Department had promoted a crook to the office of consul general in Shanghai and had covered up Mosby's letter during his Senate confirmation. Bailey must be fired and the movement to impeach George Seward must be revived in the House. Therefore, he sent a copy of his February 21 letter to the newspapers, and it appeared on the same day, August 18, in both the *Washington Post* and the *New York Times*. An accompanying editorial in the *Times* stated that the letter was "said to have been purposefully withheld by the State Department" and pointed out that publication of it now would revive the impeachment of George Seward.[28]

Then Mosby secretly called in the heavy artillery; he challenged Democrats in the House of Representatives to join the effort. In a letter to an unidentified friend in the United States who was personally acquainted with the Democrats, he repeated the charges against the Ring and reported that Stahel would be forced by the evidence to report Bailey guilty. He accused George Seward of placing Bailey in Shanghai to cover his tracks and Bailey of trying to place Loring in Hong Kong to shield him. He asked the friend to give this information to the Democrats for impeaching George Seward "and also ask them to call on the state department for all the dispatches I have sent them on the subject." And, he declared, "I want you to push this matter at your end of the line, and I will keep up the fight out here. I am in for the war, and intend either to purge the public service of these scoundrels or go out myself." This letter was later published in the newspapers, but for now it remained confidential.[29]

Regarding the publication of the February 21 letter, the State Department had no comment except that a source said that Stahel's report would take care of the problem and that the Department had answered Mosby's questions about regulations without delay. The letter hit the news on August 18, and on September 2 Hayes personally handed to "WH," probably Second Assistant Secretary of State William Hunter, another letter from Mosby to the White House, dated July 13, soundly condemning the Ring, including George Seward. Mosby had no way of knowing it, but Hayes was doing his part with this quiet, behind-the-scenes action.[30]

Stahel finished his investigation on September 22, 1879, but Mosby did all the work and wrote the report and signed it; Stahel regretfully consented that Mosby's documentary evidence was overwhelming. Mosby sent copies to the State Department and White House, but his real audience was American newspaper readers. He released it himself, and it made the greatest splash in news coverage of his Hong Kong years. With irrefutable documentary evidence, the report convicted Bailey of embezzling $38,376: $28,465 in emigration fees, $5,911 for signing invoices, and $4,000 in miscellaneous fees. And Mosby wisely delayed presenting his revelations on extra wages for almost a month, until October 21, when the publicity had lessened, and then he released a supplemental Stahel Report, giving the news a one-two punch.[31]

The story of the first report was so sensational that Mosby expected to be recalled by the next steamer with mail. Under the banner "Mosby Rampaging about the Orient," one editor rebuked him for appointing himself a reformer, violating regulations by releasing official reports to the press, ignoring orders from his "boss," and forgetting that he "was no longer engaged in the partisan ranger business." He had "inserted his nose into the business of his fellow consuls in the Orient," scolded another. "He has been rampaging around like the fabled bull in the China shop," raising a "great stink."[32]

But the overwhelming sentiment was that Mosby was a champion of genuine reform. Editors declared the State Department guilty of covering up Mosby's February 21 letter and explained that now they knew why—it was to shield George Seward from impeachment. They pointed out that now it was understandable why George refused to turn over his accounts to Congress; he would have been impeached. The *Philadelphia Times* found it singular that in this "Diplomatic Scandal" a Confederate veteran was finally delivering reform of the diplomatic service in China. The *Louisville Courier-Journal* demanded Seward's impeachment and imprisonment, and the *Milwaukee Sentinel* demanded that the administration stop protecting George Seward and the "nest of rascals" and bring the criminals to trial.[33]

A rumor went abroad that Secretary of State Evarts would recall Mosby any moment, particularly after the publication on October 7 of Mosby's letter enlisting Congressional Democrats. News commentators concluded however that Mosby had Evarts in a dilemma, and it would be worse to remove him and bring him home to testify than it would be to leave him in Hong Kong. "People would honor Mosby for the course he has taken, and coming home with a fist full of facts he would become an exceedingly troublesome customer for the Seward family," declared an editor. "No; we do not think Mosby will be dismissed just at present." Another concluded, "Mosby will prove an ugly customer to deal with," and predicted that Evarts would leave him in office. But they were overlooking the crux of the situation: Mosby had an ally in the White House. No matter how Hayes had to compromise in other areas, he was thrilled that he and Mosby were producing pure reform. He and his staff clipped the stories of the controversy and pasted them in his scrapbooks, and, reading them, he silently cheered.[34]

Still, the Ring was untouched until Mosby released the supplemental Stahel report. It proved that Bailey had stolen from seamen thirty-five to forty thousand dollars in extra wages; and, when everything was totaled from the two reports, it came to over a hundred thousand dollars in seven years. Mosby signed the supplemental report on October 21, and ten days later Fred Seward resigned. He left quietly, without damage to his reputation, but Mosby was convinced that Hayes fired him. In December Eppa Hunton introduced a resolution that passed in the House demanding that the State Department send copies of all correspondence between Mosby and the department. On December 27, Evarts recalled George Seward. Bailey had been removed by February 25, 1880, and Sickels by May 12, 1880. Mosby wrote James A. Garfield, "The President has at last swept the China Coast which I wrote him to do a year ago."[35]

Mosby's informal power as Hayes's champion in the Far East placed Secretary of State Evarts in a difficult position. When challenged on whether he had seen Mosby's February 21 letter before Bailey's confirmation, he issued a press release that he knew nothing of the allegations when the nomination was made. The New York Sun recognized this as "mere subterfuge"; of course, Mosby had not yet written the letter at the time of the nomination. Evarts would not acknowledge that he had received the Stahel Report; and when the supplement appeared, even though it was already in the newspapers, he refused to release it as "incompatible with the public interests." Then he telegraphed Mosby asking for a second copy; the department had lost the original. "Every obstacle was thrown in my way by the State Department to prevent me from exposing the frauds," Mosby wrote.[36]

With a deep sense of probity, Hayes identified with Mosby's honesty; and, while the President's natural decorum prevented him from seeking publicity himself, he fully supported Mosby. He was of course vital to Mosby's success. He appointed Mosby rather than Loring. He supported Mosby's charges by forwarding the letters Mosby addressed to his office to the State Department, without written comment. By the regulations he could have permitted Evarts to recall Mosby for openly writing the president on March 19, 1879, requesting a ruling on "unofficial fees,"[37] writing letters to the president attacking colleagues, sending a telegram to the president during the opium crisis, writing a letter that was published in which he demanded a Congressional investigation of his own department, and releasing the Stahel Report and its supplement to the press. Hayes and Mosby, two honest lawyers, made quite a team: the bombastic whistle-blower from Virginia and the Victorian gentleman from Ohio. Hayes sent Mosby no direct communication, no message of encouragement or congratulation. He made no public announcements, and Mosby had no word from him until the war was over. But finally, in March 1880, Garfield wrote that Hayes found no fault in Mosby's conduct.

He continued on duty as consul through the administrations of Hayes, Garfield, and Chester A. Arthur and was replaced in July 1885 by Grover Cleveland. There was not much comment in the United States, but he left Hong Kong as a hero. Gen. Li Hung Chang, the most powerful man in China, the father of the national union and victor over the great Tai Rebellion, had sent Mosby a telegram on December 17, 1884, inviting him to recruit several hundred Confederate veterans and lead them in fighting for China against France in the Sino-French War in Annam, today's Vietnam. The Hong Kong newspapers praised him for honesty and efficiency and for redeeming the American consulate from the depths of degradation. "In this colony Colonel Mosby has won and retained the confidence and respect of all who knew him."[38]

On the day that he and Beverly departed, Maj. Gen. W.G. Cameron, acting administrator of the colony, honored them with a luncheon and at 2:00 P.M. escorted them to Government Wharf, where a large crowd of businessmen and officials gathered to honor Mosby. They stepped into a Government House steam launch, and, accompanied by several launches of Russell and Company, the governor and several friends accompanied them aboard their passenger steamer. Throughout, Mosby looked "deeply affected." He had in his belongings a poem written in his honor and given to him by the Chinese merchants of Hong Kong, and it included the following:

> You are both pure and clear.
> An example instructive, . . .
> Incorruptible and courteous to people
> Thus should an official be.[39]

# 21

# Stuart and Gettysburg

One of the quickest paths to dishonor in the South in the late nineteenth century was to disparage the memory of Robert E. Lee, the idol of the Lost Cause. "You know Genl. Lee is worshiped as a divinity in Virginia," Mosby said. Reconciling defeat, Lost Cause advocates postulated that, even though Confederate soldiers were overwhelmed by greater numbers and resources, the South had Lee as a symbol of the superiority of Southern civilization. He was a Christian gentleman and a military genius, and, since he never made a mistake, he could not have lost the battle of Gettysburg; someone else had to be blamed. First they placed most of the taint on Longstreet, but when they shifted to Stuart, Mosby declared war on what he called "the fashionable cult" behind the Lee myth. He counterattacked so ferociously that it frightened the Stuart family and for years they would not pronounce Jeb's name in his presence.[1]

Mosby's defense of Stuart gave him needed conflict during the years of quiet in his employment after Hong Kong, when he worked as attorney for the Southern Pacific Railroad. He had been relieved of duty as consul on April 28, 1885, and, before departing Hong Kong on July 29, had written to Grant requesting work in the legal department of some corporation. He had no money saved and still had three children under the age of twenty-one. Grant was dying of throat cancer, but the day before he died wrote to his friend Leland Stanford, president of the Southern Pacific Railroad, asking him to employ Mosby. As soon as his ship docked in San Francisco, a messenger met him with a letter from Stanford offering him a position. Mosby accepted and for over fifteen years worked in San Francisco, still separated from his children except for visits to the East coast. By the time William McKinley appointed him to the Department of Interior, August 3, 1901, he was sixty-seven years old, and Ada was thirty.[2]

From Hong Kong to San Francisco, Mosby went from reformer into the bosom of "the Octopus" of Frank Norris's novel, the most cruel and corrupt monopoly in America. The Southern Pacific Railroad controlled the transportation systems and the governments on the West Coast; and Collis P. Huntington, president after 1890 and Mosby's special protector, was "as ruthless as a crocodile." Under laissez faire, Congress gave the railroads a free hand; and when Southern Pacific lawyers appeared before the Supreme Court it was like a men's club reunion. Several of the justices had been corporate lawyers themselves and like Mosby they believed that as long as corporations did not steal from the public treasury they could spend their private money to corrupt elected officials all they wanted.[3]

The records of the Southern Pacific were burned in the earthquake and fire of April 18, 1906, but obviously Mosby's duty was light, and he had much free time. His office was in the Law Department at company headquarters in San Francisco, and he made business trips to Mexico, El Paso, Los Angeles, and other locations. Eventually he longed for more of a challenge and decided to support William McKinley for president in 1896 and return to the consular service. He became one of Republican candidate William McKinley's "gold bugs" in favor of the gold standard and opposed to bimetallism and free silver. "I am for *gold* & civilization vs: Silver & barbarism," he wrote privately. As he had for Hayes, he published an essay championing this key issue, and it made a splash in the news and was reprinted as a campaign broadside. In the essay he wrote that while traveling on business in Mexico he had noticed that silver coins had driven gold out of circulation, and the same would occur in the United States if bimetallism were adopted. And even worse, the free coinage of silver advocated by McKinley's opponent William Jennings Bryan would threaten civilization. If the voters elected Bryan he would lead the nation straight to Avernus, the sulphurous lake at the entrance of the underworld in ancient literature. The essay and other writings made him visible enough in the campaign that a pro–Republican political cartoon portrayed McKinley and Mosby, united as symbols of honesty and integrity, warmly clasping hands—not across the bloody chasm of Civil War—but with Rebel Mosby standing firmly on the side of gold with McKinley.[4]

Eight days after McKinley's inauguration Mosby visited the White House to seek an office. McKinley had served on the staff of Hayes in the Civil War, and he warmly welcomed Mosby, joking that Mosby's men had made life miserable for him in the Shenandoah Valley. They became friends, and Mosby's patrons in the Senate informed him that McKinley promised a first-rate consulate. The newspapers reported that he would have a place in China or South America. There were many openings because in his tenure McKinley replaced 238 of the 272 salaried consuls.[5]

But mysteriously, the appointment never came, and Mosby concluded that someone in the administration had blocked it, probably Secretary of War Russell A. Alger. He heard that Alger had been making negative remarks about him; and one day when Mosby said hello, Alger turned away and insulted Mosby by refusing to return the greeting. After that, when they happened upon each other on the sidewalk in Washington, Alger would pause, raise his hat, and bow flauntingly; and Mosby would ignore him. Alger had been colonel of the 5th Michigan Cavalry, and Mosby decided this must be the problem: "His hostility grows out of the fact that my men came upon his regiment burning houses in the Shenandoah Valley, & shot all they caught—*which I wd. do again.*" However, there is no evidence that Alger was the culprit. More likely it was John Sherman, friend of David H. Bailey, and now Secretary of State. Consuls were in Sherman's department, not Alger's, and for Bailey he may have taken revenge on Mosby.[6]

In the meantime, Mosby had used some of his free time to represent himself as a lawyer before the Supreme Court in *John S. Mosby v. The United States.* He sued the government for the unofficial fees that he had deposited in Hong Kong and argued before the Court of Claims so effectively that one of the judges told him that he made "the strongest, clearest and most cultivated speech that he had heard for many years— that it was so *exhaustive* as to give the court no excuse for questions." He claimed $15,867.01, including $5,147 in emigration fees for emigrants on foreign ships. The government attorneys claimed that when he voluntarily paid the money into the Treasury he surrendered his right to claim it later. Ruling against the government on December 3, 1888, the Court of Claims rendered judgment that he was entitled to $13,839.21, disallowing $435.80 for certain notarial fees and $1,592 for signing a type of invoice, ruling these official fees. It was one of the most satisfying victories in Mosby's life; he won eighty-seven percent of his request, and a headline trumpeted: "Mosby Victorious."[7]

The government appealed, and before the Supreme Court Mosby again served as his own lawyer. The case was argued on January 17, 1890, and decided on February 3. Justice Samuel Blatchford, an expert on admiralty law from New York City, wrote the opinion of the Court. He commended Mosby for acting "with propriety, and with a high sense of honor," and agreed with the Court of Claims that Mosby did not surrender his right to the funds when he made the deposits. He pointed out that Mosby's letters at the time constituted formal protest and proved that he was not donating the money to the Treasury. The Court upheld the Court of Claims except that it awarded Mosby $39.29 for notarial actions excluded by the Court of Claims and overturned the award of $2,095 for certifying invoices for free goods, leaving him a net loss of $2,055.71 but a final reimbursement of $11,783.50. Because of his honesty he had turned down about $100,000 in bribes and boodle, and passing his fees through government accounting he lost $4,083.51 that consuls normally kept for themselves.[8]

But he was filled with pride, and in applying for another consulate he offered the Supreme Court decision on Hong Kong as his best recommendation: "It is an epitome of the history of my administration there." In a similar case he appeared before the Court of Claims and the Supreme Court as attorney for the estate of Thomas B. Van Buren, consul general in Yokohama, 1874-85. Van Buren had deposited $4,115 in unofficial fees; and since he was deceased, based on the precedent of the Mosby case, the Court of Claims awarded Van Buren's estate that amount. But on November 29, 1897, the Supreme Court overruled. Van Buren had not deposited the funds under protest and therefore had surrendered his title. Mosby lost, but the ruling confirmed his wisdom in documenting his own protest.[9]

He occupied himself as well writing and speaking about the Civil War. Magazines and newspapers were in a golden age, and readers had an almost insatiable appetite for articles by veterans. In July 1886 a literary agent invited him to write a series of articles on his war experiences for the *Boston Herald* and the *New York Sunday Mercury*, and Mosby accepted to make money for the children's education. The articles were well received, and the Boston post of the Grand Army of the Republic, the largest Union veteran organization, invited him to speak at Tremont Temple. This was quite an honor; Tremont Temple was a historic building on Tremont Street near Boston Common. By this time it had become a Baptist church but originally was a theater that had featured such famous personalities as Jenny Lind and Charles Dickens.[10]

That evening in late November or early December 1886, a crowd of about a thousand people filled the temple, and Mosby's stage fright exaggerated the number in his mind: "I had practiced law for twenty years," he said, "but had never delivered a lecture in my life and I entered Tremont hall by a side door and found there were 4,000 present. I was scared nearly to death and hoped the building would fall down on us before I had to make my appearance." He walked on stage, and the audience rose to their feet, applauded, and cheered. He thanked them and delivered an address on Stuart's cavalry and the raid around McClellan on the Peninsula, and when he finished the applause was thunderous. The next evening, William Forbes gave him a dinner attended by James Russell Lowell and Oliver Wendell Holmes. Mosby hardly tasted the food, but never forgot the conversation: "It was a feast of the gods." His agent scheduled the lecture in seventeen other venues, including Brockton, Massachusetts, on December 4, 1886.[11]

The agent had copyrighted the articles, and when Mosby was in New England he reported that Dodd, Mead & Company of New York were preparing to publish them as a book. "I never dreamed of their assuming a book form," he reflected. "They were nearly all dashed off at a single sitting—& without being copied, or corrected mailed on the same day to Boston so as to get the money as soon as possible." His war with the Lee cult had not yet begun; and, warmed by the realization that he was making money for his children, he allowed his gentle nature to prevail and wrote at his best. It was similar to giving interviews; at such times, he would come alive, bringing back old memories and feelings and sharing his sense of humor and colorful, warm personality, features that he usually reserved for his inner circle of friends. This is why the first twelve chapters of *Reminiscences* are among his best published war recollections. When he took time to edit, especially during literary conflict, the fighter dominated, and his pen became a weapon. For example, in the book chapter thirteen was a version of his first significant salvo in the war to defend Stuart, and its belligerence stands in contrast to the tone of the previous chapters. Chapter fourteen, the final chapter, was his Boston speech; and while it is more moderate, it is also more formal, carefully avoiding revelation of inner thoughts or feelings. A reporter commented that the book was "vividly, concisely, and most entertainingly written," with "charming glimpses" of his career.[12]

He donated the royalties of the book to John Junior and upon every opportunity visited him and the other children. In the spring of 1897, after meeting with McKinley, he and Pauline and Ada went together to the University of Virginia to attend a benefit performance of the drama,

"The Flirt," a social satire written by John Junior while studying at the university. He had since begun work as a lawyer in Denver. Before the evening of the performance, Mosby and his daughters visited friends, and he invited Mrs. Emma Robertson DuBose, thirty-two years old and daughter of his former prosecutor, Judge Robertson, for a carriage ride. On Friday afternoon, April 23, at 5:00 P.M., they were riding on the road west of Carr's Hill, just within the university, when the harness became disarranged and he leaned forward to adjust it and the dashboard gave way. He fell into the horse, and the startled animal kicked him in the head, knocking him unconscious. Emma ran for help, and some students came with a stretcher and took him to the infirmary.[13]

Surgeons from the medical school operated and determined that his skull was fractured, his brain injured, and his left eye shattered. He was sixty-three years old and in a fight for his life. Modern surgeons who studied the details of his injury for the author report that with this type of injury it was unlikely that swelling would occur that would cause a dangerous increase in intracranial pressure. Therefore, Mosby's life was not threatened by cerebral swelling, but in that era before antisepsis, he might have died of infection. Considerable morbidity usually accompanies eye loss, and often the patient must battle depression, which can slow recovery.[14]

Pauline and Ada came to the infirmary immediately, but he was unconscious and covered with dust and blood, and they were not allowed to see him until after the operation. The medical team gave him a fifty-fifty chance of surviving, based on the odds of infection, and told Pauline and Ada to summon his family and friends. One of the Rangers wired another, "Come at once. We fear the worse [sic] for our noble chief." The news spread throughout the nation, and the New York World published his obituary as "The Last of the Partisans." Newspapers in Virginia carried daily updates, and on the fourth day he was better and on the fifth day decidedly improved. When they told him he had lost an eye, he recited from Byron's Childe Harold: "Blind old Dandolo! Th' octogenarian chief, Byzantium's conquering foe."[15]

Expressions of concern deluged his room in the infirmary. William Forbes sent a hundred dollars and many flowers, and Vermont governor Grout, wounded at Miskel's Farm, sent a letter. Mosby appreciated the sympathy of his Northern friends, but he was deeply moved by the kindness of Virginians and people at the university. Perhaps someday they might be reconciled and he could come home. He avoided depression, rapidly recovered, and on June 7, about six weeks after the accident, with his head in bandages, he visited McKinley at the White House. Through the summer he stayed with his children and went back to California in the fall. He now had an artificial eye and felt very relieved that his face was not disfigured.[16]

Someone in the McKinley administration had apparently thwarted his application for a consulate, and it happened again the next spring in the Spanish-American War. On April 22, 1898, two days before Spain declared war on the United States, he telegraphed General in Chief Nelson A. Miles requesting authority to raise a battalion or regiment for the Cuban invasion. He was sixty-four years old and in good physical condition, except for the lost eye. Confederate general and now U.S. senator Matthew C. Butler of South Carolina was sixty-two years old, and he served as a major general even though he had lost his right foot in the Civil War. Mosby seriously wanted a commission. He knew that the image of Rebel veterans in U.S. uniforms would be a powerful symbol of reconciliation.[17]

He had been assured that Miles was his friend and would support his request, but Miles sent him a telegram: "I would be very glad to have your services, but think it will require some influence. Suggest that you communicate with your senators." Mosby read the message and assumed that Alger had stopped him again, and this time he was probably correct because this situation involved Alger's department. He fired back: "Your telegram received. I have no influence except my military record," and released both messages to the press. This was the heyday of yellow journalism, and reporters sensationalized the story, a "Tilt" between the high command and an old Rebel who wanted to serve, not from ambition but as "evidence of a united country." One headline asked: "What is your 'Pull?'" In an interview Mosby said, "I cannot imagine what any Congressman could say that would add anything to the indorsements I have received from General Grant and General Robert E. Lee." So Alger went to war without Mosby and, encountering huge supply problems, saw "Algerism" become the byword for bureaucratic incompetence and had to resign under a cloud.[18]

Rejected for the war in Cuba, Mosby meanwhile put his soul into the fight with the Lee cult. In Richmond, Jubal Early was president of the Southern Historical Society, the most powerful organization of the Lost Cause, and J. William Jones edited *The Southern Historical Society Papers* (SHSP), a periodical with a national audience. Along with Lee's wartime staff, Colonels Charles Marshall, Walter Taylor, Armistead L. Long, Charles Venable, and others, they conspired to create historical "truth" that, according to Jefferson Davis, eulogized Lee on "a foundation of fiction in disparagement of others." Mosby labeled the conspiracy against Stuart "one of the great crimes of history" and declared, "They make history in Richmond like they make shoes—*to order.*"[19]

Until the end of his life, Early dominated the Lost Cause and focused the Society's efforts on assassinating the character of Longstreet and other commanders while leaving Jeb Stuart relatively unharmed. John Esten Cooke and others eulogized Stuart, and by 1885 he was viewed as a knightly cavalier. There were a few criticisms in the SHSP and elsewhere, but Early was forced into a trap in which he had to agree to defend Stuart. Maj. Henry B. McClellan, Stuart's adjutant and a cousin of Union general George B. McClellan, threatened to expose Early for publishing a draft of Stuart's Gettysburg report in the SHSP and deleting Stuart's criticism of Early for not linking with him in Pennsylvania. Early agreed to defend Stuart, and McClellan in turn refrained from attacking Early or Lee in his 1885 biography of Stuart.[20]

The Early-McClellan bargain shielded Stuart and provided Mosby a debating advantage for years. During Early's presidency no really skillful writer attacked Stuart. In 1886 Armistead L. Long broke from Early's ranks with a widely read book that mostly maligned Longstreet for Gettysburg but also censured Stuart for separating from Lee, either from a misunderstanding or love of raiding. And Longstreet, defending himself in an article in the popular Civil War series in *Century* magazine, wrote that he had ordered Stuart to ride on his right flank, but Stuart disobeyed and instead undertook "another wild ride around the Federal army." Mosby researched the Confederate archives and discovered contemporary correspondence, including Longstreet's, proving that Lee gave Stuart discretionary orders authorizing Stuart's raid and at the time, regardless of his memory loss, Longstreet had approved. Mosby published the letters in *Century* and in his *Reminiscences.* In clearing Stuart, he shifted the blame for Lee's lack of cavalry to Confederate general Beverly H. Robertson. Stuart had ordered Robertson, in command of two brigades of cavalry in the Valley, to follow Lee's army, keeping on his right-rear and conducting reconnaissance. Instead, Robertson had remained behind until it was too late.[21]

Then in 1889 the Gettysburg volumes of the *Official Records* were published, and in studying them Mosby discovered a stronger line of defense for Stuart. So far he had proved that Stuart did not disobey orders but had admitted that Lee was harmed by the lack of cavalry and had blamed Robertson for that failure. Now he created his Hill-Heth thesis that Lee was doing fine without cavalry: his army was in place and on schedule, moving toward a concentration at Cashtown or some other high ground where he could concentrate and fight from a strong defensive position. But before he could move into place, on July 1, Gen. Henry Heth's division in Gen. Ambrose P. Hill's corps marched into Gettysburg, not on a reconnaissance and not to obtain shoes, but to fight and capture prisoners and have a glorious day. Without Lee's orders they precipitated the battle, committing Lee to fight on ground he had not selected. Mosby published this in *Belford's Monthly* magazine in 1891, opening with: "A TRUE history of the campaign of Gettysburg has never been written."[22]

Early died in 1894, and by this time one of the highest commemorative events in the Lost Cause was the annual celebration of Lee's birthday. On January 19, 1896, Charles Marshall delivered the Lee birthday address for the Confederate Veteran Association in Washington, D.C. The speech was one of the most comprehensive attacks ever made on Stuart; it cleared Lee of any fault whatsoever and gave none of the blame to Longstreet or anyone else—Marshall placed the entire onus for Gettysburg on Stuart. It was published in the *Richmond Dispatch* and the SHSP and was so influential that it pressured Mosby into writing a book and publicly disagreeing with Lee's official reports. Like Mosby, Marshall used contemporary correspondence, and he was an outstanding writer and talented lawyer. He wrote his speech as a prosecuting attorney writing an indictment. And what he said took on meaning because of who he was. He had been so close to Lee that he seemed like a member of Lee's family. During nearly the entire war he was Lee's adjutant and closest confidant, and after the war he helped Lee collect information for an autobiography that was never written. After Lee's death, the family selected him to write Lee's biography. He was highly intelligent and before the war had taught at Indiana University and practiced law in Baltimore.[23]

Marshall hated Stuart, and if Early had not prevented it he would have blamed Stuart all along. During the Civil War he wrote nearly all of Lee's important letters and reports, and he wrote Lee's two Gettysburg reports of July 31, 1863, and January 1864. As he and Lee reviewed the campaign, he told Lee that Stuart "ought to be shot" and urged Lee to court-martial him. He included in a rough draft of Lee's second report the charge that Stuart disobeyed orders, but, before signing, Lee had him strike the words. Even so, both reports were so critical of Stuart and so contradictory with Lee's letters and other primary documents that Mosby finally concluded that Lee must have signed them without reading them. Mosby took no satisfaction in being critical of Lee, and as the conflict unfolded he refrained as long as he could from publicly admitting that he challenged Lee's reports but finally did in 1898.[24]

Lee's first report stated that Lee directed Stuart to judge whether he should enter Maryland east or west of the Blue Ridge Mountains and then "take position on the right of our column as it advanced." Instead, Stuart became separated and his absence made it impossible for Lee to obtain accurate intelligence. Lee received no report from Stuart or any other source that the Union army had crossed the Potomac River until a scout or spy of Longstreet arrived at Chambersburg on the night of June 28, 1863, with that news. Surprised, Lee directed his three corps to march "to Gettysburg" and there "unexpectedly" confronted the Union army and battle was "in a measure, unavoidable." The second report stated that Lee gave Stuart discretion to select his route, but, if he perceived the enemy moving northward, he was to place himself "on the right" of Lee's column. But Stuart departed from Lee, and Lee was unable to ascertain the enemy's intentions. Therefore the scout's report caused Lee to concentrate east of the mountains. Heth's July 1 march to Gettysburg was a reconnaissance "to ascertain the strength of the enemy," and when Heth came "unexpectedly upon the whole Federal Army," battle was "unavoidable."[25]

Mosby ably charged that Marshall wrote the reports as "a great sophist,—an able and astute lawyer. It is a fine example of special pleading, and the composition shows that the author possessed far more of the qualities of an advocate than of a judge." Special pleading in law is an argument that omits what is unfavorable and develops only what is favorable to the case. In indicting Stuart for disobeying orders, for example, Marshall used special pleading when he omitted the fact that Lee had given Stuart authority "to judge whether you can pass around their army without hinderance," and instead the first report falsely suggested that, whichever route Stuart chose, Lee ordered him to "take position on the right of our column as it advanced" and the second suggested falsely that Lee positively ordered Stuart to withdraw and unite with the infantry "as soon as he should perceive the enemy moving northward." The reports omitted the fact that Stuart left two brigades under Robertson in Lee's rear with orders to screen and conduct reconnaissance in Lee's right-rear as he advanced. The reports omitted the fact that the timing of Lee's final order giving Stuart discretion to ride around the enemy army, signed at 5:00 P.M., June 23, meant that previous orders to move on Ewell's right and the order in this letter to "feel the right of Ewell's troops" were rendered impractical. By the time that Stuart could receive the final order and begin marching, Ewell's corps was in Pennsylvania, and, as Mosby pointed out, it would have taken the magic of Merlin or Aladdin's genie to be in two places at once. And the reports omitted that Lee's orders to Stuart were confusing and unclear—instead the reports give the impression that Lee's instructions were precise.[26]

In his 1896 speech, Marshall again demonstrated his literary skill and brilliance as an attorney. With a tone of scholarly restraint, he claimed to present only the facts known by Lee at the time, and he quoted contemporary letters, including the final order from Lee to Stuart. He charged that Stuart disobeyed positive orders to turn back if he met a hindrance and to march through Maryland on Ewell's right. Disobeying, Stuart deprived Lee of cavalry; and, at Chambersburg when Lee still had heard nothing from Stuart, Lee told Marshall more than once that he feared that Hooker was gone toward Richmond. When the spy came, Stuart's silence caused Lee to move his army to Gettysburg and fight at a disadvantage on ground that he did not choose. Marshall emphasized the hindrance theme and the spy story to indict Stuart of causing Lee's defeat.[27]

"It is the argument of an astute advocate and sophist, and utterly destitute of judicial candor," Mosby reacted. "He was guilty of both the suppressio veri & the suggestio false." Marshall again left out the fact that Lee gave Stuart authority to judge whether there was a hindrance and again made no mention that the timing made it impossible to ride on Ewell's right flank through Maryland. He stated that Robertson was left behind with two brigades to guard Lee's rear but did not include Stuart's June 24 orders to Robertson to provide reconnaissance.[28]

But Mosby believed that he had already argued down the charge that Stuart disobeyed orders. What concerned him now was Marshall's emphasis on the spy story. He decided to write a book to reveal one more example of Marshall's special pleading and to explode the thesis of the spy. He would use another contemporary Lee letter to contradict what Marshall had written in Lee's reports and in his address. Marshall had not mentioned that in Lee's headquarters letter-book in Marshall's possession and in the published *Official Records* there was a letter from Lee at Chambersburg to Ewell in Carlisle, dated June 28, 7:30 A.M. The letter became famous as the Chambersburg letter because it contradicted Lee's reports and Marshall's speech. In the letter Lee informed Ewell that he had written him the night before, on the night of June 27, that the enemy army was reported to have crossed the Potomac River and that he had ordered him to move his forces to Chambersburg. Lee's reports stated the scout arrived on the night of the 28th. If this letter was authentic and dated correctly, it would prove that Marshall had omitted part of the *res gestae*, the facts of the case, and it would prove that Lee was not surprised by the spy's report and did not concentrate his army because of the spy but from information gained earlier. This made Stuart's absence less vital and became the foundation for Mosby's further emphasis on the Hill-Heth thesis that Lee's campaign was on track until Hill and Heth threw it off by going to Gettysburg.[29]

But Lee's Chambersburg letter clearly contradicted Lee's reports, and, as Mosby wrote, "To say in the South that every line of Genl. Lee's reports is not correct is a good deal like telling an Arab there are things in the Koran one can't believe." Nevertheless, he published the letter in a newspaper article in March 1896. He claimed to refute the spy story, but Stuart's detractors questioned the date on the letter, insisting that it was written weeks later by a staff officer and inserted in the letter-book. A footnote in the *Official Records* stated, "Noted in letter-book as copied from memory." The implication was that the writer forgot the date and instead of writing June 29, which would agree with Marshall and Lee's reports, had written June 28 by mistake.[30]

For ten years Mosby attempted to have a glimpse at Lee's letter-book to determine whether the letter was authentic, but Marshall and the Southern Historical Society refused to let him see it even for a few minutes. "I was as long seeking it as the Knights of the Round Table were in quest of the Holy Grail," he sighed. Marshall had it and refused to answer two letters on Mosby's behalf from former Confederate general Marcus J. Wright, agent for the collection of Confederate documents for the *Official Records*. Marshall died in 1902, and Mosby heard that a committee of the Southern Historical Society had it; he made a formal request with them, and they refused. Finally, the book came into the possession of Gordon McCabe, a friend of Joseph Bryan in Richmond, and, while McCabe stated that he was forbidden to allow Mosby to see it, he answered Mosby's queries in two letters in December 1905 and January 1906. Then one day in early February 1906, Bryan drove Mosby to McCabe's house, and McCabe yielded. Mosby was seventy-two years old, and, when the book was laid before him, he had not been this excited since discovering Bailey's receipts in the trash in Hong Kong. "It did not take me a minute to find what I wanted," he wrote. "It knocks the foundation from under all the histories of Gettysburg."[31]

He saw that the Chambersburg letter was not inserted but written in the book in sequence, and he confirmed for himself what McCabe had written in one of his letters, that it was in the handwriting of Colonel Venable, of Lee's staff. And he noted that Marshall's handwriting was on the letter in the book immediately preceding the Chambersburg letter and the one following. "He had this [Chambersburg] letter in his possession when he delivered his philippic on Lee's birthday in 1896 against Stuart; but he did not refer to it," Mosby pointed out. Glancing at other letters, he saw the handwriting of other staff members who had censured "Stuart for obeying the instructions which they wrote him at Lee's dictation." Mocking the astounding forgetfulness of Lee's staff, he wrote that they reminded him of the mythical people in the *Odyssey* who had amnesia from eating the lotus fruit: "The Homeric legend of the Lotus-eaters who lost their memories seems to be no longer a romance but a reality."[32]

In *Stuart's Cavalry in the Gettysburg Campaign,* published in 1908, he proclaimed the purpose of clearing the "great injustice" wrought on Stuart by Lee biographers and staff members and proving that Lee's Gettysburg reports were contradicted by contemporary correspondence and were therefore in error. After an introduction on the battle of Chancellorsville and a chapter on Brandy Station, in the second and final chapter he discussed Gettysburg and his war with the Lee cult, interspersed with autobiographical narrative on his own role in events from mid-June to June 25, 1863.[33]

It was the first book to defend Stuart with contemporary correspondence and the first to challenge Lee's reports. Historians today generally agree with the book's demonstration that Lee gave Stuart discretionary authority to make his raid. Mosby repeated his Hill-Heth thesis; and whereas most of today's historians do not place all of the blame on Hill and Heth like Mosby did, they generally accept that Lee did not send Hill and Heth to Gettysburg on a reconnaissance and that their fight on July 1 altered Lee's plan and committed him to battle on a site that he did not select. Later, in his *Memoirs,* Mosby mentioned that Hill's report stated that on June 30 Hill notified Lee that the enemy held Gettysburg. Historian Gary W. Gallagher has emphasized that Lee's reception of this message makes Lee responsible for the fighting on July 1 and not Hill and Heth.[34] But the spy thesis is another matter. In the 1908 book Mosby accepted that a Longstreet scout came, not on June 28, but rather on June 30, and he did not bring news of the Union army's crossing the Potomac but word that Meade had replaced Hooker. Thus, the spy arrived too late to cause Lee to change his plan of campaign. Mosby argued that Marshall and others antedated the spy's appearance to make him Lee's chief of cavalry so that they could blame Stuart for being absent. For years Mosby attempted to corroborate the Chambersburg letter by analyzing times, distances, and marches made by Ewell's corps in response to Lee's orders, but he had to fall back on circumstantial evidence and never clinched the nail like he wanted.[35]

Most historians today disagree with Mosby's use of the letter and still accept Marshall's version in Lee's reports. They generally agree with the conclusion in Edwin B. Coddington's standard study that Venable made a clerical error and should have written June 29 on the letter. Coddington accepted Marshall's statements that the scout forced Lee to change his plan from foraging toward Harrisburg to concentrating at Cashtown. On the other hand, Coddington included Mosby's interpretation in an endnote, and Alan T. Nolan agreed with Mosby that Lee knew Hooker was over the river before the scout arrived. Lee biographer Emory M. Thomas also concluded that Lee had word of the Potomac crossing before the spy came and that the man brought word of Meade's accession to command and approximate location.[36]

Mosby believed that he had fully cleared Stuart and himself of any blame for the loss of the battle of Gettysburg. But both he and Marshall had impossible goals: Marshall had to prove that Lee had no fault at all, and Mosby had to prove that Lee was not harmed by the absence of his great cavalry chief. The consensus today agrees with Coddington that Lee gave Stuart "a free hand," as long as he could pass without hindrance, but, as Coddington wrote, Stuart failed to judiciously use that discretion, meaning that he should have turned back when his route was blocked by the enemy army.[37]

Mosby realized that the hindrance theme was the strongest charge in Marshall's indictment and reacted with special pleading of his own. Lee's final order had this sentence: "You will however be able to judge whether you can pass around their army without hinderance, doing them all the damage you can, & cross the river east of the mountains." In *Stuart's Cavalry*, Mosby quoted the sentence that followed but left out the hindrance sentence, and when he discussed Stuart's decision he omitted discussion of the hindrance statement. He wrote that Stuart had "received General Lee's order of 5 P.M., of the 23d, to start the next day and put himself on Ewell's right on the Susquehanna." With this statement, not only was he ignoring the hindrance charge, this was one of several instances when he used the art of suggestion to overstate his case on the change in Stuart's instructions due to timing. Mosby was correct that, if Stuart used his discretionary authority to raid, Stuart could not proceed through Maryland with Ewell because Ewell would be gone. But again and again the book suggests that Lee ordered Stuart to join Ewell "on" the Susquehanna River, rather than moving on Ewell's flank "towards" the Susquehanna as the orders stated. Mosby even wrote, "General Lee told Stuart he must leave him and go to Ewell," when earlier in the book he had written that Lee's final order gave him a choice of going with Lee or "by Hooker's rear."[38]

The book is disorganized and spliced together; Mosby abruptly shifted back and forth between narrating his own role and refuting Stuart's critics. Lengthy passages from secondary sources are quoted along with several entire primary documents. Mosby practiced guerrilla history by intruding his own emphasis into the documents through frequent italicization of selected phrases and sentences. At least twenty-two times he apologized to the reader, but at least twelve additional times he italicized with no apology. He condemned Heth not only of losing the battle but accused him of covering up his guilt in his report. The book is so aggressive that Douglas S. Freeman considered it "an intemperate book" and "the fullest defense of Stuart, a defense carried beyond sound argument." James I. "Bud" Robertson wrote that it is "hysterical in places."[39]

Mosby the history writer was not as interested in determining truth as he was in destroying his opponents. He rejoiced that a three-part article in the Sunday *Richmond Times* on the campaign against Sheridan gave "'Little Phil' unshirted hell," reducing him to the dimensions of Tom Thumb, the circus personality. The iconoclast in Mosby delighted in being "first" with an interpretation. He claimed to be first to tell the truth about Sheridan's Valley campaign, the Front Royal hangings, and Gettysburg. "I will knock all the Gettysburg writing into a *coelbesit* [a hole where it belonged] & reconstruct the campaign for it has never been understood & all accounts are incorrect," he wrote.[40]

The Gettysburg war was long, bitter, and bellicose. He described how he planned to assail, assault, or strike the heads of his enemies, drawing and returning fire. "My magazine is full of ammunition," he boasted, preparing to explode some accepted history, to knock it "all to pieces." Having just completed an article, he informed a friend: "In the language of Mr. Fitzsimmons [professional boxer Robert "Bob" Fitzsimmons] I think I have put Heth-Longstreet-& Marshall 'to sleep.'"[41]

Mosby's gentle side, on the other hand, suffered the torment of disapproval from the people of Virginia and the South, and it felt the same as when they had ostracized him for supporting Grant. He believed that Southerners hated him as completely as Northerners had at the end of the Civil War and that now Southern mothers were using his name to quiet their children like women had in Scotland with the name of warrior Sir William Douglas: "It has always fallen my lot like that of the Black Douglas, to have to *'bell the cat.'* People who agree with me in the Gettysburg controversy are afraid to say so; or speak with bated breath." It was unpleasant and made him sad, but he felt it a sacred duty to do justice for Stuart. Identifying with the suffering of Christ in the Garden, he lamented, "It is a cup which I wish might have passed from me."[42]

In Mosby's mind, the Stuart family were his mentors, especially Jeb's widow, Flora, and his brother William A. Stuart, a prosperous businessman and large cattle rancher in southwest Virginia. William contacted Mosby when the criticism first began and remained solidly behind him until he died in 1893. Mosby considered the Stuarts within his inner circle of friends, and it was painful when in 1887 Flora learned from Henry McClellan that Mosby was about to publish the letters contradicting Lee's reports, and she asked him to withdraw them. She wrote that she agreed with McClellan that controversy might damage Stuart's memory and she feared the "strife & bitter feeling" that would result. Mosby knew that McClellan had bargained with Early and that McClellan had read the letters in the Confederate archives but had not mentioned them in his book. He refused Flora's request, answering in the chilly tenor he usually reserved for his enemies: "I cannot recognize Genl. Stuart's fame as being the exclusive property of anyone." She relented and gave her approval but sighed: "I shrink from the bitter discussion & recrimination that *I fear* will be called forth."[43]

William and his son Henry C. Stuart were disappointed with McClellan's biography and asked Mosby to write one with a stronger defense of Jeb. Therefore, when Mosby began writing his book in 1896, he considered them his mentors and valued their encouragement. Then in 1899, Flora asked him to forgive McClellan, and Mosby replied with one of the coldest letters that he ever wrote. He described McClellan's "infamy & treachery" and declared that he would not forgive. "Why don't you ask McClellan why he tried to use you to suppress these letters?" He continued on friendly terms with Henry and with Jeb Stuart Jr., and, by the publication of the book, Henry had organized the Stuart Land and Cattle Company and had large investments in banking and real estate. He had been eleven years old when he had met his Uncle Jeb during the war, and he loved to hear Mosby's war stories. But when the book appeared, he stopped pronouncing Jeb's name in Mosby's presence. When he went to Mosby's apartment in Washington to take him for rides in his automobile, he would not mention Uncle Jeb. One day Mosby pointed to the general's portrait on the wall, and Henry looked at it but said nothing. "Now my book frightened the Stuart family," Mosby wrote.[44]

In 1913 Henry was elected governor of Virginia, and on May 29, 1915, he received a letter from him mentioning the book and inviting him to a reunion as his guest. The book had been out for seven years, and it was the first time a member of the Stuart family had recognized its existence to Mosby. He declined the invitation and wrote to a correspondent: "Too late!! too late!!" But then Henry requested a copy of his speech defending Stuart, and Mosby asked his friends to call on the governor on his behalf. In June 1915, Mosby corresponded with Flora, giving her the details of McClellan's deceitful actions and explaining why he had to contradict Lee's reports. In March 1916, when he was in St. Vincent's Hospital in Norfolk, Jeb Stuart Jr.'s wife visited him, and Mosby planned to go with a friend to visit Flora before he left Norfolk.[45]

By the last few months of Mosby's life, the Stuart family had reconciled with him, and he felt that his vindication of Stuart in the Gettysburg campaign was now complete. He realized that Southerners in his day rejected his ideas, but he was certain that future generations would agree with him.[46] Today he would be pleased that he is recognized as the first Civil War writer to use contemporary letters to refute the charge by Charles Marshall and others that Stuart disobeyed orders. He would be pleased that his proffering of an alibi for Stuart by blaming Hill and Heth for precipitating the battle has been accepted to an extent—historians agree that Hill and Heth deserve some blame, but this does not absolve Stuart. And he would be delighted to know that a few twentieth-century historians have challenged the spy thesis that Lee was surprised to learn on June 28, 1863, that the enemy army had moved. Mosby and Marshall applied the adversarial system to the history of Gettysburg and left it to future objective historians to discern the truth.

# 22

# Roosevelt's Land Agent in the Sand Hills

When Mosby was laid off from the Southern Pacific Railroad on the death of President Huntington, he had no money saved, only a small life insurance policy. It was "gall & wormwood," but he pleaded with McKinley one more time for an appointment and on August 3, 1901, at sixty-seven years of age, became special agent in the General Land Office in the Department of the Interior. At a salary of a hundred dollars per month, he had responsibility for investigating and reporting violations of federal land laws in three districts in Colorado and Nebraska. When he arrived at his headquarters in Akron, Colorado, he rented a horse and carriage and rode out on the range. He wore a black suit and his hair was white, but his step was light and quick and his eye bright and alert.[1]

He soon discovered that cattle ranchers were illegally enclosing public land. "Do you know, sir," he told a reporter, "that many of these cattle kings have fenced in and appropriated to their own use tracts of land larger than that governed by many a German prince?" For over a year he created a sensation as President Theodore Roosevelt's sword of reform and champion of the small homesteader. Again, as in Hong Kong, he used the newspapers to gain informal power, this time beyond the reach of the political influence of the stock growers. But he proved his own worst enemy and made a slip of the tongue that forced the president to muzzle and transfer him.[2]

The thrill of conflict and outdoor life on the plains compensated for his continuing exile from Virginia and from his children and now grandchildren. Beverly and John Junior had studied at the University of Virginia and had become lawyers, John still in Denver and Beverly in Salt

Lake City. May had married Robert R. Campbell, a lawyer and Republican Party leader; after he died in 1900, she supported herself and two sons, John Mosby Campbell and Alexander Spottswood Campbell, by working as postmaster of Warrenton. Stuart became an accomplished freelance writer of Civil War articles and interviews for the *Philadelphia Times* and other newspapers. She married Watson E. Coleman, a lawyer from Pennsylvania, and they lived in Washington and had two children: Beverly Mosby Coleman and Pauline Coleman. Pauline and Ada worked as nurses in Baltimore.[3]

Mosby was proud that his children identified with and benefited from his Civil War career. May kept scrapbooks of his clippings and correspondence, and now they are a valuable source on microfilm at the University of Virginia. In her home she displayed a Jeb Stuart letter and a Grant document, framed and hanging on the wall. Mosby wrote a series of articles for Stuart to syndicate in the newspapers, and she collected his cavalry hat and other artifacts. Her name, Virginia Stuart Mosby Coleman, was unsurpassed for a Southern Civil War writer. Mosby was proud that, when his men held a reunion at Salem in August 1895, all four daughters and May's sons attended. The veterans elected Pauline "Daughter of Mosby's Confederacy," as Winnie Davis was "Daughter of the Confederacy." Pauline was selected in honor of her mother and namesake.[4]

In the Land Office from his headquarters in Akron, Mosby had Akron and Sterling land districts northeast of Denver and the McCook district in southern Nebraska. First he found violations of the Timber Culture Act of 1873, where claimants had not planted the required trees, and he had their entries suspended. Then, on October 23, 1901, he reported that residents in Morgan County, Colorado, had complained about fences on public lands. The department directed him to investigate, and on November 11 he reported that yes, the Pawnee Cattle Company had erected a drift fence twenty miles long on federal land, and he asked how to proceed. Land Office Commissioner Binger Hermann, Mosby's supervisor, replied with instructions and issued a circular directing all special agents to work for "a speedy removal" of the illegal fences.[5]

Cattlemen had preceded farmers and sheep herders on the frontier in the arid West, and they learned that ten to thirty acres of land were required to furnish enough grass for one steer. For a viable ranch, at least twenty-five hundred acres were needed. They had bills introduced in Congress to increase the acreage allowed under the homestead laws, but

2,500 acres seemed excessive to eastern legislators when they compared it to the regular 160 acres. Obviously, the land was too dry for farming, and the ranchers stayed, raising beef cattle on their own small homestead entries and grazing and cutting hay on the vast public domain. At first the government allowed it, as long as the land was open to all.[6]

But the use of the public range in common failed when the cattle industry expanded in the two decades after the Civil War. Common property generally results in overuse and exhaustion of resources, and this happened. With no one in control, by 1883 ranchers had overgrazed the common grassland, and to remain in operation they enclosed sections with barbed wire. This enabled an individual to control the number of cattle grazing on his enclosure and prevented overgrazing, which destroyed the grass for everyone. The other essential was water, and the ranchers filed homestead entries for land around the lakes and along the streams. In order to control enough water for large herds, they filed many fraudulent homestead entries.[7]

From the viewpoint of the ranchers, the fences were in defense of the environment on which they depended, and the illegal entries were an adaptation to a western environment that Congress did not understand. But to the farmers and shepherds who came for a small homestead, it was shameful land-grabbing, especially when a homesteader found his claim within one of the "monopoly" enclosures of a cattle ranch. The U.S. Senate ordered a Land Office investigation in 1884 that revealed two cattle companies with fences around land amounting to over a million acres each. Farmers in eastern Nebraska and the influential *Omaha Evening Bee* supported the homesteaders.[8]

Nebraska senator Charles H. Van Wyck, a former Union general, represented the farmers by sponsoring the Van Wyck Fencing Act, which passed in Congress on February 25, 1885. It authorized the Interior and Justice Departments to prosecute ranchers with fences on public lands. The law and its regulations provided that, upon a complaint, a special agent of the Land Office would investigate, obtain affidavits, and warn violators that they had sixty days to remove the fences. If they were not taken down, the agent was to present the evidence to a federal district attorney, who was to file a lawsuit compelling removal of the enclosure. This was strictly a judicial action; no use of force was authorized.[9]

In his first year as president, Grover Cleveland issued a proclamation that the law would be enforced and the fences would come down. But in their enthusiasm Land Office officials suspended the processing of land claims to allow time to investigate fraud, and that angered prospective homesteaders. Reacting to criticism, in 1887 Cleveland dropped enforcement of the Van Wyck Act, and it was not emphasized again by the Land Office until Mosby inspired Hermann's circular. Meanwhile, the harsh winter of 1885-86 demonstrated the need for winter pastures and hay, and this caused more fraudulent entries as ranchers extended their holdings.[10]

Before the great expansion in the cattle industry, ranchers had favored revising land laws to allow large homesteads. In 1878 geologist James W. Powell reported to the Interior Department that in certain districts there should be 80-acre irrigated farms and 2,560-acre ranches. A Congressional Commission in 1879 endorsed Powell's proposal as practical but impolitic because a majority of Western voters opposed large homesteads. Therefore, Congress did not enact two bills embodying the idea. With expansion came greater competition and the ranchers changed to prefer the idea of paying a grazing fee for ten-year leases on public land, and when Theodore Roosevelt became president they expected his support.[11]

In 1884 Roosevelt had been devastated by the tragic deaths of his wife and mother on the same day and had adjusted by leaving New York City and living as a rancher for two years in North Dakota. In his 1888 book *Ranch Life and the Hunting-Trail*, he described how he "toiled over the melancholy wastes of sage brush and alkali" and reported that twenty-five acres of arid land were required to support one cow and overstocking was the great threat to the plains cattle industry. However, he stated in the book that he supported distribution of the land to as many owners as possible.[12]

The Nebraska Stock Growers Association responded to Mosby's reawakening of the issue by calling a special meeting in Alliance on February 18, 1902. They had already appointed a committee to draft a bill for ten-year leases, and now they reaffirmed their support and with the support of the American Cattle Growers Association sent a delegation to meet with Roosevelt and testify in hearings conducted by the House Committee on Public Lands. The head of the committee was Bartlett Richards, the largest cattleman in Nebraska. "Well, well, I'm glad to see you," said Roosevelt, welcoming them to the White House in May. "I am always delighted to meet the boys from the plains." Then, turning to the Nebraska senators with them, he said, "You can always depend on men like these. They are genuine." They presented him a petition, and he considered the matter for three days and saw them again. He said that there were so many letters from the West opposing large ranches that he could not support the lease bill. "Gentlemen, the fences must come down," he said. He gave them fair warning; and for the remainder of his administration, even though he refrained from prosecuting U.S. Senator Francis E. Warren of Wyoming, who was charged with illegal enclosures, he generally enforced the law with vigor.[13]

Meanwhile, Mosby continued investigating fences and fraud in his districts into August 1902, when the Land Office sent him on temporary duty to Alliance, Nebraska. Special Agent W.R. Lesser, with headquarters in North Platte, had requested assistance in removing the fences in the Sand Hills region east of Alliance. Mosby found the hunting so much more fruitful that on August 26 the office reassigned him to Alliance and placed him in charge of three districts that entirely encompassed the Sand Hills.[14]

This new assignment placed Mosby in the very center of the conflict between the cattlemen and homesteaders and at the forefront of Roosevelt's law enforcement. The Sand Hills, a grassland biome, an ecological system ideal for cattle but suitable for no other productive effort, brought the issue into clear relief and outlined the problem in black and white more clearly than anywhere else. The Sand Hills is nineteen thousand square miles of sand dunes covering one-fourth of Nebraska and making the state still today one of the largest beef producers in the United States. It is unsuitable for farming because, when a plow breaks the topsoil and removes the grass, the sand blows away, leaving a "blowout," a hole in the ground. Ranchers said the grain harvested from a Sand Hills farm would not feed a flock of canaries through the winter. It was unsuitable for sheep because the grass was too tall.[15]

The sand dunes have the forbidding appearance of waves on a stormy sea, and the first cattlemen avoided it, assuming that stray cattle that wandered in and never came out had died. Then after a blizzard in the winter of 1878-79, two cowboys rode in and found a herd of fat cattle thriving on the rich grass, plentiful ground water and thirteen hundred small lakes, and natural shelter from the windchill provided by the dunes. "We rounded up this bunch of cattle and were certainly two surprised cowboys," one wrote. Bartlett Richards, who had moved to the Sand Hills for a safe winter range and fields to produce hay, said in 1902, "We have the safest as well as the cheapest home for cattle in the world. . . . Nature seems to have fashioned it for the bovine race alone."[16]

And if the nation's land laws were unrealistic anywhere, they were in the Sand Hills. A rancher needed twenty acres to pasture one steer; and in order to avoid overgrazing and provide hay and winter pasture, one had to use part of the public domain. But the homesteaders in eastern Nebraska disagreed. "Let the government by all means move the unlawful fences and cancel the fraudulent homesteads," demanded the *Rushville Standard,* or else Nebraska would end up with a few millionaires and thousands of tramps.[17]

Mosby had been in Alliance only a short time when he saw an unusual number of women passengers going through on the Chicago, Burlington & Quincy Railroad. He inquired and determined that they were widows of Union veterans from Iowa and Kansas on their way to Wyoming to enter fraudulent homestead claims for large cattle companies. Under the law, widows had the right to make entries without residence but were required in their absence to make improvements and cultivate the land. They were receiving fifty dollars and expenses and in return committing perjury and fraud by filing a claim and signing a ten-year lease and contract to sell after the ten years. Mosby heard about a group of such women who had been in Alliance a few weeks before, and he went to the Land Office and discovered the names of sixty-two widows who had filed fraudulent entries in his districts. He reported this, and Hermann commended his zeal and told him to proceed on both fronts, the widows and the fences.[18]

Immediately, he attracted the attention of the two senators from Nebraska who had taken the cattlemen to the White House and were very pro-rancher. Senator Charles H. Dietrich, a banker in Hastings, and Senator Joseph H. Millard, a banker in Omaha, both sent for him to come meet with them. He was unable to meet with Dietrich, but the next time he was in Omaha he called on Millard. The senator told Mosby to suspend enforcement of the fence law until he could get a bill passed allowing the fences. "I told him I had no power to ignore the law, that the President himself could not do that," Mosby said. Millard suggested that Mosby go to Washington to explain the situation.[19]

Instead Mosby returned to work and investigated Bart Richards's Spade Ranch. He was preparing a fence removal order when on September 30 fifteen widows came to Alliance and filed fraudulent entries, some of them for Bart. Now he had evidence of both illegal fencing and fraud against Bart, but the next day he was recalled to report to the president. Richards was the king of the Sand Hills and probably the most powerful rancher in the nation. His brother DeForest was governor of Wyoming, and Dietrich and Millard and other powerful politicians were solidly behind him.[20]

Bart was born in Vermont, son of a Congregational minister, and at age eighteen in 1879 moved to Cheyenne in Wyoming Territory. He had chronic indigestion, and his doctor recommended that the rugged life of the cowboy might offer relief. He soon wrote to his mother that the "*broiling* sensation" was gone from his throat and his digestive system was working as well as a grist mill. He invested in land and cattle, and in 1885 DeForest joined him; together they went into banking in Wyoming and Nebraska.[21]

By the time of Mosby's investigation, Bart's Nebraska Land and Feeding Company controlled over five hundred thousand acres in the Sand Hills. Part was legal, part was with fraudulent titles, and most was government land fenced with 292 miles of barbed wire. Headquarters was Spade Ranch, twenty-five miles north of Ellsworth, and Bart had a summer mansion in Ellsworth and a winter home in Coronado, California. He and his wife, Inez, also his niece, had been married in Berlin, Germany, and had four children. He was successful because he used the Sand Hills effectively. Spade Ranch had fifty-six drilled wells with windmills so that a cow never had to walk more than a mile and a half for water. His partner, William G. Comstock, was a good manager, and Bart was great at buying cattle in Texas, New Mexico, and Mexico.[22]

When Mosby arrived in Washington, the Nebraska senators found what it was like to have him in the capital blowing the whistle of reform. The storm of sensationalism that the State Department had tempered by keeping him in Hong Kong now swept over the nation. Newspaper articles made him the sheriff of the United States, called out to the violent cattle frontier to enforce federal laws. It was well known that there had been bitter conflict between the cattle growers and the farmers and shepherds. In 1892 President Benjamin Harrison had sent the cavalry into Johnson County, Wyoming, to restore order. Recently in Wyoming thirteen-year-old Willie Nickell had been ambushed and killed riding horseback a few yards from the gate of his father's sheep ranch. Tom Horn, a detective for the cattlemen, had been arrested and charged with murder, and his two-week trial and conviction made headline news while Mosby was in Washington.[23]

Several newspapers connected Mosby's law enforcement with Willie's murder and reported that Mosby's life was threatened and the cattle barons might hire someone to shoot him. One report had him missing, a victim of foul play. Someone asked if he was afraid, and he answered, "Why, if these fellows kill me, everybody will know who did it, and why." In truth, he was in no danger, for as the pro-cattlemen *Alliance Times* accurately stated, Bart and Comstock were "too sensible to threaten violence to a kitten." The *Lincoln Daily Star* ridiculed Mosby by describing him as sharpening his "nippers," or wire cutters, to make way for "chimerical 'home builders,'" imaginary creatures who would not be able to make a living in the Sand Hills and would starve. When he threatened to bring in the cavalry, the paper exclaimed, "Once a guerilla always a guerilla," and in an article titled "MOSBY AND BLOOD," ridiculed him for declaring "war to the nippers and nippers to the hilt." "Colonel Mosby seems to love to pose as a David who, with his little nippers, will face the cattlemen with their Winchesters."[24]

An unidentified joker for the stockmen wrote a bogus letter, supposedly written by Mosby to his friend Senator Daniel, requesting that Daniel support a six-month or one-year suspension of the Van Wyck Act and vote for larger homestead entries for ranchers. "In an agricultural country a homestead of 160 acres may support a family, but it will not where land is not worth much for anything but grazing," the letter declared. "I hope to see you soon. I am out on the prairie enjoying Arctic weather."[25]

During about seven weeks in Washington, Mosby not only blew the whistle on the cattle kings, he exposed the crimes of his predecessor in the Sand Hills, Agent W.R. Lesser. "Colonel Mosby was sent to help me," Lesser said. "Instead of doing so, he immediately began hunting for trouble internally. He seemed to think he had come here to make a personal investigation of my conduct, when nothing of the kind was intended." It was true; while investigating the cattlemen and widows, Mosby had learned that Lesser had not been on duty. Instead of working at his headquarters in North Platte as his weekly reports indicated, Lesser had resided at home in Tama, Iowa, and had submitted fictional reports postmarked on a train. Mosby determined that Lesser had been in North Platte only nine days in the four months prior to July 1, 1902, and not at all during the month of July. Lesser was suspended on November 1, 1902, by Secretary of the Interior Ethan A. Hitchcock.[26]

In Washington Mosby met with Hermann, Hitchcock, and Roosevelt; and they said they were firmly behind him. When the round of meetings closed, Roosevelt told him, in news that made headlines, to go back to Nebraska and enforce the law. "Those fences must come down or there will be trouble," he said. The *Detroit Free Press* praised Roosevelt for sending "the fighting old Confederate . . . to go out there and clean up," and the *Syracuse (N.Y.) Sunday Herald* congratulated Mosby: "He goes back to his post with the scalp of the special agent Lesser at his belt, with his knife under the hair of the District Attorney and with the material at hand to do up the cattlemen." The *Omaha Evening Bee,* a homestead newspaper, exalted: "MOSBY BRINGS HIS BROOM. Bears from Washington Instructions to Sweep Away Illegal Fences."[27]

Mosby had won the war; but on his trip back to Nebraska, in the train station in Chicago, several reporters gathered around, asking questions. Enjoying the attention and savoring the fight, he went over a line that he had never crossed in his Hong Kong reform—he criticized the two Nebraska senators: "Every effort has been made to protect the cattle barons in their occupancy of the lands. Senators Millard and Dietrich are interested in aiding the barons because both are at the head of national banks which hold heavy mortgages on the stock of the ranges." He said the two men had asked him to discontinue his enforcement and he had refused. He spoke the truth, but there was no reason to say this; he had already neutralized the political influence of Millard and Dietrich.[28]

He arrived in Omaha on the night of November 27, 1902, and the next morning in the district attorney's office attempted to correct himself: "What I did say was that I had been told that both the senators were presidents of national banks which hold chattel mortgages on large numbers of cattle in the western part of the state and that it is to the interests of the banks to have the fences remain as they are. I did not state it as a fact, but said that I had been told so." One day later, on November 29, he received a telegram from Hermann: "Submit to no more newspaper interviews relative to your official work, but proceed quietly with same."[29]

By mid-December he was withdrawn. Roosevelt could not allow a land agent to publicly accuse two senators of conflict of interest. Secretary Hitchcock denied that Mosby was in bad odor and said that he had "accomplished a good work" and finished his task. But the cattle kings celebrated, for Mosby had destroyed himself and been transferred, according to the *Lincoln Daily Star,* "probably to keep him from being eaten, blood, boots, nippers and all, by the ferocious tribesmen who inhabit the sandhill regions in western Nebraska." Mosby was extremely disappointed; he despised having to leave an unfinished fight. The Land Office would not permit him to testify in the trials that followed and forbade him to give advice or consult with district attorneys on the cases.[30]

Without Mosby the administration prosecuted the cattlemen and, in November 1905 in Omaha, Richards and Comstock pleaded guilty of illegally fencing 212,000 acres of public land. Federal Judge William H. Munger fined them each three hundred dollars and court costs and sentenced them to six hours in custody of the U.S. Marshal, who turned them over to their lawyer. According to the national news they spent the six hours having dinner at the cattlemen's Omaha Club. Roosevelt was furious and determined to make examples of Richards and Comstock. He removed the district attorney and U.S. marshal and ordered a second trial, this time not for fencing but for fraudulent widow entries. This trial lasted 24 days, and the government called 132 witnesses. The two men were found guilty and fined fifteen hundred dollars each and given one year in the Adams County jail in Hastings. In jail Bart's stomach trouble returned, and he had surgery on his gall bladder at the Mayo Clinic. He returned to jail but did not recover from the operation and died September 4, 1911, at the age of fifty, with less than one month remaining in his sentence. People who never knew him stereotyped him as an arrogant monopolist, but when one of his friends heard of his death he wrote to another: "Bart. was sound all thru; you know it and I know it, and it is an infinite pity he had to die under an apparent cloud."[31]

Ironically, after Bart's conviction and before he went to jail, Roosevelt wrote in a private letter on February 11, 1907, that he now agreed with the idea of Bart's leasing plan. He wrote that he now believed that everyone on the range, including the homesteaders that he still favored, would benefit by the control and order of leasing. He had appointed a public lands commission and was agreeing with their recommendation of a lease law with a small grazing fee and local control of the range. Congress failed to enact the plan, however, and there was no change until Franklin D. Roosevelt's New Deal. In 1934 leasing was enacted in the Taylor Grazing Act. It was the first federal land law to recognize the arid West's cattle-raising problem. Today Bart's idea continues in effect in the Sand Hills and throughout the arid plains, with ranchers leasing and fencing public land for a grazing fee. Bart Richards was an entrepreneur ahead of his time, and in 1970 he was named to the Cowboy Hall of Fame in Oklahoma City, Oklahoma, in recognition of his contribution to the development of the West.[32]

Roosevelt did not remove Mosby from his job but kept him in Washington until April 2, 1903, and then he was assigned to the Land Office in Montgomery, Alabama. In May 1904 Roosevelt would approve Mosby's new position in the Justice Department, and when he went out of office told him, "Colonel Mosby! I shall always be proud that you served under my Administration." In Alabama Mosby investigated trespass on the federal pine forest and reported illegal cutting of trees and extraction of turpentine from pine trees. The people were very kind; but the work was routine and boring, and he felt humiliated for being removed from the war against the cattlemen. "I am really in exile now," he complained.[33]

He worked in Alabama one year and during that time concentrated his energy on getting an appointment as lawyer in the Justice Department under Attorney General Philander C. Knox. The antitrust division was growing and hiring attorneys to investigate trusts, and this would return him to Washington. He was so miserable that his best friend, Joseph Bryan, laid aside his abhorrence of politics and led a lobbying campaign. Bryan met with Roosevelt and took three of Mosby's friends with him: Senator John Daniel; William E. Peters, professor of Latin at the University of Virginia; and famous author Thomas Nelson Page. Bryan notified friends of Mosby in the North as well, and among those who contacted Roosevelt were Oliver Wendell Holmes Jr., Charles Francis Adams, and Henry Cabot Lodge.[34]

By May 1904, Bryan's campaign seemed ready for culmination, and Mosby went to Washington. He went to the White House, and Roosevelt treated him with respect, taking him into a private room and telling him that he approved but Knox was not satisfied with Mosby's legal qualifications, which meant that Knox feared that Mosby would stir up trouble like he had in Hong Kong and Nebraska. Roosevelt asked him to visit Knox and then come back and he would write a letter of appointment. Mosby thanked him and left but refused to go see Knox. He said that he would rather go back to Alabama than suffer such humiliation. A few days later, he learned that Knox had said he would hire Mosby if Mosby's brother-in-law, Charles W. Russell, in the department, would accept him in his bureau and control him. Russell was special assistant attorney in charge of the Bureau of Insular and Territorial Affairs. He had married Mosby's sister Lucy, and after she died married another sister, Lelia. He was a respected lawyer and was presently in Paris, France, arranging the transfer of the French Panama Canal Company to the United States. Mosby was staying with Lelia while in the city, and he and Russell respected each other. After a few days of suspense, Russell returned and agreed, and Mosby became an assistant attorney at a salary of $2,400, double what he had earned in the Land Office.[35]

He was seventy years old and felt that he had returned home at last. He continued living with Lelia and Charles for the next several months but listed his address as Warrenton. "I have been a wanderer—a Childe Harold—for 26 years & have now come back to rest & spend my last days with my friends in Old Virginia," he wrote. When things settled down, he moved in with his daughter Stuart and her family in their apartment at 1514 K Street, Northwest, about a minute's walk from his office in the Justice Department. Russell sent him on a successful "secret" mission to investigate Republican Party officials in Alabama. But when he assigned Mosby to investigate corruption of government officials in charge of Indian affairs in the Territory of Oklahoma in June 1905, within two weeks a grand jury had indicted three prominent administrators, a bank president, and three attorneys for fraud against the Chickasaw Nation. Russell sent him a telegram asking him to give a square deal to the three lawyers because they had cooperated with the Justice Department in the past. Mosby answered, "I feel very sure that if there is a square deal they will land in the penitentiary." Shocked, Russell decided that once Mosby finished in Oklahoma he would give him no more assignments. They "kept the lid on me," he recalled, "and never afterward gave me any work, but completely ignored me in the Department."[36]

For more than four years he remained on the payroll, in essence drawing a government pension and using free office space. He spent most of his time fighting the Gettysburg literary war and writing and defending his Stuart book. In 1909 he joined the protest against college football. That season a student-athlete on the University of Virginia team, Archer Christian, was killed in a game against Georgetown University. There had been changes to make the game less brutal, such as the addition of the forward pass and exclusion of the "flying wedge" in which the offensive line formed a phalanx by holding onto handles sewn on each other's trousers. But linemen were still allowed to lock arm-in-arm and run down the field in lockstep. Christian was one of twenty-seven students killed in the nation by the end of 1909.[37]

Mosby wrote two letters demanding that the University of Virginia abolish the game and released them to the newspapers. To him this was a continuation of his lifetime conflict with bullies and bruisers and reflected his disapproval of sports in general. "I had no taste for athletics and have never seen a ball game," he wrote, reflecting on his youth. He denied that brute force had anything to do with heroic masculinity. "My idea of manhood is a sense of honor and courage; such qualities may exist in a weak body." He declared that football murdered young Christian and the faculty who approved the games were "accessories before the fact." He compared football to cock-fighting and charged that the teams were "largely composed of professional mercenaries who are hired to advertise colleges. Gate money is the valuable consideration. There is no sentiment of Romance or Chivalry about them." Mosby's letters probably had no impact, but in 1910 the mass play with interlocking arms was banned.[38]

President William H. Taft's attorney general, George W. Wickersham, tolerated Mosby for over a year; but in December 1909 Russell left as minister to Persia, and Wickersham asked Mosby to resign, effective July 1, 1910. At the age of seventy-six he knew it was time to retire, took it gracefully, and was sincere in forbidding his friends to intervene. However, he said that he had lived too long, that he had expected to die in office. He had saved nothing and had no retirement plan. This caused a rumor, carried by the Associated Press, that he required charity. "COLONEL MOSBY REDUCED TO POVERTY" reported the *Confederate Veteran*, and stories spread that he was penniless, cooking on a small alcohol stove, unable to afford tea for his guests, and wandering around Washington in bedroom slippers. Some said he was homeless and others had him living in one of the worst neighborhoods in Washington.[39]

He read a newspaper article describing him as in tears over his discharge, and he struck back by inviting an unidentified woman reporter from Baltimore to his room in Stuart's apartment for an interview. He showed her his spacious, book-lined room, with windows offering a view of the trees along the street below, and he explained that his tiny alcohol stove was just for making coffee; he had most of his meals at restaurants because he enjoyed dining out. "I thought you were an old man!" she said, and he roared: "I am NOT!" He brought up the story about the weeping and said, "I've wept many a time in war when my men were killed or wounded, but I want you to understand, young lady, and everybody else, that I never yet cried over myself." She concluded that he had not been laid off because of advanced age because "he's TOO strong."[40]

His main income in retirement was from lectures. In 1906 he had given a second speech in Boston, and in 1910 he spoke in New Haven and other locations in Connecticut. In 1914 he lectured at the Toronto Military Institute, and in March 1915 for the Quill Club in New York

City. In December 1915, at the age of eighty-two, he rode in a Pullman car to Bristol and spoke for two hundred dollars.[41] His theme was still the defense of Stuart, but in the speech that was most meaningful to him, at the University of Virginia, he shared some of his own Civil War experiences.

For several years the university had wanted to honor and clear him of guilt for shooting Turpin, but it was difficult arranging an appropriate occasion. He had educated both of his sons at the university and, by now, his two older grandsons. He had visited the campus several times, including the occasion of his accident and grandson Mosby's graduation in 1904. His friends knew that he hated banquets and toasting and refused to be placed on display. "I do not choose to be an imitator of Fitz Lee & Buffalo Bill—put myself on exhibition," he said.[42]

Early in 1915 University President Edwin A. Alderman thought he had found a solution. He would invite Mosby to attend a ceremony in honor of Mosby and President Taft, whom Mosby had served under. Mosby accepted, but when he heard that Alderman planned to read a commendation, he canceled. "The reason I didn't go was that . . . they intended to give me a testimonial that would be an atonement for their having expelled me from the University for shooting a bully. That determined me not to go. It is crucifixion to me to undergo any kind of a ceremonial." He considered it a "pardon" for a guilty offender, reminding him of his jail sentence and expulsion. He was innocent and in no need of pardon. After the event, Alderman sent the medal and testimonial signed by the faculty, and Mosby saw that he had responded correctly—these were atonements for the expulsion.[43]

Then the Colonnade Club invited him to speak on campus on his war remembrances for an honorarium of $150, and this struck exactly the right tone—this was a true honor for a worthy alumnus who did not need to be pardoned—he accepted immediately. He wrote a new lecture, and Stuart was typing it two weeks before the date when he wrote to grandson Mosby, "I didn't mind going to Canada & New York—but I shed my blood for her people [Virginia's] & you know what I got in return. It is too late for them to atone for it now. It is however, very gratifying for my old men to go there to meet me." The big day was Saturday, May 1, 1915, and Cabell Hall was crowded. On stage he was joined by nine of his Rangers, including William Chapman, Dolly Richards, and surgeon William Dunn, who had in his pocket the lancet he had used to cut the bullet from Mosby that morning at Glascock's. Alderman introduced him, and the talk was well received. He knew the invitation to speak on himself was a request not to criticize Lee, like he usually unavoidably did in his talks in the North defending Stuart. He complied, and nothing spoiled the harmonious spirit of the occasion.[44]

Finally, Mosby was extending his circle of friendship into society at large. For the Quill Club lecture he required that no reporters be admitted, and he attempted to avoid them and to shun publicity. For the University of Virginia talk he excluded the press. He was finished with controversy and wanted to view himself as a symbol of reconciliation between the North and South, and on a deeper level he was realizing the integration of his bipolar personalities. Back home after the University of Virginia visit he wrote, "One of the first things that I said to Stuart was that for the first time in my life I felt that I was a rich man—that the kindness & consideration shown me where I was raised & educated convinced me that I possessed something that gold could not buy & that I have not lived in vain." To grandson Spottswood he wrote, "The reception I got at the University is the proudest recollection of my life." He sealed the reconciliation nearly six months later by donating to the university fifty copies of Jeb Stuart's congratulatory order on the Stoughton Raid.[45]

## 23

# The Gray Ghost
# of Television and Film

Mosby was famous beginning with the capture of Stoughton and, by the end of the Civil War, was easily among the ten most-popular Confederate heroes. He continued to attract attention wherever he appeared, but his popularity waned after he stumped for Grant in 1872 and did not recover until about 1900. Then Southerners began speaking positively of him again, and he became the subject of three silent films, one featuring Mosby playing himself. When he died in 1916 eulogies exalted him as the most famous Confederate raider, a guerrilla who defied death innumerable times, skillfully bedeviled the Union, and made his name a terror to children. Southerners overlooked his Republicanism, and in the South he reappeared among the most popular Confederate personalities. Then, in 1957 the Columbia Broadcasting System featured him in a weekly syndicated television series, and for a generation of Americans he became "The Gray Ghost."

But as Mosby and Longstreet experienced, even if you were a Confederate hero, in the Lost Cause era if you switched to the Republican Party you sacrificed the prosperity that fame might have produced. Mosby had little interest in saving or investing money and instead took great pleasure in giving everything to his family. He gave his interest in his grandfather's land in Nelson County to his sister Blakely. Once he sent daughter Ada sixty dollars and daughter Stuart ten dollars and lamented, "I couldn't send more because I had to pay Life Insurance." He received an advance on the publication of his memoirs and refused it; but when Moffat, Yard & Company sent the check again and insisted that he keep it, he gave it to Ada for clothes. Little, Brown & Company paid him an advance of four hundred dollars for the same book, and he deposited it, planning to use it eventually to move into a retirement home. But John Junior developed throat cancer, and he spent the money on the son's surgery. "I paid it out without *a murmur*," he stated. May died on November 24, 1904; and when John Junior failed to recover and died on August 26, 1915, Mosby stood by the new grave of a nuclear family member for the fifth time.[1]

He considered it humiliating to borrow from a family member but borrowed hundreds of dollars from Joe Bryan to educate May's sons at the University of Virginia. After Joe died, he borrowed money on his Mutual Life Insurance Company policy to loan to Spottswood for living expenses to get established in New York City. He gladly accepted cash from friends, considering it compensation for his Civil War service, which is probably how he viewed his salary from the federal government the last few years. In retirement, with income from his lectures and donations from friends in both the South and the North, he paid for his room-and-board with Stuart. When he died, he was paid up, one month in advance.[2]

His four grandchildren called him "Grandpapa" or "Grandpa," and they loved him. He encouraged them to read and rewarded them with fifty cents and later one dollar for finishing a book. He wanted Mosby to attend West Point, but he chose the University of Virginia and engineering. He expected Beverly to become a patent lawyer and would have been gratified to know that he graduated from the U.S. Naval Academy in 1922, became an attorney, and served in the Navy with distinction in World War II and the Korean War, rising to rank of Rear Admiral. Mosby wrote, "I am certainly very proud of my four grandchildren."[3]

He lived in the home of the two younger ones for eleven years on a daily basis, moving in with their family when Pauline was about four years old and Beverly about six. He took them on vacations in the Shenandoah Valley and went with them to a horse show and on a scenic carriage ride. Near the end of the Roosevelt presidency, he took them to the White House and introduced them to the president. By then one of the favorite children's dolls was the "Teddy Bear," created in honor of Roosevelt's saving the life of a bear cub on a hunting trip. A hunter had captured the animal and brought it to him but, rather than shoot it, as the news trumpeted, he set it free. Pauline was eight years old, and, when Mosby introduced her, he said that the teddy bear was her favorite toy and that he had asked her once where teddy bear lived and she answered,

"In the White House." Roosevelt roared with laughter and told Pauline that he felt honored.[4]

Mosby was very sensitive toward the women of his family, often complimenting their appearance and boosting their self-esteem. When Pauline had surgery for appendicitis in her early teen years and he visited her in the hospital, he told her that she had never looked this pretty before. Pauline collected horseshoes and other Civil War artifacts, and Beverly accompanied his grandfather on a tour of the battlefield at Manassas. They both attended several reunions of the Rangers. One year when Buffalo Bill's Wild West Circus came to town and Mosby and Beverly made plans to attend, Beverly mentioned that he would like to ride in the Wells Fargo stagecoach in the scene when it was attacked by Indians. Finally, William F. Cody arrived, and Mosby took Beverly to the Willard Hotel, introduced him to the famous showman, and mentioned Beverly's fantasy. Cody wrote a note to the stage crew, gave it to Beverly, and told him how to proceed backstage. At the show he rode in the coach and returned to his seat beside his grandfather, one happy grandson.[5]

It seems unbelievable, but years later I met and talked with Beverly Mosby Coleman, the grandson of Mosby who lived with Mosby for eleven years. On the afternoon of July 28, 1991, during one of our research trips to Virginia, my wife, Ann, and I visited him and his wife in their apartment in "The Virginian" retirement community in Fairfax. We walked into the parlor of the elegant building, and they told us at the reception desk that we could go right up; they would call him on the phone. We took the elevator to the second floor; and, when the doors opened, there he was, standing on a bright-red carpet, smiling, and extending his hand in a most cordial manner. We greeted each other, and he took Ann's hand and walked us to his door.

He had been in the hospital and had been forced to cancel our previous appointment, and I inquired about his health. He answered that he was now feeling well: "The Old Devil is not ready for me yet," he said, a twinkle in his eyes. He introduced us to Mrs. Coleman, took a seat across from us, and answered all of my questions. He remembered that his grandfather had white hair, a sparkling eye, and a warm, kind tone of voice. He remembered that Mosby was nearly always the first one up each morning, and he loved coffee and buttermilk and spent most of his time writing letters. Beverly carried his grandfather's luggage to the train station when he left on trips, and Mosby would stop frequently along the way to discuss politics with his friends.

He recalled the day when he was home and a guest came and Mosby met with him for some time and then came to his room and invited him to the parlor. "I want you to meet Mr. Daley, the drummer boy," he said. In relating this, Admiral Coleman rose from his chair and went over to the wall, where he reached up and took down a walking cane and handed it to me. "This is the engraved cane that Daley gave my Grandfather that day," he said. James Daley was, of course, the Union drummer boy that Mosby had excluded from the Berryville hangings. When our interview concluded, he showed us into the next room to say farewell to Mrs. Coleman. "You have given Bev a wonderful afternoon," she remarked. "That's what he enjoys doing, talking." He walked us to the elevator and we left, feeling that we had experienced a warm echo of the gentle side of Grandfather Mosby.

By the time of Admiral Coleman's childhood, Mosby was one of the picturesque personalities on the streets of Washington. Weather permitting, he would walk in the afternoon on Pennsylvania Avenue, and residents became familiar with his keen eye, thin figure, and white hair shooting off in several directions at once. He would pause frequently to talk, and people would gather around to hear his comments on the latest news. Years before electronic media, he gave "sound bites"—brief statements, clear and to the point. For example, on trench warfare in World War I, he said that Lee or Jackson "would have done something long before this. As it is, the forces are just killing. The object of war is not to kill. It is to disable the military power."[6]

Since the end of the Civil War his popularity had declined and ascended. In the first two years after Appomattox, he came to realize that the fear he had caused in the minds of Northerners was transforming into admiration and hero worship. A tailor from Philadelphia in business in Washington came to Warrenton and asked to measure him for a free suit of clothing. He visited New York City in November 1867, posed for Mathew Brady, and nearly everyone wanted to give him something. A man handed him theater tickets; someone paid his hack bills; and, astoundingly, a Columbia College professor bought his dinner. When he went to the financial district and walked into the gold market, trading stopped and the members divided: one group hissed and shouted for his expulsion and the other cheered and clamored to shake his hand. "My friends say that my breaking up the Gold Board is my greatest exploit," he wrote Pauline.[7]

In the mind of one Southern artist, at the end of the Civil War he ranked among the six most popular heroes of the Confederacy. In February 1865 in Richmond he sat for French painter Louis Mathieu Didier Guillaume, as one of six heroes considered by Guillaume to be famous enough to sell engravings. He painted Mosby on horseback in a series of equestrian portraits that also included Jackson, Lee, Davis, Beauregard, and Joseph E. Johnston, and planned to have mezzotint engravings made in France for sale in America. He finished the paintings, but the market was disappointing in the postwar South, and he terminated the project after producing engravings of Jackson and Lee.[8]

Remarkably, two of the artistic renderings of Mosby's likeness that he posed for at the age of thirty-one in 1865 captured the opposing sides of his personality. In February, about the same time that he sat for Guillaume, he also posed for Edward Caledon Bruce, another of Lee's portrait painters. Bruce captured in his portrait the gentle side of Mosby. Harold Holzer and Mark E. Neely Jr., in their superb book on Civil War art, point out that Bruce portrayed him as an intelligent and sensitive aristocrat. He quietly peers out at the viewer, looking everything like a classical scholar with a high, white forehead; Roman nose; and kind, generous expression. He looks as if he is about to embrace Pauline or reach down and kiss baby May. As Holzer and Neely noted, Bruce entirely "missed or avoided altogether" Mosby's "indifference to human suffering." This is correct; Bruce's artistic eye did not see the fighter in Mosby.[9]

But sculptor Edward V. Valentine saw it vividly. Son of a prominent Richmond merchant, Valentine sculpted busts of Lee, Jackson, Stuart, and others and later became known for creating the recumbent statue of Lee for the Memorial Chapel at Washington and Lee University. Mosby sat for him in August 1865, and Valentine declared, "Yours I consider one of the most striking heads that I have modelled." He made plaster copies and sold them for twenty dollars wholesale to art dealers. When Mosby saw the bust he was ecstatic: "My friends who have seen it pronounce it a perfect facsimile of the original," he wrote Valentine. "You will please accept my sincere thanks for your kindness in presenting me with this copy and for the labor & pains you have taken to perpetuate my features."[10]

Today the bust is on display in the Valentine Museum in Richmond, and when I saw it I was astounded by how effectively it captured Mosby's inner fire, his fighting spirit. There were several other pieces with it, but Mosby's bust stood out, as if it were alive, as if the spirit inside were about to take wing and fly away. It looks like an angry eagle, young and

strong, thin and sharp-beaked, burning with an overwhelming passion
to attack and vanquish some unseen antagonist. An editor for the
*Warrenton Index* had the same reaction when it was released: "It is Mosby
confessed—not with the placid serenity of the civilian in these 'piping
times of peace,' but wearing in every lineament that stern resolve and
unflinching resolution of soul which struck terror to the hearts of the
foe."[11]

He was still one of the foremost Southern heroes when he supported Grant in 1872, and his Republicanism explains why in the next
few decades, the era of the popular print, apparently no illustrations were
sold featuring him. Nevertheless John Esten Cooke's writings continued
to appeal to a national audience, and Cooke described Mosby as a hero
in the historical novel *Surry of Eagle's-Nest* (1866) and *Wearing of the
Gray* (1867), a collection of magazine articles. In about 1904 a reporter
interviewing Mosby in Washington said that he had followed Mosby's
career with interest since he had read *Surry of Eagle's-Nest.* Mosby replied that none of the deeds in the book were real, that it was all mythical. "It isn't necessary that any history should be written; let the story
tellers invent it all." John S. Patton, later librarian at the University of
Virginia, recalled as a small boy seeing Mosby in Charlottesville on one
of his visits after Hong Kong: "I had the happiness of seeing the real,
sure-enough John Singleton Mosby. I viewed him with the tense feeling
that only boys know, but with a sense of loss. The plumed hat was gone."[12]

After the Spanish-American War and the lessening of sectional ani-
mosity by the turn of the century, his popularity rose again. It became
such an honor in Virginia to be called a Mosby veteran that elderly strangers showed up at reunions of the command and enrolled. "If all the men
claiming to have served under me had been on hand *at the time* we would
have driven Grant out of Virginia without an effort," said Mosby. An
innkeeper on Lake Erie invited him to spend a summer free of charge as
guest of honor; all he had to do was attract paying clients—no wonder
he sometimes felt like "a sort of menagerie." His Valentine bust, hat, and
uniform jacket went on display at the Smithsonian Institution. Photog-
raphers shot his former home in Warrenton and the house in Fairfax
where he captured Stoughton and printed them on postcards for sale. In
1909 Mosby's men were featured in the silent film *The Old Soldier's Story.*
Mosby was not involved, but the central character was "Zeke," an old
veteran of Mosby's command. The story begins with Zeke going to the
store to buy yeast; there he meets several other Confederate veterans and

they share war tales. Zeke tells about joining Mosby's men and volunteering to deliver a message behind enemy lines.[13]

Then Sig G. Bernstein of the Capitol Film Company of Washington, D.C., recruited Mosby to play himself in the silent film *All's Fair in Love and War* (1910), shot near Washington. He was now retired and seventy-six years old, and he accepted. He donned a Confederate uniform and took Pauline and Beverly along to watch the shooting. There are no known copies of the film extant, but an advertisement suggested, "See a real hero, a true story and the actual site of the fray," with "real war-time action," including smoke and powder rising off the battlefield. Mosby's part was in the beginning and quite brief. The film began with him in his garden, strolling with his fictional daughter Helen. Suddenly a servant rushes up and hands him a message from Lee announcing that war is declared and ordering him to bring his regiment to Richmond. Mosby leaves and soon returns, dressed in a Confederate uniform, complete with gauntlets, sash, and saber. He bids farewell and is gone from the film. Three years later Broncho productions retold the same story in *The Pride of the South,* with Joseph King playing Mosby.[14]

On the set or writing his memoirs, most of the time he enjoyed excellent health. In October 1896 he had been hospitalized in San Francisco with appendicitis. Nine months after losing his eye in 1897, he wrote, "My health was never better." On through his sixties he felt well, but then in his early seventies he developed an enlarged prostate. In May 1908, at the age of seventy-four and while still at the Justice Department, he underwent a prostatectomy in a hospital in Washington. One year later he was fully recovered, but in November 1912 had surgery again on his urinary tract. In Garfield Hospital in Washington his surgeon probably removed residual prostatic tissue. Again the operation was successful, and he was completely relieved. The day before his eighty-first birthday he reported, "Well, I never felt better in my life."[15]

But five months after that he suffered prostatitis (inflammation of the prostate) with pelvic pain for a few days; it cleared up, then returned in late January 1916, when he was eighty-two years old. He went to the Turkish baths in Washington and, for about a month in March, checked into St. Vincent's Hospital in Norfolk. He returned to Washington and was admitted to Georgetown University Hospital and then stayed about the last month of his life in Garfield Hospital. His physicians diagnosed his condition as a general breakdown from multiple problems, possibly sepsis, a toxic condition produced by abnormalities in the urinary tract.

On Sunday, May 28, he felt worse and by Monday night seemed seriously ill. The next morning his physicians decided that an operation was necessary.[16]

There were showers and thundershowers that Tuesday morning, May 30, and intermittent showers all day, with a high of seventy-eight degrees. At 9:00 A.M. when they took Mosby from his room, daughters Stuart, Pauline, and Ada were present with granddaughter Pauline and grandson Beverly. They watched as a nurse wheeled him down the hall on a gurney into the operating room, where he died during surgery. He was aware to the end and knew that it was Memorial Day. People went to the cemetery to decorate the graves of Union and Confederate dead alike; it had become a day of forgiveness and reconciliation, and he could not have wished for a more symbolic day to die.[17]

A funeral with full military honors was arranged for Thursday, June 1, and before noon about three thousand people gathered in Warrenton, the largest crowd the town had ever seen. All business closed for four hours, and people gathered at the railway station for the arrival of Mosby's special funeral train from Washington. A high, black hearse stood by on the street, and the Warrenton Rifles company of the Virginia National Guard stood in dressed ranks in parade uniforms. In the morning it was a crisp sixty-eight degrees, with an afternoon high of seventy-six, and it was sunny and bright, not a cloud in the sky.[18]

At 11:00 A.M. the train arrived, and three additional companies of the National Guard quietly disembarked and joined the Warrenton Rifles in forming the honor guard. Mosby's family and friends left the train and stood in line as veterans of Mosby's Rangers took his body from the train and placed it in the hearse. The invitation had gone out to all the Rangers to serve as pallbearers; twenty-seven came, including Fount Beattie and Samuel Chapman, most of them dressed in three-piece suits, with white beards and walking canes. The procession moved through the streets to Town Hall, where Mosby lay in state for four hours.[19]

Governor Stuart sent a wreath, placed beside the casket by his representative at the funeral, John Stewart Bryan, Joe Bryan's son and publisher of the *Richmond News Leader*. The governor had sent the family a telegram of sympathy: "I prized the friendship and affectionate regard of Colonel Mosby as that of a few men in the world. I cherished for him the highest admiration both as a man and as soldier, and considered it a privilege and honor to have known him in life, and I shall ever honor him in memory." At 3:00 P.M. the procession reformed, and the hearse moved into the cemetery to the Mosby family plot, to an open grave between Pauline and May. There on a hill overlooking the surrounding woodlands and fields, Father W.R. Gill of the Catholic church in Warrenton conducted Mosby's funeral service.[20]

University of Virginia President Alderman issued a statement: "The University of Virginia lost one of her bravest and noblest sons. The president and the faculty send expression of most profound sympathy and affection." Eulogies published across the nation outlined his Civil War career, praised his fighting spirit, and mentioned the coincidence of his death on Memorial Day. In Warrenton, the *Fauquier Democrat* reprinted a eulogy from the *Richmond Virginian* concluding: "With the bitterness of war all gone, there remains to Americans, North and South, a precious heritage of valor, of self-sacrifice, of sturdy, unflagging never-give-up spirit, a heritage which, in future days of possible stress, will prove inspiration unto us. Mosby is dead—peace to his ashes."[21]

Less than three years after Mosby died, the people of Warrenton organized a campaign to erect a monument. In March 1919 the *Confederate Veteran* published an appeal for donations to honor "one of Virginia's bravest, most gallant heroes," who "must not be forgotten—no, not by our children's children." The fund drive succeeded, and a twenty-five-foot granite monument was erected on the lawn beside the courthouse. For the dedication on June 19, 1920, a crowd filled the sidewalks and stood in windows of nearby buildings. A few Ranger veterans attended, and from the platform someone read the poem "Mosby," by Beverly R. Tucker, which closed:

> And when the children gather 'round
> Your knee at twilight hour,
> Tell them of Mosby and his men—
> Of Southern knighthood's flower.

Granddaughter Pauline pulled the cord, and the statue was unveiled.[22]

Early in 1921 in Richmond, the Confederate Memorial Association dedicated the new Battle Abbey, a commemorative building occupied today by the Virginia Historical Society. The Association commissioned French painter Charles Hoffbauer to paint a series of murals depicting the four seasons of the Confederacy. The emphasis was on military themes in the eastern theater, and fittingly Hoffbauer gave prominence to Jackson, Lee, and Stuart. Surprisingly, Jubal Early was not included, but Republicans Longstreet and Mosby were. Mosby is not in one of the main paintings but appears on a small side panel unrelated to the seasonal theme. It captures the guerrilla nature of Mosby's war—with no saber, he is leading a few men on a raid at night and is giving a hand signal for quiet, in order to surprise the enemy.[23]

Today, when Mosby's name is mentioned, almost anyone who watched television in the 1950s will say, "Oh, the Gray Ghost; I saw him on television." His fame soared to new heights with the broadcast in the 1957-58 season of *The Gray Ghost*. Once each week for thirty minutes, in thirty-nine episodes, Mosby thrilled families throughout the nation with his daring and cunning raids against the Union army. Columbia Broadcasting System produced the program and cast Tod Andrews as Mosby. He was a stage and television actor born in Buffalo, New York, and reared in Los Angeles. Virgil Carrington "Pat" Jones, author of the 1944 biography, *Ranger Mosby*, and veteran reporter of the *Wall Street Journal* and other newspapers, served as historical consultant. A CBS representative from New York accompanied him on a flight to Los Angeles, taking him to the office of the director of the show. A projector was brought in and set up, and with the wall as a screen they showed him the rough cut of the first episode. It started out with Mosby sitting in front of a tent, and Pat said, "Mosby never had a tent, and if he had, he would not have put his name on it." He made other corrections, and the changes were made. After a few days he went home, and CBS sent him scripts and he mailed his suggestions. Some were accepted and some were not, but he felt that he made a positive impact.[24]

When September 1957 came and it was time to begin the fall television season, the integration of public schools had begun. On September 24, President Dwight D. Eisenhower dispatched federal troops to Little Rock, Arkansas, to protect African American high school students. CBS executives worried that it might seem inappropriate to have a Confederate raider humiliating the Union cavalry each week on television. Three sponsors withdrew, and network heads decided the series was too controversial to broadcast on CBS; instead they released it for syndication and let the individual stations contract with sponsors. Only one CBS affiliate refused—a station in Boston decided that "portraying a rebel as a hero" was subversive. This was the only objection; there was no protest, there were no demonstrations, and the program was a ratings success, reaching an audience of 21 million people. Andrews became a celebrity and an attraction at parades and other events, particularly in the South.

The Dell Publishing Company published *The Gray Ghost* comic book based on the series. In the comic, published in 1958, Mosby wears a blue overcoat and penetrates Union lines masquerading as a Union guard. On the other hand, he has a tent and fights on horseback with a saber.[25]

*Walt Disney's Wonderful World of Color* television series presented the feature film *Willie and the Yank* on three Sunday evenings, January 8, 15, and 22, 1967.[26] Kurt Russell portrayed the fictional character Willie Prentiss, one of Mosby's men, and Jack Ging played Mosby. The film had many historical inaccuracies, but to director Michael O'Herlihy's credit the Rangers used two revolvers each and no sabers, and one fighting scene depicted Mosby and his men using the tactics of decoy and ambush in a fairly realistic reenactment. Later Disney released the film on home video as *Mosby's Marauders*. In 1993 the Arts and Entertainment Network broadcast *The Gray Ghost: John Singleton Mosby* in its *Civil War Journal* series. Historian Jeffry D. Wert was interviewed, along with John E. Divine. Time-Life Video marketed the tape in a Collector's Edition Series of the *Civil War Journal* in 1997.

In Warrenton in 1971 the Fauquier National Bank named its area for public concerts "Mosby Plaza," and in 1980 Little River Turnpike in northern Virginia was redesignated "John S. Mosby Highway." Today Mosby is a popular subject for Civil War paintings, calendars, and collectibles. Victory Games, Inc., of New York City has marketed a board game, "Mosby's Raiders: Guerrilla Warfare in the Civil War." In a parallel to Guillaume's plans including Mosby as one of the top six Confederate heroes at the end of the war, in 1995 Historical Sculptures of Cairo, New York, advertised miniature busts of eight Civil War heroes by sculptor Ron Tunison. They were Lincoln, Custer, and Joshua L. Chamberlain for the Union, and Lee, Jackson, Stuart, Nathan B. Forrest, and Mosby for the Confederacy. The judgment of the artist and decision-makers sponsoring this project was probably sound—in the public mind today Mosby's support of Grant only makes him more interesting. He has again ascended to near the top rank of the Confederate pantheon.[27]

# Conclusion

When Mosby's Civil War career is evaluated from the view of his Union opponents and in perspective of the history of guerrilla warfare, he emerges as one of the most successful guerrilla leaders in history. He accomplished the limited goals of irregular warfare in support of the regular Confederate army. With fewer than 400 men at any one time and a total of 1,570 enrolled by the end of the war, he suffered about 640 casualties and killed, wounded, or captured at least 2,900 of the enemy, more than 4 times his losses. The Union army dispatched more than seventy missions to capture or kill him or his men, and most of the expeditions had more than two hundred men. Blazer's hunter-killer team was unusual in that they fought for nearly three months with the single mission of taking out Mosby and his men. Finally, the Union cavalry on the Washington, D.C., early-warning screen, including some who had fought Mosby's guerrillas for nearly two years, determined that the only safe way to resist was to shift to tactics used by the army against Native Americans on the frontier and go on the defensive in a line of stockades.[1]

One of Mosby's goals as an irregular was to neutralize as many of the enemy's force as possible by keeping a continuous alarm and diverting men from the front to guard the rear. In quantifiable achievement, documented from the Union side, he succeeded. As has been demonstrated, during the battle of Gettysburg, he siphoned off 462 Union cavalry, 15 times his own strength. For the battle of New Market he drew eight hundred cavalry from Sigel's army, four times his number. The Wagon Raid, his most strategic achievement, diverted 1,800 infantry from the battles of Third Winchester and Fisher's Hill, 6 times his strength, and the same 1,800 infantry from Cedar Creek, 4.8 times his increased number by the time of that important battle. Sheridan had an additional thirty-six hundred in the rear during Fisher's Hill and, during Cedar

Creek, another forty-three hundred men. Mosby deserves some credit for these diversions as well, as they were unusually heavy partially because of Mosby's threat.

He and his men contributed to the heavy guarding of the Orange and Alexandria Railroad, but this achievement is complicated and less quantifiable, as other Rebel partisans were active in the region and often regular Confederate cavalry forces were within striking distance. Nevertheless, it is clear that Mosby and his men contributed to the assignment of one regiment of infantry from the Washington defenses as train guards, assisted in causing the posting of a small force of Washington-based soldiers at Burke's Station to guard woodcutters, and had a part in heavier-than-usual infantry and cavalry guarding of the railroad, with guards taken both from Washington and from the regular army at the front. Mosby's attacks on sutlers in August 1863 forced the use of Union cavalry to convoy sutler wagon trains.

As mentioned, Mosby claimed later that his greatest strategic accomplishment was his campaign against Sheridan and the Manassas Gap Railroad, which allegedly saved Richmond and added six months to the life of the Confederacy. But study from the Union side confirms the conclusion of historians Jeffry Wert and Dennis Frye that, except for diversions to the rear, Mosby had no strategic impact on Sheridan's campaign.[2] This places Mosby and his contribution in perspective—as the truest guerrilla in the Civil War, in command of a small force, his goal was not to single-handedly alter the campaign of the enemy army or save the Confederacy. Along with his resources and opportunities, Mosby's aims were limited, and only within this configuration is it fair to judge him.

Evaluated from the perspective of irregular warfare and from the vantage point of Sheridan, Mosby was highly successful. Sheridan biographer Roy Morris Jr. wrote that Mosby stung Sheridan like a wasp down his collar. Indeed, Mosby was a major embarrassment, and this took the edge off Sheridan's celebration of victories over Early. Three sensational Mosby news stories ran during Sheridan's command in the Valley—the headline-making Wagon Raid, the twin Greenback-Adamstown Raids, and Mosby's wound on December 21, 1864. Sheridan wanted a taut operation, and he despised having mail lost, official dispatches captured, and payday postponed. He grieved over the killing and capture of staff members and close friends, and it pained him when reporters ridiculed him for allegedly withdrawing from Cedar Creek because of a few guerrillas and for failing to provide safe travel along his communication line.

He hated it when Stanton scolded him for not securing the Baltimore and Ohio Railroad, and it was galling that, just as he was leaving the Valley, Stanton demanded an explanation of a rumor in Washington that Mosby's men had captured an entire cavalry detachment. As historian William C. Davis stated, Mosby was Sheridan's one great failure in the war.[3]

Mosby and his men were not armed civilians fighting a European people's war, but as raiders under the Partisan Ranger Act they accomplished the goals of guerrilla war expressed by military philosophers Clausewitz and Jomini. Mosby created what Clausewitz described as a "feeling of uneasiness and dread" in the enemy and achieved Jomini's aim of making everything outside the invaders' camp hostile and multiplying "a thousandfold the difficulties he meets at every step."[4] Tactically, Mosby's adaptation to modern weapons in casting aside sabers and using "go-through" mounted charges with revolvers was brilliant, and his capture of Stoughton was a model overnight guerrilla raid demonstrating use of an enemy deserter as guide, reconnaissance, secrecy, cover of darkness, stealth, and masquerading as the enemy.

On the Confederate side, Jeb Stuart and Robert E. Lee believed there was no better scout in the Confederate army than Mosby, and they were probably correct. Rarely in military history has a scout made as great an impact on the career of his commander as Mosby did for Stuart. Mosby's scouting gave him an axial role in the Peninsula Raid that made Stuart famous and in the Gettysburg Campaign Raid that tainted Stuart's reputation in history. Otherwise, from Lee's perspective, Mosby's scouting had a more normal effect; his reports arrived among others and were only pieces of Lee's intelligence synthesis. Even so, as demonstrated, Lee placed greater confidence in Mosby's reports than all of his other scouts combined.

Mosby and his men captured over thirty-five hundred horses and mules, a significant contribution in one of the Confederacy's most severe shortages. The sight of large herds of mules tramping into Confederate army camps and the arrival of groups of Mosby's Union prisoners in Richmond boosted Southern morale. Stories of the capture of sutler wagons almost within sight of Washington, derailment of trains, and other adventures lifted the spirits of the people. When Tee Edmonds learned of the Wagon Raid, she cheered: "Oh! but didn't we clap our hands when we heard it, for joy, joy joy. hurrah for Moseby, My dear Gallant Moseby—the guerrilla chief."[5] He touched the soul of the Southern people, and they made him a leading folk hero, the Confederacy's Prince of Guerrillas. Mosby's many small victories represented retaliation for the Yankee invasion and symbolized the hope of Confederate independence; and finally, when the cause of Confederate nationalism was lost, Mosby's irrepressible spirit and repeated success against superior forces vindicated Southern honor.

# Notes

## Abbreviations

### Manuscript Collections

B&O-MHS Baltimore and Ohio Railroad Papers, Maryland Historical Society, Baltimore, Maryland

BFP-VSA Bryan Family Papers, Archives Research Services, The Library of Virginia, Richmond, Virginia

BFP-UVA Burnley Family Papers, Special Collections Department, University of Virginia Library, Charlottesville, Virginia

BRMC-NSHS Bartlett Richards Manuscript Collection, Nebraska State Historical Society, Lincoln, Nebraska

BRP-UW Bartlett Richards Papers, American Heritage Center, University of Wyoming, Laramie, Wyoming

CMSR-NA Compiled Military Service Record, Records of the Adjutant General's Office, RG 94, National Archives, Washington, D.C.

CWMC-USAMHI Civil War Miscellaneous Collection, U.S. Army Military History Institute, Carlisle Barracks, Pennsylvania

CWTI-USAMHI *Civil War Times Illustrated* collection, U.S. Army Military History Institute

DCHK-NA Department of State, Dispatches from U.S. Consuls in Hong Kong, RG 59, National Archives

ECTP-DU Edward C. Turner Papers, Special Collections Library, Duke University, Durham, North Carolina

HCWRT-USAMHI Harrisburg Civil War Round Table Collection, U.S. Army Military History Institute

JAGP-LC James A. Garfield Papers, Library of Congress, Washington, D.C.

JBP-VHS Joseph Bryan Papers, Virginia Historical Society Library, Richmond, Virginia

JDBP-CWM James D. Blackwell Papers, Earl Gregg Swem Library, College of William and Mary, Williamsburg, Virginia

JEBSP-VHS James E.B. Stuart Papers, Virginia Historical Society Library

JJP-VSA Joseph Johnson Papers, Mosby Pardon File, Archives Research Services, The Library of Virginia

JSMBF-FCPL John S. Mosby Biographical File, The Virginia Room, Fairfax County Public Library, Fairfax, Virginia

JSMC-MC John S. Mosby Collection, Eleanor S. Brockenbrough Library, The Museum of the Confederacy, Richmond, Virginia

JSMC-UVA John S. Mosby Correspondence, University of Virginia Library

JSMF-VM John S. Mosby Newspaper Clippings, The Valentine Museum, Richmond, Virginia

JSMP-DU John Singleton Mosby Papers, Special Collections Library, Duke University

JSMP-FCPL John S. Mosby Papers, Fairfax County Public Library

JSMP-LC John S. Mosby Papers, Library of Congress

JSMP-USAMHI John S. Mosby Papers, U.S. Army Military History Institute

JSMP-UVA John S. Mosby Papers, Special Collections Department, University of Virginia Library

JSMP-VHS John S. Mosby Papers, Virginia Historical Society Library

JSMP-WFS John S. Mosby Papers, William H. White Jr. Library, Woodberry Forest School, Woodberry Forest, Virginia, copies at Special Collections Department, University of Virginia

JSMSB-UVA John S. Mosby Scrapbooks, microfilm copy, Special Collections Department, University of Virginia Library

JWDP-DU John Warwick Daniel Papers, Special Collections Library, Duke University

LLC-USAMHI Lewis Leigh Collection, U.S. Army Military History Institute

MFF-VSA McLaurine Family File, Archives Research Services, The Library of Virginia

MM-NYHS Miscellaneous Manuscripts, Mosby, John S., New York Historical Society Library, New York, New York

RBHP-HPCL Rutherford B. Hayes Papers, Rutherford B. Hayes Presidential Center, Fremont, Ohio

RCM-NA Army Court-martial Files, 1809–1894, Records of the Judge Advocate General, RG 153, National Archives

UIS-CWM Unidentified Scrapbook, 1867, Swem Library, College of William and Mary

USAMHI U.S. Army Military History Institute

WHPP-VSA William H. Payne Papers, Archives Research Services, The Library of Virginia

## People

| | |
|---|---|
| ABC | Arthur B. Clarke |
| AM | Aristides Monteiro |
| ASC | Alexander Spottswood Campbell (grandson) |
| BH | Binger Hermann |
| FWS | Frederick W. Seward |
| JB | Joseph Bryan |
| JMC | John Mosby Campbell (grandson) |
| JSM | John S. Mosby |
| JWD | John W. Daniel |
| PM | Pauline Mosby (wife) |
| SC | Samuel Chapman |
| VM | Virginia Mosby (mother) |
| WHC | William H. Chapman |

### 1. Mosby's Weapon of Fear

1. John H. Alexander, *Mosby's Men* (1907; reprint, Gaithersburg, Md., 1987), 138–39.

2. *The War of the Rebellion: A Compilation of the Official Records of the Union and Confederate Armies,* 73 vols. (Washington, D.C., 1880–1901), (ser. 1) 25(2): 856 (hereafter *OR*).

3. John Scott, *Partisan Life with Col. John S. Mosby* (1867; reprint, Gaithersburg, Md., 1985), 97, 100; JSM to James E.B. Stuart, June 4, 1863, JSMP-LC.

4. *OR* (ser. 1) 43(1): 672.

5. John S. Mosby, *Mosby's War Reminiscences and Stuart's Cavalry Campaigns* (New York, 1887), 33; Alexander, *Mosby's Men,* 45–49.

6. Diana R. Haslam, "The Military Performance of Soldiers in Continuous Operations: Exercises 'Early Call' I and II," in *Biological Rhythms, Sleep and Shift Work,* ed. Lavern C. Johnson et al., (New York, 1981), 435–58; Haslam, "Sleep loss, recovery sleep, and military performance," *Ergonomics* 25 (1982): 163–78; Timothy F. Deaconson et al., "Sleep Deprivation and Resident Performance," *The Journal of the American Medical Association* 260 (Sept. 23/30, 1988): 1721–27; Edward G. Longacre, *Mounted Raids of the Civil War* (Lincoln, Neb., 1994), 80–88, 244–46, 256; John W. Munson, *Reminiscences of a Mosby Guerrilla* (1906; reprint, Washington, D.C., 1983), 35.

7. Mosby, *Reminiscences,* 68; Walter S. Newhall, *A Memoir* (Philadelphia, 1864), 131.

8. See Chapter 12 for further discussion of Mosby's use of fear. For scholarly analysis of the debilitating effects of fear in warfare, see Richard Holmes, *Acts of War: The Behavior of Men in Battle* (New York, 1985), 204–69; Richard A. Fox Jr., *Archaeology, History, and Custer's Last Battle: The Little Big Horn Reexamined* (Norman, 1993), 46–52; and Eric T. Dean Jr., *Shook Over Hell: Post-Traumatic Stress, Vietnam, and the Civil War* (Cambridge, Mass., 1997).

9. Newhall, *Memoir,* 124–25; *Washington Star,* March 18, 1863; *Baltimore American,* May 20, Aug. 10, 1863, Oct. 15, Nov. 28, 1864; *New York Herald,* Aug. 16, 1864; *New York Times,* Aug. 29, 1864; OR (ser. 1) 29(1): 659; 37(1): 322; 37(2): 389; Scott, *Life,* 52.

10. JSM to JB, March 5, 1904, JBP-VHS; *Alexandria Gazette,* Oct. 30, 1863; *Baltimore American,* May 20, Sept. 12, 1863; *Washington Star,* Aug. 29, 1863; *New York Herald,* Oct. 17, Nov. 10, 1864; newspaper clipping, UIS-CWM (newspaper clippings are undated and unidentified unless indicated); *Literary Digest,* July 15, 1916; James J. Williamson, *Mosby's Rangers* (1896; reprint, no place, 1982), 437–38.

11. Mark E. Neely Jr., Harold Holzer, and Gabor S. Boritt, *The Confederate Image: Prints of the Lost Cause* (Chapel Hill, 1987), 205; *New York Herald,* Dec. 30, 1864, quoting *Richmond Dispatch,* Dec. 27, 1864; Charles W. Russell, ed., *The Memoirs of Colonel John S. Mosby* (1917; reprint, Gaithersburg, Md., 1987), 166–67; newspaper clipping, vol. 2, JSMSB-UVA.

12. *New York Herald,* Oct. 15, 1864.

13. *Richmond Examiner,* Sept. 7, 1864, quoted in *New York Herald,* Sept. 10, 1864; *Richmond Dispatch,* July 14, 1864, quoted in *New York Herald,* July 17, 1864.

14. *Richmond Dispatch,* Jan. 31, Feb. 2, 7, 1865; JSM to PM, Feb. 3, 1865, JSMP-VHS; Edward Younger, ed., *Inside the Confederate Government: The Diary of Robert Garlick Hill Kean* (Baton Rouge, 1993), 170. Kean was head of the Confederate Bureau of War.

15. *Richmond Whig,* Oct. 18, 1864. George Trenholm was Confederate Secretary of the Treasury, and the reference is to printing treasury notes.

16. *Richmond Dispatch,* Aug. 13, 1863; *New York Herald,* Nov. 2, 1863; Mosby, *Reminiscences,* 23; Robert P. Warren, ed., *Selected Poems of Herman Melville* (New York, 1970), 153.

17. *New York Herald,* Dec. 17, 1863; *Washington Star,* Dec. 16, 1863; *Alexandria Gazette,* Oct. 30, 1863; Joseph Schubert, handwritten memoir, Joseph Schubert Collection, USAMHI; John Y. Simon, ed., *The Personal Memoirs of Julia Dent Grant* (New York, 1975), 155–56; newspaper clipping, JSMF-VM; OR (ser. 1) 46(3): 838.

18. Scott, *Life,* 345; Charles R. Williams, ed., *Diary and Letters of Rutherford Birchard Hayes,* 5 vols. (Columbus, Ohio, 1922–1926), 2: 501–2.

19. Aristides Monteiro, *War Reminiscences by the Surgeon of Mosby's Command* (1890; reprint, Gaithersburg, Md., no date), 157–58, 180–81.

20. Ibid., 214; *New York Herald,* Jan. 30, 1864.

21. Williamson, *Rangers,* 15; newspaper clipping, UIS-CWM.

22. Monteiro, *Reminiscences,* 119.

## 2. The Weakling and the Bullies

1. Russell, *Memoirs,* 5; Harris D. Riley Jr., M.D., to author, Aug. 5, 1993. Riley is professor of Pediatrics, Vanderbilt Children's Hospital, Vanderbilt University Medical Center, Nashville, Tennessee.

2. JSM to Cornelia G. Peyton, Jan. 20, 1897, Peyton Family Papers, Virginia Historical Society Library (hereafter VHS); newspaper clippings, vol. 2, 3, JSMSB-UVA.

3. Helena M. Wall, *Fierce Communion: Family and Community in Early America* (1990; reprint, Cambridge, 1995), 139–41; Daniel B. Smith, *Inside the Great House: Planter Family Life in Eighteenth-Century Chesapeake Society* (Ithaca, 1980), 42–54; Jan Lewis, *The Pursuit of Happiness: Family and Values in Jefferson's Virginia* (Cambridge, 1983), 184–85.

4. Mosby Family Bible Record, Archives Research Services, The Library of Virginia (hereafter VSA); JSM to JB, Nov. 25, 26, 1903, JBP-VHS; Virgil C. Jones, *Ranger Mosby* (Chapel Hill, 1944), 16, 20; John L. Brinkley to author, March 8, 1993.

5. James H. Mosby, *Our Noble Heritage: The Mosby Family History* (Evansville, 1957), 117, 134, 142; Will of Nicholas Cox, Cumberland County, Va., Will Book 1: 178, VSA.

6. Richard T. Couture, *Powhatan: A Bicentennial History* (Richmond, 1980), 69–72; Edward P. Valentine, *Valentine Papers,* 4 vols. (1927; reprint, Richmond, 1954), 2: 839. The genealogical essay in the Mosby Family Bible Record at the Virginia State Archives traces John S. Mosby to Benjamin rather than Hezekiah, but wills and deeds prove that his ancestor was Hezekiah. See Will of Hezekiah Mosby, Powhatan County, Will Book 1: 138; Will of Daniel Mosby, Nelson County, Will Book B: 248–50; Will of John H. Mosby, Nelson County, Will Book E: 388; Deed, Henry Martin to John Mosby, May 29, 1789, Amherst County, Deed Book F: 349; Deed, Daniel and Sarah Mosby to Daniel Carter, May 22, 1775, Cumberland County, Deed Book 5: 360; Deed, Daniel and Sarah H. Mosby to John Mosby, May 14, 1796, Amherst County, Deed Book H: 112, VSA.

7. Will of Hezekiah Mosby; Estate Inventory of Hezekiah Mosby, Powhatan County, Will Book 1: 160; Auditor of Public Accounts (RG48), Taxes, Personal Property (hereafter Personal Property Tax Records), Albemarle County, 1782; Personal Property Tax Records, Amherst County, 1789; Auditor of Public Accounts (RG48), Taxes, Land (hereafter Land Tax Records), Amherst County, 1789; Will of Daniel Mosby, Nelson County, Will Book B: 248–50; Deed, David and Mary Montgomery to Daniel Mosby, Oct. 6, 1788, Amherst County, Deed Book F: 270–71; Deed, Daniel Mosby and Sarah H. Mosby to John Mosby, May 14, 1796, Amherst County, Deed Book H: 112, VSA.

8. Will of John H. Mosby, Nelson County, Will Book E: 388; Bond of Executors, Estate of John H. Mosby, Nelson County, Will Book E: 393; Estate Inventory of John H. Mosby, Nelson County, Will Book E: 403; Bond of Executors, John H. Mosby Estate, Nelson County, Deed Book E: 393, VSA; JSM to Annie W. Fox, March 16, 1904, JSMC-MC.

9. JSM to Lily Ann Herblin, July 5, 1899, JSMP-VHS; newspaper clipping, vol. 2, JSMSB-UVA.

10. McLaurine Family Bible Record; Southam Parish Vestry Book, 1745–1791, Powhatan County, Anglican Church Records (hereafter Powhatan Vestry Book), VSA; Albert Boggess to Mrs. William P. Jervey, Sept. 20, 1947, MFF-VSA; P. William

Filby and Mary K. Meyer, eds., *Passenger and Immigrant Lists Index,* 4 vols. (Detroit, 1982–1985), 3: 2008.

11. Will of J. Robert McLaurine, Cumberland County, Will Book 2: 104–6; Powhatan Vestry Book; Couture, *Powhatan,* 101.

12. Albert Boggess to Mrs. William P. Jervey, Sept. 20, 1947, May 6, 1950, MFF-VSA; Will of J. Robert McLaurine; interview with David Payne, Oct. 9, 1996.

13. Will of J. Robert McLaurine; Boggess to Jervey, Sept. 20, 1947, May 6, 1950; Land Tax Records, Cumberland County, 1825; Will of James McLaurine, Cumberland County, Will Book 11: 405–7; Estate Inventory of James McLaurine, Cumberland County, Will Book 11: 430–32, VSA.

14. Boggess to Jervey, Sept. 20, 1947.

15. J.W. Comfort, *Thomsonian Practice of Midwifery, and Treatment of Complaints Peculiar to Women and Children* (Philadelphia, 1845), 38–78; Jones, *Mosby,* 17–18. Eventually Edgemont passed from the family, and in the 1970s the owners subdivided the land and intended to dismantle the structure and sell the mantels and staircase on the antique market. Aldine West and her husband, Warren W. West, a fireman in Richmond, learned that one of Aldine's ancestors had ridden with Mosby in the war, and they purchased land within one mile of the site and carefully moved and restored the building for their beautiful home. On July 29, 1988, the West family, including children Florence and Warren Jr., hosted a memorable dinner for me, my wife Ann, and our friends Baxter and Stella Perkinson of Petersburg, Virginia. Before dinner the Wests gave us a tour of the house, highlighted by a visit to the upstairs bedroom where Mosby was born.

16. Personal Property Tax Records, Nelson County, 1836, VSA; Russell, *Memoirs,* 2–3; Adele H. Mitchell, ed., *The Letters of John S. Mosby,* 2d ed., (no place, 1986), 190. In his seventies Mosby drank imported wine with friends.

17. Russell, *Memoirs,* 2; John H. Moore, *Albemarle: Jefferson's County, 1727–1976* (Charlottesville, 1976), 145.

18. Deeds, Albemarle County, Deed Book 40: 315–17, 323–24; 41: 502–3, VSA.

19. Russell, *Memoirs,* 3, 6; Charles C. Wertenbaker to W. Sam Burnley, Jan. 18, 1911; typed essay by W. Sam Burnley (hereafter Burnley essay), BFP-UVA.

20. Wertenbaker to Burnley, Jan. 18, 1911, BFP-UVA; Diary of Virginia Jackson McLaurine Mosby, quoted in Russell, *Memoirs,* 354; Certificate of J.W. Poindexter, June 11, 1853, Certificate of John C. Hughes, June 11, 1853, JJP-VSA; Harris D. Riley Jr. to author, Aug. 5, 1993.

21. Eighth Census, Virginia, Population, VSA; JSM to Annie W. Fox, March 16, 1904, JSMC-MC; newspaper clipping, vol. 3, JSMSB-UVA.

22. Russell, *Memoirs,* 4; Jones, *Mosby,* 18.

23. Alexander Hunter, *The Women of the Debatable Land* (Washington, 1912), 43; Moore, *Albemarle,* 134, 137; Russell, *Memoirs,* 6; handwritten note by JSM, on back of photo, JSMP-WFS; JSM to JB, June 3, 1903, JBP-VHS.

24. Newspaper clipping, vol. 6, JSMSB-UVA; Moore, *Albemarle,* 140–41; newspaper clipping, JSMF-VM; Indictment, *Commonwealth v. John S. Mosby,* Circuit

Court of Albemarle County, 1851, copy in BFP-UVA.

25. JSM to John S. Patton, March 9, 1916, JSMP-UVA; Charles C. Wertenbaker to W. Sam Burnley, n.d.; Burnley essay, BFP-UVA. Later the name of the Brock House changed to the Cabell House.

26. State of Virginia, *Journal of the Senate*, 1853–1854, 172; Wertenbaker to Burnley, Jan. 18, 1911, BFP-UVA.

27. *Baltimore Sun,* Jan. 15, 1911; VM to Joseph Johnson, July 15, 1853, JJP-VSA; Burnley essay.

28. VM to Johnson, July 15, 1853; Burnley essay; JSM to Patton, March 9, 1916.

29. Shelton F. Leake to Joseph Johnson, June 21, 1853, JJP-VSA; JSM to Patton, March 9, 1916; JSM to Louise Cocke, Jan. 16, 1911, JSMP-UVA. At the battle of First Bull Run, Mosby met a fellow alumnus in an Alabama regiment, and he told Mosby that Turpin was dead. Burnley essay.

30. Handwritten notes by W. Sam Burnley on Albemarle County Circuit Court records (hereafter Burnley Court notes); Burnley essay, BFP-UVA; *The Code of Virginia* (Richmond, 1849), 724; Lyon G. Tyler, ed., *Encyclopedia of Virginia Biography,* 5 vols. (New York, 1915), 2: 67, 116; Lindsay R. Barnes Jr., "William J. Robertson, 1817–1898: Modesty and Achievement in Times of Turmoil and Change," *Magazine of Albemarle County History* 43 (1985): 41–61.

31. Virgil C. Jones, "Ranger Mosby in Albemarle," *Papers of the Albemarle County Historical Society* 5 (1944–1945): 40–42; Shelton F. Leake to Joseph Johnson, June 21, 1853, JJP-VSA; Burnley essay; newspaper clipping, vol. 6, JSMSB-UVA.

32. State of Virginia, *Journal of the Senate*, 1853–1854, 172; Petition of Jurymen for Pardon of John S. Mosby, n.d., JJP-VSA.

33. *The Code of Virginia* (Richmond, 1849), 750; Burnley Court notes.

34. JSM to SC, Oct. 23, 1915, JSMP-UVA; newspaper clipping, vol. 6, JSMSB-UVA; JSM to Arthur B. Clarke, May 20, 1915, JSMP-VHS.

35. Newspaper clipping, vol. 6, JSMSB-UVA; VM to Joseph Johnson, n.d., JJP-VSA.

36. Barnes, "Robertson," 49.

37. Mitchell, *Letters,* 302; *The Poetical Works of Lord Byron* (London, 1945), 405.

38. Citizens' Petition; Shelton Leake to Joseph Johnson, June 21, 1853; Alexander Rives to Joseph Johnson, June 15, 1853; Certificates by John C. Hughes, J.W. Poindexter, and W.E. Bibb, JJP-VSA. The alleged prejudicial juror was John N. Hamner, but there is no record of why he may have had a grudge against Alfred. Juror D.W. Maupin wrote the governor, denying that Hamner made any such statement. D.W. Maupin to Joseph Johnson, June 10, 1853, JJP-VSA.

39. Virginius Dabney, *Virginia: The New Dominion* (Charlottesville, 1971), 222; William M.E. Rachel, ed., "Petitions Concerning the Pardon of John S. Mosby in 1853," *Papers of the Albemarle County Historical Society* 9 (1948–1949): 13–14, 27–28, 35–36; VM to Joseph Johnson, July 15, 1853, JJP-VSA.

40. D.W. Maupin to Joseph Johnson, June 10, 1853, Joseph Points to Johnson, June 8, 1853, July 8, 1853; George W. Munford to Shelton F. Leake, Aug. 19, 1853, JJP-VSA.

41. vm to Joseph Johnson, July 15, 1853, jjp-vsa.

42. George W. Munford to vm, July 20, 1853; Shelton F. Leake to Joseph Johnson, Aug. 8, 1853; handwritten note on back of the Petition of Jurymen, Aug. 16, 1853, jjp-vsa.

43. vm to Joseph Johnson, n.d., jjp-vsa.

44. Joseph Johnson to George W. Munford, Dec. 6, 1853; vm to Munford, Dec. 16, 1853, jjp-vsa; State of Virginia, *Journal of the Senate,* 1853–1854, 142, 173, 184; *Journal of the House of Delegates,* 1853–1854, 335.

### 3. "Virginia is my mother."

1. Personal Property Tax Records, Fluvanna County, 1854, vsa; Mosby's Law License, Sept. 4, 1855, jsmp-vhs; Jones, "Mosby in Albemarle," 43.

2. *Biographical Encyclopaedia of Kentucky* (Cincinnati, 1878), 120; Linn Boyd to James Buchanan, April 9, 1857, Thomas C. McCreery to James Buchanan, March 17, 1857, Department of State, Letters of Application and Recommendation During the Administrations of Franklin Pierce and James Buchanan, 1853–1861, RG 59, National Archives (hereafter NA); Simpson County Historical Society, *Simpson County, Kentucky: Families Past and Present, 1819–1989* (Franklin, Ky., 1989), 192; Mrs. Dorothy Steers to author, Sept. 21, 1991, Oct. 10, 1991, Jan. 21, 1993.

3. *P.H. Boisseau v. Nathan Salmons Heirs,* Simpson Circuit Court, File 777–1851, Simpson County Historical Society Archives; *Frankfort Commonwealth,* Aug. 7, 1855; *Frankfort Tri-Weekly Commonwealth,* May 18, 1860; Zenobia A. Clarke to Lewis Cass, March 21, 1860, Department of State, Dispatches from United States Ministers to Central America, 1824–1906, Guatemala, vol. 3, May 10, 1850–March 25, 1860, RG 59, NA; *Biographical Encyclopaedia of Kentucky,* 120. George W. Clarke was killed fighting under John H. Morgan. *Simpson County,* 192. Marcellus Jerome Clarke, Beverly Clarke's first cousin and Pauline's first cousin once removed, served as Morgan's artillery commander and late in the war became famous as the outlaw "Sue Mundy." Mrs. Dorothy Steers to author, Jan. 21, 1993. Mosby and Pauline named their first son and second child Beverly, and Mosby's grandson, Admiral Beverly Coleman, was named for him.

4. jsm to Victoria Mosby, Dec. 17, 1856, jsmp-lc; Marriage License, Dec. 30, 1856, Davidson County Marriage Records, 1856, Tennessee State Library, Nashville; jsm to Dear Cousin, March 4, 1900, jsmp-vhs. Mosby stated that one of the invited guests was Andrew Johnson, a friend of Pauline's father. Johnson, former governor of Tennessee and at the time a U.S. senator, served in the U.S. House of Representatives with Clarke. I have discovered no confirmation that Johnson attended the wedding. Newspaper clipping, vol. 1, jsmsb-uva; Jones, *Mosby,* 28.

5. jsm to pm, Nov. 21, 1861, pm to Lizzie, Oct. 17, 1872, jsmp-vhs.

6. Newspaper clipping, vol. 6, jsmsb-uva; jsm to My dear Cousin, March 4, 1900, jsmp-vhs; jsm to jmc, Sept. 1, 1915, jsmc-uva; Jones, *Mosby,* 29.

7. V.N. "Bud" Phillips, *Bristol Tennessee/Virginia: A History—1852–1900* (Johnson City, Tenn., 1992), 49, 52, 117, 253, 362–63; interview and tour of Bristol with V.N. "Bud" Phillips, July 22, 1991; undated clipping, *Bristol News,* JSMP-VHS; Land Tax Records, Washington County, 1861, Personal Property Tax Records, Washington County, 1859, 1861, VSA. The Virginia part of Bristol was incorporated as Goodson in 1856, but the name later changed to Bristol. Phillips, *Bristol,* 42–44.

8. Undated clipping, *Leslie's Illustrated Newspaper,* vol. 5, JSMSB-UVA; JSM to Reuben Page, June 11, 1902, Douglas Southall Freeman Papers, Special Collections Department, University of Virginia Library (hereafter UVA).

9. State of Virginia, Secretary of State, Election Records, electoral returns, 1860, Washington County, VSA; JSM to JWD, May 1, 1902, JWDP-DU.

10. Russell, *Memoirs,* 16–17.

11. Lewis P. Summers, *History of Southwest Virginia, 1746–1786, Washington County, 1777–1870* (1903; reprint, Baltimore, 1971), 514; Russell, *Memoirs,* 11; William W. Blackford, *War Years with Jeb Stuart* (New York, 1945), 13–14.

12. Russell, *Memoirs,* 18.

13. JSM to Reuben Page, June 11, 1902, Douglas Southall Freeman Papers, UVA; JSM to SC, Sept. 30, 1909, JSMP-DU.

14. *Bristol Herald Courier,* June 29, 1958, clipping in Mosby Family File, Historical Society of Washington County, Abingdon, Va.; Russell, *Memoirs,* 23, 27; JSM to John C. Ropes, June 27, 1898, MM-NYHS; Blackford, *War Years,* 14. In camp in Abingdon, Mosby applied for a transfer to the infantry to join some of his friends. He later believed that if the request had been approved he would not have been more than a private. Mosby, *Reminiscences,* 8.

15. JSM to VM, June 18, 1861, JSMP-LC; JSM to PM, June (no day), 1861, JSMP- VHS.

16. JSM to PM, June (no day), July 27, Aug. 10, Sept. (no day), Nov. (no day), 1861, JSMP-VHS.

17. Staff, *Civil War Times Illustrated,* "'Grumble' Jones: A Personality Profile," *Civil War Times Illustrated* (hereafter *CWTI*), June 1968, 35–36; Summers, *Southwest Virginia,* 753.

18. Staff, *CWTI,* "Jones," 36; JSM to PM, Sept. (no day), 1861, JSMP-VHS; Longacre, *Raids,* 139.

19. Russell, *Memoirs,* 30; Mosby, *Reminiscences,* 7, 206; John S. Mosby, *Stuart's Cavalry in the Gettysburg Campaign* (1908; reprint, Gaithersburg, Md., 1987), 109, 202, 216; JSM to Reuben Page, June 11, 1902, Douglas Southall Freeman Papers, UVA.

## 4. Scouting behind Enemy Lines

1. Blackford, *War Years,* 16; Russell, *Memoirs,* 31; JSM to PM, July 12, 1861, JSMP-VHS; John S. Mosby, "Personal Recollections of General J.E.B. Stuart," *Munsey's Magazine* 49 (April 1913): 35–36.

2. J.E.B. Stuart Scrapbook, Eleanor S. Brockenbrough Library, The Museum of the Confederacy (hereafter MC); Emory M. Thomas, *Bold Dragoon: The Life of J.E.B. Stuart* (New York, 1986), 18; Blackford, *War Years,* 16; John Cheves Haskell, *The Haskell Memoirs,* ed. Gilbert E. Govan and James W. Livingood (New York, 1960), 19; Mosby, *Reminiscences,* 11–12, 206; Mosby, "Stuart," 36.

3. JSM to PM, July 12, 1861, JSMP-VHS; Mosby, *Reminiscences,* 12.

4. Russell, *Memoirs,* 47–48; newspaper clipping, vol. 1, JSMSB-UVA; Blackford, *War Years,* 23–24.

5. Thomas, *Bold Dragoon,* 78; Russell, *Memoirs,* 51–53.

6. Edwin C. Fishel, *The Secret War for the Union: The Untold Story of Military Intelligence in the Civil War* (Boston, 1996), 81–84. The battle of Balls Bluff, October 21, 1861, was a Union demonstration resulting in a minor Confederate victory.

7. Mosby, *Reminiscences,* 14; Russell, *Memoirs,* 99.

8. JSM to PM, Aug. 10, Sept. 14, Sept. (no day), Nov. (no day) 1861, JSMP-VHS.

9. Mosby, *Reminiscences,* 15–16; JSM to PM, Sept. 2, 1861, JSMP-VHS.

10. Russell, *Memoirs,* 87; JSM to PM, Sept. 2, Sept. 14, Nov. 21, 1861, JSMP-VHS; OR (ser. 1) 5: 441–43.

11. OR (ser. 1) 5: 167–84; JSM to PM, Sept. (no day) 1861, JSMP-VHS.

12. Ezra J. Warner, *Generals in Gray: Lives of the Confederate Commanders* (Baton Rouge, 1959), 178–79; Douglas S. Freeman, *R.E. Lee: A Biography,* 4 vols. (New York, 1934–1935), 1: 279; Russell, *Memoirs,* 94.

13. Thomas, *Bold Dragoon,* 83, 202; Mosby, "Stuart," 38; newspaper clipping, vol. 1, JSMSB-UVA; OR (ser. 1) 51(2): 594. Stuart's evaluation of Mosby was in his July 19, 1862, letter of recommendation to Jackson. OR (ser. 1) 51(2): 594.

14. Thomas, *Bold Dragoon,* 74–75, 120; Blackford, *War Years,* 39–40, 46; Freeman, *Lee,* 3: 239.

15. Mosby, *Reminiscences,* 20.

16. Ibid., 20–22.

17. Fishel, *Secret War,* 146.

18. Ibid.; Thomas, *Bold Dragoon,* 102–3.

19. JSM to PM, April 1, 1862, JSMP-VHS; OR (ser. 1) 12(1): 415–16, 11(3): 406–7.

20. OR (ser. 1) 11(3): 41, 45, 405–7; 12(3): 20; Craig L. Symonds, *Joseph E. Johnston: A Civil War Biography* (New York, 1992), 148.

21. OR (ser. 1) 12(1): 412–14; Mosby, "Stuart," 37; Mosby, *Reminiscences,* 215.

22. Mosby, *Reminiscences,* 215–16; OR (ser. 1) 12(1): 412–17.

23. OR (ser. 1) 12(1): 417; 11(3): 415–16; Fishel, *Secret War,* 146. The first history of Mosby's command states that Mosby made a foray to Bull Run after March 29 and captured two prisoners who stated that McClellan's main force had fallen back to Alexandria, where a large fleet of transports had gathered. Scott, *Life,* 434.

24. Richard N. Current, ed., *Encyclopedia of the Confederacy*, 4 vols. (New York, 1993), 1: 396; Freeman, *Lee,* 1: 279–80; Russell, *Memoirs,* 109. Jones left to take command of the 7th Virginia Cavalry.

25. Russell, *Memoirs,* 109; Mosby, *Reminiscences,* 22; JSM, CMSR-NA; JSM to ASC, June 23, 1915, John S. Mosby Correspondence, UVA.

26. James A. Ramage, *Rebel Raider: The Life of General John Hunt Morgan* (Lexington, 1986), 69–71; *Richmond Whig,* May 7, 1862; Russell, *Memoirs,* 125–26; newspaper clipping, vol. 1, JSMSB-UVA. On March 27, 1862, the Virginia legislature authorized the Virginia State Rangers primarily for guerrilla war in what became West Virginia. See Randall Osborne and Jeffrey C. Weaver, *The Virginia State Rangers and State Line* (Lynchburg, 1994).

27. John S. Mosby, "The Ride Around General McClellan," *Southern Historical Society Papers* (hereafter SHSP) 26: 247–48.

28. Ibid., 248; Thomas, *Bold Dragoon,* 111, 113. After the war Heros Von Borcke, the colorful Prussian soldier of fortune on Stuart's staff, claimed that on the night of June 8, 1862, he accompanied Stuart on a ride behind enemy lines to meet a spy who told of the vulnerable Union right flank. Stuart's biographer Emory M. Thomas credits the story, presenting it as another piece of intelligence that Stuart synthesized. In his *Reminiscences* Mosby declared that the spy story was as fictional as the adventures of Baron Munchausen in the literature of Von Borcke's native Prussia. But Mosby implied that he, not Stuart or Lee, first had the idea of the raid. Mosby the memorialist described events from his own single point of view to the exclusion of many other intelligence sources that Stuart and Lee had, and this caused him to form an exaggerated opinion of his own impact. In truth, Mosby did not suggest the idea of the raid, but his scouting provided a fresh, reliable intelligence foundation. Thomas, *Bold Dragoon,* 109–10; Heros Von Borcke, *Memoirs of the Confederate War for Independence,* 2 vols. (1866; reprint, New York, 1938), 1: 34–37; Mosby, *Reminiscences,* 221–22.

29. Thomas, *Bold Dragoon,* 113, 115–16; Mosby, *Reminiscences,* 222–24; OR (ser. 1) 11(1): 1036–37; Russell, *Memoirs,* 120. Latane's burial became famous through the Lost Cause print *The Burial of Latane.* Neely, Holzer, and Boritt, *Confederate Image,* ix-xiii.

30. Douglas S. Freeman, *Lee's Lieutenants: A Study in Command,* 3 vols. (New York, 1942–1944), 1: 288–89; OR (ser. 1) 11(1): 1038; Mosby, *Reminiscences,* 224.

31. Mosby, *Reminiscences,* 224–30; Russell, *Memoirs,* 114–15, 120; OR (ser. 1) 11(1): 1027–28, 1032. Scouts Redmond Burke and William D. Farley were also in the advance at Tunstall's. OR (ser. 1) 11(1): 1038.

32. See Michael C.C. Adams, *Our Masters the Rebels: A Speculation on Union Military Failure in the East, 1861–1865* (Cambridge, Mass., 1978); Mosby, "Ride," 251–52; Mosby, *Reminiscences,* 229; *Richmond Dispatch,* June 17, 1862.

33. JSM to PM, June 16, 1862, JSMP-VHS; Mosby, "Ride," 252; Mosby, *Reminiscences,* 232; Thomas, *Bold Dragoon,* 121.

34. *OR* (ser. 1) 11(1): 1041–42; Mosby, *Reminiscences*, 240; *Richmond Dispatch*, June 17, 1862; typed copy of article from *Abingdon Virginian*, June 27, 1862, vol. 4, JSMSB-UVA.

35. JSM to PM, June 16, 1862, JSMP-VHS; Russell, *Memoirs*, 121, 125; Jones, *Mosby*, 61; Mosby, *Reminiscences*, 241. Scott wrote that Mosby scouted once on the Peninsula and once toward Fredericksburg during this period. Scott, *Life*, 437–38.

36. Russell, *Memoirs*, 125–26; *OR* (ser. 1) 51(2): 594.

37. Russell, *Memoirs*, 126, 128–29; newspaper clipping, "First Meeting of Lee and Mosby," vol. 4, JSMSB-UVA (hereafter "Lee and Mosby").

38. Newspaper clipping, "Mosby and the War," JSMF-VM (hereafter "Mosby and the War"); *OR* (ser. 1) 12(3): 479, 484, 487, 490–91; Scott, *Life*, 439; Mosby, *Reminiscences*, 241.

39. Mosby, *Reminiscences*, 242; "Mosby and the War."

40. "Mosby and the War"; Mosby, *Reminiscences*, 242–43; Russell, *Memoirs*, 130; "Lee and Mosby."

41. Russell, *Memoirs*, 131; Mosby, *Reminiscences*, 243–44; "Lee and Mosby"; Freeman, *Lee*, 4: 170–71; Emory M. Thomas, *Robert E. Lee: A Biography* (New York, 1995), 125–26, 140.

42. *OR* (ser. 1) 12(3): 923; Clifford Dowdey and Louis H. Manarin, eds., *The Wartime Papers of R.E. Lee* (New York, 1961), 245.

43. "Mosby and the War"; "Lee and Mosby"; Mosby, *Reminiscences*, 244.

44. "Mosby and the War"; "Lee and Mosby"; newspaper clipping, vol. 3, JSMSB-UVA; Russell, *Memoirs*, 133.

45. *OR* (ser. 1) 12(3): 924–25; Dowdey and Manarin, *Papers*, 246–48.

46. Dowdey and Manarin, *Papers*, 247; Frank E. Vandiver, *Mighty Stonewall* (New York, 1957), 337–38.

47. Russell, *Memoirs*, 133; Mosby, *Reminiscences*, 244; "Mosby and the War"; "Lee and Mosby"; Charles P. Roland, *An American Iliad: The Story of the Civil War* (Lexington, 1991), 75.

48. Newspaper clippings, vol. 1, JSMSB-UVA; "Mosby and the War"; Thomas, *Bold Dragoon*, 141–47; Mosby, "Stuart," 39. Pauline and the children made several visits to Idle Wilde and when possible Mosby spent time with them there. On January 21, 1862, he applied for a six-day furlough, possibly to visit Pauline at Idle Wilde, but no evidence has been found to confirm that he actually made the trip. On February 24, 1862, he sent for her to come with the children to Gainesville in Prince William County, but again confirmation that she came is lacking. Mosby very much wanted Pauline with him at the front; and later, when he went independent, he brought her to northern Virginia. JSM leave application, Jan. 21, 1862, JSMP-LC; JSM to PM, Feb. 24, 1862, JSMP-VHS.

49. JSM to PM, Sept. 5, 1862, JSMP-VHS; Mosby, "Stonewall Jackson," *Munsey's Magazine* 47 (June 1912): 333–34; newspaper clipping, vol. 3, JSMSB-UVA; Isaac J. Wistar, *Autobiography of Isaac Jones Wistar, 1827–1905* (New York, 1937), 407–9, 475–76.

50. JSM to PM, Nov. 15, Dec. 9, 1862, JSMP-VHS; Scott, *Life*, 441–42; Freeman, *Lee*, 2: 429–30; *OR* (ser. 1) 21: 1019.

51. Stephen D. Engle, *Yankee Dutchman: The Life of Franz Sigel* (Fayetteville, Ark., 1993), 150–51; *OR* (ser. 1) 21: 800–801, 1027; Russell, *Memoirs*, 146; JSM to PM, Dec. 9, 1862, JSMP-VHS; *Richmond Dispatch*, Nov. 28, 1862; John Esten Cooke, *Wearing of the Gray* (1867; reprint, Bloomington, 1959), 104–5, 335.

## 5. Capturing a Yankee General in Bed

1. Benjamin F. Cooling, *Mr. Lincoln's Forts: A Guide to the Civil War Defenses of Washington* (Shippensburg, 1988), 26; Cooling, *Symbol, Sword, and Shield: Defending Washington during the Civil War* (Hamden, Conn., 1975), 140–41; *OR* (ser. 1) 21: 715–17, 939; 25(2): 504; 33: 888; Mosby, "A Bit of Partisan Service," (hereafter "Partisan Service") in *Battles and Leaders of the Civil War* (hereafter *B&L*), ed. Robert U. Johnson and Clarence C. Buel, 4 vols. (New York, 1956), 3: 148.

2. Scott, *Life*, 22–24; newspaper clipping, vol. 5, JSMSB-UVA; Hugh C. Keen and Horace Mewborn, *43rd Battalion Virginia Cavalry: Mosby's Command* (Lynchburg, 1993), 6–8, 377.

3. Mosby, handwritten, thirteen-page essay on the Aldie Mill Fight (hereafter "Mill Fight"), JSMP-DU ; Mitchell, *Letters*, 299–300; Russell, *Memoirs*, 149; JSM to Arthur B. Clarke, Jan. 24, 1915, JSMP-VHS; Scott, *Life*, 24–25.

4. William H. Martin to wife, Feb. 2, 1863, William H. Martin Papers, HCWRT-USAMHI; *OR* (ser. 1) 25(1): 5–6; Scott, *Life*, 25–26.

5. Edward G. Longacre, *Jersey Cavaliers: A History of the First New Jersey Volunteer Cavalry, 1861–1865* (Hightstown, N.J., 1992), 30–35, 45–46.

6. *OR* (ser. 1) 25(1): 5; Scott, *Life*, 26–27.

7. JSM to F.W. Powell et al., Feb. 4, 1863, JSMP-LC; William H. Martin to wife, Feb. 2, 1863, William H. Martin Papers, HCWRT-USAMHI; *OR* (ser. 1) 25(1): 5; (ser. 3) 5: 581, 583, 975; Scott, *Life*, 28–29; Russell, *Memoirs*, 152–55.

8. William H. Martin to wife, Feb. 19, 1863, HCWRT-USAMHI; O.R. Howard Thomson and William H. Rauch, *History of the "Bucktails": Kane Rifle Regiment of the Pennsylvania Reserve Corps* (Philadelphia, 1906), 11, 247–48; newspaper clipping, vol. 2, JSMSB-UVA. Mosby was absent on a raid to Dranesville, capturing fifteen men and horses. Scott, *Life*, 30–32.

9. William H. Martin to wife, Feb. 15, 27, 1863, William H. Martin Papers, HCWRT-USAMHI; Russell, *Memoirs*, 170; Scott, *Life*, 35–36.

10. *OR* (ser. 1) 25(1): 38–39, 41–42, 1121; Catherine B. Broun, *Family Events, 1859–1889*, Philip H. Broun, comp., (no place, 1959), 57; Mosby, "Mill Fight"; Scott, *Life*, 40.

11. *OR* (ser. 1) 25(1): 41–42; Mosby, "Mill Fight"; George G. Benedict, *Vermont in the Civil War*, 2 vols. (Burlington, 1886–1888), 2: 582–83; Joseph Gilmer, CMSR-NA.

12. Charles B. Chapin to Wilbur Chapin, March 7, 1863, Charles B. Chapin Papers, CWMC-USAMHI; *OR* (ser. 1) 25(1): 41–42, 1121; Benedict, *Vermont,* 2: 582–83; Mosby, "Mill Fight"; Mosby, *Reminiscences,* 51–56.

13. William R. Plum, *The Military Telegraph during the Civil War in the United States,* 2 vols. (1882; reprint, New York, 1974), 1: 361; Longacre, *Jersey Cavaliers,* 127.

14. Russell, *Memoirs,* 172; *OR* (ser. 1) 25(1): 1121–22; Mosby, "One of My War Adventures," (hereafter "Adventures") in Williamson, *Rangers,* 35–36; Williamson, *Rangers,* 29, 31; Ezra D. Simons, *A Regimental History: The One Hundred and Twenty-fifth New York State Volunteers* (New York, 1888), 58; Thomson and Rauch, *"Bucktails,"* 247; William H. Martin to wife, March 14, 1863, William H. Martin Papers, HCWRT-USAMHI. On Stoughton's capture see Howard Coffin, *Nine Months to Gettysburg: Stannard's Vermonters and the Repulse of Pickett's Charge* (Woodstock, Vt., 1997), 108–32.

15. Ezra J. Warner, *Generals in Blue: Lives of the Union Commanders* (1964; reprint, Baton Rouge, 1992), 482–83; *OR* (ser. 1) 21: 833; 25(2): 30; Thomas J. Evans and James M. Moyer, *Mosby's Confederacy: A Guide to the Roads and Sites of Colonel John Singleton Mosby* (Shippensburg, 1991), 1–6. Today Stoughton's headquarters is the office of Truro Episcopal Church.

16. *OR* (ser. 1) 21: 717–18; Benedict, *Vermont,* 2: 424, 426–27; *Baltimore American,* March 17, 1863; Evans and Moyer, *Mosby's Confederacy,* 4–5.

17. *New York Times,* March 14, 1863; Benedict, *Vermont,* 2: 430; *OR* (ser. 1) 25(2): 114–15.

18. Keen and Mewborn, *43rd Battalion,* 291; Mosby, *Reminiscences,* 63; Scott, *Life,* 33, 61–62; Williamson, *Rangers,* 29–33. Ames was killed in action October 9, 1864. Keen and Mewborn, *43rd Battalion,* 291.

19. Mosby, "Adventures," in Williamson, *Rangers,* 43; newspaper clipping, vol. 6, JSMSB-UVA.

20. Newspaper clipping, vol. 6, JSMSB-UVA; *OR* (ser. 1) 25(1): 1121–22; Mosby, "Stealing a General," typescript carbon copy, interview by James F. Breazeale, VHS.

21. Newspaper clippings, vol. 4, 6, JSMSB-UVA; Mosby, "Partisan Service," 150.

22. *OR* (ser. 1) 25(1): 43; newspaper clippings, vol. 4, 6, JSMSB-UVA; Scott, *Life,* 45; Evans and Moyer, *Mosby's Confederacy,* 6; Mosby, "Adventures," in Williamson, *Rangers,* 39.

23. Frank Moore, ed., *The Rebellion Record: A Diary of American Events,* 12 vols. (1861–1868; reprint, New York, 1977), 6: Documents, 443; Russell, *Memoirs,* 173–74; newspaper clipping, vol. 6, JSMSB-UVA.

24. Edwin H. Stoughton to JSM, June 1, 1867, JSMBF-FCPL; newspaper clipping, vol. 4, JSMSB-UVA. Lee graduated from West Point in 1856 and Stoughton in 1859.

25. Newspaper clipping, vol. 6, JSMSB-UVA.

26. Plum, *Telegraph,* 1: 360; Scott, *Life,* 49; Benedict, *Vermont,* 2: 429.

27. Mosby, "Partisan Service," 151; Keen and Mewborn, *43rd Battalion,* 36; newspaper clipping, vol. 6, JSMSB-UVA.

28. Newspaper clipping, vol. 6, JSMSB-UVA; OR (ser. 1) 25(1): 44, 1122; Plum, *Telegraph*, 1: 360.

29. Newspaper clipping, vol. 6, JSMSB-UVA; JSM to JB, May 7, 1903, Jan. 30, 1904, JBP-VHS; OR (ser. 1) 25(1): 66. When Fitz Lee wrote his book *General Lee*, Mosby politely answered his questions and found him an agent. JSM to William Chapman, July 29, 1894, JSMP-DU.

30. *Washington Star*, March 9, 14, 1863; *Baltimore American*, March 17, 1863.

31. *New York Times*, March 11, 12, 1863; *Baltimore American*, March 13, 1863.

32. Newspaper clippings, vol. 1, 4, 6, JSMSB-UVA; Edwin H. Stoughton to JSM, June 1, 1867, JSMBF-FCPL; Warner, *Generals in Blue*, 482–83; *The Poetical Works of Lord Byron* (London, 1945), 393.

33. *New York Times*, March 12, 1863; OR (ser. 1) 25(1): 43; Evans and Moyer, *Mosby's Confederacy*, 5; Robert Johnston, CMSR-NA.

34. Longacre, *Jersey Cavaliers*, 129; Stephen Z. Starr, *The Union Cavalry in the Civil War*, 3 vols. (Baton Rouge, 1972–1985), 1: 96.

35. Thomson and Rauch, *"Bucktails,"* 247; *Washington Star*, March 14, 1863; William H. Martin to wife, March 14, 23, 1863, William H. Martin Papers, HCWRT-USAMHI; Benedict, *Vermont*, 2: 430; Benedict, *Army Life in Virginia: Letters from the Twelfth Vermont Regiment* (Burlington, 1895), 127–28; James H. Kidd, *Personal Recollections of a Cavalryman* (Ionia, Mich., 1908), 96; James H. Stevenson, *"Boots and Saddles": A History of the First Volunteer Cavalry of the War known as the First New York (Lincoln) Cavalry* (Harrisburg, 1879), 162–63.

36. OR (ser. 1) 21: 939; 25(2): 56, 146, 181–83, 586; Frederick H. Dyer, *A Compendium of the War of the Rebellion*, 3 vols. (New York, 1959), 1: 375; 3: 1227; Benedict, *Vermont* 2: 430.

37. OR (ser. 1) 21: 1114–15; 25(2): 856–57; James E.B. Stuart to JSM, March 25, 1863, JSMP-LC; Mitchell, *Letters*, 250. Mosby, *Reminiscences*, 84–85; JSM Commission, Major of Partisan Rangers, March 26, 1863, JSMP-USAMHI; Scott, *Life*, 75–76. Stuart offered Mosby a commission as captain in the Virginia state forces; Mosby, realizing that was a dead end, felt offended and refused. Russell, *Memoirs*, 183–84.

38. OR (ser. 1) 25(2): 857–58; Moore, *Rebellion Record*, 6: Documents, 443–44; *Richmond Dispatch*, March 12, 13, 1863; Monteiro, *Reminiscences*, 38.

39. Simons, *Regimental History*, 62; Arabella M. Willson, *Disaster, Struggle, Triumph: The Adventures of 1000 "Boys in Blue"* (Albany, 1870), 136; *Washington Star*, March 10, 14, 17, 1863; *Baltimore American*, March 18, 1863; Mitchell, *Letters*, 105. Stuart had given Ford an honorary commission and Union officials considered it evidence that she was a spy. See Linda J. Simmons, "The Antonia Ford Mystery," *Northern Virginia Heritage* (Oct. 1985), 3–6, 20.

40. Mosby, *Reminiscences*, 69–75; Benedict, *Vermont*, 2: 583–84; OR (ser. 1) 25(1): 65–66; *Washington Star*, March 18, 1863. Lt. Edwin H. Higley, in command of the relief, pursued Mosby for four miles and halted at Horse Pen Run. He was dismissed on April 6, 1863, for cowardice and breach of duty for not

pursuing more vigorously. A military commission found him innocent and he was restored with pay. Edwin H. Higley, CMSR-NA; Benedict, *Vermont*, 2: 584.

41. OR (ser. 1) 25(1): 71–72; Mosby, *Reminiscences*, 82–84.

42. Scott, *Life*, 60–61.

43. OR (ser. 1) 25(1): 70–72; Mosby, *Reminiscences*, 88–92; Fairfax Harrison to Frank F. Abbott, Nov. 13, 1917, Fairfax Harrison Papers, VHS.

## 6. Miskel's Farm

1. *Confederate Veteran* 31 (1923): 18; newspaper clippings, vol. 1, 6, JSMSB-UVA.

2. JSM to James Seddon, Oct. 21, 1863, Confederate Records, Letters Received by the Confederate Adjutant and Inspector General, Sept.-Nov. 1863, RG 109, NA.

3. Mosby, *Reminiscences*, 99; *New York Herald*, May 5, 1863; Scott, *Life*, 59.

4. Scott, *Life*, 63; Mosby, *Reminiscences*, 101.

5. Mosby, *Reminiscences*, 103–4; newspaper clipping, vol. 5, JSMSB-UVA.

6. Scott, *Life*, 63–64.

7. Benedict, *Vermont*, 2: 540, 547, 576, 585; OR (ser. 1) 25(1): 77.

8. Benedict, *Vermont*, 2: 585; Mosby, *Reminiscences*, 109; Keen and Mewborn, *43rd Battalion*, 44–46, 350; Scott, *Life*, 65.

9. Benedict, *Vermont*, 2: 586; Mosby, *Reminiscences*, 105; Scott, *Life*, 67.

10. Scott, *Life*, 65; Mosby, *Reminiscences*, 104–5; Conrad H. Lanza, *Napoleon and Modern War: His Military Maxims* (Harrisburg, Pa., 1943), 25, 30.

11. Gerald F. Linderman, *Embattled Courage: The Experience of Combat in the American Civil War* (New York, 1987), 156; Munson, *Reminiscences*, 58; Benedict, *Vermont*, 2: 586; OR (ser. 1) 25(1): 77–78.

12. Munson, *Reminiscences*, 56–59; Mosby, *Reminiscences*, 106–7.

13. Mosby, *Reminiscences*, 107; OR (ser. 1) 25(1): 78; George H. Bean, CMSR-NA.

14. Mosby, *Reminiscences*, 110; OR (ser. 1) 25(1): 72; Benedict, *Vermont*, 2: 587.

15. Russell, *Memoirs*, 30, 284.

16. Newspaper clipping, vol. 5, JSMSB-UVA.

17. OR (ser. 1) 25(2): 860; Mosby, *Reminiscences*, 123; Scott, *Life*, 78. Fishel points out that Stuart expected Hooker to withdraw to Alexandria and reopen the Richmond front. Fishel, *Secret War*, 349.

18. Keen and Mewborn, *43rd Battalion*, 54; Mosby, *Reminiscences*, 130–35; OR (ser. 1) 25(1): 1104–7; 25(2): 861; *New York Herald*, May 5, 1863; *Washington Star*, May 5, 1863; *Baltimore American*, May 6, 1863; *New York Times*, May 5, 1863. The Union men had two dead, one mortally wounded, and fifteen wounded. OR (ser. 1) 25(1): 1105.

19. JSM to JB, Jan. 30, 1904, JBP-VHS; Scott, *Life*, 88–89; Mosby, *Reminiscences*, 139; OR (ser. 1) 25(2): 860, 862.

20. Charles A. Manson to parents, June 2, 1863, Charles A. Manson Letters, LLC-USAMHI; OR (ser. 1) 25(1): 1117–18; 25(2): 493, 499–500.

21. OR (ser. 1) 25(1): 1118; Mosby, *Reminiscences,* 142.

22. OR (ser. 1) 51(1): 1042; Mosby, *Reminiscences,* 142.

23. Keen and Mewborn, *43rd Battalion,* 59; Williamson, *Rangers,* 64; *Washington Star,* June 1, 1863.

24. *Washington Star,* June 1, 1863; Mosby, *Reminiscences,* 144; Williamson, *Rangers,* 65; Scott, *Life,* 92.

25. OR (ser. 1) 25(1): 1117.

26. Mosby, *Reminiscences,* 146–48; Munson, *Reminiscences,* 72–73, quoting Elmer Barker.

27. Mosby, *Reminiscences,* 148.

28. Munson, *Reminiscences,* 73, quoting Barker.

29. OR (ser. 1) 25(1): 1118–19; Mosby, *Reminiscences,* 150–51; Scott, *Life,* 95.

30. OR (ser. 1) 25(1): 1119; *Richmond Dispatch,* June 3, 1863; Russell, *Memoirs,* 197; *New York Times,* May 31, 1863; Moore, *Rebellion Record,* 7: Poetry and Incidents, 75; Recollection of Col. John Singleton Mosby, no date, Curt B. Miller Papers, The Western Reserve Historical Society, Cleveland, Ohio. After the war, Mosby concluded that the Catlett's Station Raid caused so much uneasiness in Washington that Stahel's "6000 sabres" were denied to Union general Alfred Pleasonton in the battle of Brandy Station, June 9, 1863. In fact, Stahel had thirty-six hundred cavalry, and they were not tied down defending from Mosby during the battle. Hooker asked Halleck to send Stahel's cavalry to hold Rappahannock fords on his right flank during the battle. But as Hooker's headquarters had requested earlier, about half of Stahel's cavalry were scouting toward the Blue Ridge Mountains. Nevertheless, on the night of June 7, Stahel concentrated his remaining force of between sixteen and seventeen hundred men and marched them to Kettle Run on the O&A Railroad, arriving at 6:00 A.M. on June 8. He met with Pleasonton, who requested him to guard the O&A, send out scouting parties, and post pickets in the rear, where Pleasonton was removing his own men in preparation for action. Stahel complied, and during the battle his men guarded the O&A as far southwest as Bealeton Station, eight and one-half miles from Brandy Station. It is inaccurate to claim that Mosby diverted Stahel's cavalry from the battle. Mosby, *Reminiscences,* 152–53; Mosby, "Partisan Service," 148–49; Mosby, *Stuart's Cavalry,* 10; OR (ser. 1) 27(1): 33, 27(3): 18–19, 25–26, 31, 33–40.

31. JSM to PM, March 16, 1863, JSMP-LC; Eighth Census: 1860, Fauquier County, Agricultural, VSA; Eighth Census, Fauquier County, Slave Schedules, NA.

32. *Washington Star,* June 12, 1863; Moore, *Rebellion Record,* 7: Documents, 281; Scott, *Life,* 91. Legend holds that Mosby was in bed with Pauline when the Federals came, and he opened a window and climbed onto a limb of a walnut tree and remained there until they departed. When Loudoun County historian John E. Divine and historian Horace Mewborn guided my wife and me on a tour of Mosby's country in 1988, we visited the Hathaway farm and saw the window and the tree, still standing. The Civil War vintage limb had been trimmed, but another limb was extending near the window, making the story seem plau-

sible. However, I have found no contemporary mention of the story. It does not appear in any of the diaries or letters that I have read, and I have seen no mention of it by Mosby. The respected *Mosby's Rangers* (1896), by former Ranger James J. Williamson includes the story in the appendix, within a quoted passage from *"Boots and Saddles"* (1879), regimental history of the 1st New York Cavalry. The author, James H. Stevenson, described the raid and the discovery of Pauline. Concerning the tree limb, he wrote, "It appears that Mosby had been in the house, but had got out of a window into the branches of a tree, from which he was quietly watching the party, and in the darkness he was not discovered." This may be genuine, but it seems strange that the story is not in John Scott's book; it is the kind of irregular ruse that Scott appreciated. Williamson, *Rangers*, 440–41; Stevenson, *"Boots and Saddles,"* 182.

33. Scott, *Life*, 77; William C. Davis, *Jefferson Davis: The Man and His Hour* (New York, 1991), 480; John B. Jones, *A Rebel War Clerk's Diary*, ed. Earl S. Miers (Baton Rouge, 1993), 121, 202, 242, 433–34; OR (ser. 4) 2: 289.

34. Scott, *Life*, 77.

35. Williamson, *Rangers*, 69; newspaper clipping, JSMF-VM; Scott, *Life*, 209.

36. Scott, *Life*, 97; JSM to J.E.B. Stuart, June 11, 1863, JSMP-LC; Russell, *Memoirs*, 199; OR (ser. 1) 27(2): 786–87; Mosby, *Reminiscences*, 160. Mosby gave Stuart a sorrel horse captured at Seneca. Mosby, *Reminiscences*, 163.

37. Mosby, *Stuart's Cavalry*, 60–62; Mosby, *Reminiscences*, 164.

38. OR (ser. 1) 27(1): 200; 27(2): 689; 27(3): 86, 176–77, 192; Mosby, *Reminiscences*, 165.

39. OR (ser. 1) 27(2): 689; 27(3): 176–77; Freeman, *Lee*, 3: 38–39; Dowdey and Manarin, *Papers*, 519.

40. *New York Herald*, June 21, 1863; *Washington Star*, June 20, 1863; OR (ser. 1) 27(3): 192, 194, 229; OR (ser. 1) 51(1): 1062.

41. OR (ser. 1) 27(2): 692; Thomas, *Bold Dragoon*, 239–40; JSM to John W. Daniel, Feb. 19, 1906, Marshall Family Papers, VHS; Mosby, *Stuart's Cavalry*, 76–78.

42. Thomas, *Bold Dragoon*, 240; Williamson, *Rangers*, 73; Mosby, *Stuart's Cavalry*, 78–81.

43. Mosby, *Reminiscences*, 177; Mosby, *Stuart's Cavalry*, 92, 174; Dowdey and Manarin, *Papers*, 526.

44. OR (ser. 1) 27(1): 143; Mosby, *Stuart's Cavalry*, 175, 177.

45. Dowdey and Manarin, *Papers*, 526.

46. Thomas, *Bold Dragoon*, 241; Williamson, *Rangers*, 80.

## 7. Featherbed Guerrillas

1. OR (ser. 1) 25(2): 858; 43(2): 909; Mosby, *Reminiscences*, 63; Williamson, *Rangers*, 98.

2. See unit roster, Keen and Mewborn, *43rd Battalion*, 290–386; Jeffry D. Wert, *Mosby's Rangers* (New York, 1990), 328–29; Bell I. Wiley, *The Life of Billy Yank: The Common Soldier of the Union* (Baton Rouge, 1986), 303.

3. Charles Dear Memorandum, Feb. 3, 1905, typed copy, BFP-VSA.

4. Scott, *Life*, 209, 395; newspaper clipping, vol. 5, JSMSB-UVA.

5. Munson, *Reminiscences*, 22; Carl Schurz, *The Autobiography of Carl Schurz*, ed. Wayne Andrews (New York, 1961), 284; Mosby, *Stuart's Cavalry*, 62–63; Francis S. Drake, ed., *Dictionary of American Biography* (1872; Chicago, 1974), 807.

6. Russell, *Memoirs*, 258; newspaper clipping, vol. 6, JSMSB-UVA; Munson, *Reminiscences*, 10; JSM to AM, Feb. 19, 1895, JSMC-MC; Monteiro, *Reminiscences*, 196; Alexander, *Mosby's Men*, 44.

7. Williamson, *Rangers*, 97.

8. Amanda V. Edmonds Chappelear Diary, Jan. 19, 1865, VHS (hereafter Edmonds Diary). See Nancy Chappelear Baird, ed., *Journals of Amanda Virginia Edmonds: Lass of the Confederacy, 1859–1867* (Stephens City, Va., 1984).

9. Walter Laqueur, *The Guerrilla Reader: A Historical Anthology* (Philadelphia, 1977), 34; newspaper clipping, vol. 6, JSMSB-UVA; Autobiography of Augustus P. Green, New York Historical Society Library; *Baltimore American*, Dec. 22, 1864; newspaper clipping, JSMF-VM. Mosby's Confederacy, the area where his men boarded, was bounded by the Bull Run Mountains, the road from Aldie to Snicker's Gap, Blue Ridge Mountains, and on the south by a line running from Manassas Gap to Thoroughfare Gap.

10. Drew G. Faust, *Mothers of Invention: Women of the Slaveholding South in the American Civil War* (Chapel Hill, 1996), 238–39, 243; William A. Blair, "Virginia's Private War: The Contours of Dissent and Loyalty in the Confederacy, 1861–1865" (Ph.D. diss., Pennsylvania State University, 1995), xi–xiii, xvi, 253–54, 262, 265–70; Daniel E. Sutherland, *Seasons of War: The Ordeal of a Confederate Community, 1861–1865* (New York, 1995), 355, 367, 382; Mary H. Lancaster and Dallas M. Lancaster, eds., *The Civil War Diary of Anne S. Frobel* (McLean, Va., 1992), 202; Broun, *Family Events*, 78. See also Noel G. Harrison, "Atop an Anvil: The Civilians' War in Fairfax and Alexandria Counties, April 1861–April 1862," *Virginia Magazine of History and Biography* 106 (Spring 1998): 133–64 (hereafter *VMHB*).

11. James A. Ramage, "Inside Mosby's Confederacy," unpublished paper for Virginia Historical Society Summer Fellowship, 1989; OR (ser. 1) 33: 9, 1252.

12. *Eighth Census, Population: 1860* (Washington, 1864); *Eighth Census, Agriculture: 1860* (Washington, 1864); Eighth Census: 1860, Loudoun County, slave schedules manuscript, NA; Ervin L. Jordan Jr., *Black Confederates and Afro-Yankees in Civil War Virginia* (Charlottesville, 1995), 8, 314; Kenneth M. Stampp, *The Peculiar Institution: Slavery in the Ante-Bellum South* (New York, 1982), 30. On antebellum Loudoun County society see Brenda E. Stevenson, *Life in Black & White: Family and Community in the Slave South* (New York, 1996).

13. Eighth Census: 1860, Fauquier County, slave schedules manuscript, NA; *Eighth Census, Mortality and Miscellaneous: 1860* (Washington, 1864); *Eighth Census, Population, Agriculture;* Jordan, *Black Confederates*, 8, 313, Stampp, *Peculiar Institution*, 32.

14. John C. Hoadley, *Memorial of Henry Sanford Gansevoort* (Boston, 1875), 48; Williamson, *Rangers,* 133–34; Munson, *Reminiscences,* 80.

15. Interview with John E. Divine, July 26, 1988; Hunter, *Women,* 229–37.

16. Russell F. Weigley, *The American Way of War: A History of United States Military Strategy* (Bloomington, 1973), 217–19.

17. Arthur L. Wagner, *Organization and Tactics* (New York, 1895), 183–88; OR (ser. 1) 27(2): 787.

18. Mosby, *Reminiscences,* 89–90; newspaper clipping, vol. 1, JSMSB-UVA; Williamson, *Rangers,* 287; OR (ser. 1) 46(1): 465.

19. Munson, *Reminiscences,* 25; newspaper clipping, vol. 2, JSMSB-UVA; Scott, *Life,* 206.

20. Newspaper clipping, vol. 5, JSMSB-UVA.

## 8. Unguarded Sutler Wagons

1. Scott, *Life,* 119; John M. Crawford, *Mosby and His Men* (New York, 1867), 154; *Washington Star,* Aug. 8, 1863.

2. Walter Laqueur, *Guerrilla: A Historical and Critical Study* (Boston, 1976), 20; Russell F. Weigley, *The Partisan War: The South Carolina Campaign of 1780–1782* (Columbia, S.C., 1970), 55; James M. Matthews, ed., *The Statutes at Large of the Confederate States of America,* 1st Cong., 1st sess., 48; OR (ser. 4) 2: 498–99.

3. JB to John R. Bryan, April 6, 1865, Bryan Family Papers, VHS; Paddy Griffith, *Battle Tactics of the Civil War* (New Haven, 1989), 81; *Washington Star,* March 18, 1863; Adolphus E. Richards, "Mosby's 'Partizan Rangers,'" in *Famous Adventures and Prison Escapes of the Civil War* (1885; reprint, New York, 1920), 113.

4. Thomas R. Phillips, trans., *Frederick the Great: Instructions to his Generals* (1944; reprint, Harrisburg, Pa., 1951), 22; Lanza, *Napoleon,* 136; OR (ser. 1) 25 (2): 858; 43(2): 909; Linderman, *Courage,* 43; Scott, *Life,* 59.

5. Alexander, *Mosby's Men,* 60; Keen and Mewborn, *43rd Battalion,* 142; newspaper clipping, vol. 1, JSMSB-UVA; Munson, *Reminiscences,* 171–72; Henry P. Moyer, *History of the Seventeenth Regiment, Pennsylvania Volunteer Cavalry* (Lebanon, Pa., 1911), 160; Scott, *Life,* 338; *Jones, Mosby,* 226; *Baltimore American,* Oct. 21, 1864.

6. Thomas, *Bold Dragoon,* 118; James I. Robertson Jr., *Soldiers: Blue and Gray* (Columbia, S.C., 1988), 72–73; Jack Coggins, *Arms and Equipment of the Civil War* (New York, 1962), 124; Munson, *Reminiscences,* 208–9.

7. Judith W. McGuire, *Diary of a Southern Refugee during the War* (1867; reprint, New York, 1972), 257; George G. Morris and Susan L. Foutz, *Lynchburg in the Civil War,* 2d ed. (Lynchburg, 1984), 21, 26, 32–33; Cornelia Peake McDonald, *A Woman's Civil War,* ed. Minrose C. Gwin (Madison, Wisc., 1972), 220; Michael Golay, *To Gettysburg and Beyond: The Parallel Lives of Joshua Lawrence Chamberlain and Edward Porter Alexander* (New York, 1994), 191, 240.

8. Williamson, *Rangers,* 107.

9. Munson, *Reminiscences,* 211; newspaper clipping, vol. 3, JSMSB-UVA; Scott, *Life,* 238.

10. JSM to PM, Oct. 1, 1863, JSMP-VHS; Russell, *Memoirs,* 314; Keen and Mewborn, *43rd Battalion,* 197; Catherine Cochran Recollections (hereafter Cochran Recollections), Oct. 17, 1864, VHS. Mosby suffered a sprained ankle when his horse was shot and fell on him in a skirmish near The Plains, October 11, 1864. Williamson, *Rangers,* 258.

11. Scott, *Life,* 109; OR (ser. 1) 27(2): 991–92; Munson *Reminiscences,* 77; *Confederate Veteran* 36 (1928): 417.

12. OR (ser. 1) 27(1): 60; 27(3): 354, 359, 380, 440, 722–23, 809.

13. Ibid., 27(2): 988–92; Scott, *Life,* 114–16.

14. Warner, *Generals in Blue,* 284–85; Charles A. Humphreys, *Field, Camp, Hospital and Prison in the Civil War, 1863–1865* (1918; reprint, Freeport, N.Y., 1971), 188.

15. Stanton Garner, *The Civil War World of Herman Melville* (Lawrence, Kans., 1993), 306; Edward W. Emerson, *Life and Letters of Charles Russell Lowell* (1907; reprint, Port Washington, N.Y., 1971), 39, 294–96; Humphreys, *Field,* 377. Effy and Charles were probably the models for the newlyweds in Melville's poem "The Scout toward Aldie." Garner, *Melville,* 306.

16. OR (ser. 1) 27(2): 990–91; Emerson, *Lowell,* 294.

17. *Washington Star,* Aug. 7, 1863; JSM to William C. Marshall, May 12, 1905, Marshall Family Papers, VHS; *New York Herald,* Aug. 5, 12, Nov. 2, 1863.

18. Scott, *Life,* 140–1; *New York Herald,* Aug. 31, 1863; *Richmond Dispatch,* Aug. 11, 27, 1863.

19. OR (ser. 1) 29(1): 69; 29(2): 79, 83.

20. Ibid., 27(2): 992; 29(2): 652–53.

21. Ibid., 29(2): 12–13, 50, 61, 88.

22. Ibid., 29(1): 80; 29(2): 399, 400, 405; *Washington Star,* Aug. 29, 1863; Starr, *Union Cavalry,* 2: 13.

23. *Baltimore American,* Aug. 29, 1863; OR 29(1): 80; 29(2): 98–99; *Washington Star,* Aug. 29, 1863.

24. Newspaper clipping, vol. 2, JSMSB-UVA; James J. Williamson, *Mosby's Rangers,* 2d ed. (New York, 1909), 495 (hereafter *Mosby's Rangers,* 1909 ed.). In California after the war Mosby saw a document indicating that Frederick F. Low, governor of California, 1863–1867, recommended a promotion for the man who had shot him. Visiting in Low's home he joked with him about this. Newspaper clipping, vol. 2, JSMSB-UVA. Keen and Mewborn identify the man as William Short, 2nd Massachusetts Cavalry. *43rd Battalion,* 78.

25. *Washington Star,* Aug. 29, 1863; *New York Herald,* Aug. 31, Sept. 9, 1863; OR 29(1): 95; 29(2): 113; Luther C. Furst Diary, Aug. 31, 1863, HCWRT-USAMHI.

26. Emerson, *Lowell,* 298–99, 311, 473; OR 29(2): 98–99.

27. JSM to PM, Oct. 1, 1863, JSMP-VHS; OR (ser. 1) 43(1): 84; 43(2): 918. Mosby considered using torpedoes by Aug. 19, 1863. OR (ser. 1) 29(2): 653.

28. JSM to PM, Oct. 1, 1863, JSMP-VHS; OR (ser. 1) 29(1): 81; 29(2): 766.

29. Williamson, *Rangers,* 92–93; OR (ser. 1) 29(1): 9, 80–81; 29(2): 161–62, 178–81, 189; 51(2): 769.

30. Williamson, *Rangers,* 93; OR (ser. 1) 29(1): 80–81, 145–46; 29(2): 172, 254, 256; Richard J. Del Vecchio, "With the First New York Dragoons: From the Letters of Jared L. Ainsworth," typed manuscript, 46, in Jared L. Ainsworth letters, HCWRT-USAMHI; Scott, *Life,* 143–44.

31. Scott, *Life,* 144; *Richmond Sentinel,* quoted in *Baltimore American,* Oct. 6, 1863.

32. Scott, *Life,* 144; Williamson, *Rangers,* 93–94; James G. Barber, *Alexandria in the Civil War* (Lynchburg, 1988), 93; Jack P. Maddex Jr., *The Virginia Conservatives, 1867–1879: A Study in Reconstruction Politics* (Chapel Hill, 1970), 26–27; OR (ser. 1) 29(1): 81; newspaper clipping, JSMF- VM.

33. Anna Pierpont Siviter, *Recollections of War and Peace* (New York, 1938), 128; Francis H. Pierpont to Edwin M. Stanton, Oct. 20, 1863, Francis H. Pierpont Papers, Governor's Office (RG#) Executive Papers, VSA.

34. Scott, *Life,* 145; Anne S. Frobel, *The Civil War Diary of Anne S. Frobel* (1986; reprint, McLean, Va., 1992), 209.

35. OR (ser. 1) 29(1): 80–81; *New York Herald,* Oct. 2, 1863; *Alexandria Gazette,* Sept. 29, 1863.

36. Scott, *Life,* 230–32; Keen and Mewborn, *43rd Battalion,* 131–32; OR (ser. 1) 37(1): 611–12.

37. Williamson, *Rangers,* 231–32; Keen and Mewborn, *43rd Battalion,* 160, 164; Munson, *Reminiscences,* 200–201.

38. William A. Tidwell, with James O. Hall and David W. Gaddy, *Come Retribution: The Confederate Secret Service and the Assassination of Lincoln* (Jackson, Miss., 1988), 140–42; OR (ser. 1) 46(2): 923–24; Keen and Mewborn, *43rd Battalion,* 299.

39. Virgil C. Jones, *Gray Ghosts and Rebel Raiders* (New York, 1956), 361; newspaper clipping, JSMF-VM.

## 9. Masquerading as the Enemy

1. OR (ser. 1) 29(1): 492; 29(2): 344–45, 350; Scott, *Life,* 146; *New York Herald,* Nov. 2, 1863.

2. OR (ser. 1) 29(1): 492; 51(2): 778–79.

3. Ibid., 29(1): 495; Williamson, *Rangers,* 102.

4. Samuel Chapman and William Chapman, CMSR-NA; Russell, *Memoirs,* 356; Mosby, *Reminiscences,* 108–9.

5. *New York Herald,* Nov. 1, 1863; OR (ser. 1) 29(1): 495; Williamson, *Rangers,* 439.

6. OR (ser. 1) 29(2): 392; *New York Herald,* Oct. 30, Nov. 2, 1863.

7. Williamson, *Rangers,* 104, 115; OR (ser. 1) 29(1): 495, 552.

8. OR (ser. 1) 29(1): 550, 552; 29(2): 423–24.

9. OR (ser. 1) 29(1): 81, 552, 662, 667; 29(2): 477.

10. *OR* (ser. 1) 29(1): 804–6; 29(2): 477.

11. *OR* (ser. 1) 29(1): 13; 826; Williamson, *Rangers,* 111–12; Scott, *Life,* 157; *Richmond Dispatch,* Nov. 30, 1863.

12. *Alexandria Gazette,* Jan. 5, 7, 8, 9, 1864; *Baltimore American,* Jan. 9, 1864.

13. *OR* (ser. 1) 11(2): 522; Keen and Mewborn, *43rd Battalion,* 372; JSM to Thomas W. Duke, April 4, 1915, UVA; James D. Peavey, *Confederate Scout: Virginia's Frank Stringfellow* (Onancock, Va., 1956), 49–51.

14. Henry A. Cole, CMSR-NA; Chester G. Hearn, *Six Years of Hell: Harpers Ferry During the Civil War* (Baton Rouge, 1996), 231–32; guided tour of site, John E. Divine and Horace Mewborn, July 27, 1988. On the Nov. 21 raid see: Scott, *Life,* 153–54; Williamson, *Rangers,* 107–9; *OR* (ser. 1) 29(1): 659–60; *New York Herald,* Nov. 23, 1863.

15. C. Armour Newcomer, *Cole's Cavalry; or Three Years in the Saddle in the Shenandoah Valley* (1895; reprint, Freeport, N.Y., 1970), 94; William A. McIlhenny Diary, William A. McIlhenny Papers, CWTI-USAMHI.

16. See Chapter 12 on the defeat of Cole's detachment on January 1, 1864.

17. *OR* (ser. 1) 33: 15; Williamson, *Mosby's Rangers,* 1909 ed., 486; Williamson, *Rangers,* 125–26.

18. *OR* (ser. 1) 33: 15; Scott, *Life,* 179–80; Williamson, *Rangers,* 127.

19. *OR* (ser. 1) 33: 17; Newcomer, *Cole's Cavalry,* 93–94; Thomas J. Evans and James M. Moyer, "Skirmish on Loudoun Heights," *Northern Virginia Heritage* (June 1986): 8; Williamson, *Rangers,* 126.

20. Newcomer, *Cole's Cavalry,* 95, 102–3, 105; McIlhenny Diary; Williamson, *Rangers,* 126–27; Evans and Moyer, "Loudoun Heights," 2, 9; *Baltimore American,* Jan. 13, 21, 1864; *Washington Star,* Jan. 13, 1864; *OR* (ser. 1) 33: 17–18. Vernon survived and was promoted to lieutenant colonel. Newcomer, *Cole's Cavalry,* 114.

21. *OR* (ser. 1) 33: 16; Sun Tzu, *The Art of War,* ed. James Clavell (New York, 1983), 37.

22. *New York Herald,* Jan. 21, 1864; *Baltimore American,* Jan. 13, 21, 1864; *Washington Star,* Jan. 11, 1864; Williamson, *Rangers,* 127; Keen and Mewborn, *43rd Battalion,* 369–70, 377.

23. *Washington Star,* Jan. 11, 1864; Newcomer, *Cole's Cavalry,* 102, 113–14; *OR* (ser. 1) 33: 17–18.

24. Munson, *Reminiscences,* 242; *OR* (ser. 1) 33: 16; JSM, CMSR-NA.

25. Tzu, *Art of War,* 17.

## 10. Seddon's Partisans

1. Rembert W. Patrick, *Jefferson Davis and His Cabinet* (Baton Rouge, 1944), 133, 337; Jones, *Clerk's Diary,* 242.

2. Patrick, *Cabinet,* 134; Current, *Encyclopedia of the Confederacy,* 3: 1383–87.

3. Roger U. Delauter Jr., *McNeill's Rangers,* 2d ed. (Lynchburg, 1986), 2, 21, 34–35; *OR* (ser. 1) 25(2): 656.

4. Ramage, *Rebel Raider,* 69; *Richmond Enquirer,* March 17, 1862.

5. *OR* (ser. 1) 5: 1090; 51(2): 526; Randall Osborne and Jeffrey C. Weaver, *The Virginia State Rangers and State Line* (Lynchburg, 1994), 10–11.

6. Jones, *Gray Ghosts,* 76; Herman Hattaway and Archer Jones, *How the North Won: A Military History of the Civil War* (Urbana, 1983), 113.

7. *OR* (ser. 4) 2: 26, 48; Jones, *Gray Ghosts,* 107; Albert B. Moore, *Conscription and Conflict in the Confederacy* (New York, 1924), 121–22. When Union officials prepared to execute two captured captains of the Virginia State Rangers, Randolph and Davis threatened to retaliate and McClellan backed down on June 20, 1862. Osborne and Weaver, *State Rangers,* 15–17.

8. *Knoxville Register,* Oct. 19, 1862; *OR* (ser. 4) 2: 289. The Virginia State Rangers and Virginia State Line, commissioned to conduct guerrilla war behind enemy lines in West Virginia, acquired such a criminal reputation that they were officially disbanded on April 1, 1863. Osborne and Weaver, *State Rangers,* 119.

9. *OR* (ser. 4) 2: 1003.

10. *OR* (ser. 4) 2: 1061–62; Current, *Encyclopedia of the Confederacy,* 3: 1347; Mark M. Boatner, III, *The Civil War Dictionary* (New York, 1991), 709–10.

11. John E. Divine, *35th Battalion Virginia Cavalry,* 2d ed. (Lynchburg, 1985), 1–2, 42, 50. In July 1864, Company B of White's battalion deserted to go home to Maryland; and in the winter of 1864–1865, all but one company deserted, and the battalion received temporary permission to operate independently. Divine, *35th Battalion,* 54, 64.

12. Jones, *Gray Ghosts,* 213; Delauter, *Rangers,* 60–61.

13. *OR* (ser. 1) 33: 1081–82.

14. Ibid., 1082.

15. Ibid., 1113, 1252–53; 29(2): 755.

16. Ibid., (ser. 1) 33: 9; (ser. 4) 3: 194.

17. *OR* (ser. 1) 33: 1252.

18. Ibid., 1253.

19. JSM to William H. Chapman, April 29, 1891, JSMP-DU; Delauter, *Rangers,* 66. John McNeill was mortally wounded in action on October 3, 1864, and died November 10, 1864. His son Lt. Jesse McNeill commanded the company to the end of the war. Delauter, *Rangers,* 80, 122.

20. Munson, *Reminiscences,* 85.

21. *OR* (ser. 1) 33: 159–60; Williamson, *Rangers,* 142; Keen and Mewborn, *43rd Battalion,* 112. In late January Mosby visited Pauline in Charlottesville and went to Richmond before returning to duty by February 20, 1864. Keen and Mewborn, *43rd Battalion,* 106. Deserter Charles Binns guided Reed's raid. Williamson, *Rangers,* 145.

22. Williamson, *Rangers,* 143; Williamson, *Mosby's Rangers,* 1909 ed., 142–43; Scott, *Life,* 201.

23. Williamson, *Mosby's Rangers,* 1909 ed., 142–43.

24. Ibid.; Scott, *Life,* 201–2; Williamson, *Rangers,* 144.

25. Williamson, *Mosby's Rangers,* 1909 ed., 143.

26. Munson, *Reminiscences,* 85–88; *Washington Star,* Feb. 23, 1864; newspaper clipping, vol. 3, JSMSB-UVA.

27. OR (ser. 1) 33: 159–60; Williamson, *Rangers,* 145.

28. OR (ser. 1) 33: 1268–69; Freeman, *Lee,* 3: 264.

29. Keen and Mewborn, *43rd Battalion,* 116–17; OR (ser. 1) 33: 1240–41. Henry B. McClellan was Stuart's adjutant.

30. Dowdey and Manarin, *Papers,* 688, 704; Engle, *Sigel,* 169–73; Franz Sigel, "Sigel, in the Shenandoah Valley in 1864," *B&L,* 4: 487; William C. Davis, *The Battle of New Market* (1975; reprint, Baton Rouge, 1983), 25.

31. Dowdey and Manarin, *Papers,* 688; William Marvel, *Burnside* (Chapel Hill, 1991), 338, 343; Jeffry D. Wert, *General James Longstreet: The Confederacy's Most Controversial Soldier—A Biography* (New York, 1993), 371.

32. OR (ser. 1) 33: 1276, 1278; 51(2): 855–56; Dowdey and Manarin, *Papers,* 692–94. Channing Smith later joined Mosby's command. Keen and Mewborn, *43rd Battalion,* 368.

33. OR (ser. 1) 33: 1268–69. Mosby had requested two thousand dollars in Secret Service money to invest in tobacco to sell for greenbacks. The transaction was pending on April 18 and it might be that Mosby was promising to pay for military intelligence. OR (ser. 1) 33: 1241; Walter E. Frankland to James A. Seddon, April 18, 1864, Confederate Records, Letters Received by the Confederate Secretary of War, 1861–1865, RG 109, NA.

34. OR (ser. 1) 33: 1276; 51(2): 856. Grant directed that all troops that could be spared from the Washington defenses be sent to Burnside in Annapolis. OR (ser. 1) 33: 879.

35. Marvel, *Burnside,* 341, 471; OR (ser. 1) 33: 946, 955.

36. OR (ser. 1) 51(2): 855–56.

37. Ibid., 33: 1278.

38. Ibid., 1276–77, 1279–80; Jones, *Clerk's Diary,* 360–62.

39. OR (ser. 1) 33: 1282–83; Dowdey and Manarin, *Papers,* 699–700.

40. OR (ser. 1) 33: 1290.

41. Ibid., 1321; Dowdey and Manarin, *Papers,* 706–7.

42. Dowdey and Manarin, *Papers,* 708–9; Douglas S. Freeman, ed., *Lee's Dispatches: Unpublished Letters of General Robert E. Lee* (New York, 1915), 172; OR (ser. 1) 33: 249.

## 11. Mosby's Clones in the Valley

1. Newspaper clipping, vol. 6, JSMSB-UVA.

2. Keen and Mewborn, *43rd Battalion,* 350; Munson, *Reminiscences,* 141, 181, 198–99; Williamson, *Rangers,* 312; OR (ser. 1) 43(1): 634. Montjoy was killed on November 28, 1864.

3. Williamson, *Rangers,* 157–58, 181, 284–85; Keen and Mewborn, *43rd Battalion,* 150, 352; JSM to Frederick F. Bowen, June 15, (no year), Frederick F. Bowen Papers, VHS. On Nelson's later defeat, see Chapter 15.

4. Engle, *Sigel,* xvi-xvii, 3–4, 66; Davis, *New Market,* 25, 39, 42–43, 65, 68–69; Delauter, *Rangers,* 68–69; OR (ser. 1) 37(1): 384, 388–89, 397, 447. In contrast to Sheridan later, Sigel forbade scouts to masquerade in Confederate uniforms. George Lyon to S. Young, April 22, 1864, Franz Sigel Papers, Western Reserve Historical Society.

5. OR (ser. 1) 37(1): 2–3, 371, 378, 384, 386, 388–89, 397, 507; Keen and Mewborn, *43rd Battalion,* 121, 125; Williamson, *Rangers,* 165–67. Lee recommended on April 1, 1864, that Gilmor's partisan battalion be disbanded under the repeal of the partisan law, but he was still operating when captured on February 5, 1865. OR (ser. 1) 33: 1252.

6. Thomas A. Lewis, *The Shenandoah in Flames* (Alexandria, Va., 1987), 39; Lee C. Drickamer and Karen D. Drickamer, eds., *Fort Lyon to Harper's Ferry: On the Border of North and South with "Rambling Jour": The Civil War Letters and Newspaper Dispatches of Charles H. Moulton* (Shippensburg, 1987), 195–96; Boatner, *Dictionary,* 418–19.

7. OR (ser. 1) 37(1): 97; Lewis, *Shenandoah,* 42; Jones, *Gray Ghosts,* 251; Edward H. Phillips, *The Lower Shenandoah Valley in the Civil War: The Impact of War Upon the Civilian Population and Upon Civil Institutions* (Lynchburg, 1993), 159.

8. OR (ser. 1) 37(1): 519, 525; Cecil D. Eby Jr., *"Porte Crayon": The Life of David Hunter Strother* (Chapel Hill, 1960), 236.

9. OR (ser. 1) 37(1): 614; Thomas F. Wildes, *Record of the One Hundred and Sixteenth Regiment, Ohio Infantry Volunteers in the War of the Rebellion* (Sandusky, 1884), 93, 102 (hereafter Wildes, *116th Ohio*); Eby, *Strother,* 270. Hunter delayed one day in Lexington for the arrival of two hundred supply wagons. OR (ser. 1) 37(1): 97.

10. OR (ser. 1) 37(1): 507, 512, 527, 532; Michael Auer, CMSR-NA.

11. Scott, *Life,* 217–18; Alexander, *Mosby's Men,* 62; OR (ser. 1) 37(1): 3, 527, 532.

12. OR (ser. 1) 37(1): 527, 532.

13. Auer, CMSR-NA; newspaper clipping, vol. 6, JSMSB-UVA.

14. OR (ser. 1) 37 (1): 528.

15. Ibid., 3, 161, 557; Wildes, *116th Ohio,* 91; Eby, *Strother,* 241; Henry A. DuPont, *The Campaign of 1864 in the Valley of Virginia and the Expedition to Lynchburg* (New York, 1925), 51.

16. OR (ser. 1) 37(1): 606.

17. Ibid., 645, 649–52; Grant's report, July 22, 1865, quoted in B&L, 4: 151.

18. Gary W. Gallagher, "The Shenandoah Valley in 1864," in *Struggle for the Shenandoah: Essays on the 1864 Valley Campaign,* ed. Gary W. Gallagher (Kent, Ohio, 1991), 9; OR (ser. 1) 37(1): 103; 37(2): 367.

19. OR (ser. 1) 37(1): 655, 667, 674–75.

20. Ibid., 674–75, 686, 694–95.

21. Keen and Mewborn, *43rd Battalion,* 364; Marshall McCormick to Claude A. Swanson, Jan. 25, 1910, John S. Russell Papers, DU.

22. Williamson, *Rangers,* 178; *New York Herald,* July 17, 1864.

23. OR (ser. 1) 37(1): 3, 692–93; Scott, *Life,* 236; Williamson, *Rangers,* 182; John L. Wilson, Report of the Master of the Road, 38th Baltimore and Ohio Railroad Annual Report, 56, Maryland Historical Society, Baltimore (hereafter Wilson, 38th B&O Report).

24. Keen and Mewborn, *43rd Battalion,* 137–38; OR (ser. 1) 37(1): 693; 37(2): 383. For a description of White's Point of Rocks raid, see Divine, *35th Battalion,* 30. The railroad tunnel now at Point of Rocks was built after the war.

25. Scott, *Life,* 239; *Baltimore American,* July 7, 1864.

26. *Baltimore American,* July 7, 1864; Keen and Mewborn, *43rd Battalion,* 139–40; OR (ser. 1) 37(2): 64; Wilson, 38th B&O Report, 57.

27. OR (ser. 1) 37(1): 36, 185; 37(2): 24, 36, 54–55; Hearn, *Harpers Ferry,* 246; *Baltimore American,* July 7, 1864.

28. *Washington Star,* July 5, 6, 1864.

29. OR (ser. 1) 37(2): 22–23, 38–39, 43, 55, 59, 81.

30. OR (ser. 1) 37(2): 59; Frank E. Vandiver, *Jubal's Raid: General Early's Famous Attack on Washington in 1864* (New York, 1960), 142–44.

31. Wilson, 38th B&O Report, 57; Scott, *Life,* 242. Mosby reported, "The magnitude of the invasion was greatly exaggerated by the fears of the enemy, and panic and alarm spread through their territory." OR (ser. 1) 37(1): 4.

32. OR (ser. 1) 37(1): 358–59; newspaper clipping, vol. 2, JSMSB-UVA; Allen Johnson and Dumas Malone, eds., *Dictionary of American Biography* (hereafter DAB), 22 vols. (New York, 1928–1944), 3: 507–9; Benjamin W. Crowninshield, *A History of the First Regiment of Massachusetts Cavalry Volunteers* (Boston, 1891), 325.

33. OR (ser. 1) 37(1): 358–59; Humphreys, *Field,* 94, 96.

34. Scott, *Life,* 247; Alexander, *Mosby's Men,* 92.

35. Humphreys, *Field,* 96; Alexander, *Mosby's Men,* 92–93; OR (ser. 1) 37(1): 359.

36. Humphreys, *Field,* 96–97; Lanza, *Napoleon,* 25.

37. Humphreys, *Field,* 98, 104; Williamson, *Rangers,* 188.

38. Keen and Mewborn, *43rd Battalion,* 145; OR (ser. 1) 37(1): 358–60; Alexander, *Mosby's Men,* 19.

39. JSM to Frederick F. Bowen, July 25, 1898, Frederick F. Bowen Papers, VHS; JSM to William B. Palmer, May 9, 1906, Albert G. Nalle Papers, VHS.

40. Charles C. Osborne, *Jubal: The Life and Times of General Jubal A. Early, CSA, Defender of the Lost Cause* (Baton Rouge, 1992), 4–52, 223; Boatner, *Dictionary,* 254–55; Warner, *Generals in Gray,* 79–80; JSM to Palmer, May 9, 1906; JSM to AM, June 5, 1890, JSMC-MC.

41. Scott, *Life,* 491–92; JSM to Frederick F. Bowen, June 12, (no year), Frederick F. Bowen Papers, VHS; Jubal A. Early, *A Memoir of the Last Year of the War for Independence in the Confederate States of America* (Lynchburg, 1867), 58; Jubal A. Early, *Lieutenant General Jubal Anderson Early, C.S.A.* (Philadelphia, 1912),

391. Beattie informed Mosby years later that Early was intoxicated at the meeting. JSM to Bowen, June 12, (no year).

42. JSM to Frederick F. Bowen, June 12, (no year), July 25, 1898, Frederick F. Bowen Papers, VHS.

43. JSM to Frederick F. Bowen, April 29, 1895, June 15, (no year), Frederick F. Bowen Papers, VHS.

44. Scott, *Life,* 492.

45. Scott, *Life,* 251; Williamson, *Rangers,* 189–91; OR (ser. 1) 37(1): 4–5; *Washington Star,* July 15, 1864; *Philadelphia Inquirer* report in *New York Times,* July 17, 1864.

46. JSM to Frederick F. Bowen, June 12, (no year), Frederick F. Bowen Papers, VHS; Williamson, *Rangers,* 192; OR (ser. 1) 37(2): 597–98.

47. Early, *Memoir,* 58; Jubal A. Early to JSM, April 21, 1867, JSMP-LC; JSM to Jubal A. Early, July 15, 1867, Early Family Papers, VHS; Scott, *Life,* 492; Osborne, *Early,* 284–86.

48. Scott, *Life,* 251; JSM to Bowen, July 25, 1898.

49. OR (ser. 1) 37(1): 4–5; 37(2): 512, 524; Williamson, *Rangers,* 197–202.

## 12. The Night Belonged to Mosby

1. Laqueur, *Guerrilla Reader,* 35; Che Guevera, *On Guerrilla War,* 6th ed. (New York, 1970), 11; Mao Tse Tung, *Mao Tse-Tung on Guerrilla Warfare,* trans. Samuel B. Griffith II (Garden City, N.Y., 1978), 20, 49–50.

2. Mao Tse Tung, in introduction to *Warfare,* 6–7.

3. Louis N. Boudrye, *Historic Records of the Fifth New York Cavalry, First Ira Harris Guard* (Albany, N.Y., 1865), 57; *Baltimore American,* July 11, 1864; Hoadley, *Gansevoort,* 149, 163.

4. Russ McClelland, "'We Were Enemies': Pennsylvanians and Virginia Guerrillas," *Civil War Times Illustrated,* Dec. 1983, 40.

5. Eugene A. Nash, *A History of the Forty-fourth Regiment, New York Infantry in the Civil War, 1861–1865* (Chicago, 1911), 179–80; William O. Lee, *Personal and Historical Sketches of the Seventh Regiment, Michigan Volunteer Cavalry* (Detroit, 1901), 138–41.

6. Samuel C. Farrar, *The Twenty-Second Pennsylvania Cavalry and the Ringgold Battalion, 1861–1865* (Pittsburg, 1911), 177–78, 284.

7. Scott, *Life,* 82; Boudrye, *Fifth New York,* 54; OR (ser. 1) 25(2): 257.

8. Mosby, *Reminiscences,* 121–22; Scott, *Life,* 80; William H. Martin to wife, April 30, 1863, typed copy, William H. Martin Papers, HCWRT-USAMHI.

9. Mosby, *Reminiscences,* 123–26; Scott, *Life,* 80–83; Boudrye, *Fifth New York,* 54; Martin to wife, April 30, 1863.

10. Scott, *Life,* 83; Cochran Recollections, April 1863.

11. OR (ser. 1) 33: 259–60; 51(1): 220–21.

12. Emily G. Ramey and John K. Gott, *The Years of Anguish: Fauquier County, Virginia, 1861–1865* (1965; reprint, Warrenton, 1987), 164–65; Newcomer, *Cole's*

*Cavalry,* 90–91; *Baltimore American,* Jan. 6, 11, 1864; Williamson, *Rangers,* 118; Hearn, *Harpers Ferry,* 232; OR (ser. 1) 33: 9.

13. Garner, *Melville,* 310. Gansevoort was absent in Washington and did not participate in the raid. Ibid., 306–10.

14. Emerson, *Lowell,* 296; Garner, *Melville,* 310–13.

15. Garner, *Melville,* 313–15; Humphreys, *Field,* 25–29.

16. OR (ser. 1) 33: 306; Humphreys, *Field,* 29–30.

17. OR (ser. 1) 33: 306; Humphreys, *Field,* 31–33.

18. OR (ser. 1) 33: 315–16.

19. Harold Holzer and Mark E. Neely Jr., *Mine Eyes Have Seen the Glory: The Civil War in Art* (New York, 1993), 163; Warren, *Poems,* 33; Garner, *Melville,* 319; Edward W. Goggin, "Confusion and Resolution in 'The Scout Toward Aldie,'" *Melville Society Extracts,* March 1993, 5, 8.

20. Warren, *Poems,* 153. In "The Armies of the Wilderness," Melville wrote, "And foxes peer within the gloom, / Till scared perchance by Mosby's prowling men, / Who ride in the rear of doom." Ibid., 132–33.

21. Ibid., 174, 382.

22. Ibid., 161.

23. Ibid., 175.

24. Ibid., 159, 167, 176, 179.

25. Ibid., 152–79.

26. Scott, *Life,* 212; Thomas W. Smith, *The Story of a Cavalry Regiment: "Scott's 900," Eleventh New York Cavalry* (Chicago, 1897), 264–65.

27. Marvin Wright to Amelia, March 29, 1863, LLC-USAMHI; Aaron E. Bachman Memoir, typed copy, HCWRT-USAMHI; Journal of John C. White, Dec. 4, 1863, Library of Congress.

28. Russell, *Memoirs,* 329; Benjamin F. Ashenfelter to Churchman Ashenfelter, March 1, 1863, Benjamin F. Ashenfelter Papers, HCWRT-USAMHI; Lee, *Seventh Regiment,* 105–6; Regimental History Committee, *History of the Third Pennsylvania Cavalry* (Philadelphia, 1905), 330; OR (ser. 1) 25(2): 149–50.

29. Frederic Denison, *Sabres and Spurs: The First Regiment Rhode Island Cavalry in the Civil War, 1861–1865* (Central Falls, R.I., 1876), 327–28; J. Michael Welton, ed., *"My Heart Is So Rebellious": The Caldwell Letters, 1861–1865* (Warrenton, no date), 188.

30. Bachman Memoir; Theodore Garrish, *Army Life: A Private's Reminiscences of the Civil War* (Portland, Maine, 1882), 154.

31. OR (ser. 1) 37(2): 83; newspaper clipping, vol. 3, JSMSB-UVA.

32. OR (ser. 1) 25(1): 1107–8; 25(2): 472–73, 482; *Washington Star,* May 13–16, 1863; *Baltimore American,* May 16, 1863; *New York Times,* May 14, 1863.

33. OR (ser. 1) 37(2): 103; Mosby, *Reminiscences,* 154; *Report of the Joint Committee on the Conduct of the War* (Washington, 1865) 1: 162–63.

34. Stephen E. Ambrose, *Halleck: Lincoln's Chief of Staff* (Baton Rouge, 1996), 6, 9–10, 14, 16; Warner, *Generals in Blue,* 195–97.

35. OR (ser. 1) 37(2): 456–57, 474.

36. OR (ser. 1) 37(2): 480, 497, 502, 504, 529; Abner Hard, *History of the Eighth Cavalry Regiment Illinois Volunteers, During the Great Rebellion* (1868; reprint, Dayton, Ohio, 1984), 307.

37. OR (ser. 1) 37(2): 499, 501, 504, 506.

38. OR (ser. 1) 37(2): 492, 502–5; telegram, Stanton to John W. Garrett, July 30, 1864, Letters to President Garrett, B&O-MHS.

39. Williamson, *Rangers,* 197; Scott, *Life,* 293–94; Divine, *35th Battalion,* 54.

40. Williamson, *Rangers,* 202; *Washington Star,* Aug. 2, 1864; *New York Times,* Aug. 3, 1864.

41. OR (ser. 1) 37(2): 560–63, 573, 576; *Washington Star,* Aug. 2, 1864; *New York Herald,* Aug. 3, 1864; *New York Times,* Aug. 3, 8, 1864; *Baltimore American,* Aug. 3, 1864.

42. OR (ser. 1) 43(2): 314–15.

43. Ibid., 322–27, 333, 343, 353.

44. *New York Herald,* Oct. 15, 1864; John H. Brinton, *Personal Memoirs of John H. Brinton: Civil War Surgeon, 1861–1865* (Carbondale, 1996), 294–95.

45. Kevin H. Siepel, *Rebel: The Life and Times of John Singleton Mosby* (New York, 1983), 160–161; Marguerite Merington, ed., *The Custer Story: The Life and Intimate Letters of General George A. Custer and His Wife Elizabeth* (Lincoln, Neb., 1950), 90, 119.

## 13. Blue Hen's Chickens and Custer's Wolverines

1. James R. Bowen, *Regimental History of the First New York Dragoons* (no place, 1900), 136; Paul A. Hutton, "Introduction," in Philip Sheridan, *Civil War Memoirs* (New York, 1991), xviii; James E. Taylor, *The James E. Taylor Sketchbook* (Dayton, Ohio, 1989), 41; OR (ser. 1) 43(2): 684.

2. Roy Morris Jr., *Sheridan: The Life and Wars of General Phil Sheridan* (New York, 1992), 46–49; Williams, *Hayes,* 2: 500.

3. OR (ser. 1) 37(1): 475; 37(2): 558.

4. Ibid., 43(1): 709–10; 727–29, 918–19.

5. Ibid., 744, 762.

6. Ibid., 18, 760.

7. Ibid., 18, 624; Jeffry D. Wert, *From Winchester to Cedar Creek: The Shenandoah Campaign of 1864* (Carlisle, 1987), 31.

8. OR (ser. 1) 37(2): 217; 43(1): 628, 772; Wagner, *Tactics,* 447.

9. OR (ser. 1) 43(1): 776.

10. Ibid., 18–19.

11. Ibid., 623–25, 630.

12. Ibid., 621–22, 624, 631–32.

13. Ibid., 484–85, 621, 623; 37(2): 217; Warner, *Generals in Blue,* 261–62; Boatner, *Dictionary,* 453–54.

14. OR (ser. 1) 43(1): 623–24.

15. Ibid., 622, 624–25.

16. Ibid., 628; Wagner, *Tactics*, 447.

17. OR (ser. 1) 43(1): 625, 629.

18. Ibid., 621, 626, 629.

19. Russell, *Memoirs*, 290; Munson, *Reminiscences*, 102–4.

20. Williamson, *Mosby's Rangers*, 1909 ed., 207, 209; OR (ser. 1) 43(1): 484, 621, 623, 627, 630–31, 634, 842; newspaper clipping, vol. 6, JSMSB-UVA; Denison, *Rhode Island Cavalry*, 376; Richards, "Partizan Rangers," 112. The Cavalry Reserve Brigade lost thirty-two wagons and the 6th New York Cavalry eight or ten. OR (ser. 1) 43(1): 484, 621, 630–31.

21. OR (ser. 1) 43(1): 77–78, 785–87, 802; 43(2): 390.

22. Ibid., 43(1): 783, 842; *New York Times*, Aug. 21, 1864; William G. Hill Diary, Aug. 14, 1864, Library of Congress.

23. *Baltimore American*, Aug. 19, 23, 1864; *New York Times*, Aug. 19, 21, 22, 1864; William H. Beach, *The First New York (Lincoln) Cavalry* (New York, 1902), 413–14.

24. OR (ser. 1) 43(1): 619–32, 842.

25. Ibid., 620.

26. Ibid., 698, 811; Mark E. Neely Jr., *The Fate of Liberty: Abraham Lincoln and Civil Liberties* (New York, 1991), 78–79. In August, during the retrograde movement, Sheridan's cavalry burned food, forage, livestock, and outbuildings from Cedar Creek to south of Winchester; in late September and early October, they burned along the upper Valley. OR (ser. 1) 43(1): 440, 442–43, 822. See Mark Grimsley, *The Hard Hand of War: Union Military Policy toward Southern Civilians, 1861–1865* (Cambridge, 1995) for analysis of the origin and development of Grant's "hard war" policy against the Southern economy and Southern civilians.

27. OR (ser. 1) 43(1): 822, 841, 880.

28. Mosby, "Communication from Colonel John S. Mosby," SHSP 27 (1899): 267, 269, 274; Russell, *Memoirs*, 368–69.

29. OR (ser. 1) 43(1): 634; Williamson, *Rangers*, 213; William Chapman, "Col. Chapman's Account of the Killing of the Picket, . . . and Events Following," in Williamson, *Mosby's Rangers*, 1909 ed., 449.

30. John W. Athearn, "The Civil War Diary of John Wilson Phillips," *Virginia Magazine of History and Biography* 62 (Jan. 1954): 117; Chapman, "Account," 451; Keen and Mewborn, *43rd Battalion*, 162.

31. Chapman, "Account," 450–51; Scott, *Life*, 281.

32. Chapman, "Account," 451; Mosby, "Communication," 275; OR (ser. 1) 43(1): 634; *New York Times*, Aug. 25, 1864.

33. OR (ser. 1) 43(1): 843–44, 860, 845, 848. The 8th Illinois Cavalry had arrested more than ninety Loudoun County males by August 31, 1864. OR (ser. 1) 43(1): 898; 43(2): 4.

34. OR (ser. 1) 43(2): 50; *Baltimore American*, Sept. 6, 8, 1864; Williamson, *Rangers*, 223–30.

35. Williamson, *Rangers*, 232; OR (ser. 1) 43(1): 616–17.

36. *OR* (ser. 1) 43(1): 617; Hoadley, *Gansevoort*, 183–84. Smith did not know it was Mosby until later; then Gansevoort promoted him to sergeant. Hoadley, *Gansevoort*, 184.

37. Mosby, *Reminiscences*, 81; Munson, *Reminiscences*, 238–39. During his recovery, Mosby posed for a photograph in Richmond.

38. Munson, *Reminiscences*, 239. Mosby left William Chapman in command. Russell, *Memoirs*, 298.

39. *OR* (ser. 1) 43(1): 865; Wesley Merritt, "Sheridan in the Shenandoah Valley," *B&L*, 4: 512–13; George H. Miller Diary, Aug. 19, 1864, CWMC-USAMHI; JSM, handwritten memo, "Oct. 31, 1864," JBP-VHS.

40. *New York Times*, Aug. 25, 31, 1864.

41. Theodore W. Bean, "Annals of War," in Moyer, *Seventeenth Regiment*, 218.

42. *OR* (ser. 1) 43(1): 428; Wert, *Creek*, 112, 129–32.

43. A.D. Slade, *A.T.A. Torbert: Southern Gentleman in Union Blue* (Dayton, Ohio, 1992), 15, 17, 26, 29; Warner, *Generals in Blue*, 508–9; *OR* (ser. 1) 43(1): 428, 441, 490.

44. Williamson, *Rangers*, 239–40; Keen and Mewborn, *43rd Battalion*, 175–76; Scott, *Life*, 319; *OR* (ser. 1) 43(1): 441; Moses Harris, "With the Reserve Brigade," *Journal of the United States Cavalry Association* 3 (Sept. 1890): 238; Roberta E. Fagan, "Custer at Front Royal: 'A Horror of the War'?" in Gregory J.W. Urwin, *Custer and His Times: Book Three* (Conway, Ark., 1987), 28, 44, 67–68. Fagan's well-researched, extremely valuable study emphasizes eyewitness accounts.

45. Fagan, "Custer," 28, 40–48; Keen and Mewborn, *43rd Battalion*, 176–78; Evans and Moyer, *Mosby's Confederacy*, 54–56; Bean, "Annals," 217–18; Williamson, *Mosby's Rangers*, 1909 ed., 502.

46. Evans and Moyer, *Mosby's Confederacy*, 55; Williamson, *Mosby's Rangers*, 1909 ed., 241; Laura V. Hale, *Four Valiant Years in the Lower Shenandoah Valley: 1861–1865* (Front Royal, 1986), 431, 433; *SHSP*, 24 (1896): 109; Bean, "Annals," 217.

47. Moyer, *Seventeenth Regiment*, 165; Lee, *Seventh Regiment*, 258; Harris, "Reserve Brigade," 238; Aldophus E. Richards, "Address for Monument Dedication," Sept. 23, 1899, *SHSP*, 27 (1899): 254; Bean, "Annals," 217; Charles H. Veil, typed memoir, CWMC-USAMHI; Thomas L. Rosser to A.E. Richards, Nov. 23, 1899, in Richards, "Major Richards Cites Authorities for His Conclusions," *SHSP*, 27 (1899): 283.

## 14. The Lottery

1. Mosby, *Reminiscences*, 81; Mitchell, *Letters*, 98.

2. Angus J. Johnston, II, *Virginia Railroads in the Civil War* (Chapel Hill, 1961), 4–5, 31, 38–40, 43, 50–54, 106–9, 171–73.

3. Russell, *Memoirs*, 328; JSM to AM, Jan. 30, Feb. 19, 1899, JSMC-MC; *OR* (ser. 1) 43(2): 249.

4. *OR* (ser. 1) 43(2): 196, 249.

5. Ibid., 210, 249, 257–58, 265–66.

6. Ibid., 268, 276, 290.

7. Williamson, *Rangers,* 250–51; Russell, *Memoirs,* 308; Scott, *Life,* 324.

8. OR (ser. 1) 43(2): 299, 301; Williamson, *Rangers,* 253; Plum, *Military Telegraph,* 2: 272–73.

9. OR (ser. 1) 43(2): 300, 310–12, 319, 334; Williamson, *Rangers,* 255.

10. Williamson, *Rangers,* 257; Plum, *Military Telegraph,* 2: 273; OR (ser. 1) 43(2): 335; (ser. 3) 5: 68; *New York Herald,* Oct. 11, 1864.

11. Newspaper clipping, vol. 1, JSMSB-UVA; OR (ser. 1) 43(2): 334–35, 388–89, 405; *Baltimore American,* Oct. 19, 1864; *New York Herald,* Oct. 18, 1864; *Washington Star,* Aug. 4, 1863; Williamson, *Rangers,* 267, 275.

12. OR (ser. 1) 43(2): 348, 415; *Washington Star,* Oct. 19, 1864.

13. OR (ser. 1) 43(2): 333–34, 340.

14. Russell, *Memoirs,* 328; newspaper clipping, vol. 1, JSMSB-UVA; OR (ser. 1) 43(2): 334.

15. Ibid., 356, 465.

16. Morris, *Sheridan,* 226. See Dennis E. Frye, "'I Resolved to Play a Bold Game': John S. Mosby as a Factor in the 1864 Valley Campaign," in Gallagher, *Shenandoah,* 107–26.

17. OR (ser. 1) 43(1): 109, 110, 125, 127, 187, 368–69; 43(2): 69, 131, 419, 427; Moyer, *Seventeenth Regiment,* 347–48.

18. OR (ser. 1) 43(1): 640; 43(2): 175, 207, 212–13, 373, 390.

19. Scott, *Life,* 334–39; John H. White, "The Greenback Raid," *Railroad History* 146 (1982): 41–46; Russell, *Memoirs,* 321; Munson, *Reminiscences,* 223; Jones, *Gray Ghosts,* 216–18; OR (ser. 1) 43(1): 633.

20. OR (ser. 1) 43(2): 63–4, 132, 373, 381, 385, 387–88; Williamson, *Rangers,* 264–65.

21. *Baltimore American,* Oct. 19, 1864; *Washington Star,* Oct. 14, 15, 1864; *New York Herald,* Oct. 19, 1864; OR (ser. 1) 43(2): 385.

22. *Richmond Whig,* Oct. 18, 1864, quoted in *New York Herald,* Oct. 21, 1864; *New York Times,* Nov. 11, 1864; *New York Herald,* Oct. 17, 1864; *Baltimore American,* Oct. 21, 1864.

23. Keen and Mewborn, *43rd Battalion,* 200; OR (ser. 1) 43(1): 618–19.

24. George B. Sanford, *Fighting Rebels and Redskins: Experiences in Army Life of Colonel George B. Sanford, 1861–1899,* ed. E.R. Hagemann (Norman, Oklahoma, 1969), 301–3; Morris, *Sheridan,* 207–8; *New York Herald,* Oct. 29, 1864.

25. Morris, *Sheridan,* 186; OR (ser. 1) 43(2): 308; Wildes, *116th Ohio,* 190–92; Sheridan, *Memoirs,* 261–62.

26. OR (ser. 1) 43(2): 330, 336, 354, 492; *New York Herald,* Oct. 9, 1864; J. Willard Brown, *The Signal Corps, U.S.A. in the War of the Rebellion* (1963; reprint, New York, 1974), 634–36; *Baltimore American,* Oct. 15, 1864; Sheridan, *Memoirs,* 271; Moyer, *Seventeenth Regiment,* 115; Autobiography of Augustus P. Green, New York Historical Society Library.

27. *OR* (ser. 1) 43(2): 351; Keen and Mewborn, *43rd Battalion,* 191; *New York Herald,* Oct. 13, 1864; *Baltimore American,* Oct. 17, 1864; newspaper clipping, vol. 3, JSMSB-UVA.

28. *New York Tribune* dispatch in *Baltimore American,* Oct. 15, 1864; *New York Herald,* Oct. 13, 1864; *OR* (ser. 1) 43(2): 339–40; Alexander Neil to Friends, Oct. 13, 1864, Alexander Neil Letters, UVA.

29. *OR* (ser. 1) 43(1): 509; Keen and Mewborn, *43rd Battalion,* 200–201.

30. *OR* (ser. 1) 43(2): 414–15; Keen and Mewborn, *43rd Battalion,* 202; Cochran Recollections, Oct. 1864.

31. *OR* (ser. 1) 43(1): 186; 43(2): 355, 466, 475; Scott, *Life,* 350; *Baltimore American,* Nov. 1, 1864; *Richmond Sentinel,* Oct. 29, 1864, quoted in *Baltimore American,* Nov. 2, 1864.

32. *SHSP* 27 (1899): 270; *OR* (ser. 1) 43(2): 909–10.

33. Keen and Mewborn, *43rd Battalion,* 209; Charles Brewster, "Captured by Mosby's Guerrillas," *War Papers and Personal Reminiscences, 1861–1865, Military Order of the Loyal Legion of the United States,* Missouri (St. Louis, 1892), 1: 87–88.

34. Brewster, "Captured," 81–82, 88–92; Williamson, *Rangers,* 291; Alexander, *Mosby's Men,* 144, 146.

35. Brewster, "Captured," 92–93; Munson, *Reminiscences,* 150.

36. Fagan, "Custer," 35–36, 72; Brewster, "Captured," 103–4; Charles E. Marvin account, in Williamson, *Rangers,* 455–57; James Bennett, CMSR-NA.

37. Marvin account, 457; Bennett, CMSR-NA.

38. JSM to Landon Mason, March 29, 1912, JSMP-DU; *OR* (ser. 1) 43(2): 566; *New York Times,* Nov. 10, 12, 1864.

39. *SHSP* 27 (1899): 318; *OR* (ser. 1) 43(2): 602; Scott, *Life,* 360–61.

## 15. Sheridan's Mosby Hunt

1. Michael Fellman, *Inside War: The Guerrilla Conflict in Missouri during the American Civil War* (New York, 1989), 95–96; Grimsley, *Hard Hand,* 111–19.

2. *OR* (ser. 1) 29(1): 90; *New York Herald,* Jan. 8, 1865.

3. James M. McPherson, *Battle Cry of Freedom: The Civil War Era* (New York, 1988), 501. See Grimsley, *Hard Hand,* 38-39 for discussion of Pope's earlier use of such measures in Missouri.

4. *OR* (ser. 1) 27(3): 786–87; Herman Haupt, *Reminiscences of General Herman Haupt* (1901; reprint, New York, 1981), 250–51; Emerson, *Lowell,* 311–13.

5. *OR* (ser. 1) 29(2): 467–68; 33: 364–65.

6. Beach, *First New York,* 222–23; Stevenson, *"Boots and Saddles,"* 166–69; *OR* (ser. 1) 43(1): 818.

7. *OR* (ser. 1) 27(1): 642–43; 27(3): 289; Mosby, *Stuart's Cavalry,* 174–75.

8. *OR* (ser. 1) 27(1): 641–42; 27(3): 255; Scott, *Life,* 103–4; Mosby, *Reminiscences,* 169–70; Mosby, *Stuart's Cavalry,* 72–73.

9. *OR* (ser. 1) 27(3): 64–66, 74, 95.

10. *OR* (ser. 1) 29(1): 104; Laqueur, *Guerrilla Reader,* 43; Newhall, *Memoir,* 115–16.

11. *OR* (ser. 1) 29(1): 994–95; 29(2): 588–89.

12. Williamson, *Rangers,* 231, 308.

13. *OR* (ser. 1) 29(1): 73; 29(2): 24.

14. Neely, *Liberty,* 99–103; Welton, *Caldwell Letters,* 248; Cochran Recollections, Oct. 19, 1864; *OR* (ser. 1) 27(3): 72; Mosby, *Reminiscences,* 158.

15. Michael J. Walsh with Greg Walker, *SEAL!* (New York, 1994), 7; Emerson, *Lowell,* 294.

16. *OR* (ser. 1) 27(2): 992–94; 27(3): 805.

17. Ibid., 29(1): 658; Keen and Mewborn, *43rd Battalion,* 297; newspaper clipping, vol. 6, JSMSB-UVA.

18. Henry S. Gansevoort, CMSR-NA.

19. *OR* (ser. 1) 33: 568.

20. Williamson, *Rangers,* 136; *OR* (ser. 1) 33: 571; Regimental History Committee, *Third Pennsylvania,* 402.

21. Ibid., 399–405; Longacre, *First New Jersey,* 184–85; *OR* (ser. 1) 33: 155–56; 620.

22. *OR* (ser. 1) 33: 155–56, 570, 620.

23. Sheridan, *Memoirs,* 286; *OR* (ser. 1) 43(1): 860.

24. Richard Blazer, CMSR-NA; newspaper clipping, vol. 6, JSMSB-UVA; Michael J. Martin, "A Match for Mosby?" *America's Civil War* (July 1994): 28.

25. Newspaper clipping, vol. 6, JSMSB-UVA; John N. Opie, *A Rebel Cavalryman with Lee, Stuart and Jackson* (1899; reprint, Dayton, Ohio, 1972), 276.

26. Scott, *Life,* 289–90; *OR* (ser. 1) 43(1): 23, 615–16; Williamson, *Rangers,* 226–28, 302; Martin, "Match," 28–29.

27. Keen and Mewborn, *43rd Battalion,* 215–16; Williamson, *Rangers,* 299–300; *OR* (ser. 1) 43(2): 654; newspaper clipping, vol. 6, JSMSB-UVA.

28. Williamson, *Rangers,* 302; newspaper clipping, vol. 6, JSMSB-UVA; Munson, *Reminiscences,* 118.

29. Williamson, *Mosby's Rangers,* 1909 ed., 496; Williamson, *Rangers,* 302–3.

30. Alexander, *Mosby's Men,* 122.

31. Ibid., 123–24; Williamson, *Rangers,* 304–6.

32. Williamson, *Rangers,* 305; Scott, *Life,* 368–69, 371; *OR* (ser. 1) 43(2): 654.

33. Blazer, CMSR-NA; *OR* (ser. 1) 43(2): 654; Williamson, *Mosby's Rangers,* 1909 ed., 496. Blazer returned to Gallipolis, Ohio, after the war, and he and his wife had six children. He served four years as sheriff of Gallia County, but his ailment left him unwell. He died October 29, 1878, at about forty-eight years of age; rumor claimed that yellow fever took his life. However, the symptoms reported by physicians in his pension records indicate that his death was probably from kidney disease. Blazer, CMSR-NA; Harris D. Riley Jr. to author, Oct. 29, 1994.

### 16. Sheridan's Burning Raid

1. *OR* (ser. 1) 43(1): 671–72; Frobel, *Diary,* 246; Drickamer and Drickamer, *Moulton,* 218.

2. Broun, *Family Events,* 74; *OR* (ser. 1) 43(2): 672; Edmonds Diary, Nov. 28, 1864.

3. *OR* (ser. 1) 43(1): 811; 43(2): 679–80.

4. Committee on Regimental History, *History of the Sixth New York Cavalry (Second Ira Harris Guard)* (Worcester, Mass., 1908), 243, 391–93; Treasury Department, Records of the Southern Claims Commission, RG 217, Box 378, Loudoun County, Claim of John F. Waters, NA; *Baltimore American,* Dec. 16, 1864.

5. Samuel M. Janney, *Memoirs of Samuel M. Janney* (Philadelphia, 1881), 230–31.

6. Committee, *Sixth New York,* 391–92.

7. *Baltimore American,* Dec. 16, 28, 1864. Beginning about six weeks later the Quakers petitioned Congress for redress, and in 1871, when the Southern Claims Commission was created to reimburse Southern Unionists for property taken for use by the Union army, many filed claims. It was an involved process, and they built up hope, but the Claims Commission denied their claims because the army had turned most of their livestock over to treasury agents who sold them at public auction in York, Pennsylvania; the army had not used the animals nor the burned buildings or crops. Then the Quakers and other Unionists petitioned Congress for two special bills, one for the livestock and the other for the burned property. The livestock bill provided reimbursement of $61,821.13 to the loyal Loudoun County citizens who had filed claims. The House Committee of Claims recommended the bill based on a Treasury Department report that during the five-month period when the animals were sold the government received $84,865.65 in sales of captured animals. Concluding that the payments would be simply returning the funds from the treasury to the former owners of the animals, Congress passed the bill on January 23, 1873, and the payments were made. However, Congress agreed with the Southern Claims Commission that the claims for $199,220.24 in burned property fell under losses sustained by the fortunes of war and could not be reimbursed. *Congressional Globe,* 42d Cong., 2d sess., April 8, 1872, 2260; 3rd sess., Jan. 17, 1873, 680–81, appendix, 314–16; Charles P. Poland Jr., *From Frontier to Suburbia* (Marceline, Mo., 1976), 225. See Frank W. Klingberg, *The Southern Claims Commission* (Berkeley, 1955) on the history of Southern claims.

8. *OR* (ser. 1) 43(2): 730.

9. Treasury Department, *Commercial Intercourse with and in States Declared in Insurrection* (Washington, 1863), 9–30; Treasury Department, Records of the Civil War Official Agencies of the Treasury Department, Records of the Seventh Special Agency, RG 366, NA.

10. *OR* (ser. 1) 43(2): 680–81, 731, 733, 741, 764, 771.

11. Ibid., 43(2): 679; 43(1): 672.

12. Ibid., 43(2): 64, 679, 688–89.

13. Ibid., 688–89, 698, 709, 712, 731; Scott, *Life*, 374.

14. JSM to JB, Nov. 25, 1903, JBP-VHS.

15. *OR* (ser. 1) 43(2): 937; Williamson, *Rangers*, 339–40; Scott, *Life*, 397–98.

16. *OR* (ser. 1) 43(2): 806.

17. Ibid., 806–7; Russell, *Memoirs*, 335.

18. Keen and Mewborn, *43rd Battalion*, 340; newspaper clipping, vol. 1, JSMSB-UVA; Scott, *Life*, 387. Mosby wore a scarlet-lined cape and black plumed hat and rode a gray horse while hovering Cole's Cavalry on February 20, 1864. Scott, *Life*, 199.

19. Russell, *Memoirs*, 335–36.

20. Keen and Mewborn, *43rd Battalion*, 237, 339, 342, 368; newspaper clipping, vol. 1, JSMSB-UVA.

21. Russell, *Memoirs*, 337–38; newspaper clippings, vol. 1, 3, 6, JSMSB- UVA; *OR* (ser. 1) 43(2): 843.

22. Russell, *Memoirs*, 338–39; newspaper clipping, vol. 3, JSMSB-UVA; *Cincinnati Enquirer*, May 31, 1916.

23. *OR* (ser. 1) 43(2): 843; Russell, *Memoirs*, 341.

24. Harris D. Riley Jr. to author, Oct. 29, 1994.

25. Evans and Moyer, *Mosby's Confederacy*, 114; Russell, *Memoirs*, 344–45; Riley to author, Oct. 29, 1994.

26. Newspaper clipping, vol. 1, JSMSB-UVA; Russell, *Memoirs*, 345–46, 354; *OR* (ser. 1) 43(2): 832–33, 840, 844; Scott, *Life*, 390.

27. *Richmond Dispatch*, Dec. 27, 1864, quoted in *Baltimore American*, Dec. 31, 1864; *New York Herald*, Dec. 28, 29, 30, 1864; *Baltimore American*, Dec. 28, 1864. Missouri guerrilla William Anderson was killed October 24, 1864.

28. *Baltimore American*, Dec. 30, 1864, Jan. 2, 1865; *New York Herald*, Dec. 31, 1864.

29. *Richmond Sentinel*, Jan. 7, 1865, quoted in *New York Herald*, Jan. 11, 1865; *Richmond Dispatch*, Jan. 4, 1865.

30. *Richmond Whig*, Jan. 10, 1865, quoted in *New York Herald*, Jan. 13, 1865; *Richmond Whig*, Jan. 28, 1865, quoted in *Washington Chronicle*, Feb. 1, 1865; Edmonds Diary, Dec. 22, 1864.

31. *OR* (ser. 1) 43(2): 838–40, 843–44.

32. Ibid., 843–44; Douglas Frazar, CMSR-NA

33. *OR* (ser. 1) 43(2): 791, 835, 840, 843–45; Committee, *Sixth New York*, 247–51; *OR* (ser. 1) 46(2): 385, 387, 412, 560, 702.

34. *OR* (ser. 1) 46(2): 49–50, 182–83, 188, 265; Scott, *Life*, 444; John L. Wilson, Report of the Master of the Road, 39th Baltimore and Ohio Railroad Annual Report, Maryland Historical Society; Jan. 18, 1865, 41; telegram, William Bryan to F. Perkins, Jan. 19, 1865, Letters to President Garrett, B&O-MHS.

35. *OR* (ser. 1) 46(1): 455; 46(2): 384, 387, 411–13, 455, 539.

36. *OR* (ser. 1) 46(1): 462–63.

37. Ibid., 463–64, 467; Scott, *Life*, 447.

38. Ibid., 46(1): 464.

39. Scott, *Life*, 448; Williamson, *Rangers,* 349.

40. *OR* (ser. 1) 46(1): 464–66; 46(2): 1245; Mitchell, *Letters,* 144.

41. *OR* (ser. 1) 46(2): 605, 608.

42. Ibid., 683, 702.

43. *OR* (ser. 1) 43(1): 55.

44. Sheridan, *Memoirs,* 222, 226, 236; Mosby, "Retaliation," *SHSP* 27 (1899): 315; newspaper clipping of John S. Mosby, UVA. Actually Early had thirteen to fourteen thousand and Sheridan about forty-eight thousand in the Valley at the time. Wert, *Creek,* 22, 26.

45. Hoadley, *Gansevoort,* 50; Boudrye, *Fifth New York,* 48; Garner, *Melville,* 7. Mark Grimsley concluded that Sheridan, Grant, and the Union high command in the last year of the war tempered their operations with deliberate restraint in recognition of political realities. He wrote that Sheridan's Valley Burn, similar in level of destruction to the Loudoun Burn, "was probably one of the more controlled acts of destruction during the war's final year." Grimsley, *Hard Hand,* 178.

## 17. Apache Ambuscades, Stockades, and Prisons

1. Glenn Tucker, *Hancock the Superb* (Dayton, Ohio, 1980), 263–66; Warner, *Generals in Blue,* 202–4.

2. *OR* (ser. 1) 46(2): 798, 822, 839.

3. Ibid., 46(1): 526, 535–36; 46(3): 94, 96, 108.

4. Ibid., 46(1): 535.

5. Ibid., 535–36; Keen and Mewborn, *43rd Battalion,* 252–53; Williamson, *Rangers,* 355–58.

6. *OR* (ser. 1) 46(1): 526, 536; Keen and Mewborn, *43rd Battalion,* 254; Williamson, *Rangers,* 358–60; Monteiro, *Reminiscences,* 155–56.

7. *OR* (ser. 1) 46(1): 526; 46(3): 329–30, 391, 540–42, 570–71.

8. George Baylor, *Bull Run to Bull Run: or, Four Years in the Army of Northern Virginia* (1900; reprint, Washington, D.C., 1983), 311–16; Briscoe Goodhart, *History of the Independent Loudoun Virginia Rangers* (1896; reprint, Gaithersburg, Md., no date), 195–96.

9. Williamson, *Rangers,* 366–71; *Washington Chronicle,* April 11, 1865; *OR* (ser. 1) 46(1): 1309–10; 46(3): 700–701, 715; Keen and Mewborn, *43rd Battalion,* 264–66; Baylor, *Bull Run,* 322–26, 328; handwritten note on back of Mosby's Farewell Address, Bryan Family Papers, VSA. Authors of two books have theorized that Baylor's mission was not to capture mules but to blow up the White House and kill Lincoln and his Cabinet. See Tidwell, Hall and Gaddy, *Come Retribution,* and William A. Tidwell, *April '65: Confederate Covert Action in the American Civil War* (Kent, Ohio, 1995), and see book review by James A. Ramage of *April '65* in *The Journal of Southern History* 62(1996): 595–96. The raid had the

characteristics of a normal Mosby expedition, and I found no evidence of any strategic purpose other than to capture mules.

10. Newspaper clippings, vol. 1, 6, JSMSB-UVA; *Alexandria Gazette* clipping, undated, JSMBF-FCPL.

11. OR (ser. 1) 27(3): 354, 380.

12. OR (ser. 1) 37(2): 388–89; 43(1): 902.

13. George W. Cullum, *Biographical Register of the Officers and Graduates of the U.S. Military Academy* (West Point, 1920), 636; OR (ser. 1) 37(2): 388–90.

14. Williamson, *Rangers,* 218; Williamson, *Mosby's Rangers,* 1909 ed., 218–20; OR (ser. 1) 43(1): 638, 900–901; 43(2): 5, 23.

15. OR (ser. 1) 43(1): 901, 910; 43(2): 5; *Washington Star,* Aug. 15, 1864.

16. OR (ser. 1) 37(2): 388, 511; 43(2): 403; Hoadley, *Gansevoort,* 165–66.

17. OR (ser. 1) 43(2): 645–46; Warner, *Generals in Blue,* 165–66; Boatner, *Dictionary,* 322. Gamble was brevetted brigadier general after the war, dating from December 14, 1864. Warner, *Generals in Blue,* 166.

18. OR (ser. 1) 43(2): 782; 46(1): 546–48, 551; 46(2): 882, 955.

19. OR (ser. 1) 46(1): 546–48, 551, 1307–9; 46(2): 821, 942–43, 955.

20. Neely, *Liberty,* 35, 42–44; OR (ser. 2) 6: 1–2.

21. Henry W. Halleck, *Halleck's International Law,* 2 vols. (London, 1878), 2: 6–9; Richard S. Hartigan, *Lieber's Code and the Law of War* (Chicago, 1983), 2, 6–7; Grimsley, *Hard Hand,* 148.

22. OR (ser. 3) 3: 148–64; Grimsley, *Hard Hand,* 145, 148–49.

23. Neely, *Liberty,* 42–43, 169–70.

24. James P. Trammell, CMSR-NA; Case MM 1271, RCM-NA; Halleck, *Law,* 2: 44.

25. Case MM 1271, RCM-NA.

26. Ibid.; Neely, *Liberty,* 41; William Winthrop, *Military Law and Precedents,* 2d ed. (Washington, 1920), 166.

27. Case MM 1271, RCM-NA.

28. Ibid.

29. Ibid. The court acquitted Trammell of the specific charge of stealing from the U.S. government.

30. Keen and Mewborn, *43rd Battalion,* 294; Case MM 1271, RCM; Case NN 1280, RCM-NA. Trammell's case file contains a copy of the printed orders for Barnes's case.

31. Case NN 1280, RCM-NA; Trammell, CMSR-NA; John H. Barnes, CMSR-NA.

32. OR (ser. 3) 3: 91; 4: 505. On April 6, 1864, Gen. William T. Sherman requested authority to quickly hang spies and guerrillas convicted by military commission, and Holt replied that commanders had no such authority. OR (ser. 2) 7: 18–20. This act fulfilled Sherman's request; hangings could begin.

33. Case NN 2163, RCM-NA. On March 10, 1866, Andrew Johnson, on Grant's request, remitted Harrover's sentence and accepted his surrender. Ibid. The trial record lists Colonel Dulaney's name as John F.D. Dulaney.

34. Charles F. Beavers, CMSR-NA; *New York Herald,* Aug. 27, 1864; *New York Times,* Aug. 28, 1864.

35. *OR* (ser. 1) 43(1): 910–11; (ser. 2) 7: 792–93.

36. Crowninshield, *Massachusetts Cavalry,* 325; *OR* (ser. 2) 7: 1113, 1190–91; 8: 87; JSM to Robert Ould, April 4, 1865, JSMP-LC; Keen and Mewborn, *43rd Battalion,* 346. On March 29, 1865, Mosby's private John W. McCue was captured, convicted of murder by a military commission, and sent to prison in Clinton, New York. On November 8, 1865, upon Grant's demand, Andrew Johnson paroled and released him. Order for the Release of John W. McCue, Nov. 8, 1865, Orders and Endorsements Sent by the Secretary of War, RG 107, NA.

37. William B. Hesseltine, *Civil War Prisons: A Study in War Psychology* (1930; reprint, New York, 1964), 229–30, 232; William Marvel, *Andersonville: The Last Depot* (Chapel Hill, 1994), 234; *OR* (ser. 2) 5: 628, 632, 651–52.

38. *OR* (ser. 2) 7: 112.

39. Keen and Mewborn, *43rd Battalion,* 363, 371, 374; Minor H. McLain, "The Military Prison at Fort Warren," in *Civil War Prisons,* ed. William B. Hesseltine (Kent, Ohio, 1962), 32–47.

40. *OR* (ser. 2) 8: 93; *New York Herald,* Feb. 8, 1865; *Washington Chronicle,* Feb. 8, 9, 1865; *Baltimore American,* Feb. 9, 1865; newspaper clipping, vol. 1, JSMSB-UVA; Williamson, *Rangers,* 461.

41. *Washington Star,* March 3, 1865; *Washington Chronicle,* March 3, 1865; *OR* (ser. 2) 8: 432; JSM to Ould, April 4, 1865, JSMP-LC; Keen and Mewborn, *43rd Battalion,* 290–386; Williamson, *Rangers,* 461–63; Russell, *Memoirs,* 371.

42. Broun, *Family Events,* 78.

## 18. "All that the proud can feel of pain"

1. Monteiro, *Reminiscences,* 126–29; newspaper clipping, vol. 2, JSMSB- UVA.

2. *OR* (ser. 1) 46(3): 685, 699, 714; Circular by Hancock, April 10, 1865, JSMP-LC.

3. Circular by Hancock, April 13, 1865, JSMP-LC; *OR* (ser. 1) 46(1): 526–27; 46(3): 750–56, 767.

4. *Confederate Veteran* 35 (1927): 327; *OR* (ser. 1) 46(3): 765–66; Monteiro, *Reminiscences,* 147–60.

5. Monteiro, *Reminiscences,* 174–75; *Confederate Veteran* 35 (1927): 327.

6. *OR* (ser. 1) 46(3): 800; Warner, *Generals in Blue,* 80.

7. *OR* (ser. 1) 46(3): 830–31.

8. *OR* (ser. 1) 46(3): 830–31, 839. At 10:45 A.M. on April 19, Stanton wired Hancock that Mosby had known of John Wilkes Booth's plan to assassinate Lincoln and that Mosby had been in Washington with Booth at the time and Booth was attempting to enlist Mosby's men in the escape. Hancock had an aide pass this along to his commanders and ordered them to watch for escaping assassins. Then, dismissing the allegations against Mosby as ridiculous, he went on with the next day's meeting. *OR* (ser. 1) 46(3): 838, 840.

9. Monteiro, *Reminiscences,* 206–7; *OR* (ser. 1) 46(3): 868; JSM to H.C. Jordan, Aug. 23, 1909, JSMP-DU.

10. Munson, *Reminiscences,* 270.

11. Ibid., 271. Several of Mosby's men had already surrendered. At the disbanding, William Chapman called a meeting for the next day, April 22, in Paris, for all who desired to surrender in a group. Many responded, and they rode to Winchester and surrendered. Williamson, *Rangers,* 395–96.

12. Munson, *Reminiscences,* 274–77.

13. Ibid., 271–73.

14. *SHSP* 27 (1899): 322; *OR* (ser. 1) 46(3): 830, 897.

15. Ibid., 1080, 1157; *New York Herald,* May 1, 4, 1865.

16. Newspaper clipping, vol. 6, JSMSB-UVA; typed account by W. Sam Burnley, BFP-UVA; R.T.W. Duke Jr., "Col. John S. Mosby," *The Magazine of Albemarle County History* 22: 83–84; speech of Judge Duke, typed ms., Confederate Veteran Papers, Biographical, DU; Jones, *Mosby,* 323. McGuffey wrote the famous McGuffey Readers.

17. Robert E. Lee to George S. Palmer, June 6, 1865, Robert E. Lee Family Collection, MC.

18. Freeman, *Lee,* 4: 200–207; Thomas, *Lee,* 370–71.

19. Williamson, *Mosby's Rangers,* 1909 ed., 398; JSM to John W. Daniel, April 13, 1904, JWDP-DU; JSM to Aristides Monteiro, June 28, 1879, March 25, 1890, Aug. 7, 1894, JSMC-MC; JSM to JB, Feb. 5, 1904, JBP-VHS; Albert Ordway to Alexander P. Duncan, June 13, 1865; Telegram, Albert Ordway to John C. Kelton, June 14, 1865; Alexander P. Duncan to Albert Ordway, June 14, 1865, Confederate Records, Miscellaneous unfiled slips and papers, M347, NA; JSM to Sam Chapman, Jan. 12, 1907, Thomas Nelson Page Papers, DU.

20. JSM to Sam Chapman, Jan. 12, 1907, Thomas Nelson Page Papers, DU; newspaper clipping, vol. 6, JSMSB-UVA. Willie, Mosby's adjutant, was paroled.

21. Duncan to Ordway, June 14, 1865; JSM to Chapman, Jan. 12, 1907, Thomas Nelson Page Papers, DU. The *Lynchburg Republican* endorsed a June 16 petition to parole Mosby. *Lynchburg Republican,* June 17, 1865, quoted in *Baltimore American,* June 29, 1865.

22. *OR* (ser. 1) 46(3): 853; JSM to John W. Daniel, April 13, 1904, JWDP- DU.

23. Undated clipping, *Cincinnati Daily Commercial,* VHS; *Washington Star,* Aug. 11, 1865; newspaper clippings, vol. 6, JSMSB-UVA; *Baltimore American,* Aug. 12, 1865; *Alexandria Journal,* Aug. 10, 1865, quoted in *Baltimore American,* Aug. 12, 1865; JSM to PM, Jan. 8, 1866, JSMP-LC.

24. JSM to Daniel, April 13, 1904; James Keith to JB, Jan. 27, 1904, in "Col. Mosby and Grant," pamphlet reprint from *Richmond Times-Dispatch,* Jan. 31, 1904, JSMP-DU; JSM to JB, Jan. 30, 1904, JBP-VHS; Russell, *Memoirs,* 393–94; Grant's order, Feb. 2, 1866, typed copy, and inscribed note by Mosby, JSMP-DU.

25. Inscribed note by JSM, on Grant's order, Feb. 2, 1866, JSMP-DU.

## 19. Grant's Partisan in Virginia

1. *Washington Star,* Oct. 24, 1867, quoted in Jones, *Mosby,* 282.

2. JSM to JB, Jan. 30, March 5, 1904, JBP-VHS.

3. Newspaper clipping, vol. 3, JSMSB-UVA; *New Orleans Picayune,* April 29, 1866.

4. Personal Property Tax Records, Fauquier County, 1866, 1868, 1871, VSA; Jones, *Mosby,* 281; JSM to AM, Dec. 1, 1866, JSMC-MC.

5. Siepel, *Rebel,* 174. On Virginia politics see Hamilton J. Eckenrode, *The Political History of Virginia during Reconstruction* (Freeport, N.Y., 1971).

6. Russell, *Memoirs,* xv; Jones, *Mosby,* 283–84.

7. Russell, *Memoirs,* 380–82; JSM to Eppa Hunton, March 25, 1911, typed copy, Archibald G. Robertson Papers, VHS.

8. Dabney, *Virginia,* 374–78; Jack P. Maddex Jr., *The Virginia Conservatives, 1867–1879: A Study in Reconstruction Politics* (Chapel Hill, 1970), 100–101, 133–34.

9. JSM to JB, Feb. 6, 1904, JBP-VHS; *New York Times,* Aug. 21, 1892.

10. *Richmond Times-Dispatch,* Jan. 31, 1904; *New York Times,* Aug. 21, 1892; JSM, memorandum on Wade Hampton's Dec. 11, 1876, telegram, typed copy, JWDP-DU (hereafter JSM's Hampton memo).

11. *Washington Star,* May 8, 1872, quoted in Jones, *Mosby,* 286; *Bristol News,* May 17, 31, 1872; newspaper clipping, vol. 2, JSMSB-UVA.

12. *Washington Star,* May 8, 1872, quoted in Jones, *Mosby,* 287.

13. Ulysses S. Grant, *Personal Memoirs of U.S. Grant,* 2 vols. (New York, 1885–1886), 2: 142; newspaper clipping, vol. 5, JSMSB-UVA.

14. *New York Times,* Aug. 21, 1892.

15. JSM to John S. Wise, July 1, 1872, John S. Wise Papers, Swem Library, College of William and Mary.

16. Newspaper clipping, Aug. 4, 1872, vol. 2, JSMSB-UVA; Warner, *Generals in Gray,* 146.

17. Newspaper clipping, vol. 2, JSMSB-UVA.

18. Ibid., *Washington Star,* Aug. 9, 1872, quoted in Siepel, *Rebel,* 180.

19. Newspaper clipping, vol. 2, JSMSB-UVA.

20. Siepel, *Rebel,* 182; Maddex, *Conservatives,* 134.

21. Russell, *Memoirs,* 387–89.

22. Dabney, *Virginia,* 378; JSM to U.S. Grant, Aug. 31, 1873, in *Richmond Times-Dispatch,* Jan. 31, 1904.

23. Mitchell, *Letters,* 48–49.

24. JSM to Grant, Aug. 31, 1873; Siepel, *Rebel,* 185–86; JSM's Hampton memo.

25. Siepel, *Rebel,* 186.

26. Jones, *Mosby,* 295; Siepel, *Rebel,* 186.

27. JSM to G.B. Samuels, Aug. 4, 1874; JSM to Alexander D.F. Payne, Aug. 20, 1874; Payne to JSM, Aug. 20, 1874; William H. Payne memorandum, Aug. 27, 1874, WHPP-VSA; Virginia *Sentinel,* Aug. 21, 1874.

28. JSM to Edward C. Turner, Oct., 24, c. Oct. 25, 1874, ECTP-DU; newspaper clipping, WHPP-VSA.

29. JSM to JB, Jan. 5, 1904, JBP-VHS.

30. JSM to JB, March 5, 1904, JBP-VHS; Russell, *Memoirs,* 394.

31. Siepel, *Rebel,* 189; JSM to Edward C. Turner, Nov. 21, 1876, ECTP-DU; PM to Lizzie, Oct. 17, 1872, JSMP-VHS; Jones, *Mosby,* 295; grave markers, Warrenton Cemetery.

32. Newspaper clipping, vol. 4, JSMSB-UVA.

33. Siepel, *Rebel,* 189; JSM to Rutherford B. Hayes, July 24, 1876, RBHP- HPCL.

34. *New York Herald,* Aug. 12, 1876, reprint in handout, RBHP-HPCL.

35. Ibid.

36. Ibid.

37. Ibid.; Kenneth E. Davison, *The Presidency of Rutherford B. Hayes* (Westport, Conn., 1972), 137–38. In the letter to the editor Mosby warned that if Hayes were elected with "a solid South" voting Democratic against him, the South would be left without federal aid. Later he claimed to have coined "solid South." Today's historians do not give him credit, but he probably deserves it. Mosby's letter was written August 6, 1876, and published August 12, 1876, and the next earliest use of the term seen by the author was in the *New York Times* on October 20, 1876.

38. Undated clipping, *Warrenton Index,* WHPP-VSA; William H. Payne memorandum, undated, WHPP-VSA.

39. *New York Times,* Oct. 20, 1879; JSM to JB, Jan. 30, 1904, JBP-VHS; JSM to Edward C. Turner, March 20, 1874, ECTP-DU; JSM to S.V. Southall, June 13, 1898, typed copy, JSMP-DU; JSM to Samuel Chapman, Jan. 12, 1907, Thomas Nelson Page Papers, DU; *New York Times,* Aug. 21, 1892; Mitchell, *Letters,* 47; Siepel, *Rebel,* 224. Grant appointed William Chapman special agent of the Internal Revenue Service and Fount Beattie deputy collector of Internal Revenue. Russell apparently refused Mosby's offer; he worked as a farmer near Berryville, where he died February 21, 1932, at the age of ninety.

40. Maddex, *Conservatives,* 138; JSM to Edward C. Turner, Nov. 21, 1876, ECTP-DU.

41. Personal Property Tax Records, Fauquier County, 1871, 1876, 1878, VSA; JSM to Edward C. Turner, Nov. 21, 1876, ECTP-DU; Jones, *Mosby,* 289.

42. Siepel, *Rebel,* 179.

## 20. Hayes's Reformer in Hong Kong

1. JSM to James D. Blackwell, Sept. 6, 1879, JDBP-CWM.

2. Ibid.

3. JSM to Edward M. Spilman, Jan. 13, 1880, JSMP-VHS.

4. Rutherford B. Hayes to William M. Evarts, Aug. 22, 1878, typed copy, RBHP-HPCL.

5. Ibid. He was confirmed in the senate on December 17, 1878, and his salary was four thousand dollars per year. Department of State, List of Consular Officers, 1789–1939, RG 59, NA; JSM to FWS, Sept. 22, 1879, DCHK-NA.

6. JSM to FWS, Feb. 4, 1879, DCHK-NA; G.B. Endacott, *A History of Hong Kong,* 2d ed. (Hong Kong, 1964), 194–95.

7. Graham H. Stuart, *American Diplomatic and Consular Practice,* 2d ed. (New York, 1952), 311, 315–20.

8. Ibid., 86–90; newspaper clipping, vol. 1, JSMSB-UVA; JSM to Charles Payson, Nov. 7, 1879, DCHK-NA. The only way to employ consuls in the Barbary states was to pay them. Stuart, *Consular Practice,* 86.

9. JSM to FWS, Feb. 17, 21, 1879, DCHK-NA.

10. JSM to FWS, July 25, Oct. 21, and attached accounts of wages, Dec. 1, 1879; JSM to William M. Evarts, Jan. 10, 1880, DCHK-NA.

11. JSM to Rutherford B. Hayes, March 19, 1879; JSM to John Hay, Dec. 31, 1880, DCHK-NA.

12. JSM to FWS, July 13, 25, 1879, DCHK-NA. Smith sued Mosby for slander, and Mosby defended himself so humorously that the entire court, including Smith, broke down in laughter. Siepel, *Rebel,* 230.

13. JSM to FWS, Sept. 22, 1879, DCHK-NA.

14. JSM to FWS, July 15, Sept. 29, 1879; JSM to William K. Rogers, July 13, 1879; FWS to JSM, Sept. 29, 1879, DCHK-NA; *John S. Mosby v. the United States,* 24 U.S. Court of Claims Reports 5 (1888–1889).

15. JSM to FWS, July 25, Oct. 21, 1879; JSM to J.C.B. Davis, May 23, 1882, DCHK-NA.

16. Glenn Sonnedecker, *Kremers and Urdang's History of Pharmacy,* 4th ed. (Madison, Wisc., 1976), 133; Virginia Berridge, "Opium Over the Counter in Nineteenth Century England," *Pharmacy in History* 20 (1978): 96.

17. *Hong Kong China Mail,* Sept. 20, 23, 1879; J.M.D. Alenadoe Castro to JSM, Sept. 13, 1879; JSM to William Evarts, Jan. 10, 1880; JSM to T.C.H. Smith, March 6, p.s. of March 11, 1879, DCHK-NA.

18. JSM to Charles Payson, Dec. 17, 1880; J.M.D. Alenadoe Castro to JSM, Sept. 13, 1879; JSM to William K. Rogers, Sept. 29, 1879; JSM to J.M. Marsh, Sept. 13, 1879, DCHK-NA; *Hong Kong China Mail,* Sept. 20, 23, 1879.

19. Undated clipping, *Hong Kong China Mail* in JSM to FWS, July 25, 1879; JSM to FWS, July 25, 1879; H. Seldon Loring to FWS, February 5, 1879; JSM to John Hay, Jan. 17, 1880; JSM to T.C.H. Smith, March 6, 1879; JSM to William K. Rogers, July 13, 1879, DCHK-NA.

20. DAB, 8: 613–14; Ari Hoogenboom, *The Presidency of Rutherford B. Hayes* (Lawrence, Kans., 1988), 181; *Biographical Directory of the American Congress, 1774–1961* (Washington, D.C., 1961), 1793; newspaper clippings, White House Scrapbooks, vol. 63, RBHP-HPCL.

21. JSM to FWS, Feb. 21, 1879, DCHK-NA; Philip Marshall Brown, "Frederick Theodore Frelinghuysen," in *The American Secretaries of State and Their Diplomacy,* 17 vols, ed. Samuel F. Bemis (New York, 1927–1967), 8: 6.

22. JSM to T.C.H. Smith, March 6, 1879, DCHK-NA.

23. JSM to William K. Rogers, May 19, 1879, DCHK-NA. Dick Turpin and William Kidd were popular heroes in British history. Turpin was a highwayman, and Kidd was a pirate.

24. JSM to William Hunter, Dec. 22, 1879, DCHK-NA; newspaper clipping, White House Scrapbooks, vol. 62, RBHP-HPCL; newspaper clipping, vol. 4, JSMSB- UVA; *New York Times,* July 13, 1879.

25. JSM to FWS, Oct. 18, 1879, DCHK-NA; JSM to James A. Garfield, March 18, 1880, JAGP-LC.

26. Hoogenboom, *Hayes,* 183; JSM to Stilson Hutchins, June 29, 1879, John S. Mosby Letters, UVA.

27. JSM to FWS, July 25, 1879, DCHK-NA; JSM to "My Dear Sir," Aug. 17, 1879, in newspaper clipping, White House Scrapbooks, vol. 63, RBHP-HPCL.

28. *New York Times,* Aug. 18, 1879; *Washington Post,* Aug. 18, 1879.

29. JSM to "My Dear Sir," Aug. 17, 1879, in newspaper clipping, White House Scrapbooks, vol. 63, RBHP-HPCL. The recipient may have been his friend, Democratic congressman Eppa Hunton.

30. *New York Times,* Aug. 19, 1879; handwritten note on and text of JSM to William K. Rogers, July 13, 1879, DCHK-NA.

31. JSM to FWS, Sept. 22, 1879, DCHK-NA.

32. Newspaper clippings, vol. 63, White House Scrapbooks, RBHP-HPCL.

33. *Philadelphia Times,* Oct. 26, 1879; *Louisville Courier-Journal,* Oct. 5, 15, 1879; *Milwaukee Sentinel,* Sept. 27, 1879; newspaper clippings, vol. 63, White House Scrapbooks, RBHP-HPCL.

34. *Hartford Evening Post,* Sept. 29, 1879; newspaper clipping, vol. 63, White House Scrapbooks, RBHP-HPCL.

35. JSM to FWS, Oct. 21, 1879; JSM to John Hay, February 25, 1880, DCHK-NA; JSM to John W. Daniel, May 9, 1902, JWDP-DU; *New York Times,* Jan. 3, 1880; Hoogenboom, *Hayes,* 183; JSM to James A. Garfield, May 12, 1880, JAGP-LC.

36. Newspaper clipping, vol. 63, White House Scrapbooks, RBHP-HPCL; *New York Times,* Jan. 3, 1880; JSM to William M. Evarts, Jan. 10, 1880, DCHK-NA; JSM to Edward M. Spilman, Jan. 13, 1880, JSMP-VHS.

37. JSM to Rutherford B. Hayes, March 19, 1879, DCHK-NA.

38. Newspaper clipping, vol. 1, JSMSB-UVA; *Hong Kong Telegram,* July 20, 1885.

39. *Hong Kong China Mail,* July 29, 1885, typed copy in vol. 4, JSMSB-UVA; JSM to FWS, May 7, 1879, DCHK-NA. On April 5, 1906, Congress passed an act ending all unofficial fees. All fees for notarial services were to be deposited in the Treasury. Mosby had recommended this on May 7, 1879, nearly twenty-seven years earlier. The same law gave the president authority to appoint inspectors to make regular inspections of consulates. On June 27, 1906, Theodore Roosevelt brought consuls under the merit system of the Civil Service Act by executive order. Stuart, *Consular Practice,* 94.

## 21. Stuart and Gettysburg

1. JSM to ABC, Aug. 8, 1914, JSMP-VHS; *Richmond Times-Dispatch,* Feb. 2, 1910. See William G. Piston, *Lee's Tarnished Lieutenant: James Longstreet and His Place in Southern History* (Athens, Ga., 1987) on the attack on Longstreet.

2. *Confederate Veteran* 18 (1910): 201–2.

3. Oscar Lewis, *The Big Four: The Story of Huntington, Stanford, Hopkins, and Crocker, and the Building of the Central Pacific* (New York, 1969), 211.

4. JSM to JWD, Jan. 21 (no year), JWDP-DU; *New York Times,* Aug. 23, 1896; Siepel, *Rebel,* 248–49; newspaper cartoon, vol. 3, JSMSB-UVA. According to biographer Ladislas Farago, one of Mosby's leisure-time activities was visiting with young George S. Patton Jr. (1885–1945) on the Patton ranch near San Gabriel, California. Ladislas Farago, *Patton: Ordeal and Triumph* (New York, 1963), 50–51.

5. JSM to JB, March 12, 1897, BFP-VSA; *Richmond Times,* June 20, 26, 1897; Stuart, *Consular Practice,* 92.

6. JSM to JWD, Aug. 7, 1898, JWDP-DU.

7. W.H. Payne to JSM, Feb. 25, 1888, in vol. 5, JSMSB-UVA; *John S. Mosby v. the United States,* 24 U.S. Court of Claims Reports 1–18 (1888–1889); newspaper clipping, vol. 1, JSMSB-UVA.

8. *United States v. Mosby,* 133 U.S. 273-89 (1889).

9. *Edgar M. Wilson, Administrator of Van Buren, v. the United States,* 32 U.S. Court of Claims Reports 64–68 (1896–1897); *United States v. Wilson,* 168 U.S. 273–78 (1897); JSM to JWD, April 21, 1902, JWDP-DU.

10. Newspaper clipping, vol. 1, JSMSB-UVA. The building in which Mosby spoke burned; today's structure dates to 1896 and is the home of Tremont Temple Baptist Church, 88 Tremont Street.

11. Ibid., JSM to John C. Ropes, June 27, 1898, MM-NYHS; JSM to Francis R. Lassiter, Dec. 3, 1886, Daniel William, Francis Rives, and Charles Trotter Lassiter Papers, DU.

12. JSM to WHC, Nov. 6, 1897, JSMP-DU; newspaper clipping, vol. 6, JSMSB- UVA.

13. *Richmond Times,* April 24, 1897; newspaper clippings, vol. 2, 5, JSMSB-UVA.

14. Harris D. Riley Jr. to author, Sept. 28, 1996; newspaper clipping, vol. 2, JSMSB-UVA.

15. Newspaper clippings, vol. 2, 6, JSMSB-UVA.

16. JSM to Benton Chinn, Oct. 17, 1897, photocopy, JSMP-FCPL; newspaper clipping, vol. 2, JSMSB-UVA; *Richmond Times,* June 8, 1897.

17. JSM to Nelson A. Miles, April 22, 1898, in vol. 6, JSMSB-UVA; Warner, *Generals in Gray,* 40–41.

18. Nelson A. Miles to JSM, May 4, 1898, JSM to Nelson A. Miles, May 4, 1898, in vol. 2, JSMSB-UVA; newspaper clippings, vol. 1, 2, JSMSB-UVA. Two of Mosby's Rangers were in the army: Samuel F. Chapman, chaplain, 4th U.S. Infantry and John C. Edmonds, colonel, 4th Texas Infantry. Francis B. Heitman, *Historical Register and Dictionary of the United States Army,* 2 vols. (Washington, 1903), 2: 199, 208.

19. Thomas L. Connelly, *The Marble Man: Robert E. Lee and His Image in American Society* (New York, 1977), 27; JSM to Flora Stuart, March 15, 1899, JEBSP-VHS; JSM to ABC, Dec. 22, 1914, JSMP-VHS.

20. Paul D. Escott, "The Uses of Gallantry: Virginians and the Origins of J.E.B. Stuart's Historical Image," *Virginia Magazine of History and Biography* 103 (1995):

63; *SHSP* 2 (1876): 76; Connelly, *Lee,* 88–89; Henry B. McClellan, *The Life and Campaigns of Major-General J.E.B. Stuart* (Boston, 1885).

21. Armistead L. Long, *Memoirs of Robert E. Lee: His Military and Personal History* (New York, 1886), 271–80; James Longstreet, "Lee's Invasion of Pennsylvania," *B&L* 3: 251; Mosby, *Reminiscences,* 178–204; Mosby, "The Confederate Cavalry in the Gettysburg Campaign," *B&L* 3: 251–53. Walter H. Taylor's *Four Years with General Lee* (New York, 1877) also criticized Stuart.

22. Mosby, "Stuart's Cavalry in the Gettysburg Campaign," *Belford's Monthly,* Oct. 1891, 149–63; Nov. 1891, 261–75.

23. Charles Marshall, "Events Leading up to the Battle of Gettysburg," *SHSP* 23 (1895): 205–29; Connelly, *Lee,* 49. Marshall's unfinished manuscript on Lee was published in Frederick Maurice, ed., *An Aide-de-Camp of Lee* (Boston, 1927).

24. Maurice, *Aide-de-Camp,* 209–11, 214–16, 220–24; David G. McIntosh, "Review of the Gettysburg Campaign," *SHSP* 37 (1909): 94–95; Mosby, *Stuart's Cavalry,* 203.

25. *OR* (ser. 1) 27(2): 306–8, 316–18.

26. Mosby, *Stuart's Cavalry,* 209; Dowdey and Manarin, *Papers,* 526; *OR* (ser. 1) 27(2): 306, 316; Edwin B. Coddington, *The Gettysburg Campaign* (1968; reprint, Dayton, Ohio, 1994), 108.

27. Marshall, "Events."

28. Ibid., 216; *SHSP* 23 (1895): 348; JSM to Holmes Conrad, Jan. 28, 1896, Holmes Conrad Papers, VHS.

29. *OR* (ser. 1) 27(2): 307, 316; 27(3): 943–44.

30. JSM to JWD, April 26, 1896, JWDP-DU; newspaper clippings, vol. 1, JSMSB-UVA; *OR* (ser. 1) 27(3): 944. Mosby mentioned the Chambersburg letter and quoted the vital part in *Reminiscences,* 194.

31. Newspaper clipping, vol. 1, JSMSB-UVA; Mosby, *Stuart's Cavalry,* 120; JSM to William C. Marshall, Feb. 6, 1906, Marshall Family Papers, VHS.

32. Mosby, *Stuart's Cavalry,* 118–21. The next letter after the Chambersburg letter was dated July 1, 1863, leaving the possibility that Venable might have written it on June 29. Mosby, *Stuart's Cavalry,* 121.

33. Mosby, *Stuart's Cavalry,* v.

34. Gary W. Gallagher, "Confederate Corps Leadership on the First Day at Gettysburg" in *The First Day at Gettysburg: Essays on Confederate and Union Leadership,* ed. Gary W. Gallagher (Kent, Ohio, 1992), 32, 34, 44–45; Russell, *Memoirs,* 236–37.

35. Mosby, *Stuart's Cavalry,* 121–27, 129–30; Russell, *Memoirs,* 241–44.

36. Coddington, *Gettysburg,* 181, 186–87, 189, 654; Alan T. Nolan, "R.E. Lee and July 1 at Gettysburg," in Gallagher, *First Day,* 13–14; Thomas, *Lee,* 293.

37. Coddington, *Gettysburg,* 110–11, 207–8.

38. Dowdey and Manarin, *Papers,* 526; Mosby, *Stuart's Cavalry,* 91, 119, 141, 154, 169, 179, 180, 212, 213, 216, 220.

39. Mosby, *Stuart's Cavalry,* 150–51; Freeman, *Lee,* 3: 547, and *Lee's Lieutenants,* 3: 208; James I. Robertson Jr., *General A.P. Hill: The Story of a Confederate Warrior* (New York, 1987), 214.

40. JSM to AM, Jan. 3, 30, 1895; JSMC-MC; JSM to WHC, May 20, 1891, JSMP-DU.

41. JSM to Edward C. Burks, Feb. 1, 1910, JSMP-DU; JSM to ABC, Sept. 9, 1914, JSMP-VHS; JSM to Benton Chinn, (no date), photocopy, JSMP-FCPL.

42. JSM to Edward C. Burks, Feb. 1, 1910, JSMP-DU; Mitchell, *Letters,* 155.

43. Flora Stuart to JSM, Feb. 22, 1887; JSM to Flora Stuart, Feb. 27, 1887; Flora Stuart to JSM, March 1, 1887, JEBSP-VHS.

44. JSM to ABC, Sept. 9, 1914, May 20, 1915, JSMP-VHS; JSM to Flora Stuart, April 4, 1899, JEBSP-VHS.

45. JSM to ABC, May 29, 1915, JSMP-VHS; Mitchell, *Letters,* 219–22, 245, 246.

46. JSM to John S. Russell, Aug. 11, 1909, JSMP-DU; Mitchell, *Letters,* 155.

## 22. Roosevelt's Land Agent in the Sand Hills

1. JSM to Robert S. Walker, Aug. 20, 1900, JSMP-WFS; JSM to JWD, June 4, 1902, March 24, 1904, JWDP-DU; BH to JSM, Aug. 3, 1901, Department of the Interior, General Land Office Records, Division P, Press Copies of Letters Sent to Special Agents, March 14, 1891, to Oct. 31, 1910, RG 49, NA (hereafter Land Office Records).

2. Newspaper clipping, BRP-UW.

3. Newspaper clippings, vol. 1, 2, JSMSB-UVA.

4. Williamson, *Rangers,* 499, 501.

5. BH to JSM, Nov. 12, 23, 1901, Land Office Records.

6. Ernest S. Osgood, *The Day of the Cattleman,* 2d ed. (Minneapolis, 1954), 194; Edward E. Dale, *The Range Cattle Industry: Ranching on the Great Plains from 1865 to 1925,* 2d ed. (Norman, Okla., 1960), 83; Paul W. Gates, *History of Public Land Law Development* (Washington, D.C., 1968), 466; Francis E. Warren to A. Kendall, Aug. 18, 1902, Francis E. Warren Papers, American Heritage Center, University of Wyoming.

7. Osgood, *Cattleman,* 190, 201.

8. Gates, *Land Law,* 466–67.

9. Gary D. Libecap, *Locking Up the Range: Federal Land Controls and Grazing* (San Francisco, 1981), 32–33; BH to JSM, Nov. 23, 1901, Land Office Records.

10. Libecap, *Land Controls,* 34; Gates, *Land Law,* 468; Bartlett Richards Jr. with Ruth Van Ackeren, *Bartlett Richards: Nebraska Sandhills Cattleman* (Lincoln, 1980), 101, 103.

11. Osgood, *Cattleman,* 196–99, 201–2.

12. Theodore Roosevelt, *Ranch Life and the Hunting-Trail* (1888; reprint, Ann Arbor, 1966), 18, 22, 81.

13. Richards, *Richards,* 99, 104–9, 154–55; newspaper clipping, BRP-UW; Frank Benton, "Land Leasing Speech," March 5, 1902, Wyoming Stock Growers Association Records, American Heritage Center, University of Wyoming.

14. BH to JSM, Jan. 13, 1902; Acting Commissioner to JSM, Aug. 26, 1902, Land Office Records.

15. John Madson, "Nebraska's Sand Hills: Land of Long Sunsets," *National Geographic* (Oct. 1978): 493–517; *Lincoln Daily Star*, Dec. 6, 1902.

16. Richards, *Richards*, 57, 229; Madson, "Sand Hills," 499.

17. *Rushville Standard*, Feb. 28, 1902, typed copy of clipping, BRMC-NSHS.

18. BH to JSM, Sept. 26, 1902, Land Office Records; *Omaha Daily Bee*, Nov. 12, 1902, Dec. 1, 1902.

19. James C. Olson, *History of Nebraska*, 2d ed. (Lincoln, 1966), 237–38; *Lincoln Daily Star*, Nov. 29, 1902.

20. JSM to BH, Oct. 1, 1902 in vol. 5, JSMSB-UVA.

21. Richards, *Richards*, 3, 12, 50–53.

22. Ibid., 35, 76, 80–81, 89, 95.

23. Newspaper clippings, BRMC-NSHS; newspaper clippings, BRP-UW; *Billings (Mont.) Gazette*, July 19, 1992; newspaper clippings, vol. 4, 6, JSMSB-UVA.

24. Newspaper clippings, vol. 2, 4, JSMSB-UVA; *Alliance Times*, Jan. 8, 1907; *Lincoln Daily Star*, Dec. 8, 27, 1902.

25. Newspaper clipping, vol. 6, JSMSB-UVA.

26. Newspaper clipping, BRP-UW; BH to JSM, Nov. 18, 1902, Land Office Records; *Omaha Evening Bee*, Nov. 28, 1902.

27. *Omaha Evening Bee*, Nov. 28, 1902; undated, unidentified reprints from *Detroit Free Press* and *Syracuse Sunday Herald* in vol. 6, JSMSB-UVA.

28. *Lincoln Daily Star*, Nov. 29, 1902.

29. *Omaha Evening Bee*, Nov. 28, 1902; BH to JSM, Nov. 29, 1902, Land Office Records.

30. *Omaha Evening Bee*, Dec. 16, 1902; *Lincoln Daily Star*, Dec. 17, 1902.

31. Olson, *Nebraska*, 193; Richards, *Richards*, 175, 220; E.B. Bronson to Edmund Seymour, Dec. 5, 1911, BRMC-NSHS.

32. Elting E. Morison and John Blum, eds., *The Letters of Theodore Roosevelt*, 8 vols (Cambridge, 1951–1954), 5: 583; Gates, *Land Law*, 489–91, 610–11; Richards, *Richards*, 193.

33. W.A. Richards to JSM, April 2, 1903, Land Office Records; Mitchell, *Letters*, 315; JSM to JB, June 3, 1903, JBP-VHS.

34. JB to JSM, July 7, 1903, Joseph Bryan Letterbook, VHS; newspaper clipping, vol 4, JSMSB-UVA.

35. JSM to JB, May (no day) 1904, May 15, 24, 1904, JBP-VHS; Siepel, *Rebel*, 274; *DAB*, 8: 241.

36. JSM to JB, May 26, 1904, JBP-VHS; newspaper clipping, vol. 4, JSMSB-UVA; JSM to JB, April 18, 1905, JSMC-MC; telegram, JSM to Charles Russell, June 22, 1905; telegram, Russell to JSM, June 24, 1905, vol. 1, JSMSB-UVA; JSM to Russell, June 24, 1905, JBP-VHS; JSM to E. Leroy Sweetser, July 13, 1910, JSMP-UVA; JSM to Russell, Feb. 5, 1905, Russell to JSM, Aug. 14, 1905, Department of Justice, Bureau of Insular and Territorial Affairs, Letters Sent, RG 60, NA.

37. *Louisville Courier-Journal*, Sept. 14, 1986; *Richmond News Leader*, Oct. 6, 1990.

38. Russell, *Memoirs*, 6; JSM to Eppa Hunton, Nov. 18, 1909, typed copy, Armistead C. Gordon Papers, VHS; JSM to Thomas P. Bryan, Dec. 7, 1909, typed copy, JSMP-DU.

39. *Confederate Veteran* 18 (1910): 429; Edmund Wilson, *Patriotic Gore: Studies in the Literature of the American Civil War* (New York, 1962), 323; newspaper clippings, vol. 1, 2, JSMSB-UVA.

40. *Baltimore News*, July 26, 1910.

41. JSM to ASC, July 25, Dec. 17, 1915, John S. Mosby Correspondence, UVA.

42. JSM to JB, May 7, 1903, JBP-VHS.

43. JSM to ASC, Jan. 27, 1915, John S. Mosby Correspondence, UVA; Mitchell, *Letters*, 210, 261–62.

44. JSM to ABC, March 27, May 21, 1915, JSMP-VHS; JSM to JMC, April 16, May 5, 1915, John S. Mosby Correspondence, UVA.

45. JSM to ABC, May 7, 1915, JSMP-VHS; JSM to ASC, May 30, 1915, John S. Mosby Correspondence, UVA; JSM to University of Virginia Library, Oct. 27, 1915, JSMP-UVA.

## 23. The Gray Ghost of Television and Film

1. JSM to Edward Burks, March 10, 1913, JSMP-DU; JSM to JMC, May 11, 1903, JSM to ASC, Sept. 9, 1915, JSMC-UVA; Mitchell, *Letters*, 187.

2. Mitchell, *Letters*, 175; JSM to JMC, Jan. 14, 1915, March 18, 1916, JSMC-UVA.

3. JSM to ABC, March 4, 1914, JSMP-VHS.

4. JSM to JB, April 18, 1905, JSMC-MC; Mitchell, *Letters*, 156, 159–60.

5. JSM to JMC, Jan. 29, 1916, JSMC-UVA; Pauline Coleman to Arthur (unidentified), Nov. 30, 1914, JSMP-VHS; interview with Beverly M. Coleman, July 28, 1991; JSM to Bettie P. Cocke, Sept. 23, 1914, JSMP-UVA; newspaper clipping, vol. 3, JSMSB-UVA.

6. Newspaper clipping, vol. 5, JSMSB-UVA.

7. JSM to AM, Sept. 19, 1865, JSMC-MC; JSM to PM, Nov. 20, 1867, JSMP-VHS.

8. JSM to PM, Feb. 3, 1865, JSMP-VHS; Holzer and Neely, *Art*, 66–69; Holzer and Neely, "'In the Best Possible Manner': The Equestrian Portraits of L.M.D. Guillaume," *Virginia Cavalcade*, (autumn 1993): 86–87.

9. Holzer and Neely, *Art*, 59, 64.

10. Edward V. Valentine, sculptor's notes; JSM to Edward V. Valentine, Oct. 28, 1868; Edward V. Valentine to JSM, March 16, 1877, Edward V. Valentine Manuscript Collection, The Valentine Museum.

11. Newspaper clipping quoting *Warrenton Index*, JSMF-VM.

12. Neely, Holzer, and Boritt, *Confederate Image*, 205; newspaper clipping, vol. 4, JSMSB-UVA; *Baltimore Sun*, Jan. 15, 1911.

13. Magalene McDowell to Anne Clay McDowell, undated, Henry Clay Memorial Foundation Papers, McDowell Family, Letters to Anne Clay McDowell,

Special Collections and Archives Service Center, University of Kentucky, Lexington, Ky.; JSM to JB, July 8, 1905, JBP-VHS; JSM to AM, Sept. 19, 1865, JSMC- MC; JSM to ASC, Oct. 13, 1906, JSMC-UVA; *Moving Picture World*, Feb. 27, 1909.

14. *Moving Picture World*, Oct. 8, 15, 1910, March 22, 1913; Jack Spears, *The Civil War on the Screen and Other Essays* (South Brunswick, N.J., 1977), 87.

15. *New York Times*, April 27, 1897; newspaper clippings, vol. 2, 6, JSMSB-UVA; JSM to Alice Chinn, Jan. 22, 1898, photocopy, JSMP-FCPL; Mitchell, *Letters*, 157; JSM to Edward Burks, Nov. 9, 1912, JSMP- DU; Warrenton *Fauquier Democrat*, Nov. 30, 1912; JSM to ABC, Dec. 5, 1914, JSMP-VHS; Harris D. Riley Jr. to author, March 5, 1997.

16. JSM to ASC, May 30, 1915, JSM to JMC, Jan. 29, 1916, JSMC-UVA; JSM to ABC, Feb. 25, March 21, April 16, 1916, JSMP-VHS; Evans and Moyer, *Mosby's Confederacy*, 108–9; *Washington Post*, May 30, 31, 1916; *Richmond Times-Dispatch*, May 31, 1916; Harris D. Riley Jr. to author, March 5, 1997. Mosby's death certificate is missing.

17. *Washington Post*, May 31, 1916; Evans and Moyer, *Mosby's Confederacy*, 109.

18. Siepel, *Rebel*, 291; *Richmond Times-Dispatch*, June 1, 2, 1916; Jones, *Mosby*, 308; *Washington Post*, June 2, 1916.

19. *Richmond Times-Dispatch*, June 2, 1916; Evans and Moyer, *Mosby's Confederacy*, 16.

20. *Richmond Times-Dispatch*, June 1, 2, 1916.

21. Ibid., June 1, 1916; Warrenton *Fauquier Democrat*, June 3, 1916.

22. *Confederate Veteran* 27 (1919): 116; 28 (1920): 277; Beverly R. Tucker, *Mosby*, copy in JSMC-MC.

23. William M.S. Rasmussen, "Making the Confederate Murals: Studies by Charles Hoffbauer," VMHB 101 (July 1893): 433–34, 438.

24. *New York Times*, Sept. 28, 1958; Tim Brooks and Earle Marsh, *The Complete Directory to Prime Time Network TV Shows, 1946–Present*, 4th ed. (New York, 1988), 309; interview with Virgil C. Jones, June 17, 1990. One of the highlights of the research was meeting Virgil C. "Pat" Jones in his home in Centreville, Virginia. For years I had admired his writing, having read *Ranger Mosby* when I was nineteen years old and stationed on Okinawa in the U.S. Air Force. That book and Bruce Catton's works first inspired my interest in history.

25. Greg Biggs, "The Gray Ghost Story," *Blue & Gray Magazine*, April 1994, 31–33; Brooks and Marsh, *TV Shows*, 309; *New York Times*, Sept. 28, 1958.

26. Larry J. Gianakos, *Television Drama Series Programming: A Comprehensive Chronicle, 1959–1975* (Metuchen, N.J., 1978), 118.

27. Lee Moffett, *The Diary of Court House Square: Warrenton, Virginia, U.S.A., From Early Times Through 1986* (Stephens City, Va., 1988), 341–42; advertisement, *Civil War Times Illustrated*, (Dec. 1995): 7.

## Conclusion

1. CMSR, Mosby's Command; Keen and Mewborn, *43rd Battalion*, 290–386.

2. Wert, *Mosby's Rangers*, 242–43; Frye, "Mosby as a Factor," 123–25.

3. Morris, *Sheridan*, 226. Davis commented on *The Gray Ghost: John Singleton Mosby, Civil War Journal Series*, Arts and Entertainment Network, Sept. 29, 1993.

4. Laqueur, *Guerrilla Reader*, 35, 43.

5. Edmonds Diary, Aug. 13, 1864.

# Bibliographic Essay

During Mosby's twenty-five-year exile from Virginia and for the remaining twelve years of his life, one of his favorite recreations was writing personal letters. Nearly every day he would arise before dawn, make coffee, and sit down to write. His memory remained accurate, and with vibrant nostalgia he relived the glorious times of the Civil War. His numerous letters are a biographer's dream, providing a wealth of information and insight into his personality. The John S. Mosby Papers at the Virginia Historical Society contain highly revealing letters from Mosby to his wife during the Civil War and, for the postwar years, valuable correspondence with other persons, including many letters from him to his grandsons in the last few years of his life. In addition, the Virginia Historical Society has many extremely helpful collections such as the Joseph Bryan Papers, Amanda V. Edmonds Chappelear Diary, and Catherine Cochran Recollections.

The John S. Mosby Papers in the Special Collections Department, University of Virginia Library, include postwar letters from Mosby revealing details on the war and describing his emotions and thoughts at the time. Several other helpful collections shed light on aspects of Mosby's life and career. Archives Research Services, The Library of Virginia, has vital primary sources on Mosby's family background, youth, education, trial, and pardon for shooting Turpin; and the William H. Payne Papers help clarify the issues in Mosby's postwar political career. The Eleanor S. Brockenbrough Library, The Museum of the Confederacy, made available the John S. Mosby Collection, giving insight into Mosby's Civil War activities, Gettysburg literary war, and other affairs. The collection has several letters from Mosby to his former command surgeon, Aristides Monteiro. The Special Collections Library, Duke University, has the John Singleton Mosby Papers, which contain valuable correspondence of the late nineteenth and early twentieth centuries with former Rangers Samuel and William Chapman and John S. Russell. Other collections such as the John Warwick Daniel Papers clarify the complicated issues in Mosby's postwar political career and literary war on Gettysburg.

The John S. Mosby Papers in the Library of Congress contain several Civil War letters, and the James A. Garfield Papers cast light on Mosby's consular reform. The John S. Mosby Papers and John S. Mosby Biographical File in the Virginia Room, Fairfax County Public Library, have documents relating to Stoughton's capture and correspondence of the 1890s. The Valentine Museum manuscripts provide information on Edward V. Valentine's bust of Mosby. Adele H. Mitchell's *The Letters of John S. Mosby*, 2d ed. (no place, 1986) is an excellent source, revealing valuable insights on Mosby's role in the Civil War and contributing many details on the final two decades of his life.

Several collections of government documents in the National Archives were of great value. The Army Court-martial Files, 1809–1894, Records of the Office of the Judge Advocate General, RG 153, contain vital, fascinating information on the trials of Mosby's men by military commissions. Key information on Civil War trade across the Potomac River border is contained in Treasury Department, Records of the Civil War Official Agencies of the Treasury Department, Records of the Seventh Special Agency, RG 366. Details on the impact of Sheridan's Burning Raid are available in Treasury Department, Records of the Southern Claims Commission, RG 217. The following collections enlighten Mosby's work for the federal government: Records of the Department of State, RG 59, Department of the Interior, General Land Office Records, RG 49, and Department of Justice Records, RG 60.

The Rutherford B. Hayes Papers, Rutherford B. Hayes Presidential Center, shed light on Mosby's participation in Hayes's election and administration, and Hayes's White House Scrapbooks contain many newspaper clippings on Mosby's work in Hong Kong. The Bartlett Richards Manuscript Collection, Nebraska State Historical Society, and the Bartlett Richards Papers, American Heritage Center, University of Wyoming, yield valuable information on fencing reform; both libraries have outstanding collections of contemporary newspapers.

Perspective of Mosby's warfare from the Union side is provided by eyewitness accounts of Union soldiers in the extensive collections of the Archives Branch, U.S. Army Military History Institute, Army War College and Carlisle Barracks. The *Official Records* and contemporary newspapers are gold mines of information in this regard, as are Compiled Military Service Records of Mosby's opponents in the National Archives. The Baltimore and Ohio Railroad Papers, Maryland Historical Society Library, document Mosby's impact on the railroad and reveal the reaction of company executives to his raids.

Further record of Mosby's impact is available in several strong Union Cavalry regimental histories, such as Charles A. Humphreys, *Field, Camp, Hospital and Prison in the Civil War, 1863–1865* (1918; reprint, Freeport, N.Y., 1971); and Howard Coffin, *Nine Months to Gettysburg: Stannard's Vermonters and the Repulse of Pickett's Charge* (Woodstock, Vt., 1997), considers Stoughton's capture. Edwin C. Fishel, *The Secret War for the Union: The Untold Story of Military Intelligence in the Civil War* (Boston, 1996), provides perspective on intelligence; and Mark Grimsley, *The Hard Hand of War: Union Military Policy toward Southern Civilians, 1861–1865* (Cambridge, 1995), analyzes Union policy toward civilian supporters of guerrillas. Michael C.C. Adams, *Our Masters the Rebels: A Speculation on Union Military Failure in the East, 1861–1865* (Cambridge, 1978), provides evidence of the impact of fear on Union troops.

Mark E. Neely Jr., *The Fate of Liberty: Abraham Lincoln and Civil Liberties* (New York, 1991) places Joseph Holt's military commissions in perspective. Gary W. Gallagher, ed., *Struggle for the Shenandoah: Essays on the 1864 Valley Campaign* (Kent, Ohio, 1991), evaluates Mosby's impact on Sheridan; and Gallagher, ed., *The First Day at Gettysburg: Essays on Confederate and Union Leadership* (Kent, Ohio, 1992), considers Stuart and the Gettysburg campaign. Roberta E. Fagan, "Custer at Front Royal: 'A Horror of the War'?" in *Custer and His Times: Book Three*, ed. Gregory J.W. Urwin (Conway, Ark., 1987), is a pathbreaking study of the Front Royal killings featuring eyewitness accounts from both sides.

Mosby's best Civil War essays, the first twelve chapters of his book, *Mosby's War Reminiscences and Stuart's Cavalry Campaigns* (New York, 1887), explain his emphasis on guerrilla warfare and cover his fighting through June 1863. His other book, *Stuart's Cavalry in the Gettysburg Campaign* (1908; reprint, Gaithersburg, Md., 1987), narrates his activities in June 1863, when he scouted for Stuart before the battle of Gettysburg. When he died, *The Memoirs of Colonel John S. Mosby* (1917; reprint, Gaithersburg, Md., 1987) remained unfinished, and his brother-in-law Charles W. Russell edited and published the book. It is fragmented and incomplete but includes war letters from Mosby to his wife and other useful documents and contains Mosby's recollections of his Manassas

Gap Railroad campaign, the Greenback Raid, and his December 21, 1864, wound. Among the many articles that he published, "Personal Recollections of General J.E.B. Stuart," *Munsey's Magazine* 49 (April 1913): 35–41, is a well-written description of scouting for Stuart in 1862 and features Mosby's role in the Peninsula Raid. "A Bit of Partisan Service," *Battles and Leaders of the Civil War,* ed. Robert U. Johnson and Clarence C. Buel, 4 vols. (New York, 1956), 3: 148–51, provides a detailed account of Stoughton's capture.

Other than Mosby's writings, one of the most helpful sources in analyzing his guerrilla tactics is the first history of the command, John Scott, *Partisan Life with Col. John S. Mosby* (1867; reprint, Gaithersburg, Md., 1985). Scott was not a member of Mosby's Rangers, but Mosby knew that he understood guerrilla war and, therefore, just before surrendering, invited him to write the history of the unit. Scott moved in with Mosby's family and conducted many hours of interviews with him and several of his former soldiers. The book exaggerates Mosby's impact and has incorrect dates and confused chronology, but Scott maintained intellectual freedom and did not allow Mosby to read the manuscript until it was published; then Mosby approved. *Reminiscences of a Mosby Guerrilla* (1906; reprint, Washington, D.C., 1983) by John W. Munson, a private under Mosby, also reflects an appreciation for guerrilla warfare, as does the article by Mosby's former major, Adolphus E. "Dolly" Richards, "Mosby's 'Partizan Rangers,'" *Famous Adventures and Prison Escapes of the Civil War* (1885; reprint, New York, 1920), 102–115.

Less discerning of guerrilla themes but more accurate and reliable is *Mosby's Rangers* (1896; reprint, no place, 1982) by James J. Williamson, a private in the command who wrote a war diary and studied official records in Washington. Williamson expanded the second edition (New York, 1909) with accounts by William Chapman and additional helpful documents. Former private John H. Alexander, who rode with Mosby in the last year of the war, wrote *Mosby's Men* (1907; reprint, Gaithersburg, Md., 1987), contributing perceptive comments on Mosby's leadership and describing the melee. Aristides Monteiro, *War Reminiscences by the Surgeon of Mosby's Command* (1890; reprint, Gaithersburg, Md., no date), illuminates the final few months of the war and describes Mosby's personality and despair when the war ended. Mosby read it after it was published and approved. Former private John M. Crawford's *Mosby and His Men* (New York, 1867) has value as an eyewitness memoir, but Crawford exaggerated and made many factual errors.

Thomas J. Evans and James M. Moyer, *Mosby's Confederacy: A Guide to the Roads and Sites of Colonel John Singleton Mosby* (Shippensburg, 1991), is an excellent guidebook and reference source on names and locations. Virgil C. Jones, *Gray Ghosts and Rebel Raiders* (New York, 1956), contributes an awareness of the work of other Partisan Rangers and how it related to Mosby. Emory M. Thomas, *Bold Dragoon: The Life of J.E.B. Stuart* (New York, 1986), clarifies the movements of Stuart's command. Clifford Dowdey and Louis H. Manarin, eds., *The Wartime Papers of R.E. Lee* (New York, 1961), furnish valuable Lee letters; and the best sources for keeping track of the Confederate army are Douglas S. Freeman's *R.E. Lee: A Biography,* 4 vols. (New York, 1934–1935) and Freeman's *Lee's Lieutenants: A Study in Command,* 3 vols. (New York, 1942–1944). V.N. "Bud" Phillips, *Bristol Tennessee/Virginia: A History—1852–1900* (Johnson City, Tennessee, 1992), is excellent and reliable.

Finally, the author is grateful to previous students who have focused on Mosby and researched the complicated issues of his life. Virgil C. Jones, *Ranger Mosby* (Chapel Hill, 1944), endures as a well-written classic that relies on primary research, including interviews with Mosby's children. Kevin H. Siepel, *Rebel: The Life and Times of John Singleton Mosby* (New York, 1983), paved the way in research in manuscripts at the National Archives and other libraries, and Siepel's account of Mosby's postwar career helped me define and clarify the issues. Jeffry D. Wert, in *Mosby's Rangers* (New York, 1990), gleaned additional sources on the Civil War and effectively revised Mosby's claim of adding six months to the life of the Confederacy. Hugh C. Keen and Horace Mewborn, *43rd Battalion Virginia Cavalry: Mosby's Command* (Lynchburg, 1993), contribute a sound narrative based on primary research and a firm grasp of names and locations. The emphasis is on Mosby's men, and the extremely helpful roster provides brief biographical sketches of many of the men.

# Acknowledgments

Many individuals and institutions encouraged and supported this ten-year research project. First and foremost, my wife and best friend, Ann, accompanied me on trips, proofread the manuscript, and shared my time with Mosby, always generously and with a cheerful, buoyant spirit. I am thankful to our daughter, Andrea, for sharing my enthusiasm for history, and I am honored that she followed in my footsteps as a graduate student in history at the University of Kentucky. I express gratitude to Andrea's husband, Steven M. Watkins, not only for being an ideal son-in-law but also for making a contribution to this study. As a former Navy SEAL and decorated veteran of the Persian Gulf War, Steven consulted on today's special forces and introduced me to Mike Bailey, a SEAL veteran of the Vietnam War. Steven and Mike gave me a deeper understanding of irregular warfare and a greater appreciation of Mosby's significance.

The project would not have been possible without the support of Northern Kentucky University, and I am most grateful. Northern granted travel funds and release time for research, and provided encouragement through two College of Arts and Sciences Research Grants, Summer Fellowship, Faculty Project Grant, Sabbatical Leave, and Regents Professorship. The Virginia Historical Society assisted with a Summer Fellowship for research on Mosby's civilian supporters. I thank Michael C.C. Adams and Michael A. Flannery for reading the entire manuscript and offering valuable suggestions. Steven Watkins, Mike Bailey, and Allen Ellis read portions, and Harris D. Riley Jr., M.D., read the passages on Mosby's health problems and provided professional advice on medical issues throughout the project. Flannery advised on alternative medicine and other issues, and Allen Ellis and David Payne consulted on many questions. Roger C. Adams answered questions on military life in the Civil War and, as acting curator, Northern Kentucky University Special Collections and Archives, facilitated my research in the university's extensive collection of published Civil War sources. Kent Masterson Brown gave encouragement and helpful counsel.

My mentor, W. Frank Steely, provided daily encouragement and steadfast support, and Department Chair Robert C. Vitz elevated my morale with his sense of humor and enthusiasm for the project. Marian Winner, Sharon Taylor, Philip Yannarella, and others at the Steely Library and Chase College of Law Library, Northern Kentucky University, assisted greatly. W. Baxter Perkinson Sr. and his wife, Stella, warmly welcomed Ann and me to their home near Petersburg, Virginia, during several of my research trips, accompanied us to Powhatan County, and introduced us to the Wests and Cellas. Aldine and Warren West and their children, Florence and Warren Jr., entertained us at their home, "Edgemont," Mosby's birthplace, and Aldine helped with the research. Charles P. Cella Jr. and his wife, Lucy Ann, generously conducted many hours of research on Mosby's family, and Charles guided me in using genealogical documents at the Virginia State Library and Archives. Mrs. Dorothy Steers conducted research on Pauline Clarke Mosby. Frances Pollard assisted tremendously at the Virginia Historical Society Library. Gladys Calvetti and Judith A. Sibley helped during my visit in the United States Military Academy Library, and Richard J. Sommers and Pamela A. Cheney helped greatly at Carlisle Barracks.

I am grateful for the hospitality and encouragement of Mosby's grandson, Beverly Mosby Coleman, and for the inspiration and counsel of Virgil C. "Pat" Jones, Mosby's first biographer. Nat and Sherry Morison assisted during our visit to Welbourne. John E. Divine and Horace Mewborn contributed an invaluable and comprehensive tour of Mosby's Confederacy. Mewborn gave valuable assistance, advice, and counsel. Mrs. William J. deButts welcomed us to her home, "Tudor Grove," Mosby's boyhood home in Charlottesville, and V.N. "Bud" Phillips gave us a tour of Bristol and Abingdon. Adele H. Mitchell conferred with me and contributed inspiration and assistance. James E.B. "Jeb" Stuart IV hosted my visit to the Stuart-Mosby Historical Society Museum and graciously accorded encouragement.

Among the many other individuals, including librarians and faculty colleagues, who have given assistance, I wish to mention the following: Thomas H. Appleton Jr., Jerry M. Bloomer, Leon E. Boothe, Jim Brown, Chris Burns, Bell Chevigny, John Cimprich, Brian Conley, John M. Coski, Sandra L. DeKay, Elizabeth Dunn, Jeffrey M. Flannery, Stanton

Garner, Paul L. Gaston, Perilou Goddard, George D. Goedel, James R. Harris, Margaret Heilbrun, David A. Holt, James F. Hopgood, John M. Hyson Jr., Suzanne Levy, Bill Lowe, Bruce McClure, Danny L. Miller, Dan Murphy, Mark E. Neely Jr., Roger H. Ney, Margaret M. O'Bryant, L. MacKenzie Osborne, Michael Plunkett, Brian Pohanka, Steven Poling, Anita Ramos, Rogers W. Redding, Robert T. Rhode, Teresa Roane, Joseph Robertson, Lindsay G. Robertson, Dave Roth, Jason Roth, Ann Sindelar, Guy R. Swanson, Richard Taylor, Sister Mary Philip Trauth, Sarah McNair Vosmeier, Jim Votruba, Robert Wallace, Pat Webb, Donald R. Welti, Macel M. Wheeler, and Frank Wood.

In addition, I am thankful for the assistance of other staff of the following libraries and organizations: Academy of Television Arts & Sciences; Albemarle County Historical Society; Archives Branch, U.S. Army Military History Institute, Army War College and Carlisle Barracks; *Blue & Gray Magazine;* Bristol Public Library; Colorado Historical Society; Eleanor S. Brockenbrough Library, The Museum of the Confederacy; Library of Congress; Denver Public Library; Special Collections Library, Duke University; Virginia Room, Fairfax County Public Library; Fauquier Bank; Rutherford B. Hayes Presidential Center; Kentucky Historical Society; Special Collections and Archives Service Center, University of Kentucky; Louis A. Warren Lincoln Library and Museum; Maryland Historical Society; National Archives; Nebraska State Historical Society; New York Historical Society; R.W. Norton Art Gallery; Davis Memorial Library, Patton Museum; Simpson County Historical Archives; Sky Meadows State Park; Stuart-Mosby Historical Society Museum; Tennessee State Library and Archives; U.S. Military Academy Library; The Valentine Museum; Virginia Historical Society; Archives Research Services, The Library of Virginia; Special Collections Department, University of Virginia Library; Washington County Historical Society; Western Kentucky University; Western Reserve Historical Society; Earl Gregg Swem Library, College of William and Mary; Frank & Marie-Therese Wood Print Collections; William H. White Jr. Library, Woodberry Forest School; and American Heritage Center, University of Wyoming.

# Index

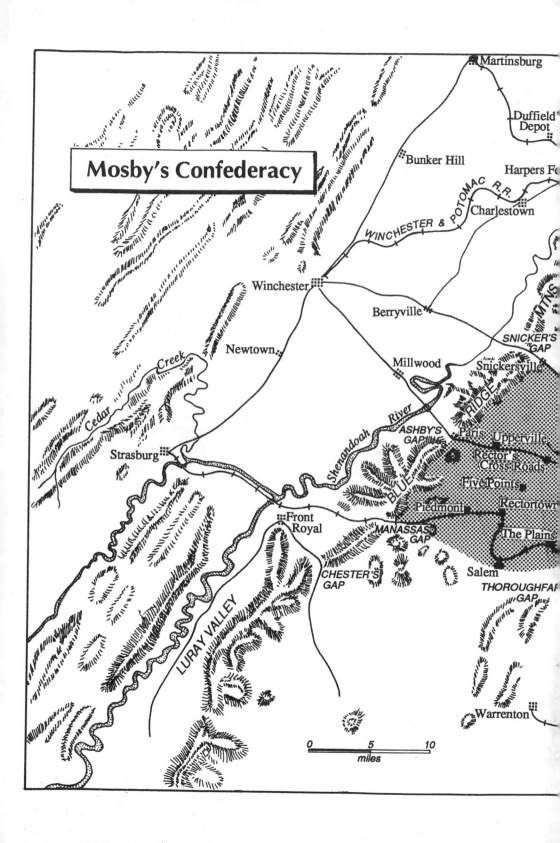

# Mosby's Confederacy

Martinsburg

Duffield Depot

Bunker Hill

Harpers Fe

WINCHESTER & POTOMAC R.R.

Charlestown

Winchester

Berryville

SNICKER'S GAP

MTNS

Newtown

Millwood

Snickersville

Creek

Cedar

Shenandoah

River

ASHBY'S GAP

RIDGE

Paris

Upperville

BLUE

Rector's Cross Roads

Strasburg

Five Points

Rectortown

Piedmont

Front Royal

MANASSAS GAP

The Plains

CHESTER'S GAP

Salem

LURAY VALLEY

THOROUGHFAR GAP

Warrenton

0        5        10
miles